W9-BFX-432

TECHNICAL ANALYSIS

TECHNICAL ANALYSIS

THE COMPLETE RESOURCE
FOR FINANCIAL MARKET TECHNICIANS

SECOND EDITION

Charles D. Kirkpatrick II, CMT
Julie Dahlquist, Ph.D., CMT

Vice President, Publisher: Tim Moore
Associate Publisher and Director of Marketing: Amy Neidlinger
Executive Editor: Jim Boyd
Editorial Assistant: Pamela Boland
Operations Manager: Gina Kanouse
Senior Marketing Manager: Julie Phifer
Publicity Manager: Laura Czaja
Assistant Marketing Manager: Megan Colvin
Cover Designer: Chuti Prasertsith
Managing Editor: Kristy Hart
Project Editor: Betsy Harris
Copy Editor: Karen Annett
Proofreader: Kathy Ruiz
Indexer: Erika Millen
Compositor: Bronkella Publishing
Manufacturing Buyer: Dan Uhrig

© 2011 by Pearson Education, Inc.
Publishing as FT Press
Upper Saddle River, New Jersey 07458

FT Press offers excellent discounts on this book when ordered in quantity for bulk purchases or special sales. For more information, please contact U.S. Corporate and Government Sales, 1-800-382-3419, orpsales@pearsontechgroup.com. For sales outside the U.S., please contact International Sales at international@pearson.com.

Company and product names mentioned herein are the trademarks or registered trademarks of their respective owners.

Printed in the United States of America

First Printing November 2010

ISBN-10: 0-13-705944-2
ISBN-13: 978-0-13-705944-7

Pearson Education LTD.
Pearson Education Australia PTY, Limited.
Pearson Education Singapore, Pte. Ltd.
Pearson Education Asia, Ltd.
Pearson Education Canada, Ltd.
Pearson Educación de Mexico, S.A. de C.V.
Pearson Education—Japan
Pearson Education Malaysia, Pte. Ltd.

Library of Congress Cataloging-in-Publication Data

Kirkpatrick, Charles D.
  Technical analysis : the complete resource for financial market technicians / Charles D. Kirkpatrick and Julie Dahlquist.
— 2nd ed.
    p. cm.
  Includes bibliographical references and index.
  ISBN 978-0-13-705944-7 (hbk. : alk. paper)
  1. Technical analysis (Investment analysis) 2. Investment analysis. I. Dahlquist, Julie R., 1962- II. Title.
  HG4529.K564 2011
  332.63'2042—dc22
                                    2010032991

To Ellie—my precious wife, long-term love and companion, and best friend.

—Charlie

To Richard, Katherine, and Sepp.

—Julie

CONTENTS

Acknowledgments xxiii

About the Authors xxv

Part I: Introduction

1   INTRODUCTION TO TECHNICAL ANALYSIS 3

2   THE BASIC PRINCIPLE OF TECHNICAL ANALYSIS—
THE TREND 9

     How Does the Technical Analyst Make Money? 10

     What Is a Trend? 11

     How Are Trends Identified? 12

     Trends Develop from Supply and Demand. 14

     What Trends Are There? 15

     What Other Assumptions Do Technical Analysts Make? 17

     Conclusion. 19

     Review Questions. 20

3   Hɪsᴛᴏʀʏ ᴏғ Tᴇᴄʜɴɪᴄᴀʟ Aɴᴀʟʏsɪs 23

     Early Financial Markets and Exchanges 23
     Modern Technical Analysis 26
     Current Advances in Technical Analysis......................30

4   Tʜᴇ Tᴇᴄʜɴɪᴄᴀʟ Aɴᴀʟʏsɪs Cᴏɴᴛʀᴏᴠᴇʀsʏ 33

     Do Markets Follow a Random Walk? 35
         Fat Tails 36
         Drawdowns..37
         Proportions of Scale 39
     Can Past Patterns Be Used to Predict the Future?..............40
     What About Market Efficiency?..............................41
         New Information..42
         Are Investors Rational? 46
         Will Arbitrage Keep Prices in Equilibrium?.....................47
     Behavioral Finance and Technical Analysis 49
     Pragmatic Criticisms of Technical Analysis...................50
     What Is the Empirical Support for Technical Analysis?........52
     Conclusion...52
     Review Questions..53

Part II: Markets and Market Indicators

5   Aɴ Oᴠᴇʀᴠɪᴇᴡ ᴏғ Mᴀʀᴋᴇᴛs 57

     In What Types of Markets Can Technical Analysis Be Used? 58
     Types of Contracts...59
         Cash Market 60
         Derivative Markets 62
         Swaps and Forwards..66

How Does a Market Work? **66**

Who Are the Market Players? **68**

How Is the Market Measured? **69**
Price-Weighted Average *70*
Market Capitalization Weighted Average *71*
Equally Weighted (or Geometric) Average *72*

Conclusion **73**

Review Questions **73**

6   DOW THEORY **75**

Dow Theory Theorems **78**
The Primary Trend *80*
The Secondary Trend *81*
The Minor Trend *81*
Concept of Confirmation *82*
Importance of Volume *83*

Criticisms of the Dow Theory **85**

Conclusion **86**

Review Questions **86**

7   SENTIMENT **89**

What Is Sentiment? **90**

Market Players and Sentiment **91**

How Does Human Bias Affect Decision Making? **92**

Crowd Behavior and the Concept of Contrary Opinion **95**

How Is Sentiment of Uninformed Players Measured? **96**
Sentiment Indicators Based on Options and Volatility *97*
Polls *102*
Other Measures of Contrary Opinion *107*
Unquantifiable Contrary Indicators *116*
Historical Indicators *117*

How Is the Sentiment of Informed Players Measured? **118**
    Insiders *118*

Sentiment in Other Markets **124**
    Treasury Bond Futures Put/Call Ratio *124*
    Treasury Bond COT Data *125*
    Treasury Bond Primary Dealer Positions *125*
    T-Bill Rate Expectations by Money Market Fund Managers *126*

Hulbert Gold Sentiment Index **128**

Conclusion **128**

Review Questions **129**

8   Mᴇᴀsᴜʀɪɴɢ Mᴀʀᴋᴇᴛ Sᴛʀᴇɴɢᴛʜ **131**

Market Breadth **133**
    The Breadth Line or Advance-Decline Line *134*
    Double Negative Divergence *136*
    Traditional Advance-Decline Methods That No Longer Are
        Profitable *138*
    Advance-Decline Line to Its 32-Week Simple Moving Average *139*
    Breadth Differences *140*
    Breadth Ratios *146*
    Breadth Thrust *147*
    Summary of Breadth Indicators *148*

Up and Down Volume Indicators **149**
    The Arms Index *149*
    Ninety Percent Downside Days (NPDD) *152*
    10-to-1 Up Volume Days and 9-to-1 Down Volume Days *153*

Net New Highs and Net New Lows **154**
    New Highs Versus New Lows *155*
    High Low Logic Index *156*
    Hindenburg Omen *157*

Using Moving Averages **157**
    Number of Stocks above Their 30-Week Moving Average *157*

Very Short-Term Indicators **159**
    Breadth and New Highs to New Lows *159*
    Net Ticks *160*

Conclusion **161**

Review Questions **162**

9 TEMPORAL PATTERNS AND CYCLES 163

Periods Longer than Four Years.............................164
  Kondratieff Waves, or K-Waves *164*
  34-Year Historical Cycles..*166*
  Decennial Pattern *168*

Periods of Four Years or Less 169
  Four-Year or Presidential Cycle.......................................*170*
  Election Year Pattern *171*
  Seasonal Patterns *172*

January Signals 174
  January Barometer *174*
  January Effect...*174*

Events...175

Conclusion..175

Review Questions..................................176

10 FLOW OF FUNDS 177

Funds in the Marketplace 178
  Money Market Funds *178*
  Margin Debt *179*
  Secondary Offerings *180*

Funds Outside the Security Market...........................181
  Household Financial Assets *182*
  Money Supply *183*
  Bank Loans...*184*

The Cost of Funds 185
  Short-Term Interest Rates...*185*
  Long-Term Interest Rates (or Inversely, the Bond Market) *187*
  Money Velocity..*187*
  Misery Index *188*

Fed Policy 190
  Fed Policy Futures...*191*
  The Federal Reserve Valuation Model..............................*192*
  Three Steps and a Stumble *193*
  Yield Curve *194*

Conclusion. 195
Review Questions. 196

Part III: Trend Analysis

11 History and Construction of Charts 199

History of Charting. 201
What Data Is Needed to Construct a Chart?. 204
What Types of Charts Do Analysts Use? 206
    Line Charts..207
    Bar Charts..210
    Candlestick Charts 211
What Type of Scale Should Be Used? 213
    Arithmetic Scale...213
    Semi-Logarithmic Scale...214
Point-and-Figure Charts 215
    One-Box (Point) Reversal...216
    Box Size 217
    Multibox Reversal..217
    Time 218
    Arithmetic Scale...220
    Logarithmic Scale..220
Conclusion. 220
Review Questions. 221

12 Trends—The Basics.....................................223

Trend—The Key to Profits. 224
Trend Terminology 225
Basis of Trend Analysis—Dow Theory .225
How Does Investor Psychology Impact Trends? 226
How Is the Trend Determined?. 227
    Peaks and Troughs..228

Determining a Trading Range.................................230
What Is Support and Resistance?.......................................*230*
Why Do Support and Resistance Occur? *230*
What About Round Numbers? *232*
How Are Important Reversal Points Determined? *232*
How Do Analysts Use Trading Ranges?.................................*236*

Directional Trends (Up and Down) 237
What Is a Directional Trend? *238*
How Is an Uptrend Spotted? *238*
Channels...*243*
Internal Trend Lines *244*
Retracements *245*
Pullbacks and Throwbacks *247*

Other Types of Trend Lines..................................247
Trend Lines on Point-and-Figure Charts...............................*248*
Speed Lines *248*
Andrews Pitchfork *249*
Gann Fan Lines *250*

Conclusion..251

Review Questions..251

13   **B**REAKOUTS, **S**TOPS, AND **R**ETRACEMENTS **255**

Breakouts...255
How Is Breakout Confirmed? *256*
Can a Breakout Be Anticipated? *262*

Stops 263
What Are Entry and Exit Stops?..*263*
Changing Stop Orders...*264*
What Are Protective Stops? *264*
What Are Trailing Stops?...*265*
What Are Time Stops?...*268*
What Are Money Stops?...*269*
How Can Stops Be Used with Breakouts?...............................*269*
Using Stops When Gaps Occur *269*
Waiting for Retracement..*270*
Calculating a Risk/Return Ratio for Breakout Trading.............*271*
Placing Stops for a False (or "Specialist") Breakout................*272*

Conclusion 273
Review Questions 274

14   MOVING AVERAGES 275

What Is a Moving Average? 276
How Is a Simple Moving Average Calculated? 276
    Length of Moving Average 279
    Using Multiple Moving Averages 280
What Other Types of Moving Averages Are Used? 281
    The Linearly Weighted Moving Average (LWMA) 282
    The Exponentially Smoothed Moving Average (EMA) 282
    Wilder Method 284
    Geometric Moving Average (GMA) 284
    Triangular Moving Average 285
    Variable EMAs 285
Strategies for Using Moving Averages 285
    Determining Trend 285
    Determining Support and Resistance 286
    Determining Price Extremes 287
    Giving Specific Signals 288
What Is Directional Movement? 288
    Constructing Directional Movement Indicators 289
    Using Directional Movement Indicators 289
What Are Envelopes, Channels, and Bands? 291
    Percentage Envelopes 291
    Bands 292
    Trading Strategies Using Bands and Envelopes 294
    Channel 295
Conclusion 296
Review Questions 297

Part IV: Chart Pattern Analysis

15 BAR CHART PATTERNS 301

    What Is a Pattern?. 302
      Common Pattern Characteristics *302*
    Do Patterns Exist?. 303
      Behavioral Finance and Pattern Recognition *304*
    Computers and Pattern Recognition. 305
    Market Structure and Pattern Recognition. 306
    Bar Charts and Patterns 307
    How Profitable Are Patterns? 308
    Classic Bar Chart Patterns 309
      Double Top and Double Bottom *309*
      Rectangle (Also "Trading Range" or "Box") *310*
      Triple Top and Triple Bottom *313*
      Standard Triangles *314*
      Descending Triangle *315*
      Ascending Triangle *317*
      Symmetrical Triangle (Also "Coil" or "Isosceles Triangle") *317*
      Broadening Patterns *320*
      Diamond Top *321*
      Wedge and Climax *322*
    Patterns with Rounded Edges—Rounding and Head-and-
      Shoulders 325
      Rounding Top, Rounding Bottom (Also "Saucer," "Bowl," or
        "Cup") *325*
      Head-and-Shoulders *326*
      Shorter Continuation Trading Patterns—Flags and Pennants
        (Also "Half-Mast Formation") *329*
    Long-Term Bar Chart Patterns with the Best Performance
      and the Lowest Risk of Failure 332
    Conclusion. 332
    Review Questions. 333

16   POINT-AND-FIGURE CHART PATTERNS **335**

What Is Different About a Point-and-Figure Chart?...........**336**
  Time and Volume Omitted...*336*
  Continuous Price Flow Necessary *336*
  "Old" and "New" Methods *337*

History of Point-and-Figure Charting.......................**337**

One-Box Reversal Point-and-Figure Charts **339**
  *Consolidation Area on the One-Box Chart (Also "Congestion
      Area")* *340*
  Trend Lines in One-Box Charts..*340*
  The Count in a One-Point Chart *341*
  Head-and-Shoulders Pattern *343*
  The Fulcrum *344*
  Action Points..*344*

Three-Point (or Box) Reversal Point-and-Figure Charts **345**
  Trend Lines with Three-Box Charts..*346*
  The Count Using Three-Box Reversal Charts *347*
  The Eight Standard Patterns for Three-Box Reversal Charts............*348*
  Other Patterns *354*

Conclusion...**357**
Review Questions...**357**

17   SHORT-TERM PATTERNS **359**

Pattern Construction and Determination.....................**362**
Traditional Short-Term Patterns **362**
  Gaps...*363*
  Spike (or Wide-Range or Large-Range Bar) *370*
  Dead Cat Bounce (DCB) *371*
  Island Reversal *373*
  One- and Two-Bar Reversal Patterns...*373*
  Multiple Bar Patterns *380*
  Volatility Patterns *384*
  Intraday Patterns *386*

Summary of Short-Term Patterns **389**

Candlestick Patterns **390**
  One- and Two-Bar Candlestick Patterns *391*
  Multiple Bar Patterns *396*
  Candlestick Pattern Results *401*

Conclusion **402**

Review Questions **402**

Part V: Trend Confirmation

18   Confirmation **407**

Analysis Methods **408**
  Overbought/Oversold *408*
  Failure Swings *409*
  Divergences *409*
  Reversals *410*
  Trend ID *410*
  Crossovers *411*
  Classic Patterns *411*

Volume Confirmation **411**
  What Is Volume? *411*
  How Is Volume Portrayed? *412*
  Do Volume Statistics Contain Valuable Information? *414*
  How Are Volume Statistics Used? *415*
  Which Indexes and Oscillators Incorporate Volume? *416*
  Volume Spikes *425*
  Examples of Volume Spikes *426*

Open Interest **427**
  What Is Open Interest? *427*
  Open Interest Indicators *428*

Price Confirmation **429**
  What Is Momentum? *430*
  How Successful Are Momentum Indicators? *431*
  Specific Indexes and Oscillators *432*

Conclusion **444**

Review Questions **445**

Part VI: Other Technical Methods and Rules

19 CYCLES **449**

What Are Cycles? **452**
    Other Aspects of Cycle Analysis *455*

Translation **457**

How Can Cycles Be Found in Market Data? **458**
    Fourier Analysis (Spectral Analysis) *458*
    Maximum Entropy Spectral Analysis *459*
    Simpler (and More Practical) Methods *459*

Projections **467**
    Projecting Period *468*
    Projecting Amplitude *470*

Conclusion **475**

Review Questions **475**

20 ELLIOTT, FIBONACCI, AND GANN **477**

Elliott Wave Theory (EWT) **477**
    Ralph Nelson Elliott *478*
    Basic Elliott Wave Theory *478*
    Impulse Waves *480*
    Corrective Waves *483*
    Guidelines and General Characteristics in EWT *486*
    Projected Targets and Retracements *488*
    Alternatives to EWT *490*
    Using EWT *491*

The Fibonacci Sequence **492**
    Fibonacci *493*
    The Fibonacci Sequence *493*
    The Golden Ratio *493*
    Price and Time Targets *495*
    W. D. Gann *497*

Conclusion **498**

Review Questions **499**

Part VII: Selection

21 SELECTION OF MARKETS AND ISSUES: TRADING AND
INVESTING **503**

Which Issues Should I Select for Trading? **503**
Choosing Between Futures Markets and Stock Markets....................*504*
Which Issues Should I Select for Investing? **506**
Top-Down Analysis **507**
Secular Emphasis *507*
Cyclical Emphasis *510*
Stock Market Industry Sectors...*515*
Bottom Up—Specific Stock Selection and Relative Strength....**516**
Relative Strength..*517*
Academic Studies of Relative Strength *517*
Measuring Relative Strength *518*
**Examples of How Selected Professionals Screen for Favorable
Stocks**..**520**
William O'Neil CANSLIM Method......................................*521*
James P. O'Shaughnessy Method *521*
Charles D. Kirkpatrick Method...*522*
Value Line Method..*522*
Richard D. Wyckoff Method *522*
Conclusion..**525**
Review Questions.......................................**525**

Part VIII: System Testing and Management

22 SYSTEM DESIGN AND TESTING **529**

Why Are Systems Necessary? **530**
Discretionary Versus Nondiscretionary Systems *530*
How Do I Design a System?................................**532**
Requirements for Designing a System...*532*
Understanding Risk *533*

Initial Decisions *534*
Types of Technical Systems *535*

How Do I Test a System? **538**
Special Data Problems for Futures Systems....................*539*
Testing Methods and Tools *540*
Test Parameter Ranges *540*

Optimization...**546**
Methods of Optimizing *546*
Measuring System Results for Robustness *549*

Conclusion...**556**

Review Questions...**557**

23   MONEY AND RISK MANAGEMENT **559**

Risk and Money Management **560**

Testing Money-Management Strategies **561**

Money-Management Risks **562**
Concepts *562*
Reward to Risk...*564*
Normal Risks *564*
Unusual Risks *570*

Money-Management Risk Strategies.......................**572**

Monitoring Systems and Portfolios **577**

If Everything Goes Wrong...................................**577**

Conclusion...**577**

Review Questions...**578**

Part IX: Appendices

A   BASIC STATISTICS **581**

Returns...**581**

Probability and Statistics...................................**582**

Descriptive Statistics **583**
Measures of Central Tendency *583*
Measures of Dispersion *585*
Relationships Between Variables *586*

Inferential Statistics **591**

Modern Portfolio Theory **594**

Performance Measurement **600**

Advanced Statistical Methods **602**

Artificial Intelligence **603**

Review Questions **604**

B   **TYPES OF ORDERS AND OTHER TRADER TERMINOLOGY** ...**607**

    An Order Ticket **609**

BIBLIOGRAPHY **611**

INDEX **637**

ACKNOWLEDGMENTS

To Richard D. Kirkpatrick, my father, and ex-portfolio manager for Fidelity beginning in the 1950s. He introduced me to technical analysis at the age of 14 by asking me to update his charts. In the year of his retirement, 1968, he managed the best-performing mutual fund in the world.

To the Market Technicians Association, through which I have met many of the best innovators and practitioners of technical analysis, and especially to staff members Cassandra Townes and Marie Penza for their support and assistance in making available the MTA library.

To Skip Cave, past dean of the Fort Lewis College School of Business Administration, for allowing me to assist him in teaching a course in technical analysis, for getting this project going by introducing me to other textbook authors, such as the Assistant Dean Roy Cook, and for providing office space during the initial writing and researching for this book.

To Thomas Harrington, past dean of the Fort Lewis College School of Business Administration, for allowing me to maintain an office at the college, for allowing me special privileges at the college library, and for asking me to continue teaching a course in technical analysis.

To my students in class BA317 at Fort Lewis College School of Business Administration, for being my teaching guinea pigs and for keeping me on my toes with questions and observations.

To my friends and colleagues at the Philadelphia Stock Exchange, specifically Vinnie Casella, past president, who taught me from the inside how markets really work.

To the dedicated people at Pearson Education, specifically Jim Boyd, executive editor; Pamela Boland, editorial assistant; Betsy Harris, production editor; Karen Annett, copy editor; and all the others behind the scenes whom I have not known directly.

To Phil Roth and Bruce Kamich, both past presidents of the Market Technicians Association, professional technical analysts, and adjunct professors teaching courses in technical analysis at universities in the New York area, for editing the material in this book and keeping me in line.

To Julie Dahlquist, my coauthor, and her husband, Richard Bauer, both professors steeped in the ways of academia, for bringing that perspective to this book.

To my wife, Ellie, who has had to put up with me for 48 years and has always done so pleasantly and with love.

To my children, Abby, Andy, Bear, and Bradlee, for their love and support.

And to my grandchildren, India and Mila, who didn't do anything for the book but who pleaded to be mentioned.

I thank you and all the many others from my lifetime of work in technical analysis for your support, friendship, and willingness to impart your knowledge of trading markets.

Charles Kirkpatrick
Kittery, Maine

The assistance and support of many people contributed to turning the dream of this book into a reality. Fred Meissner was the one who initially introduced me to my coauthor, Charlie, at a Market Technicians Association chapter meeting. After I worked with Charlie on several projects and we served together on the Market Technicians Association Educational Foundation Board, he bravely agreed to a partnership in writing this book. Charlie has been the ideal coauthor—positive, patient, and persistent. It has been an honor to work with someone so knowledgeable and an incredible experience to work with someone so willing to share his knowledge.

The faculty and staff in the Department of Finance at the University of Texas at San Antonio College of Business have been a pleasure to work with over the past couple of years while this book has been in process. Keith Fairchild, Lula Misra, and Robert Lengel have been especially supportive.

The expertise of the dedicated team at Pearson Education has been invaluable in helping Charlie and me get our ideas into this final format. Thanks to Jim Boyd, Pamela Boland, Betsy Harris, Karen Annett, and the entire Pearson Education team for their gentle prodding, their continued encouragement, and their tireless commitment to this project.

My husband, Richard Bauer, assisted in more ways than can ever be counted. He graciously wrote the Basic Statistics appendix for this book. He served as a sounding board for many of the ideas in this book. He read drafts and made many helpful suggestions to the manuscript. However, his support goes far beyond his professional expertise. Richard untiringly took care of many household tasks as I spent time working on this project. His help made it easy for me to travel to meet with Charlie and work on this project. I am blessed to receive his unwavering emotional support and encouragement.

My two children have also been a source of blessing and inspiration. They demonstrated extreme patience through this entire process. They also reminded me of the need for fun, laughter, and a good hug whenever I was tempted to work too hard. Discussing stock charts with my eleven-year-old son, Sepp, made this project much more interesting than it would have otherwise been. Writing next to my fourteen-year-old daughter and budding author, Katherine, made the countless hours of tedious work much more enjoyable.

Julie Dahlquist
San Antonio, TX

ABOUT THE AUTHORS

Charles D. Kirkpatrick II, CMT, is

> President, Kirkpatrick & Company, Inc., Kittery, Maine—a private firm specializing in technical research; editor and publisher of the Market Strategist newsletter.

> Adjunct Professor of Finance, Brandeis University International School of Business, Waltham, Massachusetts.

> Director and Vice President, Market Technicians Association Educational Foundation, Cambridge, Massachusetts—a charitable foundation dedicated to encouraging and providing educational courses in technical analysis at the college and university level.

> Past editor, *Journal of Technical Analysis*, New York, New York—the official journal of technical analysis research.

> Past director, Market Technicians Association, New York, New York—an association of professional technical analysts.

In his life in the stock and options markets, Mr. Kirkpatrick has been a hedge fund manager, investment advisor, advisor to floor and desk traders and portfolio managers, institutional stock broker, options trader, desk and large-block trader, lecturer and speaker on aspects of technical analysis to professional and academic groups, expert legal witness on the stock market, owner of several small businesses, owner of an institutional brokerage firm, and part owner of a CBOE options trading firm. His research has been published in Barron's and elsewhere. In 1993 and 2001, he won the Charles H. Dow Award for excellence in technical research, and in 2009, he won the MTA award for his contributions to technical analysis. Educated at Phillips Exeter Academy, Harvard College (A.B.) and the Wharton School of the University of Pennsylvania (M.B.A.), he was also a decorated combat officer with the 1st Cavalry Division in Vietnam. He currently resides in Maine with his wife, Ellie, and their various domestic animals.

Julie R. Dahlquist, Ph.D., received her B.B.A. in economics from University of Louisiana at Monroe, her M.A. in Theology from St. Mary's University, and her Ph.D. in economics from Texas A&M University. Currently, she is a senior lecturer, Department of Finance, at the University of Texas at San Antonio College of Business. Dr. Dahlquist is a frequent presenter at national and international conferences. She is the coauthor (with Richard Bauer) of *Technical Market Indicators: Analysis and Performance* (John Wiley & Sons). Her research has appeared in *Financial Analysts Journal*, *Journal of Technical Analysis*, *Managerial Finance*, *Applied Economics*, *Working Money*, *Financial Practices and Education*, *Active Trader*, and in the *Journal of Financial Education*. She serves on the Board of the Market Technicians Association Educational Foundation, on the editorial board of the *Southwestern Business Administration Journal*, and as a reviewer for a number of journals, including the *Journal of Technical Analysis*. She resides in San Antonio with her husband, Richard Bauer, and their two children, Katherine and Sepp.

INTRODUCTION

CHAPTER 1   INTRODUCTION TO TECHNICAL ANALYSIS

CHAPTER 2   THE BASIC PRINCIPLE OF TECHNICAL
              ANALYSIS—THE TREND

CHAPTER 3   HISTORY OF TECHNICAL ANALYSIS

CHAPTER 4   THE TECHNICAL ANALYSIS CONTROVERSY

INTRODUCTION TO TECHNICAL ANALYSIS

Technical analysis—these words may conjure up many different mental images. Perhaps you think of the stereotypical technical analyst, alone in a windowless office, slouched over stacks of hand-drawn charts of stock prices. Or, maybe you think of the sophisticated multicolored computerized chart of your favorite stock you recently saw. Perhaps you begin dreaming about all the money you could make if you knew the secrets to predicting stock prices. Or, perhaps you remember sitting in a finance class and hearing your professor say that technical analysis "is a waste of time." In this book, we examine some of the perceptions, and misperceptions, of technical analysis.

If you are new to the study of technical analysis, you might be wondering just what technical analysis is. In its basic form, technical analysis is the study of prices in freely traded markets with the intent of making profitable trading or investment decisions. Technical analysis is rooted in basic economic theory. Consider the basic assumptions presented by Robert D. Edwards and John Magee in the classic book, *Technical Analysis of Stock Trends:*

- Stock prices are determined solely by the interaction of demand and supply.
- Stock prices tend to move in trends.
- Shifts in demand and supply cause reversals in trends.
- Shifts in demand and supply can be detected in charts.
- Chart patterns tend to repeat themselves.

Technical analysts study the action of the market itself rather than the goods in which the market deals. The technical analyst believes that "the market is always correct." In other words, rather than trying to consider all the factors that will influence the demand for Gadget International's newest electronic gadget and all the items that will influence the company's cost and supply curve to determine an outlook for the stock's price, the technical analyst believes that all of these factors are already factored into the demand and supply curves and, thus, the price of the company's stock. We find that stock prices (and prices for any security in freely traded markets) are influenced by psychological factors as well, most of them indecipherable. Greed, fear, cognitive bias, misinformation, expectations, and other factors enter into the price of a security, making the analysis of the factors nearly impossible. The technical analyst, thus, disregards all these imponderables and studies how the marketplace is accepting the multitude of exogenous information and beliefs with the intention of finding secrets in that action that have predictive potential.

Students new to any discipline often ask, "How can I use the knowledge of this discipline?" Students new to technical analysis are no different. Technical analysis is used in two major ways: predictive and reactive. Those who use technical analysis for predictive purposes use the analysis to make predictions about future market moves. Generally, these individuals make money by selling their predictions to others. Market letter writers in print or on the Web and the technical market gurus who frequent the financial news fall into this category. The predictive technical analysts include the more well-known names in the industry; these individuals like publicity because it helps market their services.

On the other hand, those who use technical analysis in a reactive mode are usually not well known. Traders and investors use techniques of technical analysis to react to particular market conditions to make their decisions. For example, a trader may use a moving average crossover to signal when a long position should be taken. In other words, the trader is watching the market and reacting when a certain technical condition is met. These traders and investors are making money by making profitable trades for their own or clients' portfolios. Some of them may even find that publicity distracts them from their underlying work.

The focus of this book is to explain the basic principles and techniques for reacting to the market. We do not attempt to predict the market, nor do we provide you with the Holy Grail or a promise of a method that will make you millions overnight. Instead, we want to provide you with background, basic tools, and techniques that you will need to be a competent technical analyst.

As we will see when we study the history of technical analysis, the interest in technical analysis in the United States dates back over 150 years, when Charles H. Dow began to write newsletters that later turned into the *Wall Street Journal* and developed the various Dow averages to measure the stock market. Since that time, much has been written about technical analysis. Today, there are entire periodicals, such as the *Technical Analysis of Stock and Commodities* and the *Journal of Technical Analysis,* devoted to the study of the subject. In addition, there are many articles appearing in other publications, including academic journals. There are even a number of excellent books on the market. As you can see from this book's extensive bibliography, which is in no way a complete list of every published item on technical analysis, a massive quantity of material about technical analysis exists.

So, why does the world need another book on technical analysis? We began looking through the multitude of materials on technical analysis a few years ago, searching for resources to use in educational settings. We noticed that many specialized books existed on the topic, but there was no resource to provide the student of technical analysis with a comprehensive summation of the body of knowledge. We decided to provide a coherent, logical framework for this material that could be used as a textbook and a reference book.

Our intent in writing this book is to provide the student of technical analysis, whether a novice college student or an experienced practitioner, with a systematic study of the field of technical analysis. Over the past century, much has been written about the topic. The classic works of

Charles Dow and the timeless book by Edwards and Magee still contain valuable information for the student of technical analysis. The basic principles of these early authors are still valid today. However, the evolving financial marketplace and the availability of computer power have led to a substantial growth in the new tools and information available to the technical analyst.

Many technical analysts have learned their trade from the mentors with whom they have worked. Numerous individuals who are interested in studying technical analysis today, however, do not have access to such a mentor. In addition, as the profession has advanced, many specific techniques have developed. The result is that the techniques and methods of technical analysis often appear to be a hodgepodge of tools, ideas, and even folklore, rather than a part of a coherent body of knowledge.

Many books on the market assume a basic understanding of technical analysis or focus on particular financial markets or instruments. Our intent is to provide the reader with a basic reference to support a lifelong study of the discipline. We have attempted to provide enough background information and terminology that you can easily read this book without having to refer to other references for background information. We have also included a large number of references for further reading so that you can continue learning in the specialized areas that interest you.

Another unique characteristic of this book is the joining of the practitioner and the academic. Technical analysis is widely practiced, both by professional traders and investors and by individuals managing their own money. However, this widespread practice has not been matched by academic acknowledgment of the benefits of technical analysis. Academics have been slow to study technical analysis; most of the academic studies of technical analysis have lacked a thorough understanding of the actual practice of technical analysis. It is our hope not only to bring together a practitioner-academic author team but also to provide a book that promotes discussion and understanding between these two groups.

Whether you are a novice or experienced professional, we are confident that you will find this book helpful. For the student new to technical analysis, this book will provide you with the basic knowledge and building blocks to begin a lifelong study of technical analysis. For the more experienced technician, you will find this book to be an indispensable guide, helping you to organize your knowledge, question your assumptions and beliefs, and implement new techniques.

We begin this book with a look at the background and history of technical analysis. In this part, we discuss not only the basic principles of technical analysis but also the technical analysis controversy—the debate between academics and practitioners regarding the efficiency of financial markets and the merit of technical analysis. This background information is especially useful to those who are new to technical analysis and those who are studying the subject in an educational setting. For those with more experience with the field or with little interest in the academic arguments about market efficiency, a quick reading of this first part will probably suffice.

In the second part of the book, we focus on markets and market indicators. Chapter 5, "An Overview of Markets," provides a basic overview of how markets work. Market vocabulary and trading mechanics are introduced in this chapter. For the student who is unfamiliar with this terminology, a thorough understanding of this chapter will provide the necessary background for the remaining chapters. Our focus in Chapter 6, "Dow Theory," is on the development and principles of Dow Theory. Although Dow Theory was developed a century ago, much of modern-day technical analysis is based on these classic principles. A thorough understanding of these time-less principles helps keep the technical analyst focused on the key concepts that lead to making money in the market. In Chapter 7, "Sentiment," we focus on sentiment; the psychology of market players is a major concept in this chapter. In Chapter 8, "Measuring Market Strength," we discuss methods for gauging overall market strength. Chapter 9, "Temporal Patterns and Cycles," focuses on temporal tendencies, the tendency for the market to move in particular directions during particular times, such as election year cycles and seasonal stock market patterns. Because the main fuel for the market is money, Chapter 10, "Flow of Funds," focuses on the flow of funds. In this chapter, we look at measures of market liquidity and how the Federal Reserve can influence liquidity.

The third part of the book focuses on trend analysis. In many ways, this part can be thought of as the heart of technical analysis. If we see that the market is trending upward, we can profitably ride that trend upward. If we determine that the market is trending downward, we can even profit by taking a short position. In fact, the most difficult time to profit in the market is when there is no definitive upward or downward trend. Over the years, technical analysts have developed a number of techniques to help them visually determine when a trend is in place. These charting techniques are the focus of Chapter 11, "History and Construction of Charts." In Chapter 12, "Trends—The Basics," we discuss how to draw trend lines and determine support and resistance lines using these charts. In Chapter 13, "Breakouts, Stops, and Retracements," we focus on determining breakouts. These breakouts will help us recognize a trend change as soon as possible. We also discuss the importance of protective stops in this chapter. Moving averages, a useful mathematical technique for determining the existence of trends, are presented in Chapter 14, "Moving Averages."

The fourth part of this book focuses on chart pattern analysis—the item that first comes to mind when many people think of technical analysis. In Chapter 15, "Bar Chart Patterns," we cover classic bar chart patterns; in Chapter 16, "Point-and-Figure Chart Patterns," we focus on point-and-figure chart patterns. Short-term patterns, including candlestick patterns, are covered in Chapter 17, "Short-Term Patterns."

Part V, "Trend Confirmation," deals with the concept of confirmation. We consider price oscillators and momentum measures in Chapter 18, "Confirmation." Building upon the concept of trends from earlier chapters, we look at how volume plays a role in confirming the trend, giving us more confidence that a trend is indeed occurring. We also look at oscillators and indexes of momentum to analyze other means of confirming price trend.

Next, we turn our attention to the relationship between cycle theory and technical analysis. In Chapter 19, "Cycles," we discuss the basic principles of cycle theory and the characteristics of cycles. Some technical analysts believe that cycles seen in the stock market have a scientific basis; for example, R. N. Elliott claimed that the basic harmony found in nature occurs in the stock market. Chapter 20, "Elliott, Fibonacci, and Gann," introduces the basic concepts of Elliott Wave Theory, a school of thought that adheres to Elliott's premise that stock price movements form discernible wave patterns.

Once we know the basic techniques of technical analysis, the question becomes, "Which particular securities will we trade?" Selection decisions are the focus of Chapter 21, "Selection of Markets and Issues: Trading and Investing." In this chapter, we discuss the intermarket relationships that will help us determine on which market to focus by determining which market is most likely to show strong performance. We also discuss individual security selection, measures of relative strength, and how successful practitioners have used these methods to construct portfolios.

As technical analysts, we need methods of measuring our success. After all, our main objective is making money. Although this is a straightforward objective, determining whether we are meeting our objective is not quite so straightforward. Proper measurement of trading and investment strategies requires appropriate risk measurement and an understanding of basic statistical techniques. The last couple of chapters help put all the tools and techniques we present throughout the book into practice. Chapter 22, "System Design and Testing," is devoted to developing and testing trading systems. At this point, we look at how we can test the tools and indicators covered throughout the book to see if they will make money for us—our main objective—in the particular way we would like to trade. Finally, Chapter 23, "Money and Risk Management," deals with money management and avoiding capital loss.

For those who need a brushup in basic statistics or want to understand some of the statistical concepts introduced throughout the book, Richard J. Bauer, Jr., Ph.D., CFA, CMT (Professor of Finance, Bill Greehey School of Business, St. Mary's University, San Antonio, TX), provides a tutorial on basic statistical techniques of interest to the technical analyst in Appendix A, "Basic Statistics."

For those who are unfamiliar with the terms and language used in trading, Appendix B, "Types of Orders and Other Trader Terminology," provides brief definitions of specific order types and commonly used terms in order entry.

As with all skills, learning technical analysis requires practice. We have provided a number of review questions and problems at the end of the chapters to help you begin thinking about and applying some of the concepts on your own. The extensive bibliography will direct you to further readings in the areas of technical analysis that are of particular interest to you.

Another way of honing your technical skills is participating in a professional organization that is focused on technical analysis. In the United States, the Market Technicians Association (MTA) provides a wide variety of seminars, lectures, and publications for technical analysis professionals. The MTA also sponsors the Chartered Market Technician (CMT) program. Professionals wanting to receive the prestigious CMT designation must pass three examinations and adhere to a strict code of professional conduct. More information about the MTA and the CMT program may be found at the Web site: www.mta.org. The International Federation of Technical Analysts, Inc., (IFTA) is a global organization of market analysis societies and associations. IFTA, and its member associations worldwide, sponsor a number of seminars and publications. IFTA offers a professional certification, the Certified Financial Technician, and a masters-level degree, the Master of Financial Technical Analysis. The details of these certifications, along with contact information for IFTA's member associations around the world, can be found at their Web site: www.ifta.org.

Technical analysis is a complex, ever-expanding discipline. The globalization of markets, the creation of new securities, and the availability of inexpensive computer power are opening even more opportunities in this field. Whether you use the information professionally or for your own personal trading or investing, we hope that this book will serve as a stepping-stone to your study and exploration of the field of technical analysis.

THE BASIC PRINCIPLE OF TECHNICAL ANALYSIS—THE TREND

CHAPTER OBJECTIVES

After reading this chapter, you should be able to

- Define the term *trend*
- Explain why determining the trend is important to the technical analyst
- Distinguish between primary, secondary, short-term, and intraday trends
- Discuss some of the basic beliefs upon which technical analysis is built

> The art of technical analysis—for it is an art—is to identify trend changes at an early stage and to maintain an investment position until the weight of the evidence indicates that the trend has reversed. (Pring, 2002)

Technical analysis is based on one major assumption—trend. Markets trend. Traders and investors hope to buy a security at the beginning of an uptrend at a low price, ride the trend, and sell the security when the trend ends at a high price. Although this strategy sounds very simple, implementing it is exceedingly complex.

For example, what length trend are we discussing? The trend in stock prices since the Great Depression? The trend in gold prices since 1980? The trend in the Dow Jones Industrial Average (DJIA) in the past year? Or, the trend in Merck stock during the past week? Trends exist in all lengths, from long-term trends that occur over decades to short-term trends that occur from minute to minute.

Trends of different lengths tend to have the same characteristics. In other words, a trend in annual data will behave the same as a trend in five-minute data. Investors must choose which trend is most important for them based on their investment objectives, their personal preferences, and the amount of time they can devote to watching market prices. One investor might be more concerned about the business cycle trend that occurs over several years. Another investor might be more concerned about the trend over the next six months, while a third investor might be most concerned about the intraday trend. Although individual investors and traders have investment time horizons that vary greatly, they can use the same basic methods of analyzing trends because of the commonalities that exist among trends of different lengths.

Trends are obvious in hindsight, but ideally, we would like to spot a new trend right at its beginning, buy, then spot its end, and sell. However, this ideal never happens, except by luck. The technical analyst always runs the risk of spotting the beginning of a trend too late and missing potential profit. The analyst who does not spot the ending of the trend holds the security past the price peak and fails to capture all of the profits that were possible. On the other hand, if the analyst thinks the trend has ended before it really has and sells the security prematurely, the analyst has then lost potential profits. Therefore, the technical analyst spends a lot of time and brainpower attempting to spot as early as possible when a trend is beginning and ending. This is the reason for studying charts, moving averages, oscillators, support and resistance, and all the other techniques we explore in this book.

The fact that market prices trend has been known for thousands of years. Specific records are available from the eighteenth century in Japan. Academics have disputed that markets tend to trend because if it were true, it would spoil their theoretical models. Recent academic work has shown that the old financial models have many problems when applied to the behavior of real markets. In Chapter 4, "The Technical Analysis Controversy," we discuss some of the new academic findings about how market prices behave and some of the evidence against the old finance theories. Academics and others traditionally have scorned technical analysis as if it were a cult; as it turns out, however, the almost religious belief in the Efficient Markets Hypothesis has become a cult itself, with adherents unwilling to accept the enormous amount of evidence against it. In fact, technical analysis is very old, developed through practical experience with the trading markets, and has resulted in some sizable fortunes for those following it.

How Does the Technical Analyst Make Money?

Several requirements are needed to convert pure technical analysis into money. The first and most important, of course, is to determine when a trend is beginning or ending. The money is made by "jumping" on the trend as early as possible. Theoretically, this sounds simple, but profiting consistently is not so easy.

The indicators and measurements that technical analysts use to determine the trend are not crystal balls that perfectly predict the future. Under certain market conditions, these tools might not work. Also, a trend can suddenly change direction without warning. Thus, it is imperative that the technical investor be aware of risks and protect against such occurrences causing losses.

From a strategic standpoint, then, the technical investor must decide two things: First, the investor or trader must choose when to enter a position, and second, he or she must choose when to exit a position. Choosing when to exit a position is composed of two decisions. The investor must choose when to exit the position to capture a profit when price moves in the expected direction. The investor must also choose when to exit the position at a loss when price moves in the opposite direction from what was expected. The wise investor is aware of the risk that the trend might differ from what he or she expected. Making the decision of what price level to sell and cut losses before even entering into a position is a way in which the investor protects against large losses.

One of the great advantages in technical analysis, because it studies prices, is that a price point can be established at which the investor knows that something is wrong either with the analysis or the financial asset's price behavior. Risk of loss can therefore be determined and quantified right at the beginning of the investment. This ability is not available to other methods of investment. Finally, because actual risk can be determined, money management principles can be applied that will lessen the chance of loss and the risk of what is called "ruin."

In sum, the basic ways to make money using technical methods are

- "The trend is your friend"—Play the trend.
- Don't lose—Control capital risk of loss.
- Manage your money—Avoid ruin.

Technical analysis is used to determine the trend, when it is changing, when it has changed, when to enter a position, when to exit a position, and when the analysis is wrong and the position must be closed. It's as simple as that.

WHAT IS A TREND?

What exactly is this **trend** that the investor wants to ride to make money? A rising trend, or **uptrend**, occurs when prices reach higher peaks and higher troughs. An uptrend looks something like Chart A in Figure 2.1. A declining trend, or **downtrend**, is the opposite—when prices reach lower troughs and lower peaks. Chart B in Figure 2.1 shows this downward trend in price. A **sideways** or **flat trend** occurs when prices trade in a range without significant underlying upward or downward movement. Chart C in Figure 2.1 is an example of a sideways trend; prices move up and down but on average remain at the same level.

Figure 2.1 shows a theoretical example of an uptrend, downtrend, and sideways trend. But, defining a trend in the price of real-world securities is not quite that simple. Price movement does not follow a continuous, uninterrupted line. Small countertrend movements within a trend can make the true trend difficult to identify at times. Also, remember that there are trends of differing lengths. Shorter-term trends are parts of longer-term trends.

From a technical analyst's perspective, a trend is a directional movement of prices that remains in effect long enough to be identified and still be playable. Anything less makes technical analysis useless. If a trend is not identified until it is over, we cannot make money from it. If it is unrecognizable until too late, we cannot make money from it. In retrospect, looking at a graph of prices, for example, many trends can be identified of varying length and magnitude, but such observations are observations of history only. A trend must be recognized early and be long enough for the technician to profit.

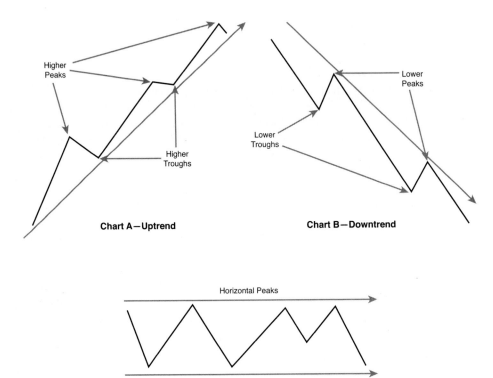

Chart A—Uptrend   Chart B—Downtrend

Chart C—Sideways Trend

FIGURE 2.1   The trend

HOW ARE TRENDS IDENTIFIED?

There are a number of ways to identify trends. One way to determine a trend in a data set is to run
a linear least-squares regression. This statistical process will provide information about the trend
in security prices. Unfortunately, this particular statistical technique is not of much use to the
technical analyst for trend analysis. The regression method is dependent on a sizable amount of
past price data for accurate results. By the time enough historical price data is accumulated, the

trend is likely beginning to change direction. Despite the tendency for trends to be persistent enough to profit from, they never last forever.

BOX 2.1 LINEAR LEAST-SQUARES REGRESSION

Most spreadsheet software includes a formula for calculating a linear regression line. It uses two sets of related variables and calculates the "best fit" between the data and an imaginary straight (linear) line drawn through the data. In standard price analysis, the two variable data sets are time and price—day d1 and price X1, day d2 and price X2, and so forth. By fitting a line that best describes the data series, we can determine a number of things. First, we can measure the amount by which the actual data varies from the line and, thus, the reliability of the line. Second, we can measure the slope of the line to determine the rate of change in prices over time, and third, we can determine when the line began. The line represents the trend in prices over the period of time studied. It has many useful properties that we will look at later, but for now, all we need to know is that the line defines the trend over the period studied. Appendix A, "Basic Statistics," provides more detailed information about least squares regression.

Many analysts use moving averages to smooth out the shorter and smaller trends within the trend of interest and identify the longer trends. Chapter 13, "Breakouts, Stops, and Retracements," discusses the use of moving averages.

Another method of identifying trends is to look at a graph of prices for extreme points, tops, and bottoms, separated by reasonable time periods, and to draw lines between these extreme points (see Figure 2.2). These lines are called **trend lines.** This traditional method is an outgrowth of the time before computer graphic software when trend lines were hand drawn. It still works, however. Using this method to define trends, you must define reversal points. Chapter 12, "Trends—The Basics," covers several methods of determining reversal points, but most such points are obvious on a graph of prices. *By drawing lines between them, top to top and bottom to bottom, we get a "feeling" of price direction and limits.* We also get a "feeling" of slope, or the rate of change in prices. Trend lines can define limits to price action, which, if broken, can warn that the trend might be changing.

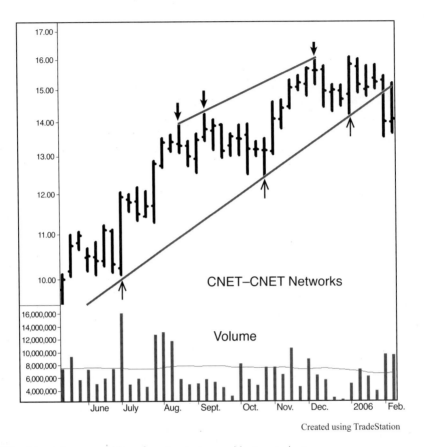

Created using TradeStation

FIGURE 2.2   Hand-drawn trend lines from top to top and bottom to bottom

TRENDS DEVELOP FROM SUPPLY AND DEMAND

As in all markets, whether used cars, grapefruit, real estate, or industrial products, the economic principle of interaction between supply and demand determines prices in trading markets. Each buyer (demand) bids for a certain quantity at a certain price, and each seller (supply) offers or "asks" for a certain quantity at a certain price. When the buyer and seller agree and transact, they establish a price for that instant in time. The reasons for buying and selling can be complex—perhaps the seller needs the money, perhaps the seller has learned of unfavorable information, perhaps the buyer heard a rumor in the golf club locker room—whatever the reason, the price is established when all of this information is collected, digested, and acted upon through the bid and offer.

Price, therefore, is the end result of all those inexact factors, and it is the result of the supply and demand at that instant in time. When prices change, the change is due to a change in demand and/or supply. The seller might be more anxious; the buyer might have more money to invest—whatever the reason, the price will change and reflect this change in supply or demand. The technical analyst, therefore, watches price and price change and does not particularly worry about the reasons, largely because they are indeterminable.

Remember that many players for many reasons determine supply and demand. In the trading markets, supply and demand may come from long-term investors accumulating or distributing a large position or from a small, short-term trader trying to scalp a few points. The number of players and the number of different reasons for their participation in supply and demand is close to infinite. Thus, the technical analyst believes it is futile to analyze the components of supply and demand except through the prices it creates. Where economic information, company information, and other information affecting prices is often vague, late, or misplaced, prices are readily available, are extremely accurate, have historic records, and are specific. What better basis is there for study than this important variable? Furthermore, when one invests or trades, the price is what determines profit or loss, not corporate earnings nor Federal Reserve policy. The bottom line, to the technical analyst, is that price is what determines success and, fortunately, for whatever reasons, prices tend to trend.

WHAT TRENDS ARE THERE?

The number of trend lengths is unlimited. Investors and traders need to determine which length they are most interested in, but the methods of determining when a trend begins and ends are the same regardless of length. This ability for trends to act similarly over different periods is called the "fractal" nature of trends. Fractal patterns or trends exist in nature along shorelines, in snowflakes, and elsewhere. For example, a snowflake is always six-sided, having six branches, if you will. Each branch has a particular, unique pattern made of smaller branches. Using a microscope to look closely at the snowflake, we see that the smaller branches off each larger branch have the same form as the larger branch. This same shape carries to even smaller and smaller branches, each of which has the same pattern as the next larger. This is the fractal nature of snowflakes. The branches, regardless of size, maintain the same pattern. Figure 2.3 shows a computer-generated fractal with each subangle an exact replica of the next larger angle.

The trading markets are similar in that any period we look at—long, medium, or very short—produces trends with the same characteristics and patterns as each other. Thus, for analysis purposes, the length of the trend is irrelevant because the technical principles are applicable to all of them. The trend length of interest is determined solely by the time horizon of the investor or trader.

This is not to say that different trend lengths should be ignored. Because shorter trends make up longer trends, any analysis of a trend of interest must include analysis of the longer and shorter trends around it. For example, the trader interested in ten-week trends should also analyze trends longer than ten weeks because a longer trend will affect the shorter trend. Likewise, a trend shorter than ten weeks should be analyzed because it will often give early signals of a change in direction in the larger, ten-week trend. Thus, whatever trend the trader or investor selects as the trend of interest, the trends of the next longer and next shorter periods should also be analyzed.

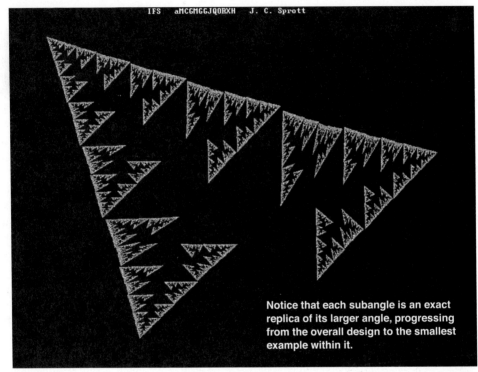

FIGURE 2.3   Example of computer-generated fractal

For identification purposes, technical analysts have divided trends into several broad, arbitrary categories. These are the primary trend (measured in months or years), the secondary or intermediate trend (measured in weeks or months), the short-term trend (measured in days), and the intraday trend (measured in minutes or hours). Except for the intraday trend, Charles H. Dow, founder of the Dow Jones Company and the *Wall Street Journal,* first advanced this division in the nineteenth century. Charles Dow also was one of the first to identify technical means of determining when the primary trend had reversed direction. Because of his major contributions to the field, Dow is known as the "Father" of technical analysis. We will look more closely at Dow's contributions in Chapter 3, "History of Technical Analysis," as we study the history of technical analysis, and in Chapter 6, "Dow Theory."

WHAT OTHER ASSUMPTIONS DO TECHNICAL ANALYSTS MAKE?

That markets trend is the basic principle underlying the theory of technical analysis. Of course, it is the price of the securities that are being monitored that form the trend. Supporting this notion of trending prices, technical analysts have made several other assumptions that we cover briefly.

First, technical analysts assume that price is determined by the interaction of supply and demand. As basic economic theory teaches, when demand increases, price goes up, and when demand decreases, price goes down. One of the factors that determine supply and demand is buyer and seller expectations. (You do not buy a stock unless you expect it to rise in price.) Expectations result from human decisions, and decisions are based on information (perceived, accurate, or otherwise), emotions (greed, fear, and hope), and cognitive limitations such as behavioral biases, emotions and feelings that originate from the chemistry and electrical connections within our brains. A new field of study called "neurofinance," an interdisciplinary study of the application of neuroscience to investment activity, is finding remarkable connections between how our brain functions and how we invest.

Second, technical analysts assume that price discounts everything. Price discounts all information, related to the security or otherwise, as well the interpretation of expectations derived from that information. This concept was first articulated by Charles H. Dow, later reemphasized by William Peter Hamilton in his *Wall Street Journal* editorials, and succinctly described by Robert Rhea (1932), a prominent Dow Theorist, when writing about stock market averages:

> The Averages discount everything: The fluctuations of the daily closing prices of the Dow-Jones rail and industrial averages afford a composition index of all the hopes, disappointments, and knowledge of everyone who knows anything of financial matters, and for that reason the effects of coming events (excluding acts of God) are always properly anticipated in their movement. The averages quickly appraise such calamities as fires and earthquakes.

This sounds a little like Eugene Fama's (1970) famous statement related to the Efficient Markets Hypothesis (EMH) that "prices fully reflect all available information." However, Fama was referring more to information on the specific security and was presuming that all interpretation of that information was immediately and rationally interpreted. Although technical assumptions include the price discount assumption of EMH adherents, they go far beyond that simplicity. They include not only information, both about the security and about all other outside factors that might influence that security price, but also the interpretation of that information, which might or might not be rational or directly related, and the expectations derived from that information. Interpretation, according to technical analysis, is subject to "irrational exuberance" and will "drive men to excess" as well as to a "corresponding depression" (Hamilton, 1922).

BOX 2.2   PROFESSOR ANDREW LO'S ADAPTIVE MARKETS HYPOTHESIS

In an attempt to reconcile the existing but different finance ideas of efficient markets and behavioral finance, Dr. Lo has proposed the "Adaptive Markets Hypothesis" (2005). Lo proposes a framework based upon the principles of evolution, competition, adaptation, and natural selection in which markets and players change over time. The risk-reward relationship is not constant, but changes with market conditions. Thus, investors do not seek to optimize their returns because to do so is too costly. Decisions instead are made based on experience and "best guesses," leaving them subject to interpretative and behavioral bias—namely emotions. As long as the markets are stable, these methods provide satisfactory results. When the economic environment changes, however, and the methods fail, the investors then have to adapt to survive. The size and strength of the different interacting player groups can cause this environmental change. An example is when the bondholders, during the 1998 Russian government debt default, sought liquidity and upset the investors in previously stable interest rate spreads, leaving them with failing and illiquid positions. Those who could rapidly adapt survived. Those who could not, failed. In sum, investment strategies change and evolve; innovation is the secret of survival; and survival is the goal rather than maximizing the utility of risk versus return.

Third, an important corollary to the notion that markets trend is the technical analyst's belief that prices are nonrandom. As we address further in Chapter 4, if prices are nonrandom, past prices potentially can be used to predict future price trends. Technical analysts reject the notion that stock prices are random.

Fourth, technical analysis assumes that history, in principle, will repeat itself (or as Mark Twain said, "History rhymes: It does not repeat"), and that humans will behave similarly to how they have in the past in similar circumstances. This similar behavior tends to form into patterns that have predictable results. These patterns are almost never identical and are, thus, subject to interpretation, with all its own bias problems, by the technical analyst. This is the most controversial aspect of technical analysis, as well as its most long-standing, and it is only recently being investigated with sophisticated statistical methods (see Chapter 4).

Fifth, technical analysts also believe that, like trend lines, these patterns are fractal (see Figure 2.4). Each investor or trader has a specific time frame in which he or she operates. Interestingly, regardless of period, patterns occur with very similar, though not identical, shapes and characteristics. Thus, an analyst who is watching five-minute bar charts will observe the same patterns that an analyst watching monthly bar charts will see. These patterns suggest that the behavior that produces them is dependent also on the participants' period of interest. A pattern in a five-minute bar chart, for example, is the result of other traders with a five-minute bar chart time horizon. Monthly investors would have very little effect on the five-minute bar chart, as five-minute traders would have almost no effect on the monthly bar chart. Thus, each group of participants, as defined by their investment horizon, has its own world of patterns that might or might not affect each other but will be similar in shape. Pattern analysis is, therefore, universal and independent of time.

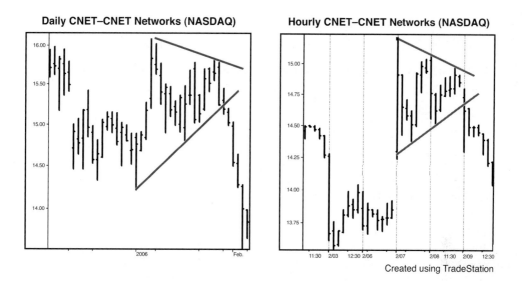

Notice that the patterns are almost identical, yet they occur over different time intervals, one with
daily bars and the other with hourly bars. The development of the pattern, the shape of the pattern,
and the final breakdown are very similar. These patterns are said to be "fractal" in that they occur
irrespective of time.

FIGURE 2.4 Daily and hourly charts in the same stock over different periods

Sixth, technical analysis is also based on the notion that emotions are affected by earlier
emotions through emotional feedback. If I buy a stock today and its price rises, I am happy and
tell others to buy the stock, or others see its price rising and also buy it, thus causing the price to
rise farther. Action in the markets, therefore, is not independent but is related instead to how the
market itself is behaving. Excessive feedback can cause "bubbles" when price behavior rises far
out of proportion to value and can cause panics when price behavior declines sharply. Technical
analysis presumes that prices will expand beyond equilibrium for emotional reasons and eventually will revert to the mean and then expand beyond the mean in the opposite direction, constantly oscillating back and forth with excessive investor sentiment.

CONCLUSION

The focus of this chapter has been on the importance of understanding price trends to the practice of technical analysis. We have introduced some of the basic assumptions and beliefs of technical analysts. As we go through the next few chapters, we address each of these assumptions in

more detail. Some of the basic beliefs that technical analysis is built on and that we build upon throughout this book are as follows:

- The interaction of supply and demand determine price.
- Supply and demand are affected by investors' emotions and biases particularly fear and greed.
- Price discounts everything.
- Prices trend.
- Recognizable patterns form within trends.
- Patterns are fractal.

REVIEW QUESTIONS

1. Explain why the notion that prices trend is central to the practice of technical analysis.
2. The earlier an uptrend can be spotted, the more money an investor can make by "riding the trend." Explain why recognizing a trend too late reduces potential profits for the investor.
3. The sooner an investor recognizes that a trend has changed, the more profitable the investor's trading will be. Explain why early recognition of trend reversals influences the investor's profitability.
4. Newton's first law of motion is inertia—an object in motion will remain in motion in the same direction unless acted upon by an unbalanced force. How does this physics principle serve as an analogy for the notion of trends in technical analysis?
5. Define primary, secondary, short-term, and intraday trends.
6. Gather monthly closing prices for the Dow Jones Industrial Average (DJIA) from 1965 until the present. One publicly available source for this data can be found electronically at http://finance.yahoo.com using the ticker symbol ^DJI. Under "quotes," choose the "historical prices" option. At this point, you will be able to choose a monthly data option and download the data into a spreadsheet.
    a. Graph the monthly data for the DJIA for the 1965 through 1980 time period. Was the market in an uptrend, downtrend, or sideways trend during that time? Explain your answer.
    b. Graph the monthly data for the DJIA for the 1980 through 1990 time period. Was the market in an uptrend, downtrend, or sideways trend during that time? Explain your answer.
    c. Graph the monthly data for the DJIA for the 1990 through 2000 time period. Was the market in an uptrend, downtrend, or sideways trend during that time? Explain your answer.

    d. Graph the monthly data for the DJIA from 2000 until the present. Has the market been in an uptrend, downtrend, or sideways trend? Explain your answer.

    e. Comparing the four charts that you have generated, what conclusions do you draw about historical market trends?

7. Choose a one-year period during each of the 1965–1980, 1980–1990, 1990–2000, and 2000–present periods. Download daily DJIA closes from the Yahoo! Finance Web site for each of these four one-year periods. Graph the daily data for each of these four periods. What types of trends do you see in these daily data graphs? Comparing these daily graphs with the monthly graphs during the same time periods, what similarities and what differences do you find?

HISTORY OF TECHNICAL ANALYSIS

CHAPTER OBJECTIVES

In this chapter, you will gain knowledge about

- The history of financial markets and exchanges
- The creation of market indices by Charles Dow
- The development of technical analysis in the United States over the past century
- The impact that academic theory and fundamental stock market analysis have had on the development and use of technical analysis
- The impact that data availability and computer power have had on the development of technical analysis

EARLY FINANCIAL MARKETS AND EXCHANGES

Though technical analysis is thought to be an ancient method of analyzing markets and prices, its history has been poorly recorded. We do not have recorded evidence of technical analysis being used in ancient times, but it is conceivable that technical analysis, in some form, was used in the distant past in freely traded markets.

Markets in one form or another have existed for centuries. For instance, we know that notes and checks between traders and bankers existed in Babylon by 2000 BC (Braudel, 1981). Currency exchange, commodities, and participations in mercantile voyages were traded in Ostia, the seaport of Rome, in the second century AD (Braudel, 1982). In the Middle Ages, wheat, bean, oat, and barley prices were available from 1160 on in Angevin, England (Farmer, 1956); and a large grain market existed in Toulouse as early as 1203 (Braudel, 1982). Publicly available evidence suggests that as early as the twelfth century, markets existed in most towns and cities and were linked in a network of arbitrage (Braudel, 1982).

Exchanges were developed later where more complicated negotiable instruments, such as state loan stocks, were invented, accepted, and traded. The earliest exchanges appeared in the fourteenth century, mostly in the Mediterranean cities of Pisa, Venice, Florence, Genoa, Valencia, and Barcelona. In fact, the *Lonja,* the first building constructed as an exchange, was built in 1393 in Barcelona (Carriere, 1973). The Lonja has been described as

> ...a whole squadron of brokers [could be seen] moving in and out of its pillars, and the people standing in little groups were *corridors d'orella,* the "brokers by ear" whose job was to listen, report, and put interested parties in touch. (Carriere, 1973)

The statutes of Verona confirm the existence of the settlement or forward market (*mercato a termine*), and a jurist named Bartolomo de Bosco is recorded as protesting against a sale of forward *loca* in Genoa in 1428 (Braudel, 1981). As early as the fifteenth century, *Kuxen* shares in German mines were quoted at the Liepzig fairs (Maschke) and stocks traded in Hanseatic towns (Sprandel, 1971). A trading market for municipal stocks known as *renes sur L'Hotel* existed in France as early as 1522 (Schnapper, 1957).

Can we assume that traders would record prices in these sophisticated markets and would attempt to derive ways to profit from those recordings? It seems very likely. Even if prices were not recorded using pencil and paper, traders mentally remembering past prices and using these memories to predict future price movements would be using a form of technical analysis.

By 1585, public quotes of over 339 items were reported as traded on the streets and in the coffee houses in Amsterdam (Boxer, 1965). Commodities had been traded there as early as 1530 (Stringham, 2003). The greatest of the early exchanges, the Amsterdam Exchange, called "The Beurs" or "Bourse," was founded in 1608. The building housing the exchange was built in 1611 and was modeled after the Antwerp Bourse of 1531 (Munro, 2005). This exchange is famous for the "Tulip Bulb Mania" of 1621. By 1722, the Amsterdam Exchange provided trading space for over 4,500 traders every day between noon and two o'clock (Ricard, 1722). Dealers, brokers, and the public traded and speculated on short sales, forwards, commodities, currencies, shares of ventures, and maritime insurance, as well as other financial instruments, such as notes, bonds, loans, and stocks. They traded grain, herring, spices, whale oil, and, of course, tulips (Kellenbenz, 1957, 1996). The principal stock traded was in the Dutch East India Company. (See Figure 3.1, which is an example of one of the oldest stock shares.) It seems likely that prices for these items were also recorded and analyzed.

In the eighteenth century, as the Dutch empire declined, the London and Paris Exchanges gradually surpassed the Amsterdam Exchange in activity and offerings. In other parts of the world, specifically in Japan, cash-only commodity markets in rice and silver were developing, usually at the docks of major seacoast cities. It is in these markets we first read about a wealthy trader who used technical analysis and trading discipline to amass a fortune.

His name was Sokyo Honma. Born in 1716 as Kosaku Kato in Sakata, Yamagata Prefecture, during the Tokugawa period, he was adopted by the Honma family and took their name. A coastal city, Sakata was a distribution center for rice. Honma became very wealthy by trading rice and was known throughout Osaka, Kyoto, and Tokyo. He was promoted to Samurai (not bad for a technical trader) and died in Tokyo at the age of 87.

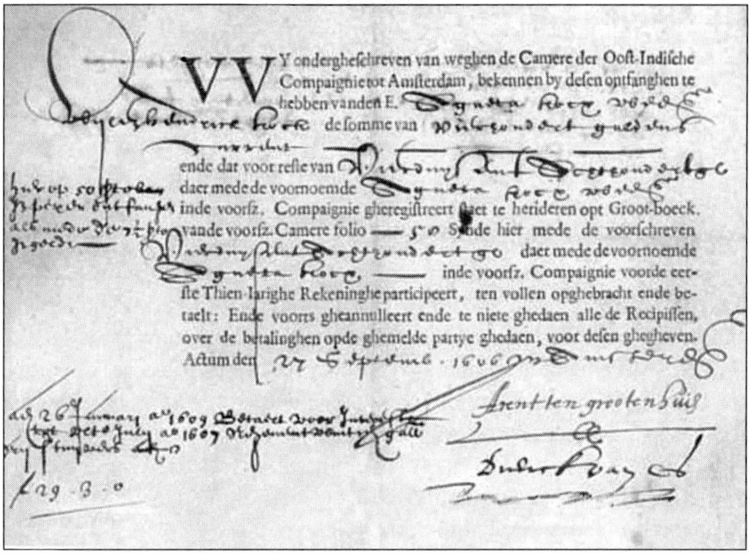

WY ondergheschreven van weghen de Camere der Oost-Indische Compaignie tot Amsterdam, bekennen by desen ontfanghen te hebben vanden E.
de somme van
ende dat voor reste van
daer mede de voornoemde
inde voorsz. Compaignie gheregistreert staet te herideren opt Groot-boeck vande voorsz. Camere folio
daer mede de voornoemde
inde voorsz. Compaignie voorde eerste Thien-Jarighe Rekeninghe participeert, ten vollen opghebracht ende betaelt: Ende voorts gheannulleert ende te niete ghedaen alle de Recipissen, over de betalinghen opde ghemelde partye ghedaen, voor desen ghegheven.
Actum den

Source: www.oldest-share.com

Dutch Vereinigte Oostindische Compaignie (VOC) share certificate # 6, down-payment on a share; issued by the Camere Amsterdam 27th September 1606. Original signatures: Arent ten Grotenhuys and Dirck van Os, company founder van Verre and after 1602 Directors of VOC Kammer Amsterdam. Source: Private collection

FIGURE 3.1 Oldest stock certificate—Dutch United East India Company (1606)

Honma's rules are recorded as the "Sakata constitution." These rules include methods of analyzing one day's price record to predict the next day's price, three days of rice prices to predict the fourth day's price, and rate of change analysis (Shimizu, 1986). None of this information was recorded on charts—they came later in Japan. Honma's rules might also be considered "trading rules" rather than "technical rules" because they had much to do with how to limit loss and when to step away from markets. Nevertheless, his methods were based on prices and, thus, largely technical, were successful, and, most important, were recorded.

Because Japan is the first place in which recorded technical rules have been found, many historians have suggested that technical analysis began in the rice markets in Japan. However, it seems inconceivable that technical analysis was not used in the more sophisticated and earlier markets and exchanges in Medieval Europe. Indeed, even in Japan, it is thought that charts were introduced first in the silver market around 1870 by an "English man" (Shimizu, 1986). Thus, technical analysis has a poorly recorded history but by inference is a very old method of analyzing trading markets and prices.

MODERN TECHNICAL ANALYSIS

Although the practice of technical analysis in some forms likely dates back many centuries, Charles Dow (1851–1902) was the first to reintroduce and comment on it in recent times. He is considered the father of "modern" technical analysis. Dow's introduction of stock indexes to measure the performance of the stock market allowed for a major advance in the sophistication of stock market participants.

Dow was a lifelong newspaper journalist. His specialization in covering financial news began with a mining story he wrote when working for the *Providence Journal* (Rhode Island) in 1879. In 1880, Dow relocated to New York, where he continued covering the mining industry. In 1882, Dow joined with Edward Jones and Charles Bergstresser to form Dow, Jones & Company. The company offices were located behind a soda shop that was located next door to the entrance of the New York Stock Exchange. The company wrote handwritten news bulletins and distributed them by messenger to customers in the Wall Street vicinity.

On July 3, 1884, Dow published his first version of a stock index in the company's "Customer's Afternoon Newsletter." Dow calculated this price-weighted average simply by summing the prices of the stocks in the index and dividing by the number of stocks. This index included a total of 11 stocks—9 railroads and 2 industrials.

Table 3.1 shows the companies that Dow included in this first index. Although this might seem to be an odd combination by today's standards, the index was consistent with the important role the railway companies played in the economy of the 1880s. In February 1885, Dow began publishing a daily index of actively traded, highly capitalized stocks. This index contained 12 railways and 2 industrial stocks. By January 1886, Dow replaced the 14-stock index with a 12-stock index, containing 10 railroads and 2 industrials. By May 1896, Dow recognized the increasing role the emerging industrial sector was playing in the U.S. economy and altered his index so that it consisted entirely of industrial stocks. The first version of the Dow Jones Industrial Average (DJIA) appeared in the *Wall Street Journal* on May 26, 1896, and included the 12 stocks listed in Table 3.2. Although all of these companies survive in some form today, only General Electric remains a component of the DJIA.

Dow's initial index of rail stocks was renamed the Railroad Average. The Railroad Average developed into the modern-day Dow Transportation Average on January 2, 1970, when it included nonrailroad stocks such as airlines and truckers. As of today, of the 20 stocks in the Transportation Average, only four are railroad stocks—Burlington Northern Santa Fe Corp., CSX Corp., Norfolk Southern Corp., and Union Pacific

TABLE 3.1   *"Customer's Afternoon Newsletter"* (Forerunner to the *Wall Street Journal*)

July 3, 1884
List of "Representative" Stocks

Chicago & North Western
D. L. & W.
Lake Shore
New York Central
St. Paul
Northern Pacific pfd.
Union Pacific
Missouri Pacific
Louisville & Nashville
Pacific Mail
Western Union

TABLE 3.2   Wall Street Journal

May 26, 1896
Original Dow Jones Industrial Average

American Cotton Oil
American Sugar
American Tobacco
Chicago Gas
Distilling & Cattle Feeding
General Electric
Laclede Gas
National Lead
North American
Tennessee Coal & Iron
U. S. Leather pfd.
U. S. Rubber

Corp. Indeed, reflecting the changes in transportation since its composition, the Transportation Average now includes two shipping companies, five airlines, three trucking companies, two leasing companies, and four air delivery and freight services.

In 1916, 14 years after Charles Dow's death, the DJIA expanded to 20 stocks. It was not until 1928 that the index further expanded to 30 stocks. Though the average has been updated to reflect the changing composition of trading-market conditions, market capitalization, and industrial composition, the practice of including 30 stocks continues today.

Dow's original intent was to use these averages as predictors of the economy, but his analysis took a life of its own, and his theories became known as the "Dow Theory." (See Chapter 6, "Dow Theory.") They are the foundation for modern technical analysis. The principles that Dow established are still valid today, albeit in a different form.

However, Dow's contribution to the field of technical analysis goes beyond the creation of indexes. The Dow Jones Company was the first in the United States to publicly report stock prices. Private subscription letters with stock prices had existed earlier but were available only to the few who paid directly for them. The reporting of prices on a consistent basis provided the "meat" for technical analysis. Motivation came from the many wide swings in prices both from legitimate news and information as well as from manipulation. By watching prices, investors and traders hoped to gather information on who was buying and selling shares and, thus, what the prospects for future prices might be. *Technical analysis is a means for the uninformed to become informed.*

With recording of prices and the calculation of averages, analysts began to see that prices often traded with certain repetitive patterns. They also noticed that market dynamics are complicated and influenced by people and their own way of looking at investments, their own time horizons, their own information, and their own emotions. Patterns in market averages, specifically the "line" and the "double" top or bottom, were first mentioned by Charles Dow and his subsequent followers, William Peter Hamilton, S. A. Nelson, and Robert Rhea, in the 1920s. Richard D. Wyckoff offered a successful correspondence course in trading and investing, principally using technical analysis theories, in 1931. Earlier, in the 1920s, he published a technical newsletter that reached over 200,000 subscribers.

Also in the 1920s and 1930s, classic indicators such as the advance-decline line (A/D line) were created. Colonel Leonard P. Ayers (1944) developed an early measure of business confidence and is considered the originator of the A/D line. Ayers ran a company called Standard Statistics. In 1941, Standard Statistics merged with a company headed by Henry Poor; this new entity became Standard and Poor's.

Richard W. Schabacker, the financial editor of *Forbes* magazine and of the *New York Times,* began to recognize individual stock patterns and observed many common characteristics between different issues. He is probably the first person to use the words "triangle," "pennant," and "head-and-shoulders" to describe chart formations we consider in future chapters. Schabacker authored *Stock Market Theory and Practice* (1930), *Technical Analysis and Market Profits* (1932), and *Stock Market Profits* (1934). The commodity markets, which had long depended on price action for their speculative activity, also evolved their share of special technical theories such as those by William Delbert Gann. This was the age of speculation, inside information, and manipulation with little regulation. Those outside the information loop were at a disadvantage. Technical analysis made the difference by using price action as a predictive tool.

During the late 1930s and much of the 1940s, little was written about stock market analysis. If we consider the business and economic climate at that time, it is not surprising that there is a void in the literature. After the Securities Act of 1933 and the Securities Exchange Act of 1934, Graham and Dodd published one of the few pieces of security analysis of the period. In their book, *Security Analysis* (1934), Graham and Dodd established the fundamental analysis side of investment analysis, which is concerned with economic conditions and company value. Although this book provides the groundwork for the development of fundamental analysis, a closer reading of it reveals that Graham and Dodd did not believe that fundamental analysis alone determined stock prices. For example, consider the following passage from their book:

> The influence of what we call analytical factors over the market price is both **partial** and **indirect**—partial, because it frequently competes with purely speculative factors which influence the price in the opposite direction; and indirect, because it acts through the intermediary of people's sentiments and decisions. In other words, the market is not a weighing machine, on which the value of each issue is recorded by an exact and impersonal mechanism, in accordance with its specific qualities. Rather we should say that the market is a voting machine, whereon countless individuals register choices which are the product of and partly of emotion. (p. 28)

It was not until 1948 that Robert Edwards (son-in-law to Schabacker) and John Magee (see Figure 3.2) published the first edition of *Technical Analysis of Stock Trends.* Edwards and Magee demonstrated the technical patterns observed in hundreds of stocks. Their interpretations are still used to this day, and technicians know their book as the "bible of technical analysis." In fact, the ninth edition of the book was published in 2009.

At first, prices were recorded and then plotted by hand. Indeed, even today, strict followers of point-and-figure technique plot their charts by hand, as do many specialists and traders who want to get the "feel" of the stocks they are trading. Chart services published books of hand-plotted charts for those who could not afford the time to check for accuracy and plot their own charts.

As technical analysts became increasingly comfortable with more complex mathematical tools, they focused on more than just the chart patterns of their predecessors. Analysts began using more advanced mathematics to describe price action. The most prominent technical analyst of the 1950s was Joseph Granville, who worked for E. F. Hutton and published a short article on the Barron's Confidence Index in *Barron's* in 1959. After this article, Granville wrote two books in which he covered on-balance volume, the 200-day moving average, and other tools and concepts that are still popular today. Some of the other great technicians during this time were Kenneth Ward, Edmund Tabell, E. S. C. Coppock, D. G. Worden, Garfield Drew, and George Lindsay.

Edwards   Magee

Source: W.H.C. Bassetti, adjunct professor Finance and Economics, Golden Gate University, San Francisco; editor John Magee Investment Series; editor and coauthor, *Edwards and Magee's Technical Analysis of Stock Trends,* ninth edition

FIGURE 3.2 Edwards and Magee

In the 1960s, the concept of rate of change (ROC), or momentum, became one of the technician's tools. By the late 1970s, computer technology was available to draw charts more accurately and with greater speed. In addition, ratios, oscillators, and other more arcane calculations could be moved from the adding machine to the computer for quicker calculation and more thorough testing. The computer changed the face of technical analysis forever.

One of the most popular technical tools developed in the 1970s was the relative strength index (RSI), created by J. Welles Wilder, Jr. (see Figure 3.3). One of the most inventive technicians, Wilder is also credited with the Directional Movement concept, the Parabolic System, and Average True Range, all still used today. Another technician and commodity trader, Richard Donchian, promoted the use of the 10-day and 20-day moving averages crossovers as buy and sell signals, as well as the "4-week" rule, whereby a price break above or below the four-week high or low indicated the initial stage of a new trend. Focusing on the options market, technician Martin Zweig examined the use of the put-call ratio. A variety of moving average indicators was developed, such as moving-average envelopes, moving-average crossover, and the Moving-Average Convergence/Divergence (MACD) oscillator, by technicians like Fred Hitschler and Gerald Appel. We mention many other inventive technical analysts in later chapters when we cover their specialties.

Just as the mathematical sophistication and computer technology was allowing for great advances in the development of technical analysis, technical analysis came under fire by the academic community. Academics argued that technical analysis was impossible because prices were randomly distributed and had no history embedded in them that could predict future prices. At the same time, proponents of the Efficient Markets Hypothesis argued that markets were efficient and that news, information, and so on was immediately and rationally discounted in the markets. Because no means of price study could anticipate such news, technical analysis was a futile study. Gradually, professional money managers, most of whom were raised and trained at business schools in this antitechnical school of thinking, closed their technical departments, and technical analysis went into a decline.

Source: J. Welles Wilder, Jr.

FIGURE 3.3   J. Welles Wilder, Jr.

However, while the academic community was discounting the use of technical analysis, the technical analyst's access to more powerful computers and better data was rapidly increasing. The fast computers and accessibility to a large data set of clean post-World War II data allowed analysts to attempt to optimize their trading strategies, taking past price data and performing numerous calculations to determine which of a number of strategies would have yielded the best profits. These optimized results could be used to develop future trading strategies, assuming that the markets would behave similarly in the future.

Ironically, although the dawning of the computer age brought new, increasingly sophisticated technical tools to the study of technical analysis, the development of these tools coincided with the introduction of an ancient technical tool to the U.S. financial markets. As we discussed earlier, Japanese candlestick charts dated back to the mid-1700s; however, the western financial markets had not had access to the Japanese writings and technical tools. Steve Nison introduced candlestick charts into U.S. technical analysis in the late 1980s. Since then, numerous other chart types like Kagi, Kase, Renko, and Ichimoku Kinko have been added to the list of visual analysis methods.

CURRENT ADVANCES IN TECHNICAL ANALYSIS

Interest in technical analysis is resurging. The Efficient Markets Hypothesis has been found to have a number of serious flaws, and stock price motion is being shown to be nonrandom. This new knowledge has cast doubt on the objections raised earlier about technical analysis, and academics are gradually beginning to perform serious studies on technical theory and indicators. Behavioral Finance, a relatively new realm of study concerned with the psychology of market participants, has shown that investors do not necessarily act rationally, as is assumed in the Efficient Markets Hypothesis. They have found instances of predictable investor behavior and are beginning to explain some of the reasons for price patterns known by technical analysts over a hundred years.

During the equity market decline from 2000 to 2002 and from 2007 to 2009, many stocks declined severely before the damaging information causing their decline became public. In the earlier period, the names of Enron, WorldCom, Tyco, HealthSouth, Qwest, and others ring in the ears of those who suffered large losses by owning these stocks and by being fooled and lied to by their managements. Although this might not have been manipulation in the old style, it nevertheless again was the uninformed being duped by the informed. In the later period, the seriousness of the mortgage-debt implosion was kept from the public to prevent panic, yet the stocks affected by the crisis took terrible beatings. For example, Citigroup, a Dow Jones Industrial Average stock, declined from $57 to less than $1, and AIG, an institutional favorite, declined from over $1,400 to $8 during the same period.

Figure 3.4 shows a monthly stock chart for Tyco. Technical analysis, if properly applied, would have protected an investor from large losses in this stock because it would have warned that the price action of these stocks was not consistent with what management was saying to the fundamental analysts. On January 9, 2002, a Prudential Securities analyst was the first large Wall Street analyst to downgrade the stock from a buy to a hold (*New York Times*). Figure 3.4 shows the price of Tyco falling while fundamental analysts were still recommending that investors buy the stock and while insiders of the company, such as the CFO, were claiming, "The more you know about our accounting, the more comfortable you will be" (*Wall Street Journal*, February 14, 2002).

In addition, falling commissions and maximum speed of communication have made technical analysis extremely useful to those who can spend the time studying it. Analysts developed trading rules that trade portfolios without human intervention. Futures markets in stock averages, currencies, and other markets have expanded and become more efficient, making competition extremely keen. Stock market trades have become almost instantaneous, and with the advent of computerized markets, intermediaries, with their delay and cost, have largely been eliminated.

Computers are now so sophisticated that almost every possible technical calculation has been tried and tested. Market participants know, as they have long suspected, that no magic formula for riches exists. The reason is that people trading and investing in an imperfect, emotionally charged world determine prices. Because technical analysis deals only with price and some other incidental trading information, it has evolved into a study of more intangible information, concerned mostly with psychology and trading behavior. *Modern computer technology has demonstrated that prices are not necessarily random, but also that they are not perfectly predictable.* The reason, of course, is that people buy and sell items based not only on what they believe are reasonable expectations but also on emotion, specifically fear and greed, inherent and learned bias, overconfidence, perception, and prejudice. Emotion has always been a large component in technical analysis studies.

Today, technical analysis covers many different time horizons: long-term investing, short-term swing, and intraday trading. The indicators and methods utilized for these horizons often have their own characteristics. In addition to time horizons, different investing or trading instruments exist. Commodities, for example, have their own technical information and peculiarities, as do currencies and financial instruments such as bonds and notes. *The subject of technical analysis is complex.* Because knowledge of all possibilities is impossible, the individual must decide the period, methods, and instruments best suited to his or her personality, ability, knowledge, and time available. Although the basic principles of technical analysis that we investigate in this book are common to all areas of markets, investors must learn by reading, studying, and experiencing the peculiarities of the markets in which they want to profit.

Created using TradeStation

FIGURE 3.4 Example of fraudulent insiders (1996–2003)

When you enter the stock market [or any other market], you are going into a competitive field in which your evaluations and opinions will be matched against some of the sharpest and toughest minds in the business. You are in a highly specialized industry in which there are many different sectors, all of which are under the intense study by men (and women) whose economic survival depends on their best judgment. You will certainly be exposed to advice, suggestions, and offers of help from all sides. Unless you are able to develop some market philosophy of your own, you will not be able to tell the good from the bad, the sound from the unsound.

—John Magee (Edwards and Magee, 2009)

CHAPTER 4

THE TECHNICAL ANALYSIS CONTROVERSY

CHAPTER OBJECTIVES

After studying this chapter, you should have a good understanding of

- The basic principles of the Random Walk Hypothesis (RWH)
- The historical distribution of stock market returns
- The basic principles of the Efficient Markets Hypothesis (EMH)
- The pragmatic criticisms of technical analysis
- How technical analysts respond to critics

Though technical analysis is widely used by practitioners, its popularity is not mirrored in the academic community. The divergence in emphasis placed on technical analysis is highlighted by a study conducted by Flanegin and Rudd (2005) in which they surveyed both college professors and practitioners. The college professors were asked how much emphasis they placed on each of 20 topics in their investment courses. These professors ranked the subject areas on a 1 to 5 scale, with "1" indicating that they spent very little time in class on the material and "5" indicating that they spent considerable time on the topic. Given the same list of 20 topics, the practitioners were asked which subject matter they utilized within the realm of their jobs on a fairly consistent basis. These professionals also ranked the topics on a 1 to 5 scale, with "1" signifying the topic was not used and "5" indicating that the subject was used all the time. Table 4.1 provides a summary of their results. The practitioners report seldom using many of the topics most thoroughly covered by the professors. Likewise, the professors in the study report very little class time is spent teaching the subject material practitioners claim to use most often.

TABLE 4.1   Importance of Financial Topics as Reported by Professors and Practitioners*

Topic	Instructors' Mean	Practioners' Mean
Portfolio Theory	3.89	2.44
Discounted Cash Flows	3.87	2.95
CAPM/Beta	3.85	2.48
Required Rate of Return	3.85	2.41
Dividend Discount Model	3.77	1.73
Efficient Markets Hypothesis	3.54	1.85
Ratio Analysis	2.70	2.56
Arbitrage Pricing	2.40	2.21
Acct. Aspect of Earnings	2.34	2.95
Crowd Psychology	1.99	3.56
Charting	1.80	3.56
EIC Analysis	1.70	2.56
Trend Lines	1.70	4.39
Support/Resistance Levels	1.68	4.41
Trading Ranges	1.66	4.37
Relative Strength Index	1.65	3.54
Stochastic	1.63	3.51
Volume Tracking	1.54	3.78
Moving Average/Convergence	1.49	3.56
Overbought/Oversold	1.46	3.93

*Adapted from Flanegin and Rudd (2005)

This divergence is not surprising given the fact that the majority of academics opposes the use of technical analysis. In fact, a study by Robert Strong (1988) showed that over 60% of PhDs do not believe that technical analysis can be used as an effective tool to enhance investment performance. Because of the view of these academics, little emphasis has been placed on technical analysis in traditional finance curriculums in recent years, as shown in the Flanegin and Rudd survey results.

Because the academic community strongly resists the use of technical analysis, we address in this chapter some of the academic community's criticisms before moving on to the specific techniques and tools of technical analysis. The principal theoretical arguments against technical analysis are the Random Walk Hypothesis (RWH) and the Efficient Markets Hypothesis (EMH). Each hypothesis makes broad assumptions that in their purest state would eliminate the possibility for technical analysis, or fundamental analysis for that matter. Let us look at each of these hypotheses a little more closely.

DO MARKETS FOLLOW A RANDOM WALK?

Opponents of technical analysis claim that looking at past technical data, such as price and volume, to help predict the future is outlandish. In the popular book, *A Random Walk Down Wall Street,* Burton Malkiel refers to technical analysis as "sharing a pedestal with alchemy." Some of these opponents believe that no underlying patterns exist in stock prices. These individuals believe that prices move in a random fashion and have no "memory." This assumption would imply that technical analysis, which depends on prices predicting prices, has no foundation because all price motion is random.

A random walk occurs when future steps cannot be predicted by observing past steps. For example, flipping a coin produces a random walk. Suppose you flip a coin once and it lands on heads; observing that the coin landed on heads does not help you predict what the outcome will be the next time the coin is flipped. Each flip of the coin is an independent event, and the outcome of one flip of the coin has no impact on the outcome of any other flip. If the stock market follows a random walk, future stock prices cannot be predicted by observing past stock price movements.

The concept that stock price returns followed a random walk was first suggested by Louis Bachelier (see Box 4.1), a French mathematician, in his PhD thesis, "The Theory of Speculation" (1900, 1906, and 1913). He commented that "the mathematical expectation of the speculator is zero." In the 1937 *Econometrica* article, "Some A Posteriori Probabilities in Stock Market Action," Alfred Cowles and Herbert E. Jones (1937) also hypothesized that the stock market prices exhibited randomness. It was Paul Cootner's 1964 book, *The Random Character of Stock Market Prices,* that popularized the random walk theory and its application in the stock market. The following year, Eugene Fama's seminal article (1965), "The Behavior of Stock Market Prices," was published in the *Journal of Business,* giving additional credence to the random walk theory.

BOX 4.1 LOUIS BACHELIER

Louis Bachelier (1870–1946) was the first person to anticipate Brownian motion, random walk of financial prices, option pricing, and martingales long before Einstein, Wiener, and Black and Scholes. Receiving high marks from his advisor, the famous mathematician, Henri Poincare, Bachelier became a lecturer at the Sorbonne and at several other universities. In 1926, he was turned down for a professorship at Dijon because of a critical letter from another famous mathematician, Paul Levy, who was unfamiliar with his earlier work. Later, in 1931, Levy learned of his work and sent an apology. Bachelier ended up as a professor in Besançon. Einstein had never heard of his work, and, finally, in the 1960s, when Professor Paul Samuelson distributed Bachelier's work among leading economists, his financial theories were "rediscovered."

Fat Tails

A normal distribution curve looks like the bell-shaped chart in Figure 4.1.

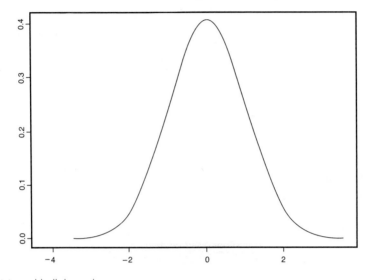

FIGURE 4.1   Normal bell-shaped curve

     Figure 4.2 shows a chart of the actual distribution of stock returns for General Electric between January 1, 2003, and November 19, 2004. Compare Figure 4.1 with Figure 4.2. Notice how the chart of real historical returns (Figure 4.2) does not perfectly match the bell-shaped curve shown in Figure 4.1. In particular, compare the outer edges, or tails, of the two charts. The tails of the normal distribution, in Figure 4.1, get thinner and thinner, approaching zero. However, in the actual stock return data in Figure 4.2, we do not see this thinning of the tails; instead, we see that the tails have bumps or remain flat. Thus "fat tails" are present in Figure 4.2 but not in Figure 4.1.

     Benoit Mandelbrot (1963) first noticed this phenomenon of fat tails, called a "leptokurtic distribution," in stock market returns in the early 1960s. Fat tails occur when one or more events cause stock prices to deviate extraordinarily from the mean.

     An example of one of these events is the large decline in stock prices that occurred on October 19, 1987. On this day, known as "Black Monday," the U.S. stock market crashed, sending the Dow Jones Industrial Average down 22.6%. What are the chances of a one-day drop of this magnitude occurring randomly? In a 1996 article appearing in the *Journal of Finance,* Jens Carsten Jackwerth and Mark Rubenstein state that if the life of the universe had been repeated one billion times and the stock market were open every day, a crash of that magnitude would still have been "unlikely." In his 2003 book, *Why Stock Markets Crash: Critical Events in Complex Financial Systems,* Didier Sornette claims that, statistically, a crash as large as was seen on Black Monday would be expected to occur only once in 520 million years. Thus, the huge negative return seen in October of 1987 is clearly an outlier.

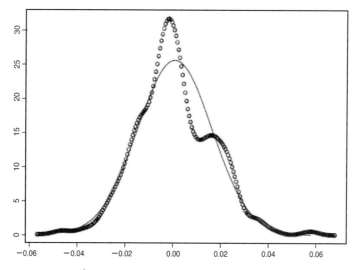

FIGURE 4.2 Density estimation for GE compared with a normal distribution (adapted from Luke Olsen, "Why Be Normal?" Society for Amateur Scientists, E-bulletin, November 21, 2003)

Drawdowns

Black Monday represented an abnormally large one-day negative return in the stock market. Although this alone was a significant deviation from the mean stock return, even more significant is the fact that October 19 was preceded by three days of market losses. Market losses were 2%, 3%, and 6% on the three previous trading days. In other words, there were four consecutive days of trading losses, resulting in a 30% decline in the market. Periods of successive losses like this are referred to as **drawdowns**.

Sornette has studied these types of drawdowns in an attempt to understand why outliers occur and how they can be integrated into the RWH. He argues that although independence can accommodate one large deviation, the probability of two or more large deviations occurring back-to-back is out in the stratosphere.

For example, the probability of a one-day decline of 10% in the stock market is approximately 1 in 1,000. In other words, a 10% drop would occur statistically once every four years. Although a drop of this magnitude would be a large deviation from the average daily stock return, it would fall within the normal distribution. If stock returns are independent, the probability of two consecutive daily drops of 10% would be the product of the probability of the two independent events occurring, or 1/1000 multiplied by 1/1000. Likewise, the probability of three consecutive 10% drops, or a 30% drawdown, is $1/1000 \times 1/1000 \times 1/1000$, or 1 in 1,000,000,000. This means, statistically, a 30% three-day drawdown could be expected to occur only once every four million years!

Historically, of course, these back-to-back events have occurred, especially in declines. Dismissing randomness under such events suggests that when sequential returns reach a critical mass, they begin to foretell future returns and are, thus, no longer random or independent. Sornette calls these periods "bursts of dependence" or "pockets of predictability." If these successive declines occur more often than what is statistically predicted, some correlation must exist between the daily stock returns, indicating that stock returns do not follow a random walk.

TABLE 4.2   Historical Drawdowns in the Dow Jones Industrial Average*

Rank	Beginning Date	Dow Jones Industrial Average	Duration (Days)	Decline (Percent)
1	10/1987	2508	4	−30.7
2	7/1914	76.7	2	−28.8
3	10/1929	301	3	−23.6
4	7/1933	109	4	−18.6
5	3/1932	77.2	8	−18.5
6	11/1929	238	4	−16.6
7	11/1929	274	2	−16.6
8	8/1932	67.5	1	−14.8
9	12/1931	90.1	7	−14.3
10	9/1932	76.6	3	−13.9
11	9/1974	674	11	−13.3
12	6/1930	240	4	−12.9
13	9/1931	110	5	−12.4
14	8/1998	8603	4	−12.4

*Adapted from Didier Sornette, 2003

As shown in Table 4.2, Sornette's research indicates that large drawdowns in the DJIA have occurred more often than can be statistically expected. When considering the three largest twentieth-century stock market declines (1914, 1929, and 1987), Sornette calculates that statistically about 50 centuries should separate crashes of these magnitudes. He concludes that three declines of this magnitude occurring within three-quarters of a century of each other are an indication that the series of returns was not completely random.

What Sornette found was that under normal circumstances, returns follow a generally normal distribution. These normal conditions represent about 99% of market drawdowns. However, there appears to be a completely different dynamic occurring in the remaining 1% of drawdowns; these drawdowns occur in the fat tails of the distribution when extraordinary market declines occur (see Figure 4.3). Interestingly, Sornette also found this drawdown, outlier behavior common to currency, gold, foreign stock markets, and the stocks of major corporations, even though individual-day declines were contained within the normal distribution.

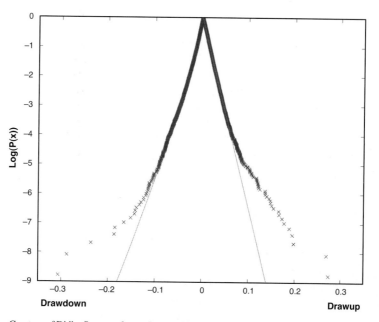

Courtesy of Didier Sornette, from a January 28, 2003 private paper: *Critical Market Crashes*

In this chart, Sornette compares the number of times particular drawdowns and drawups occurred in the DJIA during the twentieth century. Compare the actual numbers with those assumed by the null hypothesis of randomness shown by the straight lines.

FIGURE 4.3   Frequency of drawdowns and drawups in the DJIA

Proportions of Scale

A random walk is associated with a specific scaling property. Under RWH, if price change fluctuates over one series of intervals, say days, price change fluctuations over another series of intervals, say weeks, should be randomly distributed and proportional to the square root of the original interval changes. In other words, the square root of the typical amplitude of return fluctuations increases in proportion to time. If this proportional relationship does not exist, the price changes are not completely random. Furthermore, if the plot of the distribution of price changes shows any irregularity from the ideal plot of a random sequence of numbers, the assumption of randomness is challenged.

Andrew W. Lo of MIT (see Figure 4.4) and A. Craig MacKinlay of the Wharton School of Business tested to see if this proportional relationship does indeed exist. In their 1988 *Review of Financial Studies* article, "Stock Market Prices Do Not Follow Random Walks: Evidence from a Simple Specification Test," they reported that these amplitudes were not proportional for the time period from September 1962 to December 1985 and concluded that stock returns were nonrandom.

Lo and MacKinlay used a simple mathematical model to demonstrate the nonrandomness of stock prices. Surprised that such a simple proof had not been used earlier, they conducted a more thorough research of the literature. In doing so, they found that others (Larson, 1960; Alexander, 1961; Osborne, 1962; Cootner, 1962; Steiger, 1964; Niederhoffer and Osborne, 1966; and Schwartz and Whitcomb, 1977) had also demonstrated the absence of random walk in securities prices. With the exception of the Schwartz and Whitcomb article, these previous studies had been published outside of the mainstream academic finance journals and had been ignored by finance academics. Even today, many professionals, not having read the literature or heard the results from their peers, incorrectly believe that security prices follow a random walk.

> The random walk model is strongly rejected for the entire sample period (1962–1985) and for all subperiods for a variety of aggregate returns indexes and size-sorted portfolios. Although the rejections are due largely to the behavior of small stocks, they cannot be attributed completely to the effects of infrequent trading or time-varying volatilities. Moreover, the rejection of the random walk for weekly returns does not support a mean-reverting model of asset prices. (Lo and MacKinlay, 1988)

Courtesy of Professor Andrew W. Lo, MIT

FIGURE 4.4   Andrew W. Lo

In sum, evidence against the RWH has been found in many tests of independence, distribution, and proportion. The occurrence of strange outliers implies that other dynamics are occurring in freely traded markets. The evidence against the possibility of a random walk in price returns, however, does not suggest that technical analysis is an assured strategy. Yes, certain technical strategies may work, but the rejection of the RWH only suggests that because price returns are not purely randomly distributed, they may be dependent; in other words, they may have a "memory" and may provide some form of predictive power. The importance of the elimination of the RWH to technical analysis is that the profitability of technical analysis cannot be automatically dismissed as improbable. If price returns are somewhat dependent, as the tests show, then the gates are open for technical analysis to predict future prices.

CAN PAST PATTERNS BE USED TO PREDICT THE FUTURE?

Some researchers who have accepted that stock prices do not follow a random walk still do not accept the validity of technical analysts. These opponents agree that there may be patterns that can be fitted to stock price movement after the fact, but they argue that these past patterns cannot be used to predict the future. In other words, past patterns cannot be exploited to gain above-average returns. There are two major reasons why this group of opponents, especially academics, has drawn these conclusions.

First, though there may be some underlying patterns, markets are constantly being affected by new information. This new information causes enough variability in the underlying pattern that any knowledge of the underlying pattern will not be enough to exploit the knowledge for profit. For example, a recurring business cycle is a well-known and accepted economic phenomenon but not a predictable harmonic. The economy experiences expansionary periods followed by recessionary periods repeatedly. Therefore, we can expect cycles of expansions and contractions in the future. However, each of these business cycles is unique; the cycles vary in length and intensity. Thus, acknowledgment of a recurring cycle cannot be equated with the ability to predict the timing of an expansion or the intensity of a recession.

Second, even if we can use past stock market statistics, such as price and volume, to help predict future stock market movements, this information will not allow us to earn abnormal, above-average profits in the stock market. This conclusion is a result of the assumption of market efficiency. The EMH is widely accepted in the economic and finance communities, especially among academics. The EMH argues that price changes occur only on new information, immediately and rationally applied, and that any irregular price action is quickly adjusted back to true value by arbitration. Because prices change only on new information, technical analysis cannot determine future prices without that new information and is, thus, futile.

WHAT ABOUT MARKET EFFICIENCY?

Because of the central role the EMH has played in financial theory in the past 35 years, we spend a little time developing the basic ideas of the EMH and how, although it might be an interesting and thought-provoking model, it does not necessarily describe the real world of investments and markets.

> Market efficiency is a description of how prices in competitive markets respond to new information. The arrival of new information to a competitive market can be likened to the arrival of a lamb chop to a school of flesh-eating piranha, where investors are—plausibly enough—the piranha. The instant the lamb chop hits the water, there is a turmoil as the fish devour the meat. Very soon the meat is gone, leaving only the worthless bone behind, and the water returns to normal. Similarly, when new information reaches a competitive market, there is much turmoil as investors buy and sell securities in response to the news, causing prices to change. Once prices adjust, all that is left of the information is the worthless bone. No amount of gnawing on the bone will yield any more meat, and no further study of old information will yield any more valuable intelligence. (Higgins, 1992)

The EMH, which evolved in the 1960s from Eugene Fama's PhD dissertation, states that at any given time, security prices fully reflect all available information. The implication of this hypothesis is that if current prices fully reflect all information, the market price of a security will be a good estimate of its intrinsic value, and no investment strategy can be used to outperform the market.

The basis for the EMH is the economic theory of competitive markets. Basic economic theory teaches that arbitrage competition among investors and their profit motive will create efficient markets. As new information enters the marketplace, so the hypothesis states, all investors will be appraised of it immediately and will act rationally to adjust the price to the new intrinsic value of the security. Should the price deviate from its true value, so-called "noise," arbitrageurs will compete to bring that price back to that value at which the price will be in equilibrium with its value. Such is a purely efficient market. Figure 4.5 shows what would happen in a purely efficient market to a security price upon the announcement of new information. It shows a steplike progression as the price reacts instantly to that new information.

Courtesy Professor Aswath Damodaran, Stern School, New York University

This figure shows the ideal efficient market assumption of how information affects price and two other assumptions that have been shown to be more realistic.

FIGURE 4.5   The impact that new information has on security prices

Unfortunately for the hypothesis and fortunately for technical analysis, empirical evidence demonstrates that these immediate and complete reactions to new information do not occur. The problems with the hypothesis center around the assumptions that all investors will receive new information instantly, will react rationally to that new information, and that arbitrageurs will immediately and always act to adjust any deviations in the price back to its new value. Indeed, in their 1980 article "On the Impossibility of Informationally Efficient Markets," Stanford Grossman and Joseph Stiglitz argue that because information is costly for investors to obtain, prices cannot perfectly reflect all available information. If prices do perfectly reflect all available information, those who obtain costly information receive no compensation for doing so.

Even Paul Samuelson, professor at MIT and originator of the EMH, has begun to slightly change his tune.

Samuelson's Dictum:

Modern markets show considerable micro efficiency (for the reason that the minority who spot aberrations from micro efficiency can make money from those occurrences and, in doing so, they tend to wipe out any persistent inefficiencies). In no contradiction to the previous sentence, I had hypothesized considerable macro inefficiency, in the sense of long waves in the time series of aggregate indexes of security prices below and above various definitions of fundamental values. (Paul A. Samuelson in a private letter to John Campbell and Robert Shiller, from Robert J. Shiller, *Irrational Exuberance*, 2nd Edition, 2001, p 243)

New Information

Information for purposes of the EMH is any news that will affect the intrinsic value of the security. In the case of a stock, most analysts and theoreticians hypothesize that the value of a company's stock is equal to the present value of the future cash flows that the investor purchasing the stock expects to receive. This present value is a function of all of the company's future cash flows and the expected interest rate during the period that the cash flows occur. New information is any news that affects interest rates or cash flow directly or indirectly. That information can be related to the underlying company or can be any of a multitude of other news about the economy, politics, and so on. In short, it can be almost anything because almost all change has an effect on value regardless of its immediate importance.

Information itself is subject to many problems and thus brings into question the precepts about it in the EMH. A well-documented characteristic of financial markets is the presence of asymmetric information. Asymmetric information refers to a situation in which one party of a transaction has information that the other party involved in the transaction does not have. For example, the managers of a corporation have better information about how well their business is doing than the stockholders do. In addition, the company managers know whether they are being honest about their reporting of the company's financial position, but stockholders cannot immediately discern whether the managers are being honest.

As any investor knows, in the real world, all information is not disseminated instantly to all market players. A classic example of the presence of asymmetric information is the Enron debacle in 2000. The management of Enron knew for years that the fundamental numbers being reported to the public and to analysts were incorrect and were upwardly exaggerated to maintain an artificially high stock price for acquisitions (see Figure 4.6). The true information was kept inside the corporation and known by only a few insiders.

Even when the real story began to leak out and the stock price began to decline, security analysts on Wall Street continued to recommend the stock based on projections from the old, incorrect numbers. Thus, this new information was dribbled out to the public in small amounts. But, even when finally disseminated among analysts, it was not interpreted correctly. This is an extreme case, of course, but in the practical world of investments, new information gets disseminated slowly through the investment world and is acted upon with even more hesitation.

Therefore, several problems exist in the process of information dissemination. First, in its transmission, the information might be inaccurate. Second, the source might be intentionally lying, as in the case of Enron executives. Third, the information might not be disseminated immediately even though it is time sensitive. Fourth, there exists a natural lag between when the news is announced and when it is received by the last recipient, during which time the information might have changed.

Once information disseminates, the market participants must interpret the information. This interpretation can be extremely difficult and problematic. The information might be too numerous and too complex and, thus, not easily or inexpensively interpreted. The information age produces an enormous and incomprehensible amount of news and data that is impossible to assimilate. Often, information is vague and its consequences not understandable. Not enough precedent has occurred to be able to judge what potential consequences are likely from specific information. In short, information by itself is unreliable and its interpretation subject to logical errors.

Academic studies suggest that it would be extremely costly for market participants to attain and assimilate perfectly new information. In his book, *A Theory of Adaptive Economic Behavior,* Cross (1983) discusses the costliness of solving the complex statistical problems that modern economic and financial theory assume that individuals in the market are working.

> The methodological price for this approach [traditional statistical and mathematical decision analysis] has been extremely high, however, for it has become necessary to assume individuals in these markets can be represented as mathematical statisticians capable of solving specific problems that are often beyond the analytic abilities of professionals in that field. It also requires reliance on the assumptions that individuals follow optimizing rules of behavior under just those dynamic and risky types of situations for which the assumption of optimization has the least empirical support. (Cross, 1983)

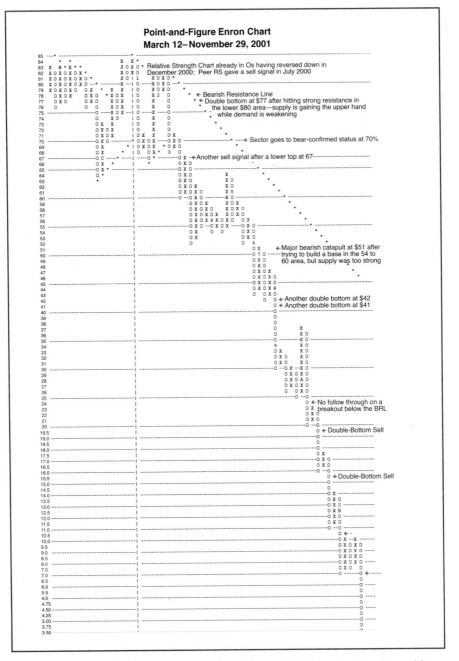

Enron chart and associated commentary courtesy of Dorsey, Wright & Associates, www.dorseywright.com

FIGURE 4.6 Point-and-figure chart of Enron stock price March 2001 through November 2001, with samples of Wall Street advisory comments on specific dates

**Advice from Major Wall Street Firms on Enron
March 12–November 29, 2001**

Date	Price		Date	Price	
3/12	$61.27	Prudential—cut upward target price	10/23	19.79	Edward Jones—cut to reduce
3/14	62.75	Commerzbank—raised to accumulate	10/24	16.41	Prudential—cut to sell
3/21	55.89	Merrill—reiterated near-term buy			JP Morgan—cut to long-term buy
3/22	55.02	Commerzbank—reiterated accumulate			Lehman—reiterated strong buy
3/29	55.31	Goldman—reiterated Recommend List			First Albany—cut to buy
4/16	59.44	Goldman—reiterated Recommend List	10/25	16.35	Banc America—cut to market perform
4/17	60.00	Merrill—reiterated near-term buy			Salomon—reiterated buy but target cut
4/18	61.62	Goldman—reiterated Recommend List			from 55 to 30
		Commerzbank—reiterated to accumulate			S&P—cuts to negative
5/21	54.99	Prudential—price target cut	11/1	11.99	Merrill—near-term neutral
6/8	51.13	Bear Sterns—reiterated attractive			CIBC—reiterated buy—but saw no
6/15	47.26	JP Morgan—reiterated buy			reason to buy the stock
6/20	45.80	Goldman—reiterated Recommend List	11/7	9.05	AG Edwards—cut to sell
6/22	44.88	AG Edwards—raised to accumulate	11/9	8.63	Commerzbank—cut to hold
6/27	46.72	Goldman—estimate raised	11/12	9.24	Prudential—raised to hold
7/10	49.22	JP Morgan—reiterated buy	11/13	9.98	Edward Jones—raised to maintain position
7/13	48.78	First Albany—estimates raised			
8/15	40.25	Banc America—reiterated strong buy	11/21	5.01	Goldman—cut to market perform
		Goldman—reiterated Recommend List			CIBC—cut to hold
		Bear Sterns—reiterated attractive			Edward Jones—cut to sell
		Merrill—cut to near-term neutral	11/28	.61	Prudential—estimates reduced
8/28	38.16	Banc America—reiterated strong buy			UBS—cut to hold
9/6	30.49	Sanders Morris—raised to buy			Commerzbank—cut to sell
9/26	25.15	AG Edwards—upgraded to strong buy	11/29	.36	Credit Suisse—cut to hold
10/3	33.49	Goldman—reiterated Recommend List			RBC Capital—cut to underperform
10/4	33.10	AG Edwards—downgraded to buy			
10/5	31.73	First Albany—reiterated strong buy			
10/9	33.39	Merrill—raised to long-term buy			
10/16	32.84	Merrill—raised to near-term accumulate			
10/17	32.20	First Albany—reiterated strong buy			
10/19	26.05	AG Edwards—cut to hold			
10/22	20.65	CIBC—downgraded to hold			
		Prudential—downgraded to hold			

Enron chart and associated commentary courtesy of Dorsey, Wright & Associates, www.dorseywright.com

Some of the optimization problems that market participants would need to be solving are beyond the analytical abilities of professional statisticians using high-speed computers. G. Hawawini and D. Keim (1994) argue that markets are not efficient because investors are prevented from optimizing by their inherent cognitive limits. Rode, et al., in a Wharton School working paper (1995) argue that there are "substantial constraints on the information processing time allowed," that "there is also a continual abundance of new information made available," and that "this flow of information easily exceeds investor's abilities to process it completely." They argue that because the object of technical analysis is to make sense out of this complex world of new and continual information, it has created rules that substitute simplified and "less complex for the intractable." Basic economic theory teaches that market players will continue the costly process of gathering and processing information only so long as the cost of doing so is less than the cost of being wrong. Technical analysis represents a rational choice for bounded rational investors; it can allow them to make reasonably well-informed decisions with relatively small information processing costs.

Interpretation is also subject to changes in risk preferences. In his 2004 article, "The Adaptive Markets Hypothesis: Market Efficiency from an Evolutionary Perspective," Andrew Lo argues that even in the rational market assumed in the EMH, risk aversion is not a constant. Risk aversion depends on the history of market behavior, and, thus, may be time-varying. For example, an investor who had never experienced a stock market collapse before might assume a different risk preference structure after losing money in the 1987 crash or the 2007–2009 decline than he or she had before. This means that even under a rational decision-making assumption, the risk parameters are not constant. Time-varying risk assumption can also develop when investors trade based on irrational expectations, and time-varying risk assumptions may arise from the interactions of heterogeneous investors. In short, the assumption that risk assessment is a constant has a few problems.

Are Investors Rational?

This brings us to the subject of rationality. The EMH assumes that investors as a group will act rationally. In its more recent version, it also assumes that there are irrational participants, called "noise" players, in the marketplace (Black, 1986). When noise players, who drive prices away from intrinsic value, are not counteracted by arbitrageurs, who are called "informed" players, the market is considered irrational. Thus, individual irrationality can exist in the marketplace, but it is usually nullified by rational arbitrage.

We will get to the subject of arbitrage shortly, but first let us look at the critiques of rationality. Most have centered on the subjects of behavior and preference of market participants.

Market participant actions depend on how individuals process information and make decisions. Information interpretation and decision making are subject to cognitive bias and limits. The science of behavioral finance studies the irrational behavior of investors and how they interpret information. Some of the results have shown illogical behavior that would be undesirable in the marketplace, such as comfort in crowds called "herding" (Huberman and Regev, 2001), overconfidence based on little information (Fischoff and Slovic, 1980; Barber and Odean, 2001; Gervais and Odean, 2001), overreaction (DeBondt and Thaler, 1985), psychological accounting

(Tversky and Kahneman, 1983), miscalibration of probabilities (Lictenstein et al., 1982), hyperbolic discounting (Laibson, 1997), and regret (Bell, 1982; Clarke et al., 1994). More and more of these kinds of studies are demonstrating that investors often act irrationally.

Preference in markets is directly related to the assumption that investors are risk averse. The EMH assumes that investors will be willing to take on more risk only if they are compensated by receiving a higher expected rate of return. Thus, the EMH assumes that investors will optimize their decisions based on their perception of and ability to assume risk. Many psychologists and experimental economists have found empirically "specific behavioral biases that are ubiquitous to human decision-making under uncertainty, several of which lead to undesirable outcomes for an individual's economic welfare…" (Lo, 2004).

The most famous early experiment was by Daniel Kahneman of the University of British Columbia and Amos Tversky (1979) of Stanford in which a number of participants were asked about preferences for different probability costs and outcomes. Invariably, they chose, when presented with potential gains, a risk-aversion strategy, and when presented with potential losses, a risk-seeking strategy. In the financial markets, this kind of decision making can be disastrous. It suggests that investors have a strong tendency to sell winning positions and to keep losing positions, quite contrary to the rationality assumption of the EMH. For the duo's work in behavioral finance, Kahneman received the Nobel Prize for Economics in 2002. Unfortunately, Tversky died in 1996 and was, therefore, ineligible.

Advocates of the EMH argue that although irrational players can sometimes affect prices for a short time, prices are quickly brought back into equilibrium to their true value by a rational arbitrage that profits at the expense of the players with irrational beliefs. Thus, prices may stray from their true value occasionally but will quickly return to them. The stray prices are "noise" about the true value and provide opportunity for the insightful arbitrageur. Prices always return to their true value, and irrationality, although it does occur, is never in control of prices because profitable, competitive arbitrage will always return those prices to their true value.

This brings us to the question of whether arbitrage actually does bring prices back to equilibrium or whether there are other forces, either of human bias or emotion, that can overwhelm the rational force of the arbitrageur.

Will Arbitrage Keep Prices in Equilibrium?

Price equilibrium at the intrinsic value of a security in the EMH relies on arbitrageurs acting on a profit motive to bring prices back to equilibrium if they should stray. In practice, the ability for arbitrage is less likely than the EMH assumes. It is too risky for reasons other than volatility.

Ideally, risk-averse arbitrage is "the simultaneous purchase and sale of the same, or essentially similar, security in two different markets at advantageously different prices" (Sharpe and Alexander, 1990). In many market instances, there is no substitutable alternative for the arbitrageur, or arbitrageurs are unable to trade alternatives for practical reasons such as lack of liquidity, lack of margin, trading costs, and so on. Arbitrage depends on sufficient liquidity for the arbitrageur to get into a position and, most important, to get out. In periods of fast markets and emotional panic, liquidity is often absent, leaving the risk to the arbitrageur that a position cannot be closed. Trading costs, in addition to slippage from illiquidity, are a concern to the arbitrageur. Trading costs must be minimal because with the small spreads involved, they can reduce a large portion of potential profit. These factors of liquidity and costs often convince the potential arbitrageur to go elsewhere to make a profit.

When there is no substitutable alternative for arbitrage, one side or the other of a run away from the theoretical intrinsic equilibrium value can continue. There is nothing to check it. The absence of a tradable vehicle to provide a risk-averse arbitrage might not be available. This is true, for example, in the entire stock and bond market. If "irrational exuberance"[1] (a term used by Yale Professor Robert Shiller) develops, as it did in the 1920s and 1990s, and prices rise significantly above their equilibrium value, there is no security that arbitrageurs can use to arbitrate prices back to their rational value without incurring substantial capital risk. Without an arbitrage vehicle, prices can trend in one direction without the arbitrage check to bring them back to rational values.

As opposed to the EMH, technical assumptions include the ability for prices to trend, in which case the arbitrageur, if he exists, may be overwhelmed by and may even join the consistent trend of prices away from true value. In addition, when a trend is completed and reverses, researchers such as DeBondt and Thaler (1985) empirically observe that those prices often trend in the opposite direction well beyond rational value. This cyclicality in price direction and extent is assumed by technical analysis to be due to irrational behavior overcoming rational arbitrage.

BOX 4.2   A CASE STUDY IN THE FAILURE OF FINANCIAL THEORY—THE LONG-TERM CAPITAL MANAGEMENT DEBACLE

The failure of rationality and arbitrage in the face of irrational behavior was empirically but unfortunately demonstrated by the collapse of Long-Term Capital Management (LTCM) in 1998. Managed by extremely knowledgeable and sophisticated professionals, this fund had two Nobel Prize winners, Scholes and Miller, on its advisory staff. It leveraged itself by avoiding Federal Reserve margin requirements and otherwise sane ratios of safety into almost 30-to-1 positions of investments to cash and controlled thereby over 300 billion dollars' worth of arbitraged positions. In addition, it held over a trillion dollars in derivative obligations that, had they failed, would have brought that amount of exposure to otherwise secure positions in the banks that were on the other side of these contracts, and it would have forced them to liquidate also. In other words, *LTCM was in a position to bring down the U.S. and perhaps world financial system if it failed.*

One of the problems of pure arbitrage is that the marketplace, over very short time periods, is efficient enough that bid-ask spreads are extremely small and the potential profit so minimal that meaningful profit can only come from a very large position, similar to a grocery store making many small profits on high turnover. Leverage

---

1. "Shiller used the phrase during testimony before the Federal Reserve, and Alan Greenspan repeated it in his famous December 1996 speech." (Interview of Professor Shiller by Chris Rugaber, Motley Fool [Fool.com], April 11, 2001). The apparent origin of the phrase, however, goes back to Hamilton (1922).

must then be used to increase the size of the position. The danger is that although leverage can increase profit, it can also increase the risk of capital loss to the point where, depending on the size of the leverage, a small movement against a position can wipe out the underlying assets. With a 30-to-1 leverage and 300 billion in contracts, a move of only 3.4% against the positions would be enough to wipe out the fund and force liquidation. This is essentially what happened to LTCM.

Here was a portfolio managed on the most modern versions of finance theory that collapsed because certain unrealistic assumptions were made, based on the EMH, and where "mispricing" became worse before it became better, forcing the covering of positions at the worst time and thus exacerbating the mispricing even more.

> Investors flocking to safety and liquidity in the aftermath of the Russian (debt) default in August 1998 were stronger, at least for several months, than the forces of rationality. (Lo, 2004)

Thus, even when a series of theoretically riskless spread positions were entered with rational expectations, the reaction to an event overwhelmed those positions, and lack of liquidity as well as the pressure of margin calls created a substantial collapse. Finally, several major banks and brokerage firms, with the insistence and support of the Federal Reserve, had to take over the assets of LTCM, force it out of business, and gradually liquidate its positions over time as the market spreads improved.

The lesson learned from this expensive adventure into the EMH was that market forces may abide by the principles of efficiency a majority of the time, but occasionally and unexpectedly, irrational forces can overwhelm rationality and cause a disaster. Several months after the LTCM debacle, arbitrage professionals analyzed the LTCM portfolio and agreed that the positions were reasonable, and after a time the spreads initiated did return to their mean. In other words, had LTCM not been so highly leveraged and had it been able to withstand the short-term losses, it would eventually have profited. To achieve a high return on capital, however, LTCM needed leverage. Leverage introduced another risk, over the risk of volatility—the risk of ruin. And when the markets ran outside the normal distribution of returns and developed a "fat tail," LTCM was out of business. This is why the assumption of a normal distribution in price returns can be hazardous. It is also why the subject of behavioral finance was born.

BEHAVIORAL FINANCE AND TECHNICAL ANALYSIS

Behavioral finance is a quickly growing subfield of the finance discipline. This branch of inquiry focuses on social and emotional factors to understand investor decision making. Behavioral finance studies have pointed to cognitive biases, such as mental accounting, framing, and over-confidence, which impact investors' decisions. These studies suggest that investors act irra-tionally, at times, and can drive prices away from the EMH true value. Investor sentiment and price anomalies, either as trends or patterns, have been the bulk of technical analysis study. Sen-timent and psychological behavior have always been the unproven but suspected reason for these trends and patterns, and human bias has always been in the province of trading system develop-ment and implementation.

The EMH is based upon a deductive reasoning process. In this deductive reasoning process, financial economists began with assumptions, such as markets are composed of rational individuals maximizing utility. Then using logic and increasingly complicated mathematical equations, they deduced theories that must follow from the assumptions. This deductive approach results in theories, but as we have seen with the EMH, these theories do not always square with observations of real-world data.

Those who practice behavioral finance follow an inductive approach of watching real-world events and looking for patterns. The inductive reasoning process is based upon observa-tion; a major drawback of the inductive process, however, is that just because a phenomenon has repeated itself and a pattern is detected, there is no guarantee that the relationship will continue in the future. To conclude that the phenomenon will continue to occur depends upon subscribing to a theory of why it would continue.

The deductive process has resulted in the EMH, a theory that has not been supported by observation. The inductive process of behavioral finance has resulted in a collection of observa-tions, many which contradict the EMH, but lacks a theory to support the usefulness of these observations in the future. The evidence presented by behavioral finance supports the use of technical analysis. However, behavioral finance lacks a theory to explain why the observations seen occur. Without such a theory, the academic world has been slow to let go of its adherence to the EMH.

Although the divide between theory and observation remains, progress is occurring as aca-demics attempt to develop theories that are consistent with market observations. For example, Andrew Lo (2004) applies principles of evolution such as competition, adaptation, and natural selection to financial interactions and proposes the Adaptive Markets Hypothesis. Lo claims that many of the observations behavioralists cite as counterexamples to the EMH are consistent with an evolutionary model of investors adapting to a changing environment using simple heuristics.

At this point, behavioral finance does not provide an alternative theory to the EMH, but empirical studies questioning the EMH in its purest form have bolstered the credibility of techni-cal analysis with more sophisticated investigations of technical rules, and they have added hope that the academic world will eventually catch up to the real world of markets.

PRAGMATIC CRITICISMS OF TECHNICAL ANALYSIS

In addition to the theoretical criticisms of technical analysis, there are some pragmatic criticisms of technical analysis.

Some investors incorrectly believe that technical analysis is only for the short-term trader and is not useful to the long-term investor. Because new and relevant fundamental information on a security doesn't change minute-by-minute or day-by-day, a short-term trader must rely more on technical analysis. The short-term trader must rely on an interpretation of market price behavior rather than on news and company announcements. In this instance, technical analysis gives the trader more of an advantage than fundamental analysis. This happenstance has led to the incorrect belief that technical analysis is only for the short-term trader. But, technical analysis is the study of price, and people determine prices. *People affect long-term prices as much as short-term prices.* Analysis of price behavior over the long term is just as valuable to the investor as analysis over the short term is to the trader. Indeed, the professional managers who have been the most successful have been so because they used technical analysis for long-term decisions.

Other opponents of technical analysis claim that if successful, technical analysis would cancel itself out by being self-fulfilling. A corollary to this claim is that technical rules that worked in the past might not work in the future. Such a criticism assumes that technical analysis will fail when all investors practice it, including the self-same critics. So far, the widespread, ubiquitous use of technical analysis is illusory. Many rules, both technical and fundamental, suffer the fate of becoming too popular. Look at the concept of "diversification" into noncorrelated assets, an idea much toted before the 2008 stock market decline took all noncorrelated assets down at the same time. Another example of this phenomenon is the small capital effect. Historically, smaller capitalized stocks tended to outperform larger capitalized stocks, but this fundamental rule no longer holds true. These are investment fads, not principles. Technical analysis, having been around for hundreds of years, is not a fad. There is no question that methods of pattern analysis seem not to work as well as in the past. This is also a problem with all investment analysis. As markets become more efficient, competition becomes more fierce and any method having some modicum of success is quickly jumped on until it becomes neutralized. Although it occurs with technical analysis, it is not unique to it. As for technical rules working in the future, who is to say? All rules are subject to change. At least technical analysis works with reliable data; most rules have been tested; and risk levels can be established to limit loss of capital.

An additional criticism of technical analysis is that most technical rules require subjective judgment and are, thus, fallible. On the other hand, what form of investment analysis doesn't require subjective judgment? Why is technical analysis singled out? Certainly, fundamental analysts must judge whether to buy, sell, hold, or ignore a security they are analyzing. It is true that technical analysis of charts is subjective, and some call it an "art" or "skill," but the demonstration of data on a chart is just another means of time-series analysis. Most theoreticians also use charts to clarify their hypotheses. One sure aspect of technical analysis, unlike others, is that the data used is as timely and accurate as any data can be. Actually, technical analysis is becoming more "mechanical" as quantitative experts use computers to determine statistical rules for action and money management. Some believe this may "blow up" and denigrate technical analysis or at least drive it back to the subjective rules, as did the LTCM debacle for the EMH about arbitrage, but for now technical analysis is becoming the less subjective of the two major forms of investment analysis.

WHAT IS THE EMPIRICAL SUPPORT FOR TECHNICAL ANALYSIS?

Despite the theoretical criticisms, can technical analysts use past price data to predict future price movement? Over the years, hundreds of studies have been conducted to test the efficacy of technical trading rules. Cheol-Ho Park and Scott Irwin conducted one of the most extensive reviews of these tests. In their 2003 report, they review 92 post-1986 academic studies that tested the profitability of technical analysis strategies.[2]

Of the 92 studies reviewed, 58 of the studies concluded that positive results could be gained from using technical analysis; only 24 of the studies concluded that the use of technical strategies led to negative results. Under the Random Walk Hypothesis, because prices returns are independent of each other, no technical trading strategy can be consistently profitable. Believers in the Random Walk Hypothesis would admit that a strategy could appear to be profitable ex-post, but that this profitability was simply due to luck, not a successful technical trading rule. However, the fact that two-thirds of the studies that Park and Irwin reviewed showed positive results could not be attributed to luck. Of course, as Park and Irwin point out, criticism can be made of some of the reviewed studies in that the various testing methods used by the researchers were in some cases subject to data snooping and ex-post selection of trading rules; some of these studies may also be flawed due to difficulties in estimating risk and transaction costs. It is unlikely, however, that all 58 positive studies are at fault for testing deficiencies. Park and Irwin's summary results at least show possible refutation of the Random Walk and the Efficient Markets Hypotheses, something that until recently had not been accomplished with rigorous testing of trading rules.

CONCLUSION

Like any practical discipline, especially one working with an indefinite and fickle subject such as the marketplace, technical analysis has problems. The Random Walk Hypothesis is not perfect; yet at many times, prices appear to behave randomly. The EMH has many holes that cannot be explained, yet prices seem to be very efficient and the possibility of profit often slim. Fundamental analysis has its problems, most of which were exaggerated during the market decline in the early 2000s and more recently in 2007–2009, but there is little question that stock prices, commodity prices, and currency rates change over the long run due to the fundamental changes in the economy and structure of markets. Technical analysis is no different. It has many flaws, is difficult to learn, is subject to error and bias, and often falls on its face. Nevertheless, technical analysis can be extremely useful to investors wanting to profit from timing and trend riding while limiting risk.

---

2. Many tests of technical trading strategies conducted before the mid-1980s focused on only one or two trading systems, did not test for statistical significance of trading profits, and did not correctly address issues of risk.

REVIEW QUESTIONS

1. You walk into a room where some friends have been playing a coin toss game. They ask you to guess whether the coin will land on heads or tails on the next toss. Does the fact that your friends have knowledge about how many heads and tails have already occurred in the game give them any advantage over you in guessing whether a coin will land on heads or tails on the next coin toss? Explain.

2. Supporters of the Random Walk Hypothesis claim that stock prices have no "memory." What do they mean by this claim?

3. What does the term *fat tails* mean? How do fat tails differ from the tails that would occur in a normal distribution?

4. If the probability of a 10% decline in stock prices occurring on any particular day is 1 in 1,000 and stock returns are random, explain why the probability of having a 10% decline in stock prices on two consecutive days is only 1 in 1,000,000.

5. What are some of the problems associated with information that bring the EMH into question?

PART II

MARKETS AND MARKET INDICATORS

CHAPTER 5   AN OVERVIEW OF MARKETS

CHAPTER 6   DOW THEORY

CHAPTER 7   SENTIMENT

CHAPTER 8   MEASURING MARKET STRENGTH

CHAPTER 9   TEMPORAL PATTERNS AND CYCLES

CHAPTER 10   FLOW OF FUNDS

CHAPTER 5

An Overview of Markets

CHAPTER OBJECTIVES

After studying this chapter, you should be familiar with

- The market characteristics required for investors to use technical analysis
- The types of markets in which technical analysis can be used
- The differences between informed, uninformed, and liquidity market players
- The differences between price-weighted, market capitalization weighted, and equally weighted averages

Technical analysis is widely used in freely traded markets. In the United States and most major industrial countries, technical analysis is used in the currency, equity, fixed income, and commodity markets. Professional traders and investors, as well as individuals who are investing their own funds, use the techniques of technical analysis. An obvious use of technical analysis is to make money. Investors attempt to buy a security at a low price and sell it at a high price; technical analysis helps identify profitable buying and selling opportunities. In addition to aiding the investor with determining profitable buying and selling opportunities, technical analysis can be used to manage risk.

For an investor to use technical analysis in a market, easy access, fungibility, sufficient liquidity, and continuous trading must characterize the market. Although there are many freely traded markets in the world in which technical analysis is used, the most common, and the one this book will most frequently address, is the U.S. stock market.

BOX 5.1 FUNGIBILITY

Fungibility is the interchangeability of financial assets on identical terms. Often a stock, future, or option will be traded on more than one exchange. It is especially important that the financial asset being purchased on one exchange and sold on another is fungible. In other words, if a trader buys an S&P contract on the Singapore exchange and sells the same contract (as defined by asset, amount, currency, and expiration) on the Chicago Mercantile Exchange, he or she must be sure that the contracts are fungible, that they are exactly interchangeable, and they can be cleared through either exchange. Some exchanges trade the same contracts, but they are not members of the same clearinghouse, the entity that makes and takes delivery. Thus, a purchase in one exchange would not be accepted for delivery in the other exchange. When trading in offshore markets, fungibility can become a serious problem.

IN WHAT TYPES OF MARKETS CAN TECHNICAL ANALYSIS BE USED?

Markets are simply meeting places of buyers and sellers. Markets can be categorized in many ways. They can be categorized by the assets being traded, the manner in which the borrowers and lenders meet, or by the type of contract that is executed. Let us begin by dividing markets into categories based on how organized or integrated the market is. Using this type of division results in four different types of markets: direct search markets, brokered markets, dealer markets, and auction markets.

The direct search market is the least organized market structure. With this type of market, buyers and sellers must seek and find each other directly. For example, suppose that Elizabeth wants to buy a used washer and dryer for her new apartment. Elizabeth might search the classified ads in her local newspaper for a seller of a washer and dryer. Generally, low-priced, nonstandard goods are traded in the direct search market. This type of market is characterized by sporadic participation by the market players.

The next level of market organization, the brokered market, addresses the direct search market problem of the buyer and seller finding each other. In markets where the volume of trading in a particular good is sufficiently high, brokers can specialize in bringing buyers and sellers together. One of the most familiar examples of a brokered market is the real estate market. Through specialization and economies of scale, the real estate broker is able to provide search and matching services to clients at a cost much lower than the clients' private search costs would be. The broker is able to earn a commission by providing these search and matching services for the buyer and seller. Brokered investment markets work similarly, with brokers matching buyers and sellers of financial assets for a commission.

A third type of market structure, the dealer market, arises when the trading in a particular type of asset becomes sufficiently heavy. Unlike brokers, dealers trade assets for their own accounts. Specializing in particular types of assets, these dealers post bid and ask prices and stand ready to buy and sell at these prices. The NASDAQ is an example of a dealer market for stocks. The dealer offers to buy securities at the **bid** price and offers to sell the securities at the **ask** price. The dealer's profit margin is known as the **bid-ask spread**. The dealer market saves market players search costs by providing readily available information about the prices at which they can buy and sell securities. The securities traded in dealer markets are usually substitutable and liquid, with the dealers standing ready to purchase or sell securities providing the liquidity. Thus, dealer markets generally have the characteristics necessary to use technical analysis.

The most highly integrated market is the auction market. In an auction market, all participants converge at one place to buy or sell a good. The centralized facility can be a location, a clearinghouse, or even a computer. An important aspect of the auction market is that all information about offers and bids is centralized where it is readily accessible to all buyers and sellers. As all of the market participants converge, buyers and sellers need not search for each other, and a mutually agreeable price can be established, eliminating the bid-ask spread. Assets such as art, jewelry, and antiques are sold in periodic auction markets. The New York Stock Exchange is an example of a continuous auction market.

Some auction markets can be studied using technical analysis, while others cannot. For example, auction markets in paintings could not be subject to technical analysis because a painting is unique and not substitutable with another painting. The auction market for U.S. Treasury bills, however, can be analyzed with the tools of technical analysis because U.S. Treasury bills are highly liquid securities and are easily substitutable. Because organized exchanges are structured for continuous trading in liquid, substitutable assets, they are usually subject to technical analysis.

TYPES OF CONTRACTS

Now let us look at categorizing markets by the type of contract that is executed. Two broad contract catgories are the cash market and the derivative market. The futures market and the option market are subcategories of the derivative market. Table 5.1 shows the types of assets that might be bought and sold in the cash, futures, and option markets.

TABLE 5.1   Asset Categories Traded in Cash, Futures, and Option Markets

Type of Asset Traded	Cash Market	Futures Market	Option Market
Common Stock	Yes	Yes	Yes
Commodities:			
Agriculturals	Yes	Yes	Yes
Metals	Yes	Yes	Yes
Interest Rates	Yes	Yes	Yes
Foreign Exchange (FOREX)	Yes	Yes	Yes
Indexes	Yes	Yes	Yes
Mutual Funds	Yes	No	No
Exchange Traded Funds (ETF)	Yes	Yes	Yes

Cash Market

The cash, or spot, market is the oldest type of market. In the cash market, a contract is entered into that will result in immediate exchange of the agreed-upon items. Different rules and conventions regarding the meaning of "immediate" apply depending upon the type of asset being traded. For example, when foreign currencies are being exchanged, delivery is usually instantaneous or at least within two days. In the case of common stock, the delivery period is three days. In the case of cash commodities, each market has its own rules and conventions. Cash indexes trade almost exactly like common stocks, and their delivery is regulated by the exchanges upon which they are traded.

The stock market, the most widely recognized cash market, is open to the public. In the cash commodities markets, the prime producers or consumers of the commodity traded often dominate. For example, Nestle is a large participant in the cocoa cash market; Exxon is a major participant in the oil cash market; Citibank is a major participant in the financial cash market (bonds, notes, fed funds, etc.); and UBS is a principal participant in the FOREX (foreign exchange) cash market.

As technical analysts, the cash markets in which we are principally interested are the common stock and index cash markets that are available on the public stock exchanges. Cash markets can be leveraged but not usually as much as the other vehicles. The amount of leverage in the stock market, as well as the option market, is controlled by the Federal Reserve and the Securities and Exchange Commission, but various ways of getting around the regulations have been developed through the use of derivative markets and private arrangements with lenders. Nevertheless, the average trader or investor is bound by the Federal Reserve regulations, which presently require that for stocks and indexes, a minimum of 50% of market value must be in cash for overnight positions and 25% for intraday positions. This means that the trader or investor can have a 2-to-1 margin for overnight holdings and a 4-to-1 margin for pattern trades intraday. For each $1, up to $2 in securities can be purchased or sold short overnight, and $4 in securities can be held within the day. There are different rules for day traders, for holders of U.S. Treasury securities, for market makers, and for shares selling under $5, and the various exchanges and brokerage firms can have tighter margin requirements if they want. Before contemplating the use of margin, the investor or trader should inquire at the intended brokerage firm what rules and regulations would be applicable to the trading or investing style desired.

Liquidity in the cash stock markets is excellent. The volume of trades and amount of money transacted each day suggest that willing buyers and sellers can always be found. The only time that the U.S. exchanges adjust trading or close down is when the exchange's computers go down, when a major event or severe weather affecting the United States occurs, or when the stock averages rise or decline a certain large amount, say in a panic. In the instance of a large price change, the NYSE reacts in two ways depending on its severity. When predetermined limits, called **circuit breakers**, based on a percentage change in the Dow Jones Industrial Average are reached, the exchange closes down all trading for a limited time. As of the first quarter of 2010, for example, should the Dow decline more than 1,050 points (10%) in a day before 2:00 p.m. EST, the exchange would close for an hour. After 2:00 p.m. but before 2:30 p.m., it would close for 1/2 hour, and after 2:30 p.m., it wouldn't close at all. Should the Dow decline 2,100 points (20%) within a day, the exchange would stop trading for two hours unless it was after 2:00

p.m., in which case it would close for the day. Should the Dow decline 3,150 (30%) points within the day, the exchange would halt trading for the remainder of the day. The limits adjust each quarter based on the Dow level for the previous quarter and have only triggered a shutdown once, on October 27, 1997, when the Dow Jones Industrial Average declined 550 points by 3:30 p.m.

BOX 5.2　EXCHANGE-TRADED FUND (ETF)

In the past 20 years, a security called an exchange-traded fund (ETF) that replicates an index fund or a basket of assets has become extremely popular as a trading and a hedging vehicle.

History—A failed attempt to create a similar investment vehicle in 1989 at the American Stock Exchange and the Philadelphia Stock Exchange was the first ETF-type security. It intended to simulate the S&P 500. A year later, the Toronto Stock Exchange successfully introduced freely traded index funds of Canadian stocks, emulating the Toronto Stock Exchange 35 and 100 averages.

Nathan Most (who died in December 2004 at the age of 90), an executive of the American Stock Exchange, seeing the success of the funds in Toronto, created in 1993 the first such fund to replicate the Standard & Poor's 500 Index. It was a Standard & Poor's Depository Receipt (SPDR), and the ticker symbol was SPY. Consequently, it earned the nickname "Spyder" that is now seen on the TV ads. It is the most traded ETF traded, even today.

Structure—ETFs hold assets, similar to a mutual fund. Ordinarily, large institutional dealers buy and sell shares directly from the ETFs in exchange for large blocks of the underlying assets in the fund. These dealers then become market makers in these ETF shares and trade them on the exchanges similarly to common stocks. Because the shares are backed by the underlying assets, arbitrage keeps their value close to the price of the underlying assets. From the retail standpoint, the ETF is then equivalent to a mutual fund with liquidity. The difference between them and mutual funds is that they trade all day, can be bought or sold at any time during the day, and unlike closed-end funds, trade with only a very small discount. (The *Wall Street Journal*, November 2008, reported an average deviation of 1% during the market turbulence of that time, and as high as 10% in some thinly traded issues.) As retail demand for the ETF increases, a small temporary premium develops that incites the dealers to exchange more assets for the ETF shares. The constant arbitrage between the assets prices and the ETF price keep the two generally in parity.

The largest ETF with the most trading volume is still the Spyder, but numerous others have come on the market. Close behind are the QQQQs (the "Cubes"), replicating the NASDAQ 100, and the DIAs ("Diamonds"), replicating the Dow Jones Industrial Average.

Advantages—In most cases, ETFs distribute dividends (or reinvest them), thus eliminating the dividend spread seen in the index futures and options markets; they

(continued)

are taxed like stocks; and they do not require an uptick to be sold short. They have a lower expense ratio than mutual funds and do not have load fees, redemption fees, or short-term trading fees. The cost of transacting them is a normal brokerage fee just as if they were stocks. Capital gains are payable upon sale of the ETF, unlike with mutual funds where a capital gain can be incurred during the ownership period. Finally, ETFs, by their nature, are transparent. You, as the investor, know exactly what assets the ETF holds, unlike a mutual fund that may buy and sell assets between reporting periods.

Styles—Replication of stock market indexes is the most common form of ETF. Next in popularity are commodities ETFs (and a variant called Exchange Traded Commodities). These invest in commodities such as precious metals, energy, and agriculturals. There are hidden dangers in holding these investment vehicles because their underlying is often a position in the futures markets and are rolled forward with each expiration, causing a "cost to roll" above the value of the underlying commodity. Finally, there are three other important styles: U.S. government bond funds, currency funds, and actively managed funds.

Leverage—ETFs can be leveraged just as if they were common stocks under the Federal Reserve margin regulations. However, in the past few years, leveraged funds appeared that promise to double or triple daily returns both upward and downward (called inverse funds). The speculator can now leverage a position beyond the margin requirements, but at the same time also expose a position to larger risk of capital loss. These leveraged funds incur additional costs during volatile markets because they are backed by various derivative positions that are bought and sold continually to balance the underlying portfolio risk.

Derivative Markets

The term **derivative** describes a financial contract that "derives" its value from some other investment vehicle, often called the **underlying**. The primary use for derivatives is to hedge against risk of loss in the underlying or to speculate with high leverage. Aside from the risk of loss from the hedge or speculation decreasing in value, both hedging and speculation take on additional risks such as **counterparty risk**, the risk that the party on the other side of the derivative contract may fail to deliver. However, most derivatives have not had this problem, and are used principally to transfer risk between investing parties. In this sense, derivatives are thought to cushion economic downturns. In specific instances, however, the derivative market increased volatility, as occurred during the "insurance programs" in 1987, when equity portfolio managers to protect against losses in their portfolios sold S&P 500 futures as the market declined and thus contributed further to the market decline that turned into a crash in prices not seen ever before.

The most common derivatives are futures, options, and swaps, traded either on exchanges, where their prices are visible, or over the counter, where their prices are hidden. The principal underlying vehicles are commodities, equities, FOREX, interest rates, and credit markets.

Futures Markets

Futures contracts that are traded in the futures markets are contracts in which the buyer and seller agree to trade at specific terms at a specific future date. Futures markets are often incorrectly called *commodity markets* more from historical usage than as a realistic description. Futures markets first developed in the agricultural markets as forward contracts, mostly in the grain markets, to provide a hedge for farmers and banks against crop failure or surplus. To understand the development of the futures market, suppose that you are a wheat farmer. You are concerned about the market price of wheat at harvest time. If the price is not as high as you anticipated because of a bumper crop of wheat, your profits will suffer. American Bread Company (ABC) is also concerned about the price of wheat, although ABC's concern is the opposite of yours. ABC's fear is that a poor wheat crop will lead to rising wheat prices, which translates into higher input costs and lower profits for ABC. You and ABC can ease your concerns by entering into a forward contract. In this forward contract, you would agree to sell a particular amount of wheat to ABC at a particular future date and at a price you set now. This reduces your risk and ABC's risk, you know what to expect as far as your income, and ABC locks in the price of its input.

Although individuals wrote forward contracts for many years, the contracts were first traded in the United States on the Chicago Board of Trade (CBOT) in 1848. However, the trading was cumbersome because the contracts were nonstandard: They each had different delivery dates and different commodity quality specifications. To address this issue, the CBOT developed the standardized contracts we know today as "futures contracts" in 1865 (Brecht, 2003).

The CBOT, often referred to as "The Board of Trade," is the oldest futures exchange in North America. Ironically, the largest is the Chicago Mercantile Exchange (CME Group), often called the "Merc," that now owns the CBOT and the NYMEX. Today, there are a number of futures exchanges throughout the world, many specializing in contracts of specific underlying assets. Futures exchanges are becoming a minigrowth industry as developing nations are organizing markets to trade especially in local products. As Table 5.2 demonstrates, some of the largest futures exchanges are outside of North America.

TABLE 5.2 Ten Largest Futures Exchanges in Derivative Trading Volume

Rank in 2008	Volume Exchange	(in Millions Contracts)
1	CME Group (includes CBOT & NYMEX)	3,278
2	Eurex (includes ISE)	3,173
3	Korea Exchange	2,865
4	NYSE Euronext (includes all EU and US)	1,676
5	CBOE (includes CFE)	1,195
6	BM&F Bovespa	742
7	Nasdaq OMX Group (includes all EU & US)	722
8	National Stock Exchange of India	590
9	JSE South Africa	514
10	Dalian Commodity Exchange	313

Source: *Futures Industry Magazine* (March/April) 2009

Futures, unlike stocks, are contracts and represent an agreement to purchase or sell a very specific amount and quality of asset at the expiration date. Most nonfinancial contracts are either closed in the marketplace by selling or buying before their first delivery day or are "delivered." For example, if you own one contract in sugar and do not sell it before the delivery day, you are obligated legally to accept delivery of several railroad boxcar loads of sugar at your railhead. Major dealers in these commodities have the facilities to take or make delivery; most speculators do not. When a trader buys a futures contract then, he does not own anything other than an obligation to take delivery on the delivery day of the commodity underlying the contract. Because the contract is not a specific title of ownership, it is never executed until the delivery day. It is traded back and forth between buyers and sellers, similar to how musical chairs are played, only the music stops on delivery day. Financial futures contracts are different from commodity futures contracts in that they settle on delivery day with cash based on the closing prices of the underlying securities or index.

When a position is initiated in a futures contract, the brokerage firm requires a **good faith deposit** that requires the trader to make good on any fluctuation in the contract price value. As the price of the contract rises and declines, the good faith deposit is increased or decreased by the amount of the price value change. When the deposit declines below a certain level, the brokerage firm requires that more funds be added to the account. Otherwise, the brokerage firm closes the position.

Margin requirements change as the price of the contract changes, as the price level or volatility changes, or if the exchange determines that the price may change significantly. Exchanges determine the minimum requirements for their contracts, and brokers may set rates higher but not lower than the exchange requirements. There are two types of margin—initial and maintenance. Initial is the amount necessary in the account before an order can be placed. Maintenance margin is the minimum amount necessary to keep an account active. This margin changes each day with the movement of the contract price.

Futures contracts trade in a series of contract months, and each is a unique contract group. The May 2005 Heating Oil futures are different from the June 2005 Heating Oil futures. They are substitutable for their specific contract months but not for each other. On a futures contract, the expiration day, the specific description of the underlying, and the contract size are constants while the price fluctuates. Financial futures are the same in this respect. Their expiration months are quarterly (March, June, September, and December) for each year.

The advantages of futures relative to stocks are many. Futures do not require an uptick for short-selling; they are highly leveraged; and they have a favorable tax benefit. Any futures trade is automatically allocated 60% to long-term gain/loss and 40% to short-term gain/loss. Furthermore, at year-end, the brokerage firm sends only one piece of paper with the net gain or loss for the year rather than a wheelbarrow full of transaction tickets needed to fill out the IRS Schedule D.

The danger of futures centers on its leverage and, in some instances, its illiquidity. Counterparty risk is alleviated through guarantees enforced by the exchanges on all participating parities. The margin requirement for most futures contracts is less than 10%. It is not required that futures traders use all their margin. Indeed, prudent money management would suggest otherwise, but the danger of trading without protective stops (see Chapters 13, "Breakouts, Stops, and Retracements," 22, "System Design and Testing," and 23, "Money and Risk Management," for usage of stop orders) and a reasonable money management method (see Chapter 23) has been the ruination of many traders. The other major danger is in more illiquid futures markets where what is called a **limit** day occurs. Some futures have daily range limits. This practice has declined over the past few years to the point where some futures have limits only for contracts older than the spot month. Nevertheless, a daily price limit, when applicable, means that once the daily range limit from open to high or low is reached, trading in that contract is shut down. If one has a stop order that was not executed when the range was exceeded and the market shut down, too bad. Sometimes several range or daily limit days occur in a row and no trading takes place at all. On a highly leveraged position on the wrong side of the market, this can be ruinous. In the liquid markets such as the financial markets, a limit day is rarely seen because the liquidity of the market is so strong. Nevertheless, a limit day is a risk to be considered.

BOX 5.3   CONCURRENT EXPIRATION OF OPTION AND FUTURES CONTRACTS

One cross-vehicle effect that can influence price action in all three market vehicles in the stock market especially is the expiration of option and futures contracts. On each concurrent expiration date or shortly before, the prices of all three vehicles can be affected by the crosscurrents between each vehicle expiring and its underlying security. This is even more complicated when the underlying security is itself a derivative. For example, options on index futures expire on the same day and are priced at the same time. Depending on the number of options being exercised on that day and the number of futures also coming due that day, the markets in the underlying can become hectic. From the viewpoint of the technical analyst, almost none of the price action from such expiration activity has any meaning for the future of the underlying prices. Nevertheless, limit and stop orders can sometimes be triggered, causing necessary adjustments in a portfolio.

Option Markets

An option contract gives the holder the right, but not the obligation, to complete the transaction stated in the contract before the expiration date of the contract. There are two basic types of options—call options and put options. The call option gives the owner the option to buy an asset at a particular price, known as the strike price, before the option expiration date. The owner of a put option has the right to sell the stated asset at the strike price before the option expiration date.

Technical analysis is useful in the cash and futures vehicles but not so much in the options markets. Option markets usually have a short life span and with certain exceptions, such as the index options, less liquidity than the other vehicles. Because options are derivatives of the cash or futures markets (the "underlying" markets), often these markets are analyzed first and then trading rules are applied to the options markets. For example, in the S&P 500 futures, a technical buy signal may be generated and the trader, instead of acting on the future, will buy the call, sell the put, or create some kind of combination of calls and puts. This is extremely dangerous for the novice because options include sizable leverage risk and other complications. Options are a subject all their own and are not covered in this book. Because options are derivatives of other vehicles, the student should well understand the cash and futures market before studying or entering the options markets.

Most options trade on exchanges. However, there are esoteric options that trade over the counter in an invisible market between large institutions. These options include the credit default options (CDO) that caused so many problems in the recent financial breakdown. These markets are not freely traded, nor are prices readily available for technical analysis. Within institutions that trade such vehicles, prices may be available for study, but for the public they are not.

Swaps and Forwards

Swaps and forwards are traded over the counter, not on exchanges where prices are continuous and visible. Often, these contracts are specific to the parties only, not transferable, not freely traded, and do not have continuous prices. For these reasons, technical analysis is impossible. Swaps are contracts between parties agreeing to swap certain investment vehicles, one interest rate vehicle for another, for example. Forwards are swap agreements to swap similar investment vehicles sometime in the future. Repurchase agreements, for example, where one agrees to sell and then repurchase Treasury bills are forward swaps. Technical analysis is inapplicable to most of these contracts because they are not freely traded or substitutable with continuous prices. Indeed, in many cases, these contracts cannot be valued.

How Does a Market Work?

To understand the principles of technical analysis, we must be familiar with how markets work and who the players might be. To better understand how market prices are set, let us begin with a hypothetical trading example. Let us assume that we are watching the trading post on the New York Stock Exchange where the stock of an imaginary company International Business Products (IBP) is being traded during normal trading hours.

Assume that a specialist who has an interest in the stock of IBP is present; this specialist's job is to stabilize the price of IBP's stock. In addition, several floor traders are present; these floor traders represent off-floor interests in the stock. The first off-floor interest is a mutual fund that wants to purchase the stock because its analyst believes the company's earnings are going to rise suddenly and rapidly. The analyst has determined this expectation from studying the financial statements of IBP and from interviewing IBP's management. The second off-floor interest is a group of investors from a golf club in New Jersey who have heard of the profits one member of the club has gained from buying IBP earlier in the year. They also are interested in buying the stock but have no other information than what they have heard about their friend's profits. The third off-floor interest is a pension fund that currently owns IBP stock. This pension fund has made a substantial profit in IBP but now wants to sell its holdings because it has determined that the stock is overpriced. The fourth off-floor interest is an estate that owns the stock and needs to liquidate the position to raise cash to pay taxes. The fifth off-floor interest is a hedge fund that has been watching the stock price change and is flexible enough to either buy or sell shares but has no particular opinion about the prospects for the company.

Thus, the players in this hypothetical marketplace can be summarized as

1. A specialist whose job is to stabilize the price of IBP
2. A mutual fund that desires to accumulate shares of IBP because it believes the earnings of IBP will improve rapidly
3. A group of investors acting on the fact that IBP's stock has risen in the past
4. A pension fund that already owns shares of IBP and believes the current price is too high
5. An estate that owns shares of IBP and must sell them to raise cash
6. A hedge fund that is attempting to trade the shares of IBP but has no opinion about the prospects for IBP as a company

Notice that the players have different sources of information, different interpretations of that information, different reasons for trading IBP's stock, different time horizons, and different expectations. The mutual fund believes in the analyst's recommendation that the prospects for the company will improve immediately and wants to buy because it expects the price to rise. On the other hand, the pension fund believes the price of the shares is already too high and wants to sell, not necessarily because it expects the price to decline but because the possibility of future rises is diminishing. One or the other will end up correct, depending on how the stock performs in the future. In addition to these major players is the estate that wants to sell the stock to raise cash. It has no interest in the company and only wants the money from the sale. Its information is the necessity to raise cash and its interpretation is to sell the stock. The specialist may have an opinion and expectations about the company, but his responsibility is to stabilize the market for its shares. He will step in and buy or sell to provide liquidity and to keep the share price from rising or declining sharply. He will thus be acting contrary to the direction of the stock price, buying when it dips and selling when it rallies. The hedge fund will try to take advantage of anomalies, times when the stock seems to be out of balance with either its trend or its value. Finally, the golf club members are interested in buying the stock only because someone they know has made money in it. They expect to realize a sizable profit.

These different types of players are just examples. In real markets, of course, the number of players is huge, and information and interpretation of that information are equally as vast. Players buy and sell based on their interpretation of information. In some cases, that information might have nothing to do with the company and might not even be accurate. The estate sale, for example, is based on information that the estate needs cash, and the golf club members are buying stock purely on the information that someone else has made money in it. It is possible that the estate does not need the cash or that the member claiming the outstanding profit is lying. Players might interpret the information incorrectly; they might not care about the company at all; or they might act strictly emotionally, based on either greed or fear (in the case of a sudden and unexpected decline). The net result is a transaction between opposing players at a specific price. That price reflects the sum of all the information and interpretation by all players at that instant in time.

Now what happens to that price when the players interact over time? Obviously, each new price reflects a new sum of interpretation. Say the last price of IBP was $50.0. The mutual fund is anxious to buy the stock and bids 50.0 for 20,000 shares. The pension fund, not being as anxious, offers 10,000 shares at 50.4 and 10,000 shares at 50.6, all it has to sell. This is a standoff, as a new price has yet to be established. The specialist, judging that the spread between the bid and offer is too wide and surmising from his information that the buyer is larger than the seller, offers 1,000 shares at 50.1 because he cannot outbid the buyer above the last price. At the same time, the golf club members enter an order to buy 1,000 shares at the market. This trades at 50.1 against the specialist's offer. Now a new price has been established at 50.1, higher than the previous price of 50.0. The sum of all expectations has changed slightly to the upside. Now the estate comes in and sells its 10,000 shares at the market, which is the 20,000-share mutual fund bid at 50.0. The new price is back to 50.0 on higher volume. The hedge fund, seeing that the 10,000 shares were easily traded at 50.0, believes there is a large buyer at 50.0 and buys the pension fund's 10,000 shares at 50.4. Remember that each time a trade occurs, one player is willing to buy at that price and another player is willing to sell an identical number of shares at the same price; there is always a buyer and a seller for every transaction that takes place. Also, it is important to remember that the individual players know their own motivation for buying and selling, but they do not know with whom they are trading or why the other party wants to enter the transaction. The players only see the price and the volume of shares traded.

Thus, we have a series of transactions at different prices and different volumes reflecting the interpretation of different information by the different players. The mutual fund and pension fund are interpreting fundamental information about the company and the value of its stock relative to that information. The specialist is using knowledge of what exists in the way of bids and offers; the hedge fund is watching the tape; and the estate and golf club members are acting without regard to price but on information having to do with practicality in the case of the estate and emotion in the case of the golf club members. As long as the players on both sides of the transaction are fairly balanced, the price of the stock will oscillate in a relatively small zone, as it has in our example. If one of the factions (buyers or sellers) overwhelms the other, the price will adjust accordingly. The reasons for the adjustment in price are unimportant. What is important to the trader or investor is that the price moves in such a manner that its direction can be determined or confirmed from past experience. This is why technical analysts study price behavior. It discounts all known information and interpretation and considers only what the price action implies about future price action.

WHO ARE THE MARKET PLAYERS?

From the preceding example, it is obvious that a number of different individuals participate in establishing the price of a security. Academia has divided these types of participants into three separate categories: informed, noise, and liquidity players.

The early Efficient Markets Hypothesis presumed that only informed investors acted within the marketplace to establish a price. These players supposedly interpreted new information rationally and adjusted the market price of a security to its equilibrium value immediately. This strict interpretation has been relaxed considerably. Now the informed investor is considered similar to the more historical type, called the "professional or smart money investor," who can be just as affected by bias and misinformation as any other investor or trader. Professional speculators, position traders, hedge fund managers, professional arbitrageurs, and insiders are considered to be in this category.

Noise is a term coined by Fisher Black (Black, 1986) and is used to describe the random activity around the equilibrium price. Academically, the uninformed market participants are the **noise players**. A more widespread and older term is the **public**. Most mutual fund managers, pension fund managers, traders, and technical analysts are considered also to be in this category, even if they are professionals. The distinction between informed and uninformed is blurry, of course, and it's only useful in certain sentiment statistics generated by each group (see Chapter 7, "Sentiment"). All types of participants are human and subject to the same universal human biases and cognitive limitations.

Liquidity players are market participants who affect prices in the markets for other reasons than investment or trading. An earlier example is the estate that wants to liquidate securities for needed cash. This type of player makes no investment decision but affects the market for a very short time with its liquidation. Another example is the index fund that is forced to buy and sell a security based on its addition to or deletion from the index that the fund is following. This causes an outside effect on each security's price with no regard for its investment value by itself.

Too often, these three participant types are considered as separate and distinct groups. However, they are changing constantly. Arbitrageurs sometimes act as uninformed players, members of the public learn and change categories, insiders misjudge the marketplace, and so on. Experience, as well as knowledge, is important and also changing. In short, the marketplace is not a stable system headed in a straight line toward equilibrium. The interaction is dynamic and nonlinear. The system is complex.

HOW IS THE MARKET MEASURED?

As more of the market players want to buy stocks and fewer want to sell their stock holdings, stock prices will be driven up. Likewise, if many market players want to sell their stocks relative to the number of participants who want to buy stocks, stock prices will fall. Looking at the increase or decrease in the price of one stock will tell us how strong the market for that one particular stock is. If we want to measure the overall direction of the stock market, however, we need a way of measuring the movement of the broad market that is composed of the stocks of many companies.

Though the origins of the U.S. stock market date back to 1792 when 24 New York City stockbrokers and merchants gathered under a buttonwood tree and signed the Buttonwood Agreement, it was almost 100 years later before the concept of a measure of overall market movement was developed. At the end of the nineteenth century, Charles H. Dow began publishing a representative average of stocks. Dow intended to gauge overall market trends by looking at the combined stock price movement of nine railroad stocks, the blue chips of the day. As we discussed in Chapter 3, "History of Technical Analysis," Dow's initial average developed into the Dow Jones Industrial Average that we have today. Dow's work also led to the development of the Dow Jones Transportation Average and the Dow Jones Utility Average.

Building on Dow's initial concept, other individuals have also developed averages, or indices, to measure market movement. Today there are almost as many averages or indices as there are stocks. Although the concept of a market average or index might be simple, choosing a method to use to construct the index is complicated. There are three major types of index construction: price weighted, market capitalization weighted, and equally weighted.

Price-Weighted Average

The Dow Jones averages are price-weighted averages. This means that the prices for each of the component stocks are added together, and the sum is divided by a divisor that has changed over the years to account for splits and stock dividends in each of the component stocks. To see how a price-weighted average is constructed, consider the four hypothetical stocks in Table 5.3. A price-weighted average for each trading day is calculated by simply adding the four prices and dividing by four. The problem with a price-weighted average is that a high-priced stock will have more influence on the average than a lower-priced stock. Note that between trading Day 1 and Day 2, the price of Alpha increased by 10%, while the price of the other three stocks remained constant; this led to a 3.8% increase in the value of the price-weighted index. On the following trading day, the price of Delta rose by 10% and the price of the other three stocks did not change. When the lower-priced Delta increased in value by 10%, the price-weighted index only changed by 0.9%. The price-weighted average does not represent the usual manner in which a portfolio is constructed. Investors rarely invest in an equal number of shares in each portfolio stock.

TABLE 5.3   Calculation of Price-Weighted, Market Capitalization, and Unweighted Indexes

Company	Alpha		Beta		Gamma		Delta		Price-Weighted Index		Market Capitalization Weighted Index		Unweighted Average	
Volume of Shares Outstanding	5,000,000		8,000,000		6,000,000		2,000,000							
	Price	Change	Price	Change	Price	Change	Price	Change	Level	Change	Level	Change	Level	Change
Day 1	80		85		25		20		52.50		100.00		100	
Day 2	88	10.00%	85	0.00%	25	0.00%	20	0.00%	54.50	3.81%	103.15	3.15%	102.50	2.5%
Day 3	88	0.00%	85	0.00%	25	0.00%	22	10.00%	55.00	0.92%	103.46	0.31%	105.06	2.5%
Day 4	88	0.00%	85	0.00%	27.5	10.00%	22	0.00%	55.62	1.14%	104.65	1.14%	107.69	2.5%

Market Capitalization Weighted Average

Another way to calculate a market index is to use market capitalization in the weighting scheme. The Standard & Poor's 500 Index is a market capitalization weighted index, in which each of the 500 stocks is weighted by its market value. The NYSE composite index, the NASDAQ composite index, and the Russell Indexes are also capitalization weighted. An interesting change in the Standard & Poor's 500 Index began in the spring of 2005. Rather than calculating the index based on the shares outstanding in each company, Standard & Poor's index now calculates based on the float of each stock. **Float** is a term used to describe the number of shares actually available to the marketplace for purchase or sale. In many companies, some stock is held in the treasury, some has been given to employees in the form of options, some has been reissued in secondary offerings, and some is held closely by entities such as pension funds, foundations, other companies, owners, or syndicates. These closely held shares are generally not available for normal day-to-day transactions and are, thus, eliminated from the calculation of the index. The purpose in this new calculation is to reduce the influence on the index by the amount of capital value that is locked up and not available to the market.

To compare how this index construction differs from price weighting, refer to Table 5.3. To begin creating a market capitalization weighted index, an initial market value of all the included stocks is calculated. In our example, this would be accomplished by multiplying each stock's price by the number of shares outstanding on Day 1. This gives a value of 1,270,000,000. This initial figure is the base and is assigned an index value, usually of 100. Then a new market value is calculated for all of the securities each trading day. This new value is compared with the initial base level to calculate a daily index value. The general formula for calculating the daily index level is

$$\text{Index}_t = \frac{\sum P_t Q_t}{\sum P_b Q_b} \times \text{Beginning Index Value}$$

Index_t = Market capitalization weighted index on Day t

P_t = Closing stock prices on Day t

Q_t = Number of outstanding shares for stocks on Day t

P_b = Closing stock prices on initial base day

Q_b = Number of outstanding shares for stocks on initial base day

Because of the weighting scheme used, stocks with a large number of shares outstanding and high prices have a disproportionate influence on a market capitalization weighted index. In the Table 5.3 sample data, one stock increased in value by 10% while all of the other stocks remained the same on Days 2, 3, and 4. Look at how much more sensitive the index was to changes when the stock had a relatively high price or number of shares outstanding. Just as the price-weighted index is not representative of how most investors purchase stocks, neither is the market capitalization weighted index. An investor seldom invests in stocks in proportion to their market capitalization.

Equally Weighted (or Geometric) Average

A third method of calculating an index uses equal weighting of all included stocks. Sometimes, the term **unweighted index** is used to refer to this type of average because all stocks carry equal weight, regardless of their price or market value. This index is calculated by averaging the percentage price changes of each of the stocks included in the group. As you can see in Table 5.3, it does not matter which stock increases by a particular percent. For each of the sample trading days, one stock increased in value by 10% while the other three stocks remained unchanged; each day, the equally weighted average index increased by 2.5%.

This index calculation is a dollar-weighted average; in other words, it assumes that an investor invests equal dollar amounts in each stock. For example, an investor with $10,000 would purchase $2,500 worth of each of the four stocks in our example. Thus, the investor would be purchasing fewer shares of the high price per share stocks and more shares of the low price per share stocks. This calculation most closely represents how the typical investor goes about organizing a portfolio.

Several of the Value Line averages are equal weighted averages that are calculated using an arithmetic average of the percent changes. However, one of the Value Line averages, the Value Line Industrials Average, and the *Financial Times* Ordinary Share Index are equally weighted averages that are constructed in a slightly different manner. These two indices are computed using a geometric average of the holding period returns. Table 5.4 demonstrates the calculation of a geometric average for the four-stock portfolio example.

TABLE 5.4   Calculation of a Geometric Average Calculation

Day	Alpha		Beta		Gamma		Delta		Geometric Average Calculation		
	Price	HPR	Price	HPR	Price	HPR	Price	HPR	$\prod_{i=1}^{n}$ HPR	$\Pi HPR^{\frac{1}{4}}$	Index Value
Day 1	80		85		25		20		(Product of HPRs)		100
Day 2	88	1.1	85	1	25	1	20	1	1.1	1.024	102.411
Day 3	88	1	85	1	25	1	22	1.1	1.1	1.024	104.881
Day 4	88	1	85	1	27.5	1.1	22	1	1.1	1.024	107.410

Comparing this geometric average with the equally weighted average calculated for the same stocks shows a downward bias when using a geometric average rather than an arithmetic average. An investor who had purchased $100 of each of these four stocks on Day 1 and held each of these stocks for all four days would have an ending wealth of $430, or 7.5% greater than the beginning wealth level of $400. The geometric weighted index shows a change of 7.41%.

CONCLUSION

In this chapter, we have explored the basics of how markets work. Because our interest lies in the area of using technical analysis, we have focused on markets in which substitutable, liquid, continuously traded assets are bought and sold. In these markets, we find informed, uninformed, and liquidity players buying and selling securities and, thus, affecting the price of these securities. As technical analysts, we are concerned with observing and predicting price movements as these various market players go about their trading. Market indices are used to measure the overall price movement in the marketplace.

As we continue through Part II, "Markets and Market Indicators," we build upon these basic ideas. The focus of Chapter 6, "Dow Theory," is Dow Theory and the basic fundamental relationships between markets and the economy. In Chapter 7, "Sentiment," we focus on the market players; we examine the notion of sentiment: how emotions and human biases impact the behavior of both the informed and uninformed market participants. Chapter 8, "Measuring Market Strength," focuses on measuring the strength of the market. Going beyond the indices we use to measure historical market performance, we examine indicators that measure the market's ability to maintain its performance into the future. Chapter 9, "Temporal Patterns and Cycles," addresses temporal tendencies; historically, analysts have found seasonal and cyclical tendencies in the marketplace that impact price movements. Finally, in Chapter 10, "Flow of Funds," we address the movement of money in the marketplace, known as the "flow of funds."

REVIEW QUESTIONS

1. For technical analysis to be used, the asset being traded must be substitutable. Explain what *fungibility* means and why fungible assets are a prerequisite for technical analysis.

2. For technical analysis to be used, the market in which the security is trading must be sufficiently liquid. Explain what *liquid* means in this context and why liquidity is a prerequisite for technical analysis.

3. Explain the differences among *informed, uninformed,* and *liquidity* market participants.

4. Classify each of the following market participants as an informed, uninformed, or liquidity player, and explain the reasons for your classification:

   a. Raymond is 18 years old and ready to begin college. His parents are selling shares of MSFT and KO to pay the tuition bill.

   b. Sandra just read a *Wall Street Journal* article about how successful Wal-Mart has been at managing costs. Impressed by what she read, she calls her broker and puts in an order to buy 100 shares of WMT.

   c. Michelle, the CEO of Led Computers, purchases 5,000 shares of LED.

5. Explain what is meant by an index being *price weighted.* In a price-weighted average, would you expect a $10 stock or a $50 stock to be more important? Why?

6. Explain how to compute a market-weighted average.

7. Explain how to calculate an unweighted average index.

8. The following table contains six daily closing prices for four stocks.

    a. Calculate the daily percentage change in price for each stock.

    b. Calculate a price-weighted average for Days 1–6.

    c. Calculate a market-weighted average for Days 1–6.

    d. Calculate an unweighted average index for Days 1–6.

    e. Compute the daily percentage change for the price-weighted, market-weighted, and unweighted average indices.

    f. Explain the differences in the results among the three types of indices.

Company	BCD		EFG		HIJ		KLM	
Volume of Shares Outstanding	2,000,000		3,000,000		7,000,000		9,000,000	
	Price	% Change	Price	% Change	Price	% Change	Price	% Change
Day 1	60		85		53		16	
Day 2	63		88		52		19	
Day 3	60		91		51		15	
Day 4	61		85		53		16	
Day 5	58		87		50		17	
Day 6	60		88		53		18	

9. Choose five stocks that are included in the DJIA. Download the daily closing prices for these five stocks for the past 30 days from the Yahoo! Finance Web site at http://finance.yahoo.com.

    a. Compute and graph a daily price-weighted index for these five stocks over the past month. What was the return on the index over the 30-day period?

    b. Find the number of shares outstanding for these five companies. Using this information, calculate a market-weighted index for the 30-day period. Graph the index and compute the return on this index over the past month.

    c. Construct and graph an unweighted average index for this five-stock portfolio. Compute the rate of return on this index for the 30-day period.

    d. Compare and contrast the graphs that you created and the 30-day returns you calculated.

    e. How do you explain the differences among the graphs and the return calculations?

CHAPTER 6

DOW THEORY

CHAPTER OBJECTIVES

By the end of this chapter, you should know

- A brief history of the development of Dow Theory and the major contributors to this development
- The three Dow Theory hypotheses presented by Rhea
- The theorems of Dow Theory
- The three types of trends—primary, secondary, and minor—of Dow Theory
- The concept of confirmation in Dow Theory
- The role of volume in Dow Theory
- The criticisms of Dow Theory

Charles H. Dow was the founder of the Dow-Jones financial news service in New York, and founder and first editor of the *Wall Street Journal.* He died in December, 1902, in his fifty-second year. He was an experienced newspaper reporter, with an early training under Samuel Bowles, the great editor of the *Springfield* [MA] *Republican.* Dow was a New Englander, intelligent, self-repressed, ultra-conservative; and he knew his business. He was almost judicially cold in the consideration of any subject, whatever the fervor of discussion. It would be less than just to say that I never saw him angry; I never saw him excited. His perfect integrity and good sense commanded the confidence of every man in Wall Street, at a time when there were few efficient newspaper men covering the financial section, and of these still fewer with any deep knowledge of finance. (Hamilton, 1922)

Charles Dow, the father of modern technical analysis, was the first to create an index that measures the overall price movement of U.S. stocks. However, he never specifically formulated what has become known as the "Dow Theory." Indeed, he likely never intended his disjointed statements and observations in the *Wall Street Journal* to become formalized. He wrote editorials about what he had learned from his experience as a reporter and advisor on Wall Street but never organized these individual pieces into a coherent theory. In fact, he only wrote for five years before his sudden death in 1902. The term "Dow Theory" was first used by Dow's friend, A. C. Nelson who wrote in 1902 an analysis of Dow's *Wall Street Journal* editorials called *The A B C of Stock Speculation.*

After Dow's death, William Peter Hamilton succeeded him as editor of the *Wall Street Journal.* For over a quarter of a century, from 1902 until his death in 1929, Hamilton continued writing *Wall Street Journal* editorials using the tenets of Dow Theory. Hamilton also described the basic elements of this theory in his book, *The Stock Market Barometer,* in 1922.

Alfred Cowles III (1937) performed the first formal test of the profitability of trading using the tenets of Dow Theory in 1934. Cowles was an early theoretician of the stock market and used statistical methods to determine if Hamilton could "beat the market." Cowles found that a portfolio based on Hamilton's theory lagged the return on a portfolio fully invested in a market index that Cowles had developed. (Cowles's index was a predecessor of the S&P 500.) Therefore, Cowles determined that Hamilton could not outperform the market and concluded that Dow Theory of market timing results in returns that lag the market. Cowles's study, considered a seminal piece in the statistical testing of market-timing strategies, provided a foundation for the Random Walk Hypothesis and the Efficient Markets Hypothesis.

In recent years, however, researchers have reexamined Cowles's work using more sophisticated statistical techniques. In the August 1998 *Journal of Finance,* an article by Brown, Goetzmann, and Kumar demonstrated that adjusted for risk (Hamilton was out of the market for a portion of his articles), Hamilton's timing strategies yield high Sharpe ratios and positive alphas for the period 1902 to 1929. In other words, contrary to Cowles's original study, Brown, Goetzmann, and Kumar conclude that Hamilton could time the market very well using Dow Theory. In addition, they found that when Hamilton's decisions were replicated in a neural network model of out-of-sample data from September 1930 through December 1997, Hamilton's methods still had validity. His methods worked especially well in sharp market declines and considerably reduced portfolio volatility.

After Hamilton's death, Robert Rhea further refined what had become known as Dow Theory. In 1932, Rhea wrote a book called *The Dow Theory: An Explanation of Its Development and an Attempt to Define Its Usefulness as an Aid to Speculation.* In this book, Rhea described Dow Theory in detail, using the articles by Hamilton, and formalized the tenets into a series of hypotheses and theorems that are outlined next.

Rhea presented three hypotheses:

1. The primary trend is inviolate.

2. The averages discount everything.

3. Dow Theory is not infallible.

The first of these hypotheses dealt with the notion of manipulation. Although Rhea believed that the secondary and the minor, day-to-day motion of the stock market averages could possibly be manipulated, he claimed that the primary trend is inviolate. The second hypothesis, that the averages discount everything, is because prices are the result of people acting on their knowledge, interpretation of information, and expectations. The third hypothesis is that Dow Theory is not infallible. Because of this, investment requires serious and impartial study.

BOX 6.1   SOME OF WILLIAM HAMILTON'S THOUGHTS ON THE STOCK MARKET AND THE DOW THEORY

The sum and tendency of the transactions in the Stock Exchange represent the sum of all Wall Street's knowledge of the past, immediate and remote, applied to the discounting of the future. (Hamilton, 1922, p 40)

The market is not saying what the condition of business is today. It is saying what that condition will be months ahead. (Hamilton, 1922, p 42)

The stock barometer [the Dow-Jones averages] is taking every conceivable thing into account, including that most fluid, inconsistent, and incalculable element, human nature itself. We cannot, therefore, expect the mechanical exactness of physical science. (Hamilton, 1922, p 152)

Let us keep in mind that Dow Theory is not a system devised for beating the speculative game, an infallible method of playing the market. The averages, indeed, must be read with a single heart. They become deceptive if and when the wish is father to the thought. We have all heard that when the neophyte meddles with the magician's wand, he is apt to raise the devil. (Hamilton, 1922, p 133)

These three hypotheses are very similar to those of technical analysis today. They show how prescient Dow was and how universal and persistent his theories have been. As markets have become more efficient, there is some question about how much manipulation can and has occurred. Recent untruths by major corporations concerning their earnings have shown that the desire to manipulate still exists. Dow's tenet, however, stated that the primary direction of stock prices could not be manipulated and, therefore, should be the primary focus of all serious investors.

The concept that prices discount everything, including expectations, to the point that they are predictive of events is the most revolutionary of Dow's hypotheses. Until then, most investors looked at individual stock prices and studied what was available about individual companies. Dow believed that the averages of stocks foretold the shape of industry and were, thus, valuable in understanding the health of the economy.

Dow was under no illusion that he had found the magic formula for profit, nor were Hamilton or Rhea. Nevertheless, they did believe that by careful and unbiased study of the market averages, they could interpret, in general terms, the likelihood of the markets continuing or reversing in direction and thereby could anticipate similar turns in the economy. Their emphasis on study and lack of emotional reaction is still important today. Ignoring this point is one of the most widespread causes for investor failure.

DOW THEORY THEOREMS

One of the theorems of Dow Theory is that the ideal market picture consists of an uptrend, top, downtrend, and bottom, interspersed with retracements and consolidations. Figure 6.1 shows what this ideal market picture would look like. This market picture, of course, is never seen in its ideal form. Consider Hamilton's quote, "A normal market is the kind that never really happens" (Hamilton, May 4, 1911). The purpose of the ideal market picture is to provide a generalized model of the stock market's price behavior over time. It is very simple and resembles a harmonic without a constant period or amplitude.

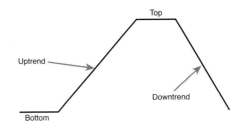

FIGURE 6.1 The Dow Theory ideal market picture

From the modern standpoint of the Efficient Markets Hypothesis (EMH), this ideal picture is interesting because it presumes that prices oscillate over long periods based on the accumulated emotion of investors as well as the facts of the business cycle. Were market prices to duplicate the business cycle precisely, prices would not oscillate as widely as they do nor lead the business cycle by as much as they do. Indeed, some theorists argue that the markets actually cause the business cycle, that confidence or lack of confidence from the markets translates into buying and selling of products (Szala and Holter, 2004). However, for Dow Theory, the picture of the ideal market remains the same regardless of cause.

A second theorem of Dow Theory is that economic rationale should be used to explain stock market action. Remember that Dow created both an industrial average and a railroad average. Although we have no record of Dow's precise reasoning for doing so, Rhea posited that Dow believed that industrial stocks represented the trend of industry profits and prospects and that railroad stocks represented railroads' profits and prospects. The profits and prospects for both of these sectors must be in accord with each other. For example, industry may be producing goods, but if railroads are not shipping these goods, then industry must slow down. Goods produced must be shipped to the customer. Railroads must confirm that produced goods are being sold and delivered. Today, of course, the railroad average has been changed to the transportation average to represent airlines, truckers, and other means of shipping goods. Nevertheless, the economic rationale of goods produced and transported is still valid in the industrial sector of the economy. Where Dow's economic rationale differs from the present is in the service and technology sectors that have become larger in dollar volume than the industrial sector. Some analysts use representations of these newer sectors to form an economic rationale for stock market action.

A third theorem of Dow Theory is that prices trend. A **trend** is defined as the general direction in which something tends to move. Because we are talking about markets, that "something" is price.

BOX 6.2 SOME OF WILLIAM HAMILTON'S THOUGHTS ON TRENDS

...on the well-tested rule of reading the averages, a major bull swing continues so long as the rally from a secondary reaction establishes new high points in both averages.... (Hamilton, December 30, 1921)

An indication [of price trend] remains in force until it is cancelled by another.... (Hamilton, September 23, 1929)

As we saw in Chapter 2, "The Basic Principle of Technical Analysis—The Trend," the concept that prices trend is one of the fundamental assumptions of technical analysis. It is the reason why technical analysts can profit. A trend is the basic pattern of all prices. A trend can be upward, downward, or sideways. Obviously, a sideways trend is more difficult to profit from than an upward or downward trend. Technical analysts endeavor to forecast the direction of the market trend. Because trends are the central principle in technical analysis, Chapters 12, "Trends— The Basics," and 14, "Moving Averages," focus on how trends are defined, measured, and analyzed by modern-day technical analysts. Right now, we focus on the notion of trend within the Dow Theory.

Dow Theory posited that there are three basic trends in price motion, each defined by time:

There are three movements of the averages, all of which may be in progress at one and the same time. The first, and most important, is the primary trend: the broad upward or downward movements known as bull or bear markets, which may be of several years duration. The second, and most deceptive movement, is the secondary reaction: an important decline in a primary bull market or a rally in a primary bear market. These reactions usually last from three weeks to as many months. The third, and usually unimportant, movement is the daily fluctuation. (Rhea, 1932)

Figure 6.2 shows graphically how these three trends are interrelated. Let us look at each of these three types of trends—the primary, secondary, and minor—a bit more closely.

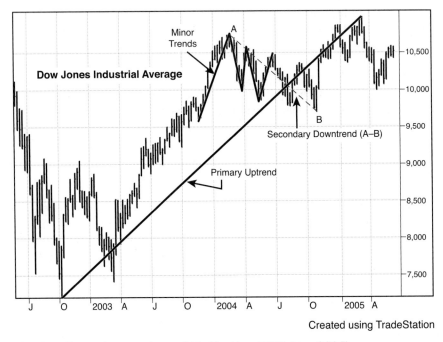

FIGURE 6.2   Dow Theory three trend types (Weekly: May 2002–May 2005)

The Primary Trend

> Correct determination of the primary movement (or trend) is the most important fac-
> tor in successful speculation. There is no known method of forecasting the extent or
> duration of a primary movement. (Rhea, 1932)

The primary trend is the longest of the three trend types. It represents the overall, broad, long-
term movement of security prices. The duration of this long-term trend can be several years. The
primary trend may be an upward trend, which is known as a primary bull trend, or it may be a
downward trend, referred to as a primary "bear" trend. The general long-run upward trend in Figure 6.2 indicates a primary "bull" trend.

Primary bull markets are characterized by three separate phases: The first represents reviving confidence from the prior primary bear market; the second phase represents the response to
increased corporate earnings; and the third is when speculation becomes dominant and prices
rise on "hopes and expectations."

Primary bear markets are long downward price movements, interrupted by occasional rallies, that continue until prices have discounted the worst that is apt to occur. They, too, are characterized by three separate phases: first, abandonment of hopes upon which stocks were

purchased; second, selling due to decreased earnings; and third, distress selling, regardless of value, by those who believe the worst is yet to come or who are forced to liquidate.

The Secondary Trend

> …a secondary reaction is considered to be an important decline in a bull market or advance in a bear market, usually lasting from three weeks to as many months, during which intervals the price movement generally retraces from 33 percent to 66 percent of the primary price change since the termination of the last preceding secondary reaction. (Rhea, 1932)

The secondary trend is an intermediate-term trend that runs counter to the primary trend. For example, during a several-year primary uptrend, prices may fall for a few weeks or a few months. During this secondary trend market decline, prices fall often, erasing 33% to 66% of the gain that has occurred since the completion of the previous secondary uptrend. Points A to B in Figure 6.2 represent a secondary downtrend.

Being able to anticipate or recognize secondary reactions increases profit capabilities by taking advantage of smaller market swings, but Dow believed this exercise was too dangerous. Because the primary trend and secondary trend reversal have similar characteristics, secondary reactions are often initially assumed as changes in primary trends or are mistakenly thought to be only reactions when the primary trend is changing.

The Minor Trend

> Inferences drawn from one day's movement of the averages are almost certain to be misleading and are of but little value except when "lines" are being formed. The day to day movement must be recorded and studied, however, because a series of charted daily movements always eventually develops into a pattern easily recognized as having a forecasting value. (Rhea, 1932)

> A line is two to three weeks of horizontal price movement in an average within a 5% range. It is usually a sign of accumulation or distribution, and a breakout above or below the range high or low respectively suggests a movement to continue in the same direction as the breakout. Movement from one average unconfirmed by the other average is generally not sustained. (Rhea, 1932)

> The portion of the Dow Theory which pertains to "lines" has proved to be so dependable as almost to deserve the designation of axiom instead of theorem. (Hamilton, September 23, 1929)

> The stock market is not logical in its movements from day to day. (Hamilton, 1929)

Dow, Hamilton, and Rhea would likely be horrified at today's preoccupation with minute-to-minute "day trading" and would likely consider such activity too risky. (Based on the percentage of day traders who currently fail, they would be right.) Their observation essentially states that prices become more random and unpredictable as the time horizon shrinks. This is certainly true today as well and is one reason why, as during Dow's, Hamilton's, and Rhea's time, investors today should concentrate on longer-term time horizons and avoid the tempting traps in short-term trading.

Concept of Confirmation

> Dow always ignored a movement of one average which was not confirmed by the other, and experience since his death has shown the wisdom of that method of checking the reading of the averages. His theory was that a downward movement of secondary, and perhaps ultimately primary importance, was established when the new lows for both averages were under the low points of the preceding reaction. (Hamilton, June 25, 1928)

In line with the economic rationale for the use of the industrial and railroad averages as proxies for the economy and state of business, Dow Theory introduced a concept that also is important today, namely the concept of **confirmation.** Confirmation has taken new directions, which this book covers later, but in Rhea's time, confirmation was the consideration of the industrial and railroad averages together. "Conclusions based upon the movement of one average, unconfirmed by the other, are almost certain to prove misleading" (Rhea, 1932).

Confirmation in the Dow Theory comes when both the industrial and railroad averages reach new highs or new lows together on a daily closing basis. These new levels do not necessarily have to be reached at exactly the same time, but for a primary reversal, it is necessary that each average reverses direction and reaches new levels before the primary reversal can be recognized (see Figure 6.3). Confirmation, therefore, is the necessary means for recognizing in what direction the primary trend is headed. Failure to reach new levels during a secondary reaction is a warning that the primary trend may be reversing. For example, when there is a primary bull market, the failure of the averages to reach new highs during a secondary advance alerts the analyst that the primary trend may be reversing to a bear market. In addition, if lower levels are reached during the secondary bear trend, it is an indication that the primary trend has changed from an upward bull trend to a downward bear trend. Thus, more extreme levels occurring during a secondary retracement in the opposite direction of the primary trend are evidence that the primary trend has changed direction. When confirmed by the other average, the technical analyst then has proof that the primary trend has reversed and can act accordingly.

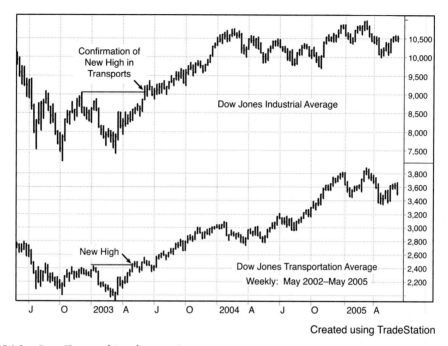

FIGURE 6.3 Dow Theory of "confirmation"

Today, because the makeup of the economy is so different than in Dow's and Hamilton's time, with the advent of a wider base of industrial stocks and technology stocks, the usual method of confirming a primary trend is to use confirmation between the two indexes: Standard & Poor's 500 and the Russell 2000. The economic rationale is that the Standard & Poor's 500 represents the largest, most highly capitalized companies in the United States, and the Russell 2000 represents smaller companies with higher growth and usually a technological base. When these two indexes confirm each other, the primary trend is confirmed. Figure 6.4 shows the more modern application of Dow's theory of confirmation.

Importance of Volume

Various meanings are ascribed to reductions in the volume of trading. One of the platitudes most constantly quoted in Wall Street is to the effect that one should never sell a dull market short. That advice is probably right oftener than it is wrong, but it is always wrong in an extended bear swing. In such a swing... the tendency is to become dull on rallies and active on declines. (Hamilton, May 21, 1909), as quoted in Rhea, 1932)

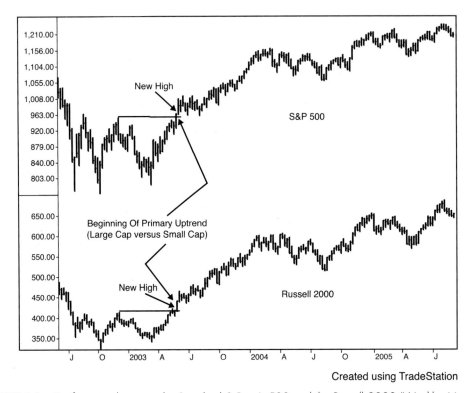

FIGURE 6.4   Confirmation between the Standard & Poor's 500 and the Russell 2000 (Weekly: May 2002–September 2005)

Although volume of transactions cannot signal a trend reversal, it is important as a secondary confirmation of trend. Excessively high market prices that are accompanied by less volume on rallies and more activity on declines usually suggest an overbought market (see Figure 6.5). Conversely, extremely low prices with dull declines and increased volume on rallies suggest an oversold market. "Bull markets terminate in a period of excessive activity and begin with comparatively light transactions" (Rhea, 1932).

The originators of Dow Theory were quick, however, not to overstate the importance of volume. Although volume was considered, it was not a primary consideration. Price trend and confirmation overrode any consideration of volume.

> The volume is much less significant than is generally supposed. It is purely relative, and what would be a large volume in one state of the market supply might well be negligible in a greatly active market. (Hamilton, 1922, p. 177)

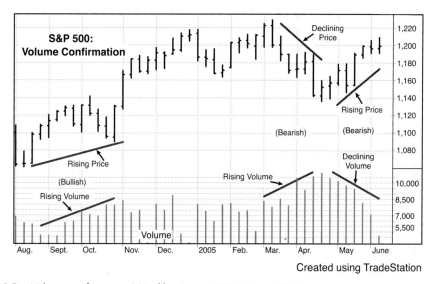

FIGURE 6.5 Volume confirmation (Weekly: August 2004–May 2005)

CRITICISMS OF THE DOW THEORY

Although Dow Theory forms the building blocks for modern-day technical analysis, this theory is not without criticisms. One of the criticisms is that following the theory will result in an investor acting after rather than before or at market tops and bottoms. With Dow Theory, there is an inevitable lag between the actual turn in the primary trend and the recognition of the change in trend. The theory does not recognize a turn until long after it has occurred and has been confirmed.

On the other hand, the theory, if properly interpreted, will recognize that primary trend change and will, thus, never allow a large loss. Dow's contention was that concentrating on any direction change of shorter duration than the primary trend increased the chances of having one's portfolio whittled away by high turnover, many errors in judgment, and increased transaction costs. Therefore, Dow Theory is biased toward late recognition of a change in trend to minimize the costs of wrongly identifying a change in trend.

A second criticism of Dow Theory is that the different trends are not strictly defined. Often the interpretation of price swings is difficult to assign to a specific trend type. Secondary trend beginnings often appear like primary trend beginnings, for example. This makes the determination of the primary trend unclear at times and can incite investment in the wrong direction.

Others, however, criticize Dow Theory for being too specific about the requirements needed to identify a change in trend. Requiring that only closing prices be used or that any break to a new level no matter how small is significant often places too much emphasis on a small change in price.

> ### SUMMARY OF DOW'S WISDOM
>
> ...the Dow-Jones averages... have a discretion not shared by all prophets. They are not talking all the time. (Hamilton, December 17, 1925)

CONCLUSION

Even though Charles Dow never formalized the Dow Theory, his work has formed the basis for modern-day technical analysis. Despite the many changes that have occurred in the securities markets over the past century, much of Dow's basic work and ideas remain pertinent today. Though Dow might be surprised at the analysis that more advanced tools and computer power allow, his classic work provides the basic theory that these contemporary models build upon. Although the specific economic relationships that were valid in Dow's lifetime, such as the relationship between industrial stocks and railroad stocks, may need to be altered to represent today's economy, basic economic relationships such as these are still fundamental to market activity. Despite the fact that today's technical analyst can build sophisticated, complex mathematical models and run complicated computer tests of trading strategies, it is important to remember that a thorough grounding in the basics of market activity is necessary for any trading philosophy to stand the test of time and remain profitable.

REVIEW QUESTIONS

1. What were the three hypotheses of Dow Theory presented by Rhea? How is each of these hypotheses relevant for the modern investor?

2. Describe what the Dow Theory ideal market pattern of an uptrend, top, downtrend, and bottom looks like.

3. Why did Dow think there was an important economic relationship between the stocks of industrial companies and the stocks of railroads? How do you think this general relationship between economic activity and sectors of the economy might be seen and measured in today's economy?

4. What are the three major trends in Dow Theory? Which is the most important? Why?

5. Dow Theory teaches that, while the investor is foregoing potential profit, the investor should avoid trying to make money by attempting to predict the secondary trend. Why did Dow and his followers think that trading with the secondary trend was too risky?

6. How would Dow and his followers react to the modern-day practice of day trading? According to Dow Theory, what trend are these day traders following?

7. What is meant by the term *confirmation* in Dow Theory?

8. What role does volume play in Dow Theory?

9. According to Dow Theory, what signals would an investor watch for that would indicate a reversal in the primary trend?

10. One of the criticisms of Dow Theory is that it calls market reversals long after they occur. Explain why Dow Theory makes these market calls late. What are the trade-offs that investors make with a system that tends to make late calls of market reversals?

SENTIMENT

CHAPTER OBJECTIVES

After studying this chapter, you should

- Understand what the term *sentiment* means
- Understand the concept of contrary opinion
- Be familiar with methods for measuring sentiment of uninformed and informed market players

As a general rule, it is foolish to do just what other people are doing, because there are almost sure to be too many people doing the same thing. (William Stanley Jevons [1835–1882], as quoted in Neill, 1997, p 13)

The focus of this chapter is market sentiment. **Market sentiment** refers to the psychology or emotions of market participants. At times, investors are acting on feelings of fear and pessimism. At other times, hope, overconfidence, and greed characterize **investor psychology.** Investors react emotionally to the market, and these reactions affect the market. Thus, investor psychology is both influenced by and an influencer of market activity.

From a simplistic standpoint, consider a bull market in which stock prices have been advancing. Investors see their portfolio values increasing. Those who have been sitting on the sidelines hear how their friends have made money in the stock market. Not wanting to miss out on these returns, they join in. The average investor is hopeful and confident that the trend of rising stock prices will continue. Of course, as these investors place more and more money in the market, stock prices do rise; in economic jargon: As the quantity of investors in the marketplace increases, the demand for stocks increases, driving stock prices higher. The optimistic view of the market participants drives prices even higher. Seeing that they were correct, investors eventually become overconfident and greedy, and purchase even more stocks irrespective of "value." At the peak of optimism, investors have placed most of their available money in the stock market. At this point, there are dwindling amounts of money available to fuel the demand that has been driving price upward. There is no more fuel to keep stock prices rising, and the stock market reaches a peak.

Conversely, when investors are pessimistic and fearful, they begin to sell stock. As the level of pessimism rises in the market and more investors sell, stock prices fall. These falling prices lead more and more investors to feel fearful and to sell their shares. When investors are the most pessimistic and fearful, they have withdrawn much of their money from the market. The downward trend exacerbated by investors leaving the market ends, and the market reaches a bottom.

WHAT IS SENTIMENT?

Sentiment is defined as the net amount of any group of market players' optimism or pessimism reflected in any asset or market price at a particular time. When a stock or commodity is trading at a price considerably above or below its intrinsic value, something we will not know until considerably later, the difference or deviation from that value often will be accounted for by sentiment. It is the collective emotion and other intangible factors that come from the human interaction involved in determining a price over or under the supposed value. It is the subject of study by behavioral finance departments, which are interested in the ways that human cognitive bias and brain activity affect financial decisions, and it is a staple in technical analysis, for technical analysts have long held that prices are a combination of fact and emotion. When emotion becomes excessive and prices thereby deviate substantially from the norm, a price reversal is usually due, a reversion at least to the mean and sometimes beyond. It is, thus, important for the technical analyst to know when prices are reflecting emotional extremes.

BOX 7.1   THE THEORY OF CONTRARIAN INVESTING

Whenever nonprofessional investors become "significantly" one-sided in their expectations about the future course of stock prices, the market will move in the direction opposite to that which is anticipated by the masses.

Suppose the overwhelming numbers of investors (call them "nonprofessionals") become rampantly bullish on the market. The logical extension of highly bullish expectations results in the purchase of stocks right up to the respective financial limits of the masses. At the very moment when the masses become most bullish, they will be very nearly fully invested! They won't have the financial capacity to do more buying. Who then is left to create demand? Certainly not the minority of investors we call professionals. It is that group which recognizes over-valuations and presumably has been the supplier of stock to the nonprofessionals during the time that both prices and the optimism of the masses were rising.

> Thus, when the crowd has become extraordinarily bullish, a dearth of demand exists. The nonprofessionals are loaded with stocks and are cash-poor, while the professionals are liquid, but in no frame to buy. Demand is saturated, and even minor increases in supply will cause stock prices to tumble. At this point, prices are a strong bet to go (nowhere) but down. (Marty Zweig in the foreword to Ned Davis' The Triumph of Contrarian Investing, McGraw-Hill, New York, 2004.)

MARKET PLAYERS AND SENTIMENT

The appropriate corresponding timing strategy is to follow informed trader sentiment, act against positive feedback trader sentiment, and ignore liquidity trader sentiment. (Wang, 2000)

Remember from Chapter 5, "An Overview of Markets," that there are three types of players in any market: the informed, the uninformed, and the liquidity players. The estate that needed to sell stock to raise cash in the discussion of market players in Chapter 5 was an example of a liquidity player. Liquidity players have only a cursory interest in the markets and do not have an important role in determining price trends. They affect the market minimally. On the other hand, informed and uninformed players are the market. Because the interactions between the informed and uninformed players determine prices, we will focus our discussion on those two groups.

The uninformed players are those participants who, being ruled by their emotions and biases, act irrationally. They tend to be optimistic after a market rise and buy, thus creating market peaks, and to be pessimistic during a market decline and sell, thus creating market bottoms. Though the uninformed players are often called the "public," even professionals can be part of this group. It is not simply the profession or career standing of a market player that classifies an individual as an informed or uninformed player, it is the timing of the player's optimistic buying and pessimistic selling relative to market highs and lows. Research has found that even professionals such as mutual fund managers, Wall Street strategists, and investment-advisory newsletter writers often behave as uninformed participants. In other words, *the majority of market players are uninformed players.*

The informed market players tend to act in a way that is contrary to the majority. That is, the informed market participants tend to sell at the top, when the majority is optimistic, and buy at the bottom, when the majority is fearful and selling. Just as uninformed players need not be amateurs, informed players need not be professionals. They can be corporate insiders or day traders sitting in their dens in the Caribbean.

By and large, the uninformed players have considerably more money than the informed players. While day to day the informed players stabilize the markets by spotting and acting upon small anomalies in prices or as contrarian investors invest in undervalued assets, over longer periods, the uninformed tend to overwhelm the price action with their positive feedback, in many instances, forcing the informed to ride with the trend of emotion.

Because maximum optimism and pessimism tend to occur at market price extremes, and because this emotional background is principally the provenance of the uninformed player, if the technical analyst can determine how each group is acting, some knowledge of the future direction of prices can be gained. Presumably, the informed professional will act correctly, and the uninformed public will act incorrectly, especially at emotional extremes. If we know that a majority of those participating in the market are extremely optimistic about stock prices continuing on an upward trend, we can conclude that these investors are near fully invested in the market and that stock prices are close to a peak. The sentiment indicators that we discuss in this chapter are designed to measure the extent of investor optimism or pessimism. By using sentiment indicators, the technical analyst is attempting to separate the opinions and actions of the informed players from the uninformed players. The analyst wants to make investment decisions contrary to those that the uninformed group is making and wants to mimic the actions of the informed players.

BOX 7.2   NEUROCHEMISTRY AFFECT ON HUMAN THINKING

Neurotransmitters affect emotion and behavior. At present there have been discovered over 108 different neurotransmitters that interact, stimulating and inhibiting the activities of each other. "Five of these neurotransmitters act throughout most of the brain: Histamine, serotonin, dopamine, gamma-aminobutyric acid (GABA), and acetylcholine." (Peterson, 2007 [*Inside the Investor's Brain: The Power of Mind Over Money*], p. 48) "Additionally, local actions of opiods, norepineprhine, stress hormones, and omega-3 fatty acids affect behavior and decision making. And if that weren't enough, common medications, street drugs, and foods also should be considered for the neural effects on judgment." (Peterson, p. 50)

"Many pathological mood states (such as depression, mania, anxiety, and obsession), neurological conditions (such as Parkinson's disease and Alzheimer's disease), and impulse-control disorders (such as kleptomania, compulsive shopping, and pathological gambling) are known to affect financial decision making: depression is associated with risk aversion, mania with investing overconfidence, anxiety with "analysis paralysis," and compulsions with overtrading. Interestingly, the financial symptoms of these illnesses can be reduced by medications." (Peterson, p. 47)

HOW DOES HUMAN BIAS AFFECT DECISION MAKING?

Remember, the Efficient Markets Hypothesis (EMH) suggests that enough investors are acting rationally at any particular point in time to make it impossible for a technical analyst to profit from security mispricing due to the emotions of the uninformed players. However, the field of behavioral finance has defined numerous ways in which investors act less than rational. These biases are common not just to the occasional investor or uninformed public but to professionals as well. Just look at how many professional securities analysts were caught in the late 1990s stock market euphoria. These were not stupid, irrational people, but their inherent biases, those common to all humans, overcame their ability to reason, and they became caught up in the optimism of the time, to tragic effect.

BOX 7.3 INVESTORS ARE THEIR OWN WORST ENEMIES

From Zweig (2007)

- Everyone knows that you should buy low and sell high—and yet, all too often, we buy high and sell low.
- Everyone knows that beating the market is nearly impossible—but just about everyone thinks he can do it.
- Everyone knows that panic selling is a bad idea—but a company that announces it earned 23 cents per share instead of 24 cents per share can lose $5 billion of market value in a minute-and-a-half.
- Everyone knows that Wall Street strategists can't predict what the market is about to do—but investors still hang on every word from the financial pundits who prognosticate on TV.
- Everyone knows that chasing hot stocks or mutual funds is a sure way to get burned—yet millions of investors flock back to the flame every year. Many do so though they swore, just a year or two before, never to get burned again.

…our brains often drive us to do things that make no logical sense—but make perfect emotional sense.

Those who study behavioral finance attribute some of the biased behavior of financial market players to crowd behavior. These researchers have found that crowd opinions are formed by several biases. People tend to conform to their group, making the taking of an opposite opinion sometimes difficult and dangerous. People do not like rejection or ridicule and will stay quiet to avoid such pressure. People often meet hostility when going against a crowd. Another bias is that people gain confidence by extrapolating past trends, even when doing so is irrational, and, thus, they tend to switch their opinions slowly. Also, people feel secure in accepting the opinions of others, especially "experts," and tend to believe the establishment will take care of them.

Understanding that investor emotion and bias affect investment decisions is important for two reasons. First, understanding the links between emotions, investment behavior, and security prices can help the technical analyst profit by spotting market extremes. Second, technical analysts must remember that they are subject to the same human biases as other investors. This set of human biases is so strong that even those who recognize them still are affected by them and must constantly fight against them. Successful traders and investors often say that the worst enemy in investment is oneself. Technical analysts hope to profit from understanding how human bias can cause people to pay prices greater than the intrinsic value for a stock, but if they are not careful, their own biases may cause them to do the same.

For example, the behavioral finance principle of "representation" suggests that people often recognize patterns where they do not actually exist. Although it is the technical analyst's strategy to attempt to recognize patterns, an analyst must be certain not to "see" patterns that do not really exist. Therefore, an investor or trader must not only understand our human foibles but must also find a way to either fight against them or avoid them.

At times, emotional excess leads to extraordinary rises in prices (and sometimes to extraordinary declines, called **crashes** or **panics**). These periods of extraordinary price increases, whether in the stock market, gold, or tulip bulbs, are called **bubbles.** During a bubble, stock market returns are much higher than the mean, or average, return. Bubbles are part of that fat tail mentioned in the discussion of the nonrandomness of prices in Chapter 4, "The Technical Analysis Controversy." Although bubbles occur infrequently, they occur considerably more often than would be expected under an ideal random walk model.

For the current discussion, the existence of bubbles is proof that prices are not always determined rationally; emotion can get hold of the market and, through positive feedback, run prices far beyond any reasonable value before reversing. This type of bubble is visible in Figure 7.1. During the late 1990s, security prices were rapidly increasing. By 2000, security prices were extremely high, especially in the technology sector. The price earnings ratios for many companies were at record highs. For some companies, the price earnings ratios were infinite because there were no earnings at all. In fact, investors would have to assume that earnings would grow at an astounding 100% per year for 20 years to justify the stock prices using traditional stock valuation models. According to investment analyst David Dreman, "This seems to be a classic pattern of investor overreaction" (Dreman, 2002, p. 4). Nevertheless, the bubble occurred, indicating that investors of all kinds can become blind to reality when greed and other psychological biases influence decision making.

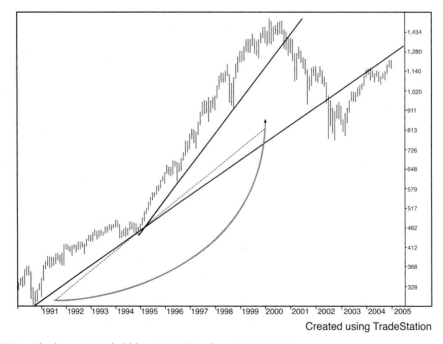

Created using TradeStation

FIGURE 7.1   The late 1990s bubble (S&P 500 Index: 1990–2004)

BOX 7.4 BOOKS ON THE HISTORY OF MANIAS AND PANICS

A number of excellent books have been written about the manias and panics that characterize the financial markets. For further information about this phenomenon, you can read the following:

Ahamed, Liaquat. *Lords of Finance: The Bankers Who Broke the World*. New York, NY: Penguin, 2009.

Allen, Fredrick Lewis. *Only Yesterday*. New York, NY: First Perennial Classics, 2000.

Amyx, Jennifer. *Japan's Financial Crisis: Institutional Rigidity and Reluctant Change*. Princeton, NJ: Princeton University Press, 2004.

Bruner, Robert F. and Sean D. Carr. *The Panic of 1907: Lessons Learned from the Market's Perfect Storm*. New York, NY: John Wiley & Sons, Inc., 2009.

Galbraith, John K. *A Short History of Financial Euphoria*. New York, NY: Penguin House, 1994.

Kindlelberger, Charles P. *Manias, Panics, and Crashes: A History of Financial Crises*. New York, NY: John Wiley & Sons, Inc., 2005.

Mackay, Charles. *Extraordinary Popular Delusions and the Madness of Crowds*. Petersfield, Hampshire, UK: Harriman House, 2003.

Reinhard, Carmen M. and Kenneth Rogoff. *This Time is Different: Eight Centuries of Financial Folly*. Princeton, NJ: Princeton University Press, 2009.

Sobel, Robert. *Panic on Wall Street: A History of America's Financial Disasters*. New York, NY: Macmillan, 1968.

Wicker, Elmus. *Banking Panics of the Guilded Age*. UK: Cambridge University Press, 2008.

CROWD BEHAVIOR AND THE CONCEPT OF CONTRARY OPINION

The art of contrary thinking may be stated simply: Thrust your thoughts out of a rut. In a word, be a **nonconformist** when using your mind.

Sameness of thinking is a natural attribute. So you must expect to practice a little to get into the habit of throwing your mind into directions that are opposite to the obvious.

Obvious thinking—or thinking the same way in which everyone else is thinking—commonly leads to wrong judgments and wrong conclusions.

Let me give you an easily remembered epigram to sum up this thought:

When everyone thinks alike, everyone is likely to be wrong. (Neill, 1997, p. 1)

When individuals think by themselves, they can be very logical and reasonable, but when joined with a crowd, they tend to let certain cognitive biases affect their decision making. History is replete with examples of financial manias, those periods when, in retrospect, the crowd of investors became overly irrational. During those periods, the irrationality is met with a new hysteria, the belief that "things are different this time." We have seen this emotional excess just recently in the Internet stock-price bubble in the late 1990s and in the real estate bubble in the early 2000s. At those times, it was very difficult to argue, much less invest, against the prevailing trend of emotion. Too many were making too much money regardless of their reasoning. Of course, such times eventually reverse and return to normal and often decline to an opposite excess. Not believing that they are personally caught in a mania, when prices reverse, people blame others for their own irrationality. Denying their own responsibility for being duped by the emotions of the crowd, they demand new laws be passed to prevent "evil" corporations or government laxity or fads as derivatives from causing another bubble. Such behavior is not limited to financial markets. Manias occur in politics, religion, philosophy, education—almost every human endeavor. They are often man-made, as in either the Tulip Bulb mania or as in politics through propaganda and "spin." The Theory of Contrary Opinion is an attempt to teach individuals how to recognize and profit from such excesses in emotional fervor and to look at all sides of a belief before committing to it or rejecting it.

> A "crowd" thinks with its heart (that is, is influenced by emotions) while an individual thinks with his brain. (Neill, 1997, p. 3)

> Contrary opinion is a "way of thinking…It is more of an antidote to general forecasting than a system for forecasting. In a few words, it is a thinking tool, not a crystal ball" (Neill, 1997, p. 9). To be a contrarian, an investor must sell (be pessimistic) when the overall market mood is grossly optimistic and buy (be optimistic) when most investors are pessimistic and in a panic. Although this might sound easy enough, the problem with implementing a contrarian strategy is that it is indefinite. Remember that one of the basic tenets of Dow Theory is that prices trend. When prices are trending upward, we want to be in a long position, riding the trend. The goal of understanding sentiment is to discern when that trend is losing energy and will reverse. Therefore, the task of the contrarian player is to find a way in which to quantify which direction the majority of market players is headed and to question whether there is enough remaining energy to keep the market moving in that direction. Remember that so long as players still have money to invest in the market, their optimism will drive prices higher. It is only when players are fully invested that their optimism will not be accompanied by security purchases. At this point, the market is at an excess, and the trend often ends. To quantify these excesses, the technical analyst uses publicly available data to construct indicators of emotional excess. Now that we have looked at some of the theoretical underpinnings, let us look at how these sentiment indicators are typically constructed and evaluated.

HOW IS SENTIMENT OF UNINFORMED PLAYERS MEASURED?

> A top in the market is the point of maximum optimism, and a bottom in the market is the point of maximum pessimism. (Davis, 2003, p. 9)

Sentiment indicators are data series that give the technical analyst some feeling for how much prices are at an excessively emotional level. With that information, potential future reversals in trend can be better anticipated. Generally, sentiment indicators are more useful in analyzing markets than individual issues. Individual issue prices have their emotional component, of course, but ways to measure that component are much less reliable than those of measuring overall market sentiment. Therefore, we focus our discussion on indicators that reflect overall market optimism.

Remember, we are interested in the two broad categories of players—the uninformed and the informed. Most sentiment indicators focus on the uninformed. These uninformed players are usually wrong at major market turns. Therefore, if we know what the uninformed are doing, we have a clue about what *not* to do. On the other hand, some sentiment indicators attempt to measure the action of informed players, who generally are accurate in their assessment of market prospects. These indicators are based on watching professional traders and corporate insiders and following their lead.

Fear and greed are not mirror images of one another. Emotional excess is often the sharpest at market bottoms when panic has occurred. On the other hand, optimism can last for a long while. Most sentiment indicators are, therefore, useful in determining market bottoms when the fear reaches its highest level. These indicators can often be deceiving on the rise in prices, however, because the extreme in greed, the converse of fear in markets, will place them at high levels during which the market will continue to rise. A sell signal generated by a specific sentiment indicator is, thus, less likely to be as valid as a buy signal.

Sentiment Indicators Based on Options and Volatility

To glean some information about what uninformed traders are doing, analysts often consider option trading activity and volatility measures. Option trading can be a sign of market speculation, and volatility can be an indication of the anxiousness of market players. Let's look at some of these measures.

Option Trading and Sentiment

Traditionally, odd lot statistics were reliable indicators of the sentiment of uninformed, small investors. That small investors, who did not have enough capital to purchase round, 100-share lots, were heavily buying stocks was an indication that the uninformed public was overly optimistic. When small, uninformed investors were highly pessimistic, they would short sell odd lots. The odd lot figures represented a measure of uninformed, public speculation, which tended to be highest at market turning points.

Today, listed options data has replaced the old odd-lot figures as one of the best measures of public speculation. A call option is an option to buy an asset, usually a stock or commodity, at a fixed price for a specific period. A put option is an option to sell an asset at a fixed price for a specific period of time. Some options, by expanding on the basics of time and price, can become very complex. However, the standard call and put option is the most widely traded and has the highest volume of any option type. The option market, by its very nature, is a speculative market.

It depends on leverage for maximum gains, and positions can close worthless on the expiration of options. As such, it has become a speculative vehicle for the uninformed public.

Let us look at how the options market can measure sentiment. Let us assume that Jerry thinks that the price of stock XYZ will increase above its current level of $20 per share. Jerry can purchase a call option in which he has the option to buy 100 shares of XYZ at a price of $20 per share anytime in the next three months. The option price and premium—say, $2 per share—is much less than the outright purchase price of the stock. If the price of XYZ rises above $20, Jerry can exercise his option and purchase shares at the guaranteed, and now very favorable, $20. If instead, the price of XYZ declines or remains flat during the three-month period, Jerry will allow the option to expire and he will lose his investment. Thus, the option market gives Jerry, an uninformed player, a way to speculate about the movement of the price of a stock by paying a small fee for the option. When investors think that stock prices will rise, they speculate by purchasing call options. When investors are bearish, they speculate by purchasing put options. When investors are very bullish, they buy out-of-the-money call options—those that have a striking price above the current stock price—because they trade at very low prices.

Owners will exercise their call options when they correctly project price increases and their put options when they correctly anticipate price decreases. When investors incorrectly predict market moves, exercising their options is unprofitable. If the owner of an option does not exercise the option by the expiration date, then the option expires worthless.[1]

Because the purchase of a call represents one who believes the stock market will rise and a put reflects a bearish opinion, the ratio of calls to puts represents the relative demand for options by speculators and, thus, is a hint as to their disposition toward the market. The more call buyers relative to put buyers, the more optimistic are the speculators.

Using Put/Call Ratios to Gauge Sentiment

There are several ways to calculate a ratio between puts and calls. Some have used a ratio of the average premium paid for calls versus the average premium paid for puts. In theory, the premium represents the anxiousness of the option buyer and the reticence of the option seller. Statistically, however, this has not been reliable for indicating sentiment. Some analysts have added the price of all options traded each day multiplied by the volume of each trade to arrive at a dollar volume ratio between calls and puts. Not only does this calculation require accurate data and significant computing power, but the information provided by this calculation also has not seemed to be particularly useful. Others have calculated a ratio based on the open interest in calls and puts. Unfortunately, this has also turned out to be a mediocre indicator of contrary opinion.

---

1. It has long been thought that most options expire worthless, indicating that most people purchasing options have incorrectly predicted the direction of market moves. However, recent research indicates that more are exercised than had been thought. In the November 2004 issue of *Technical Analysis of Stocks and Commodities,* Tom Gentile reports on a study of 30 years of option data conducted by Alex Johnson of the International Securities Exchange who found that only 30% of options expire worthless. Roughly 10% are exercised, and the remaining 60% are closed through offsetting transactions. The percentage expiring worthless, nevertheless, is large and still suggests that many option buyers are uninformed.

The final, simplest, and most consistent method of calculating puts to calls is to calculate a ratio of the total volume of puts traded in a day versus the total volume of calls (McMillan, 1996). For the stock market, the raw volume statistics as well as the ratio are available in Microsoft Excel format on the Web site of the Chicago Board Options Exchange (www.cboe.com), known as the CBOE, the largest options exchange in the world according to the Futures Industry Association. One unique way of measuring option-player sentiment is the International Securities Exchange (ISE) Sentiment Index. The ISE (www.ise.com) is the largest electronic options exchange in the United States, and offers trading in over 2,000 equity, ETF, index, and foreign exchange products. Their Sentiment Index, based on the idea that investors will often buy call and put options to express their market view of a stock, uses opening long position volume only. Because they are not considered representative of true market sentiment due to their specialized nature, firm trades and market markers are excluded from the calculation.

Option volume ratios have changed over the 35 years that options have been traded in exchanges. It is, thus, imperative to smooth the raw volume data using moving averages to reduce the effect of this long-term relationship change. Ned Davis Research, Inc. (www.ndr.com), using the ISE Sentiment Index, discovered a technique to take advantage of short-term stock market moves. They calculated a ratio of the 13-day simple moving average to the 20-day simple moving average of the index. When the ratio rose above 1.02, a buy signal was generated, and when the ratio declined below 0.98, a sell signal was generated. Figure 7.2 displays and summarizes the results of these signals. They are high-turnover signals with an average of 12.5 trades per year.

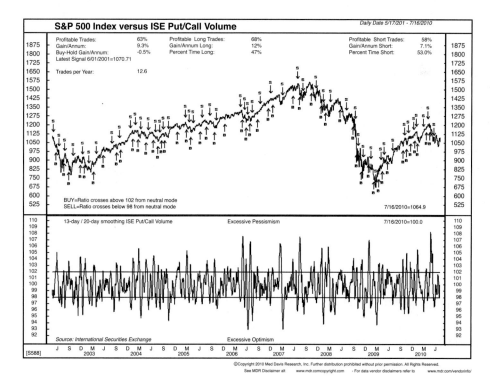

FIGURE 7.2   ISE Sentiment Index and the S&P 500 (daily: May 17, 2002–July 16, 2010)

Ken Tower, CMT, chief market strategist at Quantitative Analysis Services, Inc., uses a ratio of the 10-day moving average of the put/call volume to the 126-day moving average, roughly equivalent to a 2-week versus a 26-week moving average. Deviations between these two averages determine the extremes in option emotion. A high ratio suggests more put buyers than call buyers, indicating that the uninformed players are pessimistic. Because this ratio is a contrarian indicator, a high put/call ratio is generally favorable for the future market direction. By combining futures premium/cash ratios on the NASDAQ and S&P 500 futures with CBOE put/call volume, Ned Davis Research, Inc., found another superior method with excellent trade performance, as shown in Figure 7.3. This combination of contrary opinion indicators produced a 26.6% gain per annum when favorable and a 17.8% loss when unfavorable. It appears that option volume and futures premiums are excellent methods of measuring speculator opinion.

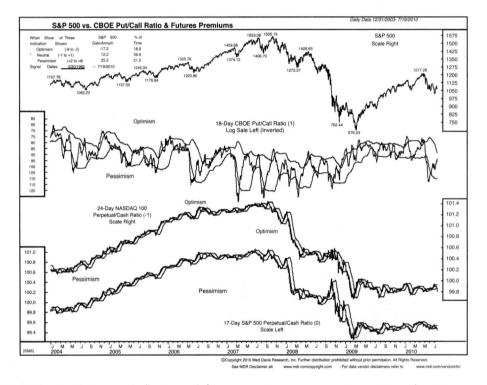

FIGURE 7.3 Combining put/call ratios with futures premium to gauge sentiment (December 31, 2003–July 19, 2010)

Volatility and Sentiment

Another strategy for analyzing the behavior of the uninformed market participants is looking at volatility. Volatility is a measure of the amount by which a security price oscillates, usually about its mean, without regard to its trend over a specified period. The most common calculation for volatility is the standard deviation about the mean. Historical volatility is the standard deviation of prices in the underlying security about its mean over some past period. The 100-day volatility, for example, is the amount by which a security oscillated over the past 100 days about its mean.

Volatility is mean reverting. Therefore, when it gets out of alignment with what it has been on average, we can assume that it will return to its mean. As in security returns, however, this is not an absolute. Just as there are fat tails in the distribution of price returns, fat tails also occur in volatility distributions. Another common assumption is that volatility is independent of price return. In other words, adherents to this assumption claim that the ability to predict the volatility of a security will not aid in predicting the future price direction or return. Some evidence refutes this hypothesis. Volatility is often a measure of the anxiousness of the players in the security market, increasing as they become nervous and decreasing as they become complacent. Because the players act as a crowd and are often uninformed, volatility can be a predictive factor in markets. Let us look at some of the ways to measure volatility.

Using Volatility to Measure Sentiment

VIX is the exchange symbol for a percentage indicator of implied volatility in Standard & Poor's 500 options. Volatility in the NASDAQ Composite and the S&P 100 Index are represented by VXN and VXO, respectively. VIX, VXN, and VXO are traded on the CBOE as futures and options. Instead of measuring historical volatility, these indicators measure what is known as **implied volatility.** Historic volatility is past volatility and generally oscillates with past anxiousness. By looking at implied volatility, the analyst hopes to measure market participants' anxiousness about the future.

Implied volatility is a figure derived from the Black-Scholes option formula. The Black-Scholes option-pricing model suggests that the price of an option is a function of the spread between the underlying security price and the strike price of the option, the time remaining in the option, the prevailing interest rate, and the volatility of the underlying security. If we know the price of an option, the option strike price, the price of the underlying security, the interest rate, and the time remaining in the options, we can calculate the only missing variable—the implied volatility. Thus, implied volatility is the volatility implied by the option traders in their pricing of the options in the marketplace. Implied as well as historic volatility correlates to some extent with market prices. High volatility tends to occur at periods of stress, emotion, uncertainty, fear, and nervousness, most often peaking at a panic bottom. On the other hand, low volatility seems to occur during market rises and market peaks when emotions are calm, content, and relaxed. By looking for extremes in implied volatility then, because implied volatility expresses the expectations of those option traders, we can determine market emotion. VIX is the most common measure of implied market volatility, and its predictive ability is demonstrated in Figure 7.4.

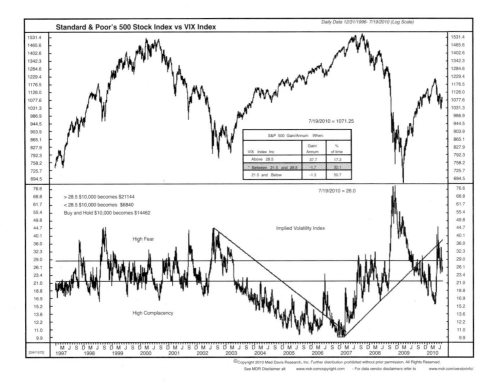

FIGURE 7.4 The S&P 500 and VIX (December 1996–July 2010)

Combining Put/Call Ratio and Volatility

One final method of using option data is using the CBOE put/call volume ratio for all stocks and the VXO, the implied volatility index for the Standard & Poor's 100 Index, the OEX. By calculating the ratio of a 10-day moving average to a 65-day moving average for each figure to normalize the data and averaging it by summing the two calculations and dividing by two, Kaeppel (2004) developed an option sentiment index that signaled intermediate market turns during the period from January 1997 through February 2003. As with many other indicators, the long, sustained rise into 2000 was partially missed with early sell signals. Option sentiment and other measures of sentiment tend to work more reliably at bottoms when investors panic than during an advance when greed develops more slowly.

Polls

One way to measure the sentiment of market participants is simply to ask the players if they are bearish or bullish. Although this might appear to be the most straightforward way of gathering information about expectations, sampling problems and other biases associated with poll taking exist. Despite these biases, poll results, if measured over a constant time interval, can give some idea of the public mood. Poll results are contrary indicators because they express optimism at market tops and pessimism at market bottoms. Polls, thus, gather information and measure the sentiment of uninformed investors. Several different companies collect and publish sentiment information based on polls. Let us look at a few of these.

Advisory Opinion

Investors Intelligence (www.investorsintelligence.com), a wholly-owned U.S. subsidiary of Stockcube Plc, a U.K. company, located in New Rochelle, New York, provides sentiment information in its Advisory Service Sentiment survey. Since 1963, the company has read approximately 120 independent ("not affiliated with brokers or mutual funds") investment-advisory newsletters every week and determined the percentage of those that are bullish, bearish, or expecting a correction. Intuitively, it seems that newsletter writers would be more sophisticated and, thus, more in tune with the market than the public they advise, but the numbers over the past 40 years instead show a tendency to be incorrect, especially at market extremes. Thus, this survey provides information about the uninformed players and works as a contrarian indicator. What they have found is that when the percentage of bearish advisors is greater than 50 and the percentage of bullish advisors is less than 25, a buy signal occurs in the general stock market. On the other hand, when the percentage of bearish advisors declines below 20 and the percentage of bullish advisors exceeds 55–60, a sell signal occurs. They neglect showing any tests of these levels, and have derived them purely from observation of the statistics over 45+ years.

The profitability of using this information to make trading decisions is questionable. Solt and Statman (1988) found no statistically significant relation between the sentiment of investment newsletters and stock returns: The raw numbers and several ways of looking at them have not proven to be informative in the past. Colby (2003) found no profitable results in the crossing of advisory data exponential moving averages between 1 and 1,000 weeks.

However, several studies by others have shown that with certain modifications, the advisory sentiment in the past has been a somewhat reliable indicator of future stock market price action. A standard calculation of advisory sentiment is the ratio of the percentage of bullish advisors to the total of the percentages of bullish and bearish advisors. This is then plotted (see Figure 7.5) and the signal levels are determined. Ned Davis Research, Inc., used a ten-week simple moving average of this ratio and determined that a rise above 69% in the ratio resulted in a loss/year of 0.6%, and a decline below 53% produced a gain/year of 11.5% over the period September 18, 1970 through February 12, 2010. These are credible results.

To improve these results, they added a monetary background component, as displayed in Figure 7.6. They based the monetary background on a 26-week rate of change in three-year U.S. Treasury bill yields and Moody's BAA bond yields from January 1965 through February 12, 2010, and produced a gain/annum of 13.1% versus a buy-and-hold gain of 5.8%.

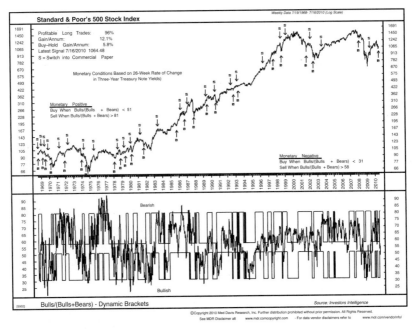

Data source: Investors Intelligence

FIGURE 7.5 Advisory opinion—Percentage bullish/[percentage bullish + percentage bearish] (July 1968–July 2010)

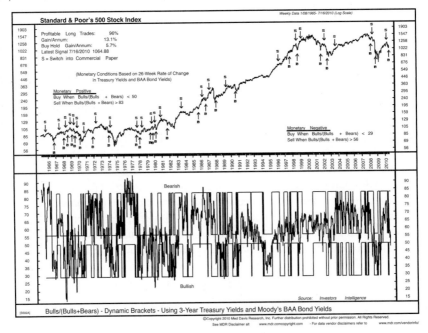

Data source: Investors Intelligence, Moody's, U.S. Treasury

FIGURE 7.6 Advisory opinion with monetary component (January 1965–July 2010)

Colby (2003) also suggests that when a large percentage of advisors are bearish, market prices will rise. He suggests using advisory sentiment to find these periods of extreme pessimism by using an optimistically skewed decision rule. In this decision rule, investors take a short position whenever the percentage of bearish newsletters is greater than the 54-week exponential moving average of bears plus ten percentage points. Following this strategy over the 1982–2001 period would have resulted in a net profit of 70.3% over the profits of a buy-and-hold strategy.

American Association of Individual Investors

The American Association of Individual Investors (AAII; www.aaii.com) compiles a daily poll from its 150,000 members on what they believe the stock market will do over the next six months. DeBondt (1993) found that the members polled by the AAII tended to forecast as though they expected a continuation of the past stock returns. Ned Davis Research, Inc., found that over the July 1987–February 2010 period, when a two-week moving average of the bullish investor percentage divided by the sum of the bullish and bearish percentages rose above 65.0 (that is, the AAII investors were too optimistic), the stock market had a tendency to decline 2.8% per annum. When the ratio declined below 59.5, the stock market had a tendency to rise 9.9% per annum (see Figure 7.7).

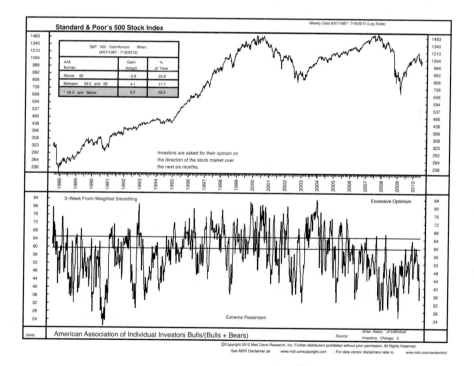

FIGURE 7.7 American Association of Individual Investors bulls and bears (August 1987– July 2010)

Consensus Bullish Sentiment Index

Consensus, Inc., (www.consensus-inc.com) of Independence, Missouri, draws from a mix of brokerage house analysts and independent advisory services to compile the Consensus Bullish Sentiment Index. The data covers a broad spectrum of approaches to the market, including the fundamental, technical, and cyclical. Consensus, Inc., considers only opinions that have been publicized.

Market Vane

Market Vane Corporation (www.marketvane.net) of Pasadena, California, polls 100 leading commodity trading advisors every day for their opinions of the futures markets, principally: stock indexes, T-bonds, gold, silver, Yen, crude oil, soybeans, live cattle, sugar, and others. This data is then used to construct the bullish consensus statistics published in *Barron's* every week.

The Sentix Sentiment Index

Originated in February 2001, the relatively new Sentix Index (www.sentix.de) is a comprehensive poll of German investors about their opinion of the markets, including the U.S. stock and bond markets. The poll is taken every week on Friday, and the results are published each Monday morning in Germany. About 3,100 people (among them more than 690 institutional investors) are asked about their opinion on 12 different markets: DAX-Index, TecDAX (German technology stocks), EuroSTOXX 50, S&P 500, NASDAQ Composite, Nikkei-Index, Bund-Future, T-Bond-Future, EUR-USD currency, USD-JPY currency, gold, and oil. The poll includes the investors' expectations for one month (short-term) and six months (medium-term). Hubner (2008) has described several uses of the Sentix data for anticipating market direction, and van Daele (2005) used the Sentix data for his PhD thesis on why "noise traders" act the way they do.

Consumer Confidence Index

The Conference Board (www.conference-board.org), producers of the index of leading economic indicators and the help-wanted index, reports on consumer confidence each month. The Consumer Confidence Index is based on a representative sample of 5,000 U.S. households. The survey is based on consumer expectations for the U.S. economy. Like most other opinion polls, the survey has been a contrary indicator to the stock market. As seen in Figure 7.8, Ned Davis Research, Inc., found that between 1969 and 2010, when the survey number rose above 110, demonstrating that consumers were overly optimistic, the stock market remained relatively flat (-0.2% per year). However, when consumers were predominately pessimistic and the survey number declined to below 66, the stock market rose on average 14.6% per annum.

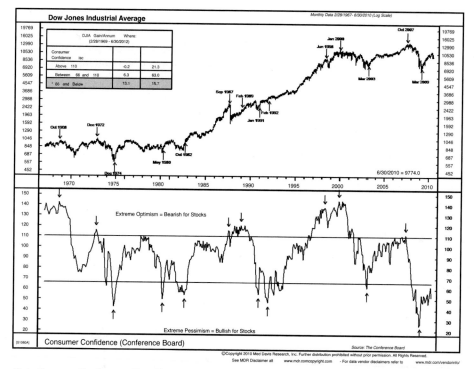

Data Source: Conference Board

FIGURE 7.8   The Consumer Confidence Index (February 1967–June 2010)

Other Measures of Contrary Opinion

The poll-based measures of market sentiment that we have just discussed are based upon what market participants say their market opinions are. Of course, we are not so much interested in whether market participants say they are optimistic; what were are really interested in is how much is their level of optimism resulting in buying and security price increases. Now we consider some other measures of contrary opinion that are based upon movement of money within the markets.

Buying and Selling Climaxes

Investors Intelligence uses the term **climax** to describe a specific event that occurs over a 1-week period. A buying climax occurs when a stock makes a new 52-week high but then closes below the previous week's close. A selling climax occurs when a stock makes a new 52-week low and then closes above the previous week's close. "The reason for such a rigid definition for climaxes is that this enables us to classify accurately and consistently what is and what isn't a climax. This is important as we maintain historic records of the climaxes generated each week and have noted that important market turning points are often accompanied by a sudden rise in the number of buying or selling climaxes," states Investors Intelligence (www.investorsintelligence.com). Figure 7.9 shows the buying and selling climaxes from March 2009 through the beginning of February 2010. Their work shows that sellers into buying climaxes and buyers into selling climaxes are correct in direction about 80% of the time after four months.

Data source: Investors Intelligence

FIGURE 7.9   Buy and sell climaxes (March 2009–February 2010)

Mutual Fund Statistics

Because mutual fund investors are mostly from the uninformed public sector, mutual fund statistics can often be useful in determining what the uninformed is thinking and doing. The most reliable statistic is the cash reserves in stock mutual funds as a percentage of the assets and adjusted for interest rates.

Mutual Fund Cash as a Percentage of Assets
It has long been known that mutual fund cash holdings are contrary indicators for the stock market. There are many reasons for mutual funds to hold cash, but the bottom line is that high levels of cash usually occur at stock market bottoms. Jason Goepfert (2004), in his Charles H. Dow Award paper, building on earlier work by Fosback (1976) and Ned Davis Research, Inc., found that adjusting mutual fund cash for the interest rate is an even more reliable indicator than the cash percent position by itself. He found that when mutual fund cash, adjusted for interest rates,

during the period from January 1981 through June 2004, declined to below its lowest threshold, the stock market rose on average 8.1% over the following year. When the cash level was at its highest, the stock market declined by an average 6.1% over the following year.

Ned Davis Research, Inc., found essentially the same relationship with mutual fund cash percentage, adjusted for interest rates, and the stock market (see Figure 7.10). By measuring the deviation from the 13-month average of the stock mutual fund cash/assets ratio, adjusted for interest rates and during the period from 1965 through February 2010, a level above 0.1 produced an annual gain of 8.4%, and a level below –0.7 produced a gain of only 0.3%.

In neither instance are the results exceptional. Although some watch the mutual fund cash/assets ratio, it appears to be only a marginal indicator of uninformed sentiment.

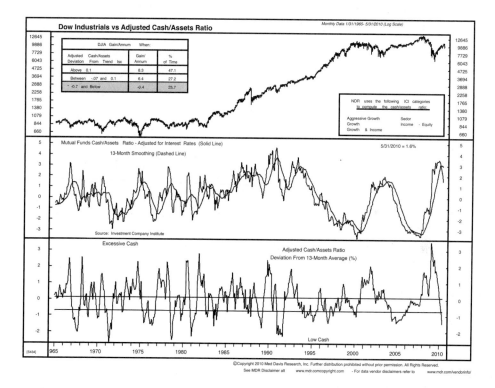

FIGURE 7.10 Mutual fund cash positions adjusted for interest rates (January 1965–February 2010)

Rydex Funds

Mutual fund management companies within the past few years have presented both style and leverage to their public offerings. Rydex Global Advisors (www.rudexfunds.com) has been particularly inventive in its styles. Not only do these include standard long-only stock mutual funds, but also funds that replicate market averages, such as the S&P 500 and the Russell 2000, and others that add leverage to the portfolios. These are called bull funds because they increase in value when the stock market rises. Contrarily, Rydex offers inverse funds in the same style that are short the averages and other indexes. These are called bear funds because they increase when the stock market declines. If the public expects the market to rise, they will purchase the bull funds and sell the bear funds, and vice versa. The ratio of the assets held by these two funds, thus, provides an indication of what direction the uninformed investors in the funds expect the market will travel.

Ned Davis Research, Inc., found that when these investors become optimistic, invariably the market performs oppositely. Indeed, from January 1994 through July 2010, when the ratio rose above 82.5, when more people were purchasing the bull funds than the bear funds, the stock market declined 16.4% per annum, and when these investors loaded up on the bear funds, the stock market advanced 51.7% (see Figure 7.11). These results show an outstanding relationship between sentiment and future market direction.

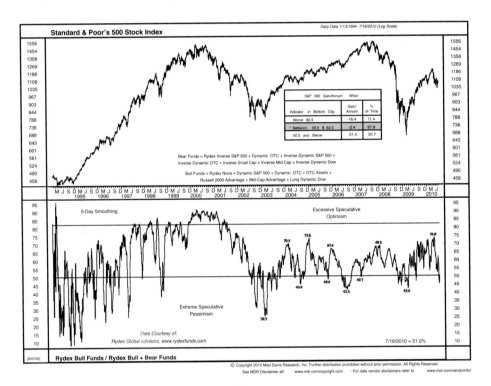

FIGURE 7.11 Rydex Global Advisors bull and bear mutual funds (January 1994–July 2010)

Margin Balances

Each week, *Barron's* reports the NYSE margin debt for the previous month. Traditionally, analysts have considered margin balances evidence of what the uninformed speculator is doing, especially at market peaks. Remember that when uninformed investors are most optimistic, they have placed most of their capital in the market and, thus, may buy stocks on margin to leverage their position. More recently, margin debt reflects professional speculators and might not be as useful as before. Taking away from the usefulness of margin debt for market forecasting is the ability through derivatives of holding positions outside the Federal Reserve requirements for margin, which only apply to banks. Part of the risk incurred by the Long Term Capital Management (LTCM) operation was over a trillion dollars in derivative contracts, most of which required very little margin. Thus, *Barron's* weekly report of margin debt, which at one time was a very reliable indicator, is no longer an accurate gauge of market sentiment. The relationship between margin debt and the S&P 500 from 1970 through 2010 is shown in Figure 7.12.

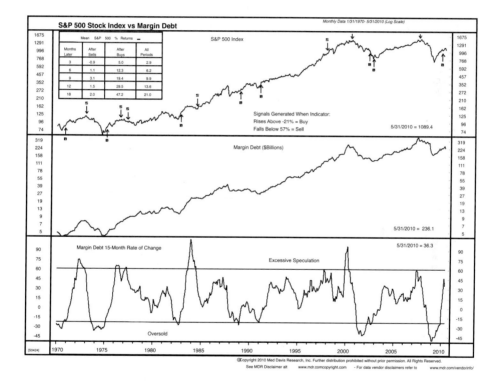

FIGURE 7.12 Margin debt and the S&P 500 (January 1970–May 2010)

Money Market Fund Assets

Where margin debt looks at speculators who are borrowing money to leverage their positions, money market funds are the repository of funds when uninformed players decide to pull back from the markets and hold cash equivalents. As a contrary opinion indicator, we would expect that money market fund assets would increase as investors become more pessimistic and that would, thus, be a sign that the market is bottoming. Ned Davis Research, Inc., found exactly that relationship in the percentage of money market assets to total stock market value (see Figure 7.13). When the percentage increased above 10.8 and uninformed investors were, thus, bearish, the subsequent market rise was 10.9% per annum. When the percentage declined to and below 10.8, the annual loss per annum was 12.5%.

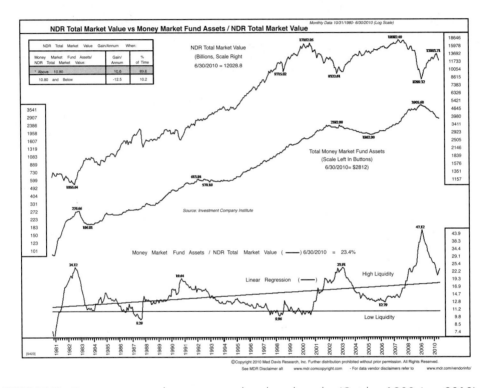

FIGURE 17.13   Percent money market assets to total stock market value (October 1980–June 2010)

Relative Volume

Another reliable indicator of uninformed sentiment is the ratio of NASDAQ to NYSE volume (see Figure 7.14). This ratio gradually increases as public enthusiasm for speculative stocks on the NASDAQ increases, and NASDAQ volume increases relative to NYSE volume. The peak in a trend seems to occur when the ratio peaks, and the bottom of the trend occurs after the bottom in the ratio. Ned Davis Research, Inc., during the period August 1998 through January 2010 (see Figure 7.14), found that when the volume ratio increased above 1.4, the S&P 500 lost 20.9% per annum, and when the ratio declined below 1.1, the S&P 500 gained 30.0% per annum, making this an easy-to-calculate indicator with a profitable history.

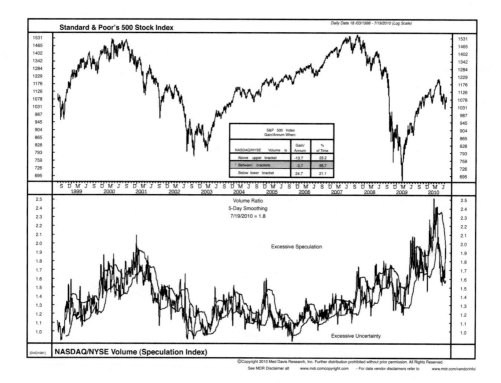

FIGURE 7.14 Ratio of NASDAQ volume to NYSE volume (August 1998–July 2010)

Uninformed Short Selling

Historically, short selling has been predominately a professional activity. It is even more so today with the many derivative securities traded. The modern use of derivatives requires short selling to reduce risk. Thus, the old relationship of short selling having to do solely with opinion about the prospect for companies has diminished. On the other hand, the total amount of short selling seems to increase with an increase in the market direction and is, thus, a contrary opinion indicator.

The Short Interest Ratio is calculated from data provided by the major exchanges, traditionally the New York Stock Exchange, on a monthly basis, and reported in *Barron's* and other financial papers. It is calculated by taking the total amount of stocks sold short as of the specific day of the report divided by the average volume for the month. Colby (2003) reports that over the 69 years of data from 1932 to 2000, using a buy signal when the current ratio was greater than its 74-month exponential moving average, and a sell signal when the 74-month average was broken, a sizable return resulted but it still underperformed the buy-and-hold strategy. This signal worked only for long positions and was out of the market for 457 months, more than half the time.

Ned Davis Research, Inc., (see Figure 7.15) found that the ratio of the 3-month simple moving average to the 45-month simple moving average of short interest was a useful indicator market performance during the 1945–2010 period. When the ratio rose above 1.5 and investors were generally pessimistic, the market advanced 15.2% per annum, and when the spread declined to and below 1.04, the market only declined 4.4% per annum. Interestingly, these results occurred during the recent periods of derivative use when short selling was an active part of the hedging process.

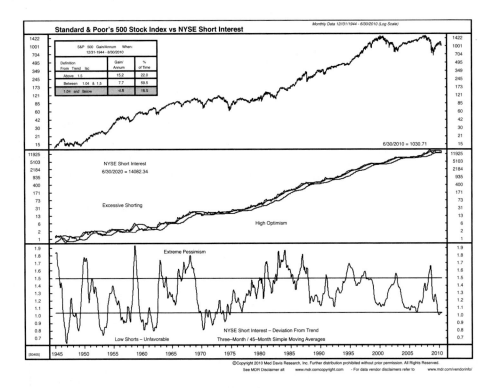

FIGURE 7.15   Short interest ratio and the S&P 500 (December 1945–June 2010)

As for the usefulness of short selling data on individual stocks and determining the potential for a "short squeeze," which is the rapid rise in a stock's price as short sellers scramble to cover, data on individual stocks is available but is often clouded by many variables. To get at information that is more useful on a company basis, considerable digging and filtering must be done to eliminate the influence of derivative transactions that may have little to do with the prospects for the firms. Phil Erlanger (www.erlanger.com) accomplishes a considerable amount of work in this area and publishes results periodically on his Web site. He has found several filters that must be applied to individual stock short sale data: (1) The data must be adjusted for splits—not only price adjustments, but also volume and short interest; (2) it must be normalized to adjust for short-term volume fluctuations; and (3) it must be normalized to adjust for historic volatility. A ranking is established, placing the stock within its smoothed, historical context over a five-year period. This ratio establishes the potential attractiveness of the stock. This number should not be used as a mechanical buy signal, however, because the short sellers may be correct in anticipating the stock to decline.

Odd-Lot Short-Selling

Earlier in this chapter, we discussed how odd-lot statistics have generally fallen out of favor as a measure of uninformed sentiment because the option markets have now replaced small stock orders as a means of speculation. The only odd-lot statistic to have some validity today is the odd-lot short sale data. Traditionally, short selling is considered a speculative endeavor. Most trading in the stock markets, but the commodity markets, is done on the long side, either initiating an invested position or selling that position. A short sale is a trade that anticipates a downward price swing, requires margin, and has infinite risk of loss. It is, thus, used mostly by speculators. Odd-lot short sellers are, therefore, speculators and their position sizes suggest a lack of sophistication. It turns out that, indeed, they are an excellent indicator of uninformed sentiment and, thus, an excellent contrary indicator of market direction.

Ned Davis Research, Inc., found that odd-lot statistics still have some predictive ability. Figure 7.16 shows the results from combining two odd-lot ratios with a put/call ratio into a contrary indicator of market direction. For the period January 2002 through mid-July 2010, the indicator when showing a preponderance of optimism, resulted in a 6.2% decline per annum, and when showing a preponderance of pessimism, resulted in a 27.3% advance. These are impressive results and show that the odd-lot trader is still with us and still acts in an uninformed manner.

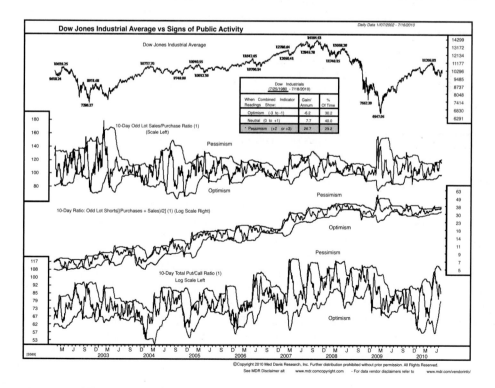

FIGURE 7.16 Odd-lot statistics (January 2002–July 2010)

Unquantifiable Contrary Indicators

Over the years, analysts have watched a number of developments in the society around them in an attempt to gauge the overall mood, emotion, and sentiment of market participants. Many of these indicators are qualitative and not quantitative. Although these indicators are not easily quantifiable and do not lend themselves to traditional statistical testing, they still provide important information to the technical analyst.

One of these unquantifiable indicators is the magazine covers theory. The media covers the news but with a strong bias. It is selling news to those who are interested. If the stock market is high and ready to decline, the media would be unlikely to report the danger even if they know it. Instead, they will emphasize the fact that the market has risen and is strong. They want people to listen, to subscribe, and to read their output, and they will not get business if they report contrary to the popular beliefs of the day. Their business is providing their subscribers with what they want. Thus, when major news magazines such as *Time, Newsweek, U.S. News and World Report, Barron's,* the *Economist,* or *BusinessWeek* include on their cover an article on the stock market, up or down, they are emphasizing what the public believes and already knows—and as has been shown previously, the public is generally wrong, at least at extremes. For this reason, these stories usually occur at or before major turning points in the stock market.

Paul Macrae Montgomery, currently with Universal Economics, has studied magazine covers back at least to 1923. He has observed that after a positive major magazine cover story on the stock market, 60% to 65% of the time the market has gained about 30% per annum over the first one to eight weeks. Eighty percent of the time, however, the market has then reversed within a year and sustained significant losses (Baum, 2000).

In 2007, University of Richmond Professors Arnold, Earl, and North (2007) published in the *Journal of Finance* a study on the market action of the stock of companies featured as cover stories in *BusinessWeek, Fortune,* and *Forbes* between 1983 and 2002. They found that the cover feature article usually followed the stock performance rather than the reverse. A negative story, for example, tended to occur after the decline in the company's stock, and a positive story occurred after a stock rise. They did not find any statistically significant results in postarticle performance, either momentum or contrary (with or against the previous trend). They concluded that if one has a position in a stock that had a good run up or down and a cover story appeared in one of those magazines explaining the reason for the price move, it was probably time to close the position.

Not only does the media report about the market (which provides some idea about the sentiment of the market players), but the reports of the media also impact the mood and emotions of investors. A study commissioned by the *Wall Street Journal* (Klein and Prestbo, 1974, as reported in Kaufman, 1998), found that 99% of financial analysts read a newspaper regularly. Ninety-two percent of these analysts considered the newspaper the "most valuable" publication they read. Obviously, the news is important. However, rapid and correct interpretation of facts is difficult. Sometimes factual news is immediately interpreted by the market incorrectly. For example, when Saddam Hussein was captured, the stock market opened up with a large gap just from the joy of the news. When investors thought about the consequences of that news, they realized it did not change anything, and the stock market closed down that day. Informed traders in a method called "event trading" likely sold into this emotional opening. It is a method of rapidly gauging the sentiment produced by a news announcement, determining whether the market is overacting, and if it is, acting contrarily. Another aspect of event trading is gauging whether the market or a stock is acting as it should on particular news, and if it is not, perhaps the news was already discounted in the price and a change in direction is due. Event trading or news trading is a very short-term use of contrary opinion.

BOX 7.4   ECCENTRIC SENTIMENT INDICATORS

Over the years, stock market followers have developed a number of "eccentric indicators" to predict stock market movements. Not based on economic or financial data, these indicators are "feel-good" or "hype" indicators that attempt to measure the overall morale of the investing population. One of the oldest feel-good indicators, first suggested by either the late Ralph Rotnem of Harris, Upham & Company (now, after a long string of mergers, Citibank) or Ira Cobleigh & DeAngelis (1983), followed women's hemlines: As hemlines rose, so did the stock market, and as hemlines fell, so did the stock market. Consider the Roaring 20s, when women wore short flapper skirts and a stock market rise followed. When the stock market crashed during the great depression, long, modest skirts followed. The hemline index implies that as people become more exuberant, stock prices rise and clothing becomes more daring, and as society becomes more pessimistic, people become more conservative with their clothing and investment choices. Market and economy watchers have also considered beer versus wine sales (people drink more beer when the market is down and approaching a low), sedans versus coupes (people buy more sedans and fewer coupes when the market is down), lipstick sales (when the market is down, women buy cheaper brands), aspirin (a rise in sales correlates with distress about the market), and the number of golf balls left at the driving range (people don't leave balls when the market is declining).

It must be emphasized that none of these indicators has an effect on stock prices. If a direct relationship exists, it exists only as correlation without a direct link to the markets. Indicators, to be truly useful, must have a rationale for their existence. Correlations may be purely accidental and, thus, meaningless. For a discussion of how some of these offbeat indicators have performed, go to www.Forbes.com/2001/06/28/exotics.html.

Historical Indicators

There are several indicators that technical analysts have used historically that you may see discussed in the literature. Although these indicators have little relevance today, at one time they played a prominent historical role in the measurement of market sentiment.

The first is NYSE member and nonmember statistics. The advent of off-board trading and of electronic trading, complicated by the use of derivatives for hedging, marginalized the usefulness of this data. At one time, the various ratios (nonmember short sale ratio, public to specialist short sale ratio, and specialist short sale ratio) had some useful, predictive meaning in the stock market. No longer, however, do these figures mean anything. Because the marketplace itself has changed so drastically, the member figures have gone out of use and are considered unreliable.

The second historically important sentiment indicator to have fallen from favor is the *Barron's* Confidence Index. This index, developed in 1932, measures the ratio of yields on high-grade bonds versus yields on speculative bonds. Although it is still published today, it seems no longer to have relevance for measuring stock market sentiment.

HOW IS THE SENTIMENT OF INFORMED PLAYERS MEASURED?

Thus far, we have focused mainly on the sentiment of the uninformed market players. Remember that these market participants often make incorrect market decisions, especially at market extremes. Therefore, the sentiment of the uninformed players is used in a contrarian strategy. Now, we center our attention on the sentiment of informed players—those most likely to make correct market decisions.

Insiders

The ultimate informed player, at least in individual stocks or commodities, is the insider. An insider is anyone who is a knowledgeable member of a firm that either trades in the commodity underlying the future most important to the firm's business, such as oil to an oil company or cocoa to a candy company, or who has knowledge of a company's internal business prospects and results and is a stockholder. Naturally, these people will act for their own benefit, hopefully within the law, and buy and sell based on their knowledge. Under SEC regulations, corporate insiders must report any stock transactions they make within a month, and in turn the SEC reports these transactions weekly. Because insiders are not allowed to profit from transactions in their company's stock for six months, their actions are a long-term indicator of prospects for the company beyond six months. Investors Intelligence and Vickers Stock Research have found that the compilation of all insider transactions is useful for forecasting the stock market a year out from the reports.

Sell/Buy Ratio

The Sell/Buy ratio is compiled by Vickers Stock Research Corporation, a subsidiary of Argus Research Group (www.argusgroup.com). It takes into account the total number of insider buy and sell transactions for each company, the percentage of change in insider holdings, the unanimity of the transactions within each company, reversals in transaction patterns, and very large transactions. A plot of the Sell/Buy ratio for 2006 is shown in Figure 7.17.

Vickers considers a ratio under 2.25 a portent of a higher stock market, and a ratio greater than 2.25 as a sign of impending market problems. Colby (2003) found that between 1971 and 2000, the ratio averaged over five weeks produced for longs only when the smoothed ratio declined below 2.25, a 29.2% profit over buy-and-hold. Bjorgen and Leuthold (2002), using only large insider block transactions, found that from 1983 to 1999, only a small percentage of the time do insiders transact their shares in a one-sided direction, but the three times that they showed excessive buying, the stock market bottomed within several weeks. On the sell side, when excessive selling occurred, the market peaked, and it either declined or consolidated approximately a year later, thus confirming the observations of Investors Intelligence outlined next.

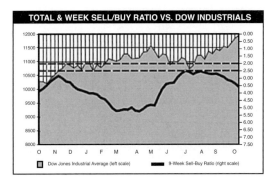

© Vickers Stock Research Corporation

FIGURE 7.17   Insider Sell/Buy ratio (October 2005–October 2006)

Investors Intelligence Method

Investors Intelligence (www.investorsintelligence.com) follows insider activity in two ways. First, for over 1,600 stocks they calculate the total insider buy and sell transactions over the previous nine months. This figure is then compared with the same figure three months prior. This gives them an estimate of the recent direction that insiders are taking with their stock. Second, they break down insider activity into industry groups and compile group rankings that they find often precede the directional movement of stocks within each group. An example of this analysis is shown in Figure 17.18.

Secondary Offerings

As the stock market rises and long-term interest rates increase, companies tend to offer secondary offerings of stock. Sometimes insiders wanting to sell stock cause this, and sometimes it is caused by a desire to raise cheap capital for expansion. Whatever the reason, increased secondary offerings of stock should increase as the market rises and give warning of a peak. Conversely, when insiders are staying away from the secondary market, the stock market is likely at or close to a bottom. Ned Davis Research, Inc., looked into this phenomena and found a weak correlation that confirmed the previous thesis. By calculating a ratio of the 5-month simple moving average of secondary offerings to the 45-month moving average, they found that when the ratio rose above 1.47, the percentage gain per year following was 0.7, whereas when the ratio declined to 109 and below, the gain per year increased to 12.9% (see Figure 7.19).

The **Entertainment Industry** showed a modest ranking retreat. There was a much larger percentage increase for the total sells compared with the increase for the total buys. Only one of the twelve stocks shows favorable insider buying.

	Last quarter	This quarter	Change
Buying decisions	9	12	+3
Selling decisions	26	49	+23
Surplus buying	-17	-37	-20

That positive stock was **Sinclair Broadcasting SBGI** (4 buys, 1 sell). They own 58 television stations in 35, mostly, medium sized markets. Revenues have begun to rebound but poor recent results forced them to increase their debt load to a very risky level. The chart shows Feb and Jul 09 lows below $1 and then a great percentage move up to $5 in Oct-09 and $5.50 this month. That is the area of the long-term down trend line, extended from the April 2007 peak at $17.50. We suggested longs three months ago on the upturn to $4, after the pullback on the first test of resistance.

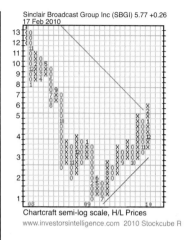

Sinclair Broadcast Group Inc (SBGI) 5.77 +0.26
17 Feb 2010
Chartcraft semi-log scale, H/L Prices
www.investorsintelligence.com 2010 Stockcube R

FIGURE 17.18 Example of Investors Intelligence industry insider analysis, February 16, 2010

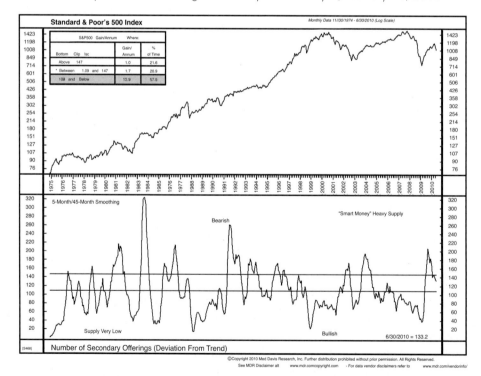

FIGURE 7.19 Secondary offerings (November 1974–June 2010)

Large Blocks

Large blocks tend to be transacted on behalf of professionals. There are several ways that large block data is used. The first is the use of the total number of large block volume relative to the total volume traded. This figure gives an indication of when the large block trader is transacting the most number of shares relative to the market as a whole. Colby (2003) found that when the large block ratio crossed above its 104-week exponential moving average, a buy signal was generated that was profitable 70% of the time with a net profit of 511% over the period from 1983 to 2001. This strategy was only successful on the long side. The short side, which was triggered by the ratio declining below its 104-week average, ended with a loss.

The anxiousness with which stocks are traded is shown by whether buyers trade on upticks or downticks. Aggressive buyers anxious to get a position in a stock will buy large blocks on upticks. The ratio of blocks traded on upticks to those on downticks is, therefore, an indicator of this professional interest in owning stocks.

Ned Davis Research, Inc., found that when large blocks transact predominately on downticks and then reverse direction, a profitable signal was generated in a study from January 1978 through February 2010 (see Figure 7.20). This seems to suggest that although large blocks trade at a market bottom on downticks during the latter stages of panic, when that panic is over and substantial investors begin to take offers on upticks, they know what they are doing and the stock market is invariably at a bottom. The results of the study showed an annual gain of 15.0% over the buy-and-hold of 9.9% per annum on the long side only. Using large block tick data on the short side was unproductive, thus confirming the directional bias observed by Colby (2003).

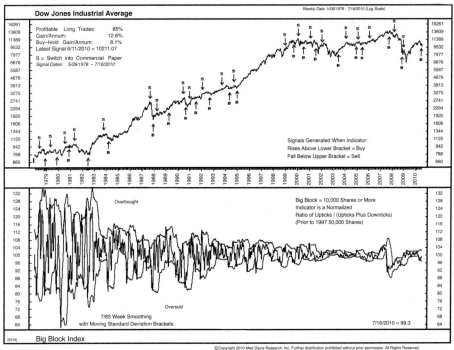

FIGURE 7.20 Big block trades from January 1978–July 2010

Art Merrill studied transactions of large blocks of 50,000 or more shares. Merrill divided the blocks into categories of upticks, downticks, and flat, smoothing each category's data. He ran a ratio of the uptick average to the downtick average, smoothing that ratio over 52 weeks and calculating the running standard deviation from the smoothed average. This provided significant directional signals of 66%, 81%, and 76% over the next 13 weeks, 26 weeks, and 52 weeks, respectively (Colby 2003).

Commitment of Traders (COT) Reports

This study examines whether actual trader position-based sentiment index is useful for predicting returns in the S&P 500 index futures market. The results show that large speculator sentiment is a price continuation indicator, whereas large hedger sentiment is a contrary indicator. Small trader sentiment hardly forecasts future market movements. Moreover, extreme large trader sentiments and the combination of extreme large trader sentiments tend to provide more reliable forecasts. These findings suggest that large speculators possess superior timing ability in the market. (Wang, 2003, p. 891)

With regard to S&P 500 Index futures, we find that large speculator sentiment is a price continuation indicator, whereas large hedger sentiment is a weak contrary indicator. Small trader sentiment does not forecast returns. We show that extreme levels and the combination of extreme levels of sentiments of the two types of large traders may provide a more reliable tool for forecasting. Our result suggests that large speculators may be associated with superior forecasting ability, large hedgers behave like positive feedback traders, and small traders are liquidity traders. (Wang, 2000)

In 1974, Congress created the Commodity Futures Trading Commission (CFTC; www.cftc.gov) to do the following: (1) "protect market users and the public from fraud, manipulation, and abusive practices related to the sale of commodity and financial futures and options" and (2) to "foster open, competitive, and financially sound futures and option markets."

Each week, the CFTC reports on the large positions held in 22 different futures markets, including stock and bond futures, metals, currency exchange rates, and agriculturals. The reports, called the Commitments of Traders or COT, are for positions held as of Tuesday's close and are published on Friday. Only those markets with 20 or more traders holding positions large enough to meet the CFTC requirements are included in the reports.

The "public" position is then taken as the difference between total open interest in each future less those positions held by the traders required to report. The trading positions are divided into two major categories: commercial and noncommercial. This nomenclature is an outgrowth of the agricultural origins of the reports. In the financial markets, the commercial traders, individual or institutional, are those who operate in the cash market and are thus called hedgers. The noncommercial participants take speculative positions, change positions more frequently, and are called large speculators. Traditionally and empirically, in the stock market, the large speculators have a better record of anticipating market moves, whereas the hedgers tend to lag behind and follow the trend (Wang, 2000). Thus, an indicator should consider the spread between the large speculator and the hedger. The small speculators tend to be dysfunctional, and their statistics are of little value.

With respect to the S&P 500 futures, Ned Davis Research, Inc., considered only the commercial (hedger) positions and found a correlation between their changes in position and the subsequent market gain or loss (see Figure 7.21). They took the net position of commercial traders as a percentage of the 78-week range, smoothed over six weeks. Later, you will be exposed to an oscillator called the stochastic. This NDR calculation is a long-term stochastic. When the stochastic advances above overbought at 55%, i.e., when the commercials have large positions, the S&P 500 futures tended to rise 16.0% per annum. When the commercials were bearish and the stochastic declined to 31.5% and below, the market declined 9.0%. This method is the most reliable one of understanding what the professional, informed traders are doing.

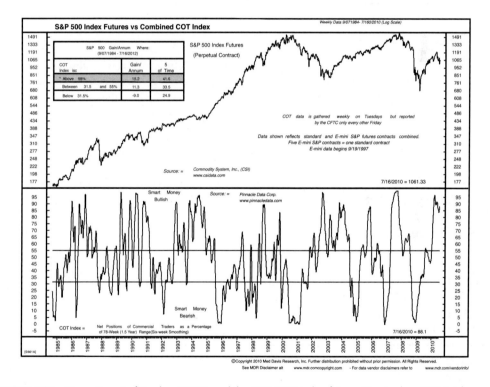

FIGURE 7.21 Commitment of Traders (COT) and the S&P 500 Index futures (September 1984–July 2010)

Because the futures market in the stock market is fractionalized by hedging between markets and other financial instruments, the COT figures for any one market might not be reliable. Tom McClellan, editor of the *McClellan Market Report* (www.mcoscillator.com), combines all the stock futures data into one series of indicators on a dollar-weighted basis and then watches the commercials (hedgers) net long positions as a percentage of the total. He finds that it has recently had a three-week lead to cash stock prices.

A number of tests have used COT data in stock futures, as well as data reported by the CFTC. The most workable systems appear to use smoothed data to normalize the longer-term trends and find that the relationship between commercials and noncommercials are different over time and between futures contracts. It thus behooves the technical analyst to experiment with the different methods for each future contract to see what works best and to update that work continually to expose any changes in relationships between the major players in each market.

SENTIMENT IN OTHER MARKETS

Given the subject matter of this book, our focus thus far in this chapter has been on the stock market. However, we complete our discussion of sentiment by presenting a few major measures of sentiment in other markets.

Treasury Bond Futures Put/Call Ratio

The advent of an options market in futures has created a whole world of new sentiment indicators for these futures markets. The most widely traded are the options of Treasury Bond futures. The chart in Figure 7.22 shows the latest study by Ned Davis Research, Inc., of the predictive ability of these options using the standard put/call volume ratio as a proxy for speculation in the Treasury Bond market. What they found was that when ratio advanced above 1.03, the market had too much pessimism and that the subsequent advance per annum averaged 5.7%. On the other hand, when the ratio declined below .66, the market was too euphoric and subsequently declined 9.1% per annum.

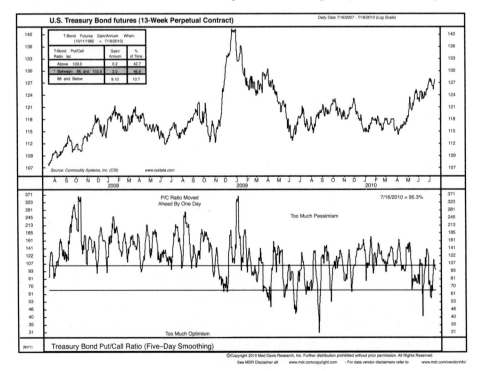

FIGURE 7.22 Treasury Bond futures put/call ratio (July 2007–July 2010)

Treasury Bond COT Data

The spread between large speculators and commercial hedgers is positively correlated with bond prices and inversely related to long-term interest rates (see Figure 7.23). Ned Davis Research, Inc., found that in the period between August 1992 and February 2010, when large speculators were net long, the bond market rose on average 4.8% per year and declined 4.7% per year when the relationship inverted.

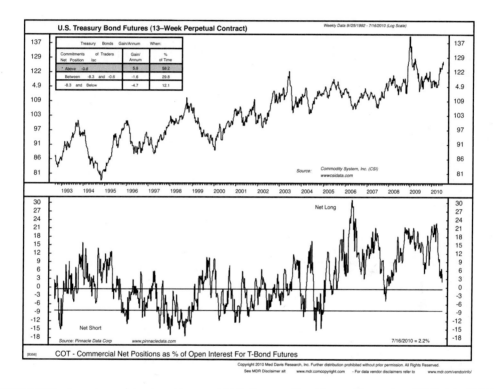

FIGURE 7.23 Large speculators' positions and U.S. Treasury Bond futures (September 1992–July 2010)

Treasury Bond Primary Dealer Positions

Contradicting the preceding relationship between commercials and the future for the bond market is the relationship between primary dealer inventories and the future for bond prices. One would think that primary dealers in bonds, those who can deal with the Treasury Department directly, would have hedged inventory positions in long-term bonds and would thus be considered part of the commercial hedger designation by the CFTC in the COT reports. Further, this would suggest that the dealers would be net long at bond market bottoms and net short at tops. The opposite seems to be the case. Primary dealers have tended to have the most long positions at tops and the most short positions at bottoms (see Figure 7.24). The reason for this logical disparity is likely that dealers must anticipate customer demands. They buy issues from the auction and then sell them to customers. If customers have been bullish, dealers must have an inventory. Thus, they tend to be long at the top when they believe their customers are bullish and willing to pay extra for bonds. Likewise, when pessimism reigns, dealers are hesitant to build inventory and instead hold net short positions, believing that the pessimism will cause customers to sell to them. Thus, at bottoms, dealers become net short.

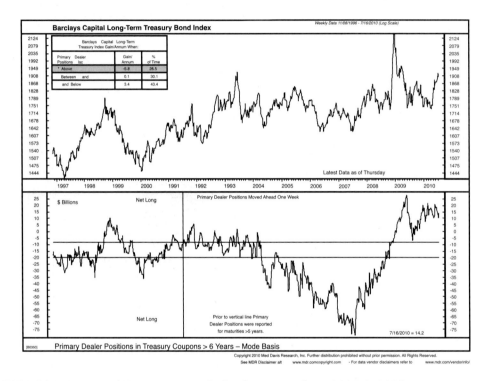

FIGURE 7.24 Positions of Treasury primary dealers from November 1996–July 2010

Ned Davis Research, Inc., found that when dealers were net short, bonds advanced 3.4% per annum, when dealers were essentially neutral, bonds advanced 6.1% per annum, and when dealers were net long, bonds declined 9.1%.

T-Bill Rate Expectations by Money Market Fund Managers

The money market fund business is highly competitive. Money managers, in order to compete on yield, tend to anticipate future short-term interest rates by lengthening or shortening the duration of their T-bill positions. Longer maturity positions suggest that money managers believe that short-term rates will decline, and shorter positions indicate a belief that short-term interest rates will rise. This has turned out to be a contrary indicator for the T-bill market yield. Money managers have tended to be generally incorrect in their assessment of the future for short-term rates. As seen in Figure 7.25, when money managers increase the maturity of their positions in anticipation of lower rates, the rates generally rise instead, and vice versa when they shorten their positions in anticipation of a rise in rates.

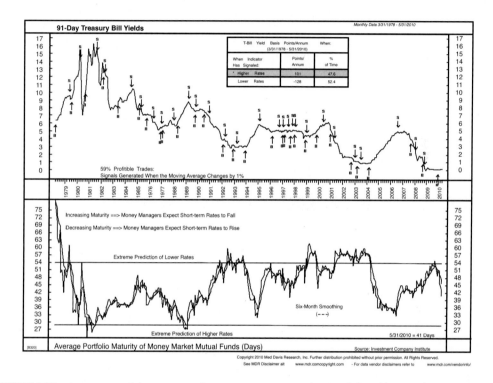

FIGURE 7.25 Average portfolio maturity of money managers and U.S. T-bill yields (March 1978–May 2010)

Figure 7.25 shows the results of a Ned Davis Research, Inc., study of money fund managers and found that when the average maturity in days rose above its six-month simple moving average, the 91-day Treasury bill rate advanced 102 basis points per annum. This measure then is a contrary indicator because when rates are expected to rise, managers should be shortening their maturity length to await the higher rates. Instead, when they believe the rates will go down, it appears they lengthen their maturity, and the T-bill market does just the opposite of their expectations. When the maturity length declines below its six-month simple moving average, the rate tends to advance, making this calculation a good contrary indicator of Treasury bill rates.

HULBERT GOLD SENTIMENT INDEX

Mark Hulbert publishes a newsletter, the *Hulbert Financial Digest*, a subsidiary of MarketWatch, that follows the performance of other investment newsletters. He has been doing this since 1980. His methods are similar to those of Investors Intelligence. A number of these newsletters discuss the price of gold. Using this information, Hulbert calculates an index of gold market sentiment. As with other measures of investment-advisory newsletters, the performance results prove to be an excellent contrary indicator of the market's future direction. Ned Davis Research, Inc., looked at this data and concluded that when the percentage of gold bulls advanced above 59, the price of the XAU, a gold mining stock index, plunged 47.6% per annum, and when the percentage declined below 7, the XAU advanced 91.9% per annum. The results are shown in Figure 7.26.

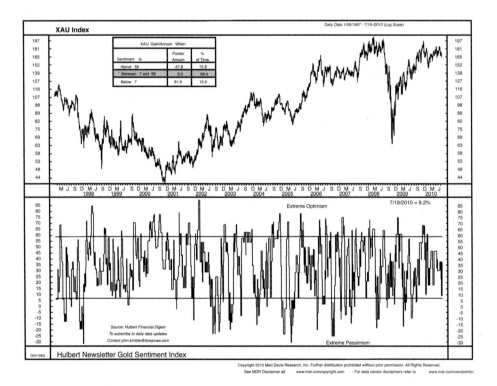

FIGURE 7.26   Hulbert Newsletter Gold Sentiment Index (January 1997–July 2010)

CONCLUSION

In this chapter, we have focused on the idea of market sentiment—the overall psychology of the market players. Emotions play an important role in determining the actions of market participants. Market participants demonstrate periods of both extreme optimism, when bubbles occur, and periods of extreme pessimism, when crashes or panics occur. The uninformed market players tend to be most optimistic as the market reaches a peak. These same individuals tend to be most pessimistic when the market is at its lowest point in a downturn. In other words, most investors are fully invested just at the time they should liquidate their holdings and out of the market just at the point when they could be buying stocks at a low price. Sentiment indicators help the technical analyst pick these market extremes. By following a contrarian strategy, the technical analyst hopes to act opposite of the uninformed, majority of market players.

REVIEW QUESTIONS

1. How would you define the term *sentiment* as it relates to the financial markets?

2. Warren is searching for a good trading rule to follow. He says, "I would be just as happy to get information from someone who always makes the wrong investment decision as someone who always makes the right investment decision to use in devising my trading strategy." Explain why Warren would find it helpful to have information about someone's bad trading decisions.

3. Explain why extremely high investor optimism is associated with market peaks.

4. Sandra thinks Microsoft (MSFT) is currently overpriced, while Tony thinks MSFT is underpriced. Which of these two investors would be more likely to buy a put, and which one would be more likely to buy a call? Explain your answer.

5. You hear a report that the ratio of put-to-call volume is extremely high. How would you interpret this high put/call ratio? What would you conclude about investor sentiment given this high ratio? What investment strategy would you want to follow given this high ratio?

6. Explain what is meant by a contrarian investment strategy. What are some market signs that the contrarian investor might watch for?

7. What information might polls give you about sentiment? What are some sources of poll data, and what general conclusions can you make about how to use poll data?

8. What type of relationship is generally seen between news reporting and market sentiment?

MEASURING MARKET STRENGTH

CHAPTER OBJECTIVES

By the end of this chapter, you should

- Understand the importance of measuring internal market strength
- Understand what is meant by market breadth
- Be familiar with how the advance-decline line measures market breadth
- Be familiar with how up and down volumes relate to market strength
- Be familiar with how new high and new low statistics measure market strength
- Be familiar with the relationship between the number of stocks above their historical moving average and market strength

In the previous chapter, we looked at the importance of market player sentiment in determining potential market trends. In addition to measuring the attitudes of market players, the technical analyst needs to look at the internal strength of a market. By looking at data specific to each market, the analyst determines whether the internal strength of the respective market is improving or deteriorating. In this chapter, we examine how the analyst looks at market data such as the number of stocks advancing and declining, the volume of the winners and losers, the new 52-week highs and lows, and the position of the averages relative to moving averages. These measures help to gauge the stock market's underpinnings. The data needed to calculate the indicators studied in this chapter is publicly available in most financial newspapers.

BOX 8.1   WHAT IS DIVERGENCE?

The most important technical concept for confirmation of a trend is called a **divergence.** As long as an indicator—especially one that measures the rate of change of price or other data (called **momentum**)—corresponds with the price trend, the indicator is said to "confirm" the price trend. When an indicator or oscillator fails to confirm the trend, it is called a **negative divergence** or **positive divergence,** depending on whether peaks or bottoms, respectively, fail to confirm price peaks or bottoms. A divergence is an early warning of a potential trend change. It means the analyst must watch the price data more closely than when the indicators and oscillators are confirming new highs and lows. Divergence analysis is used between almost all indicators and prices; a divergence can occur more than one time before a price reversal.

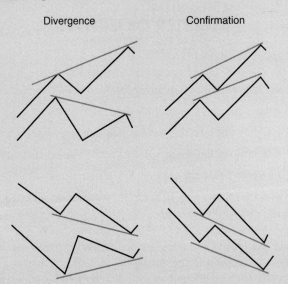

Divergence   Confirmation

As an example, one of the tenets used in analyzing trading volume is that in a rising trend, volume should expand with the price rise. If at a new short-term peak in prices the trading volume fails to expand above its earlier, time-equivalent high, a negative divergence has occurred that should warn the analyst that the new price high is occurring on less enthusiasm, as measured by volume, and that the uptrend may soon be ending.

It should be noted that knowledge of a wide array of technical indicators does not make an analyst valuable or cause him or her to profit, but knowing when to apply which indicator does. Because it is almost impossible to understand all indicators, the technical analyst often selects just a few and studies them intently.

When looking at indicators, the analyst is generally looking for confirmation or divergence. Confirmation occurs when prices are rising and these indicators rise, signaling strong market internals. Confirmation also occurs when falling prices are accompanied by an indication of weak market internals. In other words, confirmation occurs when price movement and market internals appear to agree.

When a market indicator does not support the direction of price movement, the analyst has a strong warning that the trend may be in the process of reversing. This lack of confirmation is referred to as a **divergence**.

One quick example is an indicator called the rate of change indicator (ROC). It is merely a plot of the ratio or difference between today's closing price and the closing price at some specified time in the past, such as 20 days. When the market or stock is hitting a new high and the 20-day ROC is hitting a new high, we have a confirmation of the price action. Should the ROC not be hitting a new high at the same time as the market or stock, we have a negative divergence, a warning that the upward momentum in price is slowing down.

There is another type of divergence called a **reversal** suggested by Constance Brown (1999). This occurs when the oscillator or indicator, in a **positive reversal,** reaches a second low that is not confirmed by another new low in prices. The opposite, the **negative reversal,** occurs when the oscillator reaches a new high but prices do not. Both cases are just variations of a divergence, and as in a normal divergence, each occurrence signals a potential change in market direction.

MARKET BREADTH

On any given day, a stock price can do one of three things—close higher, lower, or unchanged from the previous day's close. If a closing price is above its previous close, it is considered to be advancing, or an **advance.** Similarly, a stock that closes below the previous day's close is a declining stock, or a **decline.** A stock that closes at the exact price it closed the day before is called **unchanged.**

Prior to July 2000, all less than one dollar (or point) changes in common stock prices were in fractions based on the pre-Revolutionary practice of cutting Spanish Doubloons into eighths to make change. By February 2001, the old system of quarters, eighths, and sixteenths was replaced with the decimal system. The use of decimals may have affected some historic relationships. The resulting smaller bid-ask spreads may have reduced the number of stocks that are unchanged at the day's end.

Advance/decline data is called the **breadth** of the stock market. The indicators we focus on in this section measure the internal strength of the market by considering whether stocks are gaining or losing in price. In this section, we consider the cumulative breadth line, the advance-decline ratio, breadth differences, and the breadth thrust.

Before we begin looking more closely at these particular indicators, we must, however, mention a change that has recently occurred. Since 2000, the parameters of many breadth indicators thought to provide accurate signals have changed significantly. Applying standards that had excellent records for identifying stock market reversals now proves to be less than satisfactory. There is likely more than one reason for this sudden change, and some reasons are unknown.

One factor that has caused the old parameters to change is the proliferation on the New York Stock Exchange of ETFs, bond funds, Real Estate Investment Trusts (REITs), preferred shares, and American Depository Receipts (ADRs) of foreign stocks. These do not represent domestic operating companies and, therefore, are not directly subject to the level of corporate economic activity. They are subject to a wide variety of influences not necessarily connected with the stock market, which means they are not reflecting the market's traditional discounting mechanism.

Another possible factor is the implementation of the aforementioned decimalization. Many of the indicators using advances and declines are calculated as they were before decimalization, even though their optimal parameters may have changed. Another possibility, one more likely, is that the aberrant indicators were tested mostly during the long bull market from 1982 through 2000. The important lesson for the technical analyst, however, is that indicators do not remain the same. Parameters for known indicators change over time and with structural changes in the markets. The analyst must frequently test indicators and make appropriate adjustments in the types and parameters used.

The Breadth Line or Advance-Decline Line

The breadth line, also known as the advance-decline line, is one of the most common and best ways of measuring breadth and internal market strength. This line is the cumulative sum of advances minus declines. The standard formula for the breadth line is as follows:

$$\text{Breadth Line Value}_{\text{Day T}} = (\text{\# of Advancing Stocks}_{\text{Day T}} - \text{\# of Declining Stocks}_{\text{Day T}}) +$$
$$\text{Breadth Line Value}_{\text{Day T}-1}$$

On days when the number of advancing stocks exceeds the number of declining stocks, the breadth line will rise. On days when more stocks are declining than advancing, the line will fall.

A breadth line can be constructed for any index, industry group, exchange, or basket of stocks. In addition to being calculated using daily data, it can be calculated weekly or for any other period for which breadth data is available. It is not often applicable to the commodity markets where baskets or indices of commodities rarely are traded, though this is changing with the advent of the Commodities Research Bureau (CRB), Goldman Sachs, and Dow Jones futures index markets.

Ordinarily, the plot of the breadth line should roughly replicate the stock market averages. In other words, when the stock market averages are rising, the breadth line should rise. This indicates that a market rally is associated with the majority of the stocks rising.

The importance to technical analysts of the breadth line is the time when it fails to replicate the averages and, thus, diverges. For example, if the stock market average is rising but the advance-decline line is falling, only a few stocks are fueling the rally, but the majority of stocks are either not participating or declining in value.

Analysts point to several reasons why breadth divergence might not be as powerful of an indicator in the future as it has been in the past. The first reason is the previously discussed proliferation of nonoperating company listings. To deal with the issue of the bias from including stocks that do not represent ownership in operating companies, technical analysts often use only those breadth figures from common stocks that represent companies that actually produce a product or a service. For example, the New York Stock Exchange also reports breadth statistics for only common stocks, disregarding the numerous mutual funds, preferred stocks, and so on. This additional breadth information is available daily in most financial newspapers. The breadth line derived from this list of common stocks generally has been more reliable than the one including all stocks.

However, a major change recently occurred in how the NYSE reports breadth statistics for common stocks. Beginning in February 2005, the NYSE decided to include only those stocks with three or less letters in their stock symbols and those that are included in the NYSE Composite Index, its common stock list. Because of this change, figures since that decision will be incompatible with the prior figures.

Instead of relying on the publicly available statistics, proprietary breadth statistics also are available on a subscription basis. For example, Lowry's Reports, Inc., (www.lowrysreports.com) calculates proprietary breadth statistics that eliminate all the preferred stocks, ADRs, closed-end mutual funds, REITs, and others representing nonproductive companies.

Another difficulty with the breadth has arisen since the year 2000 according to Colby (2003) and others using data up through 2000. Trading rules used with the publicly available breadth statistics before then, despite the known problems with the types of stocks listed, showed relatively attractive results. However, using those same rules since the year 2000, we find much less attractive results in many of these indicators. Indeed, the difference is so large and consistent throughout the trading methods mentioned by Colby that it could not be attributed to the trading rules themselves or to problems connected with optimizing. The difference between then and more recently must have to do with a change in background, character, leadership, or historic relationships.

Why this change? The most obvious economic change is that of the decoupling of the stock market from long-term interest rates. From the Great Depression of the 1930s to the last decade of the last century, the business cycle was characterized by the bond market and the stock market reaching bottoms at roughly the same time, and the bond market reaching peaks earlier than the stock market reached peaks. In the late 1990s, this business-cycle relationship broke down, switching to almost the exact opposite relationship, whereby the bond market tended to trend oppositely from the stock market. Because the breadth statistics include a large number of interest-related stocks that are not included in the popular averages, this change in relationship may be the cause for the difference in trading rules using breadth, giving the breadth line more strength at tops and more weakness at bottoms.

In the NASDAQ, a cumulative breadth line constructed of only NASDAQ stocks advances, declines, and unchanged has been declining at least since 1983 (earlier figures are difficult to obtain), and even when looked at over shorter periods seems to have a very strong negative bias. This negative bias is likely due to the "survivor effect," whereby from 1996 to 2005, stocks listed on the NASDAQ declined from 6,136 to 3,440. The loss of issues from the list suggests that a large number of listings went broke during that time and were trending downward even when the larger survivors were advancing and were unavailable during the rebound in stock prices from 2002 through 2005. The NASDAQ index is a capitalization-weighted index where the survivors have considerable influence on price but little influence on breadth. This weighting bias implies that a NASDAQ breadth line is useless as a divergence indicator in its absolute form and must be analyzed instead for changes in acceleration rather than direction.

Several indicators using the advance-decline line concept appear in the classic technical analysis literature. Although these indicators have not performed well in recent market conditions, it is important for the student of technical analysis to be aware of these traditional indicators because they may become productive sometime in the future.

Double Negative Divergence

When the averages are reaching new price highs and the breadth line is not, a **negative divergence** is occurring (see Figure 8.1). This signals weak market internals and that the market uptrend is in a late phase and may soon end. In 1926, Colonel Leonard P. Ayres (1940) of the Cleveland Trust Company was one of the first to calculate a breadth line and the first to notice the importance of a negative breadth divergence from the averages. His theory was that very highly capitalized stocks influence the averages, while the breadth line includes all stocks regardless of capitalization. Sometimes at the end of a bull market, the large stocks continue to rise, and the smaller stocks begin to falter.

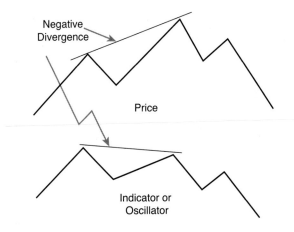

FIGURE 8.1 What does negative divergence look like?

Other market analysts, such as James F. Hughes (Merrill, *Stocks and Commodities Magazine* V6: 9, p 354–5), argued that the rise in interest rates accompanying an economic expansion reflected in the stock market causes the interest-related stocks—such as utilities, which have large capital borrowing costs and of which there are many—to falter and, thus, causes the breadth line to lose momentum. Regardless of the cause, since May 1928, when a negative breadth divergence warned of the 1929 crash more than a year later, the observance of a negative divergence has invariably signaled an impending stock market top.

Although a negative divergence signals a market top, a primary stock market top can occur without a divergence. In other words, a breadth divergence is not necessary for a market peak.

The peaks in 1937 and 1980, for example, occurred without a breadth divergence. After a sizable, lengthy advance, participants should be on guard and use a breadth divergence to help spot a potential market reversal. However, an analyst should not be adamant about requiring a breadth divergence to occur prior to a market peak.

At market bottoms, especially those that are characterized by climactic price action, a positive divergence in the cumulative breadth line rarely has been reliable in signaling a major reversal upward. However, there have been positive breadth divergences on either tests of major lows or so-called secondary lows that were useful signals of increasing market strength.

A characteristic of the breadth line that the analyst needs to recognize is that there is a downward bias to the line. Therefore, a new cumulative breadth line, one that has no relationship to the previous breadth line, begins once the market reaches a major low. For example, calculating a historical cumulative breadth line for the NYSE data resulted in an all-time peak in 1959. Although the cumulative breadth line has never reached the same 1959 level, there was a considerable rise in the market averages through 2000. This does not indicate a very large negative divergence over a 40-year time span. The cumulative breadth line, for divergence analysis, starts again once a major decline has occurred. When the market declines into a major low, one of the four-year varieties (see Chapter 9, "Temporal Patterns and Cycles"), analysis of the cumulative breadth line begins anew, and the line has no relationship to the peak of the previous major market cycle. It is as if a major decline wipes out the history of past declines, and the market then begins a new breadth cycle and new history.

A negative divergence, while not being required, has been the most successful method over the past 50 or more years for warning of a major market top. As with most indicators, different technicians use the breadth indicators in slightly different ways. For example, James F. Hughes, who published a market letter in the 1930s, learned of the breadth divergence concept from Col. Ayres (Harlow, 1968; Hughes, 1951). He used the negative breadth divergences as a major input to his stock market forecasting. Hughes required that at least two consecutive negative breadth divergences, called **double divergences** (see Figure 8.2), must occur before a major top was signaled. This requirement prevented mistakes in forecasting from the appearance of a single minor divergence that could later be nullified by a new high in both the averages and the breadth line. Often, more than two divergences occur at major market tops.

When the double breadth divergence warning occurs, it traditionally signals an actual market price peak within a year. Beginning with 1987, for example, a double breadth divergence correctly anticipated the 1987 crash when the breadth line peaked in April 1987, and five months later, in September, the market peaked and then collapsed. The breadth line peaked in the fall of 1989 followed by a peak in the average in July 1990. The most recent breadth peak signaled by a double breadth divergence was the 2007 peak in breadth and the 2008 peak in the averages, as shown in Figure 8.2. Similar to the 1928–1929 double divergence, the time between the breadth peak and the market peak stretched to 21 months, considerably longer than the traditional ten months. As Figure 8.2 shows, however, the double negative divergence in 2007 foretold the coming stock market collapse in 2008–2009. The lag between the divergence and the final low is not constant, but the theory of a double divergence warning of a major market decline is still valid.

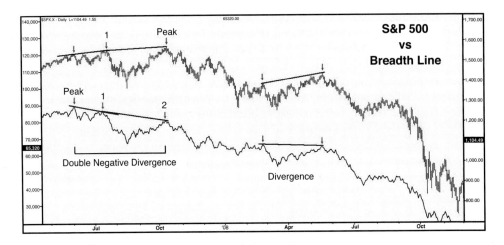

Created using TradeStation

FIGURE 8.2   S&P 500 vs. breadth line, double negative divergence and subsequent single negative divergence (April 2007–December 2009)

Traditional Advance-Decline Methods That No Longer Are Profitable

Over the past ten years the market has changed, rendering the old methods of using moving averages and reversals as signals no longer reliable. Consider the following evidence that traditional advance-decline methods are no longer profitable:

- *Advance-decline line moving average*—Colby mentions this as a profitable method prior to 2000. It is calculated by calculating a 30-day moving average of both the Standard & Poor's 500 and the breadth line. When both the index and the line are above their moving averages, the market is bought, and vice versa when they are both below their moving averages. In an optimization program, we found the 30-day moving average period unreliable and that the period of the moving average should be increased to the vicinity of 75 days. Even so, profitability only began after 2007.

- *One-day change in advance-decline line*—The simplest signal occurs when the advance-decline line changes direction in one day. However, this method also has become unprofitable since 2000. Again, using an optimization program, we found that reversals after 75 days proved the most profitable but only beginning in 2007.

   This is useful information in that it warns students of the markets that the methods of analysis are fluid, constantly changing, and should be thoroughly tested before implemented in an investment plan.

John Stack in an interview with Technical Analysis of Stocks & Commodities (Hartle, 1994) mentions using an index that compares the breadth line and a major market index. His purpose is to reduce the necessity of looking at an overlay of an indicator on the price chart to discern when a divergence has occurred. Instead, he calculates an index that tells whether breadth is improving or diverging from the market index and, thus, whether a warning of impending trouble is developing. Arthur Merrill (1990) also devised a numerical method to determine the relative slope of the breadth line versus a market index. By following the slope over time, we can calculate periods in which the breadth line is gaining or losing momentum. The advantageous aspect of this type of indicator is that it also measures the relative momentum when prices are declining.

BOX 8.2   WHAT IS AN OSCILLATOR?

At times, you will see us referring to a particular indicator as an **oscillator.** Oscillators are indicators that are designed to determine whether a market is "overbought" or "oversold." Usually, an oscillator will be plotted at the bottom of a graph, below the price action, as shown in Figure 8.3. As the name implies, an oscillator is an indicator that goes back and forth within a range. Overbought and oversold conditions (the market extremes) are indicated by the extreme values of the oscillator. In other words, as the market moves from overbought, to fairly valued, to oversold, the value of the oscillator moves from one extreme to the other. Different oscillator indicators have different ranges in which they vary. Often, the oscillator will be scaled to range from 100 to –100 or 1 to –1, but it can also be open-ended.

Advance-Decline Line to Its 32-Week Simple Moving Average

Analysts have developed several variations of using the advance-decline line. One method is to compare it with its own moving average to give buy and sell signals for the market and, thus, create an oscillator. Ned Davis Research, Inc., used a ratio of the NYSE advance-decline line to its 32-week simple moving average. They found that from 1965 to 2010 when the ratio rises above 1.04, the per annum increase in stock prices as measured by the NYSE Composite Index was 19.3%, and when it declined below 0.97, the stock market declined 11.2% per annum. This oscillator is pictured in Figure 8.3.

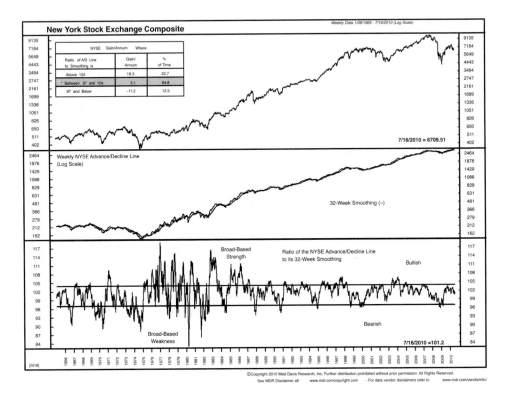

FIGURE 8.3 Advance-decline line to its 32-week simple moving average vs. NYSE Composite Index (January 1965–July 2010)

Breadth Differences

Indicators using breadth differences are calculated as the net of advances minus declines, either with the resulting sign or with an absolute number. The primary problem with using breadth differences is that the number of issues traded has expanded over time. For example, in the 40-year time period from 1960 to 2000, the number of issues on the New York Stock Exchange doubled from 1,528 issues to 3,083 issues. By 2010, the number had increased to 3,200 issues. More issues means larger potential differences between the number of advances and declines. Any indicator using differences must, therefore, have its parameters periodically adjusted for the increase in issues traded. Examples of indicators using breadth differences are listed next.

Haurlan Index

Peter N. Haurlan worked as a rocket scientist for the Jet Propulsion Laboratory in the 1960s, where he projected trajectories of satellites. Haurlan was one of the first to use a computer to analyze stock data. Combining his knowledge of mathematics, his access to a computer (which was extremely rare at the time), and his interest in the stock market, Haurlan began calculating exponential moving averages (EMAs; see Chapter 14, "Moving Averages") in stock data. Haurlan published his methodology in a pamphlet ("Measuring Trend Values") and began privately publishing the *Trade Levels Reports.*

The Haurlan Index is calculated very simply. The basic index is daily advances minus declines exponentially smoothed with a 3-day exponential moving average (Haurlan, 1968). Haurlan generated trading rules with this oscillator. His original rules were to buy and sell on the crossing of the zero line in the oscillator. Haurlan also considered several longer-term exponential moving averages. He calculated a 20-day exponential moving average of advances minus declines data to identify divergences. He also considered a 200-day exponential moving average to determine the primary trend. He did not use these longer averages, however, to generate mechanical trading signals.

Paul Carroll, in an article in *Stocks & Commodities* (1994) indicates that crossovers in each of the Haurlan averages through zero give reliable signals. He also indicates that reliable extreme signals occurred at specific levels in each average. These levels were +/–200 for the 20-day and +/–550 for the 200-day. A buy signal occurred when the EMA crossed above the upper level, and a sell signal occurred when the EMA declined below the lower limit. Since then, however, the changes in the breadth statistics from more stocks being listed and from decimalization have upset the reliability of the old rules. Indeed, the 3-day EMA is no longer valid at all. As shown in Figure 8.4, the 20-day has positive results when the outer limits are extended to +/–500, and ironically, better results occur when the buy signal occurs at the EMA breaking down from the upper limit, and the sell signal when the EMA breaks upward from the lower limit. The tenuous nature of this method because it depends on the characteristics of the breadth statistics suggests that it should be used with extreme caution.

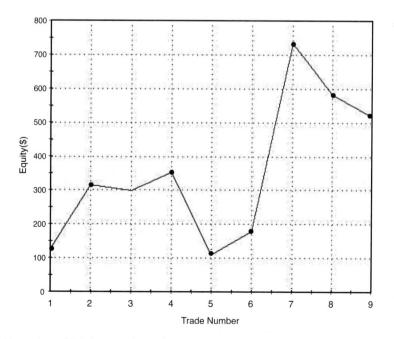

Equity Curve Line - $SPX.X Daily (01/03/00 16:00 - 03/01/10 16:00)

FIGURE 8.4 Equity line of 20-day Haurlan Index (January 2000–February 2010)

Part II Markets and Market Indicators

> ## BOX 8.3 WHAT IS AN EQUITY LINE?
>
> An **equity line** is a graph of a potential account value beginning at any time adjusted for each successive trade profit or loss. It is used to measure the success of a trading system. Ideally, each trade is profitable and adds to the value of the account each time a trade is closed. Any deviation from the ideal line is a sign of drawdown, volatility, or account loss, all of which are unavoidable problems with any trading or investment system. For profitable systems, the equity line should rise from left to right with a minimum number of corrections. For more information about equity lines, see Chapter 22, "System Design and Testing."

McClellan Oscillator

In 1969, based on Haurlan's use of advance and decline data, Sherman and Marian McClellan developed the McClellan Oscillator. This oscillator is the difference between two exponential moving averages of advances minus declines. The two averages are an exponential equivalent to a 19-day and 39-day moving average. Extremes in the oscillator occur at the +100 or +150 and −100 or −150 levels, indicating respectively an overbought and oversold stock market.

> ## BOX 8.4 MCCLELLAN MTA AWARD
>
> In 2004, Sherman and Marian McClellan were honored as recipients of the Market Technicians Lifetime Achievement Award. For more information about the McClellans' work, go to www.mcoscillator.com/user/McClellan_MTAaward.pdf.

The rationale for this oscillator is that in intermediate-term overbought and oversold periods, shorter moving averages tend to rise faster than longer-term moving averages. However, if the investor waits for the moving average to reverse direction, a large portion of the price move has already taken place. A ratio of two moving averages is much more sensitive than a single average and will often reverse direction coincident to, or before, the reverse in prices, especially when the ratio has reached an extreme.

Mechanical signals occur either in exiting one of these extreme levels or in crossing the zero line. A test of the zero crossing by the authors for the period April 2000 to February 2005, to see if the apparent changes in the breadth statistics had any effect on the oscillator, proved to be profitable. A test of crossing the +100 and −100 levels proved to be unprofitable largely because these extremes were not always met. By using stops, however, the performance improved. Divergences at market tops and bottoms were also informative. The first overbought level in the McClellan Oscillator often indicates the initial stage of an intermediate-term stock market rise rather than a top. Subsequently, a rise that is accompanied by less breadth momentum and, thus, a lower peak in the oscillator is suspect. At market bottoms, the opposite appears to be true and reliable. Finally, trend lines can be drawn between successive lows and highs that, when penetrated, often give excellent signals similar to trend line penetrations in prices.

McClellan Ratio-Adjusted Oscillator

Because he recognized that the use of advances minus declines alone can be influenced by the number of issues traded, McClellan devised a ratio to adjust and to replace the old difference calculation. This ratio is the net of advances minus declines divided by the total of advances plus declines. As the number of issues changes, the divisor will adjust the ratio accordingly. This ratio is usually multiplied by 1,000 to make it easier to read. The adjusted ratio is then calculated using the same exponential moving averages as in the earlier version of the oscillator. In a study of the usefulness of this oscillator, we optimized the possible overbought and oversold levels and found that +/–35 was the best level. Indeed, we found that the trading rule required a sell when the oversold level was penetrated from above, and the opposite buy rule for overbought. This produced over the period March 2000–February 2010, a 265% return for the period over a buy-and-hold loss of 24%. Figure 8.5 shows the equity line for this study.

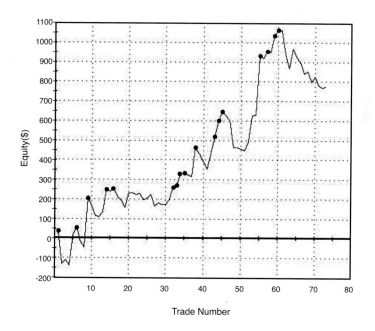

Equity Curve Line - $SPX.X Daily (01/03/00 16:00 - 03/01/10 16:00)

FIGURE 8.5 Equity line of McClellan Ratio-Adjusted Oscillator with +/−35 overbought/oversold (March 2000–February 2010)

McClellan Summation Index

The McClellan summation index is essentially a measure of the area under the curve of the McClellan Oscillator. It is calculated by accumulating the daily McClellan Oscillator figures into a cumulative index. The McClellans found that the index has an average range of 2,000 and added 1,000 points to the index such that it now oscillates generally between 0 and 2,000, and neutral is at 1,000. Originally, the summation index was calculated with the differences between advances and declines, but to eliminate the effect of increased number of issues, the adjusted ratio is now used. This is called the ratio-adjusted summation index (RASI). It has zero as its neutral level and generally oscillates between +500 and –500, which the McClellans consider to be overbought and oversold, respectively. Although no mechanical signals are suggested, the McClellans have mentioned that overbought readings are usually followed by a short correction that is followed by new highs. A failure to reach above the overbought level is a negative divergence and, thus, a sign that a market top is forming. Colby reports that only on the long side do intermediate-term signals profit (with an average holding of 172 days) given when the summation index changes direction.

Plurality Index

This index is calculated by taking the 25-day sum of the absolute difference between advances and declines. Because the calculation accounts only for the net amount of change independent of the directional sign, it is always a positive number. The stock market has a tendency to decline rapidly and rise slowly. Therefore, high numbers in the plurality index are usually a sign of an impending market bottom, and lower numbers suggest an impending top. Most signals have been reliable only on the long side because lower readings can occur early in an advance and give premature signals. Traditionally, the signal levels for this indicator were 12,000 and 6,000, but the increase in the number of issues has made these signal numbers obsolete (Colby, 2003). Colby uses a long-term (324-day) Bollinger Band (see Chapter 14) breakout of the upper two standard deviations for buys and below two standard deviations for a sell to close. This method produced admirable results and has continued to do so since 2000. There are very few signals, and a 15- or 30-day time stop should be used for longs only.

One additional suggestion for eliminating the effect of the increase in the number of issues listed over time is to use the McClellan ratio method of dividing the numerator by the sum of the advances and declines. Thus, the 25-day plurality index raw number becomes the absolute value of the advances minus declines divided by the sum of the advances and declines. This can then be summed over 25 days. One problem both for accuracy of testing and for usefulness of the plurality index is that very few trades are initiated or held for long, and not all major market bottoms are signaled.

Absolute Breadth Index

Whereas the Hughes breadth oscillator uses a ratio of the raw difference between advances and decline divided by the total issues traded, the absolute breadth index uses the absolute difference of the advances minus declines divided by the total issues traded. Thus, the index is always a positive number. By experiment, Colby (2003) found that from 1932 to 2000, a profitable signal was generated when this index crossed the previous day's 2-day exponential moving average plus

81%. His report for longs only, which were held for an average of 13 days, only beat the buy-and-hold by 35.1% over the entire 68-year period, without commissions or slippage. Ned Davis Research, Inc., (see Figure 8.6) found an 11.7% annual gain versus a buy-and-hold gain of 7.7% per annum in long trades only between February 1977 and February 2010 using a 10-day moving average. Using the Colby method since 2000, however, we found the long trades occurred less frequently and were held only an average of 2 days. In the entire period, only 20 long trades were made. However, 60% of these trades were profitable and returned a total 608% versus a 17.75% loss with buy-and-hold. The major problem with this method is that only 3 of the 20 trades were outstanding over the 10-year period, and only 2 trades per year were made on average. This means a long wait before a profitable trade and numerous small trades of little consequence in between. Most investors or traders do not have the patience for this type of system.

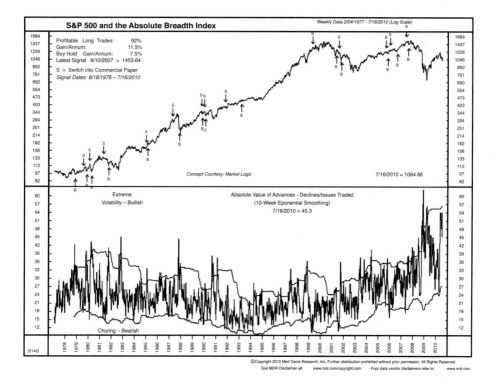

FIGURE 8.6   Absolute Breadth Index (February 1977–July 2010)

Unchanged Issues Index

The unchanged issues index uses a ratio of the number of unchanged stocks to the total traded. The theory behind it is that during periods of high directional activity, the number of unchanged declines. Unfortunately, with the decimalization of the stock quotes, the number of unchanged has declined, and the ratio now appears to have almost no predictive power. Testing this indicator, we have found negative results in almost all instances since April 2000.

Breadth Ratios

Instead of using the difference between daily or weekly advances and declines, which can be overly influenced by the increase or decrease in the number of issues listed, breadth ratios use a ratio between various configurations of advances, declines, and unchanged to develop trading indicators and systems for the markets. Using ratios has the advantage of reducing any long-term bias in the breadth statistics. These ratios usually project very short-term market directional changes and are of little value for the long-term investor. They have also changed character and reliability since the year 2000.

Advance-Decline Ratio

This ratio is determined by dividing the number of advances by the number of declines. The ratio or its components are then smoothed over some specific time to dampen the oscillations. Figure 8.7 presents testing of the success of using the advance-decline ratio over the 1947 to 2010 period by Ned Davis Research. Using daily breadth statistics, 30 buy signals were generated when the ratio of ten-day advances to ten-day declines exceeded 1.91. These signals averaged a 17.9% return over the following year. In only one of the 30 instances did the signal fail, and the loss then was only 5.6%.

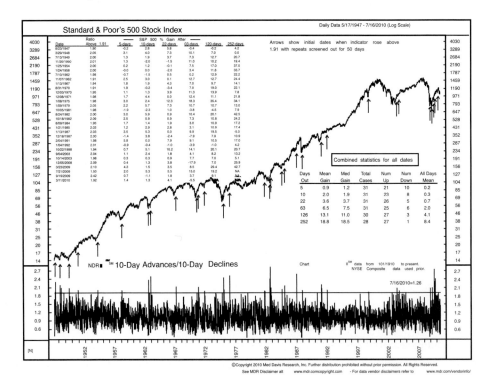

FIGURE 8.7 Advance-decline ratio—ten-day moving average (May 1947–July 2010)

Colby (2003) reports that taking a one-day advance-decline ratio and buying the Dow Jones Industrial Average (DJIA) when the ratio crossed above 1.018 and selling it when the ratio declined below 1.018, in the period from March 1932 to August 2000, would have turned $100 into $884,717,056, assuming no commissions, slippage, or dividends. Turnover, of course, would have been excessive—an average of one trade every 3.47 days—but the results were excellent for both longs and shorts. We tested this system for the period from April 2000 to February 2010 and found that until 2005, the results were still credible. However, since 2005, the equity line collapsed (see Figure 8.8). This negates, for now, the one-day method of trading the advance-decline ratio.

Equity Curve Line - $INDU Daily (01/03/00 16:00 - 03/01/10 16:00)

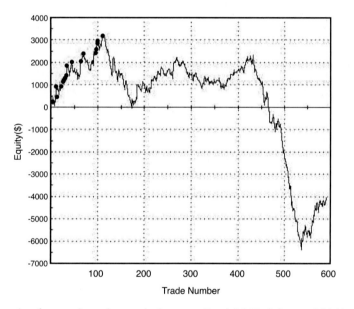

FIGURE 8.8   Equity line for one-day advance-decline ratio (April 2000–February 2010)

Breadth Thrust

A **thrust** is when a deviation from the norm is sufficiently large to be noticeable and when that deviation signals the beginning of a new trend, usually upward. Figure 8.9 shows that during the period from 1979 to 2010, when the breadth ratio thrust above 1.65, the stock market rose an average of 17.6% over the next 52 weeks. The thrust in this example is calculated as the five-week total of the weekly advances to total issues ratio less the weekly declines to total issues ratio. It appears still to be valid in 2010.

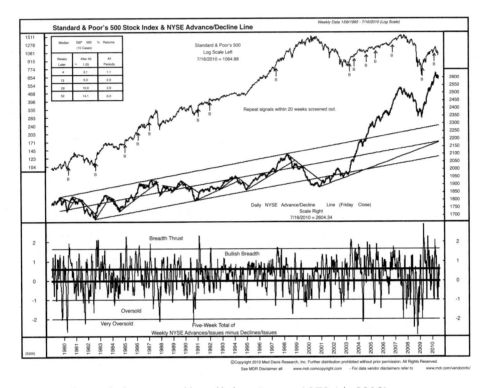

FIGURE 8.9   Advance-decline ratio and breadth thrust (January 1979–July 2010)

Martin Zweig devised the most common breadth thrust indicator, calculating a ten-day simple moving average of advances divided by the sum of advances and declines. Traditionally, the long-only signal levels in this oscillator were to buy when the index rose above 0.659 and sell when it declined below 0.366. With these limits, however, this method has not had a signal since 1994. In testing the calculation using a moving average between four and six days, we found that the original signal limits were profitable again for longs only. Why did the results for this indicator suddenly change in 1994? We do not know. Again, these changes are excellent examples of why the analyst must frequently review the reliability of any indicator being used.

One other way to use Zweig's calculation is to generate a signal when the ratio reverses direction (Colby, 2003). Although this method continues to be profitable, it suffered a severe drawdown from October 2002 to October 2003, bringing into question its long-term viability.

Summary of Breadth Indicators

It appears that since 2000, a period of declining then rising stock prices, the breadth indictors for short-term signals that had previously had admirable records mostly failed. These failures are the reason why technical analysts must constantly test and review their indicators. Many changes occur in the marketplace, both structurally—as, for example, the change to decimalization and the inclusion of many nonproducing stocks in the breadth statistics—and marketwise—as, for example, the disconnection between stock prices and interest rates. No indicator remains profitable forever, both because of these internal changes, as well as the overuse by technical analysts who recognize their value. Apparently, the best remaining breadth usage is the old Ayres-Hughes double negative divergence analysis and the ten-day advance-decline ratio. They have had minimal failures for over 60 years. Before an indicator is used in practice, however, it must be tested objectively. No indicator should be used just because it has demonstrated positive results in the immediate past.

UP AND DOWN VOLUME INDICATORS

Breadth indicators assess market strength by counting the number of stocks that traded up or down on a particular day. An alternative way to gauge market internals is to measure the up volume and down volume. Daily up volume is volume traded in declining stocks. Up and down volume figures are reported in most financial media.

Considering the volume, rather than only the number of shares traded, places more emphasis on stocks that are actively trading. With the breadth indicators, a stock that moves up on very light trading is given equal importance to one that moves up on heavy trading. By adding volume measures, the lightly traded stock does not have as much influence on the indicator as a heavily traded stock. The one caveat with using volume is that occasionally an enormous trade in a low-priced stock will upset the daily figures. This happened on December 9, 2009, when 3.76 billion Citigroup shares traded. The up and down volume statistics for that day were useless. Finally, the use of dark pools, off-exchange trading, and other methods of avoiding the reporting of transactions as well as the increase in trading in stocks that are part of ETFs have upset the earlier balance between volume and the individual investor. Many stocks are traded today as commodities in an index, for example, not because they are worthwhile investments. Volume as a statistic has, thus, become another aspect of change in the marketplace, and its use for technical indicators is changing and should be approached with caution.

The Arms Index

One of the most popular up and down volume indicators is the Arms Index, created by Richard W. Arms, Jr. (winner of the MTA 1995 Annual Award). The Arms Index (Arms, 1989), also known by its quote machine symbols of TRIN and MKDS, is reported daily in the financial media.

The Arms Index measures the relative volume in advancing stocks versus declining stocks. When a large amount of volume in declining stock occurs, the market is likely at or close to a bottom. Conversely, heavy volume in advancing stocks is usually healthy for the market. The Arms Index is actually a ratio of two ratios, as follows:

$$\text{Arms Index} = \frac{\dfrac{\text{Advances}}{\text{Declines}}}{\dfrac{\text{UpVolume}}{\text{DownVolume}}}$$

The numerator is the ratio of the advances to declines, and the denominator is the ratio of the up volume to the down volume. If the absolute number of advancing shares increases on low volume, the ratio will rise. This higher level of the Arms Index would indicate that although the number of shares advancing is rising, the market is not strong because there is relatively low volume to support the price increases. This ratio, thus, travels inversely to market prices (unless plotted inversely), tending to peak at market bottoms and bottom at market peaks. This inverse relationship can initially be confusing to the chart reader.

Similar to breadth ratios, the Arms Index can be smoothed using moving averages and tested for parameters at which positions can be entered. An Arms Index greater than 1.0 is considered to be a bearish signal, with lower levels of the index indicating a more favorable market outlook. In our experiments, however, for the period February 2000 through February 2010, we found that when the Arms Index rose above 1.0, it was a short-term buy signal. The trick was not the entry per se but the exit. Using the Diamonds (ETF for the DJIA) and after optimizing for the exit, we used a stop loss of 0.53, a breakeven of 0.01, and a trailing stop of 0.48 points, respectively. This produced a return on account of 5,334% versus a buy-and-hold of a 7% loss for the period. Because the sell stops reduced capital risk, the maximum drawdown was negligible. However, it was only invested in the DIA 8% of the period.

Equity Curve Line - $SPX.X Daily (01/03/00 16:00 - 03/01/10 16:00)

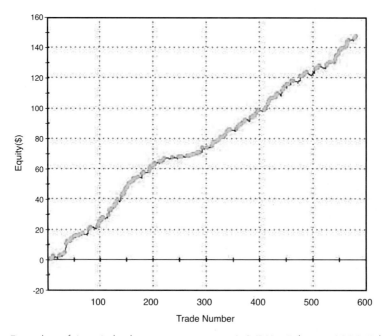

FIGURE 8.10 Equity line of Arms Index buy on crossing over 1.0 (DIA—February 2000–February 2010)

Colby (2003) introduced a number of calculations that showed promise until the year 2000. A long-standing panic signal, devised by Alphier and Kuhn (1987), is to buy the stock market when the Arms Index exceeds 2.65 and hold it for a year. This signal has occurred twice since 2000, with one win and one loss. The win, however, was considerably larger than the loss.

When we shortened the holding period to 40 days rather than the original 252 days, the performance of the signals was outstanding, a return of 97% versus a 1.8% buy-and-hold. It appears, then, that the signal is still valid, but the analyst must watch the holding period after the signal.

Ned Davis Research, Inc., found a way to use the Arms Index for selling as well as buying. They calculated a 40-day moving average and various thresholds (shown in Figure 8.11) for buying and selling. Their performance showed an 11.2% annual gain versus an 8.4% annual gain from a buy-and-hold strategy.

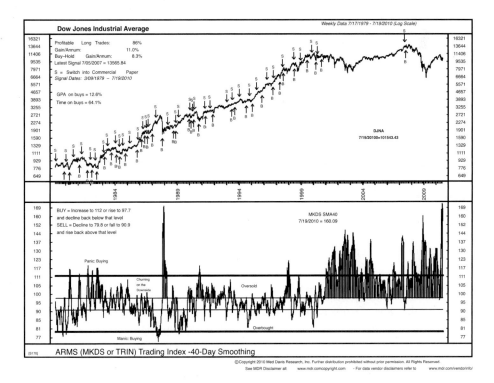

FIGURE 8.11 Arms Index 40-day moving average (February 1979–July 2010)

Modified Arms Index

Generally, a high number above 1.0 in the Arms Index is bearish and a low number bullish. However, take an example of a hypothetical day when 1,000 issues advance and 100 decline with 1m up volume and 200,000 down volume. From these numbers, the Arms Index would be calculated as 2.00, a bearish number, yet the market action was obviously bullish (1,000/100 advances to decline). To combat this problem, Dave Steckler calculates a modified index by multiplying advance issues times advancing volume and subtracting from that figure the product of declining issues times declining volume. This index can sometimes be negative. Then he sums the modified index over 11 days, smoothes the total with a 10-day moving average, and plots the result. He claims that it often diverges a few days earlier at market tops and bottoms.

Ninety Percent Downside Days (NPDD)

Paul F. Desmond in his Charles H. Dow Award paper (Desmond, 2002) presents a reliable method for identifying major stock market bottoms that uses daily upside and downside volume as well as daily points gained and points lost. The volume figures are reported in the financial media, as are the stock tables. Unfortunately, the sum of points gained and lost is not reported publicly and requires considerable handwork or a computer. A 90% downside day occurs when on a particular day, the percentage of downside volume exceeds the total of upside and downside volume by 90% *and* the percentage of downside points exceeds the total of gained points and lost points by 90%. A 90% upside day occurs when both the upside volume and points gained are 90% of their respective totals. What he found was that

- An NPDD in isolation is only a warning of potential danger ahead, suggesting, "Investors are in a mood to panic" (Desmond, 2002, p. 38).
- An NPDD occurring right after a new market high or on a surprise negative news announcement is usually associated with a short-term correction.
- When two or more NPDDs occur, additional NPDDs occur, often 30 trading days or more apart.
- Big volume rally periods of two to seven days often follow an NPDD and can be profitable for agile traders but not for investors.
- A major reversal is signaled when an NPDD is followed by a 90% upside day or two 80% upside days back-to-back.
- In half the cases, the upside reversal occurred within five trading days of the low. The longer it takes for the upside day reversal, the more skeptical the investor should be.
- Investors should be careful when only one of the two upside components reaches 90%. Such rallies are usually short.
- Back-to-back 90% upside days are relatively rare but usually are long-term bullish.

10-to-1 Up Volume Days and 9-to-1 Down Volume Days

Whereas Desmond combines breadth and volume for his panic indicator, Ned Davis Research, Inc., studied up and down volume alone without confirmation from breadth. Their rules are a little complicated, a sign that the analyst should beware. Complicated rules are usually those that are constructed from curve fitting and might not be viable in the future because they only fit past data. However, the results of these studies were impressive and just demonstrated the contrary opinion thesis that panics are often times to buy and sharp, steep rises from lows especially often signal the end of a decline.

Specifically what they found was that roughly six months after a 10-to-1 up volume day, the market was 9% higher (see Figure 8.12), and that after roughly six months following a 9-to-1 down volume day, the market was 6% higher (see Figure 8.13). Shorter periods after each signal were also higher but not by the same percentage. In other words, each of these events suggested a panic bottom.

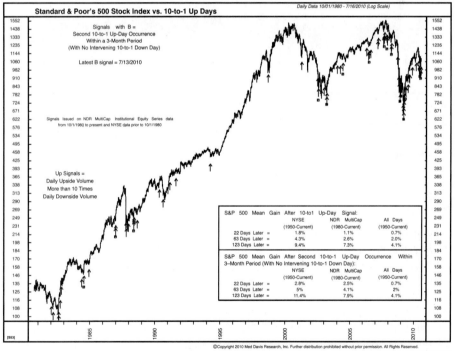

FIGURE 8.12   10-to-1 up days (October 1980–July2010)

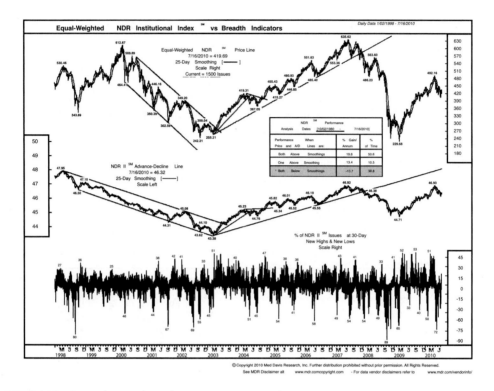

FIGURE 8.13 9-to-1 down volume days (January 1998–July 2010)

NET NEW HIGHS AND NET NEW LOWS

When the stock market is rising, it is only reasonable to assume that individual stocks are making new highs. Conversely, stock market declines are associated with stocks making new lows.

Generally, a stock is considered to reach a new high if the day's price is higher than the price has been over the past year. Prior to 1978, new highs and new lows were measured from January of the current year only, but in 1978, the New York Stock Exchange began determining new highs and new lows based on trailing 52-week prices. Other exchanges also adjusted their reporting at that time for consistency with the NYSE figures. Thus, a stock reaches a new high when the price is higher than it has been anytime during the previous 52 weeks, not necessarily when it has reached a new all-time high.

The financial press reports 52-week highs and lows, but the period of 52 weeks is not sacred. Analysts calculate many other periods based on their individual investment horizons. For short-term breakouts, for example, 10 or 21 days are used. In any case, the number of new highs and new lows is a useful measure of the number of stocks participating in an advance or decline. It is, thus, an indicator of a continuing trend and usually subject to divergence analysis, similar to breadth statistics.

The raw data of new highs and new lows is subject to the same problems as breadth in that the number of issues listed on an exchange will often change over time and make indicators using differences between highs and lows unreliable and subject to constant change in indicator parameters. As in breadth indicators, the way around this difficulty is to divide the difference between the new highs and lows by the total issues traded on the exchange, thus eliminating any bias from the changing number of listings.

New Highs Versus New Lows

The most straightforward, and probably useful, index is to buy when the number of new highs exceeds the number of new lows on a daily basis and to sell when the opposite occurs. Colby (2003) reports very favorable results on both sides of the market, long or short, but the holding period is relatively short. One interesting aspect of net new weekly highs and lows (see Figure 8.14) is that they generally peak before the market peaks, similar to the breadth line. This extremely reliable observation can warn us when we see a negative divergence in weekly high-low data that a correction is due soon. (Average lead is 33 weeks with a wide error.)

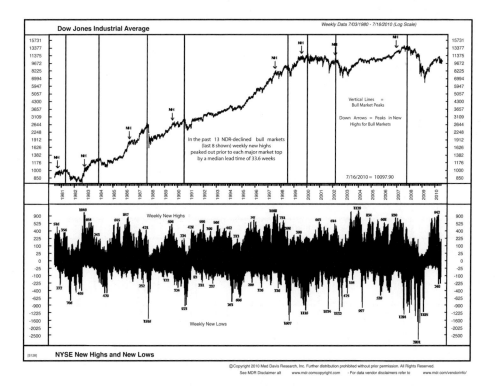

FIGURE 8.14 Five-day-smoothed new highs minus new lows divided by issues traded (July 1980–July 2010)

High Low Logic Index

Norman Fosback (1976) is the developer of the high-low logic index. This index is defined as the lesser of two ratios: the number of weekly new highs to total issues or the number of weekly new lows to total issues. Low index levels tend to suggest a strongly trending market. A low number would indicate that either a low number of new highs and/or a low number of new lows are occurring. A high index level implies mixed market because the index can only be high when the number of both new highs and new lows is large.

Analysts traditionally smooth this index over ten weeks with a moving average (see Chapter 14). With either the raw or smoothed data, levels are then determined at which a signal is generated. Generally, high levels are bearish and low levels are bullish. In the first edition of *The Encyclopedia of Technical Market Indicators*, authors Robert Colby and Thomas Meyers (1988) reported that from 1937 to 1987, the results from such indicators were highly significant to the 99.9% confidence level. Their thresholds for raw data were above 0.020 for a down market one to three months later, and below 0.002 for an up market one to six months later. For the ten-week smoothed index, a downward market was signaled above 0.058 for three months, and an upward market was signaled below 0.005 for three and twelve months later. Figure 8.15 shows Ned Davis Research, Inc., data and their thresholds for buying and selling. It is obvious that the buys are more reliable than the sells.

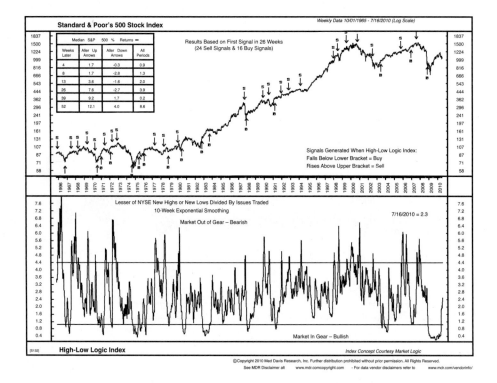

FIGURE 8.15 High-low logic index (October 1965–July 2010)

Hindenburg Omen

Many indicators use a combination of other indicators to derive a signal. The Hindenburg Omen is such an indicator. Very similar to Fosback's high-low logic index, this indicator was devised by Jim Mikkea and was named by Kennedy Gammage (Colby, 2003) after the Hindenburg Dirigible disaster of 1937. Obviously, it signals a market reversal downward and includes:

- The 52-week highs and lows are each greater than 2.2% of total issues.

- The small number of new highs or new lows is greater than 75.

- The ten-week moving average of the NYSE Composite Index is rising.

- The McClellan Oscillator is negative.

- New highs cannot be more than two times the number of new lows (OK for new lows to be two times the number of highs).

- Confirmation, defined as two or more occurrences within a 36-day period, exists.

  (Source: Robert M. McHugh, PhD, article in www.safehaven.com/showarticle.cfm?id=3880)

This indicator reportedly occurred prior to every major crash since 1985 (including the 1987 crash). Twenty-seven confirmed omens have occurred with only two failing to be followed by a decline of 2% or more. The other subsequent declines were not all crashes because the omen often gives false signals for crashes. However, the odds of a crash (down more than 15%) are about 27% after a confirmed signal. Clusters of signals don't seem to have any correlation to the extent of the subsequent decline. One major problem with the derivation of this indicator is that it is so complex. As mentioned earlier, complexity usually comes from curve fitting and is, thus, potentially unreliable. The Hindenburg Omen, however, is based on technical logic and is certainly something to follow.

USING MOVING AVERAGES

The indication of a trending stock usually is gauged by whether the stock price is above or below a moving average. The longer the moving average, the longer the trend the relationship represents. Looking at how many stocks are trending gives us a measure of market strength.

Number of Stocks above Their 30-Week Moving Average

One indicator of overbought and oversold markets, as pictured in Figure 8.16, is the number of stocks above or below their 30-week moving averages. This indicator essentially measures the number of stocks in uptrends and downtrends. It is a contrary indicator, however, in that when the percentage of stocks above their 30-week moving averages reaches above 70%, the market is inevitably overbought and ready for a correction. Conversely, when the percentage of stocks below their 30-week moving average declines below 30%, the market is at or close to a bottom. Investors Intelligence, Inc., popularized this indicator. They have developed other rules for action between the 30% and 70% levels that follow intermediate-trend turns.

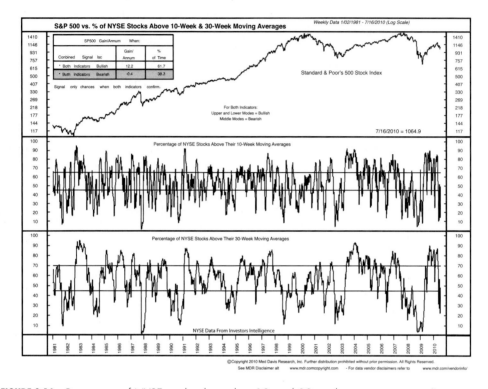

FIGURE 8.16 Percentage of NYSE stocks above their 10- and 30-week moving averages (January 1981–July 2010)

The 80/60 Rule

One interesting variation in the use of stocks above their 30-week moving average is the 80/60 rule. This rule states that when the percentage of stocks above their 30-week moving average has been greater than 80% and then declines below 60%, the percentage will decline to or close to 30%. In other words, a serious decline will likely follow such a signal. Figure 8.17 by Ned Davis Research, Inc., suggests that of the 13 instances of this occurring since 1968, 12 resulted in a general market decline. The one exception was in 1991 during the protracted bull market of the 1990s.

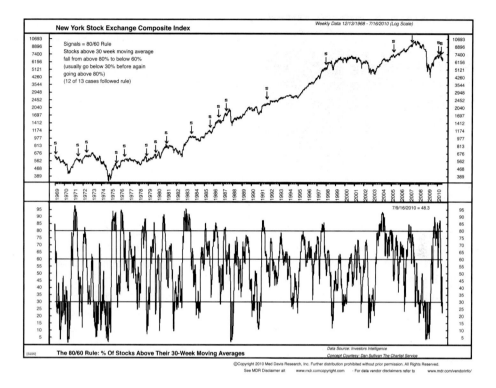

FIGURE 8.17   The 80/60 rule in stocks above their 30-week moving average (December 1968–July 2010)

VERY SHORT-TERM INDICATORS

Although market sentiment indicators generally focus on spotting long-term trend reversals, the concept of sentiment can be used as a short-term contrarian indicator. Let's look at a few ways in which following these indicators might provide clues to short-term trading opportunities.

Breadth and New Highs to New Lows

Although breadth and new high-low data tend to be indicators of trend, and divergence analysis is useful in determining when a known trend may be reversing, short-term readings of breadth and new high-low data are often contrary indicators. For example, when the daily breadth ratio of advances to declines rises to 2/1 or 3/1, the subsequent market direction is more often down than up. The opposite is also true for days in which the advance-decline ratio is 2/1 or 3/1 on the downside. It often provides excellent buying opportunities for the very short term (that is, the next week).

New highs and new lows show the same results. Trading with the longer-term trend is the best method of maximizing profits. To enter the trend right after it has been recognized, however, is often not profitable, at least until prices have retraced from their initial reaction. Thus, for example, if the market is above its 200-day moving average and is presumably in a longer-term uptrend, whenever the averages break to new 10-day lows is an excellent time to go long. Oppositely, when the market is below its 200-day moving average and thus in a longer-term downtrend, whenever rallies take prices above their 10-day highs is when the best opportunity to sell short exists. In this manner, the use of new highs and new lows, thus, can be used as a contrary signal within the major trend and a way of profiting from price dispersions from the mean trend.

Net Ticks

Ticks represent actual trades. When a stock changes price, even by the smallest amount either an uptick or downtick is produced. If the stock trades at its previous price, a zero-tick is produced. By summing at any one instant the number of upticks versus downticks, the day trader has an indicator of market action across the board. It is similar to an advance-decline ratio or difference except that it is based on much more sensitive intraday data.

Generally, tick data is used as a contrary indicator because it measures very short-term bursts of enthusiasm or fear. Extreme readings may indicate a longer-term change in trend, but usually the tick ratio oscillates within bounds throughout the day. When it is oversold, traders will buy into the short-term fear, and when it is overbought, they will sell into the temporary enthusiasm. Ratios and moving averages are used with this data in a similar manner as with breadth statistics. Ticks can also be calculated for averages and indices such as the Dow Jones Industrial, where only the stocks included in the average are measured.

Closing ticks can also be used similar to daily breadth statistics. Closing ticks represent the trading action just at the close of trading and show whether traders are anxious or ambivalent. In Figure 8.18, a ten-day moving average of net ticks shows oscillations in line with the averages. Combining this indicator with one of the Arms Index (MKDS) and the NYSE Composite, Ned Davis Research, Inc., found specific levels at which significant market moves could develop.

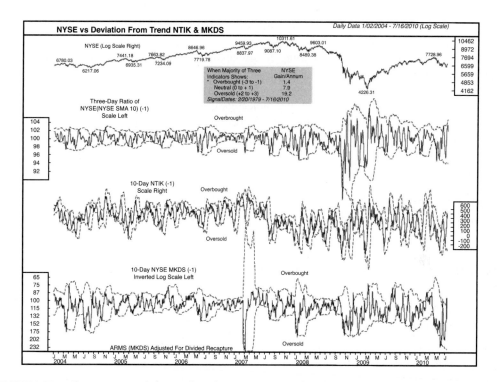

FIGURE 8.18   Short-term signals from tick and arms (MKDS) indicators (January 2004–July 2010)

CONCLUSION

In this chapter, we focused on the measurement of market internal strength. One important factor in measuring market internals is the calculation of market breadth line (advance-decline line). Market breadth is a measure of how widely a market move is spread throughout the stock market. In other words, measuring breadth tells the analyst whether an increase in the market index is characterized by a large increase in the price of a few stocks or a smaller increase in the price of the majority of the market stocks. Is the typical stock moving the same way that the market index (which can be influenced by big moves in a few stocks) is moving? If so, the market direction is confirmed by the internals. If not, the internals and the index are diverging, indicating that internal strength is changing.

Another way of looking at internal market strength is to look at up and down volume. Instead of looking at the number of issues that advanced or declined on a particular day, look at up and down volume measures. Using this type of measure, each stock issue is not given equal weight. Instead, stocks with heavy trading volume are given more weight and play a more important role in gauging internal market strength.

A third major way to gauge internal market strength is to compare the current price of each stock with its historical price. Looking at how many stocks are being traded at price extremes can do this—that is, looking at stocks trading at new highs and new lows. Alternatively, it can be done simply by comparing the current price with a historical average price of each issue to see how many stocks seem to be moving in the same direction as the market index.

Whatever method is being used, the indicators presented in this chapter are designed to measure whether there is enough strength internally to predict that the market trend will continue in the direction it has been. Understanding how internal strength relates to broader market movement is important. Unfortunately, we have seen many of the traditional indicators perform poorly during the past few years. Only time will tell if the traditional indicators with their traditional parameters will perform satisfactorily in the future. In the meantime, analysts continue to develop, test, and refine ways to measure market internal strength. It is the job of the technician to find what works best for the appropriate trading or investment time horizon.

REVIEW QUESTIONS

1. Explain what the term *market breadth* means.

2. Explain what the terms *positive divergence* and *negative divergence* mean.

3. An analyst appearing on the financial news made the following statement:

   "Since the recent run-up in the S&P 500 has been accompanied by weak internals, I do not have much confidence that the uptrend in the S&P 500 will continue much longer."

   Explain what the analyst means by *weak internals*. What types of statistics has the analyst been looking at to determine that the market internals were weak?

4. Explain how looking at *new highs* and *new lows* can help an analyst determine internal market strength.

5. Assume that market indices are all trending upward. What type of market internals would you like to see to confirm these trends?

6. The Web site http://finance.yahoo.com reports useful information about market internals every day. This information can be found under the heading Today's Markets by clicking on the Investing option. Look up the information for today's trading. What would you conclude about the internal market strength today? Explain what information leads you to your conclusion.

7. Use the information you gathered for Question 6 to calculate the Arms Index and the Modified Arms Index for the day. What information does each of these indicators give you?

TEMPORAL PATTERNS AND CYCLES

CHAPTER OBJECTIVES

By the end of this chapter, you should be familiar with

- The long (50-60-year) Kondratieff wave cycle
- The 34-year cycle
- The decennial cycle
- Four-year cycles, including the election year pattern
- Seasonal tendencies in stock performance
- The relationship between January stock market performance and the rest of the year
- The relationship between events and stock market performance

In the previous two chapters, we looked at ways to measure the sentiment of market players and the internal strength of the stock market. In those chapters, we saw that the market alternates between periods of strength and weakness. A major market cycle appears when market players become more and more optimistic, sometimes to a point of euphoria, followed by a period of market weakness, which is associated with increasing investor fear and panic. Seeing how this is a repeated pattern, some analysts have focused their attention on attempting to predict these patterns using cycle theory that is often similar to the cycle theory of the natural scientists. In Chapter 19, "Cycles," we cover how to analyze market data of unconventional cycles, but we now look at cycles appearing to occur for understandable reasons.

Is there a time of the year that is the best to buy stocks? Do stocks perform better in one month or season of the year than another? Does it matter what day of the month I buy stocks? Should I buy stocks on a certain day of the week? How do stocks perform when there is an upcoming presidential election? Does the weather affect stock performance? These are all examples of the types of questions that must be asked.

Although a rigid cycle that would result in a specific, narrow rule (e.g., always buy stocks on the first day of the month or never buy stocks in December) does not appear, the effects of time do seem to display themselves in price patterns and cycles of varying shapes and lengths. In many cases, the origin or cause of these cycles is unknown. Some analysts attempt to correlate a variety of cycles to either economic events or stock prices, and these apparent relationships range from the plausible to the ludicrous. Researchers have considered sunspots, rainfall in New York City, phases of the moon, various planet positions, tilt of the earth, lynx populations in Canada, tree rings, and elections, to name only a few of the possible causes.

Like the periodicity of the sun and moon to Stone Age man, the observations are unquestioned but the reasons are unknown. So far, only coincidental cycles have been found. Edward R. Dewey (1947, 1971) founder of the Foundation for the Study of Cycles, tabulated these coincidental periodic peaks and troughs, beginning in the 1940s. The records and past journals of the Foundation, in which many of these cycles are tabulated, have now been integrated with the library of the Market Technicians Association. In this chapter, we discuss the most dominant of these temporal effects associated with the stock market.

PERIODS LONGER THAN FOUR YEARS

Let's begin by looking at cycles occurring over a long period (over four years) of time. These cycles include Kondratieff waves, 34-year historical cycles, and decennial cycles.

Kondratieff Waves, or K-Waves

Nicolas D. Kondratieff, an economist who lived in Communist Russia, studied historical commodity prices in the 1920s. He analyzed European agricultural prices and copper prices from the late eighteenth century to his time and noticed a periodicity in these prices of approximately 50 years. He then hypothesized that there were long cycles in economic activity in capitalist nations that evolved and self-corrected and that the Marxist hopes for an approaching collapse of capitalism were misdirected. He was sent to a Siberian concentration camp, presumably for these views, where he died in 1938.

Few of Kondratieff's papers were originally published in the West, but more recently, a large number have been collected and translated into a book, *The Long Wave Cycle.* The long 50–60 year cycle that he measured, known as the Kondratieff wave (or K-wave), is an economic phenomenon that is not necessarily observable in commodity or stock prices.

It was Harvard economics professor Joseph A. Schumpeter, endorsing Kondratieff's ideas in the 1930s, who first used the name "Kondratieff wave" to refer to the cycle that Kondratieff uncovered. The K-wave theory remained in academic contention, largely because of the few-recorded instances, until the 1970s and 1980s, when the world economy slowed down and new research on the importance of innovation added substance to the theory of K-waves. Today there is a reasonable academic body of knowledge attached to K-wave theory. George Modelski and William Thompson have written extensively on the topic. In their book, *Leading Sectors and*

World Powers: The Coevolution of Global Economics and Politics, Modelski and Thompson point to the following important aspects of the K-wave theory:

- Waves are attributes of the world economy led by a major national economy.

- Waves concern *output rather than prices*—sector output surges rather than general macroeconomic performance.

- Waves unfold as *phased processes*, implying an S-shaped growth curve sequence rather than mechanical and precise periodic cycles.

- *Waves arise from bunching of innovations* in product, services, technology, methods of production, new markets, new sources of raw materials, and new forms of business organization (from Schumpeter). This innovation spurt comes from earlier economic slowdown, and its predominant innovative character (see Table 9.1) can identify each wave.

- *Each* K-wave has its *characteristic location*—cotton in Manchester, Great Britain, or technology in Orange County, California—and a clear location in time that can be dated. World systems theorists can now date the theory back 19 separate waves to Sung China, more than a thousand years ago.

- *Each* K-wave *affects the structure of the world economy into the future.*

- The long *start-up* of a K-wave is *often accompanied by a major war.*

- A *significant relationship* exists *between the K-wave and the rise and fall of world powers.* A new K-wave in a new and different location suggests the next location for global leadership. The K-wave grows out of necessity and innovation and then influences global power and politics as they evolve to accept the new economics.

The Kondratieff wave, therefore, is an interesting long-term phenomenon in economics and world politics, but it has only marginal use in the stock, bond, and commodities markets. In the 1970s, K-wave cycle theory increased in popularity as many people began watching what would happen as the fiftieth anniversary of the 1929 stock market crash and Great Depression approached. However, the rise out of the 1981–1982 stock market bottom, with the DJIA quickly breaking the 1,000 level, which continued until the year 2000, eliminated interest in the K-wave theory as applied to the stock market.

Because double K-waves seem to develop into even longer cycles of economic power and global leadership and the United States is in the second cycle, the prospects for U.S. markets are seemingly favorable for a third period of about 17 years after 2026, when the next wave is scheduled to begin. Of course, this period may, and likely will be, punctuated by wars and at least one economic depression, but the U.S. prospects are still relatively favorable, even if replaced by another innovative period somewhere else, with the K-wave cycle theory predicting at least a trading market for the next 50 years in the United States.

TABLE 9.1   *K-Wave Cycles and the Associated Global Leading Sectors (Table adapted from Modelski & Thompson, 1996)*

Date	Long Cycles	K-Waves	World Powers	Global Leading Sectors
930	LC1	K1	Northern Sung	Printing and paper
990		K2		National market
1060	LC2	K3	Southern Sung	Fiscal framework
1120		K4		Maritime trade expansion
1190	LC3	K5	Genoa	Champagne fairs
1250		K6		Black Sea trade
1300	LC4	K7	Venice	Galley fleets
1350		K8		Pepper
1420	LC5	K9	Portugal	Guinea gold
1492		K10		Spices
1540	LC6	K11	Dutch Republic	Baltic trade
1580		K12		Asian trade
1640	LC7	K13	Britain I	American plantations
1680		K14		Amerasian trade
1740	LC8	K15	Britain II	Cotton, iron
1792		K16		Railroads
1850	LC9	K17	USA	Electric power, steel
1914		K18		Electronics, motor vehicles
1973	LC10	K19	USA II	Information industries
2026		K20		

Confirming the prediction of the start of a new K-wave period beginning around the year 2026 is the relationship researchers have found between the U.S. birthrate and the stock market. A high correlation exists between the U.S. birthrate and U.S. stock market performance 46 years later. As seen in Figure 9.1, this correlation has been very close since the mid 1950s. Should this relationship continue, the birthrate data projects a major stock market bottom around 2020 followed by another major, but slightly weaker rise than the 1980–2000 rise, into about the year 2050. The birthrate projection, of course, can change over the next 50 years, but for now, it appears to confirm the projections of the K-wave.

34-Year Historical Cycles

Historical data suggests that 34-year cycles, composed of a 17-year period of dormancy followed by a 17-year period of intensity, also appear to exist. Figure 9.2, for example, shows a 17-year dormant period beginning in the mid 1930s in which movement in the Dow Jones Industrial Average (DJIA) was sideways. This trading range period was followed by a 17-year upward trend period in the DJIA. The upward movement in the DJIA ended in the late 1960s. Then another 17-year flat period followed into the mid 1980s and that also was followed by an upward trend into the turn of the century. The market is currently in another flat period, presumably of 17 years that began than and will likely end between 2015 and 2020, which coincides with the Kondratieff bottom expected from birth statistics mentioned previously.

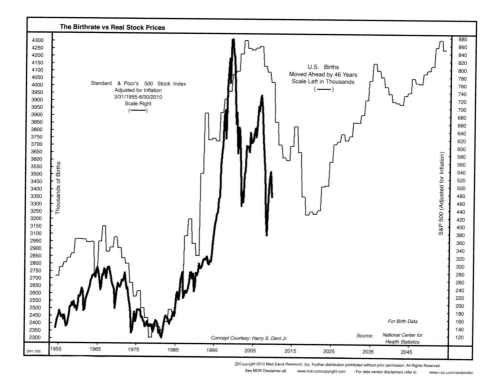

FIGURE 9.1   U.S. birthrate versus real stock prices (March 1966–June 2010)

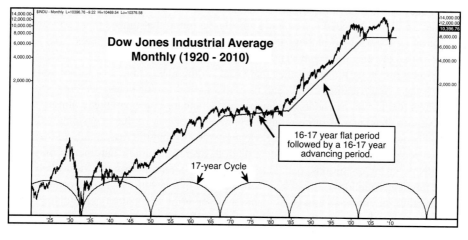

FIGURE 9.2   34-year historical cycle of the Dow Jones Industrial Average in 17-year alternating trends (1920–2010)

Notice that during the mid-1930s to mid-1940s and mid-1960s to the early 1980s and since 2000 within the flat periods that volatility was very high. Declines of 35% and 50% occurred within these periods, as well as sharp advances, yet the overall, longer-term trends remained relatively flat. These are periods when technical analysts outshine fundamental analysts because the buy-and-hold philosophy breaks down. In the intensive periods between the mid-1940s and mid-1960s and early 1980s and early 2000s, the buy-and-hold investment philosophy returned as prices generally rose, and profits were made regardless of analytical method. Since the turn of the century in 2000, another dormant but volatile period began in which buy-and-hold strategies are failing and technical analysis is returning as the most successful analytic method.

Warren Buffett, one of the wealthiest men in the world, is not widely known to use technical methods; however, it is interesting to note that he has long used the 17-year cycle in his investment planning. Buffet does not attribute the cycle to growth in the GNP, noting that in the dormant cycle from the mid-1960s to the early 1980s, the GNP grew at twice the rate as during the intensive early 1980s to the turn of the century. Instead, he attributes the different periods to changes in interest rates, corporate profits, and investor confidence in the economy, ideas he learned from reading the book *Common Stocks as Long-Term Investments* by Edgar Lawrence Smith (1928), which he claims most influenced his investment philosophy (Loomis, 2001).

Decennial Pattern

In his book *Tides and the Affairs of Men* (1939), Edgar Lawrence Smith presented the notion of a ten-year stock market cycle. Smith's theory resulted from combining two other theories, Wesley Mitchell's 40-month cycle theory and the theory of seasonality, both of which we cover in the shorter-term cycles later in this chapter. Combining these two periods, Smith theorized that there must be a ten-year, or 120-month, cycle. This would result from ten 12-month, annual cycles and three 40-month cycles coinciding every ten years.

When Smith investigated prices more closely, he found that indeed there appeared to be a price pattern in the stock market that had similar characteristics every ten years. This pattern has since been called the **decennial pattern.**

The decennial pattern theory states that years ending in 3, 7, and 10 (and sometimes 6) are often down years. Years ending in 5, 8, and most of 9 are advancing years (see Figure 9.3). Smith did not follow the normal calendar year beginning in January but found that counting the beginning of a year in October was more reliable. He also hypothesized that occasionally a 9-year or 11-year cycle overlaid the decennial cycle. He attempted to find the reason behind the decennial pattern and looked at sunspots and solar radiation, average rainfall, barometric pressure, and other weather-causing conditions, believing that weather patterns were the most likely cause of change in human psychology. It was then well accepted that weather had an effect on health and disease, and thus on optimism and pessimism, an observation first mentioned by Hippocrates.

The decennial pattern continues to have an excellent history. For example, the fifth-year advance has been observed for well over 100 years to never have failed 12 out of 12 times, though there is some question about whether 2005 advanced. Some market indexes were up slightly, and some were down. Most foreign stock markets advanced.

One problem with the theory is that a large enough sample is not possible yet, and that such projections could be the result of chance. It is something to keep in the back of an investor's mind but not something to use alone to commit funds to the stock market.

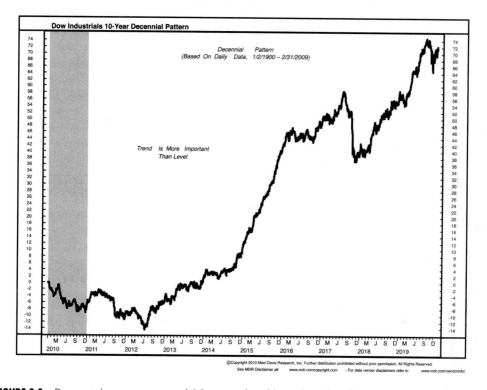

FIGURE 9.3 Decennial pattern projected 10 years ahead based on data from January 1900 through December 2009

PERIODS OF FOUR YEARS OR LESS

A day is a definite period of time. A year, within small limits, is also definite. A month, however, may be lunar or solar; it may also be a number of other things. Hence 40 months of our present calendar must remain an approximation and certainly not an exact measure of the duration of cycles, if, as we shall be led to believe, natural phenomena have some part in determining the pattern of their recurrence. (Smith, 1939, p 20)

Four-Year or Presidential Cycle

Wesley C. Mitchell (1874–1948), economics professor and one of the founders of the National Bureau of Economic Research (NBER), was the originator of the 40-month cycle theory. He empirically discovered that the U.S. economy from 1796 to 1923 suffered a recession, on average and excluding four wars, every 40 months, or approximately every four years.

Today, the four-year cycle, from price bottom to price bottom, is the most widely accepted and most easily recognized cycle in the stock market. Occasionally it strays from four years, but only by a portion of a year (see Figure 9.4). This is a remarkably consistent series.

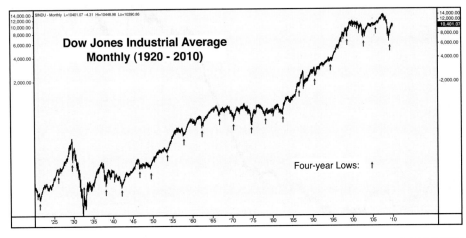

Created using TradeStation

FIGURE 9.4   Four-year cycle lows in the Dow Jones Industrial Average (1920–2010)

Almost all cycles are measured from bottom to bottom. Tops fail to occur as regularly, but, of course, their average interval is also four years (see Table 9.2). Some analysts have argued that because the U.S. presidential elections are also four years apart, the cycle is due to the election cycle (see the next section, "Election Year Pattern"). It is, thus, often called the "presidential cycle." However, this cycle also occurs in countries that do not have four-year elections, such as Great Britain. It may be that U.S. economic strength is so huge and so globally powerful that other countries are forced to follow its stock market cycles, or it may be that the 40-month (almost four years) economic cycle Wesley Mitchell discovered 80 years ago is still dominant but has been slightly stretched by economic and the Federal Reserve policy action. Whatever the reason for its existence, the four-year cycle is obviously a very strong, important, and reliable cycle.

TABLE 9.2   *Four-Year Cycle in the Dow Jones Industrial (1896–2010)*
(Adapted from Bressert, 1991)

Date of Low	Low Close	% Decline from High to Next Low	Date of High Close	High Close	% Advance to High	Months Low to Low	Months Low to High	Months High to Next Low
August 8, 1896	28	−31.2%	April 25, 1899	77	175.0%	49.0	32.0	17.0
September 24, 1900	53	−46.2%	June 17, 1901	78	47.2%	38.0	8.9	29.2
November 9, 1903	42	−48.5%	January 19, 1906	103	145.2%	48.9	26.7	22.2
November 15, 1907	53	−27.7%	November 19, 1909	101	90.6%	47.0	24.5	22.5
September 25, 1911	73	−43.6%	September 30, 1912	94	28.8%	39.5	12.4	27.2
December 24, 1914	53	−40.0%	November 21, 1916	110	107.5%	36.4	23.3	13.1
December 19, 1917	66	−46.7%	November 3, 1919	120	81.8%	44.8	22.8	22.0
August 24, 1921	64	−16.7%	February 11, 1926	162	153.1%	56.0	54.4	1.6
March 30, 1926	135	−47.8%	September 3, 1929	381	182.2%	44.1	41.8	2.4
November 13, 1929	199	−86.1%	April 17, 1930	294	47.7%	32.3	5.2	27.1
July 8, 1932	41	−49.0%	March 10, 1937	194	373.2%	69.7	56.9	12.9
March 31, 1938	99	−40.4%	September 12, 1939	156	57.6%	49.6	17.7	32.0
April 28, 1942	93	−23.5%	May 26, 1946	213	129.0%	54.2	49.6	4.5
October 9, 1946	163	−16.1%	June 15, 1948	193	18.4%	32.6	20.5	12.1
June 13, 1949	162	−12.9%	January 5, 1953	294	81.5%	51.8	43.4	8.4
September 14, 1953	256	−19.5%	April 6, 1956	522	103.9%	50.0	31.2	18.8
October 22, 1957	420	−27.1%	December 13, 1961	735	75.0%	56.9	50.4	6.5
June 26, 1962	536	−25.2%	February 9, 1966	995	85.6%	52.1	44.1	8.0
October 7, 1966	744	−35.9%	December 3, 1968	985	32.4%	44.2	26.3	18.0
May 26, 1970	631	−45.1%	January 11, 1973	1052	66.7%	55.2	32.0	23.1
December 6, 1974	578	−26.9%	September 12, 1976	1015	75.6%	39.3	21.5	17.8
February 28, 1976	742	−24.1%	April 27, 1981	1024	38.0%	54.2	38.5	15.7
August 12, 1982	777	−36.1%	August 25, 1987	2722	250.3%	63.1	61.3	1.8
October 19, 1987	1739	−21.2%	July 17, 1990	3000	72.5%	36.3	33.4	2.9
October 11, 1990	2365	−9.7%	January 31, 1994	3978	68.2%	42.4	40.3	2.1
April 4, 1994	3593	−18.5%	July 17, 1998	9338	159.9%	54.0	52.2	1.8
September 10, 1998	7615	−37.8%	January 14, 2000	11723	53.9%	61.9	16.4	45.5
October 10, 2003	7286	−6.6%	March 4, 2005	10941	50.2%	24.5	17.0	7.4
October 13, 2005	10217	−53.8%	October 9, 2007	14165	38.6%	41.3	24.2	17.1
March 5, 2009	6454							
Averages		**−33.3%**			**99.6%**	**47.2**	**32.0**	**15.2**

Election Year Pattern

Yale Hirsch, editor of the *Stock Trader's Almanac* (www.stocktradersalmanac.com), has compiled statistics on the four-year U.S. presidential election cycle and broken it down into the characteristics that have occurred each year for the period that a president is in office. Since 1832, the market has risen a total of 557% during the last two years of each administration and only 81% during the first two years. This amounts to an average of 13.6% per year for each of the last two years of an administration and only 2.0% for each of the first two years. Indeed, since 1965, none of the 13 major lows occurred in the fourth year of a presidency, and more than half (9) occurred in the second year. Hirsh's presumption is that the incumbent party wants to appear in a favorable light during the last two years, and especially in the last year of an administration, in order to be reelected. To do this, aside from providing the normal "spin" about their accomplishments, they force interest rates lower and stimulate the economy. At least, history shows that interest rates are inversely correlated with the stock market during those latter two years. How the administration in power can force them lower is subject to conjecture.

In any case, this is a reasonable and relatively consistent pattern. Some would argue that it is confusing "cause" with "correlation" and that there may not be a direct causal link between politics and the stock market. Such an argument can be made about many occurrences in nature and in man that appear to cause the stock market to react. The human mind often requires an explanation for stock market behavior. It will invent causal relationships where they do not exist. This mental tendency is something for the technical analyst to be mindful of and is the primary reason that concentration always should be focused on price action rather than on speculating about what might or might not be the cause for its behavior.

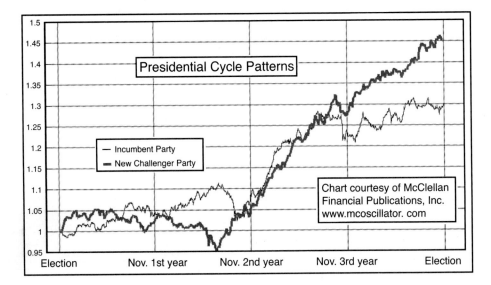

FIGURE 9.5   Presidential pattern ©McClellan Financial Publications, Inc.

Seasonal Patterns

A seasonal pattern in agricultural prices has been known for centuries. More recently, interest rates have followed a seasonal pattern as money was borrowed for seed and returned when the crops were gathered. It turns out that seasonality exists in almost all economic statistics, and most producers of economic statistics, such as the Treasury, Federal Reserve, National Bureau of

Economic Research, The Conference Board, and many others, adjust their numbers for seasonality. Technical analysts sometimes frown upon this practice because it distorts real figures with adjusted figures. However, it is an admission that seasonality is an important factor in economic statistics and that the earth's tilt and travel around its orbit have a substantial effect on prices, markets, and economic activity.

The U.S. Treasury Bond market has seasonal tendencies. In Figure 9.6, the performance by month of Treasury Bonds is averaged to show that the latter part of the year is the strongest period for the bond market, whereas the winter through spring is the weakest. This means that long-term interest rates, which travel inversely to bond prices, will tend to decline in the summer and fall and rise in the winter and spring.

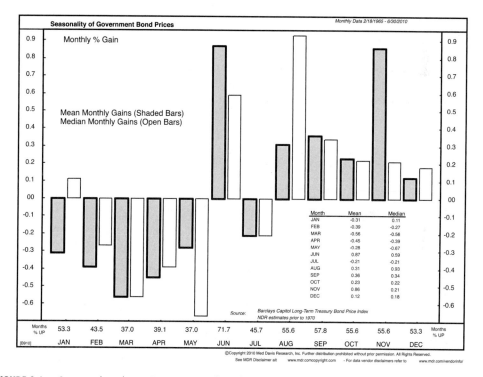

FIGURE 9.6 Seasonal cycles in Treasury Bonds (February 1965–June 2010)

In the commodity markets, such products as corn, hogs, and oil are those most affected by seasonality. However, changes are occurring in the seasonality in the agricultural sector because many food products are now produced in and shipped from the southern hemisphere in the "off-season." However, "seasonal" does not mean that from a trading or investment standpoint, a position should be held for many months. In oil, for example, since 1983, the best performance months are July through September, and the weakest is usually October ("Futures Insight: Crude Oil," *Active Trader Magazine*, July 2004, p 70). In orange juice contracts, for example, a seasonal trade for 35 years has been 74% profitable for short trades initiated on June 4 and closed on

July 1 (Momsen, 2004). Almost all commodity and stocks have seasonal components that once recognized can be profitable. This is called "entry date/exit date" trading. Price action at or near each date should be analyzed closely because dates are only arbitrary, but once a seasonal pattern is recognized, with proper discipline and observation, it can be very profitable over time.

"Sell in May and go away" (usually until October 1) refers to the tendency for the stock market to decline from May to September and rise from October to April. In the past ten years, August and September have been the worst months for performance, and October, November, and January have the best gains, with another small rise in April. According to this model, May is the month to sell, and August is the month to start looking for a bottom. This model has been very consistent. Notice in Table 9.2 that 17 out of 30, or 57%, of the four-year cycle bottoms occurred in September, October, November, or December. Only one peak occurred in October since 1896. Only one peak occurred in August and only four in September. No peaks have occurred in January. In other words, in stock prices, there seems to be a downward bias in the late spring and summer and an upward bias in the late fall and winter. In a study by *Active Trader Magazine* ("May-October System, The Trading System Lab," *Active Trader Magazine*, July 2003, p 42), the results of buying on October 1 and selling short on May 15 for ten years, January 1993 through March 2003, showed excellent results. The only problem was the occurrence of large drawdowns on the short side during the speculative bubble in 1997 and 1998. The recovery from such drawdowns was quick, however, and the possibility of another speculative bubble in the immediate future is remote. Thus, this simple seasonal system seems to have merit, even if it is only used as a guide as to when to be aggressive and when to be cautious.

JANUARY SIGNALS

January Barometer

"As the Standard & Poor's goes in January, so goes the year" is a basic contention proposed by the Hirsch's of *Stock Trader's Almanac.* Statistical problems arise with this indicator, despite its popularity. First, if January is up, for example, the year starts with an advance and already has a leg up. Second, because the stock market has had a positive bias over the years, January usually is up as is the market for the year. When the periods and odds are broken down, the predictive value of the January barometer comes within normal statistical probabilities and is without predictive value.

January Effect

The January effect was a condition that lasted for many years. During January, small-cap stocks had a tendency to have abnormal strength. Although some analysts attributed this effect to investors timing trades for tax reasons in December and January, no one could explain why the January effect occurred in the magnitude it did. As a result, it became the darling of anti-random-walk theorists as an example of how the market can establish patterns that are profitable. In recent years, however, the January effect has not worked very well. Some say it has been arbitraged out of business.

EVENTS

Short-term traders sometimes practice what is called **event trading.** This is when either a news announcement is due, a surprise news announcement occurs, or a holiday is soon to occur. Holidays are seasonal and, thus, included here.

The major holidays during the year have shown to have recurring patterns. For example, some analysts have observed an Independence Day pattern. Stock market performance tends to be the strongest five days prior to Independence Day. Diminishing average performance generally occurs the five days following Independence Day. The sixth day after Independence Day is associated with very strong stock market performance. Another example of a holiday pattern is that the two weeks before Thanksgiving seem always to be positive. However, as we have seen in the "Seasonal Patterns" section, November is generally one of the strongest months anyway. Thus, when we deduct for November's habitual strength, the pre-Thanksgiving strength becomes more random and less useful. Is this type of information useful to the individual trader? The answer is up to the individual trader. In most cases, the observed pattern is well within expected statistically random results and is, thus, not helpful.

Another often-heard rule of thumb is to "Buy stocks on Monday and sell stocks on Friday." However, monthly, weekly, and daily patterns have the same statistical problems as holidays. Any observed patterns, once adjusted for underlying trend and for randomness, show little in the way of consistent return. Testing any simple trading rule that has been popularized in current market conditions is important. In a recent study, Dahlquist ("Blue Monday Goes Green," *Active Trader Magazine,* November 2009, p 28) finds a striking deterioration in the statistical significance and profitability of this trading strategy over the past three decades. In recent years, there is no evidence that Monday returns are any different from any other day of the week.

CONCLUSION

Although the statistical methods demonstrating some of the temporal patterns are flawed, several appear to have some merit. Though not something to depend strictly upon, they are consistent enough to be considered when timing long-term investments. These are the long-term Kondratieff cycle, the alternating 17-year cycle of dormancy and intensity, the 4-year cycle, and the seasonal cycle. Each has been relatively reliable, statistically sound, with some generous and occasional adjustments, and if applied mechanically have produced substantial results. The other cycles and patterns may occasionally prove to have merit, but the technical analyst should approach their use with great caution.

REVIEW QUESTIONS

1. Consider K-wave cycle theory, 34-year cycle theory, and the relationship between birthrates and the stock market. Plot on a timeline what each of these theories suggests stock market performance will be over the next 50 years. Do the predictions tend to agree and reinforce each other, or do they tend to contradict each other?

2. Consider the four-year cycle. Plot out the pattern this theory would suggest for the stock market over the next ten years. How well does your plot match what the decennial pattern theory would suggest would be positive years for stock returns?

3. Rosa said that over the past three years, she has invested all of her money in an S&P 500 index fund on October 1 and sold the fund 7 1/2 months later on May 15, remaining out of the market until the next October 1. Why do you think Rosa followed this strategy? How well has Rosa done following this strategy over the past three years?

4. Calculate the monthly rate of return in the S&P 500 for the past two years. What about your results is in line with what you would have predicted given the information about seasonality in this chapter? What about your results seems to be contrary to the seasonality theory in this chapter?

FLOW OF FUNDS

CHAPTER OBJECTIVES

By the end of this chapter, you should

- Understand why knowledge of the flow of funds is important to determining stock market valuation
- Understand why liquidity plays an important role in potential stock market valuation
- Be familiar with measurements of market liquidity
- Understand the relationship between Federal Reserve policy and the cost of funds

Thus far, we have covered four of the five necessary ingredients for making a reasonable assessment of the market's future direction. We have looked at the primary trend, as defined in the Dow Theory; at sentiment, to see how different types of investors are thinking and acting; at market indicators, as confirmation of or divergence from the trend; at seasonality; and at other temporal tendencies. In this chapter, we look at the fifth ingredient. Our focus is on what propels markets in one direction or the other—money, traditionally called the "flow of funds."

For supply and demand to work in any market, money must be available. Money is both the fuel and the lubricant that facilitates transactions. Bartering for stock shares would be ponderous and unwieldy. When money is unavailable or expensive, the supply of stock available for sale increases as investors sell their stocks to raise funds for other purposes. When money is available and relatively inexpensive, it is available for investment in the markets. Accessible money does not necessarily imply a strong market because the available money may be invested elsewhere or just put under a mattress. However, available money seeks the most attractive return, and if the markets are advancing, as confidence in the markets builds, more money is funneled into the markets. Finally, if money is limited or becomes excessively expensive, the stock market has the conditions for a decline.

We will look at four major topics in our study of the flow of funds. First, we look at the money that is available and can be measured internally within the financial marketplace, such as money market funds, margin debt, and secondary offerings. Second, we look at the availability of funds not currently invested within the financial markets, such as household liquid assets, liquidity, money supply, and loan demand, including consumer credit. Third, we focus on the cost of funds, looking at short-term interest rates like the fed funds rate and the prime rate and long-term interest rates in the bond market. Fourth, we consider the important influence that Federal Reserve policy has on all of these variables.

As we look at the indicators in this chapter, you will see that many conventional signals turned out to be incorrect or were outweighed by other indicators during the speculative bubble from 1998 to 2000 and the subsequent collapse between 2000 and 2002, and again during the stock market advance into 2008 and the subsequent collapse to new lows in 2009. Interestingly, it appears that flow of funds signals work poorly during such emotional times, presumably because stock prices appear to divorce themselves from economics. However, now that the speculative period is over, the flow of funds signals may return to favor and should not be ignored just because of their shortcomings during that earlier period. After all, the flow of funds indicators have a history and a logical reason for existence that goes back 50 to 60 years. Their recent failures are more likely due to an anomaly than to a permanent change in the relationship of money and the stock market.

FUNDS IN THE MARKETPLACE

Let's begin by looking at the money that is available within the financial marketplace. Two of the topics we consider, money market funds and margin debt, measure the amount of funds available within the market to flow toward additional stock purchases. The third topic we consider is secondary offerings; secondary offerings represent increased stock supply to which investor money might flow.

Money Market Funds

When aggressive investors or traders become nervous about the stock market, they usually sell stocks and place the funds into money market mutual funds. The amount of money market fund assets is, therefore, a potential source of funds for reinvestment into the stock market. Because investors and traders also tend to be wrong at market extremes, the level of money fund assets can be a contrary opinion sentiment indicator.

One method of looking at the relationship between assets in money market funds and the stock market is shown in Figure 10.1. It shows that when money market mutual fund assets exceed 10.8% of Ned Davis Research total market value, on average the market advanced approximately 10.5% per annum. This is reliable when the figure is first recorded at 10.8%. Conversely, when the percentage declines to below 10.8%, the stock market has a tendency to decline 12.5% as less money is available and investors are excessively optimistic. This indicator does not give actual buy and sell signals because it shows only the liquidity or illiquidity available to the stock market. It shows the conditions existing that may have an effect on the stock market but is not a mechanical signal generator. Just because there is money in money market mutual funds does not necessarily imply that the money will eventually flow into the stock market. The indicator states only that such money is available for commitment somewhere, perhaps in the stock market.

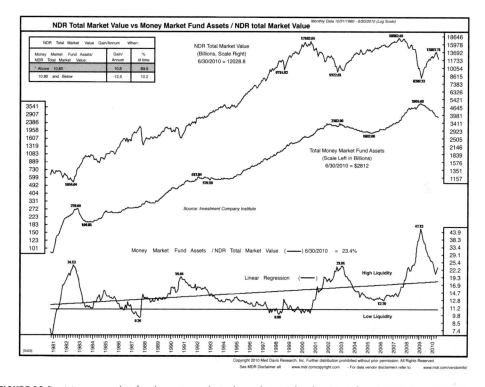

FIGURE 10.1 Money market fund assets and stock market total value (October 1980–June 2010)

Margin Debt

Margin debt, the amount of funds that customers at brokerage houses borrow for commitments in stocks, has historically been considered a sentiment indicator. The theory was that when markets became speculative and attracted the less-sophisticated and less-knowledgeable investors and traders, who began to trade on margin, the market was near a top. Although this relationship might still be partially true, margin debt as an all-encompassing figure of investor debt might have become obsolete. Today's speculator, instead of borrowing from his brokerage firm, can purchase and sell various highly leveraged derivatives such as options and futures that avoid being reported to the exchanges as margin debt. Thus, the market debt figures may be changing, and certainly an indicator based on them should continually be adjusted.

One way of looking at margin debt is shown in Figure 10.2. It uses a 15-month rate of change as the indicator of margin debt excess. When, over this period, the indicator crosses above −21%, a buy signal is generated, and when it crosses below 57%, a sell signal is generated. Eighteen months after a buy signal, the stock market has advanced on average 47.2%, and on sell signals it only advanced 2.0%. This has worked well in the period from 1970 through 2010, but potential change in the parameters must be considered for the future.

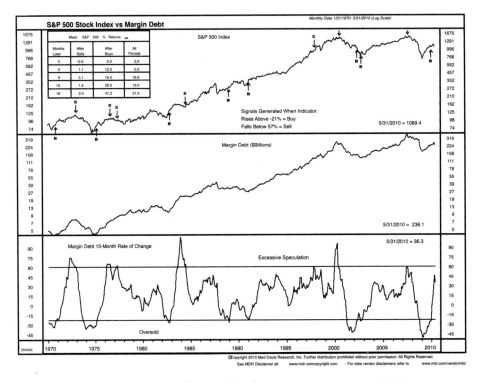

FIGURE 10.2 Margin debt and the S&P 500 stock index (January 1970–May 2010)

Secondary Offerings

The number of secondary offerings is a sign of increasing supply of stock being sold on the market. A secondary offering is the offering of additional shares of stock in a company that is already publicly traded, as opposed to a primary offering which occurs when stock in a newly publicly traded company is offered. This is usually a bearish sign for two reasons. First, it is a sign that more supply is coming into the marketplace, soaking up available funds. Following the basic principles of economics, as the supply of stock increases, the price of stock will fall. Second, the sellers, usually insiders, are liquidating. These insiders will try to sell stock at times when they think the price is relatively high. Thus, an increase in public offerings is directly related to supply and demand for stock and is also a sentiment indicator.

Ned Davis Research uses the number of offerings rather than the dollar amount so that the figures are not dominated by only a few huge offerings. The number relates more to the broadness of the tendency to sell out than to the actual money being soaked up, making it a more reliable figure of broad insider sentiment. They have found that when the 5-month moving average of the number of secondary offerings exceeds its 45-month moving average by 147, the stock market only advances another 1.0%. When the short average deviates from the long average by only 109 or less, the market advances 12.9% per annum (see Figure 10.3).

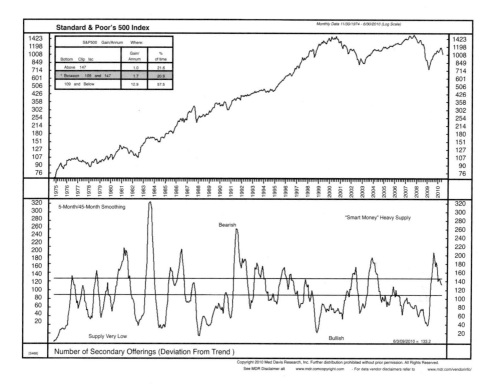

FIGURE 10.3   Secondary offerings (November 1974–June 2010)

FUNDS OUTSIDE THE SECURITY MARKET

Funds that are currently in the financial market are undoubtedly important, but the availability of funds outside the financial market also plays an important role in determining market conditions. The value of and the liquidity of household financial assets are important considerations when measuring how much money households might move into the security market. Money supply measures and bank loan activity are also important when considering how much money might flow into the financial markets.

Household Financial Assets

Households, like corporations and governments, have different kinds of assets. They have both physical assets, such as cars and houses, as well as financial assets, such as stocks, bonds, mutual funds, and banking accounts. Some of their financial assets are liquid and some are not. Liquid assets can be converted to cash quickly; cash, bank deposits, money market mutual funds, U.S. Treasury bonds, notes, and bills are liquid financial assets. Other financial assets cannot always be converted to cash quickly; stocks generally are considered to be more liquid than other financial assets, such as pension funds, retirement accounts, profit-sharing accounts, unincorporated business ownership, trusts, mortgages, and life insurance.

A ratio of liquid financial assets to total assets shows how "liquid" households are—in other words, how easily they can raise cash if they need it. Generally, the more liquid households are, the more able they are to invest in stocks. When household liquidity is high, it is, therefore, favorable for the stock market, whereas low liquidity is negative for the stock market.

The data presented in Figure 10.4 shows a substantial decline in household liquidity in the 1990s. This is one reason why consumer debt rose so strongly and why households were unable to withstand the severe economic contraction. During severe economic contractions, one major source of funds for cash-strapped households is the stock market. Thus, this indicator, although it does not give mechanical signals, does measure the potential funds for stock demand or supply.

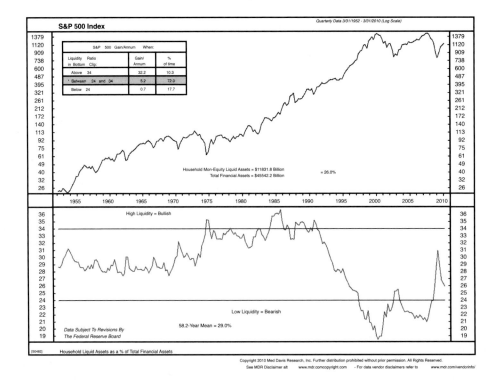

FIGURE 10.4 Household liquidity (March 1952–March 2010)

Money Supply

Expansion in the money supply is a measure of potential demand for stock, as well as other assets, and is, thus, a rough measure of the potential for business and stock market expansion. Increases in the money supply have been historically associated with increases in economic growth and productivity. Although this economic theory is straightforward, quantifying actual money supply growth is not as easy as it seems. Measuring the amount of money in the economy depends upon knowing what money is. If I ask you how much money you have, you would certainly count the currency and coins in your wallet. However, you would also probably think about the money you have in your checking account. Then, there is also the money you have in a savings account or money market mutual fund. Thus, the definition of money, and what to include in a measurement of money, is not as straightforward as it would initially seem.

The Federal Reserve measures money supply in a number of ways. Table 10.1 shows the various measurements of money that the Federal Reserve uses. The categories are based on liquidity, or the ease in which the financial assets can be converted into cash.

TABLE 10.1   Measurements of the Money Supply (May 2010)

Billions of Dollars

M1 = Currency in circulation	882.3
+ Travelers' checks	4.9
+ Demand deposits	451.1
+ Other checkable deposits	373.5
Total M1	1,711.8
M2 = M1	
+ Small-denomination time deposits	1,069.4
+ Savings deposits including money-market deposit accounts	5,071.6
+ Retail money-market mutual fund shares	746.0
Total M2	8,598.8

Source: www.federalreserve.gov/releases/h6/

M1, the narrowest definition of money, is a measure of the most liquid assets in the financial system. It includes currency and the various deposit accounts on which individuals can write checks. M2 is a slightly broader measure of money, which includes various forms of savings accounts. The additional components of M2 are slightly less liquid than the financial assets of M1. Today, the most commonly quoted monetary aggregate is M2 because its movements appear to be most closely related to interest rates and economic growth.

When M2 is measured relative to the total market value of stocks, it tells us the percentage of money available outside the stock market. A high percentage, then, tells us that there is plenty of money around to go into the stock market and is, thus, an indicator of potential funds for stocks. Ned Davis Research has found that when this ratio exceeds 143, the amount of money available is large, and, consequently, the stock market tends to rise on average 13.0% per year versus an average 5.3% buy-and-hold average annual increase. On the other hand, when the ratio dips to 89 and below, money is scarce, and the stock market tends to decline. This relationship is highlighted in Figure 10.5.

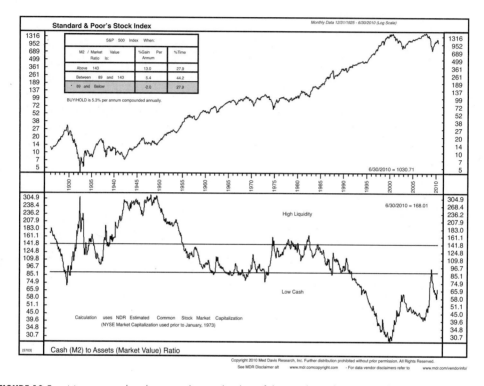

FIGURE 10.5 Money supply relative to the total value of the stock market (December 1925–June 2010)

Bank Loans

Generally, an increase in loan activity, the amount of loans being created and existing, is a sign of increased business activity. It can also be a sign of increased speculation and/or a particular period when banks, because the yield curve is so much in their favor, become less prudent in their lending policies. When loan demand increases, it puts upward pressure on interest rates. Conversely, a decrease in loan demand puts downward pressure on interest rates.

The growth and contraction of bank loans has a bearing on interest rates and on the stock market. As shown in Figure 10.6, Ned Davis Research found that since 1948, a year-to-year rise in bank loans (and leases) greater than 13% indicated an overheated economy and a high likelihood of a stock market decline. When bank loans only expanded at 5.5% or lower, the economy was healthier, and the stock market rose on average 11.5% per year on average.

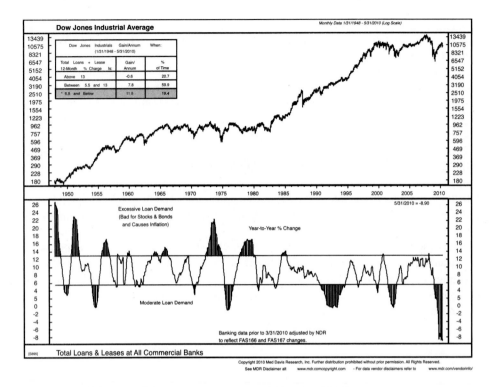

FIGURE 10.6   Bank loans and the S&P 500 (January 1948–May 2010)

THE COST OF FUNDS

The interest rate represents the price of borrowing funds. It is the cost that borrowers have to pay to use money; the higher the price, the less likely borrowers are to borrow. It is also the reward that lenders receive for letting someone borrow their money; investors compare this return with the expected return in other markets, such as the stock market, when they decide where to allocate their funds.

Short-Term Interest Rates

The theory behind using short-term interest rates as stock market signals is based on two assumptions. First, interest-bearing investments are alternatives to stock investments. In other words, savers make choices about placing their investment funds in interest-bearing securities or the stock market. When interest rates are relatively high, the interest-bearing securities look relatively more enticing. Second, interest rates directly affect costs for corporations and, thus, corporate earnings. However, the interest rate itself is important because the expected rate of return in the stock market must be greater than the short-term interest rate for investors to invest. When interest rates begin to rise, while the stock market languishes, investment outlooks begin to change. On the corporate and personal level, rising rates translate into rising costs. Whether it is working capital borrowing or adjustable rate mortgage payments, increases in short-term rates have a negative effect on net income and, by extension, on confidence. Alternatively, when rates decline, costs also decline and confidence builds. Furthermore, and regardless of potential reasons, short-term interest rates correlate very closely but inversely with stock market behavior. To know when a major switch in direction in short-term interest rates has occurred is important knowledge as to a probable switch in stock market direction.

Federal Reserve policy indicators and short-term interest rates are generally very accurate, though often early, as a predictor of stock market direction. Figure 10.7 shows the relationship between short-term interest rate movements and the S&P500. During the speculative bubble in 1998 to 2000 and its collapse into 2002, however, interest rates had little effect upon the market's direction. Emotion had overcome logic, and the relationship between short-term interest rates and the market was abandoned for greed to make easy money and fear of missing the next upward wave in stock prices. Again, in the period between 2007 and 2009, when the stock market collapsed to a new 10-year low, lower short-term interest rates had no positive effect on the stock market. Financial jargon calls this behavior "pushing on a string," when short-term rates do not cause incentives to buy stocks. The last time rates did not work was in the 1920s speculative bubble and early 1930s collapse. They were reliable for more than 50 years thereafter.

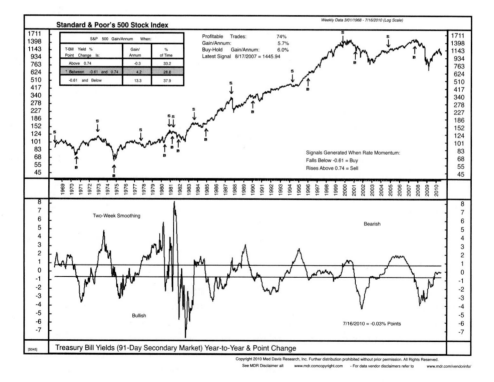

FIGURE 10.7   91-day Treasury bill rates points change (March 1968–July 2010)

Long-Term Interest Rates (or Inversely, the Bond Market)

Long-term interest rates are related to, but not perfectly correlated to, short-term interest rates. The Federal Reserve effectively controls short-term interest rates through its various policy measures, but it does not have as tight control of the long-term market. When we speak of long-term interest rates, we speak of the bond market. Long-term interest rates and bond prices are inversely related. When long-term interest rates rise, bond prices fall, and when long-term interest rates fall, bond prices rise.

Relationships between the bond market (or long-term interest rates) and the stock market also exist. The relationships between bonds and stocks have much to do with the payout for security holders, coupon payments for bondholders, and dividends for stockholders. Generally, investors view bonds as long-term investments with a steady, fixed coupon return, whereas stocks are long-term investments with a variable, less-predictable return. Both markets, however, can fluctuate widely.

For long-term outlooks (as opposed to long-term interest rates), therefore, it is important to know the historical relationship between these investments. As a rule, long-term bonds have tended to move in the same direction as the stock market. In other words, long-term interest rates have tended to move in the opposite direction from the stock market. As the bond market makes a major bottom, the stock market often makes a major bottom also. At tops, the bond market tends to lead the stock market and is, thus, very often, an early indicator of trouble ahead for the stock market. As in short-term interest rates, this relationship broke down during the period of the speculative bubble and collapse between 1998 and 2002 and between 2007 and 2009. Prior to those periods, the relationship had been steady for over 50 years and will likely return. See Figure 10.8 for the relationship between long-term Treasury bond yields and the S&P500 over the past 40 years.

Ned Davis Research developed a simple trading rule for long-term interest rates. It is the amount of points a three-week moving average changes, up or down. If the long-rate measure declines by 8.7% from a weekly peak, a buy signal is generated. On the other hand, a sell signal is generated when the long-term rate average advances 11.7% from a weekly low. The performance history of this simple method produced an average annual return of 9.9% in the S&P 500 over the past 45 years. This is compared with a buy-and-hold gain of only 5.7%.

Money Velocity

The velocity of money is a measure of how fast money turns over in the economy. It is calculated as a ratio of personal income to M2. Historically, money velocity is related to inflation, as the faster money circulates, the more pressure exists on prices, and as a leading indicator of long-term interest rates, again because it reflects inflationary pressure. In terms of being an indicator for the stock market, Ned Davis Research has found that when money velocity (a monthly figure) rises above its 13-month moving average, the stock market has advanced 3.4% per annum on average. When money velocity declines below its 13-month moving average, the stock market has advanced 10.1% per annum. This relationship is shown in Figure 10.9. Clearly, inflationary pressures from increased money velocity put a damper on stock market prices.

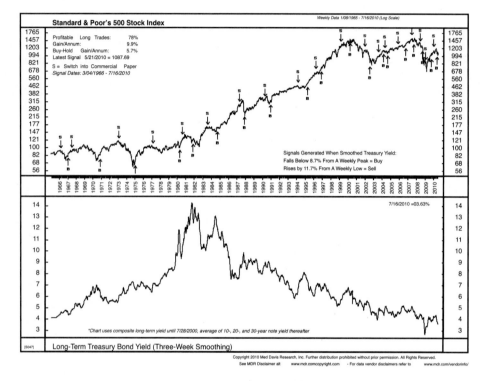

FIGURE 10.8 Long-term Treasury bond yield (January 1965–July 2010)

Misery Index

The economist Arthur Okum designed the Misery Index in the 1960s during the Johnson administration when inflation was a special concern. Inflation, coupled with high unemployment, resulted in what economists call **stagflation.** Okum created the index in an attempt to measure the social and economic cost of high inflation and high unemployment. A high Misery Index indicated that the combination of inflation and unemployment was high and that investors were experiencing a more stressful economic environment.

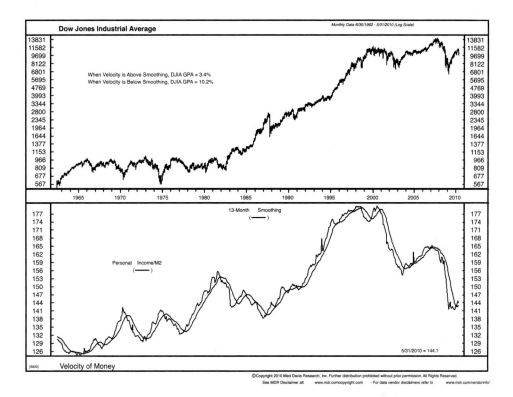

FIGURE 10.9 Money velocity (June 1962–May 2010)

The Misery Index is a universal index that can be calculated for any country by simply summing the country's inflation and unemployment rates together. The original Misery Index has been modified to create the American Misery Index. The American Misery Index is calculated by adding the inflation, unemployment, and interest rates. Figure 10.10 shows how the level of the American Misery Index has related to the performance of the DJIA since 1966. This figure shows the results of buying the DJIA whenever the American Misery Index falls by 0.3 points and selling the DJIA whenever the index rises by 3.2 points. The trading accuracy of this system is 75% favorable, and its gain per annum is greater than the buy-and-hold gain per annum by over 4%. Because the calculation of the Misery Index is easy and low-cost, the profitable results of this trading system appear valuable.

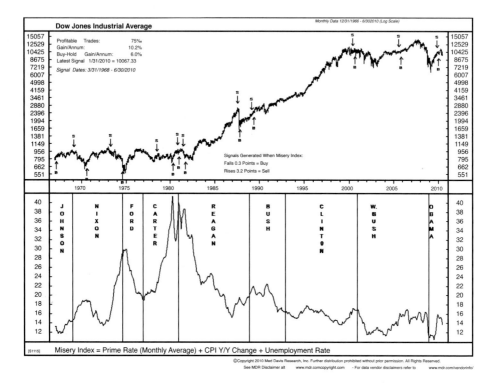

FIGURE 10.10 The Misery Index and the DJIA (December 1966–June 2010)

FED POLICY

The Federal Reserve System (www.federalreserve.gov), often referred to as "the Fed," is the independent federal organization that determines and implements monetary policy for the United States. The Federal Reserve's policy regarding the money supply is the principal determinant of short-term interest rates. The Federal Reserve has three main tools for adjusting the money supply: changing the amount of reserves that banks are required to hold, changing the discount rate, and buying and selling U.S. Treasury and federal agency securities through its open market operations. The third tool (open market operations) is the one that the Fed most often uses.

When the Federal Reserve purchases securities, it adds money to the banking system. Because banks then have more cash in reserve, they are more likely to make loans, and interest rates tend to fall. Another way to look at this relationship is that the Fed's purchase of bills represents increased demand for bills. As the demand for bills rises, bill prices rise and short-term interest rates decline.

Fed selling of government securities has exactly the opposite impact. As money is used to pay for these securities, reserves are drained from the banking system. When there is less money in the banking system, banks can make fewer loans, and interest rates tend to rise. Fed selling of government securities represents an increased supply of securities in the marketplace, and, thus, the price of these securities falls. As bill prices fall, interest rates rise.

The Fed uses open market operations to reach a federal funds rate target. The federal funds rate is the interest rate at which banks borrow from each other. Although the federal funds rate is not set by the Federal Reserve, Fed action greatly impacts this rate. If the Federal Reserve makes open market purchases, banks will have more money in reserve. Fewer banks will need to borrow reserves from other banks, and more banks will have excess reserves that they want to lend. This, in turn, places downward pressure on the federal funds rate. When the Fed sells securities, bank reserves decrease, and as bank reserves decline, more banks want to borrow and fewer banks want to lend in the federal funds market. Thus, the federal funds rate will rise.

The Federal Open Market Committee (FOMC) meets about every six weeks. At these meetings, the FOMC establishes a federal funds target rate. Although the minutes of each FOMC meeting are not made available to the general public until three weeks after the meeting, the FOMC announces its federal funds target rate at the conclusion of the meeting. By implication, this federal funds rate target tells the public whether the Federal Reserve is pursuing a restrictive or expansionist policy. Because short-term interest rates are so important to business and the stock market, and because the Federal Reserve has such a large impact on short-term interest rates, it is important for the analyst to be aware of Fed policy and the subtle changes in that policy.

Fed Policy Futures

The FOMC meets in private and only provides a brief announcement about its strategy immediately following its meeting. Because a change in Fed policy can have a significant impact on the financial markets, people try to anticipate and predict Fed policy changes. The faculty at The University of Iowa Tippie College of Business operate a small-scale (maximum investment of $500) futures market known as the Iowa Electronic Markets (IEM; www.biz.uiowa.edu/iem/markets/fedpolicyb.html). One of the IEM markets is on the prospects for the Federal Reserve to change the federal funds target rate at their next several scheduled meetings. As seen in Figure 10.11, this futures market has been very reliable in predicting, up to a month or more before, the direction of Federal Reserve policy with respect to the direction of its target rates.

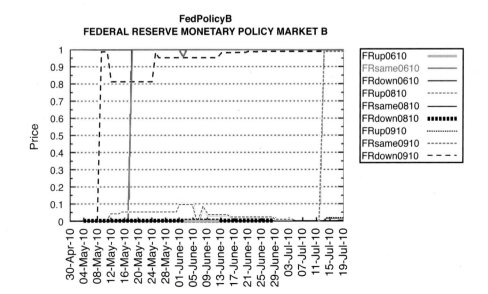

FIGURE 10.11   Iowa Electronic Futures Market, Federal Reserve policy (July 2010)

The Federal Reserve Valuation Model

Even though the Federal Reserve is in charge of monetary policy and is concerned with the overall health of the economy and the financial markets, the Federal Reserve seldom makes direct comments about the health of the stock market. However, economist Ed Yardeni (www.yardeni.com), in the back pages of a Fed report, discovered the Greenspan Model, also known as the Fed's Stock Valuation Model. As shown in Figure 10.12, this model gives a general indication of whether the Federal Reserve sees the stock market as overvalued or undervalued. It is a valuation model that determines if the stock market is too high or low based on the stock market earnings yield relative to yield on the ten-year U.S. note. Although this is an extremely easy-to-calculate indicator of general market value, there are several criticisms of this model. The principal criticisms of the model are that (1) it is too simplistic, (2) a better correlation exists between actual reported earnings than estimated earnings, and (3) it doesn't include inflation, an important factor in determining long-term interest rates.

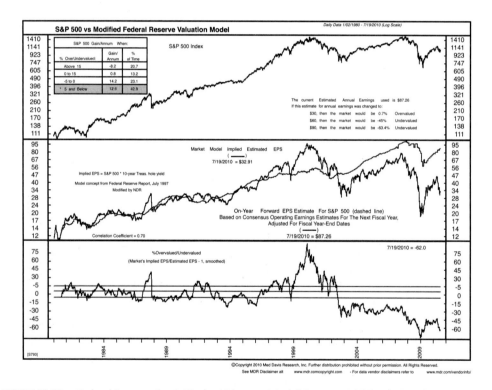

FIGURE 10.12   Federal Reserve Stock Market Valuation Model (January 1980–July 2010)

Three Steps and a Stumble

In line with the desire to measure when the Federal Reserve is tightening credit, Edson Gould, a legendary technical analyst from the 1930s through the 1970s, developed a simple rule about Federal Reserve policy that has an excellent record of foretelling a stock market decline. The rules states that "whenever the Federal Reserve raises either the federal funds target rate, margin requirements, or reserve requirements three consecutive times without a decline, the stock market is likely to suffer a substantial, perhaps serious, setback" (Schade, 2004, p. 68). This simple rule is still relevant. Although it tends to lead a market top, it is something that should not be disregarded. As shown in Figure 10.13, the rule has been followed by a median decline of 17%. Only two possible incorrect signals were given since 1915: The 1928 signal, prior to the 1929 crash, was possibly too early, and the 1978 signal was probably too late. Thus, this signal has an accuracy record of at least 87.5%.

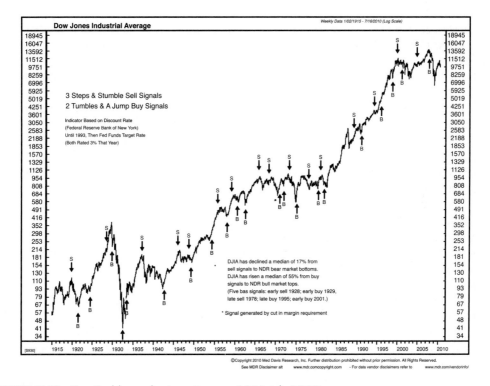

FIGURE 10.13 Two Tumbles and a Jump (January 1915–July 2010)

The Two Tumbles and a Jump indicator was first mentioned in Fosback's 1973 edition of *Market Logic*. It is essentially the opposite of Gould's Three-Steps rule. Although it uses changes in the Federal Reserve funds target rate, margin requirements, and reserve requirements, it looks for two consecutive declines, or tumbles, in any of these policy variables. It has an excellent history of predicting the stock market rises. As Figure 10.13 demonstrates, the percentage of accuracy since 1915 is 84%, with some of the errors considered questionable.

One way to use these two interest rate indicators, which the evidence shows to be superior, is to take them as warnings of important changes in market direction. They are not necessarily strict signals by themselves. However, if direction action is taken based on one of them, a reversal in direction from the signal direction would be signaled if the market exceeded its earlier high or low. Thus, if the Three-Steps rule gives a sell signal and the market begins to decline, a buy signal would be generated if either the market broke above its earlier highs or a Two-Tumble signal occurred. The same protection could be used for the Two-Tumble rule in the opposite direction. Essentially, these are "stops" that would prevent any major loss from future incorrect signals, rare as they may be.

Yield Curve

The **yield curve** is a graphical relationship of the yield on bonds with various lengths of time to maturity. Yield curve information is often summarized as a ratio or difference between a short-term and long-term interest rate over time. Figure 10.14 shows the difference between the three-month Treasury bill rate and the 30-year Treasury bond yield from 1948 through mid-2010.

Banks traditionally practice maturity intermediation, borrowing short-term funds and lending to corporations or individuals over longer periods. Thus, they are said to "borrow short, and lend long." Their profit depends on the spread between the cost of funds, the short-term interest rate, and the return from loaned funds, the long-term interest rate. As short-term interest rates rise, presumably from Federal Reserve policy action and long-term interest rates remain steady or decline, the yield curve becomes flatter and the banks are unable to profit as much from the spread. The yield curve, therefore, is a crude measurement of bank potential profitability. Bank profitability affects interest rates, and interest rates affect the stock market. Thus, the yield curve is a forecaster of stock market direction, and, historically, it has had an acceptable record of anticipating major turns in the stock market.

The "normal" relationship between interest-bearing instruments of the same quality is for longer rates to be higher than shorter rates. This is presumably because over time there is a risk of inflation, default, and other economic problems, the risk of which the holder of the long-term interest rate instrument wants to be compensated. This results in a positively sloped yield curve when plotting a graph with the time to maturity on the horizontal axis and the interest rate on the vertical axis for these securities.

The yield curve becomes abnormally steep when long-term rates rise considerably higher relative to short-term rates than the historic average of around 200 basis points. Although this can occur because of upward movement in the long-term rate or downward movement in the short-term rate, it is usually caused by the Fed lowering short-term rates to expand economic activity.

At times, short-term interest rates rise above long-term interest rates and the yield curve becomes inverted. This yield curve usually has dire consequences for the economy because it curtails the incentive of banks and other lending institutions that borrow money at short-term rates to make loans at long-term rates. The Federal Reserve estimates that an **inverted yield curve** predicts recessions two to six quarters ahead. Figure 10.14 shows the history of the yield curve and how it tends to forecast the direction of the stock market. Ned Davis Research found that when the long-rates advanced 1.1 percentage points above short-rates, the stock market advanced 10.8% per annum on average. Contrarily, when the yield curve inverted, the stock market declined on average 7.2% per annum.

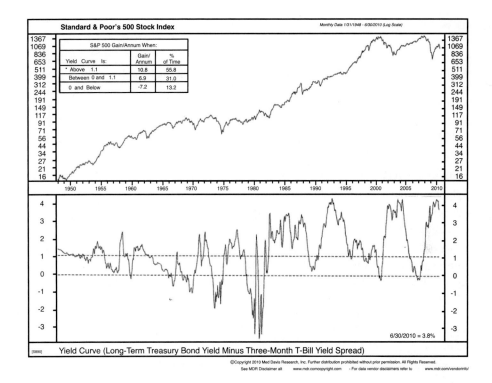

FIGURE 10.14   The yield curve as a forecast of stock market direction (January 1949–June 2010)

CONCLUSION

Flow of funds indicators, with the exception of the time during the speculative bubble from 1998 through its collapse in 2002, are a good means of assessing the available funds for investment. We have looked at some indicators of funds within the marketplace, from outside the marketplace, and their interest rates. The most reliable signals seem to come from interest rates. Some technical analysts believe that the study of the flow of funds is best left to quantitative analysts or quants, who closely follow the historic relationships between equities and fixed income securities. It may be many years for even those who subscribe to the flow of funds concept to believe in their monetary indicators after the experience of the late 1990s and early 2000s period.

REVIEW QUESTIONS

1. Explain how the amount of money in money market mutual funds can be a predictor of stock market performance. Calculate the ratio of money market mutual fund assets to the Wiltshire 5000 Index using the most recent statistics available. (Money market mutual fund asset statistics are included in the Federal Reserve Flow of Funds Report Z.1 in Chart L.122, available electronically at www.federalreserve.gov/releases/.) What does this ratio suggest about future stock market performance?

2. Why would many public offerings occur at market tops (and few at market bottoms)?

3. Why might household liquidity be related to stock market performance?

4. What has happened to the federal funds target rate over the past year? What does this suggest about stock market performance?

5. Determine the shape of the yield curve during the 2006–2007 time period. You can gather information to construct the yield curve from the Federal Reserve Web site. Alternatively, many Web sites, such as stockcharts.com (http://stockcharts.com/charts/YieldCurve.html), provide pictures of historical yield curves. Looking at this yield curve, do you think that the weak economic conditions and market downturn that began in the fall of 2008 were a surprise to an alert observer?

6. Gather data for the yield curve this week and for the yield curve one year ago. What changes do you notice? What impact do you think this will have on the stock market?

PART III

TREND ANALYSIS

CHAPTER 11 HISTORY AND CONSTRUCTION OF CHARTS

CHAPTER 12 TRENDS—THE BASICS

CHAPTER 13 BREAKOUTS, STOPS, AND RETRACEMENTS

CHAPTER 14 MOVING AVERAGES

HISTORY AND CONSTRUCTION OF CHARTS

CHAPTER OBJECTIVES

By the end of this chapter, you should be familiar with

- The advantages of presenting price information in a picture, or chart, format
- The construction of line charts
- The construction of bar charts
- The construction of candlestick charts
- The construction of point-and-figure charts
- The differences between arithmetic and logarithmic scales

A chart is like a cat's whiskers. A cat's whiskers tell the cat which way the mouse will turn and thus which way to pounce. The mouse doesn't think about which way it will turn, but the cat must anticipate that direction. Likewise, the market doesn't know which way it will turn, but the speculator must anticipate that turn regardless. He uses a chart as his whiskers. (Sieki Shimizu, 1986)

A chart is the traditional tool of the technical analyst. Charts are merely graphical displays of data. Many chart varieties have evolved over the centuries, but the basic principle of graphing price and other important information is the cornerstone of technical analysis. Indeed, in many countries, technical analysts are still called "chartists," even though hand-drawn charts have become somewhat antiquated because computers display and, in some programs, analyze the price data more quickly and efficiently. Nevertheless, some specialists, floor traders, market makers, and technical analysis departments for brokerage and management firms still maintain hand-drawn charts. These analysts believe that by drawing a chart, rather than allowing a computer to draw a chart or a publishing service to deliver a chart, the fine points of price changes, trends, and patterns become more visible. By taking the time and effort to draw each day's activity, a personal "feeling" for the price action develops that is more intimate than that gained from a mechanical drawing.

From these charts, technical analysts recognize patterns and trends that can be useful in trading and investing. Of course, the chart method is also subject to considerable criticism largely because the recognition of patterns and trends is subjective, based on the analyst's skill and experience. These human attributes are difficult to quantify and, thus, difficult to test.

Interestingly, a recent, unpublished study by Hasanhodzic, Lo, and Viola (2010) showed that humans, when confronted with graphic data in a "video game" format, can "distinguish between actual financial returns from random temporal permutations of those returns." They found "overwhelming statistical evidence (p-values no greater than 0.5%) that subjects can consistently distinguish between the two types of time series, thereby refuting the widespread belief that financial markets 'look random.' A key feature of the experiment is that subjects are given immediate feedback regarding the validity of their choices, allowing them to learn and adapt" (p. 1).

Some analysts are now using pattern-recognition systems and other sophisticated computerized methods, and early results have demonstrated that, indeed, many of the traditional chart patterns have some predictive value. Charts have other uses, however, if only to quickly observe the history of prices. The benefits of chart use outweigh the problems associated with their interpretation.

BOX 11.1 BENEFITS OF USING CHARTS

In his book, *Technical Analysis,* Jack Schwager (1996) outlines numerous benefits to the investor of using charts. These benefits include the following:

- Charts provide a concise price history—an essential item of information for any trader (or investor).

- Charts can provide the trader or investor with a good sense of the market's volatility—an important consideration in assessing risk.

- Charts can be a very useful tool to the fundamental analyst. Long-term price charts enable the fundamentalist to isolate quickly the periods of major price moves. By determining the fundamental conditions or events that were peculiar to those periods, the fundamentalist can identify the key price-influencing factors. This information can then be used to construct a price behavior model.

- Charts can serve as a timing tool, even by traders who base their decisions on other information (e.g., fundamentals).

- Charts can be used as a money management tool by helping to define meaningful and realistic stop points.

- Charts reflect market behavior that is subject to certain repetitive patterns. Given sufficient experience, some traders will uncover an innate ability to use charts successfully as a method of anticipating price moves.

- An understanding of chart concepts is probably an essential prerequisite for developing profitable technical trading systems.

- Cynics take notice: Under specific circumstances, a contrarian approach to classical chart signals can lead to very profitable trading opportunities (when those signals fail).

HISTORY OF CHARTING

According to exhaustive research on technical analysis by Lo and Hasanhodzic (2010), the earliest known recording of commodity prices with the intent to predict from them was in ancient Babylonia in the first millennium B.C. These recording were diaries of traders and astronomers who were attempting to correlate astrology with price changes. By the fifth and sixth centuries A.D., price charts, similar to those used presently, were developed in China, Europe, and Japan. The Chinese were interested in cyclicality of prices; the Europeans were interested in astrology; and the Japanese developed the candlestick chart that is still in use today. The "opening of commodity exchanges in Western Europe (1561) and Japan (1654) provided the necessary environment for the development of the chart" (Shimizu, 1986, p 14). At the time of these exchanges, freely trading markets had become sophisticated enough to produce multiple prices during a trading day and, thus, the requirement for recording the high, low, and close price of each commodity traded on the exchange. It was only natural that this information was portrayed in graphic form. By the 1830s, just before the invention of the ticker tape for the stock exchanges, several chart vendors in New York sold published charts on stock and commodity prices.

The information charted and the method of charting often flows from how the market being analyzed operates. For example, the current use of high and low in a bar chart is not feasible in those trading markets that settle a price only once a day.

Plausibly, the first type of chart was just a simple plot on paper of a number, either amount or price, and a date. In early Japan, for example, rice was traded by amount. Instead of a price per bag, it was the number of bags per price that was recorded by the famous rice trader Sokyu Honma in the 1750s. As markets began to trade more frequently during the day, the chart became more complex. A high and low price could be recorded, and eventually as multiple trades occurred, an open and close price could be added. Volume was recorded much later when more complete and public records were available. At first, witnesses located in the marketplace recorded prices. Eventually, markets became better organized, and prices and amounts were publicly available.

> The growth of this business is of great monument to the stock exchange, for it is through the instant dissemination of the quotations made on its floor that the active and continuous interest in the markets is sustained. (Horace L. Hotchkiss, founder of the Gold Stock and Telegraph Company)

The invention of the ticker and the ticker tape revolutionized technical analysis and charting. Shortly after Thomas Edison invented a machine called the Edison Telegraph Printer to print messages from a telegraph, in 1867 Edward A. Calahan, an employee of the American Telegraph Company, invented the ticker tape. Eventually, it was improved upon and patented by Thomas Edison in 1871. This invention not only made conventional charting easier but also allowed for point-and-figure charting, because such charts required knowledge of every price at which an item had traded during the day. Without the ticker tape, the gathering of this information would have been difficult in markets with multiple trades during a day.

BOX 11.2   WHAT IS A TICKER TAPE?

A **tick** is any change, up or down, in the price of a stock (or any other traded security). Information regarding stock transactions is recorded on a ticker tape. By watching the ticker tape, an investor is able to keep abreast of changes in stock prices. The first ticker tape was developed in 1867, following the invention of the telegraph machine. This technology allowed information to be printed in a shorthand format on a narrow strip of paper, or tape. Messengers would run a circuit between the New York Stock Exchange (NYSE) trading floor to brokers' offices, delivering tapes of the most recent transactions. Brokers would place an office near the NYSE because the closer they were to the trading floor, the more quickly they could get ticker tapes and the more up to date their information about recent stock transactions would be. Technology improved over the years, providing faster access to stock transaction data. In the hectic trading days of the late 1960s and early 1970s, the ticker could not keep up with trading, and there was a period when the markets were closed on Wednesdays to facilitate the clearing of trades. Not until 1996 did the real-time electronic ticker provide up-to-the-minute transaction data. Today, you will see immediate stock market transaction figures on TV news shows and Web sites. Although these figures are reported electronically, and the actual tape is no longer used, the name "ticker tape" is still used when a running list of trades is shown on TV or a quote machine.

When you are watching a ticker tape, you will see information recorded in a format such as:

$$HPQ_{2K}@23.16 \blacktriangle 1.09$$

or

Ticker Symbol $_{Shares\ Traded}$@Price Traded, Change Direction, Change Amount

The first information given is the ticker symbol; these unique characters identify a particular company's stock. In the preceding example, HPQ indicates that this information is for the common stock of Hewlett-Packard Co. Next, the volume of shares traded appears. 2K indicates that 2,000 shares were traded. The price per share for the particular trade is then quoted. Next, an up or down triangle appears, indicating whether this trading price is higher or lower than the previous day's closing price. Finally, the difference between the current trading price and the previous closing price is reported. Reading this ticker tape, we can tell that 2,000 shares of Hewlett-Packard stock just traded at $23.16 a share. We can also tell that this is $1.09 higher than the previous day's closing price of $22.07.

Modern technology has greatly simplified the task of chart construction. Computer power has replaced much of the tedious human work. Now, even basic home computers have spreadsheet programs, such as Microsoft Excel, that can store daily stock price data and create a variety of charts used by technical analysts. In addition, other sophisticated software programs that are specifically designed for technical analysis are readily available. These programs not only plot charts and indicators or oscillators but also can test trading rules. Examples are TradeStation (www.tradestation.com), Metastock (www.equis.com), High Growth Stock Investors (www.hgsi.com), and Amibroker (www.amibroker.com). In addition to charting software, the Web hosts many charting sites, examples of which are StockCharts.com, www.bigcharts.com, finance.yahoo.com, and freestockcharts.com. Today, the technical analyst can focus much more time and attention on analysis and much less on chart construction.

Over the years, technicians developed several different approaches to chart construction. The four main categories of charting that we discuss in this chapter are line charts, bar charts, candlestick charts, and point-and-figure charts. Each approach has its own features, benefits, and drawbacks. Whichever method a technical analyst chooses to use, charts serve as the technical analyst's road map. Charts give a quick and concise picture of past price action.

For example, look at Table 11.1. This table contains the closing price for Alcoa for the month of February 2010.

TABLE 11.1 Stock Price Data for AA in Tabular Form

Date	Open	High	Low	Close	Volume
2/1/2010	12.99	13.39	12.91	13.36	40,076,300
2/2/2010	13.76	13.90	13.52	13.67	50,545,100
2/3/2010	13.60	13.89	13.43	13.49	36,035,900
2/4/2010	13.29	13.29	12.90	12.91	44,587,200
2/5/2010	12.91	13.19	12.61	13.18	43,984,100
2/8/2010	13.18	13.53	12.93	13.06	39,405,800
2/9/2010	13.36	13.50	13.10	13.28	44,023,100
2/10/2010	13.31	13.34	13.00	13.16	33,049,100
2/11/2010	13.19	13.65	13.12	13.58	34,224,500
2/12/2010	13.33	13.42	13.19	13.28	46,158,500
2/16/2010	13.53	13.75	13.35	13.74	37,189,200
2/17/2010	13.89	13.90	13.51	13.60	26,052,800
2/18/2010	13.45	13.66	13.42	13.61	27,540,300
2/19/2010	13.55	13.69	13.45	13.53	28,570,000
2/22/2010	13.68	13.70	13.44	13.54	23,186,500
2/23/2010	13.44	13.52	13.05	13.18	35,032,000
2/24/2010	13.18	13.29	12.95	13.06	36,244,500
2/25/2010	12.90	13.33	12.80	13.31	39,552,000
2/26/2010	13.36	13.37	13.12	13.30	24,756,200

Source: www.finance.yahoo.com

It is difficult to look at the 19 closing prices in this table and get an idea of whether the stock price trend is up, down, or sideways. Now look at Figure 11.1.

This chart contains the same information as Table 11.1. Notice how much easier it is to process the information when it is provided in the picture form of Figure 11.1 rather than in tabular form. As the old saying goes, "A picture is worth a thousand words." With just a glance at the chart, you have a road map of where prices have been; in a fraction of a second, you can easily spot the highest prices and lowest prices that occurred during the period. A chart quickly transforms a table of data into a clear visual representation of the information.

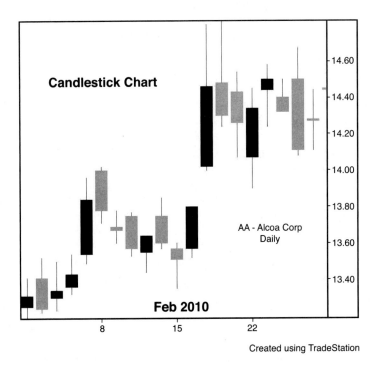

Created using TradeStation

FIGURE 11.1   Stock price information for AA in chart form (daily: February 1, 2010–February 26, 2010)

WHAT DATA IS NEEDED TO CONSTRUCT A CHART?

To construct reliable charts, the technical analyst must be sure of the trustworthiness of the data. During a normal trading day, many errors appear on the tape, from which most data originates, that someone must screen out and adjust. Some trade reports show the wrong price or volume; some trades are in error and must be broken; and some trades occur out of order. When a price error occurs at a high or a low for the trading day, the error is especially troublesome because it affects daily calculations of averages and oscillators using highs and lows. It is, therefore, very important that any data used for charting is extremely "clean" and reliable.

In addition to trading errors, other data errors can occur through stock splits, dividends, offerings, and distributions. In the commodities markets, because contracts have a settlement date at which trading halts, incorrect calculation of the time and price linkage between contracts may affect longer-term technical patterns and trends. Calculation of these linkages into time series data for a longer-term perspective is never precise. The results are called either "nearest future," "perpetual series," or "continuous series" and are provided by many data vendors and exchanges (see Box 11.3). There are other methods of joining the different contracts into a continuous series, but all have serious problems for the analyst wanting to test longer periods of data. Schwager (1996) recommends the continuous contract as the best method for such tests.

BOX 11.3 LINKED CONTRACTS

For very short-term testing and analysis of futures contracts, you can use the actual contract data. The test period must be extremely short, however, because the liquid portion of any contract, the period when active trading occurs, is only a portion of the contract time span. Thus, the data available for realistic study is short, and to test a number of signals, it must be separated at very short intervals.

Once the trading signal horizon exceeds an hour, however, one must calculate a linked contract to provide sufficient data for testing. There are three basic types of linked contracts: the nearest future, the perpetual, and the continuous. Each has its advantages and disadvantages.

The nearest future method is just a plot of each futures contract as it expires and is replaced by a new contract. Unfortunately, during the transition between old and new contract, a gap always exists at the rollover into the new contract. Thus, this method is useless for testing trading systems, even though the contracts plotted are historically correct. It is the least preferable method of analyzing longer-term futures price moves.

The perpetual contract (also known as the "constant-forward"), to avoid the nearest future rollover problem, uses a constant forward price, namely the anticipated price some specific period ahead. This forward contract comes from the interest and foreign exchange markets where constant-forward contracts are traded. The adjustment to the futures markets assumes a price that adjusts for the time between a contract series that is current and one that is beyond the specific constant-forward period. The perpetual price then is the price of the current contract and the forward contract each weighted by the amount of time remaining in the hypothetical forward period. Thus, the perpetual price avoids the problem of the rollover by smoothing the two contract prices, one near and one far out, in a gradual manner as time progresses. The problem with this method is that it is not real. The actual prices recorded in the perpetual contract never occurred. It is, thus, not a suitable method for testing a technical trading system.

continues

continued

The third method, the continuous contract, is more realistic but is useless for calculating percentage changes over time. It adjusts for the premium difference between the current contract prices—the price of the previous contract and the contract into which the trader rolls his position at a specific rollover date, say 15 days before expiration—to avoid the trading bias that occurs as the contract nears its end. This continuous contract then carries the adjustment into the future. It reflects exactly what would have occurred to a portfolio that invested in the first contract and rolled over each contract at its rollover date. It is, thus, a realistic expression of the history of the futures contract and can be used for testing past data. It has two problems, however. One is that because the adjustments are additive, it cannot be used for percentage returns; and two, the ending price of the continuous contract is not the same as the current price of the current contract. The continuous contract is the primary contract used for testing trading systems.

WHAT TYPES OF CHARTS DO ANALYSTS USE?

In early markets, when the price for a security or good might be established only once or twice a day, the chart was extremely simple. It was merely a graph of closing prices connected by a line, sometimes directly connected, and sometimes connected by perpendicular lines. In Japan, this type of chart was called a "tome" chart from the word "tomene," which means "close." In the Western world, this type of chart is still used and is called a "line" chart.

When trades became more frequent, chart forms took two paths. The first and still most common style was borrowed from the bar graph or stick graph and portrayed the high and low with a "floating" vertical line not connected to the base line. These were called bar charts or vertical line charts. Interestingly, in Japan, where many chart types were developed, the original plotting of price data was from right to left rather than the now-universal method of plotting from left to right. This bar style then evolved into the candlestick chart, which uses the same information as the bar chart but has a more appealing appearance to the eye. The other path was called the price movement line, where prices were recorded as they occurred, and only the ones that deviated from earlier prices by a specified amount were graphed in a line. This method of price plotting is the forerunner to the modern point-and-figure chart.

Today, the three most common types of charts that record prices at given time intervals (such as hourly, daily, weekly, or monthly) are line charts, bar charts, and candlestick charts. Let us look at each of these charts and see how they differ.

Line Charts

Figure 11.2 is an example of a line chart. These simple charts provide information about two variables, price and time. In Figure 11.2, the price variable is the daily closing price for AA (Alcoa Corporation). A line chart has price data on the vertical, or y, axis. On the horizontal, or x, axis it has a time measure (hours, days, weeks, etc.).

Simple line charts are especially useful when studying long-term trends. Because line charts display summary statistics, they are often used when information about several different variables is being plotted in the same graph. For example, in Figure 11.3, three line charts are used to plot the daily close of the Dow Jones Industrial Average, the S&P 500, and NASDAQ for the past four years. Journalists often use line charts to give the reader a quick, concise picture of the variables being discussed.

Figure 11.3 represents daily data. Line charts, however, can be used to present data collected at any time interval. More frequent data collection will lead to a more detailed, but more cluttered, graphical presentation. Especially when studying long-term trends, these extra details muddy the picture and obscure basic trends. For example, compare Figures 11.4, 11.5, and 11.6. Each of these charts represents trading data for JNJ (Johnson & Johnson) over the four-year time period from July 2006 through June 2010. The first chart uses daily data, the second chart displays weekly data, and the third chart presents monthly data. See how broader, longer-term movements in the stock price are more easily discernable in the third graph, which relies on less-frequent data observations.

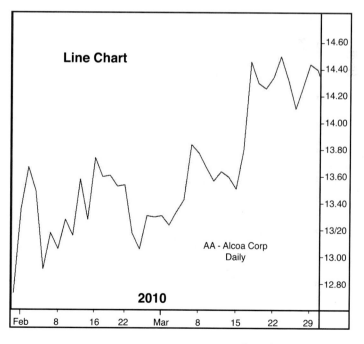

Created using TradeStation

FIGURE 11.2 Line chart of AA daily closing prices (daily: January 31, 2010–June 29, 2010)

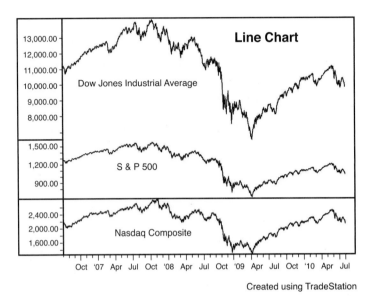

Created using TradeStation

FIGURE 11.3   Line charts of the daily closing prices of DJIA, S&P 500, and NASDAQ Composite
(daily: June 30, 2006–June 29, 2010)

Created using TradeStation

FIGURE 11.4   Line chart of daily close for JNJ (June 30, 2006–June 29, 2010)

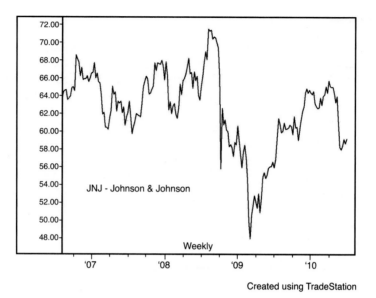

Created using TradeStation

FIGURE 11.5   Line chart of weekly closes for JNJ (June 30, 2006–June 29, 2010)

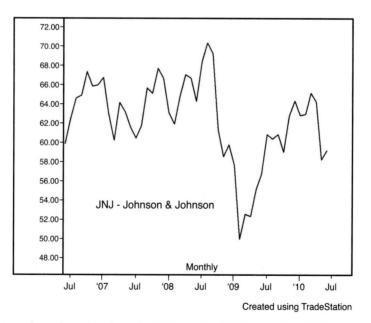

Created using TradeStation

FIGURE 11.6   Line chart of monthly closes for JNJ (June 30, 2006–June 29, 2010)

Bar Charts

Although the line chart visually displays one piece of information for each time interval, a bar chart shows at least three pieces of information: the high, the low, and the closing price for each time interval. Some bar charts also contain a fourth piece of price information, the opening price. Each time interval (that is, day, week, or five-minutes) is represented by one bar.

Figure 11.7 is an example of a daily bar chart. Each bar represents one day's price action. Just as with the line chart, price data is placed on the vertical axis, and time is measured on the horizontal axis. A vertical line shows the trading range for that day. The top of this vertical line represents the highest price at which the security traded on that day; the bottom of the bar represents the lowest trading price of the day. A longer line denotes a wider trading range during the day. Likewise, a short bar means that the spread between the highest price during the day and the lowest price during the day was small. A small tick mark on the right side of the bar indicates the closing price for the day. If the opening price for the day is recorded on the bar chart, it is represented by a small tick mark to the left side of the bar.

Created using TradeStation

FIGURE 11.7   Daily bar chart (arithmetic scale) for AA (March 31, 2010–June 29, 2010)

We see that the first bar in Figure 11.7 represents trading information for AA on March 31, 2010. The lowest point of the bar is 14.22, which is the lowest price that a share of AA traded for on that day. The highest price anyone paid for a share of AA that day was $14.44, represented by the top of the bar. The difference between the high and low price in any bar is called the **range.** The opening price for AA was $14.30, represented by the left hash mark. The right hash mark at $14.24 represents the closing price.

We can glean a lot of information from a quick visual observation of the bar chart. For example, the fact that the bar for trading day 2 is much longer than the bar for trading day 1 in Figure 11.7 indicates that the range on April 1, 2010, was much larger than the range on March 31. Another quick observation is that the bar for trading day 9, April 13, lies completely below that of the previous trading day. Thus, the bar chart makes it easy to spot days when the trading range lies completely outside of the previous day's trading range.

Just as with the line chart, bar charts can be constructed for various intervals of data collection. For example, Figure 11.8 presents a weekly bar chart for AA for the same period as Figure 11.7. As we use longer and longer intervals to gather information for our bar charts, we lose some of the details but will have a less-cluttered chart that offers more of a broad stroke picture of past price movement.

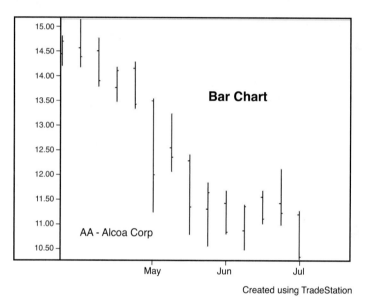

FIGURE 11.8 Weekly bar chart for AA (March 31, 2010–June 29, 2010)

Candlestick Charts

As mentioned in Chapter 3, "History of Technical Analysis," candlestick charts originated in Japan. This charting method was used as early as the mid-1600s to trade rice futures in the Japanese markets and continues to be the most popular form of technical analysis in Japan.

These techniques have been widely used in the Far East for many generations, but not until the publication of the book *Japanese Candlestick Charting Techniques* by Steve Nison in 1991 were Western traders introduced to candlestick charts. Before the publication of Nison's book, very few U.S. and European services offered candlestick charts. Today, almost every technical analysis software package and technical service offers candlestick charts. You can even create candlestick charts through the charting options in Excel.

Candlestick charts are similar to bar charts in their construction. Both charts use the high price, low price, and closing price, but candlestick charts always include the opening price. To construct a candlestick chart, the low and high prices are plotted on a thin bar, just as they would be for the bar chart we just discussed. A box is used to represent the opening and closing prices. To create this box, a horizontal mark is made at both the opening and closing prices; a rectangle is formed using these two horizontal marks. This rectangular box is called the *real body* of the candlestick. If the security closed at a higher price than it opened, the real body is white (gray in the charts here) or open. These white, or "open," real body candlesticks indicate price advances from the opening. Conversely, if the closing price falls below the opening price, the real body of the candlestick is shaded black. These candlesticks with a "closed," or black, real body designate price declines from the opening.

Figure 11.9 is a candlestick chart of daily prices during the second quarter of 2010 (the same as for Figure 11.7 and Figure 11.8) for AA. Much more colorful than the bar chart, the candlestick chart makes it easy to spot immediately days in which AA closed at a higher price than it opened. For example, the candle for the first trading day of the chart, March 31, has a gray body, indicating that the stock closed at a higher price than it opened. The following day, however, we see a black-bodied candlestick, indicating that the stock closed lower than it opened that day even though it close higher than the first day.

Created using TradeStation

FIGURE 11.9   Daily candlestick chart for AA (March 31, 2010–June 29, 2010)

As you can see in Figure 11.9, candlesticks come in a variety of shapes and sizes. If the real body of the candlestick is tall, the opening price and closing price were relatively far apart. Shorter real bodies indicate opening and closing prices that were very similar. In the extreme, the real body can be so short that it is just a horizontal line, indicating that the opening and closing prices were identical.

The thin vertical bars, representing the price extremes of the trading session, are called the **shadows.** The shadow above the real body is called the upper shadow; the shadow below the real body is called the lower shadow. You can easily see how the candlestick chart got its name; many times, the real body will look like a candle and the upper shadow will look like the wick.

Looking at the second candlestick in Figure 11.9, which represents price information for October 4, we see that this candlestick has relatively short upper and lower shadows. This, along with the black body, indicates that AA opened near the high and closed near the low of the day. We see this same type of trading pattern four days later on April 8. We can also see candlesticks with very long shadows. For example, in the candlestick for May 6, we see that its long shadow represents a relatively wide trading range for the day. The highest price that AA traded on that day was $12.64 and the lowest price was $11.25; the difference between these two extreme prices gives us a thin vertical bar of $1.39, a swing of over 10% that day (the day of the famous "flash crash"). Because the stock opened at $12.34 per share and closed at $11.94, the body of the candle is only $0.40 tall, leaving a particularly long lower shadow.

In fact, individual candlesticks can take on a variety of interesting sizes. If the opening price of the stock equals the low price for the trading session, a lower shadow will not exist on that day. Likewise, if the security closes at its high price for the day, there will be no upper shadow. Examples of this type of candlestick can be seen on May 4, May 14, and May 28. On some days, the opening and closing prices represent the entire trading range for the day.

Because candlestick charts contain all the information that a bar chart contains, all of the technical tools that are used with bar charts can also be used with candlestick charts. In addition, some technical tools rely on the color and size of individual candlesticks to signal trades. We study the trading techniques that are peculiar to candlestick charts in Chapter 17, "Short-Term Patterns."

WHAT TYPE OF SCALE SHOULD BE USED?

Price units are generally plotted on the vertical axis of stock charts. The analyst must determine the scale, or the distance between these price units, to use. Generally, two types of scales are used: an arithmetic scale and a semi-logarithmic scale.

Arithmetic Scale

For all the charts we have examined so far, we—along with most technical analysts—have used arithmetic (or linear) scales. A plot with an arithmetic scale shows the price units along the vertical scale at the same price intervals. For example, the vertical plot distance of a change of $1 to $2 would be the same as the plot distance from 10 to 11 or 100 to 101. In other words, using regular evenly divided grid paper, we plot each box vertically as the same dollar amount.

Semi-Logarithmic Scale

Although the arithmetic scale is the scale most often used, sometimes adjustments need to be made, especially when observing long-term price movements. For example, compare Figure 11.10 with Figure 11.11.

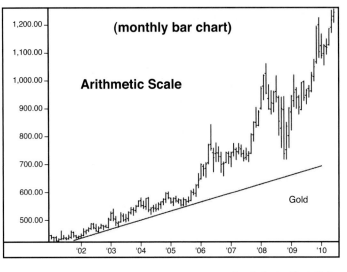

Created using TradeStation

FIGURE 11.10   Monthly bar chart for gold using arithmetic scale (December 2000–June 2010)

Both these charts plot the monthly price of gold for December 2000–June 2010. In April 2001, gold was trading for under $420 an ounce; at that time, a $42 increase in price would represent approximately a 10% gain for the investor. By June 2010, the gold price had advanced to almost $1250 a share. At that point, a $42 price increase represented only about a 3% gain for an investor owning gold. On the arithmetic scale, in Figure 11.10, a $100 price movement is visually the same whether it is a move from $400 to $500 or a move from $1100 to $1200. This type of scale can be somewhat deceptive; a $100 move is much more significant to an investor if the price of a security is $400 than if the price of the security is $1000. The logarithmic scale addresses this issue.

On the logarithmic scale, the vertical distance represents the same *percentage* change in price. Look at Figure 11.11. In this logarithmically scaled graph, the vertical distance between $500 and $600 is the same as that between $1000 and $1200 or $100 and $200, respectively. This vertical distance always represents a 100% increase in price rather than a particular dollar amount increase in price. The rule of thumb for when to use an arithmetic or logarithmic scale is that when the security's price range over the period being investigated is greater than 20%, a logarithmic scale is more accurate and useful. As a rule, the truly long-term charts (more than a few years) should always be plotted on logarithmic scales.

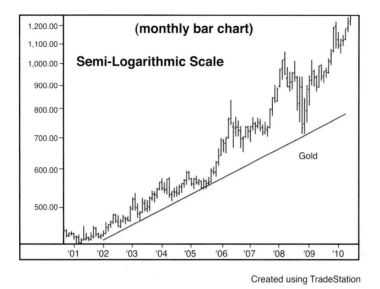

FIGURE 11.11 Monthly bar chart for gold using a logarithmic scale (December 2000–June 2010)

POINT-AND-FIGURE CHARTS

The point-and-figure chart records price data using a very different technique than line, bar, and candlestick charts. At first, it may appear that the construction of these charts is somewhat tedious. In addition, these kinds of charts are rarely published or discussed in the popular financial news. Because many of the point-and-figure charts are constructed using intraday trading data, use of these charts was historically limited to professional analysts who had access to intraday data. However, with some practice, you will see that point-and-figure chart construction is not that difficult and provides an interesting and accurate method of price analysis.

Point-and-figure charts account for price change only. Volume is excluded; and although time can be annotated on the chart, it is not integral to the chart. The original point-and-figure charts took prices directly from the tape as they were reported in the "Fitch Sheets" and by services prepared especially for point-and-figure plotting, such as Morgan, Rogers, and Roberts. Most of these services were put out of business by the computer and the use of the three-box reversal charts. The reading of each stock or commodity trade by trade was a laborious process. Today, very few services provide the data to plot one-point reversal charts.

The origin of point-and-figure charts is unknown, but we know they were used at the time of Charles Dow around the late nineteenth century. Some have thought that "point" came from the direction of the entries on the chart, pointing either up or down, but more likely "point" refers to the location of the price plot, which at first was just a pencil-point mark. "Figure" comes from the ability to figure from the points the target price.

Construction of a point-and-figure chart is very simple because only prices are used. Even then, only the prices that meet the "box" size and "reversal" size are included. Finally, the chart reflects the high and low of the period, whenever it is important. Many technicians believe that the high and low of the day are important numbers determined by supply and demand and are more important than the opening or closing prices, which occur at single, arbitrary moments in time.

As with all of the charting methods, different analysts use variations of point-and-figure charting to best meet their particular needs. We begin our discussion of point-and-figure chart construction by looking at the oldest method, referred to as the one-point reversal point-and-figure method. Further information about these one-point reversal charts can be found in reprints of Alexander Whelan's *Study Helps in Point and Figure Technique.*

One-Box (Point) Reversal

All point-and-figure charts are plotted on graph paper with squares that form a grid. There should be enough squares to include a significant period of trading activity. Early charts had a special outline around the rows ending in 0 and 5, just for clarity. As with the other types of charts, we will plot price on the vertical axis, but the bottom axis is not time scaled with the point-and-figure graph.

The best way to learn to read a point-and-figure graph is to walk through an example of how this type of graph is constructed. Let us begin by taking a series of price changes in a stock of 43.95, 44.10, 44.3, 44.15, 44.5, 44.7, 44.9, 44.85, 44.95, 45.00, 45.05, 44.4, and 43.9. Each square (now called a "box") on the graph paper will represent one point in the price. In point-and-figure charting, the plot is made only when the actual price of the box is touched or traded through. In this example, 43 would not be plotted because the price never reached 43 exactly or traded through to below 43. Forty-four would be plotted because the price ran from 43.95 to 44.10, trading through 44.00. Thus, our first plot for the point-and-figure chart would be placing an X in the 44 box when the price of 44.10 is observed, resulting in a chart that looks like Figure 11.12, Plot 1. For the next seven reported prices, no mark is made on the chart because all of these trades are between 44 and 45. When the tenth price, 45.00 is observed, a second X is plotted because the price actually touched 45. This X is plotted in the 45 box in the same column, resulting in a chart that looks like Figure 11.12, Plot 2. We now know that this first column is recording an uptrend in the stock price.

As long as the observed prices range above 44 and below 46, no more marks are made on the graph. For example, the next prices recorded in our sample data are 45.05 and 44.4. Because neither the next higher number (46) nor the next lower number (44) has been reached, no mark is made to represent this price observation. These trades are considered "noise" and the point-and-figure chart eliminates the plotting of this noise data.

It is not until the next price of 43.9 is observed that another mark is plotted. The price has now reversed downward through 44. Obviously, there is already an X at 44 in Column 1. Column 1 represented an uptrend in the price, and only price increases can be recorded in it. Therefore, we move to Column 2 and place an X at 44, as is shown in Figure 11.12, Plot 3. At this point, we don't know whether the trend in Column 2 is upward or downward. The second posting in this column will tell us. If the price should now rise to 45 again, we would place an X at 45, and Column 2 would record rising prices. If the price should decline to 43, we would place an X at 43, and Column 2 would record falling prices.

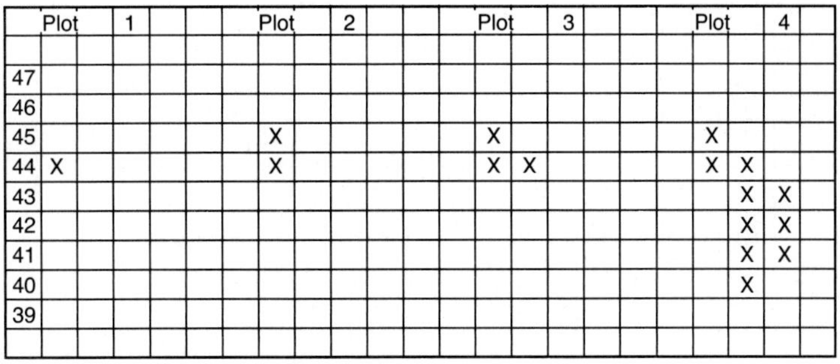

	Plot	1				Plot	2				Plot	3				Plot	4		
47																			
46																			
45						X					X					X			
44	X					X					X	X				X	X		
43																X	X		
42																X	X		
41																X	X		
40																X			
39																			

FIGURE 11.12 One-box reversal point-and-figure chart

Let us say that the price declines in a steady stream with no one-box reversals to 39.65, and then it rallies back in a steady stream to 43.15. This would be represented as in Figure 11.12, Plot 4. A plot is made only in a new box when the price is trending in one direction and is then moved over and plotted in the next column when that price reverses by a box size and cannot be plotted in the same column. Remember that a particular column can record only price increases or price declines; in our example, Columns 1 and 3 represent price increases and Column 2 plots price declines.

Box Size

From this basic method of plotting prices come many variations. Box size can be expanded, as in our example in Figure 11.13, where the box size is expanded to two points and labeled 48, 50, 52, and so on. Then a two-point change in direction would be required before prices moved to the next column. As shown in Figure 11.13, by increasing the size of the box, we reduce the amount of noise even further. Gradually, as the box size increases, the amount of price history becomes smaller and the chart becomes squeezed to the left, as fewer columns are necessary. The elimination of the noise makes the chart more useful to traders or investors interested in longer periods of time and activity. On the other hand, if a pattern appears to be developing in the longer-term chart, the box size can be reduced to give more detail near the potential longer-term change in direction. This more detailed view can give early signals based on what the longer-term pattern is forming.

Multibox Reversal

The other variable in a point-and-figure chart is the reversal amount. In our previous example, we used one point for both the box plot and the reversal amount. We could have expanded that reversal amount to three or five boxes, however. In other words, we could keep the one-point box scale but only record a reversal to the next column when the price reversed by three boxes. This also cuts down on the noise in price action and lengthens the time over which price action is recorded.

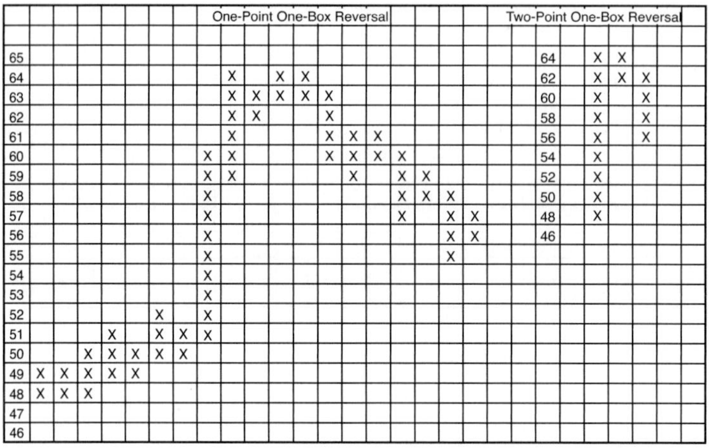

	One-Point One-Box Reversal																		Two-Point One-Box Reversal				
65																			64	X	X		
64							X		X	X									62	X	X	X	
63							X	X	X	X	X								60	X		X	
62							X	X			X								58	X		X	
61							X			X	X	X							56	X		X	
60					X	X				X	X	X	X						54	X			
59					X	X					X		X	X					52	X			
58					X						X	X	X						50	X			
57					X						X		X	X					48	X			
56					X							X	X						46				
55					X							X											
54					X																		
53					X																		
52			X		X																		
51		X		X	X	X																	
50		X	X	X	X	X																	
49	X	X	X	X	X																		
48	X	X	X																				
47																							
46																								

FIGURE 11.13 Box size and the point-and-figure chart

As an example, Figure 11.14 shows a one-point, three-box reversal chart of crude oil prices (perpetual futures contract from January 1, 2010, through June 30, 2010). The plot itself is a little different from the pure one-point, one-box reversal chart. Xs are used for the column in which prices are rising, and Os are used for the column in which prices are declining. This gives an easier-to-read picture of the price history.

The three-box reversal method gained popularity when Abe Cohen and Earl Blumenthal of *Chartcraft* publicized it in the 1950s. More recently, Tom Dorsey has popularized this method in his book *Point and Figure Charting,* and the majority of point-and-figure analysts now use the three-box reversal method. Because the three-box reversal method is less concerned about small, intraday changes in prices, it is especially useful when daily summary (H, L, C) price data is being used.

Time

In some point-and-figure charts, when a new price is first recorded for a new month, the first letter or the number of the month is plotted in place of the X or O. In other instances, the month is recorded at the bottom of the column in which a price is first recorded for that month. We can plot years, weeks, and days similarly, depending on how sensitive the chart may be to price changes. Both methods can be used concurrently. Often, when years and months are the principal periods recorded, the year will be plotted on the bottom of the column and the month number (1 for January, 2 for February, etc.) will be plotted instead of the X or O. Figure 11.15 shows the same three-box, one-point reversal chart as Figure 11.14, with the dates included. Time is of little importance in point-and-figure chart analysis. In many cases, it is plotted only to see how long it takes for a formation or pattern to form.

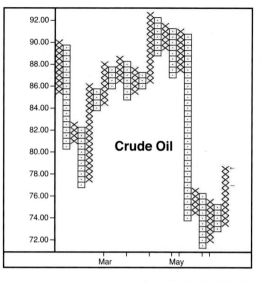

Created using TradeStation

FIGURE 11.14   One-point, three-box reversal, point-and-figure chart for crude oil (perpetual contract January 1, 2010–June 30, 2010)

65		
64	X	
63	3	O
62	X	O
61	X	O
60	X	4
59	X	O
58	X	O
57	X	O
56	X	O
55	X	O
54	X	
53	X	
52	2	
51	12	
50	11	
49	10	
48	9	
47		
46	2	2
	0	0
	0	0
	4	5

FIGURE 11.15   One-point, three-box reversal, point-and-figure chart with date notations included

Arithmetic Scale

Scale becomes a problem in plotting point-and-figure charts, especially when the price rises or falls a significant distance. Obviously, when a stock is trading at $70, a one-point move is less significant than if it was trading at $7. Blumenthal first introduced the solution to this problem in three-box reversal charts. He suggested that the chart scale be one point per box for prices between $20 and $100, one-half point per box for prices between $5 and $19.50, one-quarter point per box for stocks trading below $5, and two points per box for stocks trading above $100. This scale has since become standard in most three-box reversal charts. However, depending on the behavior of the stock price, the scale can be adjusted, and of course, it is useless in the futures markets where prices are considerably different.

Logarithmic Scale

As in bar charts, when long periods of trading activity are plotted, distortion arises from the fact that most charts are plotted on an arithmetic scale. Low-price action does not look as active as high-price action. Logarithmic scale changes the plot to include percentage change rather than absolute price change. Thus, the low-price action in percentage terms may appear more variable than the high-price action, and often is. To account for percentage change in point-and-figure charts, prices are converted into their logarithmic equivalent and plotted as a logarithmic number. This makes immediate interpretation difficult unless a table of logarithmic equivalents is immediately handy, because most analysts cannot convert the logarithmic number into the actual price in their heads.

This scale, however, should be used only for long periods of price data in which considerable volatility has made an arithmetic scale meaningless. For most investment and trading, the arithmetic scale is not only just as useful, but it is also easier to read and to convert to actual prices.

CONCLUSION

In this chapter, we have studied several different methods that technical analysts use to create charts. Line charts, which plot a single statistic, are the simplest of these methods. Bar charts and the more colorful Japanese candlestick charts provide more summary information, such as the opening price, the closing price, and the price range for a particular trading period. Point-and-figure charts provide a much different approach to graphing price data; with this method, sequential trading data is plotted with price trends and reversals emphasized.

All types of charts can include data of varying frequency: monthly, weekly, daily, and even intraday data. The frequency that an analyst will choose will depend upon the type of analysis and the period being explored. Analysts may choose to use an arithmetic scale, where the vertical distance on the graph always represents the same dollar amount, or an analyst may prefer a logarithmic scale so that the vertical distance in the chart always represents the same percentage change. We address these issues throughout the book as we look at various techniques of technical analysis. Remember that the chart is a tool of technical analysts, not an end in and of itself.

Therefore, there is not one correct charting technique but several that can meet a variety of analysts' needs.

REVIEW QUESTIONS

1. Melinda is analyzing Wal-Mart's stock over the past three months and notices that the price has ranged from $51 to $53 per share. Joshua is analyzing Merck's stock over the past five years and notices that the price has ranged from $20 to $65 a share over that period. Which analyst would be more likely to use an arithmetic scale, and which analyst would be more likely to use a logarithmic scale to analyze price information? Explain your reasoning.

2. Gather open, high, low, and closing prices for Valero Energy Corp (VLO) for the period from September 2007 to September 2010. Gather this data for daily, weekly, and monthly quotes. http://finance.yahoo.com provides this information; just put in the ticker symbol VLO and click the Historical Prices option. This data can be downloaded into a spreadsheet for easy manipulation. Be aware that the period specified starts with the newest figures first. If you want to read the data sequentially in time, the data must be sorted by date.

    a. Graph a line chart using an arithmetic scale for VLO using the daily closing prices.

    b. Graph a line chart using an arithmetic scale for VLO using the weekly closing prices.

    c. Graph a line chart using an arithmetic scale for VLO using the monthly closing prices.

    d. What type of information can you gather about VLO stock by looking at these three graphs?

    e. What differences do you notice in the three charts that you created?

3. Repeat parts a, b, and c in Question 2 using a logarithmic scale. What differences do you notice between the graphs you have created in this question and the graphs you created in Question 2?

4. Using the same data that you gathered for Question 2, create two candlestick charts for Valero using weekly data and monthly data. What type of information can you gather about VLO stock by looking at these two graphs?

5. Not having intraday, sequential trade data, instead, using the daily closing prices that you gathered for Question 2, create a one-point one-box reversal point-and-figure chart for VLO for September 2009–September 2010.

6. As in Question 5, using the daily closing prices that you gathered for Question 2, create a two-point one-box reversal point-and-figure chart for VLO for September 2009–September 2010.

7. As in Question 5, using the daily closing prices that you gathered for Question 2, create a one-point three-box reversal point-and-figure chart for VLO for September 2009–September 2010.

TRENDS—THE BASICS

CHAPTER OBJECTIVES

By the end of this chapter, you should

* Know why identifying trends is paramount to profits in securities
* Be able to recognize an uptrend, downtrend, and a trading range
* Understand the concept of support and resistance
* Be familiar with the major methods of determining trends
* Be familiar with the major signals that a trend is reversing

We are now entering into the more controversial aspects of technical analysis: the analysis of trends and in Part IV, "Chart Pattern Analysis," the analysis of patterns. This is the "fuzzy" aspect of technical analysis. Because the observations or rules are not specific, they discourage most students very quickly. Rules in technical analysis come from many, many observations by many traders and investors. In general, the rules have remained unchanged since Dow's time, and in reading some of the old masters back in the 1930s, one sees the same observations today. The advent of the computer has speeded the process and has often eliminated rules that are quantifiable but turn out to be unprofitable. However, the basics remain essentially the same. The markets have near, intermediate, and long-term trends. Patterns still form in much the same manner as 50 or 100 years ago, and analysts interpret them in the same manner as in the past. The details may be different, and perhaps the methods of profiting are dependent on various trade-offs between risk and reward, but still the analyst must use the rules and decide on the entry and exit points. The difficulty of profiting from technical analysis is not with the rules themselves but with their application.

In all the following chapters in this book, it is important to remember that the observations and statements we make derive from our observations and those of other practitioners of technical analysis. Most trends and patterns are not mechanical methods that can be easily programmed and tested on computers. Generally, they take long periods—sometimes years of practice—to be fully recognized. One of the major criticisms of technical analysis is that it has yet to be thoroughly computerized and tested. As we saw in Part II, "Markets and Market Indicators," many relationships have been tested in the past but then break down as the future unfolds. The only constants, it seems, are that trends occur and that they are the source of profit when recognized and properly utilized.

All analysts occasionally make statements that appear to be fact, but in many cases, they are statements based on subjective observations and should never be blindly relied upon without a thorough investigation. Our discussion of trend, support and resistance, and pattern nuances will show where they can be in error or where interpretation can be particularly difficult. Rules have developed over the years that will help with interpretation. Nevertheless, the student, when he can, should test and experiment. Nothing in technical analysis, or any other investment analysis approach, is foolproof. Indeed, it is surprising how much money is invested using fundamental and technical theories that have not been tested or have proven to be unprofitable. Most professionals, who have spent their lifetime in the study and practice of technical analysis, will assert, "There is no easy, magic formula for wealth!" Do not, therefore, expect the following observations and rules to be an easy means to profit. Study, have patience, and study some more. We suggest that the student trade on paper, and finally with small amounts of money. There is no need to rush. The markets are always there.

TREND—THE KEY TO PROFITS

Remember that profit with minimum capital risk in the securities markets is the sole objective, and technical analysis is an effective way to profit as well as to control risk. In earlier chapters, we emphasized the importance of determining and riding the directional trend in the security markets. The key to profiting in the securities market is to follow these three steps:

1. Determine, with minimum risk of error, when a trend has begun, at its earliest time and price.

2. Select and enter a position in the trend that is appropriate to the existing trend, regardless of direction (i.e., trade with the trend—long in upward trends and short or in cash in downward trends).

3. Close those positions when the trend is ending.

Trending is very simple in concept, but it is difficult in practice. Almost all successful mechanical trading systems that have made millions and millions for their investors have been based on the simple concept of jumping on a trend and riding it to its inevitable end. We discuss the principles behind some of these methods later in this chapter and in following chapters.

The principal caveat, however, in technical analysis, as mentioned previously, is that although the trend concept is easy to understand, its application is difficult largely because the determination of trend and trend reversal is, in many instances, a subjective decision that depends on one's skill and experience in the securities markets and one's ability to control one's own emotions. Practice and mental anguish are the background of any successful technical analyst. The most expensive education in the world is likely the money lost in incorrect, sloppy, and undisciplined decisions. All market participants make mistakes, but the regimented professionals correct theirs quickly.

When we arrive at Chapter 15, "Bar Chart Patterns," and discuss the various price patterns that have been observed, we will note that all patterns are a combination of trend lines—up, down, or sideways. It is, therefore, imperative first to understand trends and trend lines. In addition, all patterns are used to either confirm that a longer trend is still in control or warn that such a trend is changing. Patterns are, therefore, not trade signals explicitly in themselves, but they are the means of taking advantage of the underlying and, perhaps, changing trends.

TREND TERMINOLOGY

Trends define a direction in prices. When we refer to a trend, we describe a directional trend, one of rising or falling prices from which a profit can be generated with a trend-following method. We refer to a sideways trend as a **trading range** or **neutral** area. These are the recognized terms for describing different types of trends. Trend-following techniques work poorly in nontrending markets. Most technicians prefer to use price oscillators when dealing with such patterns.

In the next several chapters, we look at prices from the positive, advancing perspective. By that, we mean that when we discuss trends per se, we assume an upward trend (an uptrend). In most cases, the description and rules of a downtrend are exactly opposite from those of an uptrend. It does not make sense to duplicate every statement for both trend directions. Likewise, when we discuss support and resistance, we discuss support and make the assumption, unless otherwise noted, that resistance is the exact opposite but in an opposing direction. We do this for readability and because most investors prefer to look at rising prices anyway, even though there is no rational reason for doing so.

BASIS OF TREND ANALYSIS—DOW THEORY

As we learned in Chapter 6, "Dow Theory," Charles Dow was one of the first of the modern technicians to write about the fact that stock market prices trade in trends. Virtually all items that trade in free, liquid markets trade in trends. As noted by Dow, investors or traders must concentrate on the time horizon most favorable to their circumstances.

Trends are fractal, in that their behavior is the same regardless of the period. Minute-to-minute trends behave exactly like day-to-day trends with only minor differences because of the understandable variation in liquidity over the shorter periods. Dow suggested there were three principal time horizons—the primary, the intermediate, and the minor—that he likened to tides, waves, and ripples. In fact, there are considerably more trend periods. He focused on the first two because he apparently believed no one could analyze the ripples. Today, some technicians recognize considerably more trends than Dow observed, but then he did not have the advantage of a computer that could track prices trade by trade.

Dow's final, and perhaps most important, observation was that by their very nature, *trends tend to continue rather than reverse.* If it were otherwise, first, there would not be a trend, and second, the trend could not be used for profit. This seems like a silly and perhaps too obvious statement, but it underlies almost everything the technician assumes when looking for the beginning or end of trends. It also vexes the academic theoretician who believes that price changes are random.

Any particular trend is influenced by its next larger and next smaller trend. For example, in Figure 12.1, we can see a well-defined uptrend in the stock of JNJ (Johnson & Johnson). It is not a straight line upward, however. Within the rising trend are many smaller trends, both down and up, and if we look more closely, there are even smaller down- and uptrends within these. This is the fractal nature of trends. Notice also that the next set of trends below the long uptrend have larger rises and smaller declines. This is the effect the larger trend is having on the smaller trends. It is why the analyst, when studying any particular length trend, must be aware of the next longer and shorter trend directions. The longer trends will influence the strength of the trend of interest, and the shorter trends will often give early signs of turning in the longer. By definition, short-term trends reverse before medium-term, and medium-term trends reverse before long-term.

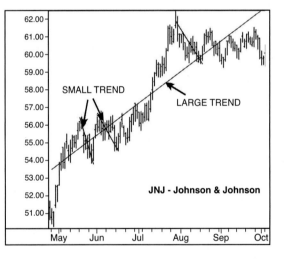

Created using TradeStation

FIGURE 12.1   Large and small trend (JNJ, daily: April 24, 2009–October 6, 2009)

HOW DOES INVESTOR PSYCHOLOGY IMPACT TRENDS?

As we know from basic economics, supply and demand establishes the price of any good. It is no different in the securities markets. Supply and demand, when sellers and buyers agree on a trade, determines prices. What does price, and especially price change, tell us? Presumably, if a substantial number of transactions occur at one price, the price is telling us that supply and demand are in a temporary equilibrium and that both buyers and sellers are satisfied. Of course, in the financial markets, long-term equilibrium is rarely reached. Prices constantly change, if only by miniscule amounts, as they move *toward* a theoretical equilibrium. They can oscillate in small increments or large; they can go up and/or down; or they can do both. Whatever the price movement, it is ultimately determined by the expectations and power of the buyers and sellers. If broad expectations are for a higher price in the future but with little or no capital to act, prices will remain as they are or even decline. Of course, expectations change, as does the power to act. Nothing is perfectly stable or constant in the markets.

When prices travel in a trend, called **trending,** they remain headed in one direction, and they tell us that there is an imbalance of demand and supply. Some will incorrectly say that there are more buyers than sellers or vice versa. However, in every transaction, there are an equal number of shares transacted, and, thus, there is always temporary equilibrium between buyers and sellers at that instant in time. What makes a trend is the power of the buyers or sellers—do they have enough stock or money?—and the aggressiveness or anxiousness of buyers and sellers—do they have specific information or deductions, rational or irrational, or are emotions of fear or greed propelling their action?

We know from behavioral studies that, psychologically, a positive feedback mechanism in our minds tends collectively to maintain that trend. In an uptrend, for example, buyers who have profited tend to continue being buyers, and new buyers, seeing what they have missed, also buy. The price trend continues upward. Eventually, over a longer period, prices revert to some kind of mean or value, but meanwhile, they trend, up, down, or sideways. If, for example, prices are gradually rising, then buyers must have stronger positive expectations and be willing and able to place more money in the security. Contrarily, if prices are declining, sellers must have stronger negative expectations and larger positions to sell. The price trend, thus, tells us the amount of power, aggressiveness, and anxiousness there is in the marketplace to buy or sell each security. To the technical analyst, the basis for the expectations—and there are many—as well as the source of power, money, or stock, is largely irrelevant. The anticipating and "riding" a trend in prices, as long as it continues, is how the technician profits.

HOW IS THE TREND DETERMINED?

Of course, the trend is never a straight line. Then it would be too easy to tell that it had reversed. Instead, the *trend is a direction rather than a line.* Many doubting participants often accompany this direction. Sometimes, it can be arbitrageurs, who bet against the trend or who are merely trading the spread. More likely, it is investors or traders running out of money or stock or just holding back for a little while, hoping that the price will retrace back toward their orders. In other words, the security price oscillates back and forth in smaller trends along its travel in the larger trend. This makes determining when that larger trend is reversing a difficult decision because any signs of reversal may only be for smaller trends within the larger trend. Additionally, securities occasionally "rest" during a trend and move sideways as the earlier rise or fall is "digested" by all the different players. The psychology of what causes these spurts, stops, and retracements is an interesting study by itself, but again it is irrelevant for our present discussion. We simply want to know what our trend of interest is, and are there signs of it ending or changing direction?

Peaks and Troughs

What is the simplest way to look at prices and determine the trend? The easiest is to look for peaks and troughs within a series of price oscillations. If the peaks tend to be higher than the earlier peaks, and the troughs tend to be higher than the previous troughs, the trend must be upward. As you see in Figure 12.2, it is that simple. If peaks and troughs are lower than previously, the trend must be downward. If the peaks and troughs are scattered, the trend is undeterminable, and if the peaks and troughs occur at the same relative levels, the trend must be a trading range.

Created using TradeStation

FIGURE 12.2   Peaks and troughs used to determine trend (JNJ weekly: November 7, 2008–July 2, 2010)

It is much easier to look at price trends on a chart. As the previous chapter demonstrated, a table of data makes recognition of price order of any sort very difficult. Most technicians use either bar or candlestick charts to draw lines representing trends (see Figures 12.3 and 12.4). There are many ways to do this that are discussed later in the chapter. For now, let us begin with discussing sideways trends because they display very clearly an important technical concept called **support** and **resistance.**

Created using TradeStation

FIGURE 12.3 Trend line drawn through troughs (JNJ weekly: November 7, 2008–July 2, 2010)

Created using TradeStation

FIGURE 12.4 Trend lines in candlestick chart (JNJ weekly: November 7, 2008–July 2, 2010)

DETERMINING A TRADING RANGE

Trading ranges (or sideways trends) occur when peaks and troughs appear roughly at similar levels. The peaks cluster at a certain price level, and the troughs cluster at a certain price level below the peaks. The configuration usually occurs after a larger trend has come to a temporary halt. A trading range also is called a **consolidation** or **congestion area** or a **rectangle formation.** Charles Dow called very small lateral patterns a **line formation** and using it in the Dow Jones Averages had very specific rules by which the averages had to abide for that designation. William Hamilton, Dow's successor editor at the *Wall Street Journal,* thought the line formation was the only price formation with any predictive power.

What Is Support and Resistance?

When prices have been rising and then reverse downward, the highest point in the rise, the peak, is referred to as a **resistance point,** a level at which the advance has met with selling "resistance." It is the level at which sellers are as powerful and aggressive as the buyers and halt the advance. When the sellers (supply) become more powerful and aggressive than the buyers (demand), the result is a subsequent price decline from the peak. A resistance level becomes a **resistance zone** when more than one resistance level occurs at roughly the same price. Prices rarely rise and stop at exactly the same level. A single, high-volume, price peak often defines a resistance point, but even then, because the high volume, especially if it is preceded by a sharp price rise, is a sign of speculation and emotion, and the price where large sellers actually begin to enter the market is unclear.

A **support point** is the opposite of a resistance point in that it is a single trough. At the support point, buyers become as powerful or aggressive as the sellers and halt a price decline.

The concept of support and resistance presumes that in the future prices will stop at these recorded levels or zones and that they represent a remembered psychological barrier for prices. The zones will carry through time and become barriers to future price action. Not only will the zones carry through time, but also, once they are broken through, they will switch functions: Previous support will become resistance, and previous resistance will become support.

Why Do Support and Resistance Occur?

Have you ever bought a stock, watched it decline in price, and yearned to sell out for what you paid for it? Have you ever sold a stock, watched it go up after you had sold it, and wished you had the opportunity to buy it again? Well, you are not alone. These are common human reactions, and they show up on the stock charts by creating **support** and **resistance.** (Jiler, 1962)

Let us look at the presumed psychology behind a support level and see why it might carry into the future.

There is little question that a price trough is a point where buyers overwhelmed sellers. In Figure 12.5, JNJ peaked at $56.50 on May 20 (a), a potential resistance level, and then declined touching $53.86 on May 28 (b), at which point it reversed upward. This support-point price becomes a support level. It is almost exactly the same level as support point (z), which bottomed at $53.90. Subsequently, the stock price rallied back to $56.50 on June 6 (c), the exact same level as the earlier May 20 (a) resistance point. We now have two, well-defined resistance points and two support points: $56.50 and $53.90.

We can assume there are the potential buyers at $53.90 because:

1. In the next sell-off, those who sold short at $56.50 will be covering because they have seen that the price halted its earlier decline at $53.90 (b and z) and do not want to take the risk that it will rally again to $56.50 and wipe out their profits.

2. Those who had been watching the stock but did not buy it at $53.90 earlier and will be satisfied that the decline to $53.90 is back to where they earlier had wanted to purchase it but "missed it."

3. Those who sold the stock at the low of $53.90, when it declined from $56.50, saw the price immediately rise thereafter, and wish to reenter a position at the price they sold it earlier.

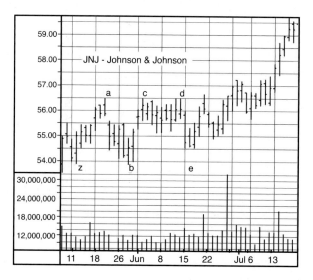

Created using TradeStation

FIGURE 12.5 Support and resistance zones (JNJ daily: May 7, 2009–July 17, 2009)

Notice that none of these players is using a fundamental or other informational reasons for buying the stock at $53.90. The reasons are purely psychological, but they are strong reasons by themselves. The presumption for technical analysts is that $53.90 has now become a support zone and that prices will stop declining at that level in the future. The presumption is that the more frequently prices halt at a zone, the stronger and more important that zone will likely be in the future.

A resistance zone will likely now also exist at $56.50 for similar reasons because sellers at that price wish to sell: sellers who missed $56.50 before, sellers who bought at $56.50 and want their money back, and sellers who want to short the stock at $56.50 where it halted earlier. Support and resistance zones, therefore, are price levels where supply and demand reach equilibrium for unusual but persistent psychological reasons.

What About Round Numbers?

Ironically, when prices reach round numbers, the tendency to buy and sell increases. As an example, Figure 12.5 of JNJ shows a strong support and resistance level at $53.9 (almost $54.00). People think in terms of round numbers. Otherwise, why would Wal-Mart sell a shirt for $29.95 rather than $30? They know people subconsciously will associate with the "29" and will believe they are getting a $29 shirt rather than a $30 one. People think in terms of round numbers and act accordingly in the securities markets as well. The current problem with the concept of round numbers is that knowledge of that tendency is widespread. From the standpoint of entering orders then, it is best to determine entry and exit points based on the technical situation rather than worry about round numbers.

How Are Important Reversal Points Determined?

The more important the reversal point, the more important the support or resistance level. There are a number of ways to identify a significant reversal point. Let us look at some of them.[1]

DeMark or Williams Method

Tom DeMark and Larry Williams each have a method of determining a reversal point by using the number of bars (in a bar chart) on either side of a suspected reversal point. In a low bar, for example, the analyst may look for two bars with higher lows directly on either side of the suspected trough bar. The number of bars on either side can be increased to increase the importance of the trough, but the number of troughs will be sacrificed. The higher the number of confirming lows necessary, the more important the trough.

As an example, look at Figure 12.6. Each of the two-bar lows and highs are marked with an arrow. Point (a) is not a trough because it does not have at least two bars on either side of it with higher lows. Likewise, Point (b) is not a peak. It does not have two bars on either side of it with lower highs. Is Point (c) a peak? We do not know because we can't see if there are two bars to the left of the high to judge Point (c).

---

1. In this section, we focus primarily on how to determine significant troughs and support levels. Of course, significant peaks and resistance levels would be determined in the same fashion, only in the opposite direction.

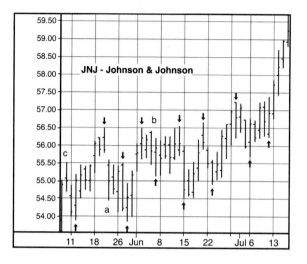

Created using TradeStation

FIGURE 12.6 DeMark-Williams reversal points (JNJ daily: May 7, 2009–July 16, 2009)

Percentage Method

Another method of identifying significant troughs is by deciding beforehand how much the price should decline and rally into the trough. A percentage is usually used. Using 1%, for example, any time the price declines more than 1%, makes a low, and then rallies more than 1% will define a significant trough. The larger the percentage used, the more important but less frequent the reversal point.

Gann Two-Day Swing Method

W. D. Gann's swing method is very similar to the DeMark or Williams method. To find a support point, or trough, a low bar is identified. Once the low bar is identified, the two following trading days are observed. If these two days have higher highs than the low bar, then the low bar is a support point. Originally, Gann used the three following trading days to determine a support point, but more recently, it has been switched to two days (Krausz, 1998). Likewise, a resistance point is defined as any high bar during an uptrend that is followed by two successive bars with lower lows. Figure 12.7 is identical to Figure 12.6, except that the reversal points are determined using the Gann rule. The difference between the two charts is that at Point (a), (b), and (c), the reversal points as defined by the Gann rule do not occur at the DeMark/Williams reversal points. The reasons are that the days of the actual reversal points were not followed by the required two successive days. Thus, by Gann's rule, the reversal may not occur on the actual high or low bar.

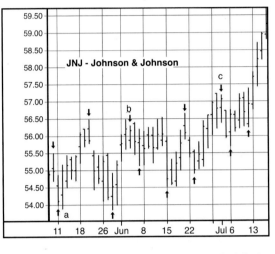

Created using TradeStation

FIGURE 12.7   Gann two-bar swing points (JNJ daily: May 7, 2009–July 16, 2009)

High Volume Method

Very large volume can also identify a significant reversal point. High volume indicates that larger than usual activity occurred on that trading day. Figure 12.8 shows a one-day reversal on high volume at a high, creating a significant reversal point and resistance level that stopped the subsequent rally.

Figure 12.8 illustrates a one-day and a two-day reversal. A two-day reversal looks the same as a one-day reversal except that it takes place over two days. These one- or two-day patterns can occur at peaks or troughs. When these occur on high volume, they usually signify important reversal points. Because these formations usually occur at a stage of high emotion, they signify either a panic or a speculative bubble. As such, the actual price level at which the reversal took place is not identifiable on a large bar chart. Sometimes intraday action must be inspected to see at just what price level the majority of buying and selling occurred.

How Are Support and Resistance Zones Drawn?

To construct a support (or resistance) zone, simply draw a horizontal line through each significant trough (or peak) into the future. These lines can be drawn through the respective bar lows or, as Jiler (1962) suggests, using the bar's close because this is what most investors read in the paper. These lines should also be extended into the past to see if earlier price declines stopped at the same price level. Where these horizontal lines bunch together, sometimes overlapping at the same price level is a support or resistance zone. This zone is usually stronger the more horizontal lines there are within it. In other words, the more times the price level has halted previous advances or supported previous declines, the stronger will be the resistance or support in the future. Because all previous significant troughs have not likely occurred at exactly the same price level, an area called a **zone** is constructed between the highest and lowest horizontal line. This defines the actual support or resistance area clearly.

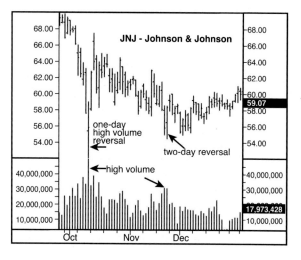

Created using TradeStation

FIGURE 12.8 One- and two-bar reversals (JNJ daily: September 25, 2008–January 5, 2009)

Figure 12.9 shows how support and resistance lines are drawn. Notice that the line just under $44 was first a support line, holding the decline from $46 for almost a week, and then became a resistance line when the price later rallied from below several times and halted at that level. Notice also that the rally above $44 in late September matched the rally to the same level in early September. These two resistance lines create a resistance zone. Notice also the support line between $38 and $40. This was touched three times before prices broke below it in early November.

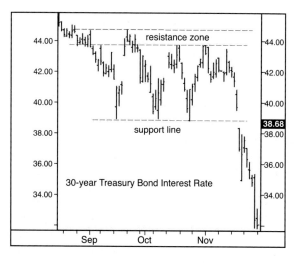

Created using TradeStation

FIGURE 12.9 Support and resistance lines (TYX daily: August 14, 2008–December 3, 2008)

If a horizontal line is by itself with no other horizontal lines close to it, it is likely an independent support or resistance level. Such levels, unless accompanied by extraordinary volume, usually do not have the same strength in the future that a combination of horizontal lines might have within a zone.

In the future, prices will tend to halt at these zones, and occasionally at a single level. Prices will often enter the zone but will not break out of the outer horizontal line of the zone. If they do break that level, we have what is called a "breakout" that has important consequences. A price break below the support zone implies that buyers are satiated at that level. See the downward breakout in Figure 12.9 in November at the support line. In this instance, the break left a vacuum of buyers, and the sellers, at least at that price, now control the stock. If there is another support zone at some distance below the current broken zone, prices will generally trade down to that next lower zone. Thus, a support zone in a declining market can become a price objective once a higher support zone is broken. Support zones exist at all horizons—day, week, or even minute-to-minute. Some traders only trade stocks or futures, especially e-mini futures, between these zones often on an intraday basis between very, very short-term support and resistance zones.

What we have said about resistance zones is equally applicable to support zones. Horizontal lines at significant troughs will show the existence of these zones, and extended into the future, they will become zones of support to price decline. In addition, as time goes on, the importance of past horizontal lines diminishes for both support and resistance zones. More recent price reversals are more important. Human memory fades quickly.

How Do Analysts Use Trading Ranges?

Getting back to our earlier introduction of sideways trends, a trading range, as shown in Figure 12.9, is a price level where both support and resistance zones are relatively close together, and prices "bounce" between them until finally breaking out in one or the other direction. Some traders will trade the "bounces" between support and resistance, but this is usually very dangerous and requires very low operating costs and constant attention (Schwager, 1996). The most profitable and reliable way to use the trading range is to practice "breakout" trading. Let us look at each of these strategies a little more closely.

Range Trading

Trading within a range is difficult. Although many books suggest it as a strategy, it is almost impossible for the nonprofessional to profit through range trading. First, it is difficult to recognize that prices are trading in a range until after a considerable amount of trading and time has passed. It is, therefore, largely in retrospect that the opportunities are recognized. In addition, operating costs, such as commissions and slippage, must be small and execution efficient, else any potential profit will be overwhelmed by transactions costs. Because the bounds of a trading range are often zones rather than specific price levels, the point at which an execution order, either buy or sell, should be placed is indefinite. Finally, the location for a protective stop-loss order to prevent a breakout from ruining trading profits is difficult to determine. By the time all these costs and execution levels are recognized, the potential for profit has diminished considerably, making any profit versus risk unlikely. Thus, most traders stay away from trading within a trading range and instead wait for the inevitable breakout and beginning of a trend.

The one exception to range trading is channel trading. A **channel** is a trading range tipped at an angle such that it trends upward or downward. Trend lines define the bounds of the channel just as support and resistance lines define the trading range. One can trade these channels back and forth but only in the direction of the channel trend. In other words, for example, if the channel is trending upward, only long positions are taken at the lower bounds and sold at the upper bounds, but no short position is taken contrary to the channel trend. As mentioned earlier, upward trends have longer upward subtrends and shorter downward subtrends. To a certain extent, depending on the slope of the channel trend, the subtrends in the direction of the trend reduce the difficulty seen in trading ranges.

Breakout Trading

Breakout trading is as old as technical analysis and likely the most successful. Remember that a trading range is somewhat like a battleground, where the buyers and sellers are warring for dominance. Most chart patterns are combinations of trend lines and, thus, are battlegrounds also. Before the war is over, it is almost impossible to determine who will win. It is usually wiser, and more profitable, to wait rather than to guess. Once, however, prices break out of the trading range, the investor has information about who has won the war. If the breakout is to the upside, buyers are driving price up; if the breakout occurs to the downside, sellers are overwhelming buyers. Trading on this breakout is probably the most profitable and reliable strategy for the investor faced with a trading range or pattern.

Breakout trading can be used in many different ways other than for just trading ranges. One of the most famous is the Donchian breakout method, also called the "four-week breakout system," originated by Richard Donchian and later improved upon by Richard Dennis. It still appears to work. A recent study by *Active Trader Magazine* (Kurczek and Knapp, 2003) indicates that even though the method is popular and has been widely known for many years, it still produces profits, especially in the commodities futures markets. Its calculation is absurdly simple. Buy when the highest high over the past four weeks is broken, and sell when the lowest low over the past four weeks is broken. A "stop-and-reverse" strategy requires a position, long or short, at all times.

A breakout is a powerful signal. It indicates that the balance between demand and supply has been settled, usually violently, and, thus, is an indication of the initiation or continuation of a directional trend. The subject of breakouts and stops is covered in the next chapter.

DIRECTIONAL TRENDS (UP AND DOWN)

We have just considered trading ranges in which successive peaks and troughs occur at roughly the same price level. This results in a flat or sideways trend in prices. Whenever reversal points are occurring at higher (lower levels) than the previous reversal points then price is trending upward (downward).

What Is a Directional Trend?

When a peak and trough occur at higher price levels than the immediately previous peak and trough, the trend has turned upward. Conversely, for a peak and trough lower than their previous peak and trough, the trend has turned down. The angle of the trend, therefore, is determined by the amount by which the peaks and troughs are higher or lower than their previous levels. To see this more clearly, a chart is almost a necessity. Figure 12.2 at the beginning of this chapter shows an upward trend in JNJ weekly from 2008 through 2010. The principles of trends are applicable regardless of direction.

Quite obviously, the steeper the angle of the trend, the more powerful is the buyer or seller group. It means that the one group is overwhelming the other group at a faster pace. In a decline, sellers are willing to receive lower and lower prices before becoming temporarily exhausted at a trough. In an advance, buyers are more and more anxious and willing to pay higher prices. This is the time when an investor who is long the security is happiest. It is a trend and is what the technician is looking for in indicators and charts. The corollary, however, is that the steeper the angle of ascent or descent, the less sustainable it becomes.

An uptrend, therefore, is a display of the eagerness of the buyers versus the eagerness of the sellers. It is similar to the concept of support and resistance except that the support and resistance are changing in a specific direction. Because all the stock desired by the buyers and sold by the sellers is not transacted at one time and at one price level but over a time as news leaks out and positive feedback affects other players, the price trend continues until it has reached a point of exhaustion. At that level, the price trend either flattens out in a congestion or consolidation area or reverses direction into a declining trend. Some analysts argue that an actual trend only lasts a short time, approximately 20% of the trading period, and during the remaining time prices remain in a consolidation or pattern formation with an indefinite trend. No one has demonstrated the validity of this percentage, however. It was estimated only by counting the time that an ADX indicator (a measure of trending tendency—see Chapter 14, "Moving Averages") shows that a trend exists in varying markets, periods, and circumstances.

It is undeniable, however, that the majority of profits come from correctly anticipating and acting upon a trend, and for this reason, almost all technical study is devoted toward early anticipation of a trend.

How Is an Uptrend Spotted?

In retrospect, a trend is easy to spot, especially on a price chart. Without being specific, it is usually easy to see reversal points and the general direction of historical prices. The difficulty, from an analysis standpoint, comes in being specific enough to determine when the signs of a trend change are occurring. To do this, the technical analyst uses several tools: (1) the regression line, (2) the trend line, and (3) moving averages. In this chapter, we discuss the regression line but focus the majority of our attention on the trend line. We focus on the use of moving averages in Chapter 14.

Using a Regression Line

Mathematic formulas can fit two sets of data, such as price and time, to a straight line. This method is called **linear regression,** and the line derived from this formula is called a **regression line.** This line has two variables—its starting point and its slope. Where the data begins and ends determines both variables. The technical analyst is interested in the regression line's location on the chart and to some degree its slope. In the example in Figure 12.10, the regression line from the bottom price to the top price travels through a majority of the data. Indeed, the mathematical equation used to determine the line minimizes the distance between all the data points and the theoretical line. The line is said to be the "best fit" to the data.

We can also calculate standard deviations about this best fit line that will encompass most of the data. Outliers, those prices that occur outside of the standard deviation lines, are considered as either anomalies or, to the technical analyst, if they occur in the most recent data, signs that the trend may be changing. In Figure 12.10, the right-hand, most recent, price plots are outside the standard deviation of the line. These, having occurred recently, are a clue that the regression line slope may be flattening.

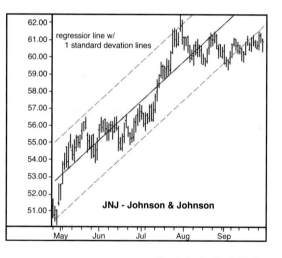

Created using TradeStation

FIGURE 12.10 Regression line and one standard deviation (JNJ daily: April 29, 2009–September 15, 2009)

Using Trend Lines

The oldest and easiest method of determining the trend of prices is with a trend line. Trend lines are drawn with just a ruler and the use of one's eyes rather than a fancy mathematical formula. All that is needed is two support reversal points or two resistance reversal points. A line is drawn between the reversal points, as shown in Figure 12.11.

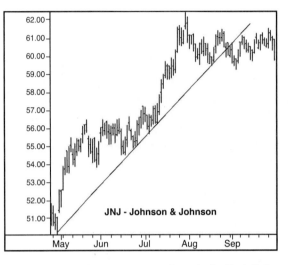

FIGURE 12.11   Trend line (JNJ daily: April 29, 2009–September 15, 2009)

The important lesson to learn is that the lines are generally drawn between lows (support) when the price is rising and between tops (resistance) when the price is declining. The lines that connect the lows or highs extend into the future so that the analyst can tell when the trend line is broken. Remember, the purpose of the trend line is to provide a signal of a change in trend. For example, in Figure 12.11, price movement appeared to be in the upward direction. Therefore, a trend line was drawn that connected the major troughs in May, June, July, and August and continued to the right. In late August, when prices broke below the trend line, analysts had a clue that the trend was changing.

Scale and Trend Lines

The problem of scale sometimes arises in the plotting of trend lines as it does with prices. Generally, on an arithmetic scaled chart in which the prices are displayed within a 20%–40% range, a trend line can be drawn with accuracy. When price changes have occurred over a wider range, the logarithmic scaled chart is necessary. In this case, the trend line represents a percentage change in prices rather than a point change. Over long periods, this is the preferred method because it represents better how investors look at a stock price. Generally, over long periods, investors think in terms of percentages, whereas over shorter periods, they may think more in terms of points.

Accelerating Trend Lines

Another problem with trend lines is that they might not be straight lines. Often prices, especially in a speculative bubble or in a panic, will accelerate upward or downward and run away from a standard, straight trend line. In this case, the trend line must be adjusted continually to account for the price action's acceleration. This phenomenon is shown graphically in Figure 12.12.

An accelerating trend line, of course, is unsustainable because eventually it would reach an infinite slope. If the acceleration can be calculated through mathematical means, the expected time for the infinite slope will be the time by which the price must reach its zenith. It is a means of determining when the latest time for the eventual reversal will occur. As we will see in the chapters on patterns, an accelerating price trend has very profitable, as well as dangerous, implications.

Decelerating Trend Lines

The opposite of an accelerating trend line is the decelerating trend line. This is called a **fan line.** In the chart, the fan lines are shown as regular trend lines that are being broken without an obvious reversal in direction and then being redrawn to account for each new support level. Figure 12.13 shows the fanning effect that decelerating trend lines give.

These lines can go on forever in theory, but practitioners have generally stated that the maximum to be expected is three fan lines before a reversal in direction is to be expected. These three fan lines often are accompanied by some kind of standard pattern. Of course, if an earlier support zone is broken as well as a trend, it is a stronger implication that the trend has reversed direction.

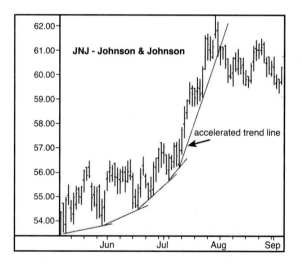

Created using TradeStation

FIGURE 12.12 Accelerating trend line (JNJ daily: May 5, 2009–September 4, 2009)

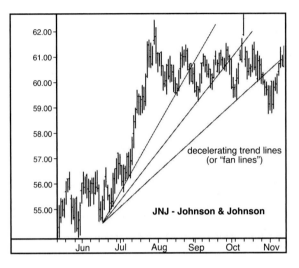

Created using TradeStation

FIGURE 12.13   Decelerating trend or fan lines (JNJ daily: May 11, 2009–November 12, 2009)

General Rules for Trend Lines

Several standard rules have been developed about trend lines. *One is that the longer and the more times that the drawn line is touched by prices, the more significant it is when the line is finally broken.* Another is that the steeper the trend line, the sooner it will be broken. This is obvious in an accelerating trend line but is equally true in a steep, straight trend line.

Sometimes a trend line is broken slightly by intraday price action, as shown in Figure 12.14. This action provides a problem for the analyst who must determine whether the break is permanent and indicative of a trend change, or whether it is an anomaly. Should it be ignored, or should the trend line be adjusted slightly to accommodate the new level? The question here is whether the break of the trend line is significant or just minor. Trend lines should never be considered exact, largely because price action within a bar may be influenced for a very short time by exogenous factors that have nothing to do with the trend. Some analysts, for example, draw trend lines between peak and trough closing prices rather than intraday highs and lows. They argue that because intraday traders usually must close their positions by day's end and are out of the market by then, the closing price represents longer-term players' determination of supply and demand and is, thus, a truer figure for drawing longer trend lines. By using the closing prices, the number of false breakouts is usually reduced. We discuss these issues regarding the rules for breakouts more thoroughly in the next chapter.

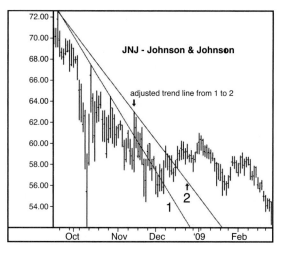

Created using TradeStation

FIGURE 12.14   Adjustment in trend line (daily: September 17, 2008–February 26, 2009)

Channels

Remember that uptrend lines should be plotted between support troughs, and downtrend lines should be plotted between resistance peaks. In other words, when prices are trending upward, the trend line will lie below the price action, and when prices are trending downward, the trend line will appear above the price action.

Sometimes, as in Figure 12.15, prices appear to travel in a "channel." A line is plotted through resistance reversal points and is parallel to the underlying uptrend line. This forms a channel. These channels often contain price motion just as the congestion area or rectangle formation contains prices when the trend is sideways. Remember that a trend is a direction of supply and demand. In an uptrend, the lower line represents the increasing demand for the security, and often the supply of the security is traveling parallel but above the demand. Thus, prices tend to "bounce" off this rising upper channel line as if supply were present at these moving intervals and rising at the same rate as demand. Indeed, when we see that a resistance reversal point is no longer parallel on the channel line (see Figure 12.15), but beginning to close on the underlying trend line, we know that supply is getting just a little more anxious and that the price is likely approaching a reversal point. Final proof that the channel has ended is when the price breaks the trend line. The same channel rules apply in downtrends.

A channel line can be drawn almost immediately after two troughs and their intervening peaks are recognized. A line is drawn parallel to the trend line through the intervening peak and projected into the future. This line now becomes a target line for subsequent rallies within the channel. In Figure 12.16, for example, the channel line (dashed line) could have been drawn as soon as the second trough in July had been recognized, by drawing a parallel line through the May peak. Projected into the future, that channel line was a level at which subsequent rallies would be expected to reach, just as the next one did at the peak in July.

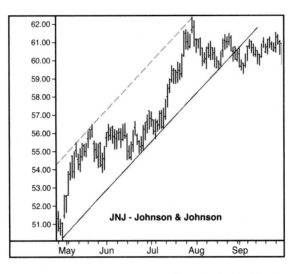

Created using TradeStation

FIGURE 12.15   Trend line with channel line (JNJ daily: April 29, 2009–September 15, 2009)

Another potential signal with channel lines is when, in an uptrend, for example, the price breaks above the channel line rather than being contained by it. This is a sign that the underlying trend is accelerating and that its end is coming closer. Such occurrences also occur during a downtrend and signal that a major price bottom is not far ahead. Any kind of acceleration is a sign of pure emotionalism and, thus, a potential sign of an impending reversal. Practically speaking, however, the investor or trader should never attempt to anticipate the reversal. A change in direction may occur soon, but because the price is changing so rapidly, an attempt to anticipate the actual price reversal can be disastrous. It is much wiser to watch for the actual reversal and then act with the comfort of trading with the new trend, rather than against the old one.

Internal Trend Lines

There is also what is called an **internal trend line.** This line is more difficult to recognize and has only limited value. Generally, it is a line drawn through trending price action such that a large number of minor reversals touch the line both from above and below. An example of an internal trend line is shown in Figure 12.16. In some ways, it appears similar to a regression line that travels through the majority of prices, and in some ways, it appears like a midpoint line between the two boundaries of a channel. In any case, though it is interesting and occurs often, its use for trading or investing is limited. The observation that prices often bounce off an internal trend line may be somewhat useful for very short-term trading, but moving averages provide a better means of measuring the midpoint in prices as they travel through time.

Retracements

The final subject relating to trends is retracements. As mentioned and observed previously, a trend rarely follows a line without including a number of smaller trends. The smaller countertrends are called **retracements,** and several rules have been developed concerning them.

Retracements are always corrections to the principal trend. As prices rise, for example, in a strong uptrend, the rise is interrupted periodically by downward corrections. In an uptrend, the beginning of these corrections is always a resistance point, and the bottom of the retracement is always a support point. The lower support point is where a new trend line can be plotted from a previous support point. Thus, a retracement is a smaller trend itself and runs counter to the principal trend.

For example, consider the price movement pictured in Figure 12.17. Obviously, the principal trend for JNJ (Johnson & Johnson) is upward. From late May to early June, the prices follow this trend, moving upward. However, for most of June, the prices are trending downward in a countertrend, retracing a portion of the price gain.

Created using TradeStation

FIGURE 12.16 Internal trend line (JNJ daily: September 21, 2009–May 5, 2010)

A retracement can be analyzed in the same way as the longer trend. It is, in fact, a trend in itself but with a direction opposite from the principal trend and with a shorter period and length. Within a trend, many retracements of different amounts and periods can occur. Because the end of a retracement usually is the support or resistance point for the longer trend, the length and time of a retracement can tell us something about the longer trend. For example, in a sharply rising uptrend, you would expect the retracements to be short and not "retrace" a large percentage of the earlier rise. Indeed, the general rule is that a strong uptrend requires retracements of less than 50% of the previous uptrend. The same is true for downtrends. Should the retracement in an uptrend decline more than 50%, the trend line in the longer uptrend would likely be in jeopardy. Figure 12.17 shows a 50% in the initial upward leg of a longer uptrend in the TYX (30-year U.S. Treasury Bond interest rate). Thus, the amount of retracement is an indication of the larger trend's strength.

Created using TradeStation

FIGURE 12.17   Retracement (TYX daily: August 6, 2009–January 14, 2010)

A retracement, in a healthy trend, can also present an opportunity for the trend follower who missed the earlier stages of the trend to jump on the longer trend. A retracement, as long as it holds above the longer trend line and does not retrace more than 50%, is usually an opportunity for the trend follower to act in the direction of the larger trend.

Unfortunately, retracements rarely reach an exact percentage. Some analysts believe that percentage retracements provide a good entry point. Many articles and books have hypothesized that in an uptrend or downtrend, prices will tend to retrace a certain percentage. The most common mentioned are 33 1/3%, 50%, 66 2/3%, and the Fibonacci percentages of 38.2% and 61.8%. The late Art Merrill, a well-respected technical analyst, in a paper published in the *Journal of Technical Analysis* (August 1989), found that the amount by which prices retrace in the Dow Jones Industrial Average during an advance or decline did not concentrate about any of these percentages.

Anticipating retracement levels, therefore, can be somewhat hazardous, and the trade-off between the amount of retracement desired and what may actually occur is usually unanticipated. Thus, a rough estimate from previous retracements, support and resistance zones, and the location of the longer trend line is probably the best information for an estimate rather than the mechanical percentage numbers derived from various formulas.

Pullbacks and Throwbacks

Variations of retracements that occur after a breakout, usually from a horizontal support or resistance zone but sometimes from a trend line, are called **pullbacks** or **throwbacks** depending on whether the breakout was downward or upward. When the price retraces quickly back to the breakout zone from an upward breakout, it is called a throwback, and conversely, the quick retracement from a break downward is called a pullback (Edwards and Magee, 2007). Figure 12.18 shows a pullback in the U.S. Treasury Bond interest rate. These retracement variations will become more important when we discuss chart patterns, but they often are found in any breakout, especially in one from a rectangle formation or congestion area. These retracements may not abide by normal retracement percentages if they are blocked by the support or resistance level from which they broke. They tend to be very short in time and distance but often provide a second, lesser-risk opportunity for a breakout trader to enter a position.

Created using TradeStation

FIGURE 12.18   Pullback (TYX daily: November 18, 2009–July 1, 2010)

OTHER TYPES OF TREND LINES

The concept of trend is central to the field of technical analysis. Therefore, analysts have developed a number of applications and variations of trend lines. Trend lines are not just useful with bar charts; analysts using point-and-figure charts make use of trend lines. Speed lines, Andrews Pitchfork, and Gann fan lines are all example of types of trend lines technical analysts use.

Trend Lines on Point-and-Figure Charts

A trend line may be drawn between successive lows or highs in the standard, old-style, point-and-figure charts, just as they are drawn in a bar or candlestick chart. There is one variation, however, that occurs in the three-box reversal method. For this type of chart, trend lines are drawn at 45-degree angles (see Figure 12.19). Upward trend lines, called **bullish support lines,** are drawn at a 45-degree angle from the lowest low, and downward trend lines, called **bearish resistance lines,** are drawn from the last peak. These lines are not really trend lines in the sense that we have covered earlier, but price penetration through them has very specific meaning. We cover these in · more detail in Chapter 16, "Point-and-Figure Chart Patterns."

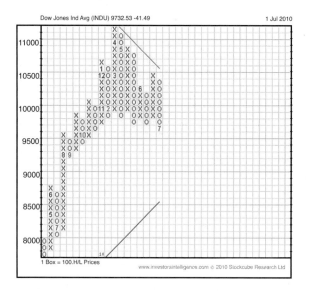

FIGURE 12.19   Bullish support and bearish resistance lines on a point-and-figure chart (DJIA through July 1, 2010)

Speed Lines

The late Edson Gould, an early proponent of technical analysis who did extensive market research, developed a means of estimating future support and resistance by what he called **speed lines.** Speed lines are calculated in the instance of an uptrend by taking the low point of the advance and the high point and creating a box whereby the low point is the lower-left corner and the high point is the upper-right corner. Alternatively, as shown in Figure 12.20, during a downtrend, the beginning of the decline (the high point) is the upper-left corner of the box and the low point is the lower-right corner of the box. The vertical line from the high to the low straight down from the high is then marked at each third and at the halfway level, and a "speed" line is drawn from the actual low in the lower-left corner through each of the two marks on the right side and projected into the future. His hypothesis was that these speed lines were natural levels of support, and the prices would retrace to them. Modern methods have included marking the Fibonacci ratio numbers of 38.2% and 61.8% and drawing the speed lines through them. As retracements do not seem to follow a consistent percentage, it seems doubtful that much merit should be applied to speed lines, but they are often seen in the literature on technical analysis.

Created using TradeStation

FIGURE 12.20   Speed resistance lines (TYX daily: September 15, 2009–February 24, 2010)

Andrews Pitchfork

Developed by Dr. Alan Andrews, the pitchfork, in a downtrend (see Figure 12.21), takes the earliest high (1), the next minor low (2), and the first major retracement high (3), and then draws a line between the low and the retracement high (2–3). It then marks the halfway point on that line, draws a trend line through the earlier high and that mark, extending it into the future, and also draws parallel lines to that new line from the minor low and from the retracement high. It sounds complicated, and like the speed line, apparently has limited value in projecting future support and resistance levels. Users claim that 80% of the time after the pitchfork is formed, prices will retrace to the middle line (1–A). This has not been tested, however. The method is often seen in press articles, likely because of the name (similar to candlestick patterns that also have catchy names), but its usefulness is suspect.

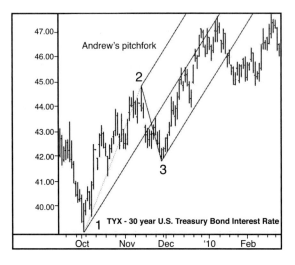

FIGURE 12.21   Andrews pitchfork (TYX daily: September 15, 2009–February 24, 2010)

Gann Fan Lines

William Delbert Gann, known as W. D. Gann, was a famous commodities trader and book writer on trading tactics. He developed a number of technical methods (see Chapter 20, "Elliott, Fibonacci, and Gann") that are still used by some practitioners. His invention of fan lines came from his belief that prices and time were related in a geometric pattern. To construct these lines, he used nine basic angles of trend lines based on the simple arithmetic relationship between the numbers 1, 2, 3, 4, and 8. By relating these numbers to a theoretical triangle beginning at an important price turning point, he could draw a series of trend lines that he thought had meaning. The angle of the trend line was always a ratio of the numbers converted into degrees. For example, he believed that 1 by 1 was the most basic ratio and converted into 45 degrees. From there to 1 by 2 was 63.75 degrees; 1 by 3 was 71.25 degrees, and so forth. Figure 12.22 shows the Gann fan lines drawn on the TYX chart used earlier for the Andrew's pitchfork and the Fibonacci speed lines to give you a comparison between approaches. There is little statistical support for any of these methods, and you can see that the lines are very similar regardless of the method used. There appears to be no foolproof method of anticipating trend lines, and the best method is still to draw a line through the actual price data.

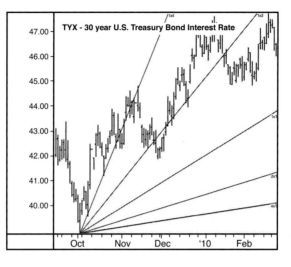

Created using TradeStation

FIGURE 12.22 Gann fan lines (TYX daily: September 15, 2009–February 24, 2010)

Conclusion

The trend of prices is the most important variable in profiting from technical analysis. The trend can sometimes be obvious and sometimes be elusive. The most useful trends are those identified the earliest, ridden as long as they last, and the inevitable end recognized. The first step in this process is observing what trends currently exist. Support and resistance zones determine when trends have reversed in the past and are a clue as to when they will reverse in the future. Support and resistance produces troughs and peaks. By connecting with a line from trough to trough and peak to peak, we can easily plot trend lines that represent past trends and extend them into the future. From retracements and the breaking of these extended trend lines, we can also spot when a trend may be changing direction. In the next two chapters, we continue with the discussion of trends, introducing other methods of measuring them and other signals that can warn of impending change in price direction.

Review Questions

1. Explain what the term *trading range* means. Why is it hard for a trader to make money when the market is in a trading range?

2. What does the term *support* mean? How is support generally drawn on a chart?

3. What does the term *resistance* mean? How is resistance generally drawn on a chart?

4. Explain the psychology behind support and resistance levels.

5. Jonathon is watching the stock of his favorite company trade in a congestion area. He is watching closely for a breakout to jump into the market. He says he does not want to miss the breakout, but he is cautious not to assume a breakout prematurely.

   a. Why do you think Jonathon is sitting on the sidelines while the stock is trading in the congestion area?

   b. How might Jonathon recognize a breakout?

   c. Explain the trade-off Jonathon is facing about being cautious regarding prematurely assuming a breakout, but at the same time being careful not to miss the breakout.

6. Below is a daily bar chart for MSFT for April 28, 1999–June 30, 1999. Much of this chart represents a trading range area.

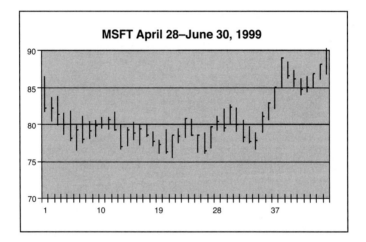

   a. Make a photocopy of this chart and mark the peaks and troughs on the chart.

   b. Which of the peaks and troughs that you marked fulfill the two-bar reversal point criterion?

   c. Which of the peaks and troughs that you marked fulfill the Gann two-day swing criterion?

   d. Draw support and resistance lines (or zones) on the graph.

   e. When does a breakout from the trading range occur?

7. Using the data that you gathered and the graphs that you created in Chapter 11, "History and Construction of Charts," for VLO (September 2007–September 2010), find the following items:

    a. Find a period of congestion on the graph. What were the levels of support and resistance during this trading range? In what direction did a breakout occur? What story does this breakout tell about the war between buyers and sellers?

    b. Locate a period when an accelerating uptrend occurs on the graph. When does a reversal occur?

    c. Locate a period when a decelerating uptrend occurs on the graph. When does a reversal occur?

    d. Find a period on the graph when the major trend is upward, but a retracement occurs.

BREAKOUTS, STOPS, AND RETRACEMENTS

CHAPTER OBJECTIVES

By the end of this chapter, you should

- Understand what a breakout is
- Be familiar with the major methods of identifying a breakout
- Be familiar with the purpose of entry and exit stops
- Be familiar with the major methods of setting entry and exit stops

In Chapter 12, "Trends—The Basics," we discussed the importance of trends for profiting from price action, and we observed several ways in which trends can be recognized. We also learned that to maximize profit, we must join a trend at its earliest, safest point, and ride it until it shows signs of changing direction against us. To do this, we mentioned that a trend will begin often from a breakout of a support or resistance level and sometimes from a trend line. In this chapter, we discuss breakouts and stops. They are never exact levels and require certain rules for us to have confidence in their validity. Stops are useful for both entry and exit strategies, and protective stops are prices at which investors must admit, as difficult as that might be, that their analysis is wrong and that the best solution is to exit from the position. Breakouts and stops are somewhat similar, although stops need not be as stringent.

BREAKOUTS

A breakout occurs most often when a price "breaks out" through a prior support or resistance level or zone. A breakout often signals that a significant change in supply and demand has occurred and that a new price trend is beginning. For this reason alone, a breakout is an extremely important signal to the investor or trader. A breakout can also occur at a trend line, which as the previous chapter noted, is just a moving support or resistance level. A breakout in the direction of the previous trend is a confirmation that the trend still exists, and a breakout in the opposite direction of a previous trend suggests that the trend is reversing and that a position should be closed and possibly reversed. Breakouts occur when prices pass through specific levels. Because these levels are often somewhat unclear zones and because false breakouts are common, the point at which a breakout occurs is extremely important. Often there must be a trade-off between speed and conviction. Speed of action is necessary just as a price breaks a level, and conviction is necessary to be sure that the breakout is real. There are a number of ways to accomplish both, but there is always the trade-off between risk and reward. More conviction that the breakout is real reduces the potential reward, and less conviction, though potentially more profitable, increases the risk that the breakout is false.

How Is Breakout Confirmed?

The first requirement for a breakout is a penetration of a previous trend line, or support or resistance zone. The next requirement is confirmation that the penetration is a real breakout, not a false one.

When the exact breakout level is not clear, as in a support or resistance zone, the extreme level of the zone is considered the breakout level. For example, in a trading range with a wide support zone of horizontal lines from previous support points, the lowest support line would be the breakout level. The other horizontal lines are also parts of the zone, but prices will often recede into the support zone without breaking through it entirely. Thus, a break of the lowest support point is evidence that the entire support zone has been penetrated. A trend line is a more definite breakout level because it is a line, but even with a trend line, a false breakout often occurs and requires redrawing of the trend line. In both these instances, a penetration of the breakout level or trend line requires confirmation. Penetrations often occur on an intra-bar basis, and then the price closes back on the nonbreakout side of the breakout level or trend line. For an example of an intra-bar penetration, see Figure 13.1. Notice that in late February, the price rose above the resistance level in intraday trading but closed below. Penetrations of this type are usually false.

Close Filter

The major problem from the analyst's standpoint is that when the penetration is occurring, there is usually no other confirming evidence until after the close of trading. Some analysts will act immediately on the penetration and wait for the confirmation later. This is dangerous because the odds of a false breakout are greater with just an intra-bar penetration, but the entry can be protected with a nearby stop. The least risky confirmation is to wait for the closing price to see if, perhaps, the penetration was just due to an intra-bar exogenous occurrence that had little longer-term meaning. If the price ends up on the nonbreakout side of the breakout level at the close of trading, it is plain that the intra-day penetration was likely false and new lines might have to be drawn to account for it. On the other hand, if the closing price is through the breakout level, the odds are higher that the breakout is real (see Figure 13.2).

Some traders even wait for two bar closes beyond the breakout level for confirmation. This increases the risk that some part of the move subsequent to the breakout will be missed, but on the other hand, it increases the possibility that the breakout is real.

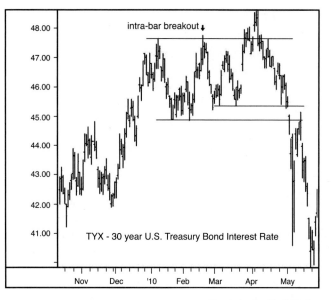

Created using TradeStation

FIGURE 13.1   Intra-bar breakout (TYX daily: October 13, 2009–May 27, 2010)

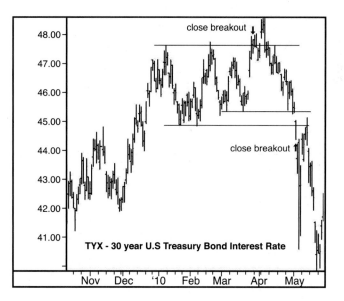

Created using TradeStation

FIGURE 13.2   Close breakout (TYX daily: October 13, 2009–May 27, 2010)

Point or Percent Filter

Another confirmation method is to establish a breakout zone either a certain number or fraction of points or percentage beyond the breakout level, as pictured in Figure 13.3. The theory is that if the price can penetrate the breakout level and a prescribed zone beyond it, the penetration must be real. The number of points or percentage is determined before the penetration and is helpful in computerized models where a definite breakout price needs to be established. Waiting for the close after an intra-bar breakout is more difficult to program. The number of points or percentage can be arbitrarily or empirically derived. Although the signal can use any percent or number of points, the most commonly used is a 3% rule, a level 3% from the ideal breakout point.

Time

Rather than looking simply at price, this method looks at time since the penetration. The basis is that if the penetration remains outside the breakout zone for a certain time, it must be real. The usual time period is two bars, but it can be any length of time. The price must remain beyond, or at least close beyond, the breakout level for the required number of bars. A combination of the time rule and the close rule uses both rules. This method requires a penetration and close beyond the breakout level, and then a second bar in which the price penetrates even further beyond the breakout level. For example, in a breakout down, the close must be below the breakout level, and the next bar must have a trade below the previous bar's low for confirmation of the breakout down. Figure 13.3 demonstrates this type of breakout to the upside.

Created using TradeStation

FIGURE 13.3   Breakout filter (TYX daily: October 13, 2009–May 27, 2010)

Volume

Increased volume of trading often occurs with a breakout. Heavier trading demonstrates that other market players are acting in the direction of the new trend and that there is sufficient power behind the penetration. Jiler (1962), however, observes, and cannot explain why, that volume can dramatically decline on a breakout, and the breakout is still valid. Usually, volume then increases as the trend develops. In Chapter 15, "Bar Chart Patterns," we look at volume behavior on the breakouts from different chart patterns.

Volatility

All of the preceding price rules have obvious drawbacks. The principal drawback to most of these methods is that they don't account for the price volatility of the security. By nature, some stocks tend to be characterized by more volatile trading; for these stocks, a more significant price move can be expected without it signaling a breakout. Remember that a filter using just the close doesn't require that the close be any distance from the breakout level. In highly volatile stocks, for example, the close can vary from a trend line or breakout level by a considerable amount and still not be a valid breakout.

A filter rule that uses some arbitrary point or percentage rule is likely to be broken by a highly volatile security before a true breakout occurs. In this case, analysts may consider the price volatility of the security when determining what the filter for a legitimate breakout should be. Three means of calculating volatility are most often used; these are beta, standard deviation of price, and Average True Range (ATR).

Beta is a calculation of the standard deviation of price relative to a market proxy, usually the S&P 500. It is not useful in commodities because commodities have little useful correlation to the stock market or a commodity average. Indeed, beta's use has diminished over the years, as the underlying assumption that it is a valid measure of risk has been questioned. It does have one advantage in that it eliminates the trend of the market from the volatility calculation.

Standard deviation of price is the basis for most option and other derivative models and uses the complete set of prices over some past period in time. Its usefulness as a breakout filter is diminished by the fact that it includes the trend of the security in its calculation. The breakout filter must use the volatility about the trend and not include the trend itself. Otherwise, a strongly trending stock with little volatility about its trend would have a higher filter than a flat-trending stock with wide fluctuations about its mean.

ATR is a derivation of the Average Range, which is just the average of the difference between each bar high and low over some past period. The ATR is calculated using a special formula devised by Wilder himself to reduce the effects of older data (see Chapter 14, "Moving Averages"). The ATR is an average of the True Range bar's close (Wilder, 1978). In doing so, it includes whatever effect a price gap between bars might have on the security's volatility. The True Range is the greatest of

- The difference between the current bar high and low
- The absolute value of the difference between the prior bar close and the current bar high

- The absolute value of the difference between the prior bar close and the current bar low

The ATR is the average of the True Range over some time period. Being dependent solely on the price of the security, the ATR is not influenced by any other average or security and is, thus, pure to the security's own action. It includes the recent trend only so far as the trend has had an effect on the range of prices. ATR is an excellent measure of volatility and is used in many indicators as well as breakout and stop-loss formulas.

As a price filter for confirmation of a breakout, by including a multiple of the ATR, the breakout level is adjusted for the volatility of the security. As you can see in Figure 13.4, an ATR filter expands and contracts over time as price volatility changes. For example, if price volatility increases, daily True Ranges will expand, and the ATR will be larger, making it less likely to have a false breakout due to the increased price volatility. This means that a highly volatile security will have a wider filter to account for its likelihood of making false breakouts just because of its higher volatility. On the other hand, a dull security that has few wild moves will have a narrow filter that will trigger the breakout with only a minimum deviation from its usual range.

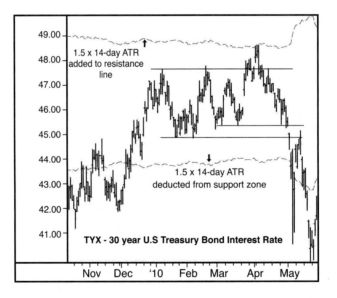

Created using TradeStation

FIGURE 13.4 ATR breakout filter (TYX daily: October 13, 2009–May 27, 2010)

Pivot Point Technique

The Pivot Point Technique is a method of determining likely support and resistance levels. It is widely used by day traders to establish potential price ranges for the day, and it is used as confirmation for breakouts (see Figure 13.5).

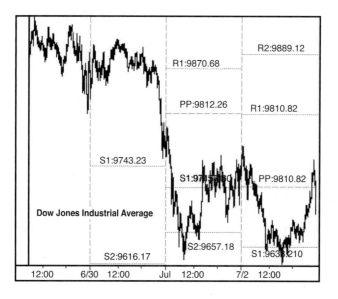

Created using TradeStation

FIGURE 13.5   Pivot Point technique filter (DJIA intra-day: June 29, 2010–July 2, 2010)

This technique uses the previous bar's high, low, and close to establish support and resistance levels for the current bar. Some formulas use the open as well. A series of points called **pivot points** for the current bar are calculated from price points derived from the previous bar. The theory behind using this technique is that as time goes on, the effect of past prices on current prices diminishes. Thus, the most recent, previous bar's action is the best predictor of the current bar's action.

This technique uses the following formula (Kaufman, 1998):

P (pivot point) = (High previous bar + Low previous bar + Close previous bar) ÷ 3

R1 (first resistance) = (2 × P) – Low previous bar

S1 (first support) = (2 × P) – High previous bar

R2 (second resistance) = (P + High previous bar – Low previous bar)

S2 (second support) = (P – High previous bar + Low previous bar)

These calculations establish upper and lower levels at which prices are expected to meet resistance or support based on the previous period's action. Floor traders will then enter or exit trades around these calculated pivot levels. The use of this formula is, of course, questionable because the logic behind it is questionable. The reason that so many intraday price reversals occur at pivot points is likely because so many traders use them, and, thus, they become self-fulfilling. In Figure 13.5, you can see that for the three days shown, the pivot points did not provide much guidance.

Traders looking for the validity of daily breakouts, on the other hand, will use the previous week or month action to establish current expected resistance and support levels; a price break through a current actual resistance or support level would be confirmed if it also broke a pivot resistance or support level. As a method of confirming breakouts, the logic behind their use is a little more solid. The formula is essentially a measure of the previous day's volatility projected into the following day. Volatility, as we have seen previously, is a useful method for determining accurate breakout confirmations.

Alternative pivot point calculations exist as well as the standard above. Tom DeMark developed a means of predicting support and resistance based on adding the relationship between the open and close price. There are also Woodie's and Camarilla pivot point formulas. When all of these methods are compared, not one seems to be consistent or accurately estimate future support or resistance levels.

Can a Breakout Be Anticipated?

So far, we have looked at ways of confirming a breakout *after* it has occurred. Is it possible to determine that a breakout is about to occur *before* it actually does? Sometimes it is possible to anticipate a breakout. Often, volume is a clue that a breakout is about to occur. As we will learn later, volume often accompanies the trend. In other words, an increase in volume with a trend is supportive of that trend. Thus, when prices are oscillating, for example, beneath a resistance zone and volume increases on every small up leg and decreases with every small down leg, the odds favor that the price will eventually break up through the resistance zone.

Prices can also give a hint as to their next directional move. For example, in a trading range, if prices begin to reverse upward at a level slightly above the lower boundary of the range and then reverse downward right at the resistance zone, it indicates that buyers are becoming a little more aggressive with every minor correction and are willing to pay just a little more for the security. If this tendency to have slightly rising lows is accompanied by increasing volume on the rallies, the probability of an upward breakout through resistance increases.

Figure 13.6 gives a hypothetical example of price activity hinting that a breakout may soon occur. Resistance has existed in the past and has stopped the first price rally. A downward reversal takes place to the point marked C. If volume increased on the initial rise to resistance but declined on the correction to C, C becomes a possible entry point in anticipation of a breakout above resistance. This is a low-odds, riskier entry point because the chances of it failing to follow with an actual breakout are considerably greater than after an actual breakout has occurred, but the price at which entry is made is lower, and, thus, the trade, if it works out, is potentially more profitable. A trade-off exists between the higher risk of entry prior to the breakout and the higher reward of a cheaper entry price. At B, assuming again that volume has increased with the small rally, the odds of a breakout have increased over C, but the price is not quite as advantageous. At A, we know that a breakout has occurred, and, thus, our risk of a failure has diminished (but has not been eliminated because false breakouts can still occur), but the price of entry is considerably higher than the other possible entry points. This trade-off between risk and reward is a constant problem for the analyst, and the decision as to which breakout method to use is entirely at the analyst's discretion, based on individual reward/risk tolerance. Deciding on the most comfortable relation between risk and reward is a problem that will arise in almost every technical situation, from breakouts to money management, and it is one of the reasons that evaluating technical systems is so difficult.

Anticipating a Breakout

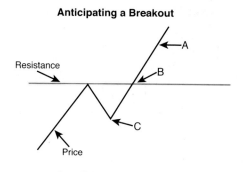

Possible Point of Entry

FIGURE 13.6   Anticipating a breakout

STOPS

A stop order is an order to buy or sell once a specific price has been reached. For example, a buy stop would be an order to buy a security at a specified price above the current price. Should the price rise to the specified buy stop price, it will be bought at the market. Conversely, a sell stop is an order to sell a security at a specified price below the current price when reached.

What Are Entry and Exit Stops?

Stop orders, also called "stops," can be used to enter a position or to exit a position. For example, if a price is approaching a resistance level above which a new trend is expected to develop, a buy stop order could be placed to be triggered if the resistance level is penetrated in a breakout. Or conversely, at a support level, the entry stop order could be placed to sell short once the specified level had been breached. These examples are entry stops. Exit stops are used either to protect capital from further loss, what Edwards and Magee (2007) call **protective stops,** or to protect profits from deteriorating back into a loss, usually called **trailing stops.** These stops are defensive in nature and are an absolute necessity once a trade entry has occurred.

Breakout levels and stop-loss levels or zones are very similar. Exit stop levels are levels that signal the analysis might be incorrect or at least that the analysis is uncertain and that a position should be exited to protect capital but not necessarily reentered in the opposite direction. Entry stop levels are positioned using the preceding rules for establishing a breakout level or zone or anticipation of a breakout through those levels or zones. The methods described previously for confirming breakouts are equally useful in confirming stop levels.

In an entry stop at a breakout level, an investor is committing new money and taking the risk that the breakout is valid. In an exit stop, an investor is closing a position and, thus, not decreasing risk. This is not to say that stops should be used carelessly. Indeed, by placing stops too close to current price action, an investor can be easily "whipsawed." A whipsaw occurs when an investor buys a security, the security price falls, the investor sells the security, and then the security price goes up above the original purchase price. The investor's original opinion was correct, but he or she still lost money. The word "whipsaw" comes from the timber industry where a long, thin, two-man wood saw would often get caught in a log, if not properly handled, and whip the sawyers back and forth without cutting the wood and subjecting them to "two damaging and usually opposing forces at the same time" (www.Randomhouse.com). The whipsaw resulted from lack of analysis and lack of patience, just as in investing.

Changing Stop Orders

The most important underlying principle for defensive stops, because they protect one's capital but at the same time may imply the original analysis was wrong, is that they should never be moved away from the trend of the security. In other words, if one is long a security and has placed a stop at a reasonable level below the current price, he should never cancel or reduce the stop order. Its purpose is to keep the investor honest. By changing or canceling the stop, especially when the security is trading at a loss, the investor is losing discipline and reacting to emotional pressures having to do with not desiring to admit an error, a natural and strong human emotion, but unrelated to the rational assessment of the price action. If a decision about the security originally is made with the best logic and information available and a stop is placed at that time at the point at which the analysis will obviously be incorrect, changing it or canceling it negates all the original thought and analysis. The stop may be adjusted along with price as a trailing stop or one that follows each successive change in support or resistance in the direction of the trend as the position progresses profitably, but it should never be canceled or changed against the trend.

Many investors and traders place stops too close to the current price of the security in which they have a position. This often causes whipsaws, even when the stop is adjusted for volatility. A defensive stop is a protection device. It is not necessary for short-term trading. Often, because they don't want to lose any amount of profit, investors will place a stop too close to the current price and get closed out too early in a longer move. A better method is to allow the security "breathing" room and place the protective stop below where the breathing room correction would be serious. We know that security prices retrace their advances in a progression of steps along the trend, and we know that we will never buy and sell at the absolute peak or trough. We also know that we have to decide upon what time horizon we want to play. Once that is decided, to place a stop based on a shorter time period only invites whipsaws. It is better to wait for the retracement and let the security "breathe."

On the other hand, if the situation is such that the overall market appears ready to reverse, and one's security has run along with the market but is also showing signs of fatigue, a trailing stop very close to the current price is sometimes warranted. When the situation is such that a position will likely be closed soon anyway, for whatever reason, tightening the stop just allows the marketplace to make the decision rather than the investor or trader.

What Are Protective Stops?

Whenever a position is initiated, usually even before initiation, a protective exit stop level must be determined and placed with the entry order. The reasons are twofold. First, the protective stop protects capital. Not every entry is correct and ends up with a profit. Indeed, many traders have more losing trades than winning trades, but they are able to profit because of the judicious use of their stops. They place protective stops at a level at which they know the trade will have been unsuccessful, and when a trade works, they run with the profits until the trend appears to be reversing. The protective stop, therefore, is necessary in any investment endeavor. Even standard fundamental analysis should use some kind of stop. It is ridiculous to think that when entering a trade or investment that it will always be successful and that risk of loss should be disregarded.

The second reason a protective stop is necessary is to determine what capital risk the trader or investor is accepting in the trade. By establishing a stop level (and placing an order to that effect), the investors now know exactly what capital risk is being taken. Assume that a stock breaks upward out of a resistance zone at $20, and the entry stop is triggered so that the investor is now invested in the stock at $20. By analyzing previous support, trend lines, and other technical data, the investor determines that if the stock should sink to $17 (perhaps that is a support level or a trend line level adjusted for confirmation), there is something wrong with the analysis that suggested that the price would be rising. *The need to know what is wrong is unnecessary because the stock price action itself is suggesting that something is wrong.* Rational investment management would then be to get out of the stock until what is wrong is understood and evaluated. Technical analysis tells the investor at what price this exit should be made. Once the $17 price is determined as the exit point, the risk of the trade has been determined to be $3, the difference between the entry and potential exit prices. Knowing that the risk is $3 makes the money management problem considerably easier. Say the investor has $100,000 and never wants to risk more than 10% of capital in any one investment. A 3,300 share position with the risk of losing $3 is a $10,000 risk in a $100,000 portfolio, or 10%. No other investment method is as useful for measuring risk of loss. If the best exit point was $16 rather than $17, the risk would be $4 per share and the ideal position to limit loss to 10% of the portfolio would then have been 2,500 shares. By knowing the risk level, the investor can adjust the amount of shares to be purchased. This method provides a tremendous advantage in reducing risk.

All stops should be placed based on the price action of the security and the level at which a reversal in trend is likely. Generally, these are trend lines or support or resistance levels. The methods using percentages or points from entry do not address the action of the price and are not adjusted to it. Instead, these levels are purely arbitrary. These rules will often stop out a position before a crucial level is reached or long after it has been penetrated. Exits always should be placed at logical levels of price based on the analysis of trend, support and resistance, volatility, and pattern, not on the peculiarities of a particular portfolio or on an arbitrary rule.

What Are Trailing Stops?

When a security is in a recognizable trend, a trailing stop can be used to avoid the potential loss of profits. Edwards and Magee called these stops "progressive" stops. These trailing stops are necessary because, for instance, in a significant uptrend, the prior support or resistance level may become a substantial price distance from the current price. For example, consider Figure 13.7. Assume that you initially enter a long position in October, with a protective stop placed at the low October price. As the stock continues trading in an uptrend over time, the price gets further and further from this initial stop point. By December, you have made a substantial profit. Setting a trailing stop will help you lock in that profit if the uptrend reverses. If you kept the stop at the original October level, you could watch the price fall by a large amount, and your profits would disappear before the protective stop was activated.

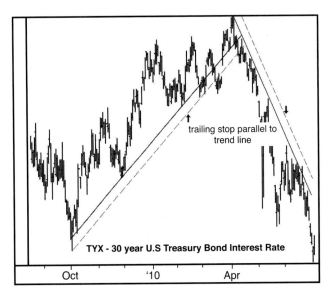

Created using TradeStation

FIGURE 13.7   Trend line trailing stop (TYX daily: August 17, 2009–July 2, 2010)

Trailing Stops Using a Trend Line

The easiest method of establishing a trailing stop is to follow the trend line with a confirmation filter similar to those used in standard breakouts, as shown in Figure 13.7. For example, an uptrending stock has a definite, well-defined, standard trend line drawn beneath the recent price history. By setting a stop level below the trend line, to prevent false signals, using the amount determined from any of the preceding breakout confirmation methods—for example, a 3% filter—you establish a trailing stop. It must be adjusted with every new bar to travel along with the trend line. If it is triggered and the position closed, profits already accrued would not be appreciably affected, at least not as much as waiting for a previous support or resistance level to be broken would adversely affect them, yet the stop level is far enough away from the trend line so as not to be triggered with a false breakout.

Another method of trailing stop designed to account for the intrinsic volatility of the security is to measure some fraction of the security's ATR from its latest reversal point. This method is called a "Chandelier Exit." For example, assume you are long a security rising on an accelerated trend that reaches $50. The 14-day ATR for this stock is $2.50. Based on an evaluation of the market strength, you decide to place a stop three times the ATR below the recent highest high. (Usually a multiple of 2.5 to 4.0 times the ATR is used.) Therefore, you place a sell stop at $42.50. You don't consider the trend line or the previous support level, which may be considerably below the current price. This method provides a stop based purely on the price and volatility of the security.

When price rises above $50, the stop moves up with the price rise to three times its new ATR below the new high. Figure 13.8 shows what using the Chandelier Exit looks like. Using this method reduces the likelihood that a false breakdown will occur because you are adjusting the stop for the security's volatility. This method is especially useful when other levels such as a trend line or support level are considerably distant from the current price, and the security is following an accelerated upward trend whose end is difficult to predict.

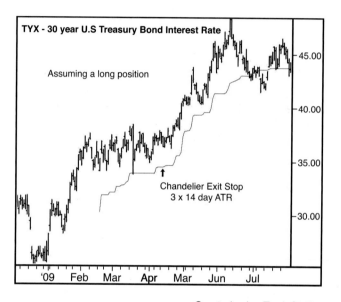

Created using TradeStation

FIGURE 13.8 Chandelier Exit (TYX daily: December 3, 2008–August 3, 2009)

Trailing Stops Using Parabolic SAR

Another trend-following method for setting stops is the Parabolic SAR. (SAR stands for "Stop and Reversal.") Developed by Welles Wilder (1978), it was initially intended as a trading system because it required a long or short position. However, it has become not only a breakout confirmation rule, but also an excellent, but sometimes very sensitive, stop rule.

The Parabolic is calculated by using an "acceleration factor" that increases as the price moves along its trend. Thus, the name "parabolic" is used because the stop level follows a parabolic curve, as shown in Figure 13.9. The weakness of the formula is that it doesn't include the security's volatility and is thus subject to many whipsaws. The acceleration factor is arbitrary and requires some testing for each security to find the best level with the least whipsaws. The concept of a parabolic curve for a stop level is an interesting one, however, and once adjusted for a security's volatility may have more value.

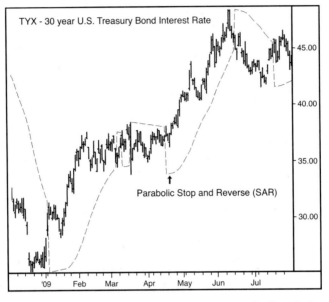

Created using TradeStation

FIGURE 13.9   Parabolic SAR (TYX daily: December 3, 2008–August 3, 2009)

Trailing Stops Using Percentage of Gain

One final method of determining trailing stops is to place stops at a percentage of each leg in the direction of the trend. This requires that a profit is accruing. On the initial favorable leg, for example, a stop can be placed at 50% of the gain and moved with the gain until after the first retracement. The stop can then be raised as a higher fraction of each successive favorable leg. This method is generally inferior to those methods based on the actual price action.

What Are Time Stops?

Time stops are exit stops used to close a position after a predetermined period of time has passed. *Time is an investor's enemy. Uncertainty increases in future time.* The longer we look into the future, the less accurate our projections are. This uncertainty is one reason why long-term interest rates are usually higher than short-term interest rates—to account for the risk of something adverse happening over time. When a trading model or investment method determines that a position should be entered, for whatever reason, the longer that time goes on without a profitable reaction to the position entry, the higher are the chances that the entered position will be unprofitable. Technical analysis is a method of timing investments or trades. To maximize return on capital, capital should not be idle. For this reason, technical analysts often use a time stop to exit a position after a predetermined time, especially if the position is not profitable. Time stops are also useful in testing mechanical trading methods. All positions must have an entry and exit. Often one is unrelated to the other, but without the ability to analyze both the entry and exit, their respective strengths and weaknesses are unknown. To analyze the signal entry, a time stop gives equal weight to all the entry signals being tested.

What Are Money Stops?

Instead of using price points at which risk of significant loss is possible, some traders and investors use a money stop. This stop is based on the risk one is willing to take in terms of money. For example, in the previous description of the protective stop, the investor was willing to risk $10,000. Instead of determining from the analysis at what point the security is at risk of major loss, the investor determines how far down the security may decline before the $10,000 is lost. With this method, investors enter into an arbitrary number of shares at their choosing without any analysis of the price point at which the position should be closed and then allow the balance in their investment account to tell them when to sell. From the strategic and money management viewpoint, this method is a poor way to establish a protective stop. The better method is to determine the risk points in the security and work from there. A money stop is based not only on the price change but also on the amount of securities or contracts entered. It is, thus, not a good method of determining when the chance of further loss has increased and will often cause expensive whipsaws, especially if the position has a large number of shares or contracts and is exited after only a small change in price.

As you can see, there are numerous variations of stops. The technical analyst usually tests a variety on the securities being traded and sticks with the most successful method.

How Can Stops Be Used with Breakouts?

A breakout above resistance or below support signals a change, usually in trend direction. A trend line breakout is a warning of change but not necessarily of a reversal in direction. The most used breakout is the breakout from support or resistance. In Chapter 15, we cover chart patterns. Almost all patterns are made of trend lines and support or resistance lines. The most reliable chart patterns are completed on a breakout, usually through support or resistance. Most strategies utilizing chart patterns, therefore, must have a way of recognizing a breakout, measuring its importance, and confirming it.

Using Stops When Gaps Occur

Some traders act directly on the breakout and are willing to pay the extra price generated by the enthusiasm associated with the breakout. This is usually a wise decision when the breakout creates a gap (see Gap A in Figure 13.10). A *gap* occurs when a security opens and trades at a range totally outside the previous day's range. In other words, there is no overlap between one day's trading prices and the previous day's trading prices, and a gap appears between the bars for the two days on a chart. A gap is usually a sign that important information was released during the period between the bars that had an extraordinary effect on the buyers and sellers. Usually, if the reason for the gap is legitimate, the price continues in the direction in which it broke out. When the gap is closed ("covered" or "filled"), however, there is the danger that the gap was false and prices will reverse their trend. Thus, a protection stop should be placed below the gap opening. We discuss the different kinds of gaps in Chapter 17, "Short-Term Patterns."

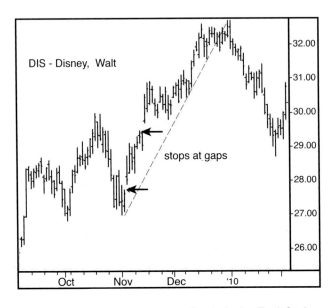

Created using TradeStation

FIGURE 13.10 Gaps (DIS daily: September 4, 2009–February 3, 2010)

Waiting for Retracement

When a breakout occurs, but a gap is not present, some traders will wait for the pullback or throwback before entering a position. To do this, they wait for the initial run from the breakout to exhaust itself, calculate a percentage—usually 50%—retracement from the breakout to the high or low, and place a limit order at that level. A breakout followed by a pullback is pictured in Figure 13.11. Studies have shown (Thom Hartle, *Active Trader Magazine,* March 2004) that the percentage retracement is not predictable and varies widely. Thus, these traders run the risk that the security will not retrace the percentage or will retrace the percentage and continue correcting back to the original stop level. To prevent this, once the percentage retracement level is determined and the limit order is placed, the stop is adjusted to just behind the limit order to prevent the retracement from becoming a large loss if it continues. Often the trader will also enter a partial position on the breakout and a partial position at the expected retracement level with a stop for the entire position just behind it. This way, the risk of missing the security continuing beyond its breakout without a retracement is reduced, and should the retracement occur, a full position will be entered at a lower average price.

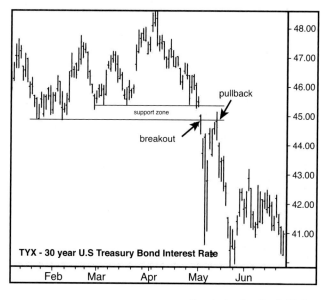

Created using TradeStation

FIGURE 13.11   Breakout and pullback (TYX daily: January 5, 2010–June 24, 2010)

Calculating a Risk/Return Ratio for Breakout Trading

Usually breakouts from support or resistance run to the next zone of support or resistance. This gives the investor or trader a price objective for the breakout. From that price objective, a risk/return ratio can be calculated. The return is the difference between the entry price and the price objective. The risk is the amount the price must go against the entry price before exited on a stop, usually some price on the other side of the breakout. Traditionally, the reward/risk ratio should be a minimum of three to one. This gives the investor the odds of making money even when two out of three trades fail, assuming the third action provides a three-to-one gain. In Chapter 15, "Bar Chart Patterns," and Chapter 16, "Point-and-Figure Chart Patterns," we learn other methods of determining a price objective. This three-to-one guideline, however, should always be the minimum reward/risk ratio. Anything less than three to one increases the odds of losing money beyond acceptable amounts.

In Figure 13.12, we show the support levels and how the price subsequent to a downward breakout tends to run to the next support level. Once a downward breakout occurs, the objective is the next support level from the previous advance. Depending on where the trade is entered and what level is necessary for a stop, a calculation can easily be made as to the reward/risk of the trade. Notice in this chart that the trader had a second chance on every downward breakout. The price rallied back to the breakout almost immediately in a pullback, and then it declined again to the next support level. Such pullbacks do not occur frequently, but the odds of returning to an earlier support level are generally good.

Created using TradeStation

FIGURE 13.12   Breakouts to support levels (X daily: January 15, 2010–July 2, 2010)

Placing Stops for a False (or "Specialist") Breakout

Figure 13.13 shows an example of a downward "specialist breakout." This false breakout triggers all the sell stops placed to protect against a loss from a reversal in upward trend or to enter a new short position. Prices, with no follow-through, then reverse again, and they break back up through the earlier breakout level, leaving many investors with a loss. Those who sold their longs on a protective stop no longer have a position, and those who entered a short position now have a loss. The false breakout down caught them. It is often called a specialist breakout from the days when specialists and market makers would create false breakouts at prices known to be strong support or resistance levels and establish a position with the longer trend—in the example, the uptrend. Thus, the breakout downward in Figure 13.13, against the longer upward trend, triggered sellers who sold their stock to the specialists or market makers, who then held for the continuation of the earlier trend. Whether these false breakouts are manipulations today is somewhat irrelevant, but they do occur quite frequently and, if not protected against, can be very painful.

To protect against these losses, the astute investor or trader will place another, close buy stop (in the example) slightly above the high of the breakout bar, as drawn on the chart. If prices quickly reverse upward, the trader will cover losses and make a profit from the second stop being triggered, and the earlier long investor will be long again.

The reaction to a specialist breakout is often so strong and dramatic because it has trapped investors in the wrong direction. In itself, it is a tradable formation. In the chart example, should the trader have no position but see the downward breakout, rather than trade the breakout, he or she could place a stop above the breakout bar in case the breakout is false. If the breakout is false and triggers the trader's entry stop, he or she makes a quick profit, and if it does not trigger, he or she doesn't lose anything. A trader who was fooled by the false breakout could also use this procedure for a stop and reverse. If the short is entered on the downward breakout, the buy stop would be placed at the upper level of the breakout bar to close the short position and to enter a long position. In the example, you can see that the triggered stop would have produced a sizable profit.

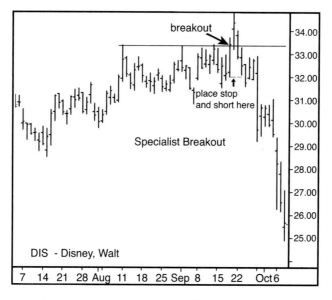

Created using TradeStation

FIGURE 13.13 *Stop for specialist breakout (DIS daily: July 2, 2008–October 9, 2008)*

The most important point about trailing stops, or any kind of stop, is to test the method first. It is remarkable how much a stop, if properly placed, can improve performance over that from just an arbitrary stop placement.

CONCLUSION

Breakouts from support, resistance, or trend lines are the primary signal that the price has changed direction or is reaccelerating in its original direction. As such, breakouts are usually the first signal to act. Because breakouts can be false, and often are, some means of confirming a breakout is necessary. We have covered a few methods but none of them is foolproof. The technical analyst must experiment with different methods and find those most satisfactory to his method of trading or investing. The same can be said for stops. Although stops need not be as precise, they are always necessary when a position has been entered, and they must never be canceled or changed until they are triggered or the position is closed. Their purpose is to keep the investor honest and solvent. The rules for breakouts apply equally to stops. They should account for either previous support or resistance or trend, should adjust for the security's volatility, and should not be placed too close to the current price as to invite a false signal or whipsaw.

REVIEW QUESTIONS

1. Explain what is meant by the term *whipsaw*. What could cause an investor to experience a lot of whipsaws?

2. The daily open, high, low, and close for two stocks, Biosite Inc. (BSTE) and Coca-Cola (KO), for April 15–May 13, 2005 are given in the following table.

   a. Calculate the five-day ATR for the two stocks for this time period.

   b. Compare the volatility of the two stocks given the ATR.

   c. How would these ATRs impact the filter you would want to use for a breakout for each of these stocks?

	KO				BSTE			
Date	Open	High	Low	Close	Open	High	Low	Close
15-Apr-05	42.08	42.13	41.15	41.29	58.65	60.26	58.18	58.35
18-Apr-05	41.12	41.33	40.74	40.97	58.33	58.81	57.52	58.42
19-Apr-05	42.7	42.92	42.06	42.4	58.33	59.92	58.14	59.82
20-Apr-05	42.52	42.55	41.63	41.88	60	60.85	58.97	59.3
21-Apr-05	42.3	42.3	41.74	41.98	59.4	60.89	59.29	60.8
22-Apr-05	41.95	42.56	41.89	42.13	58.03	62.5	58	58.89
25-Apr-05	42.43	42.73	42.11	42.68	59.51	60.2	59.09	59.77
26-Apr-05	42.68	43.31	42.6	42.96	59.35	59.69	58.15	58.4
27-Apr-05	42.89	42.95	42.48	42.82	58.55	58.55	57.15	57.75
28-Apr-05	42.63	42.92	42.62	42.69	58.04	58.04	55.99	55.99
29-Apr-05	42.71	43.5	42.6	43.44	56.46	57	55.45	57
2-May-05	43.49	43.62	43.24	43.57	56.61	56.85	55.76	56.64
3-May-05	43.57	44.02	43.52	43.76	56.78	57.06	56.01	56.26
4-May-05	43.98	44.24	43.69	43.93	56.56	57.82	56.55	57.61
5-May-05	43.78	44.24	43.76	44.15	57.59	57.96	56.81	57.42
6-May-05	44.22	44.53	44.1	44.19	57.87	57.99	56.11	56.76
9-May-05	44.2	44.6	44.1	44.57	56.65	57.7	56.27	57.47
10-May-05	44.12	44.41	44.02	44.23	57.18	57.65	57	57.21
11-May-05	44.13	44.32	43.79	44.27	57.01	57.37	55.9	56.73
12-May-05	44.17	44.75	43.75	44.17	56.7	57.87	56.51	57.65
13-May-05	44.47	44.47	43.87	44.11	57.52	58.26	56.91	57.58

3. Using the same data that you used in Question 2, calculate the daily pivot points for the two stocks. Explain how these results can be used to determine points of resistance and support or breakouts.

4. Explain why, during an uptrend, an investor would want to use trailing stops rather than setting one constant stop level.

5. Explain the advantages and disadvantages of using time stops and money stops.

MOVING AVERAGES

CHAPTER OBJECTIVES

By the end of this chapter, you should

* Be aware of how moving averages are used to identify trends
* Be able to calculate a simple moving average
* Be able to calculate an exponential moving average
* Be familiar with the concept of directional movement
* Be familiar with the construction of envelopes, bands, and price channels

One of the most successful methods of identifying and profiting from trends is the use of moving averages. A moving average is a constant period average, usually of prices, that is calculated for each successive chart period interval. The result, when plotted on a price chart, shows a smooth line representing the successive, average prices. Moving averages dampen the effects of short-term oscillations. Many of the most successful technical investment managers use moving averages to determine when trends are changing direction. Moving averages are especially useful in markets that have a tendency to trend.

Moving averages have been tested by academics and shown to have statistical significance. Brock, Lakonishok, and LeBaron (1992) were the first to demonstrate, using modern statistical bias-reducing methods, that moving average crossover signals have intrinsic value. As with most academic studies, the results of Brock, Lakonishok, and LeBaron's have been somewhat controversial. Even though some have since criticized their study, other researchers have validated their results. (Incidentally, the Brock, Lakonishok, and LeBaron study provides one of the more useful arguments against the Random Walk and Efficient Markets hypotheses.) Although the Brock, Lakonishok, and LeBaron study focused on the Dow Jones Industrials, later studies have used moving average crossover systems for market data in other countries with generally the same positive results. Detry and Gregoire (2001) provided a summary of these studies.

There obviously is something to moving averages. Traders and trend investors, of course, have known all this for many years, but technical analysts now feel more comfort in what they have been doing. In this chapter, we discuss some of the moving average methods and strategies that technical analysts use, as well as introduce some variations on moving averages, such as Bollinger Bands, envelopes, and directional movement indicators.

WHAT IS A MOVING AVERAGE?

The moving average is one of the oldest tools used by technical analysts. Daily fluctuations in stock prices, commodity prices, and foreign exchange rates can be large. Moving averages tone down these fluctuations—deemphasizing but sometimes distorting fluctuations. Technical analysts use moving averages to smooth erratic data, making it easier to view the true underlying trend.

The principal reason that moving averages are used is to smooth out shorter fluctuations and focus on the trend that fits with the investor's time horizon. A moving average by its nature is just one number that represents a net of certain past numbers. For example, a 20-day moving average is one number that represents all the prices for the past 20 days. As such, it filters out each one of the prices during the past 20 days and tells us how the group of 20 days is behaving, rather than its separate parts.

HOW IS A SIMPLE MOVING AVERAGE CALCULATED?

Table 14.1 contains the daily closing prices for CLB (Core Laboratories) from May 10, 2010 through July 12, 2010. Most moving averages of prices are based on closing prices, but they can be calculated on highs, lows, daily means, or any other value as long as the price type is consistent throughout the calculations. We use closing prices.

TABLE 14.1   Price Data and Moving Average Calculations for CLB Daily Price Close Between May 10, 2010 and July 12, 2010

	Date	Open	High	Low	Close	10-Day SMA	26-Day SMA	10-Day LWMA	10-Day EMA
1	5/10/2010	145.29	145.82	140.98	143.55	146.86	143.13	145.24	
2	5/11/2010	142.41	144.86	141.84	143	146.25	143.44	144.54	
3	5/12/2010	144.18	145.2	142.4	144	145.69	143.75	144.13	
4	5/13/2010	142.95	144.85	140.59	141.05	144.72	143.98	143.28	
5	5/14/2010	139.14	141.42	139.11	140.53	143.79	144.17	142.52	
6	5/17/2010	141.71	142.17	138.85	141.04	142.7	144.39	142.02	
7	5/18/2010	142.3	145.74	140.65	141.57	142.18	144.6	141.82	
8	5/19/2010	141.58	142.16	138.7	139.91	141.74	144.77	141.4	

	Date	Open	High	Low	Close	10-Day SMA	26-Day SMA	10-Day LWMA	10-Day EMA
9	5/20/2010	138.05	138.05	133.18	133.46	140.83	144.6	139.9	
10	5/21/2010	131.57	135	131.51	133.48	140.16	144.39	138.56	
11	5/24/2010	132.99	133.64	130.5	130.52	138.86	143.88	136.81	138.41
12	5/25/2010	127.36	131.7	126.01	131.61	137.72	143.51	135.49	137.17
13	5/26/2010	132.78	134.86	132.24	134.17	136.73	143.12	134.85	136.63
14	5/27/2010	137	140.9	136.45	140.35	136.66	142.99	135.5	137.30
15	5/28/2010	140	140	135.55	135.98	136.21	142.47	135.38	137.06
16	6/1/2010	134.69	134.69	128.72	129.46	135.05	141.58	134.15	135.68
17	6/2/2010	130.2	136.21	130.2	136.12	134.51	140.95	134.35	135.76
18	6/3/2010	135.55	142.27	135.55	141.94	134.71	140.68	135.7	136.88
19	6/4/2010	140.76	140.76	136	137.16	135.08	140.2	136.14	136.93
20	6/7/2010	136.84	139.95	134.99	135.33	135.26	139.61	136.19	136.64
21	6/8/2010	134.86	137.34	134.1	136.22	135.83	139.08	136.36	136.57
22	6/9/2010	137.5	141.69	137.13	138.19	136.49	138.56	136.79	136.86
23	6/10/2010	139.73	143.77	139.73	143.74	137.45	138.44	138.11	138.11
24	6/11/2010	142.13	146.53	142.13	146.27	138.04	138.51	139.71	139.59
25	6/14/2010	148.89	148.91	145	145.58	139	138.63	141.08	140.68
26	6/15/2010	146.9	150.04	146.9	149.99	141.05	139.01	143.08	142.37
27	6/16/2010	150.45	152.29	148.81	149.64	142.41	139.24	144.64	143.70
28	6/17/2010	150.74	152.62	149.34	152.27	143.44	139.6	146.44	145.25
29	6/18/2010	152.93	155.48	152.23	155	145.22	140.02	148.54	147.03
30	6/21/2010	157.9	157.9	155.32	156.52	147.34	140.62	150.59	148.75
31	6/22/2010	157.49	158.79	152.28	152.98	149.02	141.1	151.62	149.52
32	6/23/2010	153	153	150.51	150.93	150.29	141.48	151.97	149.78
33	6/24/2010	150	153.1	148.89	152.63	151.18	141.9	152.39	150.30
34	6/25/2010	151.2	155.02	150.01	151.8	151.73	142.36	152.5	150.57
35	6/28/2010	153	154.15	152.55	153.69	152.55	143.14	152.86	151.14
36	6/29/2010	151.78	151.8	148.1	148.29	152.38	143.71	152.08	150.62
37	6/30/2010	148.95	150.06	146.92	147.61	152.17	144.36	151.22	150.07
38	7/1/2010	147.38	148.87	145.33	147.54	151.7	144.98	150.38	149.61
39	7/2/2010	147.73	149.29	146.29	147.25	150.92	145.48	149.57	149.18
40	7/6/2010	149.42	150.6	148.75	150.6	150.33	145.87	149.51	149.44
41	7/7/2010	152.92	156.3	151.08	156.24	150.66	146.65	150.58	150.68
42	7/8/2010	156.25	158.1	155.05	156	151.17	147.67	151.55	151.64
43	7/9/2010	156.02	157.52	154.66	157.22	151.62	148.49	152.65	152.66
44	7/12/2010	157.46	158.78	155.68	158.46	152.29	149.12	153.9	153.71

Source: http://finance.yahoo.com

The most commonly used type of moving average is the simple moving average (SMA), sometimes referred to as an **arithmetic moving average.** An SMA is constructed by adding a set of data and then dividing by the number of observations in the period being examined. For example, look at the ten-day SMA in Table 14.1. We begin by summing the closing prices for the first ten days. We then divide this sum by 10 to give us the mean price for that ten-day period. Thus, on the tenth day, the ten-day simple moving average would be the mean closing price for CLB for Days 1 through 10, or $140.16.[1]

On Day 11, the moving average changes. To calculate the moving average for Day 11, we calculate the mean price for Days 2 through 11. In other words, the closing price for Day 1 is dropped from the data set, while the price for Day 11 is added. The formula for calculating a ten-day simple moving average is as follows:

$$\text{SMA}_{10} = \sum_{i=1}^{10} \text{data}_i \, / \, 10$$

Of course, we can construct moving averages of different lengths. In Table 14.1, you can also see a 26-day moving average. This SMA is simply calculated by adding the 26 most recent closing prices and dividing by 26.

Although a moving average can smooth prices over any desired period, some of the more popular daily moving averages are for the periods 200, 60, 50, 30, 20, and 10 days. These periods are somewhat arbitrary and were chosen in the days before computers when the calculations had to be done by hand or on a crank adding machine. Gartley (1935), for example, used the 200-day moving average in his work. Simple, round numbers were easier to calculate. Also, the 10-day, 20-day, and 60-day moving averages summarize approximately two weeks, one month, and three months (one fiscal quarter) of trading data, respectively.

Once calculated, moving averages are plotted on a price chart. Figure 14.1 shows a plot of the 26-day simple moving average for CLB. From mid-June through mid-July, the moving average is an upward sloping curve, indicating an upward trend in Core Labs's price. The daily fluctuations are smoothed by the moving average so that the analyst can see the underlying trend without being distracted by the small, daily movements.

A rising moving average indicates an upward trend, while a falling moving average indicates a downward trend. Although the moving average helps us discern a trend, it does so after the trend has begun. Thus, the moving average is a lagging indicator. By definition, the moving average is an indicator that is based on past prices. For example, Figure 14.1 shows an upward trend in CLB beginning in late May. However, an upward movement in the SMA does not occur until approximately mid-June. Remember that according to technical analysis principles, we want to be trading with the trend. Using a moving average will always give us some delay in signaling a change in trend.

---

1. Of course, being able to calculate a ten-day average requires ten days of data. Data occurring before the period shown in the chart was used to calculate the ten-day moving average for May 10–May 20. Our discussion centers on the calculation of the moving average for Day 10 so that the reader can follow the steps necessary to do such a calculation.

Created using TradeStation

FIGURE 14.1   Simple moving average (CLB daily: May 10, 2010–July 13, 2010)

Length of Moving Average

Because moving averages can be calculated for various lengths of time, which length is best to use? Of course, a longer time period includes more data observations, and, thus, more information. By including more data in the calculation of the moving average, each day's data becomes relatively less important in the calculation. Therefore, a large change in the value on one day does not have a large impact on the longer moving average. This can be an advantage if this large change is a one-day, irregular outlier in the data.

However, if this large move represents the beginning of a significant change in the trend, it takes longer for the underlying trend change to be discernable. Thus, the longer moving average is slower to pick up trend changes but less likely to falsely indicate a trend change due to a short-term blip in the data.

Figure 14.2, for example, shows both a 13-day and a 26-day SMA plotted for CLB. Notice how the shorter, 13-day moving average shows more variability than the longer, 26-day moving average. The 26-day moving average is said to be the "slower" moving average. Although it provides more smoothing, the 26-day smoothing average is also slower at signaling underlying trend changes. Notice how the 13-day SMA troughs in early June, signaling a change in trend; a week later, the slower, 26-day SMA is flat but and gradually turning upward. Thus, the 26-day SMA is slower to indicate a trend change.

Because spotting a trend reversal as soon as possible maximizes trading profits, the 13-day SMA may first appear to give superior information; however, remember that the faster SMA has a disadvantage of potentially giving a false signal of a changing trend direction. For example, look at early July in Figure 14.2. The 13-day SMA flattens out, suggesting an end to the upward price trend. After the fact, however, we can see that a trend reversal did not occur in early July.

The 13-day SMA was overly sensitive to a temporary decrease in price. During this period, the slower 26-day SMA continued to signal correctly an upward trend.

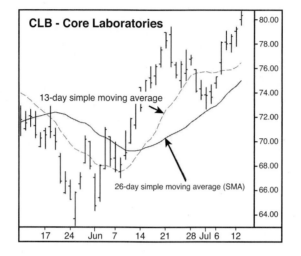

Created using TradeStation

FIGURE 14.2 Two moving averages—crossover as support and resistance zone (CLB daily: May 10, 2010–July 13, 2010)

Using Multiple Moving Averages

Analysis is not limited to the information provided by a single moving average. Considering various moving averages of various lengths simultaneously can increase the analysts' information set. For example, as shown in Figure 14.2, a support or resistance level often occurs where two moving averages cross. Where the shorter moving average crosses above the longer is often taken as a mechanical buy signal, or at least a sign that the price trend is upward. Likewise, it is considered a sell signal when the shorter declines below the longer. Many successful moving average strategies use moving averages as the principal determinant of trend and then use shorter-term moving averages either as trailing stops or as signals. In some instances, moving averages are used to determine trend, and then chart patterns are used as entry and exit signals.

Using these types of dual moving average signals during a sideways trend in prices, however, can result in a number of whipsaws. This problem can be seen in Figure 14.3. This is essentially the same problem that occurs during the standard sideways trend in a congestion area. It is very difficult to determine from such action in which way prices are going to break out, and meanwhile they oscillate back and forth within the support and resistance levels. A moving average provides no additional information on which way the trend will eventually break. Indeed, a moving average requires a trend for a crossover to be profitable. This means that the analyst must be sure that a trend exists before using moving average crossovers for signals. Otherwise—and some traders are willing to take the risk of short-term whipsaws in order not to miss the major trend—a plurality of signals will be incorrect and produce small losses while waiting for the one signal that will produce the large profit. This can be a highly profitable method provided the analyst has the stomach and discipline to continue with the small losses, and it often is the basis for many long-term trend systems. It also demonstrates how, with proper discipline, one can profit while still losing on a majority of small trades.

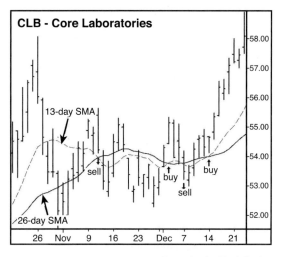

Created using TradeStation

FIGURE 14.3 Moving average crossovers causing whipsaws in a flat trend (CLB daily: October 19, 2009–December 23, 2009)

WHAT OTHER TYPES OF MOVING AVERAGES ARE USED?

Although we have discussed various lengths of moving averages, up to this point our discussion has centered on the most basic type of moving average calculation—the SMA. Remember that each day's calculation of the SMA represents adding the most recent day's price figure and dropping the earliest day's price figure. When calculating the simple moving average, equal weight is given to each daily observation. For a ten-day SMA, the information contained in the stock price for each of the ten days is given equal importance. However, in certain situations, the most recent stock price may have more bearing on the future direction of the stock than the ten-day old stock price does. If observations that are more recent contain more relevant information than earlier observations, we want to weight data in favor of the most recent observation. By calculating a weighted moving average, the most recent day's information is weighted more heavily. This weighting scheme gives the most recent observation more importance in the moving average calculation.

The Linearly Weighted Moving Average (LWMA)

Let us refer back to the example in Table 14.1 to calculate a linearly weighted moving average. A ten-day linearly weighted moving average multiplies the tenth day observation by 10, the ninth day by 9, the eighth day by 8, and so forth. The total of these numbers are added up and divided by the sum of all the multipliers. In this case, the total will be divided by the sum $10 + 9 + 8 + 7 + 6 + 5 + 4 + 3 + 2 + 1$, or 55. In Table 14.1, we find that the linearly weighted moving average for the first ten trading days is 138.56.

When using this ten-day moving average weighting scheme, the most recent trading data (Day 10) is given twice the importance of the price five days earlier (Day 5) and ten times the importance of the price ten days earlier (Day 1). As we go on to calculate the ten-day linearly weighted moving average for Day 11, the prices for trading Days 2–10 again will be weighted. Therefore, just as with the simple moving average, as the moving average is calculated for each successive day, the earliest trading day information is dropped from the data set being used in the calculation.

The Exponentially Smoothed Moving Average (EMA)

For some analysts, dropping off the earliest trading day's data that occurs with an SMA or linearly weighted moving average is problematic. If the most recent price reflects little change, but the earliest price, now being omitted, shows considerable change, the moving average can be unduly influenced by the discarding of the older data. A large change in the moving average that results from the deletion of early data potentially generates a false signal. This is called the "drop-off effect" (Kaufman, 1998) and is probably the most criticized aspect of a simple moving average.

Although it is easy to see how this very early data is not necessarily as important in determining future price movement as the most recent prices, it is still information that may have value. With both the simple moving average and the linearly weighted moving average, this older information, which lies outside of the length of the moving average, is being totally ignored. To address this issue and maintain this older information in the moving average calculation, analysts use the **exponential moving average.**

To see how the exponential moving average is calculated, let us again refer to the example in Table 14.1. The simple ten-day moving average on Day 10 was 140.16. The closing price on Day 11 was 130.52, a lower value than the mean value for the previous ten days. To calculate the exponential moving average, we will use both the ten-day moving average (which represents the mean exchange rate for Days 1–10) and the closing price for Day 11. Thus, we are now using 11 days of price information. If we were going to calculate an SMA using these 11 days of information, each day's exchange rate would have a weight of 1/11, or 9.09% in the calculation. Remember, however, that we want to place a larger weight on information that is more recent. If we want the exchange rate information from Day 11 to have a weight twice as great as it would have in a simple moving average, it would have a weight of 2/11, or 18.18%. Of course, the total of all the weights in the calculation of the exponential moving average must sum to 100%. This leaves 100% minus 18.18%, or 81.82% weight to be placed on the ten-day moving average.

The general formula for determining the weight of the current day's data in the exponential moving average calculation is as follows:

$$\text{WEIGHT}_{\text{current}} = 2 \div (\text{number of days in moving average} + 1)$$

In our example, the calculation gives us $\text{WEIGHT}_{\text{current}} = 2 \div (10 + 1) = 18.18$ percent. If we were using a longer moving average, this weight would decrease in value. For a 19-day EMA, the calculation would be $2 \div (19 + 1)$ or 10%; a 39-day EMA would have a weight of $2 \div (39 + 1)$, or 5%.

The general formula for determining the weight given to the moving average in the calculation of the exponential moving average is the following:

$$\text{WEIGHT}_{\text{ma}} = 100\% - \text{WEIGHT}_{\text{current}}$$

In our example, we have $\text{WEIGHT}_{\text{ma}} = 100\% - 18.18\% = 81.82\%$.

Once we have the weights, the formula for calculating the exponential moving average is as follows:

$$\text{EMA}_{\text{day i}} = \text{WEIGHT}_{\text{current}} \times \text{DATA}_{\text{day i}} + \text{WEIGHT}_{\text{ma}} \times \text{Moving Average}_{\text{day i}-1}$$

The exponential moving average for Day 11 in our example in Table 14.1 is calculated as the following:

$$\text{EMA}_{11} = .1818 \times 130.52 + .8182 \times 140.16 = 138.41$$

To calculate the exponential moving average for Day 12, we need only two pieces of information—the exponential moving average for Day 11 and the closing price for Day 12. The EMA_{12} would be calculated as follows:

$$\text{EMA}_{12} = .1818 \times 131.61 + .8182 \times 138.41 = 137.17$$

Figure 14.4 shows both a 26-day SMA and a 26-day EMA for CLB. Generally, the EMA will change direction more quickly because of the additional weighting that is placed on the most recent data. However, these two curves will usually track each other closely.

The EMA is used in a number of indicators and oscillators. In Chapter 8, "Measuring Market Strength," for example, we looked at the McClellan Index. The McClellan Index uses a 19-day and a 39-day EMA. Because the 19-bar EMA has a smoothing factor of 0.10 and the 39-bar EMA has a smoothing factor of 0.05, these calculations are relatively easy. We will see later that a number of oscillators use an EMA, most prominently the MACD. The reason for the use of an EMA is that it is easily calculated and that it weighs more strongly the prices that are more recent. It is, thus, called a **weighted moving average.**

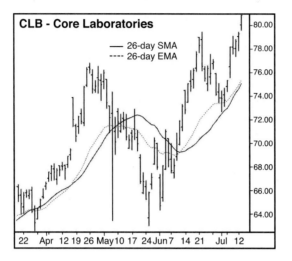

FIGURE 14.4   Exponential versus simple moving average (CLB daily: March 17, 2010–July 13, 2010)

Wilder Method

Welles Wilder (1978) used another very simple method to calculate a moving average that weights the most recent number more heavily. The formula for calculating Wilder's moving average is as follows:

$$MA_{day\ i} = ((n-1) \times MA_{i-1} + Price_{dayi}) \div n$$

For example, a 14-day Wilder moving average would be equal to the previous day's moving average figure times 13 (i.e., n – 1, where *n* is the number of items to be averaged) plus the current closing price, all divided by 14 (i.e., *n*).

Wilder's method of calculating a moving average should be used in the Average True Range (ATR), Relative Strength Index (RSI), and the Directional Movement Indicator (DMI) calculations that he invented rather than the SMA or EMA. When using Wilder's indicators that are prepackaged in available trading and charting software, one must be sure that the calculations for moving averages are Wilder's. Some software programs use just an SMA or EMA and give results inconsistent with Wilder's methods.

Geometric Moving Average (GMA)

The geometric moving average is used mostly in indexes. It is a simple moving average of the percent changes between the previous bar and the current bar over some past predetermined period. Using percentages rather than points does not change its range or dimensions like a price-based moving average. However, it still has all the other problems of equal weight and lag.

Triangular Moving Average

Taking a moving average of a moving average gives a doubly smoothed moving average. The triangular moving average begins with a simple moving average of a predetermined number of bars and then, using those results, takes a moving average of a length of half the original number of bars. An example would be a 20-day SMA of daily closes smoothed in a ten-day SMA. The result is a smoothed line that emphasizes the weight of the middle of the price series. The benefit of this method is that it doubly smoothes the data and, thus, better represents the trend. However, the double smoothing also detracts from its sensitivity to trend changes.

Variable EMAs

The use of a variable moving average is suggested by Chande and Kroll (1994). This moving average is the same as an exponential average (EMA), but the weighting scheme is adjusted based on the volatility of the price data. This is done to make the EMA shorter during trading ranges when volatility is narrow and expand the EMA when price begins to trend. The desire was to reduce the number of adverse signals during a trading range.

There are a number of variations of this theme. For example, the Kaufman Adaptive Moving Average (KAMA) involves an extremely complicated formula that adjusts an EMA for volatility and trend (Kaufman, 1998). The Volume-Adjusted Moving Average (Arms, 1989) is a somewhat complicated moving average, but its essence is that it emphasizes those bars with higher volume. In the September 2001 issue of *Stocks and Commodities Magazine,* John Ehlers presents MAMA and FAMA. MAMA, the MESA Adaptive Moving Average, and FAMA, the Following Adaptive Moving Average, are EMAs that adapt to volatility using Hilbert's Transform based on the phase change of a cycle in the data. Needless to say, the calculation of these moving averages is complicated. A buy or sell signal is generated when the MAMA crosses the FAMA. In April 2004, *Active Trader Magazine* compared the effectiveness of using the MAMA-FAMA strategy to using an SMA for 18 stocks and found that the MAMA-FAMA strategy performed only slightly better than the simple method.

STRATEGIES FOR USING MOVING AVERAGES

We have looked at a number of ways to calculate moving averages. While each of these methods has its advantages and disadvantages, our main concern is not how to calculate a moving average but how to use moving averages to make money. Moving averages are widely used in the practice of technical analysis. They are a basic tool with a broad set of uses. Technical analysts use moving averages to determine trend, to determine levels of support and resistance, to spot price extremes, and for specific trading signals.

Determining Trend

Technical analysts use moving averages in four basic ways. First, moving averages are used as a measure of trend. The most common usage is comparing the current price with the moving average that represents the investor's time horizon. For example, many investors use a 200-day moving average. If the stock or market average is above its 200-day moving average, the trend is considered upward. Conversely, if the stock or market average is below the 200-day moving average, the trend is considered downward.

Figure 14.5 includes the same data with the moving average and the trend lines we used in Chapter 12, "Trends—The Basics." You can see how the moving average tends to follow the trend line fairly well. The moving average then becomes a proxy for the trend line and can be used to determine when a trend is potentially changing direction, just as can a trend line. In the chart, for example, the later prices have held at both the trend line and the moving average.

Created using TradeStation

FIGURE 14.5   Trend line versus simple moving average (CLB daily: May 10, 2010–July 13, 2010)

Determining Support and Resistance

Second, the moving average often acts as support or resistance. As we have seen from Figure 14.5, a moving average often duplicates the trend line; therefore, it can be an easy trailing stop mechanism for determining when a position should be liquidated or reduced. In addition, prices seem to halt at the vicinity of moving averages. In Figure 14.5, for example, CLB halted its rally in mid-May at the moving average and again halted its decline at the moving average in early July.

Determining Price Extremes

Third, the moving average is an indicator of price extreme. Because the moving average is a mean, any reversion to the mean will tend to approach the moving average. For trading purposes, this reversion is sometimes profitable when the current price has deviated substantially from that mean or moving average. Price has a tendency to return to the mean. Thus, a deviation from the moving average is a measure of how much prices have risen or fallen ahead of their usual central tendency, and being likely to return to that mean, this deviation then becomes an opportunity to trade against the trend. As always, trading against the trend is dangerous and requires close stops, but the reversion also provides an opportunity to position with the trend when it occurs. In addition, when prices continue substantially away from the trend, they are often signaling that the trend is changing direction. An example is shown in Figure 14.6. This is a stock with a strong longer-term upward trend, the dominant trend. The 26-day moving average measures the minor trends within the dominant trend. When the price deviates from the 26-day SMA, it always eventually returns to that moving average. Thus, by measuring when the price is sufficiently distant from the moving average, a trade can be initiated knowing that the price will return to that mean. In the example, the minor trend turned downward in May from an overbought extreme. Because the longer trend is upward, to have shorted at that overbought extreme would have been dangerous. However, in late May, an excellent opportunity to buy in line with the longer trend occurred when the price deviated below the extreme oversold. When these opportunities are in sync with the longer trend, they provide minimum risk and excellent profit potential.

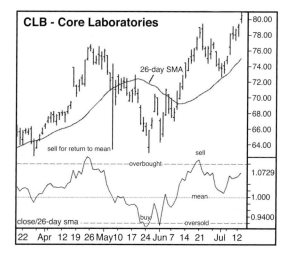

Created using TradeStation

FIGURE 14.6   Ratio of current price to moving average (CLB daily: March 18, 2010–July 13, 2010)

Giving Specific Signals

Fourth, some technical analysts use moving averages to give specific signals. These can occur when prices cross a moving average, when a shorter moving average crosses a longer moving average, and in some cases, when a third, even shorter, moving average crosses two longer ones. Generally, using two moving averages and their crossover as a signal has been successful but with substantial drawdowns in capital in sideways markets because of the many unprofitable small trades that occur from the many false signals. Methods, such as using the ADX, described in the next section, have been developed to determine if prices are trending at a rate at which a moving-average crossover system will work. The MAMA-FAMA system described previously and other methods of adapting moving averages to changes in volatility are aimed at solving this drawdown problem. However, it will not go away, and thus, though the crossover methods are profitable over time, the investor must have patience and enough capital to withstand a series of small losses until a trend develops.

Of the four strategies, the most sensible use of moving averages is trend determination. The trend is where the technical analyst profits. If the moving average can help in determining the trend, it is a useful tool. Indeed, it is only during a trending market that moving average signals are profitable. A sideways market is costly in almost all cases, but especially so if the investor depends on moving average crossovers for signals. Once a trend has been established and identified, the next best method is to use price patterns and breakouts in the direction of the trend for timing of position entries. This method will lag behind the major bottom and top of a price trend but will accrue profits and minimize losses. It is also the most popular method in professional trading systems, along with channel breakout systems such as Donchian's four-week rule that we discuss in the "Channel" section of this chapter.

WHAT IS DIRECTIONAL MOVEMENT?

One of the great contributions to the concept of trend and direction is the concept of directional movement that Welles Wilder (1978) developed in his book, *New Concepts in Technical Trading Systems.* Wilder compared a stock's trading range for one day with the trading range on the previous day to measure trend. Positive directional movement occurred when the high for a day exceeded the high of the previous day. As shown in Figure 14.7, the amount of positive directional movement (+DM) is the day's high minus the previous day's high, or the vertical distance between the top of the two bars. If the low for the day is less than the previous day's low, negative directional movement occurs. The value of the negative directional movement (–DM) is the difference between the two lows.

Days on which the range is completely within the previous day's range are ignored, and a zero is given to the range excess. In addition, one day's trading range is sometimes much larger than the previous day's trading range. This can result in both a higher high and a lower low. When this happens, the greater difference wins. In other words, only a +DM or –DM may be recorded for a particular day.

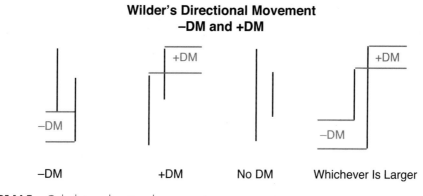

FIGURE 14.7 Calculating directional movement

Constructing Directional Movement Indicators

A moving average is calculated for both +DM and –DM, usually over 14 days, using the Wilder method of averaging. In addition, a 14-day average trading range (ATR) is calculated. Two indicators are calculated using this data. The Positive Directional Movement Indicator (DMI+) is the ratio between the smoothed +DM and the TR; this calculation gives the percentage of the true range that was above equilibrium for those 14 days. The second indicator is the negative Directional Movement Indicator (DMI–), which is calculated as the ratio between the smoothed –DM and the ATR.

Using Directional Movement Indicators

Figure 14.8 shows 14-day DMIs for Core Laboratories (CLB). Looking at this chart, an analyst sees a number of hints about trend. First, when one DMI is higher than the other, the trend is in the direction of that DMI. For example, from April through May, the DMI+ was above the DMI–, indicating that a majority of the 14-day ATR excess for CLB was on the upside during that period. When the first major crossover occurred in early May, and the DMI– crossed above the DMI+, the trend had reversed downward. At that point, a longer-term trend line would not have yet caught the switch in direction. At the point marked "1" on the chart, a downward crossover signal occurred that warned of the upcoming severe price decline. Thus, the DMI crossover is an important signal in analyzing trends.

Second, the minor crossover that occurred in March (marked with an "mc") that lasted only a day is also an important sign. It suggests that the direction of the trend is now sideways and, like a congestion area, it may break in either direction. Often, the two DMIs come to equilibrium and then part in their original direction, as happened here, in which case the earlier trend resumes. At other times, the DMIs cross more dramatically and incisively, as they did in early May, and signal a trend reversal. When the two meet, therefore, is an important period. Wilder suggested placing a buy or sell stop at the price when the two first cross. In Figure 14.8, as the two DMIs cross in March, we do not know if this is a trend reversal or not. Thus, we place a short-sell stop at a price just below the price that occurred when the two initially crossed. If the trend is reversing, the price will hit our stop, and our position will be in line with the new downward trend. If the stop is not hit, the two lines will likely diverge again, and the old trend will continue without us.

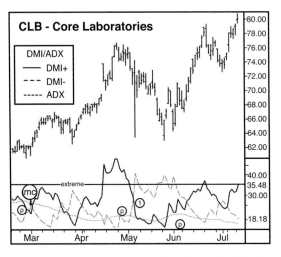

Created using TradeStation

FIGURE 14.8   Directional Movement Indicators (CLB daily: February 2010–July 2010)

Third, a DMI reaching an extreme level is often associated with a trend being at its maximum slope. When this occurs, the trend will invariably slow down and perhaps reverse. This is the best time to exit a position. In Figure 14.8, for example, peaks in the two DMIs seem to occur around 35. These levels are different for every stock or commodity and should be analyzed first. When the DMI+ rose above 35 in late April, it signaled an extreme and the best time to sell a long position. When the DMI– rose above 35 in late May, it was an extreme and the best time to cover a short.

Fourth, the DMIs can be used to create a Directional Index (DX). This DX then is used to create the average DX called the **ADX line** shown in Figure 14.8. The DX is calculated by taking the absolute difference between the values of the two DMIs and dividing it by the sum of the two DMIs. The DX is always positive and represents the tendency of the market to trend because it measures the DMIs against each other. When one DMI is very large compared with the other DMI, the market is moving strongly in one direction and the value of the DX will be large.

The ADX is the smoothed value of the DX and is plotted on Figure 14.8. When the ADX is rising, the market is increasingly trending in either direction.

The ADX indicator is valuable in determining when to apply a moving average trend-following system, for example. We know that the moving average systems have multiple whipsaws when the market is not in a directional trend but have very profitable outcomes when the market is trending in either an upward or downward direction. Many trend-following models use both of these indicators to determine when money should be committed to the markets.

Fifth, when the ADX peaks above both the DMIs, it often signals a peak in the trend. In Figure 14.8, even though the ADX never rises and peaks above both the DMIs, peaks (marked with a P) do show periods when the trend has ended, such as in February, late April, and early July.

Low levels in the ADX are also useful because they signify periods when the market has become dormant and trendless. As we know from looking at congestion areas, a dormant period is usually followed by a dynamic period. This phenomenon can be seen in Figure 14.8 with the low ADX value associated with the sideways price movement at mid May, followed by a strong upward price trend. Thus, a low ADX period is when the trader or investor should be watching price closely for a breakout in either direction. ADXs and DMIs can be used on weekly, monthly, and even shorter-term, intraday charts for clues as to trend strength and direction.

WHAT ARE ENVELOPES, CHANNELS, AND BANDS?

The simple moving average represents the center of a stock's price trend. Actual prices tend to oscillate around that moving average. The price movement is centered on the moving average but falls within a band or envelope around the moving average. By determining the band within which prices tend to oscillate, the analyst is better able to determine the range in which price may be expected to fluctuate.

Percentage Envelopes

One way of creating this type of band is to use **percentage envelopes.** This method, also known as a percentage filter, was developed in an attempt to reduce the numerous unprofitable signals from crossing a moving average when the trend is sideways. This is a popular method used in most of the academic studies on moving average crossover systems. It is calculated by taking a percentage of the moving average and plotting it above and below the moving average (see Figure 14.9)—thus the term "envelope." This plot creates two symmetrical lines, one above and one below the moving average.

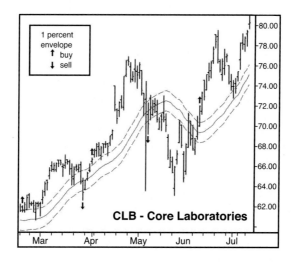

Created using TradeStation

FIGURE 14.9   Percentage envelope about a moving average (CLB daily: February 16, 2010–July 13, 2010)

This envelope then becomes the trigger for signals when it is crossed by the price rather than when the moving average is crossed. The percentage used in the calculation should be large enough that it encompasses most of the oscillations around the moving average during a sideways period and, thus, reduces the number of incorrect signals, yet small enough to give signals early enough to be profitable once a trend has been established. This percentage must be determined through experiment because a slight difference in percentage can cause a considerable difference in performance.

One of the major problems with fixed-percentage envelopes is that they do not account for the changing volatility of the underlying price. During a sideways trend, when volatility usually declines, price action can be contained within a relatively narrow band. When the trend begins, however, volatility often expands and will then create false signals using a fixed-percentage envelope. To combat this problem, the concept of bands that are adjusted for volatility developed.

Bands

Bands are also envelopes around a moving average but, rather than being fixed in size, are calculated to adjust for the price volatility around the moving average. They, thus, shrink when prices become calm and expand when prices become volatile. The most widely used band is the Bollinger Band, named after John Bollinger (2002).

Bollinger Band

As we mentioned earlier, there are two principal ways to measure price volatility. One is the standard deviation about a mean or moving average, and the other is the ATR. Bollinger Bands use the standard deviation calculation.

To construct Bollinger Bands, first calculate a simple moving average of prices. Bollinger uses the SMA because most calculations using standard deviation use an SMA. Next, draw bands a certain number of standard deviations above and below the moving average. For example, Bollinger's standard calculation, and the one most often seen in the public chart services, begins with a 20-period simple moving average. Two standard deviations are added to the SMA to plot an upper band. The lower band is constructed by subtracting two standard deviations from the SMA. The bands are self-adjusting, automatically becoming wider during periods of extreme price changes.

Figure 14.10 shows the standard Bollinger Band around the 20-period moving average. Of course, both the length of the moving average and the number of standard deviations can be adjusted. Theoretically, the plus or minus two standard deviations should account for approximately 95% of all the price action about the moving average. In fact, this is not quite true because price action is nonstationary and nonrandom and, thus, does not follow the statistical properties of the standard deviation calculation precisely. However, it is a good estimate of the majority of price action. Indeed, as the chart shows, the price action seems to oscillate between the bands quite regularly. This action is similar to the action in a congestion area or rectangle pattern (see Chapter 15, "Bar Chart Patterns"), except that prices also tend to oscillate within the band as the price trends upward and downward. This is because the moving average is replicating the trend of the prices and adjusting for them while the band is describing their normal upper and lower limits around the trend as price volatility changes.

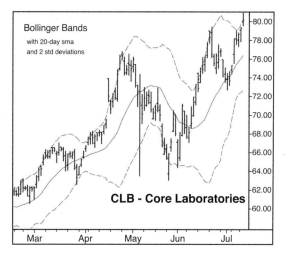

Created using TradeStation

FIGURE 14.10   Bollinger Bands (CLB daily: February 2010–July 2010)

Keltner Band

Chester Keltner (1969) introduced Keltner Bands in his book, *How to Make Money in Commodities.* To construct these bands, first calculate the "Typical Price" (Close + High + Low) ÷ 3, and calculate a ten-day SMA of the typical price. Next, calculate the band size by creating a ten-day SMA of High minus Low or bar range. The upper band is then plotted as the ten-day SMA of the typical price plus the ten-day SMA of bar range. The lower band is plotted as the ten-day SMA to the typical price minus the ten-day SMA of bar range. (When the calculation is rearranged, it is very similar to the use of an ATR, and these bands are sometimes referred to as ATR bands.)

As with most methods, different analysts prefer to modify the basic model to meet their specific needs and investment strategies. Although Keltner's original calculation used ten-day moving averages, many analysts using this method have extended the moving averages to 20 periods. The 20-period calculation is more in line with the calculation for a Bollinger Band.

STARC Band

STARC is an acronym for Stoller Average Range Channel, invented by Manning Stoller. This system uses the ATR over five periods added to and subtracted from a five-period SMA of prices. It produces a band about prices that widens and shrinks with changes in the ATR or the volatility of the price. Just as with the Keltner Bands, the length of the SMA used with STARC can be adjusted to different trading or investing time horizons.

Trading Strategies Using Bands and Envelopes

In line with the basic concept of following the trend, bands and envelopes are used to signal when a trend change has occurred and to reduce the number of whipsaws that occur within a tight trading range. While looking at the envelopes or bands on a chart, one would think that the best use of them might be to trade within them from high extreme to low extreme and back, similar to strategies for rectangle patterns. However, the trading between bands is difficult. First, by definition, except for fixed envelopes, the bands contract during a sideways, dull trend and leave little room for maneuvering at a cost-effective manner and with profitable results. Second, when prices suddenly move on a new trend, they will tend to remain close to the band in the direction of the trend and give many false exit signals. Third, when the bands expand, they show that volatility has increased, usually due to the beginning of a new trend, and any position entered in further anticipation of low volatility is quickly stopped out.

Bands, therefore, have become methods of determining the beginnings of trends and are not generally used for range trading between them. When the outer edge of a band is broken, empirical evidence suggests that the entry should be in the direction of the breakout, not unlike the breakout of a trend line or support or resistance level. A breakout from a band that contains roughly 90% of previous price action suggests that the general trend of the previous price action has changed in the direction of the breakout.

In Figure 14.10, a breakout buy signal occurs in April, when the price breaks above the upper Bollinger Band, hinting that a strong upward trend is starting. You will notice that the bands had become narrower during March. This band tightening, caused by shrinking volatility, is often followed by a sharp price move.

The only difference between a band breakout and a more conventional kind is that a band is generally more fluid. Because moving averages will often become support or resistance levels, the moving average in the Bollinger Band calculation should then become the trailing stop level for any entry that previously occurred from a breakout above or below the band. The ability of moving averages to be used as trailing stops is easily spliced into a system utilizing any kind of bands that adjust for volatility.

The other use for the moving average within a band is that because the moving average often becomes either support or resistance, it can become a retracement level for additional entry in the trend established by the direction of the moving average and the bands. With a stop only slightly below the moving average using the rules we learned in the last chapter for establishing stop levels, when the price retraces back into the area of the moving average while in a strong upward trend, an additional entry can be made where the retracement within the band is expected to halt.

In testing band breakouts, the longer the bar, it seems, the more profitable the system. Very short-term volatility, because it is proportionally more active, causes many false breakouts. Longer-term periods with less volatility per period appear to remain in trends for longer periods and are not whipsawed as much as short-term trends. The most profitable trend-following systems are long-term, and as short-term traders have learned, the ability of price to oscillate sharply is greater than when it is smoothed over longer periods. Thus, the inherent whipsaws in short-term data become reduced over longer periods, and trend-following systems tracking longer trends have fewer unprofitable signals. Bands are more successful in trending markets and are, therefore, more suitable for commodities markets than the stock market.

Another use for bands is to watch price volatility. Low volatility is generally associated with sideways to slightly slanted trends, ones where whipsaws are common and patterns fail. High volatility is generally associated with a strong trend, up or down. By watching volatility, especially for an increase in volatility, the analyst has a clue that a change in trend is forthcoming. To watch volatility, one should take a difference between the high band and low band and plot it as a line below the price action. Bollinger calls this line a **Bandwidth Indicator.** A rise in the bandwidth line, which results from increasing volatility, can be associated directly with price action. Any breakout from a pattern, support or resistance level, trend line, or moving average can be confirmed by the change in volatility. If volatility does not increase with a price breakout, the odds favor that the breakout is false. Volatility, therefore, can be used as confirmation for trend changes, or it can be used as a warning that things are about to change. This use of bands is more successful when combined with other methods of determining an actual trend change.

Channel

In discussing trend lines, we noted that a line can often be drawn parallel to a trend line that encompasses the price action in what was called a **channel.** For present purposes, that definition changes slightly by relaxing the requirement for a parallel line.

Channels have become described as something simpler than two parallel lines. For example, in Chapter 12, we mentioned the Donchian channel method that has been so successful even though it's been widely known for many years. Signals occur with the Donchian channel when the breaking above or below a high or low over some past period occurs (see Figure 14.11). This method does not require the construction of a trend line; the only requirement is a record of the highs and lows over some past period. In the case of the Donchian channel method, the period was four weeks, and the rule was to buy when the price exceeded the highest level over the past four weeks and sell when the price declined below the lowest low over the past four weeks. Such systems are usually "stop and reverse" systems that are always in the market, either long or short. As is likely imagined, the channel systems are more commonly used in the commodities markets where long and short positions are effortless and prices tend to trend much longer.

An adaptation of the standard channel breakout system is to use different periods for buy and sell signals. For example, a 200-day period of highs might be used for a buy signal, and a 20-day period might be used for a sell signal. Generally, this method works well in commodity markets where trending is stronger and longer lasting. It does not work as well in the stock market.

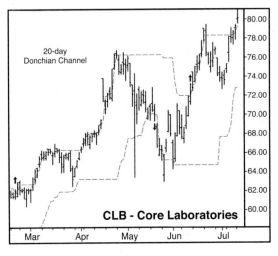

Created using TradeStation

FIGURE 14.11   Donchian Channel on daily closes (CLB daily: February 26, 2010–July 13, 2010)

CONCLUSION

The basic way the technical analyst makes profits is by identifying a trend in prices and riding that trend. At times, daily fluctuations in prices make it difficult for the analyst to view the basic underlying trend in prices. Moving averages are tools used to smooth this erratic data, making it easier to discern the genuine underlying trend.

Although there are various methods of calculating a moving average, the basic idea is to give a summary of the average or normal price history of a particular period. Because the moving averages are based on historical prices, by nature, they will be a lagging indicator of trends. The shorter the period covered by the moving average, the less of a lag there will be. However, using a shorter period also leads to more false signals. As usual, when choosing a moving average system, there is a trade-off between early trend reversal recognition and certainty of trend reversal. The use of envelopes, bands, and channels around the moving average can minimize the number of false signals by providing a larger range of price movement before a signal is triggered.

Box 14.1 gives a list of basic principles that the technical analyst should keep in mind. This list provides a summary of some of the key points we have addressed in the past three chapters.

BOX 14.1   TRADING RULES

In the past few chapters, we have covered a good deal of material regarding trends. Here are some of the key points to remember when investing:

- Riding the trend is the most profitable use of technical analysis.

- Trends can be identified with trend lines, moving averages, and relative highs and lows.

- Always pick a security that trends up and down. Flat or random trends are usually unprofitable.

- Be aware of the next longer period and shorter period trends from the one being traded.

- Always trade with the trend:
  - "Trend is your friend."
  - "Don't buck the trend."

- Breakouts from support or resistance levels, patterns, or bands usually signal a change in trend.

- A trend line breakout is at least a warning.

- The longer the trend, the more important the breakout.

- Confirm any breakout with other evidence, especially when entering a position. In exiting, confirmation is not as important.

- Always use stops, protective and trailing.
  - Do not sell profitable positions too soon; just keep trailing with stops.

REVIEW QUESTIONS

1. Explain why a rising moving average indicates an upward trend and a falling moving average indicates a downward trend in stock prices.

2. Explain why there is a lag between the time a trend reverses and when the moving average signals this reversal. Why is this lag longer for a 200-day moving average than a 10-day moving average?

3. What problems are associated with an SMA that an EMA calculation is designed to overcome?

4. Explain why a shorter-term moving average is considered to be a "faster" moving average and a longer-term moving average is considered to be a "slower" moving average.

5. Sophia says that she is watching a 10-day SMA and a 60-day SMA of her favorite stock, and she is planning to purchase the stock when the 10-day SMA crosses above the 60-day SMA. Explain the rationale for Sophia's strategy.

6. Thomas warns Sophia that her strategy can easily lead to whipsaws. Explain what Thomas means by *whipsaws,* and describe the type of market in which whipsaws are most likely to occur.

7. If Sophia is concerned about whipsaws, how might she use envelopes or bands to minimize the likelihood of whipsaws?

8. Why is choosing a stock that is trending upward or downward, rather than one that is moving sideways, an important key to trading profitability?

9. Explain what Welles Wilder means by the term *directional movement* and how this concept is important to determining price trends.

10. Why does a low value for ADX suggest a period of congestion?

11. Gather the daily high, low, and closing prices for McDonald's stock (ticker symbol MCD) for January 2009 through July 2010 from Yahoo! Finance or another electronic source.

   a. Using a spreadsheet, calculate 10-day and 60-day SMAs. Plot these two curves with a bar chart of the stock prices.

   b. Compare and contrast the 10-day and the 60-day SMA.

   c. Explain the relationship between the market trend and the 60-day SMA during the following periods:

      i. May 2004–October 2004

      ii. October 2004–May 2005

      iii. May 2005–July 2005

   d. Find a point in your graph where the faster moving average crosses the slower moving average. What type of signal would occur at this point? In hindsight, would trading on that signal have been profitable? Why or why not?

   e. Construct DMI+ and DMI– for McDonald's for the period August 2004–March 2005.

      i. Interpret DMI+ during this time.

      ii. Interpret DMI– during this time.

      iii. Compare DMI+ and DMI– with the price movement over this time. What type of relationships do you see?

PART IV

CHART PATTERN ANALYSIS

CHAPTER 15   BAR CHART PATTERNS

CHAPTER 16   POINT-AND-FIGURE CHART PATTERNS

CHAPTER 17   SHORT-TERM PATTERNS

BAR CHART PATTERNS

CHAPTER OBJECTIVES

By the end of this chapter, you should be familiar with

- Controversy over whether patterns exist
- The influence that computer technology has had on the study of patterns
- The formation of classic bar chart patterns such as triangles, flags, pennants, double tops, and head-and-shoulders
- Historical performance measures of major bar chart patterns

In the next three chapters, we discuss chart and price patterns. Traditionally, technical analysis has been closely associated with price patterns, perhaps even more than it should be. Prior to the advent of the computer, hand-drawn charts of prices were the only technical resources available. Trend lines and patterns were the principal means of analyzing price behavior. The computer has diversified technical analysis because it has made other mathematical relationships easier to calculate.

After discussing some of the basic characteristics of patterns, we look at classic bar chart patterns, those used by the majority of technical analysts and having the longest history of use, in this chapter. In Chapter 16, "Point-and-Figure Chart Patterns," we focus on point-and-figure charts. In Chapter 17, "Short-Term Patterns," we consider short-term patterns, candlesticks, one- and two-day patterns, and other patterns that are not so widely used. There are as many different patterns as the combinations of price open, high, low, and close can accommodate. Generally, shorter patterns are more common and less reliable, and longer patterns are more complex and less frequent. In addition, as a rule, the more complicated the pattern, the less likely it will be profitable, and the more frequent a pattern, the less likely it will be profitable. The best patterns seem to be in the middle of frequency and complexity. We address these. There are many reference books on other patterns that you can investigate, but most fail to give any special advantage over the classic patterns.

WHAT IS A PATTERN?

In the literature and usage of technical analysis, the terms **pattern** and **formation** are used inter-changeably. We will do the same. A *pattern* is simply a configuration of price action that is bounded, above and below, by some form of either a line or a curve.

The lines that bind price movement in a pattern can be trend lines or support/resistance lines. In this chapter, we apply the concepts and terminology that we studied in Chapter 12, "Trends—The Basics," regarding these lines. When studying patterns, we add a new concept—prices being bound by a curve instead of a straight line. A *curve* is a less-definite arc drawn with either a "smiley face" for a bottom curve or a "frown" for the top curve. The lowest level in a bottom curve is a support level, and the highest level in a top curve is a resistance level. Curves simply define a support or resistance level with curved rather than straight lines. A pattern can be bounded by any combination of curves or lines as long as the upper and lower bounds are defined well enough for a breakout level to be established.

Common Pattern Characteristics

The focus of this chapter is bar chart price configurations. Thomas N. Bulkowski has accomplished the most comprehensive modern study of bar chart patterns in his twin books, *Encyclopedia of Chart Patterns,* 2nd edition (2005) and *Trading Classic Chart Patterns* (2002). Bulkowski observed over 700 stocks over ten years on a daily basis and cataloged their results under varying conditions. In total, over two market periods he found and analyzed 12,385 chart patterns. Although his analysis of patterns was, of course, subject to his potential bias, it was consistent and included a significantly large number of examples. Much of the material—specifically the statistics—in this chapter rely on Bulkowski's work. Bulkowski has a Web site (www.thepatternsite.com) that explains in significant detail all the patterns we discuss and more. Before we begin discussing some of the particular patterns, however, we need to explain some vocabulary related to the general characteristics of bar chart patterns.

Entry and Exit

All patterns have a combination of an entry and exit. The entry describes the trend preceding the formation, and the exit is usually the signal for action. A pattern can occur after a decline, in which case, the entry is from above, or after an advance, in which case, the entry is from below. The exit, of course, can also be downward or upward. Figure 15.1, a double bottom, shows an entry from above and an upward breakout. On the other hand, a top formation has an entry from below and an exit downward. A consolidation in a larger uptrend has an entry from below and an exit upward. Thus, all patterns are described with these four variables: entry from above, entry from below, downward exit, and upward exit. These variables are important because statistically, in each pattern type, some of these characteristics are more reliable, occur more frequently, or are more profitable than others.

Fractal

The bars in a bar chart can be any period: weekly, daily, minute, and so on. Bar chart patterns are fractal. This means they can occur in any bar chart, regardless of the bar period. A triangle formation, for example, can occur in hourly bars or weekly bars. The pattern is always the same type and will always have the same general characteristics. This is odd but true. Indeed, looking at a bar chart pattern without a specified time horizon, a technical analyst who is experienced in pattern recognition cannot tell the periods of the bars.

Pullbacks and Throwbacks

Pullbacks occur when prices break out downward and then "pull back" to their breakout level. Throwbacks occur when prices break out upward and then "throw back" to their breakout level (Edwards and Magee, revised 2007). Figure 15.1 shows an example of a pullback. Neither a pullback nor a throwback is easily or precisely defined, but you know one when you see it. The interesting aspect of this price behavior is that invariably a pullback or throwback will decrease the extent of the eventual move in the direction of the breakout. Thus, although each may provide a second opportunity for action at the breakout level, the subsequent rise or fall generally will be less than if there were no pullback or throwback. Tactically, this implies that a breakout should be acted upon immediately; waiting for the retracement will diminish profitability, and you may very likely miss the entire price move.

Pullbacks seem to occur more frequently on downward breakouts with less-than-average volume, and throwbacks occur more frequently with upward breakouts on above-average volume. Because pullbacks and throwbacks seem to undermine performance, the ideal situation, as a rule, is that on an upward breakout, less volume is preferred, and on a downward breakout, more volume is preferred.

Failures

All breakouts can fail in any of the formations, some more than others. Remember that a breakout is a signal that prices are beginning to trend, either upward or downward. This is particularly frustrating to the beginner who desires perfection. As we have seen, however, perfection is not in the lexicon of technical analysis. It is favorable odds, or an "edge," for which we are looking. Bulkowski's definition of a failure, which we use, is when a breakout occurs and the price fails to move at least 5% in the direction of the breakout.

DO PATTERNS EXIST?

Some academics and investors believe that patterns do not exist. They believe either that price action is completely random or, at least, is indecipherable. We saw in Chapter 4, "The Technical Analysis Controversy," that the concept of randomness is now being questioned, leaving open the possibility that order does exist in prices. However, even if order does exist in market prices, it is possible that it cannot be recognized with present mathematical models because it is so complex. The methods used in chaos theory, neural networks, and other esoteric mathematical models may prove useful sometime in the future, but not now. Thus, there is still the realistic question of whether patterns do exist in prices. Technical analysts swear they do but in many cases analysts are not mathematically sophisticated enough to demonstrate their validity.

As mentioned in Chapter 11, "History and Construction of Charts," the unpublished article by Hasanhodzic et al. (2010) on a study of online video game players (http://arora.ccs.neu.edu) attempting to distinguish between financial market price statistics in moving chart form from random permutations of the same data with immediate feedback found that these people could "consistently distinguish between the two types of time series"(p. 1). This experiment seemed to give evidence that humans can learn to distinguish patterns and real data from random series whereas computers, so far, cannot.

If prices do have patterns, what causes them? This has been a debate for at least a century and has coalesced into a belief that patterns are the result of human behavior, which, conveniently, is indecipherable. It is, however, why technical analysts are very much interested in the new behavioral finance studies. They hope that the biases and tendencies in human behavior now being measured and gradually understood by behavioral finance students will eventually explain why price patterns seem to exist.

Behavioral Finance and Pattern Recognition

The first fact to acknowledge about chart patterns is that they have not been proven to exist or to be profitable. Although many investors and traders swear by certain formations, their evidence is largely anecdotal. Added to this is the tendency to see patterns in random data.

Humans have a tendency to want patterns in data and other information and to see them when they do not exist. Superstitions are derived from the erroneous and coincidental observations of patterns that do not exist but are created because of the desire to have a pattern. B. F. Skinner, a famous Harvard psychology professor, studied pigeon behavior in a number of stimulus-response situations to see if the pigeons would react to various stimuli and thus "learn" responses. The reward for the correct response was usually food. In one experiment, he decided to give pigeons just food without a stimulus to see what they would do. Invariably, in trying to make sense out of stimulus-response, the pigeons responded in different manners by creating their own stimulus, some bobbing, some developing strange head motions, thus creating their own superstition, when a real stimulus did not exist (Skinner, 1947).

Humans are very similar in their desire to have some kind of stimulus, even if it is a black cat crossing the road, and develop supposedly predictive relationships when none actually exists. This is a special danger in price analysis because the desire to see a pattern can occur when no pattern actually exists.

Humans are also very poor statisticians and tend to put more weight on recent history than what is statistically warranted. An experiment by Kahneman and Tversky (1982) showed that in flipping coins, which have a statistical probability of landing on their heads 50% of the time regardless of what side they landed on earlier, observers began to expect more heads in the future when the sequence of heads turned up more frequently, and they were surprised when that did not occur. Their subconscious brains expected more heads because that was the most recent history of flips, even though the odds had not changed. In the technical analysis of patterns, the analyst must guard against superstition or what is often called "market lore." Frequently these statements contradict other statements or are just plain wrong. An example is that "a descending triangle always breaks downward." You will see how this is not born out by fact when we discuss triangles. Pattern and trend analysis must be based on evidence alone.

Humans also tend to see the future as the past and look backward rather than forward. This bias is very likely the reason that trends in prices exist in the first place and why prices rise or fall until they reach some exhaustion limit rather than adjusting immediately as the EMH would suggest. For this reason, humans have difficulty in recognizing when past signs or patterns are no longer valid. Studies have shown that the human brain releases dopamine (a pleasure sensation chemical and, thus, a reward) when a human takes action that has worked before. Thus, the pleasurable action is desirable and overcomes any cognitive reasoning that might suspect the action is wrong. This problem is especially prevalent and potentially very dangerous in the financial markets where change is constant.

"In a world without change, the best way to find cheese is to return to the location where it was found previously. In a world with change, however, the best way to find cheese is to look somewhere new" Burnham (2005, p. 284), paraphrasing from Johnson (1998). In other words, the chart pattern and trend reader should look for failure rather than believe in the constancy of previous patterns. Schwager (1996) suggests that profitability from failed patterns is often greater than from correct patterns.

COMPUTERS AND PATTERN RECOGNITION

Analysts began recognizing chart patterns in the days when prices were plotted daily by hand. Aside from trend lines, patterns were the beginning of technical analysis, and for this reason, many nontechnicians mistakenly believe that patterns are all that technicians study. Floor traders and market makers still plot intraday charts of prices for their use in trading short periods, but the computer has changed technical analysis considerably. On a computer screen, charts of minute-to-minute, even tick-to-tick prices can now be displayed, and from them, various patterns can be recognized. This has led to impersonal contact with prices, different from the days when each bar was plotted individually and the "feel" for price action was more easily learned. In addition, the time horizon for traders off the floor has become shorter. The ability to see almost instantly a change in price behavior combined with lower commission costs and less slippage, all due to the introduction of computers, has led traders to speculate on shorter-term trends and patterns.

The computer did not make the study of patterns any easier, however. Patterns change and adjust to new markets. Some of the old patterns do not seem to work very well anymore, and others have taken their place. Patterns are also subjectively determined, and in many cases they are perhaps invalid. Tests are being made currently on their validity, a difficult enterprise because patterns are more visually based than mathematically based. They are peculiar to humans in that like recognizing a friend's face out of a collage of faces, a particular chart pattern must be recognized out of a series of patterns in prices. Like quantifying your friend's face, quantifying a chart pattern is not easily accomplished. Only through practice, many mistakes, and many correct interpretations that go wrong is the technical analyst consistently able to recognize patterns. This is how the art of technical analysis developed before the computer, and although the computer is now taking over both in plotting and in analyzing, the chart patterns still exist and are used by many practitioners. Recent authors of books on technical chart methods will attest to the longevity of certain patterns and their fractal nature. The analysis of price patterns remains, though less emphasis is placed on it.

The analyst using a computer is able to compute more quickly various ratios, averages, spreads, and so on. Computer usage also has the advantage of giving the technician the ability to test these new calculations as well as the old ones for accuracy and statistical significance. The old-time technical analyst had to rely on many years of experience to determine the reliability of formations and indicators and often, for example, stayed up late at night with a hand-crank adding machine calculating indicators and oscillators. As we know from studies of behavior, anecdotal experience can be deceiving, but with the advent of the computer, we can now objectively study many oscillators, averages, and other methods that before were impractical to study. The computer has "cleaned" up a lot of the folklore about patterns and trends and eliminated those that have little or no validity. It has made technical analysis more of a science than an art. Remarkably, though understandable from the previous discussion of human behavior, many of these old inaccurate methods are still used.

MARKET STRUCTURE AND PATTERN RECOGNITION

The markets, of course, have also changed since the beginning of technical analysis and the first recognition of patterns, and with this change, patterns have changed and become less accurate. First, the proliferation of technical knowledge has led to the recognition of specific patterns when they occur. Of course, once a pattern is widely recognized and acted upon, its effectiveness diminishes. Thus, patterns in widely traded securities tend to be less accurate than in those quiet trading securities that very few traders watch.

In the stock market, ownership has become concentrated in relatively few hands that tend to act in concert. These "hands" are the institutional holders of securities. They tend to act together when news is announced; thus, by their large positions and anxiousness to get in or get out, they cause patterns to self-destruct. Although it is difficult to prove, when a large institution is the dominant owner of a stock and has knowledge of technical principles, there is a temptation to "manipulate" a chart formation and cause false breakouts. This can cause havoc with the short-term trader who is watching the same patterns develop.

Finally, the advent of derivatives in large quantities has influenced the price and volume action in individual securities for reasons other than the prospects for the underlying company. Addition or deletion from a market index or basket can suddenly introduce buying or selling unrelated to the pattern developing.

BOX 15.1 FOR FURTHER READING

There are many good reference books devoted to the study of patterns in market prices. Some of these are listed here.

Bar Chart Patterns:
   Encyclopedia of Chart Patterns by Thomas N. Bulkowski
   How Charts Can Help You in the Stock Market by William Jiler
   How Technical Analysis Works by Bruce Kamich
   Profits in the Stock Market by H. M. Gartley
   Technical Analysis by Jack Schwager
   Technical Analysis Explained by Martin Pring
   Technical Analysis of Stock Trends by Robert Edwards and John Magee
   Technical Analysis of the Financial Markets by John Murphy

Point-and-Figure Patterns:
   Point and Figure Charting by Thomas J. Dorsey
   Study Helps in Point & Figure Technique by Alexander Wheelan
   The Chartcraft Method of Point and Figure Trading by Abe Cohen, Earl Blumen-
   thal, and Michael Burke
   The Definitive Guide to Point and Figure by Jeremy du Plessis

Trading—Short-Term Patterns:
   Connors on Advanced Trading Strategies by Laurence Connors
   Dave Landry's 10 Best Swing Trading Patterns and Strategies by David Landry
   Encyclopedia of Candlestick Charts by Thomas N. Bulkowski
   Japanese Candlestick Charting Techniques by Steve Nison
   Long-Term Secrets to Short-Term Trading by Larry Williams
   Market Wizards by Jack Schwager
   New Concepts in Technical Trading Systems by J. Welles Wilder, Jr.
   Street Smarts by Laurence Connors and Linda Bradford Rashke
   Trading Systems and Methods by Perry J. Kaufman

BAR CHARTS AND PATTERNS

From Chapter 11, you know how to plot a bar chart. It is the most common chart of price behavior and has been used ever since continuous trading data became available. In Chapter 12, you learned how to determine support and resistance zones and trend lines using bar charts. Bar chart patterns form by combining support and resistance zones and trend lines. In all cases, a pattern finalizes when a breakout occurs from the pattern. In some instances, a pattern will just dribble into inactivity, in which case it should be ignored, but most patterns result in a legitimate breakout in one direction or the other. The breakout may be false, of course, and we look at how to handle that occurrence. We have observed the peculiarities of drawing trend lines and establishing support and resistance zones in previous chapters, and from the previous discussion, the difficulties in recognizing patterns from imperfect data. Patterns are, thus, never exactly the same from example to example and are fit into generic categories with common characteristics based principally on the direction of internal trends and their intersections.

Traditionally, we divide patterns into two categories: continuation and reversal. This is a holdover from Schabacker (1930), and used by Edwards and Magee (revised, 2007), who needed to break patterns into easily understood and recognizable divisions. Unfortunately, as Edwards and Magee recognized, patterns cannot always easily be relegated to a specific reversal or continuation category, and such a description can often be misleading. Instead, patterns can occur in both modes. For this reason, we prefer to abandon the standard method of differentiating patterns into "continuation" and "reversal," and although we still use the terms when appropriate, we instead describe the simplest patterns first and progress to the more complex.

HOW PROFITABLE ARE PATTERNS?

Studies of chart performance and reliability are scarce. The problem, of course, is the difficulty in defining a chart pattern on a computer. In 1970, one of the authors of this book and Robert Levy (1971) devised a method to identify patterns by recording the sequence of reversal points relative to their immediate past reversal points. This sounds complex, perhaps, but using only five reversal points, almost all simple chart patterns can be identified and their results recorded. Arthur Merrill (1997) took this study method and with some variation tested it on the Dow Jones Industrial Average. In both studies, the results showed that chart patterns as defined had little predictive ability. Several patterns showed some statistical reliability, but not enough to prove the case for technical price patterns in general.

In a 1988 study by Lo and MacKinlay, more sophisticated statistical methods were used to see if patterns existed in individual prices. The study had mixed results. Although it did not negate the possibility of patterns, neither did it prove that patterns existed.

The most comprehensive study to date is that of Bulkowski (2005). Many of the statistics mentioned in each pattern section later in the chapter are taken from his more recent work on trading classic patterns (2002). The intriguing nature of Bulkowski's studies is that many of the old observations seen in the classic literature are turning out to be questionable, especially for maximum performance. As examples, volume trend within a pattern, slope of trends, and breakout volume may not be as relevant as others had originally thought.

Remember also that Bulkowski's observations are in retrospect. We can easily identify many chart patterns after they have occurred, and when we have observed the results. The real talent comes in identifying a chart pattern while it is evolving in real time and profiting from its completion. For this ability, only study, practice, and experience will suffice.

Finally, the results from Bulkowski's observations are relative only. They cannot be assumed to be profitable in the future, as they appeared to be during the trial period. The value of his study is not in determining the value of chart pattern analysis itself but in determining which of the classic patterns are more profitable with less risk. From Bulkowski's studies, it appears that pattern analysis outperforms the market (S&P 500) on average in every instance. This might or might not be true, but for our purposes, we are more interested in which patterns to study as being the most likely to profit over others.

BOX 15.2   USING BREAKOUT PRICE TO SET PRICE TARGETS

Bar charts can project price targets once a formation completes with the breakout. Most targets are measured from the breakout price. Targets are infrequently used because most technicians are satisfied with just being on the right side of the trend, want only to ride that trend, and believe that targets are generally inaccurate. In many patterns, however, this is not so. Generally, the target is calculated by taking the height of the pattern and adding it to the breakout price. In each of the following trading boxes, we describe the target peculiarities for each pattern and the success percentages.

CLASSIC BAR CHART PATTERNS

We begin by looking at classic chart patterns. These patterns generally have been recognized and used for over a hundred years. Only recently have there been tests of their reliability and profitability.

Double Top and Double Bottom

A double formation is about the simplest of the classic formations. A double top consists of only three reversal points: two peaks separated by a trough (see Figure 15.1). For it to be a true double top, the initial price must enter the pattern from below the trough price, and the exit signal must occur on the breakout below the trough low price. The two peaks must be at or within 5% of each other's price level, and the middle valley should be around 10% from the highest peak. The double top, thus, resembles the rectangle formation (described next) with less detail. The pattern forms over 2 to 7 weeks: the longer, the less reliable. The best-performing tops are with rounded peaks. These are called "Eve and Eve" double top patterns. The double bottom is the mirror image of the double top.

Newspaper and media commentators who want to sound like technical analysts frequently use the term *double* formation often when it is not a true double pattern. A true formation is only valid when the intervening reaction reversal point has been penetrated. The danger of acting prematurely is great; roughly 64% of these patterns fail to penetrate the breakout level and instead continue on their original trend. When the pattern is completed with a breakout, however, it is very accurate.

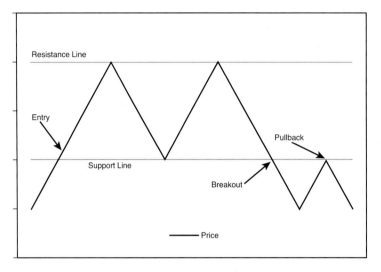

FIGURE 15.1 Double top with breakout down

The failure rates are 11%. This means that the odds of making a profit from a double top downward breakout are minimally risky. Bulkowski ranks the overall performance rank at 2 out of 21, a very high ranking. This ranking is a composition of the pattern's failure rate, average profit, pullback/throwback rate, and percent of trades reaching a price target.

BOX 15.3 TRADING DOUBLE FORMATIONS

If one observes a double pattern, several important observations must be made before acting to improve the chances of profit. First, never buy until the breakout has occurred. Second, look for flat bases either at the same level as the twin bottoms or slightly higher and earlier. Third, look for an absence of a consolidation area above the formation. Fourth, look for what is called an "Eve & Eve" variety. Volume doesn't seem to be important, though it is usually higher on the first "hump."

Rectangle (Also "Trading Range" or "Box")

In the earlier discussion on trading ranges and sideways trends, we effectively described a rectangle pattern. It is one of the simplest of patterns, consisting of a resistance line above and a support line below (see Figure 15.2). Each resistance or support line must also be a trend line, which means that it must touch roughly the same price reversal at least twice. This added requirement is what separates it from a double top or bottom formation, which only requires that three price reversals occur. Prices are bounded by and oscillate between the two lines, and eventually exit, or break out, in one direction or the other. The pattern can have a slight tilt upward or downward, but the trend lines defining the support and resistance zones are always parallel. It appears similar to a horizontal channel. It often has false or premature breakouts, neither of which is predictive of the eventual breakout direction.

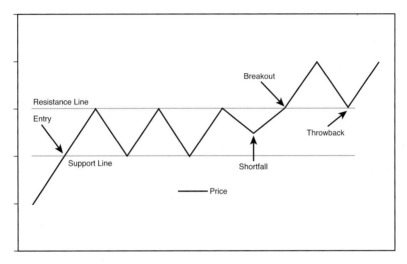

FIGURE 15.2   Rectangle with entry up and breakout up

BOX 15.4   FALSE AND PREMATURE BREAKOUTS

These breakouts are not exits from a formation but instead are minor breakouts above or below breakout levels that quickly return into the formation. They can occur at support and resistance levels as well as at trend lines. A "false" breakout is one that breaks out in the direction opposite from the direction of the final breakout, and a "premature" breakout is one that breaks in the same direction as the eventual exit breakout. In retrospect, these breakouts can have predictive value, but at the time either occurs, it is almost impossible to tell what type it is. When they occur frequently, they warn that a very strict breakout discipline must be used to avoid triggering action before the actual exit breakout.

Within the rectangle formation, prices do not necessarily always reach the two zones but may fall short (a "shortfall" or "partial"). Sometimes this is a warning as to the direction of the eventual breakout. As an example, when well along the way of the formation of a rectangle, prices begin to reverse before declining all the way to the underlying support zone; buyers are getting a little more anxious and the odds increase for a breakout upward. Bulkowski reported that such a shortfall within the latter stages of the pattern is accurate 60% to 90% of the time in predicting the direction of eventual breakout depending on the breakout direction. More than half the time, prices throw back or pull back to the breakout zone, providing another action point but one with less profit potential. Edwards and Magee estimated that about 40% of the time, a pull-back or throwback would occur. When the breakout occurs on a gap, the odds decrease that a retracement will occur.

Volume is often an important factor in any formation. In the rectangle pattern, however, a rising or declining volume trend within the pattern has little or no effect on the results after the breakout, though declining volume is more common. Results increase, however, when volume increases on the breakout itself.

Depending on the rectangle entry and exit (i.e., whether it is a reversal or continuation pattern), the failure to reach 5% was between 9% and 16%. The worst was the declining continuation pattern (entry from above, exit down). Bulkowski ranked the overall performance of rectangles in the middle of the classical pattern pack.

BOX 15.5 TRADING RECTANGLES

Edwards and Magee claimed that rectangles are more often continuation patterns, but as a reversal pattern, they occur more frequently at bottoms. This is likely why Bulkowski mostly found upward breakout rectangle patterns. An upward breakout, however, should never be assumed. Indeed, two out of three rectangles are continuation patterns, and the initial expected direction of the breakout should be in line with the previous trend.

Rectangles have the bad habit of producing false breakouts. Indeed, over 75% of early breakouts are false. This is a large enough figure to hint as to the eventual final breakout direction, but it requires very close breakout and stop discipline. Once the final breakout has occurred, the failure rate is very low. Thus, it pays to be sure that the breakout is real. Another hint is the existence of shortfalls. Shortfalls occur later in the formation and can anticipate the breakout. Use a method similar to that shown in Chapter 13, "Breakouts, Stops, and Retracements," on anticipating breakouts, and keep a close protective stop. The volume trend during the formation of the pattern gives no hint as to the breakout direction and has only a minor effect on performance.

Some traders will trade within a rectangle, buying at the support level and selling at the resistance level. This is not recommended, however, unless the rectangle is particularly wide from top to bottom. Trading has many costs inherent in acting on the buys and sells. The obvious costs are commissions, slippage, and width of the spread. Additionally, when trading within two bounds, the bounds are not exact nor will a trade be executed exactly at the bound. Thus, sell orders must be placed a certain distance, a specified filter, below a resistance zone, and buy orders a certain distance above a support zone. To be able to absorb these costs and price filters, the trader is limited to rectangles that are sufficiently high, from support to resistance. One who attempts this kind of trading must be watching the price action incessantly and be ready to scalp the few points in between the bounds and filters in an instant. Most traders and investors are unable to do this.

A target can be calculated by adding the height of the rectangle formation to the breakout price. According to Bulkowski, in rectangles, the upward target is reached or exceeded 91%–93% of the time, and in downward breakouts, the target is reached or exceeded 65%–77% of the time. The difference in percentages is based on the entry, whether upward or downward, but in all cases, the target is a relatively accurate figure and can be used for risk/reward calculations.

Triple Top and Triple Bottom

The triple top and bottom formation is just a rectangle with the number of touches to the support or resistance line being three. It is, thus, more specific than the rectangle and is less common. Each peak in the top should be at the same level and have roughly the same shape. The middle peak can be slightly lower than the other two. As in the double formations, confirmation only comes with a price breakout below the two bottoms. Throwbacks are common and diminish the breakout performance. Figure 15.3 shows a triple top with a breakout down, and Figure 15.4 shows a triple bottom with a breakout up. As you can see, they are the mirror image of each other. Sometimes in a triple bottom the second peak is slightly higher than the first. This is favorable, and the breakout is the line between the two peaks. The patterns are rare and usually depend on the underlying market trend. They rank in the top third of classic patterns. Their failure rates are very low (10% for bottoms, 4% for tops).

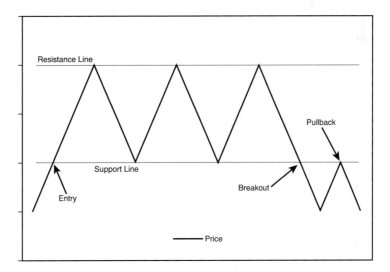

FIGURE 15.3 Triple top with breakout down

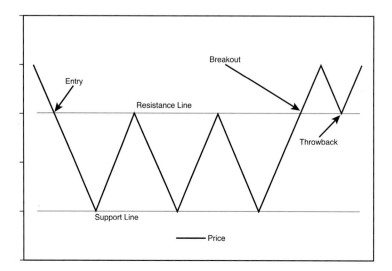

FIGURE 15.4   Triple bottom with breakout up

Standard Triangles

The rectangle pattern is bounded by parallel lines. If the same general pattern has nonparallel boundary lines such that when extended into the future they cross each other, the formation is a *triangle* pattern. Triangles can be the result of an upward-sloping lower bound or a downward-sloping upward bound. Thus, there are a number of possible combinations of the two lines.

In this section, we look only at the standard triangle patterns. In these triangles, the point at which the two lines extend and cross over each other is called the **apex** or the **cradle**, and the distance between the first high reversal point and the first low reversal point within the triangle is called the **base.**

When the lower bound is a horizontal support zone and the upper is a downward slanting trend line, it is called a **descending triangle.** When the lower trend line is rising and the upper bound is a horizontal resistance zone, it is called an **ascending triangle.** When the upper bound is declining and the lower bound is rising, it is called a **symmetrical triangle.** When both the upper bound and lower bound are slanting in the same direction and converging, it is called a **wedge,** and when the two lines are diverging regardless of slope, a reverse triangle, it is called a **broadening pattern.** When we combine a broadening pattern with a triangle, usually a symmetrical triangle, we get what is called a **diamond pattern.**

TABLE 15.1   Statistics on Triangles

	Overall Performance	Failure to reach 5%	Average Performance	Tendency to Retrace	Reaches Target Price
Descending, break up	5/23	7%	47%	37%	84%
Descending, break down	10/21	16%	16%	54%	54%
Ascending, break up	17/23	13%	35%	57%	75%
Ascending, break down	9/21	11%	19%	49%	68%
Symmetrical, break up	16/23	9%	31%	37%	66%
Symmetrical, break down	15/21	13%	17%	59%	48%
Rising Wedge, breakout up	18/23	8%	28%	73%	58%
Rising Wedge, breakout down	20/21	24%	14%	63%	46%
Declining Wedge, breakout up	20/23	11%	32%	56%	70%
Declining Wedge, breakout down	17/21	15%	15%	69%	30%
Broadening Pattern, breakout up	17–19/23	10%–15%	27%–29%	41%–54%	59%–62%
Broadening Pattern, breakout down	17–18/21	16%–18%	15%	42%–48%	37%–44%
Diamond, breakout up	8–21/23	4%–10%	27%–36%	53%–59%	69%–81%
Diamond, breakout down	1–7/21	6%–10%	21%	57%–71%	63%–76%

Source: Bulkowski (2010)

Descending Triangle

Figure 15.5 shows a descending triangle with a breakout down. Its bounds are a lower horizontal support line and a declining upper trend line; price should touch each line at least twice and should generally "fill" the triangle's space. It can be entered from any direction. The breakout is more common to the downside (64%), but the upward breakout is more reliable and profitable (47% average gain). This formation can be stretched high and wide and is sometimes difficult to recognize. The trend lines defining its boundaries are almost never exact and are loaded with false intrabar breakouts. A strict breakout strategy is required, therefore, as we discussed in Chapter 13. However, prices often explode out of it and produce sizable gains. It can also be wild and guarantee an exciting ride. It will break out and run, break out and pull back to its trend line, break out and pull back to its cradle, or break back through the cradle, create a sizable trap, and then reverse back in its original breakout direction and run. In other words, when you enter on a breakout from a descending triangle, the subsequent action must be watched carefully.

Upward breakouts on gaps add considerably to performance and are definitely something to look for. On downward breaks, gaps seem to have little effect.

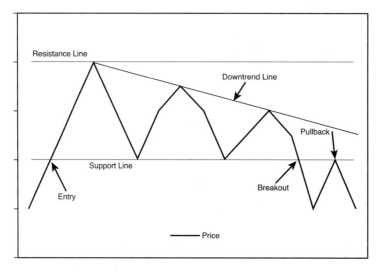

FIGURE 15.5   Descending triangle with breakout down

Figure 15.6 pictures a descending triangle with a breakout up. The typical pattern shows declining volume throughout its formation. However, increasing volume during the formation of an upward breaking descending triangle, though less frequent, is more favorable than declining volume. This contradicts the conventional opinion that advancing volume negates the pattern and represents a reason for screening it out for consideration. In the downward breakouts, declining volume during the pattern formation helps postbreakout performance only slightly. The amount of volume traded on the actual upward breakouts has little effect on the postperformance, but in downward breakouts, an increase on the breakout helps performance slightly.

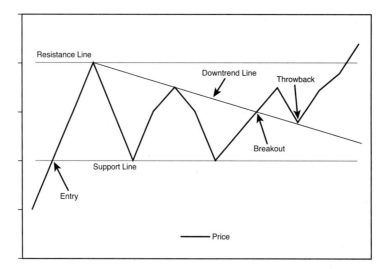

FIGURE 15.6   Descending triangle with breakout up

Ascending Triangle

A horizontal upper bound of resistance combined with an upward sloping lower bound of support defines an ascending triangle (shown in Figure 15.7 with a breakout down). The characteristics in this pattern are just as erratic as in descending triangles—lots of action up and down. Breakout points must be chosen carefully because of the pattern's nature to have many small false breakouts, and declining volume is common but not necessary. Upward breakouts occur 77% of the time, and all breakouts usually happen roughly 61% of the distance (time) from the base to the cradle. The overall performance rank is roughly in the middle of all patterns, a little more favorable for downward breakouts. Failure rates are between 11% and 13% depending on breakout direction. This is about average.

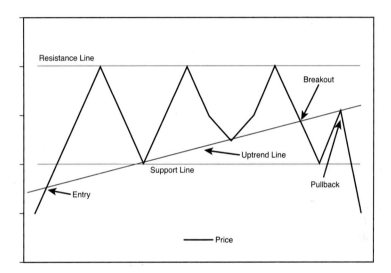

FIGURE 15.7　　Ascending triangle with breakout down

Symmetrical Triangle (Also "Coil" or "Isosceles Triangle")

When the upper bound is downward sloping and the lower bound is upward sloping, a symmetrical triangle is formed (see Figure 15.8). The term **symmetrical** gives the impression that both lines should have the same angle but in different directions. However, that the slope of the two boundaries be formed at congruent angles is not a requirement. Thus, "symmetrical" is not an accurate description but is the term most commonly in use for this pattern. The less-commonly used term **coil** is often a more accurate description.

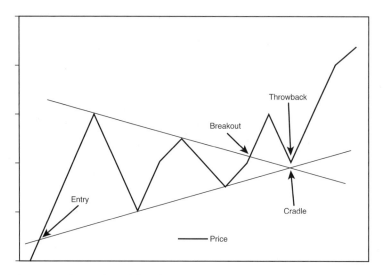

FIGURE 15.8   Symmetrical triangle with breakout up

   Like the other standard triangles, the prices must touch each border trend line at least twice and meanwhile cover the area of the triangle with price action. Volume usually trends downward during the pattern formation (86% of the time), and the breakout is usually upward (54% of the time). Symmetrical triangles have many false breakouts and must be watched carefully. A strict breakout system must be used that allows for such false moves. The breakout commonly occurs between 73% and 75% of the length of the triangle from base to cradle. This formation does not occur as frequently as the descending or ascending triangle, but it is still very common relative to other chart patterns. Throwbacks and pullbacks occur 37% and 59% of the time, respectively, and, as in most patterns, when they occur, they detract from eventual performance. This implies that for actual investment or trading, the initial breakout should be acted upon, and if a pullback or throwback occurs, the protective stop should be tightened. It does not imply that a pullback or throwback should be ignored, but that instead, performance expectations should be less than if no pullback or throwback had occurred. Gap breakouts do not seem to affect the performance on the upside but do give a few extra percentage points on the downside. Increasing volume trend seems to be associated with better results once the breakout occurs. High volume on breakouts, both upward and downward, adds considerably to the performance of the formation and is something to look for. Overall performance is slightly below the mean for classic patterns.

BOX 15.6 TRADING TRIANGLES

The ideal situation for trading triangles is a definite breakout, a high trading range within the triangle, an upward-sloping volume trend during the formation of the triangle, and especially a gap on the breakout. These patterns seem to work better with small-cap stocks in a rising market.

Triangles are plentiful. For example, the upward failure of a head-and-shoulders top before any break through the neckline is a form of an upward breaking descending triangle. This is one likely reason that such head-and-shoulder top pattern failures are so profitable.

Although triangles are plentiful, their patterns suffer from many false and premature breakouts. This requires that a very strict breakout rule be used, either a wide filter or a number of closes outside the breakout zone. It also requires a close protective stop at the breakout level in case the breakout is false. Once these defensive levels have been exceeded, and price is on its way, the trader can relax for a little while because the failure rate after a legitimate breakout is relatively low. Trailing stops should then be placed at each preceding minor reversal.

There are many old rules about when a breakout should occur within a triangle. Some, such as Murphy, say that one-half to two-thirds the distance from the base to the apex is appropriate. Others, such as Edwards and Magee, use the one-half to three-quarters rule. In fact, the breakout can occur at any time once the triangle has been defined by legitimate upper and lower converging trend lines. Edwards and Magee do point out that the longer the distance, the more likely the performance will be less, but this also is not necessarily true. The highest percentage performance does come from breakouts generally around 60%–70% of the distance from the base to the cradle. However, in symmetrical triangles, the best performance comes from late breakouts in the 73%–75% distance. Thus, the old rules are partially correct but not strictly so.

Generally, the volume trend during the formation of a triangle declines, but in the case of an upward breaking descending triangle, an ascending triangle, and a downward breaking symmetrical triangle, an upward-sloping volume trend gives better results. Declining volume is not a reason to disregard the pattern, however. Volume on the breakout seems more desirable in symmetrical triangles, but it cannot hurt in others. Gaps are better predictors of performance in the upward breaking descending triangle and the downward breaking symmetrical triangle, but they are not necessary.

An initial target for these patterns is calculated by adding the base distance—the vertical distance between the initial upper and lower reversal point prices—to the price where the breakout occurred. In an upward breaking descending triangle, for example, this target is reached better than 67% of the time. Other triangles have relatively the same success rate—higher in upward trends than in downward trends. This is why a wide trading range is preferred within the triangle—it suggests a higher target price on the breakout.

Broadening Patterns

A broadening pattern exists when we take the standard rectangle pattern and draw the bound lines diverging from each other into the future rather than converging as in a standard triangle. As pictured in Figure 15.9, the price range is increasing during the broadening pattern, as opposed to the narrowing price range that is associated with the standard triangle patterns. The terms **megaphone, funnel, reverse triangle,** and **inverted triangle** all refer to broadening patterns. The broadening pattern also comes in many variations. One is similar to ascending and descending triangles in that one of the bounds is horizontal. The other bound then slopes away from the horizontal line either above or below. A final variation is the broadening wedge. This pattern is similar to a wedge pattern (see Figure 15.9) only the bounds both trend in the same direction but diverge instead of converge as in a wedge. None of these variations seems to have any above-average performance statistics except the ascending broadening wedge, which has both bounds rising and diverging. Upward breakouts in this pattern rank 6 out of 23 in Bulkowski's scale and have failure rates at 2%, almost negligible.

Broadening formations are the least-useful patterns for a number of reasons. First, they are relatively rare in occurrence and are often difficult to identify. Second, and more important, they are difficult to profit from. Because the boundary trend lines are separating over time, the breakout lines are constantly moving away from each other. In an upward breaking broadening pattern, this means the upper breakout level is getting higher and higher along the upper trend line (see Figure 15.9). By getting higher and higher, not only is it using up much of any potential gain after a breakout, but it is also moving farther from any realistic protective stop level, thus increasing the risk. Finally, the raw performance statistics show that performance of a broadening pattern is average at best, and its failure rate is above average. One of the most profitable patterns utilizing a broadening pattern, however, is when it is combined with a symmetrical triangle into a diamond top, which we discuss next.

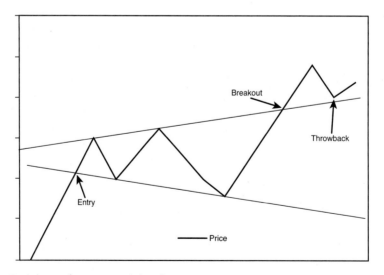

FIGURE 15.9   Broadening formation with breakout up

Diamond Top

One of the less-frequent but very profitable patterns is the diamond (see Figure 15.10). It consists of a combination of a broadening pattern and a symmetrical triangle and usually occurs at the top of a very sharp upward rise in prices. It is rare at price bottoms.

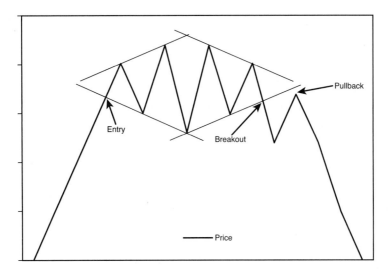

FIGURE 15.10 Diamond pattern with breakout down

Because it combines two types of triangles, the diamond is the most difficult to observe. Remember that to establish a trend line, two extreme points that a line can be drawn between must be identified. In a standard broadening formation, the upper trend line slopes upward and must, therefore, have two peaks—the latter higher than the former. Likewise, the lower trend line must have two troughs—the latter lower than the former—and each line must be formed at the same time as the other. The first reversal point depends on the entry direction, of course, and because diamonds are mostly top formations, the entry direction is generally from below. This means that the first reversal point will be a peak. After that, the first trough will appear, then the next higher peak, and then the next lower trough. When trend lines have been drawn to connect these reversal points, we have a broadening formation. Now we must observe a symmetrical triangle immediately after the broadening formation to establish a diamond pattern. The trend lines in a symmetrical triangle converge, as in all standard triangles, and must also have at least two peaks and troughs to establish each trend line. The first reversal peak and trough may be the last reversal points in the broadening formation or the next reversal points following the broadening formation. Often the trend lines in the symmetrical triangle will be parallel to the trend lines in the broadening pattern, but this is not a requirement.

Bulkowski's figures show that around 58% of the time, the preceding price action in a diamond top was a steeply rising trend. When this occurs, the odds increase that the breakout from the diamond will be downward and will be equally as steep, and 82% of the time, it will retrace the entire prior rise. These figures are only valid for downward breakouts from a top, which occur 67% of the time. Upward breakouts from a diamond top have a very poor performance history and should be avoided. Thus, action should only be taken once the pattern has been identified and the downward breakout has occurred.

Diamond bottoms have the same configuration as diamond tops and are the best patterns that Bulkowski ranks. They are number 1 in performance when they fail and break down (about 31% of the time). Even when they break upward, their ranking is 8 out of 23.

As in most patterns, volume usually declines (67% of the time) during its formation, but declining volume is not necessary. Indeed, rising volume is a plus for performance after the breakout.

Pullbacks are very common in diamond patterns, occurring more than 53% of the time. These pullbacks tend to detract from performance when they occur but are not that significant. The best combination is when downward breakout occurs on below-average breakout volume and no pullback. The failure rate is relatively low at 4%–10%. These low numbers equate, to some extent, with risk. Combined with the above-average median return, these numbers suggest that though rare, when a diamond top is identified, it has an above-average chance of being profitable with minimum risk.

BOX 15.7   TRADING DIAMONDS

The diamond formation, once properly defined, tends to have a fast-moving price run on the breakout. Indeed, if the postbreakout price behavior is sluggish, the position should likely be closed or a close trailing stop placed near the current price. The price objective is usually the distance that the entry price traveled to reach the diamond. A steep entry is usually followed by a steep exit.

Wedge and Climax

A wedge pattern is a triangle pattern with both trend lines heading in the same direction. A rising wedge has both lines headed upward, with the lower bound rising more quickly than the upper bound, as pictured in Figure 15.11. The declining wedge has both lines headed downward, with the upward bound falling more quickly than the lower bound. The lines cross in the future, just as in a standard triangle, and the nomenclature for the crossover and height is the same.

Rather than the rectangle as the basis for this formation as it is with standard triangles, consider a channel (see Chapter 12). A **channel** is two parallel trend lines either rising or declining. In the earlier discussion of channels, we noted that when the channel line, drawn parallel to the trend line through the opposite set of reversal points, begins to slope toward the trend line, it suggests that players are becoming less enthusiastic with the trend line direction. For example, in an upward-sloping channel, the channel line above the trend line connecting the downward reversal points begins as a line parallel to the upward trend line. If a later rally within the channel fails to reach the channel line, the new channel line through the new downward reversal and the last downward reversal will have a lesser slope than the underlying trend line, and if projected into the future, it will eventually meet the trend line. This new configuration of channel and trend line is a **rising wedge.** It suggests, in the example, that sellers have become a little more anxious than before, and by implication, it suggests that the trend line will soon be broken. Indeed, the statistics bear this out. Almost all declining wedges (92%) break out upward, and most rising wedges (69%) break out to the downside (Bulkowski, 2010).

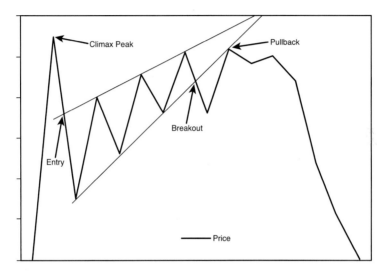

FIGURE 15.11 Rising wedge with breakout down from a climax peak

Wedges are one of a few patterns that can be consolidation patterns against the prevailing trend, consolidation patterns with the trend, or topping patterns, especially when accompanying a climax. They occur more often during consolidations but are more dramatic after a climax.

Let us look at rising wedges first. Rising wedges occur either during a long downward price trend or after an upward climax. The ones that occur during a downtrend appear as very weak rallies against the trend. As mentioned previously, they invariably break again to the downside and continue the downtrend. Declining wedges are almost the same pattern and occur under similar circumstances, only in the opposite direction.

A market climax occurs when prices accelerate, as shown in Chapter 12. At these times, the underlying trend line is gradually adjusted at a steeper slope in line with the direction of prices. In an upward accelerated trend, the support reversal points occur at levels higher than the projected trend line and cause that trend line to be adjusted to a steeper slope. This can occur several times as prices accelerate upward. The climax itself usually comes on extremely high volume and a sharp reversal. It is discussed later in Chapter 17. After a climax has occurred and prices settle down, invariably a "test" occurs that attempts to rally back through climax extreme peak. The pattern most often associated with the failure of that test—in other words, when the test fails to exceed the climax extreme or only exceeds by a small amount—is a rising wedge (refer to Figure 15.11). In the case of a climax low after a panic, the test wedge is the declining variety (see Figure 15.12).

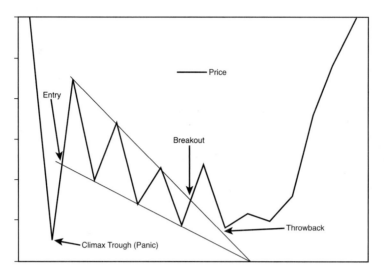

FIGURE 15.12   Declining wedge with breakout up from climax trough

At a climax peak, when the test is a rising wedge pattern, the odds are extremely high that the breakout will be downward. Because the emotion and commitment have been exhausted at the climax peak and are unable to return during the test, the downward break in the wedge pattern is the sign of a longer-term downward reversal. Thus, the wedge is a reversal pattern, even though it may not occur at the actual climax peak high.

Other rising wedges can occur as a consolidation during a sustained downward trend and occasionally will end at the top of a weakening upward trend. The latter we will see as a "fifth wave diagonal" in the discussion of Elliott Waves in Chapter 20, "Elliott, Fibonacci, and Gann."

Because trend lines often converge in the same direction when a wedge is not present, Bulkowski requires that at least five reversal points be touched to qualify the pattern as a wedge. This means three points on one trend line and at least two on the other. Otherwise, the pattern is not accurately identified and may fail to show the results seen in actual wedge patterns.

Another characteristic of wedges, in both the consolidation and reversal varieties, is declining volume during the formation of the wedge. Declining volume occurs in three-quarters of the formations, and when it does, the postperformance improves over those wedges with increasing volume. Breakout volume seems to be irrelevant to postperformance. Pullbacks and throwbacks have high odds of occurring and when present detract from subsequent performance.

The performance rank for wedges is in the lower quartile of all the other classic patterns, and its failure rate is considerably lower for upward breakouts (8%–11%) than for downward breakouts (15%–24%). The rising wedge with a downward breakout is the least reliable.

> ### BOX 15.8 TRADING WEDGES
>
> It pays to wait for that breakout and to act immediately on it. In addition, because wedges have such a high percentage of breakouts in the direction opposite from the wedge direction, the direction of breakout is clear once the wedge is forming. A rising wedge invariably will break downward, and a declining wedge upward. Whenever a climax has occurred, whether up or down, look for a wedge to form on the test. This is one of the most profitable patterns of all. Just be sure that a wedge as described previously is valid before you take any action.

PATTERNS WITH ROUNDED EDGES—ROUNDING AND HEAD-AND-SHOULDERS

The patterns we have considered up to this point have been defined by straight lines. When we begin to define patterns with curved lines, we become more indefinite than with using straight lines such as trend lines. This does not make the patterns any less useful, but it does make them more difficult to describe specifically.

Rounding Top, Rounding Bottom (Also "Saucer," "Bowl," or "Cup")

Rounding tops and bottoms occur are formed by price action that reverses slowly and gradually, rather differently from the spike with very definite and sharp reversal characteristics. Volume in the bottoms seems to follow the same trend of lessening as prices gradually approach the bottom and increasing as they gradually turn upward again. In a rounding top, volume tends to follow the same pattern of lessening as prices decelerate and increasing as prices gradually turn down. Rounding usually takes time, and within its process, it has many minor up and down, very short-term trends. Rounding is, thus, more conceptual than specific.

However, many formations depend on rounding for their description. The most famous is the "cup-and-handle" formation described in detail by O'Neil (1988) but referred to in many earlier publications. This formation, as shown in Figure 15.13, is a variation of the rounding bottom that shows a "lip" after the rise from the bottom, and a small congestion area that reverses downward for a short while called a "handle." The high of the lip establishes, in this type of rounding bottom, the resistance level to watch for an upward breakout. Sometimes the breakout never occurs, and prices keep declining in the handle, continuing to new lows. Traditionally, the cup-and-handle is considered to be a bottoming reversal pattern. However, Bulkowski has found that when it is a continuation pattern from an earlier low, it is much more reliable and profitable. It still only ranks 13 out of 23, despite its popularity.

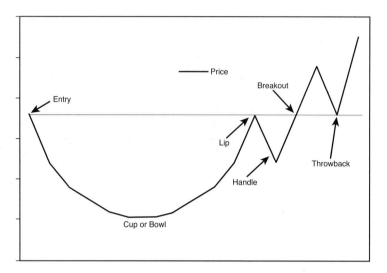

FIGURE 15.13   Cup or bowl and handle variety of a rounding bottom with breakout up

Rounded bottoms are more common than rounded tops, but neither materializes very often. They tend to be longer-term patterns, more easily identified in weekly or even monthly charts. They are reversal patterns but can also appear in very long price consolidations. Shorter-term rounded formations, often called "scallops," are usually continuation patterns and are equally difficult to define. Performance of rounded bottoms rank 5 out 23 in performance and have a low 5% failure rate. Tops have the same performance rank, when breaking downward, but a slightly higher failure rate of 9%–12%. They are difficult to recognize and often require weekly or monthly charts to identify. They are also difficult to trade. First, the breakout level is not easily defined, except in cup-and-handle patterns. Second, they are slow to develop and often fail to breakout.

Head-and-Shoulders

The head-and-shoulders pattern is probably the most famous technical pattern. Its name is often used when ridiculing technical analysis, yet its profitability is very high, relative to other patterns, and it is one of the few that the Lo, Mamaysky, and Wang (2000) study showed had statistical significance.

Head-and-shoulders is a complex pattern because it combines all three potential characteristics of a pattern: trend lines, support or resistance lines, and rounding. It is most often seen at a top or bottom, but it can occur in its normal state or as a failed formation in a consolidation. Mostly, it should be traded only after it has formed completely. Its complexity causes many impatient analysts to anticipate its formation and to act prematurely. Its performance and success rate are high, but only after it has formed completely and satisfied all its requirements. We describe the traits of a head-and-shoulders top. The bottom formation (see Figure 15.15) is the reverse in every way except where noted.

An uptrend, but not necessarily long-term trend, precedes a head-and-shoulders top. Thus, as shown in Figure 15.14, the head-and-shoulders top pattern is entered from below. (The head-and-shoulders pattern can also occur within a consolidation rather than at the end of a trend, but such occurrences are rare and more likely a series of triangles or a rectangle with a false downward breakout at the "head.")

The head-and-shoulders top pattern is a series of three well-defined peaks, either sharp or rounded. The second peak is higher than the first and third peak. This middle, higher peak is called the "head." The first peak is called the "left shoulder," and the third peak is called the "right shoulder." The left and right shoulders must both be lower than the head, but the two shoulders do not have to be the same height. In fact, a left shoulder peak slightly higher than the right shoulder peak adds a little to the postbreakout performance of a top formation. (A head-and-shoulders bottom is pictured in Figure 15.15. In the bottom pattern, a right shoulder low that is slightly lower than the left shoulder low adds to performance.)

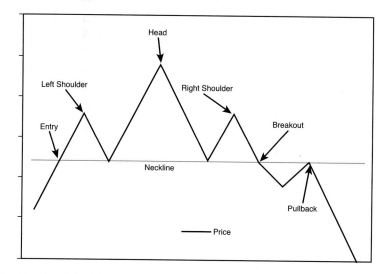

FIGURE 15.14   Head-and-shoulders top with breakout down

The peaks in the head-and-shoulders top formation are roughly equidistant from each other. The shoulders should appear roughly symmetrical about the head and should peak at roughly the same level. Symmetry is important and makes the formation more identifiable. Occasionally, more than two shoulders appear. These formations are called "complex head-and-shoulders" and have roughly the same performance and failure rates as the standard two-shoulder variety. As in the standard, the multiple shoulders appear symmetrically on both sides of the head. Rarely, a "two-headed" variety appears, and it, too, shows the same performance and failure rates as the standard. There is also the "unbalanced" version, as described by Edwards and Magee, but it is difficult to describe accurately and seems to fit only those formations that might be head-and-shoulders but cannot be formally categorized as such. The standard is the most common, and the one to look for.

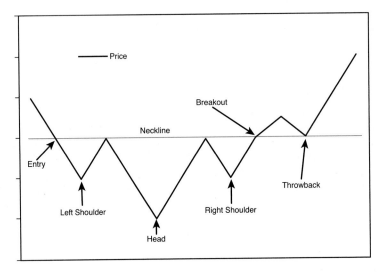

FIGURE 15.15   Head-and-shoulders bottom with breakout up

The bottoms between the peaks form a recognizable trend line. Technicians call this line the "neckline." Although the neckline is often horizontal, as in a support line, it also can be downward or upward sloping. Indeed, there is some evidence that an upward-sloping neckline in a top formation produces better performance than the standard horizontal neckline. (In a bottom formation, the same rules hold except the neckline is now resistance rather than support. In a bottom formation, a downward-sloping neckline increases postbreakout performance over an upward-sloping neckline but not over the horizontal one.) Tilting the slope of the neckline to an extreme, however, destroys the head-and-shoulders pattern and its likely consequences.

Volume is usually highest on the rise into and at the peak of the left shoulder and decreases throughout the formation. This is not a requirement, however, as those formations with decreasing volume, though slightly less frequent, seem to have a slight performance edge at tops. (Increasing volume has a slight edge in head-and-shoulders bottoms.) Higher volume on either shoulder does not affect performance at a top, but at a bottom, higher volume on the right shoulder than on the left shoulder adds considerably to postbreakout performance.

Breakout and action signals occur when prices, after completing the right shoulder, break below the neckline. The breakout is a requirement for the formation. Second-guessing before completion of the pattern can be dangerous. Sometimes, the right shoulder does not form completely, and prices fall short of breaking the neckline and rise to penetrate above the right shoulder peak. Not only is this a failure, but it also is an opportunity, provided the analyst had not anticipated a breakdown and acted prematurely. The head-and-shoulders failure of this type is very profitable, according to Schwager (1996). The standard failure, however, is when prices break below the neckline and then reverse back upward through the right shoulder. This kind of failure is relatively rare.

The breakout often occurs on increased volume, but decreased volume is not a sign of an impending failure. It just occurs less frequently. Increasing volume on a bottom formation improves performance, whereas decreasing volume on the breakout from a top pattern increases performance.

Pullbacks or throwbacks are frequent—roughly 45%–63% for bottoms and 60%–67% for tops. In summary, the head-and-shoulders pattern—aside from being the best known, even among nontechnicians—is the most reliable and profitable of the classic formations.

The performance rank for the standard head-and-shoulders top is 1, the highest ranking possible. Complex tops have a rank of 3, standard bottoms a rank of 7, and complex bottoms a rank of 9. Both top and bottom patterns, therefore, are high on the list of performance.

We have seen in most other patterns that when a pullback or throwback occurs, the comparative performance suffers. This is also true in head-and-shoulders patterns. The failure rates for both top and bottom formations are very low. Only 3%–4% failed a 5% gain or more from tops and bottoms. In short, the head-and-shoulders formation has a high rate of reliability as well as profitability.

BOX 15.9   TRADING HEAD-AND-SHOULDERS PATTERNS

Once a pattern has been observed using the preceding descriptive features, the neckline becomes the most important factor. The neckline is where the breakout level resides. Never should one act in anticipation of a break through the neckline. The risk of failure is too great, and as we have seen with the upward break of a descending triangle, the strongest upward formation, the rise from descending peaks and a flat neckline, can be substantial. This is equally true with head-and-shoulders bottom formations. The ascending triangle with a breakout down is also a powerful formation. Thus, breakout stops should be placed outside the right shoulder reversal point. Once the breakout is triggered, the risk of failure declines substantially. If the breakout is through the neckline, use the standard statistics as a guide, but if the breakout is a failed head-and-shoulders through the right shoulder extreme, use the appropriate triangle statistics as a guide.

The price target for a head-and-shoulders pattern is relatively accurate. It is calculated like the others by taking the height of the formation and projecting it up or down from the breakout price. The height is measured by drawing a vertical line from the peak of the head to where it intersects the neckline and measuring the number of points between the two. This holds for flat as well as sloping necklines.

Shorter Continuation Trading Patterns—Flags and Pennants (Also "Half-Mast Formation")

For efficient use of trading capital, consider trading with flags and pennants. They are frequent formations with extremely rapid and relatively reliable outcomes. After a breakout in either direction or either pattern, prices usually run immediately, having very few pullbacks or throwbacks and low rates of failure. Some successful traders use only flags and pennants because of these advantages. Flags and pennants are really variations of the same formation. The flag is a short channel that usually slopes in the opposite direction from the trend. The pennant is a short triangle that does the same. Both of these patterns are pictured in Figure 15.16.

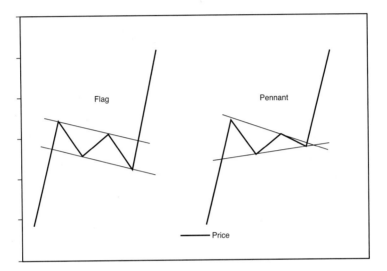

FIGURE 15.16   Flag and pennant in upward trend

Both flags and pennants are preceded by a steep, sharp price trend, best at 45 degrees rather than straight up. Flag preceded by a rise of 90% or more have almost a zero failure rate and an average return of 69%. This variety is the best of all chart patterns. Two parallel trend lines in a small channel that resembles a flag form the pattern, and the slope of the channel can be in any direction, but most commonly the best performance comes when it slopes away from the preceding trend. Flag formations occur over a short period, usually a few days to a few weeks; the best flag is less than 15 days. Volume usually declines throughout the formation of the flag. In fact, this downward trend in volume is found in almost four out of every five flags that occur.

The pennant pattern is the same as the flag except that the trend lines converge, forming a miniature triangle, instead of being parallel. The direction of the formation is usually opposite from that of the immediately preceding price trend, but in stronger moves, it can be horizontal or even trending in the same direction as the underlying trend. Pennants differ from wedges in that they are shorter in time and require a sharp move preceding them. Wedges tend to be longer-term patterns. Falling volume throughout the formation is even more common with pennants; 90% of pennants are characterized by a downward trend in volume.

Two types of failures can occur. First, a breakout in the opposite direction from the previous trend can occur. Second, a failure can occur after breakout. Because a flag or a pennant is usually a continuation formation, the breakout should be expected in the direction of the preceding trend, provided it is steep and sharp. When the breakout goes opposite to that trend, the failure invariably returns to the earlier trend, but only after a few heart palpitations have occurred first and a few protective stops have been triggered.

BOX 15.10 TRADING FLAGS AND PENNANTS—MEASURED RULE

Because these patterns have low failure rates, few pullbacks or throwbacks, short time periods, and steep trends preceding and following their occurrence, they are very good trading patterns. One of the most important identification features is the steep trend preceding the pattern. It is important to be cautious to make sure that a complete formation has occurred and to wait for the breakout. The breakout occurs when a trend line is broken, usually in the direction of the preceding trend. The price target for these patterns is calculated by taking the distance from the beginning of the sharp trend, not necessarily the beginning of the entire trend, to the first reversal in the pattern and adding it to the breakout price. This method is called the "measured rule" (see Figure 15.17) and usually only applies to flags and pennants. It implies that the formation will occur roughly halfway through the entire steep price trend; because of this, these patterns are also called "half-mast" patterns. The projection of a target is only partially accurate (about 60% of the time), but because of the steepness of the subsequent trend, close trailing stops are the best manner of protecting profits.

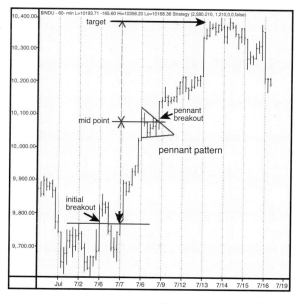

Created using TradeStation

FIGURE 15.17   The measured rule (Dow Jones Industrial Average hourly: July 1–July 16, 2010)

Long-Term Bar Chart Patterns with the Best Performance and the Lowest Risk of Failure

We have selected several patterns to highlight based upon their combination of high gains and minimum failure rates. Other patterns can also be successful if monitored closely, but the "edge" appears to be in these patterns.

According to Bulkowski (2010), the best-performing patterns, considering gain and risk, are the high-and-tight upward breaking flag, the head-and-shoulders top, top islands breaking down (to be covered in Chapter 17), and upward breaking descending triangles. A summary of these patterns is shown in Table 15.2.

TABLE 15.2   Comparative Results in Most Favorable Classic Bar Chart Patterns

	Overall Performance	Failure to Reach 5%	Average Performance	Tendency to Retrace	Reaches Target Price
Flag, rising trend, break up	1/23	0%	69%	54%	90%
Head-and-shoulders top, break down	1/21	4%	22%	50%	55%
Long island, break down	6/21	5%	22%	54%	78%
Descending triangle, break up	5/23	7%	47%	34%	84%

Source: Bulkowski (2010)

Conclusion

In summary, the profitable use of chart patterns is not easy. The potential problems with recognizing and acting upon chart patterns that we have discussed in this chapter highlight the need to know thoroughly what we are doing. There are many variables in price behavior, mostly human, and being human ourselves and subject to the same biases, we must be adaptable and recognize that chart patterns are flexible.

It is unlikely that researchers will ever be able to prove definitively that patterns exist because the mathematics are so complicated and because the marketplace is always changing. In addition, many different patterns have been recognized, and right or wrong, they have been described in the literature with nothing more than anecdotal evidence as to their reliability. If you see a pattern described with no background statistical evidence as to its usefulness, it is best not to bother with it. Today, most writers describing patterns will give some realistic evidence. Although this evidence might be flawed, it at least shows that it has been the subject of some serious study and, thus, is not merely a superstition.

The most reasonable approach for any chart reader is to take the classic patterns described in this chapter and become experienced in their use. Although the performance of these patterns will differ with different securities and with different trends in the general market, the behaviors of these patterns have remained relatively consistent for over 100 years. We have discussed general attributes of patterns that in several studies show promise, but the analyst must always adjust parameters to fit the peculiarities of the security being analyzed. Profitable chart pattern analysis is the result of determined study.

REVIEW QUESTIONS

1. A pattern is a configuration of price movement that is bounded by lines and/or curves. Explain what is meant by this definition.

2. Define each of the following terms as they relate to the characteristics and formation of patterns:

    a. Pullback

    b. Throwback

    c. Failure

3. Explain the differences among an ascending triangle, a descending triangle, and a symmetrical triangle.

4. Describe both a rising wedge and a falling wedge. What trading strategy might you follow in each of these instances?

5. Explain the difference between a flag and a pennant.

6. Flags and pennants are often said to be "half-mast" formations. Explain what is meant by this and how you would use this information to set a price target.

7. Explain the formation and characteristics of a head-and-shoulders top.

8. Explain the formation and characteristics of a head-and-shoulders bottom.

9. Select three companies, and look at the price charts for those companies over the past three months. Can you recognize any of the formations discussed in this chapter in those charts?

CHAPTER 16

POINT-AND-FIGURE CHART PATTERNS

CHAPTER OBJECTIVES

After studying this chapter, you should be familiar with

- The difference between one-point reversal and three-point reversal point-and-figure charts

- How to construct trend lines, recognize areas of consolidation, and determine the count using one-point reversal point-and-figure charts

- How to construct trend lines, recognize basic patterns, and determine the count using three-point reversal point-and-figure charts

In the previous chapter, we studied patterns that can occur when price information is displayed on a bar chart. We continue our study of patterns, but now we focus on formations that are related to point-and-figure charts. As we do this, we will notice that many of the patterns that the point-and-figure analysts use are the same as those found on bar charts. For example, we will see the head-and-shoulders pattern that we discussed in Chapter 15, "Bar Chart Patterns," appear in this chapter.

Before we delve deeply into point-and-figure chart patterns, let us take some time to review point-and-figure chart construction. We learned about basic point-and-figure chart construction in Chapter 11, "History and Construction of Charts." Because these charts are not familiar to most people, we will begin this chapter by exploring their construction in a bit more depth.

You will often see "box" and "point" used interchangeably in discussing point-and-figure charts. Although box is the proper word to use because it refers directly to the chart pattern, point also is used to represent a box. A point in point-and-figure charts is not necessarily a one-dollar price move, as in "the stock was up a point today" but represents one box on the chart. Obviously, the box size can be any consistent price difference, such as one dollar, two yen, twenty cents, and so on. We will also interchange the terms point and box.

WHAT IS DIFFERENT ABOUT A POINT-AND-FIGURE CHART?

I should say that if anybody has a good enough memory to recall thousands of changing figures, in hundreds of stocks, in a dozen averages, over a period of years, he can absolve himself from the labor of keeping charts. (de Villiers, 1933, p 16)

Time and Volume Omitted

Point-and-figure charts appear odd at first because we are accustomed to having charts with time along the horizontal axis. Those familiar with bar charts are also used to having volume plotted along the horizontal axis. Point-and-figure charts, of course, have neither time nor volume portrayed. Both are considered irrelevant to the point-and-figure advocate. Price action is all that such an analyst is interested in. Price is the focus. In this sense, a point-and-figure technical analyst is a purist. In the beginning of this book, we pointed out how price, not time nor volume, is the single result of all information. Time and volume are ancillary factors that might or might not have an effect on price. The analyst must concentrate on what a price change alone might suggest for the future.

Of course, price change is the result of changes in supply and demand. Time is but one factor, and it is not important to those utilizing point-and-figure analysis. Similarly, volume might be important but not by itself. An increase or decrease in volume is meaningless if the price remains unchanged. Only when the volume affects price change does it become important. The point-and-figure chart only plots price change, and volume and time then become unimportant.

As we saw in Chapter 15, volume is also suspect as a predictive factor for performance. Increased volume can appear or not appear, for example, on breakouts, and the results are roughly the same. Thus, the concept of volume has some weaknesses, all of which are avoided in point-and-figure charts.

Continuous Price Flow Necessary

Point-and-figure charts require a continuous price flow to be accurate. Other methods of charting prices divide price action into arbitrary periods and analyze the price action from period to period. This creates the arbitrary time of open, close, high, and low, and although depictions of these price points can be used, as we saw in the previous chapter, we must remember that they are arbitrary, human divisions of time that may be unrelated to price action. Conversely, point-and-figure analyzes all price action. In some periods, price action may be relatively dormant and meaningless, while in other periods price action may be active and meaningful. Point-and-figure relates only to that active period and disregards the inactive period. It, thus, screens out price action that has little predictive ability and concentrates on that which does.

Often, price action outside of the local normal trading day is lost when using time period charts. Requiring a continuous flow of price information, point-and-figure analysis is ideal for interpreting the 24-hour markets that do not have a beginning or end in time and can flair up into activity, especially in foreign exchange, at any time during the 24-hour period. Point-and-figure analysis disregards those periods when trading is dormant and only concentrates on those in which important activity occurs. After all, the point-and-figure method of charting developed as a result of the invention of the ticker tape, the first means by which prices were reported in a continuous flow. Until then, prices were only recorded on a daily basis, an arbitrary cutoff that could easily mask important price change information intraday or overnight. Point-and-figure is also useful in futures markets where volume is unknown and not a consideration in trading. In short, although seeming to be archaic, point-and-figure still has many uses and, as we shall see later in this chapter, has been tested and found to have statistically positive results.

"Old" and "New" Methods

Only two variables, determined by the analyst, describe a point-and-figure chart: box or point size and the number of boxes or points required for a reversal, called the **reversal amount** or **reversal size.** This is important to understand because the early point-and-figure charts were strictly one by one. In other words, the box size was one price interval such as a dollar in a stock price, and the reversal amount was one box. The patterns that evolved using this method are more complicated, are subject to analyst interpretation, and, thus, are more difficult to test statistically. They are accurate portrayals of price action, however, because they include every price transaction in the particular security. Later, the one by three point-and-figure, called a three-box reversal point-and-figure chart, became popular because it did not require as much data flow. It should be plotted, as the one-box chart, using a continuous flow of price data, but it can be estimated from daily prices in the newspaper. When estimated from daily prices alone, it loses its accuracy because intraday price action that might have been meaningful is eliminated. The three-box reversal chart does simplify analysis, however, because its method still screens out some unimportant price changes and produces an extremely simple, well-defined picture that can be tested, as we shall see later.

When discussing point-and-figure, many people confuse the two types—the old and the new—and assume that the rules and patterns for one are the same as for the other. As we will see, however, the rules and patterns are quite different. Thus, the usage of the term *point-and-figure* should always be qualified as to whether one-box reversal or three-box reversal is being discussed.

HISTORY OF POINT-AND-FIGURE CHARTING

We briefly discussed the history of the point-and-figure method in Chapter 3, "History of Technical Analysis." Unfortunately, there are only a few written references to the method, mostly books or pamphlets. Academic references are very few and generally unfavorably disposed, being still caught in the old finance theory cult and not understanding how point-and-figure is used by professionals.

Charles Dow, in 1901, mentioned a "book method" of plotting stock prices as they are printed on the ticker tape. This method and a "method of keeping records of the fluctuations in the price of stocks" (Hoyle from du Plessis, 2005) both describe a system very similar to present-day one-box point-and-figure charts. At first, these charts plotted numbers ("figures") on a graph and later a vertical scale of prices was used with the trade prices represented by checks, ticks, or crosses (Xs). The use of figures was then limited to 0 and 5 for clarity over long horizontal charts and was still described by Wheelan's textbook in 1954. Xs eventually became the standard for marking prices until Blumenthal's invention of the three-box reversal chart, when Xs were used for advancing price columns and O's for declining price columns.

The term **figure** likely came from the recording of prices. Later, in 1933, Victor De Villiers in his booklet *The Point and Figure Method of Anticipating Stock Price Movements* described both the figure method with prices in each box and the point method with Xs in each box and figures (5 or 0) in the prices rows that were multiples of 5 and 10. He mentions that figure charting was old-fashioned and preferred the point method. His later book with Owen Taylor, also in 1933, used only point charts. He summed up the advantages of using charts: They "dispense with statistics, fundamentals, values—real, absent, or presumed, news—past, present, and future, the necessity for impulsive action, decisions based on conjecture, compulsion to interpret or determine the effect before the cause, and the confusion of mental processes in the task of prematurely anticipating or discounting coming events." De Villiers sounds like a true technician. Indeed, some analysts refer to the old method of one-box reversal as the de Villiers method.

Wyckoff's *Stock Market Techniques No.2* written in 1934 also describes the one-box method. It is certain, then, that by the mid-1930s the figure method had been completely replaced by the point method.

The next published pamphlet, which is extremely useful in the description and use of one-point reversal charts, was by Wheelan (1954). It is still in print, and for anyone interested in the original method of analysis, it is a gem. Wheelan's instructional pamphlet takes the form of a lesson plan and includes many practice exercises, chart paper, and subsequent commentary. It provides the best summary of the chart patterns used in the original one-box method. Wheelan suggests that the student of point-and-figure keep an active chart on some commodity future because futures trading is so fast acting that chart patterns unfold rapidly and give rapid feedback of pattern analysis. He also suggests that two students work alongside each other because "points that are obscure to one may be clear to the other, and the opportunity to exchange ideas will greatly hasten the mastery of this analytical technique" (p. 4). His advice is still valid today.

In the 1960s, Dines, Andrews, Granville, and several others each published one-box reversal chart services. The advent of the easier three-box reversal and the beginning of computer plotting gradually put these services out of business. Until recently, several brokerage firms still kept one-box reversal charts by hand, but these firms are getting fewer and fewer because the computer has taken the job of plotting continuous data very well. Some specialists, market makers, and short-term floor traders keep a card for recording intraday price changes, which at one time the exchanges provided, that are used for short-term trading and gauging price strength and weakness. This method is also dying out, however, because these trading professions gradually are being phased out as electronic trading takes over their functions on the trading floors. "Upstairs" traders can rely on software that is designed to plot one-box charts, but they must be careful that the data flow is continuous and not just the high and low of a time bar.

The newer method of point-and-figure, the three-point reversal method, is not a true point-and-figure method because it does not rely on a continuous data stream. In some cases, only the closing prices are used, but more often the high and low are interpreted as representing price flow during the trading day.

Earl Blumenthal, the originator of the Chartcraft Service, devised and marketed the three-box reversal method starting in 1947. Blumenthal introduced the three-point reversal method in a privately published book titled *Stock Market Trading*. Updated revisions of the book were published under similar names by Abe Cohen and later, Michael Burke, subsequent owners of the Chartcraft service. In 1948, Blumenthal began the Chartcraft Weekly Service, which used three-box reversal charts to keep subscribers up to date on the most active stocks traded at that time. The service has since been sold to StockCube Ltd of Great Britain and is on the Web under the address www.investorsintelligence.com.

In 1965, Professor Robert Earl Davis of Purdue University compiled a widely quoted performance study on the eight basic three-point patterns. He examined the eight basic three-box reversal patterns for 1,100 equities between 1954 and 1964. We refer to his study later in looking at the effectiveness of this method. More recently, Dr. Carroll Aby (1996) and Thomas Dorsey (2001) have written more complete books that bring the three-box method up to date. The influence of these pioneers in the three-point method has been so successful that many analysts are unaware of the original more accurate but less definite one-point method.

Excellent compilations and descriptions of the point-and-figure method are available in Zieg and Kaufman (1975) and Murphy (1999). The performance statistics in Zieg and Kaufman are from Davis (1965). Academic literature is limited to German publications (Hauschild and Winkelman, 1985; Stottner, 1990). Also, a working paper by Professor John Anderson of Queensland University of Technology presents a study of three-point patterns on the S&P 500 futures market from 1990 to 1998. More recently, Jeremy du Plessis (2005) has written a comprehensive book on point-and-figure that has become the primary source of information about the method.

ONE-BOX REVERSAL POINT-AND-FIGURE CHARTS

Like bar chart patterns, patterns in one-box point-and-figure charts are not precise and require an experienced analyst to interpret. This is likely another reason why they have lost their popularity to the three-box version. Being imprecise also means that performance figures for patterns are almost impossible to determine. No one has done the research into interpreting one-box point-and-figure patterns as Bulkowski has in bar charts, so we are left with much conjecture and a difficult methodology.

One-box chart analysis focuses on consolidation areas, as do most chart methods, and attempts to determine the next directional move and by how much that move will likely carry. The one advantage of the one-box method is called the **count,** a means of anticipating the expected price move by measuring the width of an observed price base. We cover the count later in this chapter. In point-and-figure analysis, as in bar chart analysis, observation and analysis of patterns is largely subjective and based on the experience of the analyst. Like fundamental analysis, the experience of the analyst is the key to success.

Consolidation Area on the One-Box Chart (Also "Congestion Area")

As we know from bar chart analysis, a consolidation area is a sideways movement in prices that interrupts or reverses a trend. It is during this period of nontrending action that patterns develop that signal the new direction once a breakout occurs and potentially the extent or target price for the new directional price move. In point-and-figure, a consolidation area serves the same purpose. Various patterns have been recognized over the past that inform the analyst what is likely to occur in the future.

One observation, for example, is that when price changes occur more frequently at the lower level of a consolidation area, the odds favor a breakout to the upside. The converse is true when price changes occur frequently at the upper level of consolidation. Because one-box charts plot so much information, the consolidation areas are often very wide, being made up of many smaller price oscillations, just as in a bar chart. The important point in analyzing point-and-figure charts is to consider the consolidation area as a whole and ignore the smaller separate parts. The analyst must determine where the price change work has been done, either in the lower or upper level of the area, and place more emphasis on recent work than on past price changes. Figure 16.1 is an example of a one-box reversal chart with price action predominately in the lower level of the consolidation and a subsequent breakout upward.

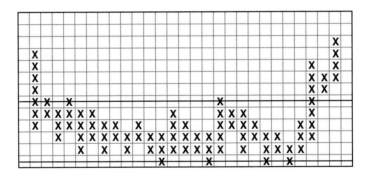

FIGURE 16.1   Consolidation area with majority of price action at lower level of area, suggesting breakout will be to the upside

Trend Lines in One-Box Charts

Trend lines are drawn on a one-box reversal chart just as they are on a bar chart, connecting highs to highs and lows to lows. These lines frequently outline standard patterns that we have seen in bar chart analysis, such as triangles, rectangles, broadening formations, wedges, and even flags and pennants. The same type of analysis used with bar charts can be applied to one-box reversal charts. Figure 16.2, for example, shows a one-box reversal chart with a triangle formed by two trend lines.

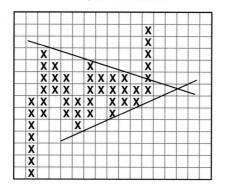

FIGURE 16.2   One-box reversal chart with a triangle

In consolidation areas, the one exception to the rule about where the majority of price changes occur, suggesting the direction of the breakout, is when a trend line is penetrated in the opposite direction from that which is developing as the most likely. Figure 16.3 shows an example of a consolidation area with the most recent and majority of action occurring at the upper end of the area, suggesting a breakout downward. However, this suggestion was negated when prices broke above the trend line.

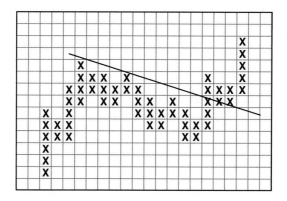

FIGURE 16.3   Consolidation area with most activity on upper level, suggesting a downward breakout, but reversed with a breakout upward through a trend line

The Count in a One-Point Chart

The count is calculated by counting the squares across a consolidation area. As shown in Figure 16.4, the price level in the consolidation area that has the most squares filled is used for the count. The count includes all squares along a horizontal price line from the left to the right of the consolidation area, including any blank squares that might occur. When each side of the consolidation is a vertical line of some proportion, called a **wall,** the determination of where to locate the horizontal line from which the count is determined is relatively easy. In most cases, a wall does not exist, however, and the analyst must judge along what price line in the consolidation the most number of filled squares occur. Figure 16.4 shows a consolidation with the left side being a wall that is relatively easy to determine, the right side with a more difficult configuration, and where the count might be applied. When the consolidation is irregular, the analyst must determine from experience with counts what the best price level to use would be.

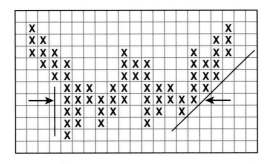

FIGURE 16.4   Determining the count in a consolidation area by using the price at which the most number of squares are filled

The count determines the approximate extent of the next move. There appears to be a direct relationship between the width of a consolidation and the vertical extent of the next rise or decline. The count is one of the most valuable features of the one-box method. The three-point method also has a count, but it is far less accurate, presumably because the three-point chart fails to represent the complete flow of prices.

Generally, the count is more accurate in those stocks and commodities with a wide public following. From the count, the analyst can estimate whether the next move will be small or large and can determine risk-reward relationships to help in deciding whether to act on the breakout signal.

Normally, the longer the consolidation area, the more difficult it is to establish a count because of the many smaller rallies and declines within the base area that obscure the real beginning and end of the consolidation area. Often a good starting point is the absolute high or low of the area, but sometimes the price has been consolidating for a while before these levels are reached. There are no definite rules for establishing the count, and academics have a fit over this because the count cannot then be analyzed and evaluated. Nevertheless, despite the count's problems, the width of the consolidation area does seem to have a relationship with the eventual distance of the next price move, and any reasonable estimate will have some value.

Once the count is determined, the distance of the count is then added to the right-hand square with the last entry in the consolidation area. This is the standard method, though there are variations. The result is as if the count line was rotated upward or downward around the last square in the count (see Figure 16.5). The resulting price level projected from the distance of the count is the objective for the next price move. It is surprising how accurate this method can be, but, of course, it should never be depended upon solely. Other factors such as market direction, change in supply or demand, or other informational changes can affect the eventual price target. It is only an approximation.

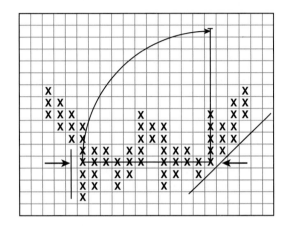

FIGURE 16.5 Target determined by rotating count around the right-hand edge in the direction of the breakout

Head-and-Shoulders Pattern

Many of the patterns observed in bar charts also occur in one-box charts. The most common is the head-and-shoulders pattern (see Figure 16.6), but the rounded, double, and triple formations are also seen. The implications of these patterns are the same as in bar charts, except that with the ability of the count to estimate a price target, the patterns are more easily assessed for reward versus risk. One-box reversal charts also have a few patterns of their own.

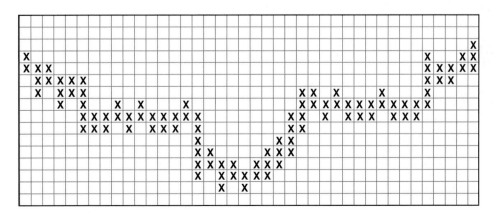

FIGURE 16.6 Head-and-shoulders bottom on a point-and-figure chart

The Fulcrum

The fulcrum is a distinctive one-box reversal chart pattern. Indeed, some analysts call all reversal patterns fulcrum, just as they call continuation patterns "semi-catapults." The fulcrum is easily recognized, occurs at both tops and bottoms, and gives a reliable count because distinct walls usually contain it. Common characteristics in the fulcrum bottom (see Figure 16.7) are the following:

1. A downward trend entering the consolidation area
2. Sideways price activity near the low of the downward trend
3. A "mid-fulcrum" rally of short duration and around 15% amplitude that sometimes is mistaken for the beginning of a larger move
4. A testing of the earlier lows with some more sideways price activity
5. A "catapult" rally above the mid-fulcrum rally

All these variables can vary, of course, but the general pattern is easily recognized. De Villiers mentioned three types of fulcrums, and Wheelan mentioned eight tops and eight bottoms. Occasionally, more than one mid-fulcrum rally occurs, and the test can occasionally break below the initial sideways price action without damaging the implications of the formation. Two fulcrums side by side is called a **compound fulcrum,** and a compound fulcrum with the second fulcrum lower than the first is called a **delayed-ending fulcrum.** These formations are more powerful than the single fulcrum once completed with the catapult breakout. Being familiar with these fulcrum patterns, an analyst can spot similar patterns even in bar charts.

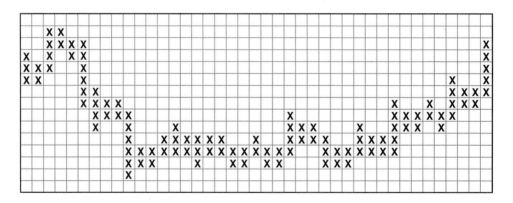

FIGURE 16.7   Fulcrum bottom (from Wheelan)

Action Points

We have looked at the characteristics of the one-box point-and-figure chart. How can this information be used to help us trade stocks? In his pamphlet, Wheelan outlines the conditions that constitute ideal buying and selling points. When all of the following appear in the one-box point-and-figure chart, the ideal buying situation exists:

1. The technical position of the market is favorable.
2. A clear and broad fulcrum appears after an extended downward trend.
3. The bottom of the fulcrum fulfills the maximum count from the previous top.
4. The bottom of the fulcrum occurs at a major support area.
5. The catapult occurs coincidently with the breaking of a downward trend line from within the fulcrum or from the previous top.
6. The catapult occurs at a price level that has little or no resistance immediately above.

The ideal selling point occurs when all of the criteria are reversed.

THREE-POINT (OR BOX) REVERSAL POINT-AND-FIGURE CHARTS

The interpretation of one-box charts is obviously difficult and takes considerable skill and experience. A more user-friendly method is the three-box reversal chart. It had the advantages of being plotted from prices in the newspaper and required the knowledge of only a few basic patterns. It appealed to academia because the patterns could be identified and tested, and it appealed to nontechnicians because it was easy.

The method for plotting three-box reversal charts became standardized to the point where the Chartcraft price scale is now referred to as "traditional." Price scales have also evolved, however, to account for percentage change rather than arithmetic change, and logarithmic scales are often a choice in the popular software programs that plot point-and-figure charts. Although the method has other peculiarities, such as trend lines at 45-degree slopes and odd-named patterns such as "high poles" and "long tails," the various tests of its success rate, though few, have shown extremely good results from following the signals on a mechanical basis.

Professor Davis (1965) studied the results from each of the eight basic patterns over ten years and 1,100 stocks. His method was to act on a signal from one of the patterns and close the position when a simple reversal signal occurred. Sometimes theoretical positions would overlap, as when more than one signal occurred before the closing criteria was met, but the data was accrued for each signal as if it were independent. Davis's results were tabulated by signal and the percentage profitable as well as the average gain or loss was recorded.

Professor Anderson used the same method on eight years of S&P 500 futures prices, by year, and tabulated the gains, losses, and percent profit from each of the eight standard patterns adjusted for different box sizes ($100 and $200) and reversal numbers (three, four, and five boxes). Unfortunately, Professor Anderson used a $100 commission rate for round-turn trades when a more accurate commission would have been closer to $5. His results show worse performance than would be expected today but even with the high commission are still largely positive. We have adjusted the overall profitability of his results, but not knowing the details of each trade, we could not adjust the profitability percentage for each signal. In both studies, Davis and Anderson, the results show very favorable results for all eight signals.

Trend Lines with Three-Box Charts

Trend lines in three-box reversal charts are drawn at 45-degree angles, as demonstrated in Figure 16.8. This method is somewhat spurious. There is little reason for drawing trend lines in this manner, but regardless, it has become the convention for these charts.

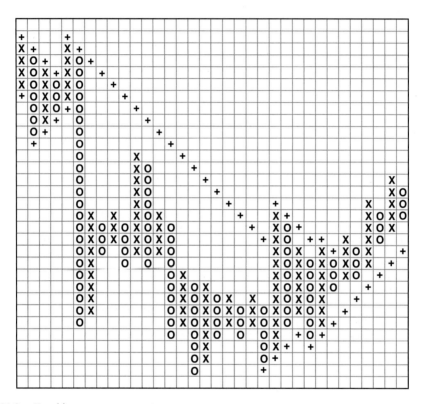

FIGURE 16.8   Trend lines

Because the method only allows one upward and one downward trend line, each has a separate name. The upward trend line, drawn one box below the last observable column (always an O column) after a buy signal from a base, is called the bullish support line. The opposite, the down trend line drawn one box above the latest top column (always an X column) after a sell signal from a top, is called the bearish resistance line. Each is treated equivalently relative to its direction.

The general rule for these lines is that one should never buy unless prices are above the bullish support line and, conversely, should never sell unless prices are below the bearish resistance line. The initial lines may last for years, depending on the slope of the subsequent advance or decline. When a price penetrates a trend line by one box at the same time that a pattern signal occurs, the signal has added importance. Unfortunately, the tests on signals did not include this qualification.

Another, even more questionable, line is drawn on three-box reversal charts. This is a line similar to the channel line in a bar chart in that it runs parallel to the trend line through the opposite extreme prices. Thus, a bullish support line that travels upward beginning at the bottom of the base can have several bullish resistance lines drawn through successive peaks in the price rise. These lines are considered to be levels at which future rallies will halt, similar again to the standard channel line.

The Count Using Three-Box Reversal Charts

Analysts use two methods of determining a target price on three-box reversal charts—the vertical and the horizontal count. However, because the three-box reversal method eliminates much of the price action that might occur within the three boxes and often does not include the continuous stream of prices, the counts are not as accurate as in the one-box method. Nevertheless, they do provide an approximate target, one that can be more confidently accepted if both the vertical and horizontal counts agree.

Calculating Horizontal Count

The horizontal count is very similar to the count in a one-box chart. The walls on either side of the base are the starting points, and the distance in boxes is measured between them. In Figure 16.9, the width of the base is 5. The distance is then multiplied by the dollars per box. In Figure 16.9, the price per box is 0.5 at the point where the base formed. The base of 5 is multiplied by the price per box of .5 to get 2.5. Next, an adjustment is made to account for the approximate loss in price action using a three-box reversal; in our example, 2.5 is multiplied by 3 because the reversal amount is three boxes, resulting in 7.5. This figure is then added to the lowest point in the formation, which in our example is 15 1/2, giving a price target on a bullish signal of 23 (15 1/2 + 7 1/2). The fact that at 23, the box sizes are one point per box is irrelevant. Remember that this is different from the count in a one-box chart, where all boxes are the same size.

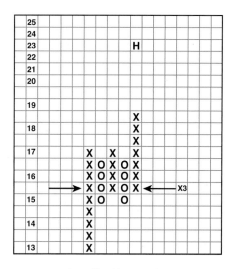

FIGURE 16.9   Horizontal count (3) x (total width of base in boxes [5] x price/box [1/2]) + lowest price in formation (15 1/2) = price target (23)

Calculating Vertical Count

The vertical count is unique to the three-box reversal. It is calculated by taking the number of boxes in the column in which an action signal has occurred, multiplying it by 3, and adding the product to the lowest box price in the column. If the box values are different because of scale changes during the column's formation, the value of the column boxes must be adjusted. In the example (see Figure 16.10), the scale does not change over the relevant range. Thus, the prices are all 1/2 point per box for seven boxes in the column in which the buy signal occurred, multiplied by 3 to adjust for the three-box reversal, which equals 10 1/2, which is then added to the lowest box price of 15 1/2 to get a vertical count of 26. In some cases, the initial signal is only a three-box column. If the base is sufficiently large, the two columns coming out of the base at the signal can be used. A special situation exists in short sales from a top. In these cases, the downward projection is a function of multiplying by 2 instead of by 3.

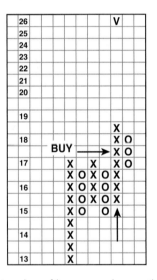

FIGURE 16.10   Vertical count (3) x (number of boxes in column with buy signal [7] x box size [1/2]) + first box in column (15 1/2) = price target (26)

The Eight Standard Patterns for Three-Box Reversal Charts

There are eight standard patterns used with three-box reversal charts. They are as follows:

- Double top or double bottom
- Rising bottom or declining top
- Triple top or triple bottom
- Ascending triple top or descending triple bottom

- Spread triple top or spread triple bottom
- Bullish or bearish triangle
- Above bullish resistance line or bearish support line
- Below bearish resistance line or bearish support line

Let us look at each of these eight patterns. Then we will look at a few additional minor three-box reversal formations.

Double Top and Double Bottom

Double tops and bottoms are the simplest of all patterns. The double pattern consists of only three columns: two X columns and one O column for the double top or two O columns and one X column for the double bottom. The nomenclature is different from both bar charts and one-box point-and-figure charts in that "top" designates the point at which a breakout occurs rather than a description of the pattern formation as being bearish. Indeed, a top—double or triple—is a bullish formation once the upward breakout occurs. The signal comes when the third column breaks above or below the first column, as shown in Figure 16.11. All other standard formations with the exception of lines have a double top or bottom within them. Davis found the double top to be profitable 80.3% of the time and the double bottom to be profitable 82.1% of the time. Anderson found their combined profitability to be tied for third best of the eight patterns, returning $1,371,810 in 18,278 trades over nine years.

FIGURE 16.11 Double top and double bottom

Rising Bottom and Declining Top

The rising bottom and declining top are variations of the double top and double bottom. Four columns are required for these formations. The rising bottom is formed by an initial X column, followed by an O column, a second X column, and then a second O column. For the pattern to be a rising bottom requirement, the first column of Os in the double top must have a lower low than the most recent column of Os. The rising bottom pattern is pictured in Figure 16.12.

Usually the first column of lows declines from a much higher lever than shown in Figure 16.12. One possible variation is for the prior column of Xs to be stronger. The declining top pattern is just the opposite of the rising bottom pattern. Figure 16.12 also shows a diagram for a declining top formation.

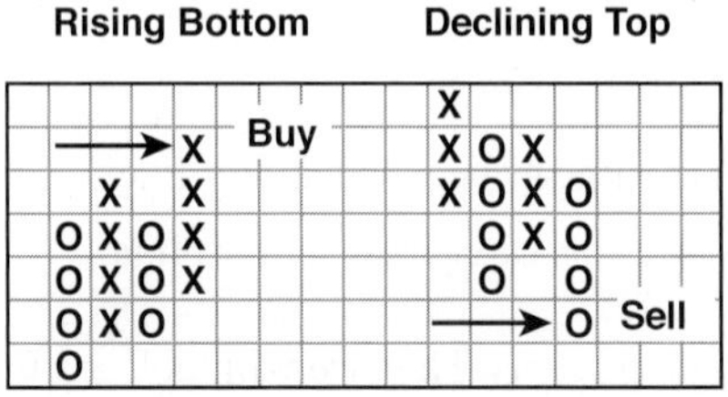

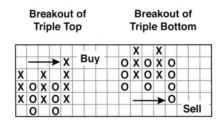

FIGURE 16.12   Rising bottom and declining top

Davis claimed that the rising bottom was profitable 80.4% of the time, and the declining top was profitable 88.6% of the time. In the Anderson study, these patterns combined tied for third best. They produced a $666,635 gain over nine years and 8,433 trades.

Triple Top and Triple Bottom

The triple top and bottom patterns require that prices break above or below two prior highs or lows. It, thus, provides more confirmation that a change in trend has occurred. As a result, it tends to be more profitable than the double top and bottom but occurs less frequently. Figure 16.13 shows a triple top and a triple bottom.

FIGURE 16.13   Triple top and triple bottom breakouts

Davis reported that the triple top formation was profitable 87.9% of the time and that the triple bottom was profitable 93% of the time. Anderson found the pattern to be the second best of the eight standard patterns and produced $320,795 over nine years and 2,201 trades for an average profit per trade of $145.70.

Ascending Triple Top and Descending Triple Bottom (Also "Diagonal" Triple Top or Bottom)

Ascending triple tops and descending triple bottoms are varieties of the triple top and bottoms. In the ascending triple top, three rows of Xs occur, with the second row of Xs breaking through the top of the first and the third row of Xs breaking through the top of the second. This is really two double top formations right after each other, denoting a strong upward price trend. An ascending triple top is shown in Figure 16.14.

The descending triple bottom is the opposite of the top. In this formation, the three rows of Os show progressively lower levels. Figure 16.14 also shows this bottom formation.

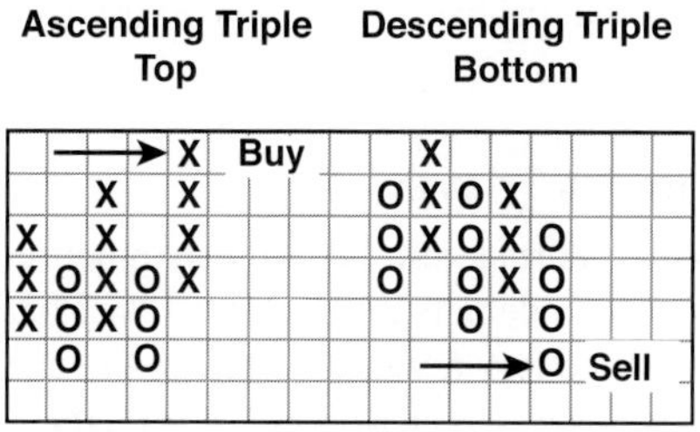

FIGURE 16.14 Ascending triple top and descending triple bottom

Davis reported that the ascending triple top was profitable 79.5% of the time, and the descending triple bottom was profitable 83.3% of the time. Anderson reported that this pattern produced profits but at a level below the average of the other eight standard patterns.

Spread Triple Top and Spread Triple Bottom

The spread triple top (bottom) is a special case of the triple top (bottom). Spread triple tops and bottoms are a little more complicated, and, thus, occur less frequently. The pattern requires at least six columns and usually more. It is somewhat similar to the fulcrum pattern in the one-box chart because it has a congestion area followed by a premature breakout and then another congestion area. The signal comes when the premature breakout is exceeded, just as in the fulcrum pattern.

Thus, in a spread triple top, there are three tops to be exceeded, with one or more lesser tops in between the major ones. A breakout must rise above all. Figure 16.15 provides a graph of a spread triple top and the spread triple bottom. You will notice that in the spread triple bottom, three major bottoms occur, with lesser bottoms between the major ones.

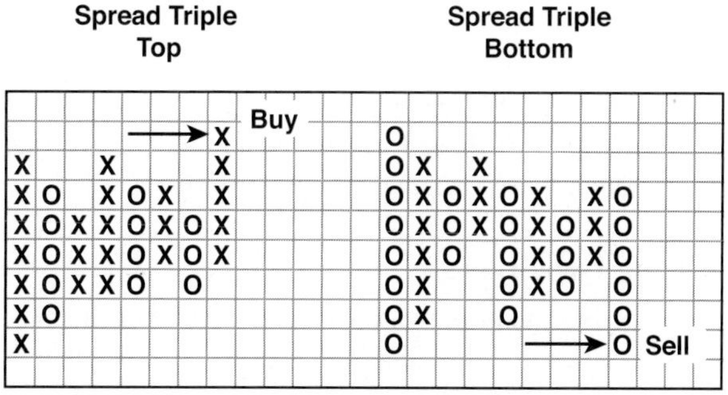

FIGURE 16.15 Spread triple top and spread triple bottom

Davis reported that the spread triple tops were profitable 85.7% of the time, and spread triple bottoms were profitable 86.5% of the time. Anderson's results were not as favorable. His report showed very small profits (only $37.9 per trade) and rare occurrences (429 over nine years). Thus, they were patterns that probably should be eliminated from the list of useful three-box reversal patterns.

Bullish Triangle and Bearish Triangle

The triangle in three-box reversal charts is similar to the symmetrical triangle we saw in bar chart patterns in Chapter 15. Figure 16.16 depicts both a bullish and bearish three-box reversal triangle. The triangle is very rare in three-box reversals, however, because it is relatively complicated and because three-box reversals cover a longer period of time than it takes for most bar chart triangles to form. The three-box reversal, therefore, only picks up those triangles that form over a longer period and that are uncommon. The pattern requires that columns converge by having successively lower highs and higher lows, as depicted in Figure 16.16.

The patterns studied by Davis and Anderson were continuation patterns because the breakout was required in the direction of the previous trend. As we know, triangles can be reversal patterns also, but these have not been analyzed for performance.

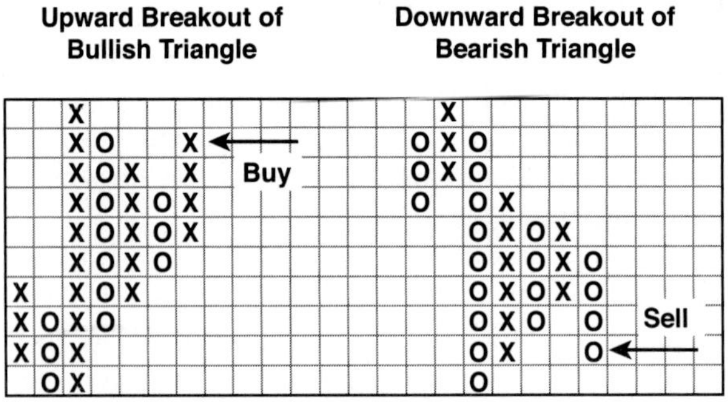

FIGURE 16.16 Bullish and bearish triangles

Davis reported that the upward breaking bullish triangle was profitable 71.4% of the time and the downward breaking bearish triangle was profitable 87.5% of the time. Anderson could only find a combined 70 examples of these formations, and their performance was a miserable $11.70 per trade. This is another pattern that could easily be disregarded.

Rising and Declining Trend Lines

In a rising trend, a trend line is usually drawn below the lows of each smaller correction within the trend. In three-box reversal charts, the trend line is drawn at a 45-degree angle from the bottom and is labeled the bullish support line. Another parallel line, similar to a channel line, is often drawn through the earliest peak in the upward trend, again at a 45-degree angle, and is called the bullish resistance line.

Prices can penetrate these lines in only two ways. They can break below the bullish support line, traditionally considered a major change in the long-term trend and called a "bullish reversed pattern" without the trend line, or prices can break above the bullish resistance line, suggesting that the upward trend has accelerated.

The upward breakout through a bullish resistance line, as shown in Figure 16.17, comes at the end of a strong move. This type of breakout is likely the last gasp in the trend direction. To be jumping on the trend at this late time is dangerous and likely wrong. On the other hand, the break of the underlying bullish support line has more validity because it signals a potential reversal in trend, just as breaking a trend line in a bar chart would imply.

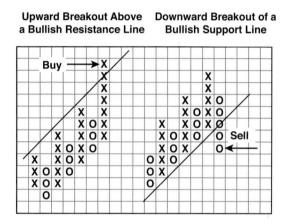

FIGURE 16.17 Breakouts from bullish resistance and bullish support lines

These breakouts are not specifically a pattern in the sense that a pattern usually is defined by two boundaries, but because of the peculiar nature of the trend being drawn at 45 degrees with little supporting evidence, the breaks have been evaluated for performance. In truth, the results from these two combinations of trend lines should not have been combined as they were. Instead, it would have been more informative to combine the channel lines together and the trend lines together. For this reason, the results from both studies are likely flawed and not good guides as to the success or failure of any of these techniques.

Nevertheless, Davis reported that the upward break profited 82.6% of the time, and the downward break profited 85.7% of the time. Anderson found only 49 examples in nine years, but these examples produced a profit per trade of $219, the highest per-trade profit of all the eight patterns. It's too bad they occur so infrequently.

Declining trend lines are just the opposite of the rising trend lines except that they appear in declining trends. There is an upper line, the bearish resistance line, and a lower line, the bearish support line. Both the bearish resistance line and the bearish support line are pictured in Figure 16.18.

Davis claimed a profit an extraordinarily high 92.0% of the time for breaking upward through the bearish resistance line, what is also called a **bearish reversed pattern** without the trend line. Zieg and Kaufman did not provide statistics from Davis's work on the profitability of a downward break. Anderson, however, found that the combination of breaks lost money. This makes sense. A 45-degree downward trend line is not usually steep enough during a decline to capture the price movement. Declines tend to occur more quickly and at a steeper slope than advances. Thus, a number of premature breakouts downward would not be surprising and seem to be what occurred in the S&P futures that Anderson monitored. The number of occurrences he noticed was only a paltry 63 over nine years.

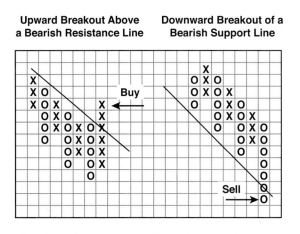

FIGURE 16.18   Breakouts from bearish resistance and bearish support lines

Other Patterns

In addition to the eight standard three-box reversal chart patterns, several other formations are of interest to the technical analyst. Three such formations to be aware of are the catapult, the spike, and the shakeout.

Catapult

Dorsey calls the catapult a "confirming" formation. It results from the pullback or throwback after the breakout from a triple top or bottom formation. Cohen maintained that a catapult would occur in roughly 50% of triple formations. As such, it is just a combination of a triple formation and a double formation.

Figure 16.19 depicts a bullish catapult. In this chart, the triple breaks out in the third column of Xs. A column of Os follows, in a throwback. As the next column of Xs occurs, a double formation then occurs.

As a formation, the bullish catapult is powerful, but it also provides a chance to enter at a slightly more favorable price. The time to enter is on the throwback, perhaps only a half position. Place a stop outside of the reversal point prior to the throwback. In the bullish catapult (see Figure 16.19), the throwback enters the triple top formation and provides a better buying price than when it originally broke out. In addition, the bottom at which a protective stop should be placed is closer, giving better risk-reward odds. Another buy order can be placed when there is a breakout from the double top.

A bearish catapult is also pictured in Figure 16.19. It is the same thing as the bullish version except in reverse. Sell orders should be handled in the same manner that buy orders were handled with the bullish catapult.

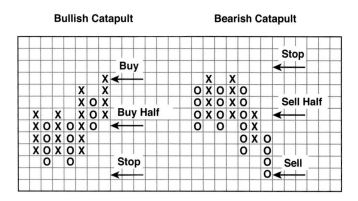

FIGURE 16.19 Bullish and bearish catapults

Spike (Also "Long Tail")

Occasionally, a price change continues in a straight line for a considerable distance on a three-box reversal chart, leading to a tall column of Xs or Os. This often occurs at a climax after an accelerated trend has reached its climax. In Figure 16.20, the long column of Os forms what looks like a long tail.

How should trading be handled when a long tail or spike occurs? Using traditional signals, the next reversal (the X column) would have to travel the entire distance back to the starting point before a signal is given. It would be fairly obvious that prices are in an uptrend, and an uptrend that the investor would want to be riding, before prices made it all the way back up the length of the tail. Therefore, different authors have tried to develop rules for trading when these tails and spikes occur.

The main question to be resolved is how far the straight line run in prices has to travel before it is considered a spike. Cohen argued that 10 boxes were sufficient to establish a spike; Blumenthal argued for 20 boxes; and Burke reported that 17 to 20 would be sufficient. Dorsey mentions a "long tail down," using a decline of 20 boxes without a reversal as his criterion; at the first reversal, he suggests a buy for a short trade on the long side. In summary, however, the answer is not clear as what the best number of boxes is, but the principle is valid especially if the overall market is at a long-term extreme.

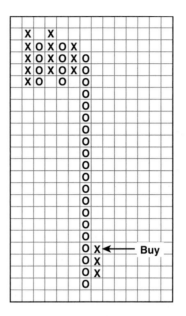

FIGURE 16.20   Spike pattern or long tail downward

Shakeout

The shakeout pattern is a deceptive pattern that plays on traders and investors who sell on the first sign of difficulty in an uptrend. It is displayed in Figure 16.21. The first column of Xs indicates a strong upward trend. Then the two columns of Os form a double bottom. This double bottom breakdown in a strong rising market often "shakes out" a number of traders and investors who have profited and want to exit the position. Under normal circumstances, the double bottom pattern would be a signal to sell, but in this case, it pays to buy instead of sell. The reason is that the trend is still upward, and the first correction is just temporary within a trend that will soon resume upward.

Trading in this situation can be tricky. It is important to remember that this pattern occurs early during a strong uptrend. Dorsey provides several rules to make sure the pattern is used correctly:

- The stock and market must be in an uptrend.
- The stock should be trading above its bullish support line.
- The stock price must form two tops at the same price.
- The reversal from these two tops gives a double bottom sell signal.
- This sell signal is the first that has occurred in the uptrend.
- The relative strength chart must be showing Xs in the recent column or be on a buy signal.

The signal to buy is on the reversal back upward from the double bottom sell signal, as shown in Figure 16.21. A protective stop can then be placed just below the prior low.

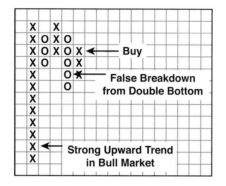

FIGURE 16.21   *Shakeout pattern*

CONCLUSION

The charts we have considered in this chapter might not look as familiar to you as the bar charts we have focused on in previous chapters. These point-and-figure charts record only price action; time and volume figures are omitted. Remember, the main objective of the technical analyst is to determine price trends in order to profit.

The original, one-point reversal point-and-figure charts require continuous price data. Many investors do not have access to this detailed intraday data. The three-point reversal point-and-figure method was developed as a way in which investors could use intermittent data, such as that reported daily in newspapers, to construct charts. Although some of the price action is lost in these charts, the three-point reversal point-and-figure chart has become the more standard type of point-and-figure charting. These charts have some unique characteristics, such as trend lines drawn at 45 degrees, which we have looked at in this chapter. Because of their uniqueness, these charts require extra study time and effort to learn; however, this study can be profitable for the serious student of technical analysis.

REVIEW QUESTIONS

1. Time and volume are not pictured on a point-and-figure chart. Explain why point-and-figure analysts might consider these two factors irrelevant to their analysis.

2. Why might one-point reversal point-and-figure charts be a useful tool for an analyst following currency trading?

3. Explain the major difference between the one-point reversal method and the three-point reversal method, highlighting the advantages to each approach.

4. Explain each of the following terms as it relates to point-and-figure charting:

    a. Congestion area

    b. Trend line

    c. Wall

    d. Count

5. How is count used in one-point reversal charts to determine a price target?

6. Explain how the term *top* is used differently with three-point reversal charts than with bar charts and one-point reversal point-and-figure charts.

7. How is horizontal count determined in a three-point reversal chart? How is vertical count determined in these charts? How would this count be used to determine a price target?

8. How do the trend lines that are drawn on three-point reversal point-and-figure charts differ from trend lines drawn on other types of charts? Describe each of the following types of trend lines on the three-point reversal chart:

    a. Bullish support line

    b. Bearish support line

    c. Bullish resistance line

    d. Bearish resistance line

SHORT-TERM PATTERNS

CHAPTER OBJECTIVES

After studying this chapter, you should be familiar with

- How short-term patterns can be used as a tool to identify reversals in longer-term trends
- The types of gaps that occur on bar charts and the significance of the various types
- Wide-range days and narrow-range days and their implications for volatility
- The formation and interpretation of the most common candlestick patterns

In previous chapters, we looked at longer-term patterns in bar charts and point-and-figure charts. We now turn our attention to short-term patterns. In this chapter, our focus is on short-term patterns on bar charts and candlestick charts. These patterns concentrate on the configuration and characteristics of individual bars, such as the height of the bar and the position of opening and closing prices on the bar. Some patterns also compare one period's bar with the preceding bar. Despite what their title suggests, short-term patterns are not limited to a particular short-term period, like one day. In this instance, "short-term" means a small number of bars. For example, on a daily bar chart, short-term patterns may form from one or two days of trading data, but on an hourly bar chart, a two-bar short-term pattern would include two hours' worth of trading data.

Although the longer-term patterns we have considered can be useful by themselves, they occur less frequently than shorter-term patterns. On the other hand, the shorter-term patterns we consider in this chapter are not useful by themselves but are very common. Why do short-term patterns occur more frequently than longer-term patterns? Think of a common bar chart; four pieces of data are represented on each bar: an open, close, high, and low. With only four pieces of information, the number of various combinations in which these variables can occur is small. Even though stretching out the pattern to several bars increases the number of possible combinations, the number is still relatively small, and these combinations occur very frequently.

Unfortunately, frequent patterns often give false signals. Although most market turning points include one or more of the short-term patterns covered in this chapter, these same patterns also occur at places where a reversal fails to follow. As Schwager (1996) states when referring to the one-day reversal pattern, it "successfully call(s) 100 out of every ten highs" (p. 89). Like Schwager, many others have been skeptical about the validity of short-term patterns. Just how useful and effective are they? Although some empirical tests suggest that these short-term patterns are not effective, many of the tests have covered longer testing periods than would be seen in practice. In most successful tests, short-term pattern entry signals are closed either at the close of the same day, the opening of the next day, the first profitable opening (called the "bailout" by Larry Williams), or the first profitable closing, which usually is only a few days later, barring the position first being stopped out. The ability to test over these short periods requires high-frequency data on a tick-to-tick basis and is usually beyond the capability of the normal investor or academic.

Nevertheless, once fully understood, short-term patterns are useful not only for trading but also for entering and exiting longer-term positions at more favorable prices. Although the average investor would not usually have the time or computer equipment and data feed to watch for short-term patterns, the professional trader certainly has the ability to watch intraday price behavior and can improve job performance and profits by understanding the nature of short-term patterns.

The basis for short-term patterns is to anticipate a sudden move, similar to the breakout concept in larger patterns, to take advantage of a period when prices have reached an emotion extreme, or to enter into a trend at an advantageous price as on a pullback or throwback. The methods usually have what is called a "setup." A setup occurs when certain known factors needed to establish the pattern have occurred, and the trader is waiting for the action signal to occur. In larger charts, we have seen this concept in patterns. When the pattern, such as a triangle, forms, the setup is the pattern formation. If this pattern formation does not abide by the rules of triangle formations during its creation, it is not a setup, and we ignore it. If it does form correctly, we wait for the breakout, which is the action signal. Traders use the short-term patterns in the same manner, but over shorter time horizons, and they use tighter stops and exit signals.

Because short-term patterns are relatively frequent and usually depend on the previous trend as well as other factors, the prior trend must be known before short-term patterns can be used. A top pattern in a downward trend is obviously meaningless, for instance, and, thus, all top patterns can be disregarded from consideration during a declining trend. This leaves only bottoming patterns to consider during a downward trend. Also, a short-term reversal pattern should only be considered necessary when prices are at some kind of support level, resistance level, or trend line. Whenever many bits of evidence occur at a particular price and time, it is called a "cluster" of evidence. Once a cluster of evidence begins to form, the analyst should begin looking for a short-term pattern. It then can be useful in signaling when and where to act as well as what the price risk might be.

Short-term patterns can also be used to determine when upward or downward momentum is slowing. In the next chapter, "Confirmation," we cover oscillators and indicators that determine momentum, but for now, remember that instead of using a momentum signal for action, using short-term patterns can often signal more precisely when to act and what risk exists once momentum begins to slow.

Although short-term patterns are usually reversal patterns, they can be used as continuation patterns in corrections within a trend. For example, in a strong upward trend, when the price corrects or retraces in a normal manner and a cluster of evidence forms that indicates the earlier, longer trend may soon continue, a short-term bottom reversal or continuation pattern may signal when to act. Usually, however, short-term patterns are best when they occur right at a peak or trough. Minimum action should be taken, however, unless there is a cluster of evidence that a longer-term reversal is due or that a strong trend is due to continue. For example, in an uptrend, if a price is near previous resistance, under but close to an important moving average, and has reached a price target, a short-term reversal top pattern is likely valid and worth acting upon. If a short-term reversal pattern of any kind occurs without supporting evidence, it might or might not signal an actual price reversal; it might simply signal that a slight consolidation period is next.

Short-term patterns are also the first sign that a reversal is nearing. They act very quickly, often occurring on the actual peak or trough day. As such, they lead most other patterns, which take time and further price action to develop. In a head-and-shoulders top pattern, for example, the analyst must wait for the actual breakout below the neckline before acting, but a short-term reversal pattern might have already indicated a potential reversal right at the top of the head.

In experimenting with short-term patterns, the technical analyst should consider several variables:

- The more complex the pattern, the less frequently it is going to occur. Some analysts have libraries of hundreds of patterns they have found useful in the past and through experimentation and use a computer-screening program that will pump out all the relevant patterns before each trading day. This gives them an edge but is impractical for most traders.

- The relationship between bars in a pattern need not be just a matter of the position of the high, low, open, and close to each other. The relation can be a proportional one rather than an exact one (Harris, 2000) where, for example, the close is in the lower 33% of the trading range, or the range that is three bars earlier is one-half the range of the last bar.

- The pattern may be split between two time periods, whereby one pattern appears at one time, and at some predetermined time later, another pattern must appear.

- The entry may be delayed by some predetermined time.

- The pattern may relate to another market entirely, whereby, for example, a pattern in the bond market may give a signal in the stock market or a currency.

These variables make the search for reliable patterns exceedingly complex and likely beyond necessity. The old principle of keeping things simple should be applied to any kind of pattern recognition search.

We divide the types of patterns into traditional bar chart patterns and candlestick patterns. Candlestick patterns portray the raw data of open, close, high, and low differently than a bar chart, but their patterns are very similar to bar chart patterns. Part of the appeal of candlestick charts is not so much the patterns but the visual ease with which the analyst can "see" intraday pressures on price and the price trend. They also have peculiar but memorable names for specific patterns that make them engaging.

As in all patterns, experience will separate the winners from the losers. Anyone using such patterns should record in a notebook the successes and failures from interpreting short-term patterns. Reviewing this recording periodically will help the investor develop a better "feel" of his ability to act profitably and learn where mistakes more frequently occur. Every trading vehicle has its own "personality." Success is often a function of understanding the peculiarities of the trading vehicle most commonly traded.

PATTERN CONSTRUCTION AND DETERMINATION

The principal data used in short-term patterns—both traditional and candlestick, regardless of bar time—is open, close, high, and low. The opening price is traditionally considered the price established from any news, emotion, anticipation, or mechanical signals that have built up overnight. Most professional day traders, scalpers, and even swing traders prefer to avoid it. They wait for some action—a gap or opening range—to take place before judging the tone of the market.

Because the closing price is the final price of the day and the one at which most margin accounts are valued, it is like a summary of the bar's activity. If the close is up, the majority and most recent action was positive; if the close is down, the majority and most recent price action was to the downside. Professionals use it as a benchmark with which to compare the next day's price action. Most people reading the financial news remember and use it to value their accounts. The closing price becomes a benchmark for future action, both long and short term. Some traders consider it the most important price of the day, even though it is somewhat arbitrary.

The high is the upper extreme reached by buyers during the bar and is, thus, a measure of buying ability and enthusiasm. On the other hand, the low is the lower extreme reached by sellers during the bar and is, thus, a measure of selling ability and fear.

The configuration, length of the bar, position on the bar, preceding bar data, and price distance between each determine the pattern. As you might guess, there is a multitude of potential combinations, and all have been investigated for ways to profit. We present next just a few of the large array of short-term patterns that have shown promise in the past.

TRADITIONAL SHORT-TERM PATTERNS

Let us look at some of the short-term patterns and their trading implications. These are patterns in use today that by themselves are warnings, at best, but not necessarily action patterns, that should be followed without a cluster of other evidence. You will notice that none of the patterns includes moving averages. Over short time periods, especially when the period is interrupted by inactivity, moving averages are not reliable. For example, when using five-minute data, the only moving average with any value would be very short because the period from one day to the next is interrupted by a long period overnight when no trading activity occurs. In 24-hour markets, short-term moving averages have more value because the markets are open continuously.

Gaps

Gaps occur when either the low for the current bar is above the high for the previous bar or the high for the current bar is lower than the low of the previous bar. Figure 17.1 pictures a gap down. The "hole" or "void" created in the price history is a "price range at which no shares changed hands" (Edwards and Magee, 2007). A price gap might or might not have significance. We have seen them before in analyzing breakouts from classic patterns, trend lines, and support or resistance zones, and in those instances, the gaps were demonstrating the beginning of a new trend. However, gap types differ based on the context in which they occur. Some are meaningful, and others can be disregarded.

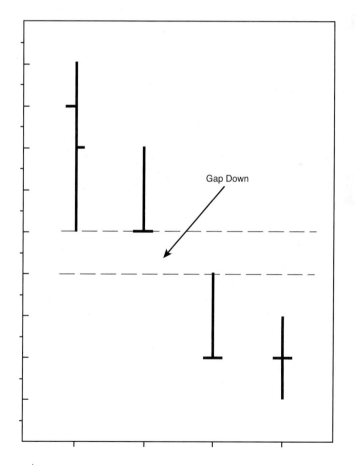

FIGURE 17.1 A gap down

Gaps often do not occur in market averages that are not themselves traded. For example, the day following Saddam Hussein's capture on December 13, 2003, a majority of stocks opened strongly upward on gaps, while the Dow Jones Industrial Average showed an opening price roughly the same as that at the close of the previous day and then rose as the prices of the component stocks gradually opened. No gap existed in the DJIA because it is an average, not a security. On the other hand, the DJIA future showed a gap because it is a traded security.

Breakaway (or Breakout) Gaps

The most profitable gaps are those that occur at the beginning of a trend, called breakaway gaps. We have seen these before when prices suddenly break through a formation boundary and a major change in trend direction begins. Breakaway gaps signal that a pattern is completed and a boundary penetrated. The size of the gap—the space between the two extremes in which no activity occurs—appears to be proportional to the strength of the subsequent price move. Heavy volume usually accompanies upward gaps but not necessarily downward gaps. The best manner of trading breakaway gaps is to wait a short while for the initial fading or profit-taking by the professionals to see if the gap is filled and if not, to enter in the direction of the gap with a stop at the point where the gap would be filled. If the gap is filled immediately, a stop and reverse might be appropriate, because a sudden failure in a gap is often followed by a large move in the opposite direction from the gap direction, similar to a Specialist's Breakout.

David Landry (2003) suggests a method of mechanizing the breakaway gap known as the "explosion gap pivot." A reversal point, often called a **pivot,** establishes not only where prices have reversed direction but also where supply and resistance are likely to occur in the future.[1] In Landry's method, a pivot low is the low of a bar that is surrounded on both sides by a bar with a higher low, as shown in Figure 17.2. This establishes a reversal point. Requirements that are more restrictive can be placed on the pivot point; for example, higher lows may be required for two or more bars on either side of the pivot point. For Landry's method, however, one on both sides is sufficient.

We know that a breakaway gap can be a false gap and that if it is "filled," the odds of it being false increase. Thus, we want a breakaway gap to establish a new high, for at least the past 20 days, and for the subsequent retracement not to fill the gap. If either of these requirements is not met, the gap is ignored. When the retracement does occur, eventually it will create a pivot low above the lower edge of the gap. Once this pivot low occurs, a buy entry stop is placed above the high of the next bar from the pivot low (the one that establishes the pivot), and a protective stop is placed just above the gap lower edge (or Landry suggests just below the pivot low). If the gap is then filled, the protective stop will exit the position. Occasionally, the pivot low will be penetrated again, but as long as the gap is not filled, the position should be kept. The reverse configuration is equally applicable to downward breakaway gaps.

---

1. This reversal "pivot" should not be confused with the "pivot point" used in intraday trading for anticipating potential support and resistance levels.

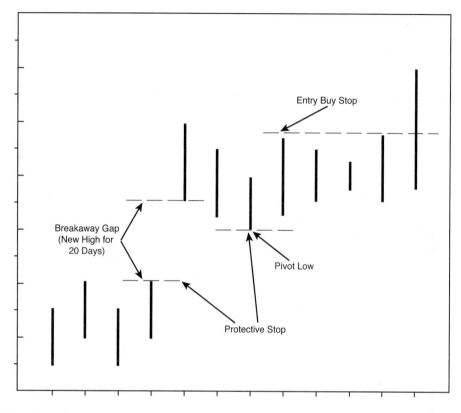

FIGURE 17.2 Explosion gap pivot

Opening Gap

When the opening price for the day is outside the range of the previous day, it is called an **opening gap.** After the opening, prices might continue in the direction of the gap, and the gap becomes a breakaway gap, or prices might retrace from the opening and fill the gap. Figure 17.3 shows an opening gap to the downside, with prices retracing and filling the gap during the day. This type of pattern is sometimes useful in determining a short-term trend reversal. The history of opening gaps in index futures suggests that they should be "faded" (or sold into) on large upward openings because they most often "fill" (retrace through the price vacuum) during the day. In downward opening gaps, a fill is not as common (Kaufman, 1998). In individual stock issues and commodities, a fill is a sign of weakness and should not occur in a breakaway gap. If the gap is not filled, usually within the first half hour, the odds of the trend continuing in the direction of the gap increase.

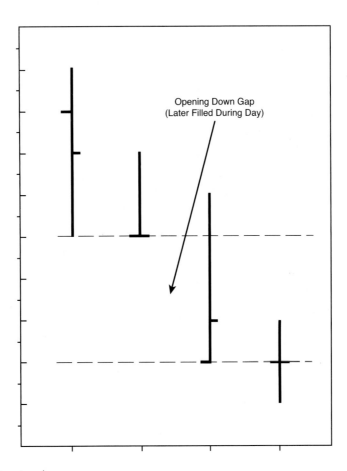

FIGURE 17.3   Opening down gap

One way potentially to profit from an opening gap is to watch the first three five-minute bars (a three-bar range) and determine the high and low of this range. A breakout of that range in the direction of the gap often indicates that the trend will continue in the gap direction; a break-out that moves in the direction of filling the gap will often continue to fill the gap. A danger is that the first run from the gap can last longer than the three bars. The three-bar range must, there-fore, be obvious, not a continued run in the gap direction. In addition, the breakout from the three-bar gap range in the direction of the gap may be false. A tight stop is necessary, or a wait for a pullback or throwback from the breakout, a narrow range bar break, or even a small cup and handle.

If the price breaks the three-bar range in the other direction toward the fill, the previous day's close, the fill line, will likely be the target. A bounce between the fill line and the range breakout line suggests that the longer-term move will be in the direction of the fill, a reversal of the gap. On the other hand, if the prices after a range break in the direction of the fill turn and retest the outer extreme of the three-bar range, the odds increase that the longer-term move will be in the direction of the gap.

Runaway Gaps (or Measuring Gaps)

Gaps that occur along a trend are called **runaway gaps.** They can appear in strong trends that have very few minor corrections and just keep rising or declining without retracements or other interruptions. They are also called **measuring gaps** because, like pennants and flags, they often occur at about the middle of a price run, and, thus, the initial distance to them can be projected above them for a target price. An upward runaway gap occurs on average 43% of the distance from the trend beginning and the eventual peak, whereas a downward gap occurs on average 57% of the distance (Bulkowski, 2010).

Exhaustion Gaps

Exhaustion gaps occur at the end of moves but are not recognized at the time because they have the same characteristics as runaway gaps. If a gap is later closed, it is likely an exhaustion gap. These gaps appear when a strong trend has reached a point where greed or fear has reached its apex. Usually they represent latecomers to the trend who are anxious to jump on or jump off. They can occur on light volume but more often occur on heavy volume.

The sign that such gaps are not runaway gaps is an immediate fill within a few bars of the gap. Remember that a runaway gap often occurs midstream in a price run. Prices should not immediately reverse and fill a gap unless the end of the run is approaching. Exhaustion gaps occur at the end of a move and signal a potential trend reversal. Usually more evidence of an exhaustion gap is necessary before an action signal can be justified. Sometimes prices reverse immediately, and sometimes they enter a congestion area.

Other Minor Gaps

Common gaps are those that occur frequently in illiquid trading vehicles, are small in relation to the price of the vehicle, or appear in very short-term trading data. They are of no consequence. Pattern gaps occasionally appear within the formation of larger patterns, and generally they are filled. Their only significance is to suggest that a congestion area is forming. Ex-dividend gaps sometimes occur in stock prices when the dividend is paid and the stock price is adjusted the following day. These have no significance and must not be misinterpreted. Often gaps occur in 24-hour futures trading when one market closes and another opens, especially if one market is electronic and the other open outcry. These are called suspension gaps and are also meaningless unless they occur as one of the four principal gaps described previously.

BOX 17.1   GAPS AND CLASSIC PATTERNS—A CASE STUDY OF APPLE COMPUTER

Figure 17.4 contains daily bar charts for Apple Computer (AAPL) for September 2009 through May 2010. What actions might we have taken in this stock, given our knowledge of classic patterns and gaps? Each paragraph number below corresponds to the number on Figure 17.4.

1. First we see a small pennant formation with an upward breakout at $167.28. We buy the stock on the breakout. Because we don't have the past history, we can't, at this point make a measured move projection of the eventual target, and we decide to just hold the stock with a protective stop below the pennant's lower bound at $164.11. Upward gap1 and gap2 appear next. We use them to place trailing stops as the price progresses upward. The pivot low after the gap1 is the first trailing stop at $169.70. We now have a locked-in profit even if the stop is triggered. Gap2 is a runaway gap. A runaway gap should not retrace back into the gap, or it is not a runaway. We, thus, raise the trailing stop to the upper edge of the gap at $177.88. Because this is a runaway gap, we can now project the target with the measured move method. We do this by measuring the price difference between the move beginning ($167.28) and the midpoint in the gap ($176.77). This $9.49 we add to the gap2 midpoint to arrive at an estimated objective of $176.77 + $9.49 = $186.25. This price is reached two days later, at which point we can sell or hang on with a close trailing stop so as not to lose the gain we have already achieved. If we sell at the target price, we will have profited by $18.97, about 11.3% in nine days.

2. The price then goes into a flag pattern and when it breaks out at $187.30, we buy it again. This breakout is accompanied by gap3, which is later filled. We place the protective stop at the low price of the flag at $180.70.

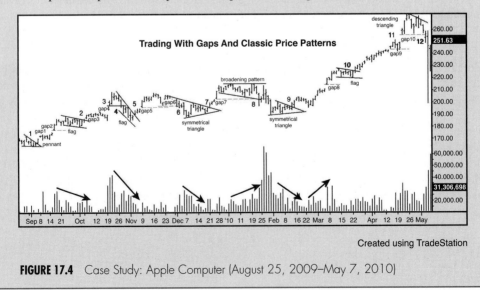

Created using TradeStation

FIGURE 17.4 Case Study: Apple Computer (August 25, 2009–May 7, 2010)

3. Gap4 occurs and has the initial appearance of a breakout or runaway gap. In neither case should prices fill such a gap, and so we move our stop to the upper limit of the gap4 at $197.85

4. Our trailing stop is triggered by an unexpected price decline that negates the earlier interpretation of gap4. We profit by $10.55.

5. The price then forms a downward flag pattern and volume confirms as it declines with price. The break upward from the flag triggers another buy at $190.73. This is followed by gap5, another likely runaway gap. The measured move projection from this gap is $200.73, which is reached on the day following gap5. We can sell at this level and reap another gain, this time of $10.00.

6. Had we not sold at the target price, we still would have placed a trailing stop at the upper level of gap5 at $196.26 and sold the stock on the retracement. We might also have sold the stock short on the trailing stop because the filling of what's thought to be a runaway gap is often an exhaustion gap and, therefore, a price trend reversal.

7. Whether we sold the stock short or not, the upward breakout from a symmetrical triangle would require another entry buy at $196.05. Following that triangle, breakout gap7 forms. This also has the appearance of a runaway gap (strong price move closing near high on increased volume), and we move a trailing stop from below the triangle to the upper edge of the gap at $203.35. We also calculate the measured move target of $209.68, which is reached two days later. If we sell at the target, we achieve on the trade a profit of $13.63.

8. If we don't sell at the target, we certainly are forced to sell when the price breaks below our trailing stop at the upper bound of gap7. This breakout is not only through the gap but also through the lower bound of a broadening pattern. Indeed, with this combination, we will short the stock at the breakout price of $203.35 and place a protective stop at the upper bound of the broadening pattern at $215.55. Following the breakout down, the price rallies in a pullback to the breakdown level but fails to penetrate back through it on the upside. However, it also fails to continue downward after the pullback and instead forms a symmetrical triangle. We place a buy stop each day along the upper bound of the triangle as our trailing stop.

9. We get stopped out with the trailing stop at $196.60, and we buy the stock on the basis of the triangle pattern confirmed with declining volume. We place a protective stop at the cradle of the triangle where the two bounds meet at $189.48 in case the breakout is false. Indeed, the price throws back shortly after the breakout but doesn't penetrate the cradle, and we remain long the stock. Gap8 comes after a healthy rise in the stock price. This also has the appearance of a runaway gap (high volume, large price move), and we move our trailing stop to the upper bound of the gap at $219.70. The measured move target from this runaway gap is $234.02. It is reached 18 days later.

continues

continued

10. We could sell at the target price, but before the target is reached, a flag pattern formed. We move our trailing stop up to the lower edge of the flag at $220.15 to protect our profit. A flag pattern is also a measured pattern that will give an additional price target. The calculation in this instance is to take the high point in the flag at $227.73 minus the starting price of the move ($196.60) for an estimated price distance of $31.13 that we add to the level at which the price breaks out of the flat ($224.64). But prices broke upward from the flag and, thus, projected $31.13 to a target of $255.77, our new target.

11. Our price target is reached 21 trading days after the upward breakout from the flag pattern on a large upward gap (gap10). There was a small gap9 preceding gap10 and a few others along the way. Each of these gaps failed to show the characteristics of a runaway gap and were, thus, ignored. But gap10, aside from reaching our objective was substantial and also likely a runaway gap, just because of the size of the gap compared with others. If we don't sell at the target price, we at least move the trailing stop to the upper level of the gap at $255.73.

12. As it turns out, gap10 was an exhaustion gap, something that can only be recognized in retrospect. However, we were stopped out of our trade at the trailing stop and perhaps went short on the exhaustion gap breakdown because this type of breakdowns often indicates a trend reversal. That the exhaustion gap occurred at the price target from the earlier flag formation confirmed the likelihood of a trend reversal. The sell stop produced a profit of $59.13, a 30% gain in less than 3 months.

The preceding example shows what can be done with just technical analysis alone. We did not act on any news or outside market behavior. We simply watched the price very closely. Stops were an important part of our strategy. If we had not moved stops when we did, we would have suffered at the upward breakout from the symmetrical triangle and from the failure of gap10. Risk control is sometimes more important than entry technique. Technical analysis takes knowledge, patience, and close watching of price action, but profits can be made.

Spike (or Wide-Range or Large-Range Bar)

Spikes are similar to gaps except that the empty space associated with a gap is a solid line (in a bar chart). Should a breakaway gap occur intraday, for example, the daily bar would not show the discontinuity from the gap but instead would show a long bar. The importance of a spike, as in a gap, depends on the context surrounding it. A spike can occur on a breakout from a formation, midpoint in a strong, accelerating trend, and as the final reversal day at the end of a trend. In the earlier discussion of breakouts, we demonstrated the Specialist Breakout. This is often a spike because it usually occurs intraday. At the ends of trends when either gross enthusiasm or panic appears, the last few bars are often spikes. At the end of an accelerated trend, the last bar within the trend is often a spike called a climax (see Figure 17.5). Thus, spikes can represent the beginning or end of a trend. On the other hand, some stocks and commodities, especially those awaiting a news announcement, will have wide-range bars that subside almost immediately within the next few days with little net change in trend direction. This behavior is generally associated with a stock or commodity that will not follow standard technical rules.

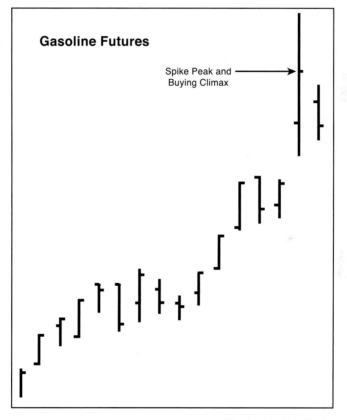

Created using TradeStation

FIGURE 17.5 Spike peak and buying climax (July 2005–September 2005)

Dead Cat Bounce (DCB)

"Dead Cat Bounce" is a graceless term for a failed rally after a sharp decline. Although the term has been used for many years on Wall Street and in Chicago, it was probably first used in print either in a 1985 *Financial Times* article by reporter Chris Sherwell in a comment on the sharp decline in the Singapore stock market or by Raymond Devoe Jr., research analyst and professional cynic, who advocated using a bumper sticker "Beware the Dead Cat Bounce" in 1986.

The DCB is most profitable and more easily recognized after a large downward breakaway gap or downward breakaway spike. The sudden downward motion is called an **event decline** because it usually occurs on an event such as a bad news announcement. It lasts just a few days (average of seven) and usually begins a longer-term downward price trend. The DCB's characteristics include a short rally of several days up to two weeks following the initial bottom from the sharp initial news event sell-off. Ideally, the rally should follow an event decline of over 20%. Normally, the larger the first decline, the higher the bounce. In Figure 17.6 of British Petroleum during the Gulf Oil disaster, the first DCB had only a very small two-day DCB before declining again. The second downward gap was followed by a larger DCB that also lasted 2 days, and the third lasted 2 days. The "bounce" comes from bargain hunters and bottom-fishing traders who are second-guessing when the actual bottom will take place. It gathers momentum from short covering and momentum signals. The buyers are usually wrong. In over 67% of DCBs (Bulkowski, 2010), the price continues to lower after the DCB and breaks the earlier news event low an average of 18%. The second decline in a DCB is characteristically less intense but equally deceiving. It also tends to be accompanied by much lower volume. Not all event declines include a DCB.

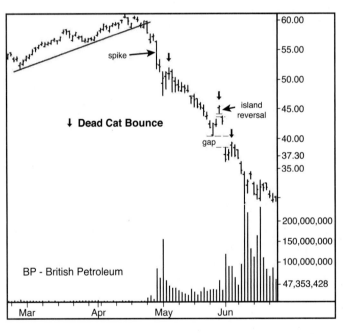

Created using TradeStation

FIGURE 17.6   Dead Cat Bounce (British Petroleum daily: February 19, 2010–June 23, 2010)

To trade the DCB, the event decline must first be recognized. This is usually easy because almost every day, somewhere, some bad news comes out about a company or commodity. Wait for the initial sell-off volume to decline and then look for a rally on lesser volume, sometimes back as far as the lower edge of the breakaway gap, and lasting only a few days. If the downward rush occurred as a spike rather than a gap (as did BP in Figure 17.6), look into the intraday trading to see where the news event gap occurred, and use that gap just as if it had occurred between the daily bars. In the British Petroleum chart (Figure 17.6), the rally did not fill the gap in all DCBs. The short-selling trading requirement then is for a topping of the bounce or a short-term top pattern, close protective stops above the entry, and a longer time horizon. For those wanting to purchase the stock, the odds are against profiting from a purchase for at least six months. Most bullish chart patterns fail during this period.

Island Reversal

An island reversal can occur at either a top or a bottom and only occurs after a relatively lengthy trend. It can occur in a congestion area, but only infrequently. It requires two gaps at roughly the same price: the first in the direction of the trend, an exhaustion gap, and the second in the reverse direction, a breakaway gap. The British Petroleum chart shown in Figure 17.6 shows an island reversal top within the context of a downward trend. The larger the gap, the more important is the formation. Between the gaps, low volatility trading can occur for a number of days or even weeks. Volume usually increases on the second gap from an island top but not necessarily from a bottom. The extreme price in the island must be either higher than previous highs at a top or lower than previous lows at a bottom. Pullbacks and throwbacks are frequent (65%–70%), and failures are low, around 13%–17%. This pattern is not very common and has terrible performance results (Bulkowski, 2010).

One- and Two-Bar Reversal Patterns

The following one- and two-bar reversal patterns are very common. Therefore, each of these patterns needs confirmation before use.

One-Bar Reversal (Also Reversal Bar, Climax, Top or Bottom Reversal Bar, Key Reversal Bar)

When a trading bar high is greater than the previous bar high and the close is down from the previous bar close, it is called a **one-bar reversal.** It is sometimes preceded by a gap, at least an opening gap, and its bar length is not as extreme or intensive as in a spike. It is not a spike, because a spike is not necessarily a reversal, but a combination of spike and reversal can elevate its meaning. This pattern will occur in reverse at a bottom. It is very common, but unfortunately, its top and bottom version will also occur within a trend, making it practically useless as a signal by itself. To be useful, but also cutting down on the number of profitable signals, it needs more stringent requirements. For example, rather than just closing down, the close may be required to exceed the previous bar low or even the low of the two previous bars. Kamich (2003) argues that a close is more reliable after a sustained advance than after a short rally. This may require that it be the highest high or lowest low over a specified period or that a series of higher highs or lower lows precede it. When combined with a cluster of other evidence, a close's significance improves. Whatever signal it gives is completely negated once prices exceed its reversal peak or trough.

Two-Bar Reversal (Also Pipe Formation)

The two-bar reversal pattern, like the one-bar reversal, occurs at the end of a trend, upward or downward, but extends the reversal over two bars. Bulkowski calls it a **pipe formation.** A two-bar reversal formation is pictured in Figure 17.7. In the bottom pattern, the first bar usually closes in the lower half of the bar, and the second bar close ends near its high. Usually high volume is seen on both bars. In its extreme and more reliable version, it consists of two side-by-side spikes, but it can also be above-average length side-by-side bars of roughly equivalent length, peaking or bottoming at close to the same price, and occurring after a lengthy trend. Following and prior to the two-bar reversal, low bar prices should be in the vicinity of the top of the bars (in a bottom, the opposite for a top). It, thus, stands out quite easily in retrospect. It is preferable for the second bar to be slightly longer than the first bar, and volume is preferably higher on the left bar than on the right. Rarely this pattern acts as a consolidation area within a trend. Many pipes occur at the end of the retracement of a longer-term move. The directional clue is the direction of the breakout from it.

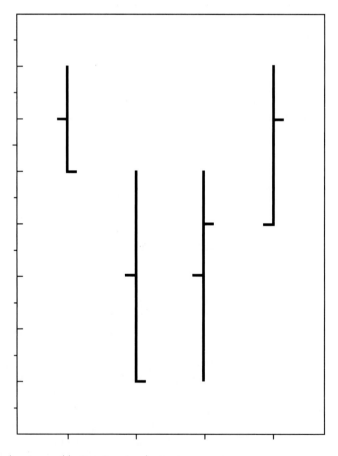

FIGURE 17.7 Two-bar reversal bottom (or pipe bottom)

Failure rates are in the 5% range, which is very low for a pattern (Bulkowski, 2010). Usually the failure occurs when the previous trend has been less than 5%. If the earlier trend is lengthy, the pattern rarely fails. Once the pattern has formed and prices have reversed direction, it is common for a test of the bars to occur soon thereafter. In most cases, the bars hold their extreme within a small percentage during the test, and this presents a good spot to place an initial protective stop. Both Kamich and Bulkowski maintain that the formation in weekly bars is more reliable than in daily bars. Bulkowski ranks it 2 out of 23 for performance in a bull market.

Horn Pattern

Bulkowski describes the horn pattern as being almost identical in behavior to the pipe except a smaller bar separates the two lengthy bars. The two long bars become the "horns" of the formation (see Figure 17.8). As in the two-bar reversal, the formation is more reliable with weekly bars and otherwise has the same characteristics as the pipe. It is not as effective as the pipe at bottoms and tops, and its failure rate increases when the trend preceding the pattern is short.

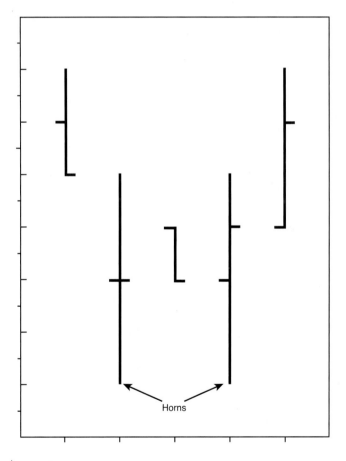

Horns

FIGURE 17.8 The horn pattern

Two-Bar Breakout

The two-bar breakout is an extremely simple pattern. Indeed, it is so simple it is hard to believe that it will work, but the testing column in *Active Trader Magazine* (November 2003) tested it and found it to be successful for stocks and commodities (more so with commodities). The rules they used and that could easily be experimented with are for longs: the next day buy on a stop one tick above today's high if (1) today's low is less than yesterday's low; (2) today's high is less than yesterday's high, and (3) today's close is less than today's open. Exit on a stop at the then-current day's low. The sell side is just the opposite. Results should be tested against a better exit strategy, but as it is, the pattern produced reasonable profits in commodities and an extremely low drawdown. In stocks, the results were not as favorable but likely could be improved upon with money management and a better exit strategy.

Inside Bar

An inside bar is a bar with a range that is smaller than and within the previous bar's range, as shown in Figure 17.9. It reflects a decline in momentum in a trend, a bar where a short-term congestion area is formed. As in most congestion areas, it reflects a pause, a period of directionless equilibrium waiting for something to happen that will signal the next trend direction. During a larger congestion pattern, such as a triangle or rectangle, an inside bar has little meaning because it is just reflecting the lack of motion in the larger pattern. Some analysts plotting larger patterns delete inside bars, especially when determining pivots, because these bars fail to represent any important price action, similar to how the point-and-figure chart eliminates dull periods. Within a trend, however, the inside bar provides some useful information and can generate profitable very short-term signals. As in the gap pattern, the context of the pattern's location is more important than the pattern configuration.

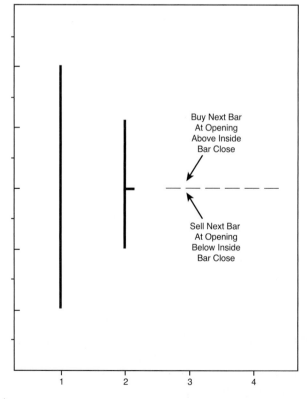

FIGURE 17.9 Inside bar

Tony Crabel (1989) found that without a cluster of other information, a number of inside bar combinations during the 1982–1986 period in the S&P futures achieved a better-than-average winning percentage. Crabel tested buying at the next opening, if it occurred above the inside bar close and selling at the next opening, if it occurred below the inside bar close (see Figure 17.10). This strategy produced a 68% winning percentage. This winning percentage could then be improved by adding even other requirements, mostly having to do with characteristics of the bars preceding the inside bar and with the preceding trend. One strategy, for example, is to buy if the inside bar close was higher than the previous day close and there is a higher open on the current bar and to sell when the inside bar close was below the previous day close and the opening on the current bar is below the inside close. For this slightly more complex strategy, a 74% winning percentage occurred.

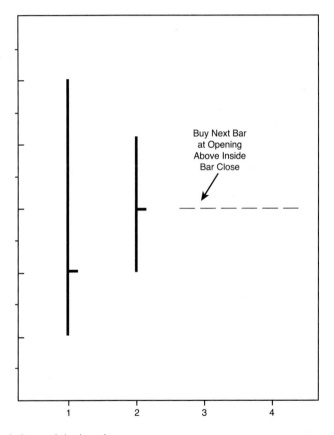

FIGURE 17.10 Inside bar with higher close

Crabel took his inside tests a little further, looking for a four-day pattern. If Day 2 had a higher low than Day 1, Day 3 was an inside day, and if Day 4 opened lower than the midrange and close of the inside day, a sell signal was generated. This strategy is pictured in Figure 17.11.

During Crabel's test period, this strategy had an 80% winning percentage. The opposite strategy would occur when Day 2 had a lower high than Day 1, Day 3 was an inside day, and Day 4 opened above the inside day close, triggering a buy signal. This strategy produced a 90% winning percentage. Although these strategies had extremely high winning percentages, they only occurred on average twice a year.

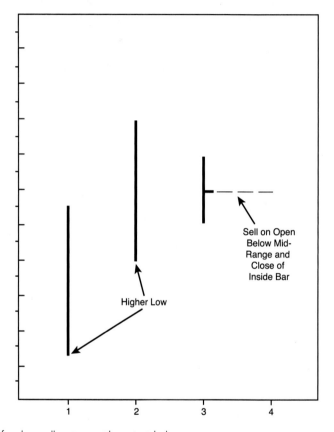

FIGURE 17.11   A four-bar sell pattern with an inside bar

What Crabel was demonstrating, regardless of the percentages, was that the opening of a bar after an inside bar shows a strong bias toward the new price direction. Granted, his testing was done during a bull market in the late 1980s and is somewhat dated today, but nevertheless, the tests showed some correlation to the inside day breakouts and future performance. His exit criterion was to close the position on the close of the day the trade was entered. This limits such trades to day traders. However, an inside bar can also occur on weekly bar charts and usually signifies a larger congestion area similar to a pennant or flag on a daily chart. In these cases, the inside week can be useful for longer-term trading.

Several other common patterns use the inside bar concept.

Hook Reversal Day

Hook is a common term for a quick loss when a profit was expected. It comes from the fishhook that the fish bites thinking that the bait is a free meal. As outlined by Kamich (2003) and Crabel (1989), a hook reversal occurs after a series of upward thrust bars, called run bars when they occur right after each other (Schwager, 1996). Then suddenly, a narrow-range bar occurs with specific characteristics. The narrow-range bar must open at above the previous high and close below the previous close. Kamich's variation is for an inside bar that opens at its high and closes at its low. This signals that the momentum built up during the run has reached a climax. A downward break would be an action signal.

Another hook formation occurs when traders are "hooked" into believing that the trend has reversed. This occurs when an open is above the previous high, but prices reverse direction and close down on the bar. This is the hook. It must have a narrower range than the previous bar, but it often fools traders into believing that a top has occurred. The action signal is when the price breaks back above the close of the first. It also works in reverse.

Naked Bar Upward Reversal

A variation of the hook, a naked bar is one that closes below a previous low (suggested by Joe Stowell and Larry Williams) and is a down bar (close less than open). It is the most bearish close possible. If an inside bar follows a naked bar with open greater than naked bar close, it is a sign that the downtrend is reversing. An upward break from the inside bar would suggest the bears are caught.

Hikkake

The hikkake is an inside bar signal that fails and become a signal itself (see Figure 17.12). As described by Daniel Chesler (2004), in Japanese, "hikkake" is a term meaning to trap, trick, or ensnare. It is a pattern that starts with an inside bar. When prices break one way or the other from an inside bar, the conventional belief is that they will continue in the same direction. The hikkake pattern occurs when the breakout fails to continue and prices in the following bars return to break in the opposite direction through the previous inside bar extreme. The reversal and opposite breakout must occur within three bars after the first breakout, and the open and close of each bar seems to be unimportant.

Outside Bar

An outside bar occurs when the high is higher than the high of the previous bar and the low is lower than the low of the previous bar. It is a specific kind of wide-range bar that "covers" all the previous bar's price action. In other words, the outside bar is longer than the previous bar and contains the entire price range of the previous bar. Traditionally, an outside bar is thought of as a bar of increased volatility, and, depending on the close, perhaps the beginning of a trend. Larry Williams (1988, 1995, 1999, 2000, 2003) has done considerable study of outside bars, and the results are available in his various books.

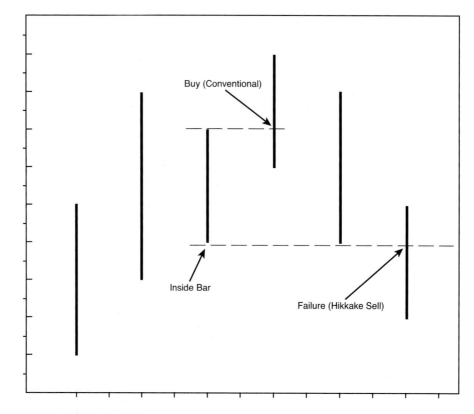

FIGURE 17.12   Hikkake buy failure

When an outside bar closes near an extreme—that is, a high or low—and above or below the previous close and its current opening, it suggests further action in the direction of the close into the following bar. Bulkowski, using daily lows observes that the close, if located within the upper or lower 25% of the range, tends to predict the future breakout upward about 66% of the time and downward 62% of the time. However, it often is a false signal. For example, one of the more reliable, though less frequently seen, setup patterns with an outside day is when the outside day closes at below the previous day's low and the next day opens lower than the outside day close. Buy the following day opening (Williams, 2000). Standard opinion would suggest that the series of lower closes was bearish, yet the setup is bullish.

Multiple Bar Patterns

Trend Correction

Many studies have shown that acting in the direction of the trend is more advantageous after waiting for a correction to that trend. The reward of catching the trend at a cheaper price as well as having a closer stop level outweigh the potential opportunity loss of missing the trend.

There are at least two different types of trend correction patterns. One is to recognize a trend and act on a percentage pullback from that trend. *Active Trader Magazine* (March, 2003) tested on 18 stocks a long-only 6% pullback system. It demonstrated during the period 1992 through 2002, a generally rising period, entering a buy at 6% below the previous bar close and exiting on the next open would produce an excellent equity curve when triggered. The gain over the period was the same as the buy-and-hold, but the market exposure was only 17% due to the limited number of trades and the quick exits.

Knockout Pattern

The knockout (or KO) pattern is another trend correction method, used by David Landry (2003). (See Figure 17.13). The first requirement for this pattern is that an extremely strong and persistent trend must be present. In an upward trend, Landry's criteria for a strong uptrend is that the stock must have risen at least ten points in the past 20 trading days and a trend line drawn through the prices touch almost all bars. Thus, if we think about a linear regression line, the bars should have a small deviation from that line, not wide swings back and forth. At some time, the stock will develop a throwback of two to five days in which two prior lows will be exceeded. Place a buy entry stop at the high of the bar with the second low. If the next bar is lower, move the buy stop to its high until the position is executed. Place a protective stop below the last low, or use any reasonable stop method. According to Landry, the reverse is equally as successful in a downtrend using the criteria in reverse. Figure 17.13 shows a steady downward trend in lumber futures with occasional two-day rallies that fulfill the requirements of the KO pattern.

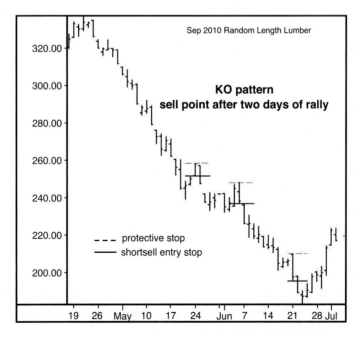

Created using TradeStation

FIGURE 17.13 Landry KO pattern (Lumber daily: April 16, 2010–July 2, 2010)

Oops!

Larry Williams (1979) coined the expression "Oops!" (see Figure 17.14). The setup for this pattern occurs when the opening price on today's bar is outside the previous day's range. Assume, for example, that a stock opens today at a price below yesterday's range. A buy stop is then placed just inside yesterday's range in case the market closes the gap, indicating a reversal. This pattern depends on traders acting in the direction of an opening gap and being caught when prices reverse.

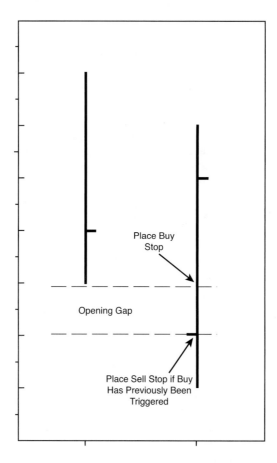

Place Buy
Stop

Opening Gap

Place Sell Stop if Buy
Has Previously Been
Triggered

FIGURE 17.14 Oops! buy pattern

Larry Connors (1998) uses a 10% qualification variation of the Larry Williams Oops! pattern. The pattern is for the first day to have a close within 10% of the low. The second day must open on a downward gap. If these conditions are met, place a buy stop at the first day's low with a sell stop near the second day's opening. A sell pattern is just the reverse on a day when the close is within 10% of its high.

Shark

The shark pattern is a three-bar pattern. The most recent bar high must be lower than the previous high and the recent low above the previous low. In other words, the recent bar is an inside bar. The previous bar must also be an inside bar. The progression in bars, therefore, is one base bar and two successive inside bars, as shown in Figure 17.15. In effect, it is a small triangle or pennant. The name "shark" comes from the pattern's finlike shape.

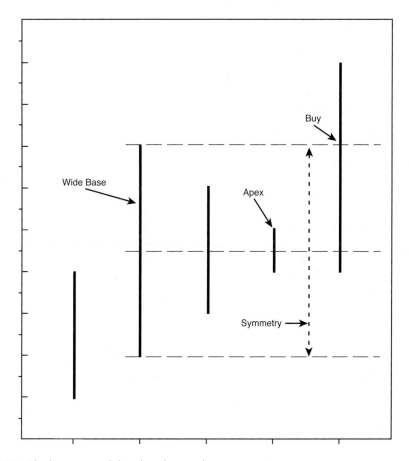

FIGURE 17.15 Shark pattern with break to the upside

In a *Stocks and Commodities* article, Walter Downs (1998) demonstrated that the short-term pattern called the Shark-32 has implications for the longer-term as well as the immediate future. This study was an interesting approach to determining the success or failure of the pattern in that Downs questioned whether the symmetry of the pattern added to or detracted from its performance. Symmetry was measured by determining the amount by which the center of the final inside day range, called the apex, deviated from the center of the base day range. Although there can be many shark patterns, Downs limited his study to those patterns that fit a specified symmetry. The test was run on Harley Davidson stock from July 1986 to April 1998, a period of generally rising stock prices. The entry was to buy on the close of the first day after a day in which the close exceeded the widest point in the pattern, usually the base day. The exit was a trailing stop or a reversal on the opposite signal.

The results of Downs' study were useful in that they suggested that the more symmetrical the shark formation, the more likely prices would continue in the same direction and improve performance at least out to 30 days thereafter. As the symmetry became very tight, the results did not change, but the number of patterns that fit into the requirements declined. One example was that if the symmetrical variance of the apex midrange was within 12% either side of the center of the base day range, the trend continued in the same direction as the prepattern direction 91% of the time, strengthened in 36% of the instances, and increased in momentum 34% of the time within 30 days.

Volatility Patterns

Most short-term patterns rely on an expansion in volatility. The inside bar strategies, for example, are based on the notion that inside bars represent low volatility and that when prices break one way or another, volatility expands. To take this concept of volatility further, many patterns look directly at volatility itself—either historical volatility as defined in the option markets, changes in trading ranges, or indicators such as the ADX. An expansion in volatility is used as a signal for action in most patterns, but sometimes a contrary action is suggested when volatility becomes extreme. Following are examples of some of these patterns.

Wide-Range Bar

A wide-range bar is a bar in which the range is "considerably" wider than the normal bar. The bars are relatively long compared with the previous bar. How large does the range have to be to be considered "wide," and how far back must the comparison be made? There are no definitive answers to these questions and, therefore, there is no specific definition of a wide-range bar other than its range is "considerably" wider than the normal bar. In any case, a wide-range bar is usually a bar with increased volatility. Increased volatility can imply the beginning of a new trend as in a breakout bar, or if the trend has been in existence for a long time and is accelerating, the wide-range bar may act like an exhaustion gap and warn of the trend's end. As a sign of impending trend reversal, it is more often seen at panic lows, as the emotions of fear accelerate prices downward. Emotional spikes and two-bar reversals are often wide-range bars. Otherwise, it is usually found on a breakout from a pattern, small or large, or as the base for a pennant or flag, indicating that the trend reached a very short-term peak and is about to consolidate. On the other hand, not all wide-range bars are meaningful. Consideration of trend, as always, areas of support and resistance, patterns, and the relative location of opens and closes are necessary before a judgment of the significance of the wide-range bar can be determined.

Larry Connors (1998) gives an example of a wide-range pattern. Connors first looks for a wide-range day in which a stock experiences a two-standard deviation decline. On the following day, if the opening is a downward gap, place a buy entry stop at the first day's close with a protection stop at the first day's low. If the buy is near the previous day's low, then lower the stop to give some room for the pattern to develop. The reverse set of signals is valid on the sell side at a top. The exit is to sell on the close, or if the close on the action day is within 10% to 15% of the high sell on the next day opening.

Narrow-Range Bar (NR)

Wide-range bars indicate high volatility; narrow-range bars indicate low volatility (see Figure 17.16). Determining narrow-range bars is useful because the low volatility will eventually switch to high volatility. As with the wide-range bar, the criteria for determining a narrow-range bar are not precise.

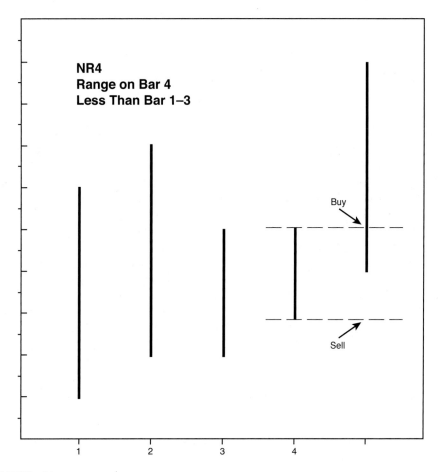

FIGURE 17.16 Narrow-range bar

Tony Crabel designed one method of defining and using narrow-range days. In his method, he determines whether the current day has a narrower range than the previous day and if so, over how many past days. For example, if the current day has a narrower range than the past three days, it is called an NR4 day (to include the current day and the past three days); in other words, the current day represents the narrowest trading range of the four days. The common narrow days of this type are the NR4 and NR7 day. Their entry signal is a breakout from the most recent narrow-range day. Thus, if today is an NR7 day, we place a buy and sell entry stop on either side to be acted upon tomorrow or the next day.

Linda Bradford Raschke (www.lbrgroup.com) is one of the leading proponents of using narrow-range days to determine low-volatility setups. Raschke adds another constraint to Crabel's method. She calculates the historic volatility of the vehicle over 6 days and over 100 days. If the 6-day historic volatility is 50% less than the 100-day, the conditions are right for either an NR4 day or inside day signal, provided today meets the criteria for each of these types of days. The buy and sell entry stops are placed at the high and low of the qualified NR4 or inside day. If the entry stop is executed, an additional exit stop is placed where the opposite entry stop currently exists. Exit the position at the close of the day if not already stopped out.

VIX

In our discussion of sentiment indicators in Chapter 7, "Sentiment," we introduced the VIX, a measure of implied volatility in the S&P 500 options. Remember that the VIX is a reflection of anxiousness in the market. Traders and investors become anxious when the market declines and become complacent when the market advances. Thus, VIX becomes a sentiment indicator. Generally, when the market is bottoming, VIX is high, because of the investor anxiousness. When the market is topping, VIX is generally low, indicating the complacency among investors.

Larry Connors (1998) introduced a number of short-term price patterns that were based on the behavior of the VIX. The principle behind these patterns was to watch for changes in VIX, as a measure of sentiment, at extremes, as for example, either after X number of days or combining with an oscillator formula to determine when VIX is overbought or oversold. A more general strategy for the VIX was to look at the deviation from a moving average (Connors, 2004). VIX has changed levels over the past decade, but a moving average dampens those changes. Connors used a 5% deviation from a 10-day simple moving average. If the VIX is below the SMA by 5% and the market is above its 200-day moving average, the odds favor a continuing upward trend but not necessarily a good time to buy except on throwbacks. When the ratio is above 5%, and even more so when it is above 10% of the SMA, the time is usually excellent to buy. Thus, the VIX in this instance gives general zones of when action in certain directions can be contemplated. The opposite relationship is valid when the market is below its 200-day moving average. Generally, bottoms are more reliably signaled by the VIX than tops.

Intraday Patterns

The opening range is the range of a daily bar that forms in the first few minutes or hour of the trading day (see Figure 17.17). It can be defined as either the high and low after a certain time, such as the high and low price that occur during the first 15 minutes of trading, or it can be a predetermined range about the opening price. A horizontal line is drawn at the opening range high and low on the intraday bar chart as a reference for the rest of the day. Other lines from the opening price, the close yesterday, the range yesterday, and so forth may also be drawn. These lines often become support or resistance levels during the day.

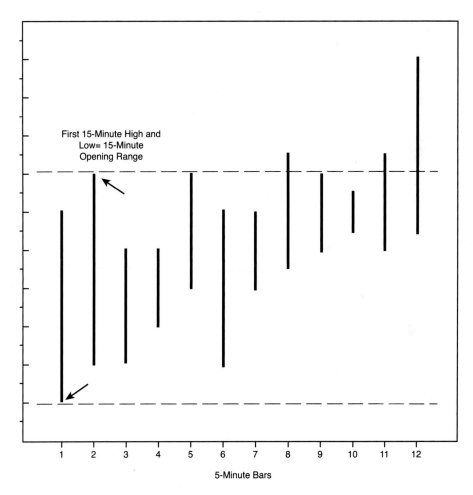

FIGURE 17.17 Opening range

The opening range breakout (ORB) is a popular method of entering a position once a setup has been established from a previous short-term pattern. As reported in *Stocks & Commodities Magazine,* Tony Crabel experimented with NR days as setups and used an ORB defined by a specified, predetermined amount above or below the opening range. He compared these results with using a wide-range day setup. He found, first, that the wide-range day setup over both four and seven days vastly underperformed the NR days over the same period, thus confirming that more profit can be obtained from an expansion in volatility than contraction. Second, he found that once the price had moved away from the open in one direction after a NR2, it normally did not return to the opening.

In a series of articles for *Stocks & Commodities Magazine,* Crabel describes methods of trading from an ORB in considerable detail. In the first article, he described how he calculates the specified amount, called the "stretch," above and below the opening that establishes the ORB. Crabel uses the ten-day average of the past differences between the open for each day and its closest extreme to the open for that day. Analysts use a number of other methods for calculating stretch, including specifying a number of ticks or calculating a range based on the ATR over some past period.

Crabel found that the use of ORBs worked well with NR4, NR7, inside days, and hook days. He found that the earlier in the day the ORB was penetrated, the better the chance for success. Even without the previously mentioned setups, trading on the ORB within the first five to ten minutes would also work, but after that short interval, if the prices have not penetrated out of the range, all orders should be canceled because the day will likely revert to a listless trading day rather than a trending day.

By analyzing the action around opening range levels, a good trader can find ways to take advantage of the tendency for these levels to act as support and resistance. One method of accomplishing this is called the "ACD method," developed by Mark Fisher (2002). This somewhat complicated method uses the opening range determined over the initial minutes of trading, an additional filter that is added to the upper bound of the range, and another subtracted from the lower edge, as shown in Figure 17.18. Entry signals occur when the outer bounds are broken during the day, and exit signals occur when the range bounds are broken. Fisher's method is not quite this simple because he uses numerous other rules and confirmations. However, Fisher, who reportedly has a trading room of over 75 day traders using this method to make their daily bread, has appeared to be very successful.

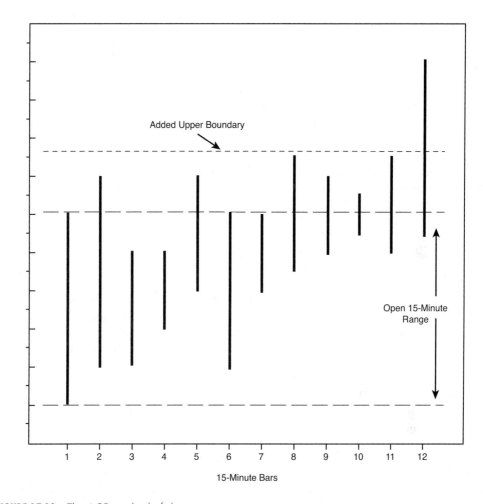

FIGURE 17.18 The ACD method of determining opening range

SUMMARY OF SHORT-TERM PATTERNS

Although there appears to be value in short-term patterns, they are not immediate sources of wealth without study, experience, and trial-and-error testing. We have only touched the edge of methods being used. Others include performance around national holidays, days of the week, time during the day, and even the new moon. There seems to be no limit. The point in this exercise, however, is to demonstrate the many ways that prices are analyzed over the short term. If interested, you can continue to experiment on your own.

CANDLESTICK PATTERNS

In Chapter 11, "History and Construction of Charts," we learned how to construct a candlestick chart. As you will recall, the raw data used in the candlestick chart is the same as the raw data used in the bar chart: open, close, high, and low price per specific period.

The candlestick chart has become popular because it represents price action in a more striking way, and furthermore, the patterns that result have interesting and novel names. One advantage of the candlestick chart is that it can still use the Western methods of analysis—patterns, trend lines, support, and resistance—yet it has a set of unique patterns of its own. These patterns are mostly short term of only one to five bars, and by themselves have not tested very well. Many patterns have their Western equivalents that we have seen before. They are generally reversal patterns and can reveal price reversals early in overbought or oversold conditions, at trend lines, or at support or resistance levels. However, they are tools, not a system. Their disadvantage is that one must wait for the close before a pattern can be recognized, and they are useless in markets that do not accurately report the opening prices. The best resource on candlesticks is *Japanese Candlestick Charting Techniques* by Steve Nison (2001), the person who introduced this ancient method to the West.

The principal analytical difference between candlestick patterns and Western bar patterns is the emphasis on the opening and close. Western traders have recognized the importance of the opening and close, but bar charts treat them without special weighting. In candlestick charts, the "real body" is the wider area between the open and close. The "shadow" is the vertical line from the real body up to the price high and down to the price low. A long shadow indicates the inability for prices to maintain their highs or lows and is, thus, a warning of trouble. The real body is a heavy color, such as black, when the close is lower than the open, and usually white when the close is higher than the open. A black body denotes, therefore, a "down" day, and a white body indicates an "up" day. (This definition is different than in the West, where a down day is a day in which the close is lower than the previous close.) A large body (in relative terms) indicates strength in the direction of the trend, and a small body indicates indecision and a potential reversal, especially after a meaningful prior trend.

Patterns are made by the relative position of the body and the shadow, the location of the candlestick in relation to its neighbors, and the confirmation the next day. Because candlestick patterns usually are defined as top or bottom patterns, the analyst must be sure that the preceding price action is in a trend, either up or down. A single pattern may or may not be meaningful depending on the direction of the previous trend. Similar to Western short-term patterns, a candlestick pattern cannot predict the extent of the subsequent move or the significance of the pattern—that is, whether it occurs at a major or minor reversal. Thus, the pattern should always be used with other evidence before action is taken. Being more often a reversal pattern, however, candlestick patterns are often useful in determining support and resistance levels on their own. At first, the analysis of these patterns seems to be filled with an endless set of rules and names, but as you become more familiar with the nomenclature, you will see that the basis of these patterns is not much different from the basis for Western short-term patterns.

There have been few tests on the effectiveness of candlestick patterns. This is odd because the patterns are easily computerized. As with tests of other short-term patterns, many of the existing studies are flawed in that the signal outcomes are often assumed to last longer than they should. Measuring the effectiveness of patterns over weeks or months is useless because these patterns are only useful in short-term situations. However, even over shorter periods, the patterns do not test well. Their profit factors are relatively low, and their drawdowns are high and in all cases greater than net profits. Some of the variables in each pattern can be tweaked to improve performance, but the basic patterns, by themselves, are not outstandingly profitable.

Two relatively recent studies with short-term results are by Caginalp and Laurent (1998) and by Schwager (1996). The Caginalp and Laurent tests included eight three-day patterns in S&P 500 stocks from 1992 to 1996. Their purpose was to demonstrate that the patterns had value above what could be expected from a random walk; however, drawdowns were not considered. Schwager tested six major patterns in ten commodities from 1990 to 1994 and included a momentum filter to account for trend, an important factor in candlestick pattern analysis. A criticism, however, is that Schwager estimated commissions and slippage to be $100 per trade, considerably higher than what can be achieved now. Both studies suffer from the type of exit method in that they depend on a holding period that is arbitrary and not based on the behavior of prices. The results could be considerably improved with testing of each pattern in combination with others and the use of protective stops. At least stops and other exit signals would reduce the extremely large drawdowns. In our presentation of the patterns covered by Schwager, we average the results from the ten commodities for each pattern and give the relative ranking rather than the raw percentages. This avoids, to some extent, the problem of commissions and slippage.

Following are some examples of the more common candlestick patterns.

One- and Two-Bar Candlestick Patterns

Candlestick patterns are short-term patterns. In fact, a number of candlestick patterns are formed by only one or two bars. Thus, on a candlestick chart of daily data, only one or two days' worth of data would be necessary to form the pattern.

Doji

A doji pattern is formed when the open and close are identical, or nearly identical. This creates a candlestick with a real body that is simply a horizontal line, as shown in Figure 17.19. It suggests that the market is in equilibrium and affected by indecision. In some respects, it is like an inside bar in its meaning because in a trend it shows a point at which the enthusiasm of the trend has stalled. It is, thus, often a warning of a reversal, but not necessarily a reversal pattern by itself. It can also occur about anywhere during a trend or within a trading range and is, thus, difficult to assess. As a result, its performance statistics were low (Schwager, 1996). It ranked at the bottom of our scale based on net profit, average trade, maximum drawdown, and percent winners.

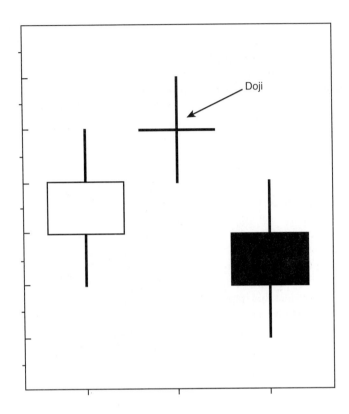

FIGURE 17.19 Doji candlestick

Windows

Windows are simply the gaps that we discussed earlier in this chapter. Nison believes they are the most reliable formations, and evidence from short-term bar patterns tends to confirm his opinion. Because the interpretation of candlestick windows is the same as for Western gaps, we will not spend time discussing them.

Harami

A harami pattern is a two-day pattern consisting of a large body of either color followed by a small body of either color that is completely within the boundaries of the large body. The harami pattern is pictured in Figure 17.20. The second candlestick pictured in the harami pattern in Figure 17.20 is called a spinning top. This second candlestick can also be a doji (resulting in a harami cross pattern), a hammer, a hanging man, or a shooting star; the only requirement is that the second candlestick body is within the first candlestick body.

The harami pattern is very similar to the inside bar pattern; however, with the harami, the range, or wick, of the second bar does not have to be within the range of the first bar. The real body of the second candle must be within the real body of the first candle. Thus, the open and close range, rather than the range, determines whether the harami criterion is met.

We know that the inside day demonstrates a contraction in volatility, and the same can be said for the harami pattern. We also know from studies of short-term bar patterns that low volatility turns into high volatility and often begins a new trend. Thus, a harami pattern can be a powerful way of signaling either the reversal of a trend or an increase in velocity of the current trend, depending on which direction prices break.

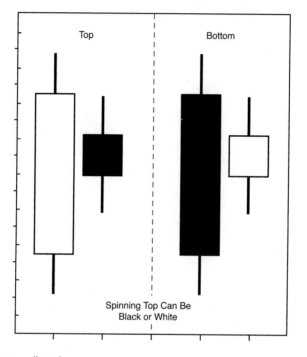

FIGURE 17.20 Harami candlestick pattern

Hammer and Hanging Man

Both the hammer and the hanging man are candlesticks in which the real body is located at the upper end of the trading range, as pictured in Figure 17.21. For these formations, the lower wick is at least twice to three times as long as the body, and the upper wick is small or nonexistent. In other words, the open and close both occur within approximately the top one-third of the bar's trading range, and either the open or close is, or nearly is, the highest price of the bar. The color of the body is irrelevant.

If this formation occurs at a peak, it is called a "hanging man." A variation is called the "kasakasa" or "paper umbrella" when the body is shorter than the shadow. When the same formation occurs at a trough, it is called a "hammer." These formations ranked best in our scale and were close to a tie with morning and evening stars.

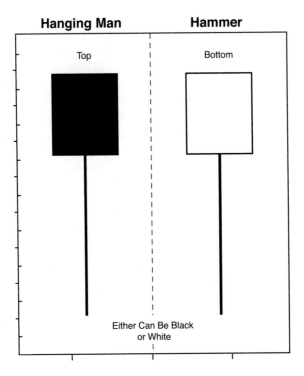

FIGURE 17.21　Hanging man and hammer

Shooting Star and Inverted Hammer

The shooting star and the inverted hammer can be thought of as an upside down hanging man or hammer. For these formations, the real body occurs in the lower end of the trading range. A shooting star occurs at peaks, and the inverted hammer occurs at bottoms. Both have long shadows above their bodies and very short or nonexistent shadows below their bodies, as shown in Figure 17.22. Again, the color of the body is irrelevant. In our ranking of patterns, they fell into the middle, nowhere near the best-performing hammer and hanging man to which they are related.

Engulfing

An engulfing pattern is a two-bar pattern in which the second body engulfs the first body (see Figure 17.23). This pattern is similar to an outside day reversal in bar patterns. Because this pattern is designed to recognize a trend reversal, there must be a clear trend preceding the engulfing pattern. In a market uptrend, a bearish engulfing pattern would indicate a market top. The bearish engulfing pattern consists of a small white-bodied candle followed by a black body that engulfs the white body. The bullish engulfing pattern would indicate that a downward trend is reversing. This bullish engulfing pattern consists of a candle with a small dark body on one bar followed by a candle with a larger white body that engulfs the dark body. For both the bearish and bullish engulfing pattern, the signal is much stronger when the first body is very small and the second body is very large. However, performance of engulfing patterns is near the bottom of the six pattern types tested by Schwager. They had the worst net profits and the largest maximum drawdowns.

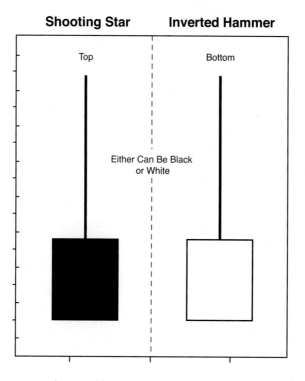

FIGURE 17.22   Shooting star and inverted hammer

Dark Cloud Cover and Piercing Line

A dark cloud cover is a two-body pattern at a top. The first body is large and white, and the second body is large and dark. The second open should be above the upper shadow of the first bar, an opening gap upward, and the close well within the first bar's white body, preferably below the 50% level. The pattern resembles the Oops! pattern in bar charts. Performance of this pattern is supposedly enhanced by a deeper penetration of the white body. (A complete penetration would be an engulfing pattern.)

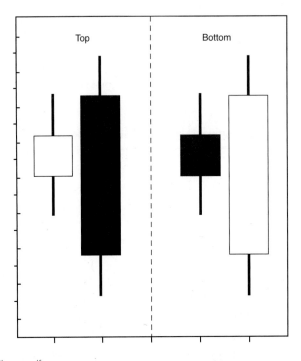

FIGURE 17.23   Candle engulfing pattern

The opposite pattern, a piercing line pattern, would indicate market bottom. The piercing line follows the same rules as the dark cloud pattern, only in reverse. Both the dark cloud cover and piercing line formations are pictured in Figure 17.24. These patterns ranked in the lower half of the six types followed. They had the second to least drawdown, lowest average profit per trade, and the lowest winning percentage.

Multiple Bar Patterns

Multiple bar candlestick patterns develop over a time period of more than two bars. A quick glance at names such as "three black crows," "three white soldiers," and "three outside up" reveals that many of the multiple bar patterns are three bar patterns.

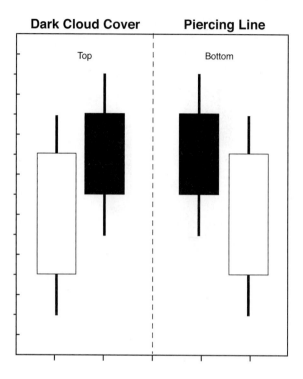

FIGURE 17.24 Dark cloud cover and piercing line

Morning and Evening Star

The evening star is a three-bar candlestick pattern that occurs at market tops, and the morning star is a three-bar, market bottom pattern. In each of these patterns, the second bar, or middle candlestick, is known as a star. A star is a candlestick that has a small body that lies outside of the range of the body before it. It implies an opening gap, as does a dark cloud and piercing line pattern, but it can later cover part of the previous bar's shadow. The important point is that its body does not overlap the previous bar's body at all. It is similar to a doji in that it represents a sudden halt in a trend and some indecision between buyers and sellers. Indeed, a doji can be a star, called a doji star, if the doji body occurs outside the body of the previous bar's body.

The evening star pattern, pictured in Figure 17.25, starts with a long white body followed by a star of either color. If the third bar forms a large black body that closes well within the body of the first bar, the pattern is confirmed. Ideally, the third body should not touch the star's body, but this rarely occurs, and it is not a necessary condition for the pattern. The amount of penetration into the first white body is more important. The evening star is similar to the island reversal bar pattern without the necessary second gap.

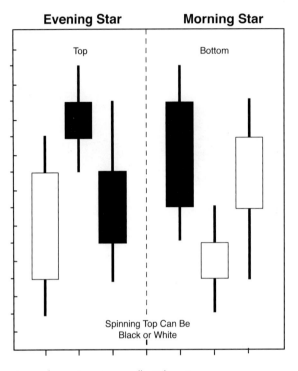

FIGURE 17.25 Evening star and morning star candlestick patterns

The morning star, which occurs at a market bottom, is the opposite formation of the evening star. As shown in Figure 17.25, it begins with a black-bodied candlestick, followed by a star. The body of the star lies completely below the body of the previous candlestick. The pattern is then confirmed if, on the third bar, a white-bodied candlestick closes well within the range of the first candlestick.

The morning and evening stars were the second-best patterns in our ranking of Schwager's tests. They were first in net profits, had the least drawdowns, and were second in the percentage of winning trades. In the Caginalp and Laurent study, the morning and evening star pattern ranked third out of the four multibar types studied.

Three Black Crows and Three White Soldiers

White soldiers are white bodies and black crows are black bodies. Three black crows is a pattern with three consecutive black bodies, preferably long, closing near their lows, openings within their previous day's body, and occurring after a meaningful upward trend. They are a top-reversal formation. As shown in Figure 17.26, three white soldiers is a bottom-reversing formation and requires the same parameters in the opposite direction.

Unfortunately, traders have difficulty profiting from these patterns because by the time they are recognized, a large portion of the new trend has already occurred. They are best played on a pullback or throwback. Nison believes that the first or second bar in the pattern is the best location for entry on the retracement. That level is often accompanied by another pattern suggesting a short reversal in the direction of the trend signaled by the major pattern.

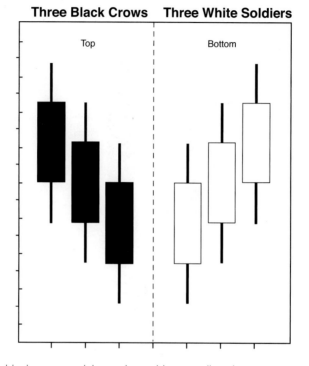

FIGURE 17.26 Three black crows and three white soldiers candlestick patterns

Three Inside Up and Three Inside Down

The three inside up pattern is a reversal pattern that occurs at the end of a declining trend. The first bar of this pattern has a large black body, and the second bar is a white spinning top (or doji) that forms a harami pattern. Then, the third bar is a large, white candle that breaks and closes above the large black body of the first bar. Although the name may sound like it, the three inside up pattern does not imply that three inside bars in a row occur, as we saw with the NR3 pattern. Instead, the three inside up pattern is similar to an upward breakout from an inside bar in a bar pattern.

As shown in Figure 17.27, the three inside down pattern is the reverse of the three inside up pattern. The three inside down pattern consists of a large white bar followed by a black spinning top and a downward break by a large black body. This pattern signals that an upward trend has ended. From the Caginalp and Laurent study, we ranked this pattern type the best. It had the highest percentage of winning trades of the four pattern types studied.

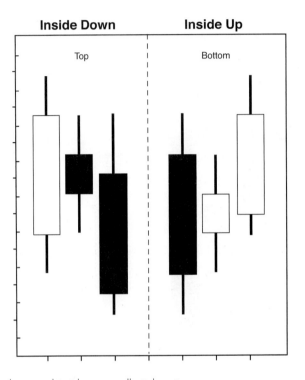

FIGURE 17.27   Inside down and inside up candlestick patterns

Three Outside Up and Three Outside Down

This pattern type starts with an engulfing pattern after a trend, just as the inside up and down started with a harami pattern. The three outside up version occurs at market bottoms. The first body is small, a spinning top, and the second body is large, engulfing the smaller previous body. The first is black and the second is white. A white body that closes above the second bar and reaches a new high above the previous two bars follows the engulfing pattern. This pattern is pictured in Figure 17.28.

Figure 17.28 also shows how the three outside down pattern is the same with opposite parameters. For the outside down pattern, the first bar is a small, white body, and the second bar is a black body that engulfs the first. The third bar is also a black body with prices moving lower than the second bar. Outside down bars occur at market tops.

From our look at short-term bar patterns, we know that outside bars are less predictable and less profitable than inside bars because the volatility has already expanded and is open to contraction at any time soon thereafter. The results of the three outside bar pattern types show the same decreased performance and were ranked fourth in our interpretation of the Caginalp and Laurent study.

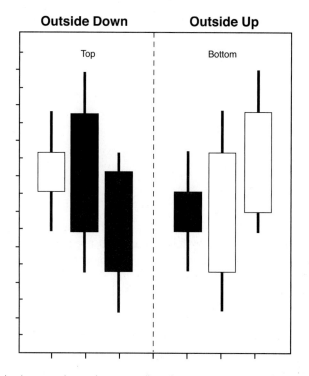

FIGURE 17.28   Outside down and outside up candlestick patterns

Candlestick Pattern Results

We have described several of the most popular candlestick patterns. Bulkowski maintains a Web site (www.thepatternsite.com) with an extensive list of candlestick patterns. Table 17.1 highlights Bulkowski's ranking of the 10 best performing candlestick patterns.

TABLE 17.1   Bulkowski Ranking of Candlestick Patterns—10 Best (Some are not shown above but may be accessed from www.thepatternsite.com.)

Pattern	Reversal or Continuation	Percent Accurate
Three line strike	Bullish reversal	84%
Three line strike	Bearish reversal	65%
Three black crows	Bearish reversal	78%
Evening star	Bearish reversal	72%
Upside Tasuki gap	Bullish continuation	57%
Hammer, inverted	Bearish continuation	65%
Matching low	Bearish continuation	61%

continues

TABLE 17.1 Continued

Pattern	Reversal or Continuation	Percent Accurate
Abandoned baby	Bullish reversal	70%
Two black gapping	Bearish continuation	68%
Breakaway	Bearish reversal	63%

Source: www.thepatternsite.com © 2008–2009 by Thomas N. Bulkowski

Conclusion

We have looked at a number of short-term patterns in this chapter on both bar charts and candle-stick charts. To use these patterns successfully, a trader must be familiar with the underlying market trend. Remember that these short-term patterns are most often reversal patterns, giving the trader a hint that the underlying trend may be changing.

Short-term patterns forming as open, high, low, and close prices occur in particular combinations during a bar or over a few bars of trading. Particular short-term patterns occur frequently. Because of the frequency with which they occur, many times they are false patterns. Traders must be aware of this and not simply rely on a particular short-term pattern to make decisions. These short-term patterns can be useful indicators, but traders need to watch for a cluster of evidence instead of relying on a short-term pattern to make decisions.

Remember that the key to making money is riding a trend. Short-term patterns are a tool to help us determine when a new trend is beginning. These formations can also help us determine when a trend is ending. This allows us to participate in the trend as soon as possible and to exit the market as quickly as possible whenever the trend has ended. Using short-term patterns and protective stops can aid traders in maximizing their gains and minimizing their risk.

Review Questions

1. Why must investors know the underlying long-term trend before using short-term patterns?
2. Explain what is meant by the term *gap*. How do breakout, runaway, and exhaustion gaps differ from each other? How would an analyst distinguish between these three types of gaps?
3. What is a spike? How is it similar to a gap?
4. In August 2005, Merck (MRK) lost an initial Vioxx product liability lawsuit. Create a daily bar chart for MRK for August 2005–September 2005. Use this chart to describe the Dead Cat Bounce. Did MRK follow the typical Dead Cat Bounce pattern?

5. Define an inside day, outside day, narrow-range day, and wide-range day. Which of these days represents increasing volatility, and which represents contracting volatility? Explain your answer.

6. Schwager (1996) states that the one-day reversal pattern "successfully call(s) 100 out of every ten highs." What does he mean by this statement, and what is the implication for traders using these reversal patterns?

7. The candlestick chart in Figure 17.29 is of AmeriSourceBergen Corp. (ABC) for August 15, 2005–October 15, 2005. Find the following patterns in this chart. Does the price behave as you would expect after each of these patterns? Explain.

   a. Morning star

   b. Doji

   c. Hammer

   d. Inverted hammer

   e. Shooting star

   f. Harami

   g. Engulfing

   h. Hanging man

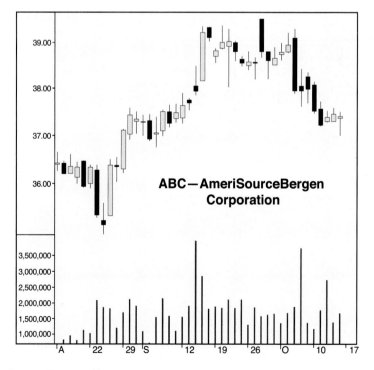

FIGURE 17.29 Review Question 7

PART V

TREND CONFIRMATION

CHAPTER 18 CONFIRMATION

CONFIRMATION

CHAPTER OBJECTIVES

By the end of this chapter, you should be familiar with

- The methods of plotting volume information on charts
- Traditional general rules for interpreting volume statistics
- The major indexes and oscillators that are designed to use volume information as confirmation
- The concept of open interest and how it might be used for confirmation
- The concept of momentum
- The major indexes and oscillators that use price data

The odds increase that a technical signal is correct if there is confirmation from another unrelated indicator. Charles Dow recognized this concept and used the confirmation of two different price averages before he recognized a legitimate market signal. In the days when only chart patterns were available as a means of interpreting price action, the technical analyst often used volume as the confirming indicator. Sometimes, depending on the calculating ability of the analyst, moving averages, rates of change, and momentum price oscillators were also used. After the introduction of the computer, the ability to calculate more complicated indicators increased. Many analysts began to use more complicated indicators as the primary source of signals and deviated from the old price pattern analysis. The number of possible combinations of prices, volume, and other factors has become almost infinite. Indeed, there is some question as to whether all this computing power has increased the ability of technical analysts to interpret price action. Some would argue that most of the indicator calculations correlate with each other, and that the market is no more understandable today than it was 50 years ago. Others maintain that the proper use of confirming indicators helps considerably in decision making, and that many successful trading models depend almost exclusively on these complex calculations.

In this chapter, we look at volume, the oldest confirming indicator, but which has developed some problems recently from the increase in program trading and other mechanical trading systems. We look at open interest in the futures markets, and then we look at price oscillators, indicators, and the discouraging evidence for their reliability in giving stand-alone signals.

ANALYSIS METHODS

The methods for analyzing confirmation rely on two main tools: indexes and oscillators. Indexes are similar to the breadth line described in the market indicators discussion in Chapter 8, "Measuring Market Strength." They are cumulative sums of data, usually some variation of volume and price, that continuously measure supply and demand over time rather than over a specific period. They do not have an upper or lower bound and are plotted with price charts where they can be compared with price action. The level of the index is irrelevant. What is relevant is the trend of the index relative to the price trend. The only useful indexes are those that begin to change direction before prices, signaling a change in trend. The analyst, thus, compares the prices with the index, looking for divergences between highs and lows in each. Although indexes can also be used with trend line, channel, and occasionally pattern analysis, their most important use is that of divergence analysis in trending markets.

Oscillators, on the other hand, are often bounded and limited to a specified past period. As shown in Figure 18.1, they tend to oscillate within these bounds and demonstrate when volume or prices are relatively high or low. These indicators show the relative changes rather than the absolute changes demonstrated in indexes and are also amenable to divergence, trend line, and pattern analysis. Oscillators are used more successfully in trading range markets.

As with many technical indicators, research has not shown that indexes and oscillators are profitable on their own. The student must judge after thorough testing and experience whether to use them as secondary indicators to price analysis.

Various visual techniques have been developed to determine some meaning from these indexes and oscillators. They are divided into methods that are peculiar to indicators, such as divergences, and those that are just an extension of classical chart pattern analysis such as trend lines and support and resistance. The principal methods unique to indicators are discussed in the following sections.

Overbought/Oversold

Oscillators can be bounded or unbounded. **Bounded** means that the oscillator swings back and forth within certain bounds or limits. These limits are the extremes to which the oscillator can reach. In most bounded and in some unbounded oscillators, a zone is chosen to represent the range near the extreme bounds. The oscillator might not reach the actual extreme bound, but might come close and by doing so have the same implications. The zone then is the range that is close enough to the extreme bound to be important. The upper zone is called overbought and the lower zone is called oversold. When a security has risen far enough that its oscillator reaches the overbought zone, it is said to be overbought, and when the price has fallen far enough that the oscillator reaches the oversold zone, it is said to be oversold.

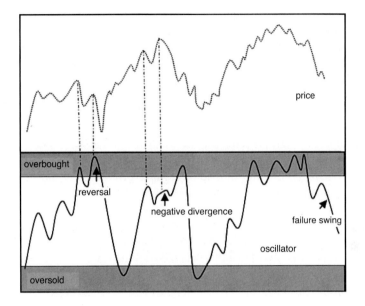

FIGURE 18.1 Example of oscillator analysis methods

In a trading range, the overbought and oversold levels are excellent indications of potential reversal levels, especially when the oscillator breaks out from the zone. The zones, however, can be deceiving in a trending market because the oscillator will remain in them during the period of the trend, and, thus, many breakouts from the zone will be false signals. In the following description of oscillators, we point out the conventional zone levels, but as always, the analyst must test for those most appropriate to the time and security being traded.

Failure Swings

A **failure swing** is a specific type of breakout from an overbought or oversold zone first described by Wilder (1978). A stronger version of the breakout, it often is the first sign of a potential reversal after a lengthy trend in which an oscillator has remained within or close to a zone. A **negative failure swing** is shown in Figure 18.1; it occurs when the oscillator breaks down out of an overbought zone, creates a reversal point, pulls back but fails to reenter the zone, and then breaks back down below the earlier reversal point. A **positive failure swing** is the opposite at an oversold zone.

Divergences

Although Wilder is also credited with discovering divergences, the concept is at least as old as Dow Theory. The basic concept is that to ensure a trend has begun or is still strong, all methods must be confirming the trend. If one index, for example, is breaking out upward but other indexes are not, the indexes are said to be diverging; in other words, they are not acting in concert with each other. A legitimate, strong trend, however, should have all indexes acting in concert. A divergence is, thus, considered to be a sign, especially after a trend has been in existence for a while, that the trend is slowing down and preparing to reverse. We saw breadth divergences in Chapter 8 and how important and reliable they have been. This is the same concept applied to oscillators and price charts.

The basic rule is that when a price reaches a new high, the oscillator should also reach a new high. Of course, this is subject to some interpretation, namely "what high is a new one?" but generally the relative highs should take place at the same time. A high on day 4 and another on day 20 should appear in both the price and the oscillator. If the price high on day 20 is higher than the high on day 4 but the oscillator high on day 20 is not higher than on day 4, the pattern is called a **negative divergence.** An example of negative divergence is shown in Figure 18.1. A **positive divergence** occurs at a series of price lows when the price reaches a new low unconfirmed by a new low in the oscillator. In a particularly strong trend, several divergences can occur and, of course, if the oscillator is bounded, it will occur more often because there is little room for the oscillator to keep making new highs or lows. This is why the first negative breadth divergence is often a false signal, but when two occur, back-to-back, the oscillator breakdown signal is more meaningful.

Reversals

Brown (1999) describes a variation of divergences known as oscillator **reversals** in detail. Like divergences, reversals have been used by technicians since oscillators were first used, but they have been popularized recently by Andrew Cardwell. A reversal differs from a divergence in that price leads the change instead of the oscillator. For example, **a negative reversal** occurs when, on day 20 the oscillator reaches a new high above that of day 4 but the price does not. As illustrated in Figure 18.1, it is sort of a divergence in reverse in that the price is showing weakness when the oscillator is not as opposed to the divergence when the price is still strong but the oscillator is not. Nevertheless, in keeping with the concept of confirmation, the two factors, price and oscillator, are not in sync and are, thus, no longer confirming the trend. A **positive reversal** is the same as the negative only at low bars. A reversal has the same implications as a divergence, namely that the trend is beginning to show signs of stress and potential reversal.

Trend ID

Brown (1999) also describes what she calls "trend id." In a trending market, oscillators will remain in one half of their range for long periods and breakout signals from the standard overbought and oversold zones are often false. For example, when a price is trending upward, the oscillator can remain at or close to the overbought zone and never reach the oversold zone to give a signal during corrections. Brown suggests that the zones should be redefined with the zone parameters raised to include those corrections at a slightly higher level. Her work centers around what is called the "RSI," a bounded oscillator that we look at later, that traditionally has an oversold zone below 30 and an overbought zone above 70. In a strongly upward trending market, the price corrections at which opportune trades might occur are never reached by the oscillator.

Thus, she suggests that during the rising trend, the oversold zone be raised to 40 and the overbought zone be raised to 90. Better signals then occur using these new levels as long as the underlying trend remains strong. In a downward trend, the zone levels can also be adjusted downward for the same reason. This adjustment of zones has no effect on divergences or reversals or any of the other chart patterns that might suggest an upcoming trend change. The analyst, however, must test for the best zones to fit the trend.

A variation of trend id that is commonly used is the standard deviation of the oscillator, similar to the use of standard deviation in Bollinger Bands. The oscillator is calculated and two bands, upper and lower, surround its plot at the level of some multiple, usually one, of the oscillator's standard deviation. This gives a "moving" overbought and oversold that trend with the oscillator and adjust to changes in the oscillator's volatility. Signals are generated when the oscillator breaks out of the overbought or oversold zone toward the center just as with the classic zones.

Crossovers

Crossovers occur when the oscillator crosses over either a particular level or another oscillator. One level that is often important is the middle value, usually either zero or one that bisects the range of the oscillator's travels. Almost by definition, when an oscillator reaches and remains above or below the midpoint in the oscillator range, it is defining the underlying trend. It is, thus, a potential trend indicator. Other oscillators have their raw figures smoothed through a moving average, and crossovers occur when the raw figure crosses over the moving average. These crossovers can either be signals to act or indications of trend change.

Classic Patterns

Strangely, oscillators and indicators often make simple patterns, such as triangles and rectangles, and produce support and resistance levels just as does price, and even have trends that can be defined by a classic trend line. These patterns have the same validity as price patterns, even when the oscillator is bounded, and can be additional evidence of trend change or short-term opportunity.

VOLUME CONFIRMATION

Volume is the classic confirming indicator. Volume measures are often portrayed on stock charts, and volume statistics are incorporated in a number of indexes and oscillators.

What Is Volume?

Volume is the number of shares or contracts traded over a specified period, usually a day, but can be one trade (called tick volume) to months or years, in any trading market—stocks, futures, and options.

In markets where considerable arbitrage exists, volume statistics can sometimes be misleading. For example, arbitrage between two differently dated commodity contracts can cause volume figures in each to be distorted due to the arbitrage and not the price trend. This arbitrage problem in volume statistics is particularly troublesome in the stock market where there is not only arbitrage against index futures markets, but also arbitrage between baskets, ETFs, and options. This arbitrage is known as "program trading," and as of 2010, it accounted for approximately 25%–50% of all traded volume on the New York Stock Exchange each day. In the heavily traded stocks included in averages and widely owned by institutions, large levels of volume may thus be due simply to arbitrage trades and not the trend direction or strength. Any analyst using these volume figures for these actively traded stocks must be aware of this potential problem in analysis.

> Indeed, one criticism of program trading voiced by professional traders is that it distorts the information typically provided by trading volume. As our analysis here suggests, introducing trading volume unrelated to the underlying information structure would surely weaken the ability of uninformed traders to interpret market information accurately. (Blume, Easley, and O'Hara, 1994, p. 178)

How Is Volume Portrayed?

Analysts display volume on a price chart in many ways. Some analysts like to see the volume statistics separately from the price statistics. Others have developed means of integrating volume data into the price chart.

Bar/Candle

The most common portrayal of volume is a vertical bar representing the total amount of volume for that period at the bottom of the price chart. A chart showing daily price data, for example, would show the volume for each day in a vertical bar below the price bar. Figure 18.2 shows volume statistics for Apple Computer using this method. This method is simple and assumes no direct relationship between price and volume. It just displays the data.

Equivolume

Many attempts have been made to integrate volume directly into a bar chart. Gartley (1935) mentions how traders before 1900 would record on a chart a vertical bar for every 100 shares traded at a certain price. For example, if 300 shares traded at a certain price, traders would record three bars at that price. A wide number of bars at a certain price showed that the majority of activity took place at that price. From this chart, traders could determine the price at which supply and demand were equalized and, thus, the support and resistance zones.

The first published service using a combination of price and volume was the Trendograph service by Edward S. Quinn (Bollinger, 2002; Gartley, 1935). Quinn produced charts using a bar for the high and low each day separated by a horizontal distance based on volume traded during the day. More recently, Richard W. Arms, Jr. (1998) designed, utilized, and reported "Equivolume" charts. These are available in some of the current charting software programs.

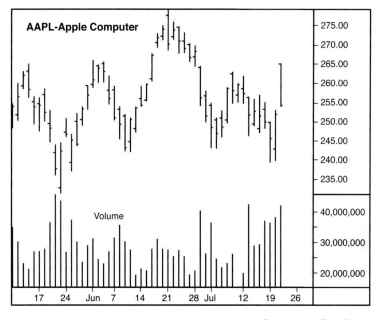

FIGURE 18.2 Price and volume (AAPL daily: May 10, 2010–July 21, 2010)

Arms' method widens the vertical price bar into a rectangle and, thus, widens the horizontal axis in proportion to the volume traded during the same period. For an example of an Equivolume shape, see Figure 18.3. The Equivolume chart resembles a regular bar chart except that the bars vary in width. Thus, wide bars portray large volume, and thin rectangles portray thin volume. The horizontal axis of the entire chart adjusts accordingly.

Arms first interpreted the Equivolume charts by considering the rectangular shapes displaying the price range by the height of the rectangle and volume by the width. For example, after a strong upward trend, the formation of a box shape or flat rectangle suggested little price motion but heavy volume. This would indicate that the trend was meeting some heavy resistance. Arms also found that the standard patterns used in bar chart analysis also occur in Equivolume charts, and interestingly, trend lines and channel lines appeared to work as well. One would think that a trend line was totally price- and time-related in a bar chart, but Arms demonstrated that trend lines in price-to-volume also occur.

More recently, with the introduction of picturesque candlestick charts, some services have adopted the principles of Equivolume to include open, close, shadows, colors, and indications of direction. (An example is the charts used in www.incrediblecharts.com.) These charts have the same rectangular appearance as the Equivolume charts but include other factors. Their interpretation is similar to Equivolume interpretation. The same trends, formations, and support and resistance levels as displayed in regular bar charts are visible.

Equivolume Shapes

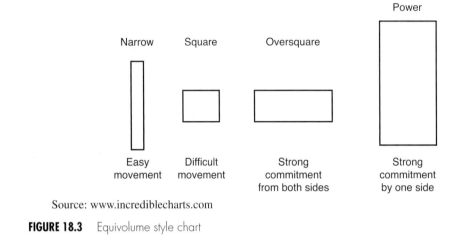

Source: www.incrediblecharts.com

FIGURE 18.3   Equivolume style chart

Point-and-Figure

Point-and-figure charts, by their nature, do not include volume. This omission has forced point-and-figure analysts who believe that volume is important to find ways to integrate volume statistics into each point-and-figure box, usually through symbols or colors. The standard method is to sum the volume that took place while each box was in effect and portray it on the chart. From this, the analyst can quickly visualize where volume occurred in the formation. The individual analyst using the method must determine whether this information is helpful. A purist in point-and-figure would argue that volume is unimportant because the price action implies it.

Do Volume Statistics Contain Valuable Information?

Academic papers using volume to confirm technical trading rules are rare. Most academic papers on volume are concerned with bid-ask spreads and intraday trading versus option trading. The intraday spread has been of interest because it is a cost of trading that has not been well quantified. Studies in this sector arose out of the legal requirement of institutions to measure the effectiveness ("best execution") of their traders and the brokerage firms that handled their orders. The difference between best execution and the execution received is a cost above the commission and slippage cost. Often, institutions traded through firms that did not receive the best execution but provided research and other benefits to the institution. The legal question was, should the customer of the institution pay an extra cost for execution through a firm that did not receive the best execution? Determining the best execution then became a major area of study that remains relatively unanswered today.

Intraday trading relative to option trading was of interest to those attempting to explain why option prices lagged behind stock prices.

Stock buyer-initiated volume (that which transacts at the ask) minus seller-initiated volume (that which transacts at the bid) has strong predictive ability for subsequent stock and option returns, but call or put net-buy volume has little predictive ability. (Chan, Chung, and Fong, 2002)

Finally, studies done on daily volume and subsequent price action came to the conclusion that volume statistics had valuable information.

Where we believe our results are most interesting is in delineating the important role played by volume. In our model, volume provides information in a way distinct from that provided by price .... Because the volume statistic is not normally distributed, if traders condition on volume, they can sort out the information implicit in volume from that implicit in price. We have shown that volume plays a role beyond simply being a descriptive parameter of the trading process. (Blume, Easley, and O'Hara, 1994, p. 177)

How Are Volume Statistics Used?

Volume indicators and signals are usually derived not from volume itself, but from a change in volume. Volume by itself may be a measure of liquidity in a security, but it is not helpful for price analysis. Volume is usually different in every security, based on factors beyond the ability for the security to rise and fall. For example, at the end of 2005, average daily volume for Wal-Mart was around 15 million shares. The average daily volume for Coca-Cola was only about half of that. The term "volume" used in conjunction with indicators and technical signals really refers to change in volume. We also use that convention.

How should a change in volume be interpreted? These general rules date back to the work of H. M. Gartley in 1935:

1. When prices are rising:
   a. Volume increasing is impressive.
   b. Volume decreasing is questionable.
2. When prices are declining:
   a. Volume increasing is impressive.
   b. Volume decreasing is questionable.
3. When a price advance halts with high volume, it is potentially a top.
4. When a price decline halts with high volume, it is potentially a bottom.

In other words, price change on high volume tends to occur in the direction of the trend, and price change on low volume tends to occur on corrective price moves. Higher volume is usually necessary in an advance because it demonstrates active and aggressive interest in owning the stock. However, higher volume is not necessary in a decline; prices can decline because of a lack of interest and, thus, potential buyers in the stock, resulting in relatively light volume.

As in all technical indicators, exceptions to the preceding rules can occur. These rules are only guides. Bulkowski, in his analysis of chart patterns, for example, found many profitable instances of patterns breaking out on low volume rather than the traditionally expected high volume. Larry Williams has reported on short-term studies of volume accompanying advances and declines and found little or no correlation. In a study of price-volume crossover patterns, Kaufman and Chaikin (1991) demonstrated that the prevailing wisdom is not always born out by fact. In a price-volume crossover chart, price closes within short trends are plotted on the vertical axis, and corresponding volume is plotted on the horizontal axis. Lines are drawn connecting these successive points, and when the lines cross, a crossover has occurred. Thus, the charts display the sequence of rising or falling price versus rising or falling volume. Kaufman and Chaikin found, for example, that rising volume in an advance was not necessarily positive, and that declines could occur on both rising and declining volume.

Nevertheless, we look at specific examples in the indicator descriptions next. We will see that volume is a secondary indicator to price analysis, and that though it is not always consistent, it can often be useful as a warning of trend change, especially on any sharp increases. As always, one must thoroughly test each assumption made about volume characteristics. The correlations between signals and price are not reliable enough to be absolute rules, and using the traditional rules too strictly can often lead to incorrect conclusions about price action.

Which Indexes and Oscillators Incorporate Volume?

Let us look at some specific examples of indicators that analysts use when looking at volume as a confirming indicator. These indicators are divided principally into two categories: indexes and oscillators.

Volume-Related Indexes

Technical analysts have developed a number of volume related indexes. On-Balance-Volume is probably the most well known of these.

On-Balance-Volume (OBV)

On-Balance-Volume (OBV) is the granddaddy of all volume indexes. Joseph Granville proposed OBV in his 1976 book, *A New Strategy of Daily Stock Market Timing for Maximum Profit.* The daily data that is cumulated into the index is the volume for the day adjusted for the direction of the price change from the day before. Thus, it is the total daily volume added to the previous day index if the price close was higher and subtracted from the previous day index if the price close was lower than that of the previous day. This index is a cumulative sum of the volume data and is plotted on a daily price chart. Figure 18.4 shows what a plot of OBV volume looks like.

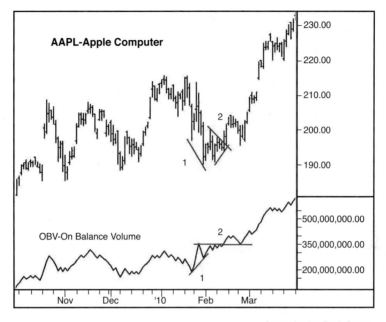

Created using TradeStation

The idea behind the OBV index is simply that high volume in one direction and low volume in the opposite direction should confirm the price trend. If high volume is not confirming the price trend, then light volume in the price trend direction and heavy volume in the opposite direction suggests an impending reversal. Observing the OBV line by itself, therefore, is not helpful, but observing its trend and its action relative to price action is. For example, in a trending market, when prices reach a new high, confirmation of the price strength comes when the OBV also reaches a new high. If the OBV does not reach a new high and confirm price strength, negative divergence has occurred, warning that the price advance may soon reverse downward. A negative divergence suggests that volume is not expanding with the price rise.

FIGURE 18.4   On-Balance-Volume (AAPL daily: October 1, 2009–March 26, 2010)

How can the OBV be used in prices that are in a consolidation pattern or trading range rather than trending? When prices are in a trading range and the OBV breaks its own support or resistance, the break often indicates the direction in which the price breakout will occur. Therefore, it gives an early warning of breakout direction from a price pattern.

Let us look a little more closely at Figure 18.4. At the beginning of the chart, prices seem to be in a trading range. Then, notice how a positive divergence developed at Marker 1. The low in the OBV did not confirm the new low in price. At Marker 2, the OBV broke above its entire trading range while price broke upward from a small pennant. The OBV thus confirmed the breakout that later formed a runaway gap and a large price rise. The "seeds" to that price rise were sown with the OBV breakout. Finally, notice that after Marker 2, each successive high in price was accompanied by an equivalent new high in the OBV, continuing to confirm the upward price trend.

Price and Volume Trend

Another way of calculating a combination of price and volume is to determine daily the percentage price change, up or down, times the total volume for the day. This figure is then cumulated into an index called the price-volume trend. This index will be more heavily impacted when large percentage price changes occur on heavy volume. Signals are triggered in the same manner as for the OBV.

In Figure 18.5, notice that this method, using the same data as Figure 18.4, shows the price-volume trend confirming only after the upward gap breakout in March. Indeed, this method in this case merely tracks the price changes and shows little in the way of signals of impending trend change.

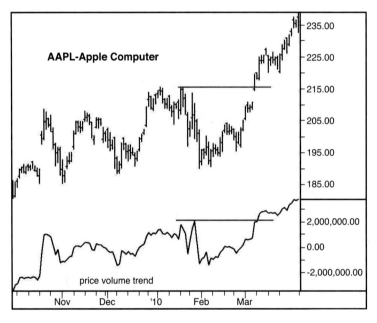

Created using TradeStation

FIGURE 18.5 Price Volume Trend (AAPL daily: October 1, 2009–April 1, 2010)

Williams Variable Accumulation Distribution (WVAD)

Larry Williams believes that the open and close prices are the most important price of the day. The Williams Variable Accumulation Distribution (WVAD) calculates the difference between the close and the open and relates it to the range as a percentage. For example, if a stock opened at its low price of the day and closed at its high price of the day, this percentage would be 100%. The other extreme would be if a stock opened at P_1, moved higher (or lower) during trading, but returned to close at P_1, then the percentage would be 0%. This percentage is then multiplied by the daily volume to estimate the amount of volume traded between the open and close.

The new volume figure is then added or subtracted from the previous day WVAD and drawn on a price chart. It can also be converted into a moving average or oscillator. Interpretation of the WVAD is identical to the other volume indexes.

Accumulation Distribution (AD)

In 1975, financial newspapers no longer published the opening prices of stocks. Marc Chaikin, using the Williams WVAD formula as a base, created the Accumulation Distribution (AD) index that uses the high, low, and close prices each day. The basic figure determines where within the daily price range the close occurs in the formula:

$$\text{Volume} \times ([\text{close} - \text{low}] - [\text{high} - \text{close}]) / (\text{high} - \text{low})$$

Thus, if the close occurs above its midpoint for the day, the result will be a positive number, called accumulation. Conversely, a negative number occurs when a stock closes below its midpoint for the day, and distribution is said to occur. Each daily figure is then cumulated into an index similar to the OBV, and the same general rules of divergences apply.

Figure 18.6 shows a plot of the AD index using Chaikin's formula. The trend was generally downward during the large consolidation period but then suddenly turned upward and broke above a lengthy trend line. This index tends to form trends and channels. The signal breakthrough anticipated the later upward break to a new high by six days.

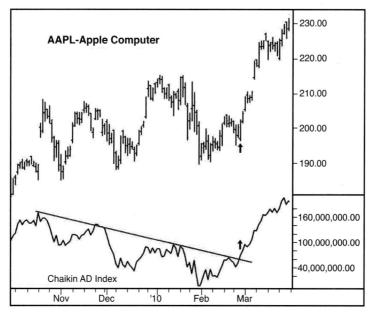

Created using TradeStation

FIGURE 18.6 Chaikin Accumulation Distribution (AAPL daily: March 1, 2009–March 26, 2010)

Williams Accumulation Distribution (WAD)

Not to be confused with the earlier Williams Variable Accumulation Distribution (WVAD) or Chaikin's Accumulation Distribution (AD), the Williams Accumulation Distribution (WAD) also eliminates the use of the open price no longer reported in the financial newspapers. This indicator uses the concept of True Range that J. Welles Wilder developed during the same general period.

The True Range uses the previous day's close as a benchmark and avoids the problems that arise when a price gaps between days. The calculations for the True Range high and low are based on a comparison. The True Range high, for example, is either the current day's high or the previous day's close, whichever is higher. The True Range low is either the current day's low or the previous day's close, whichever is lower.

In the WAD, accumulation occurs on days in which the close is greater than the previous day's close; the price move on these days is calculated as the difference between the current day close and the True Range low. Distribution occurs on a day when the close is less than the previous day's close; the price move on these days is the difference between the current day close and the True Range high, which will result in a negative number. Each price move is multiplied by the volume for the respective day, and the resulting figures are cumulated into an index, the WAD.[1]

Volume-Related Oscillators

Unlike indexes, volume-related oscillators are somewhat bounded. When an oscillator approaches the upper bound, an overbought condition occurs; when it approaches the lower bound, an oversold condition occurs. Oscillators are especially useful during trading ranges.

Volume Oscillator

The volume oscillator is the simplest of all oscillators. It is merely the ratio between two moving averages of volume. Its use is to determine when volume is expanding or contracting. Expanding volume implies strength to the existing trend, and contracting volume implies weakness in the existing trend. It is, thus, useful as a confirmation indicator for trend and for giving advanced warning in a range or consolidation formation of the direction of the next breakout. For example, if within the range, the oscillator rises during small advances and declines during small declines, it suggests that the eventual breakout will be upward.

Let us look at Figure 18.7. Like volume itself, the volume oscillator should confirm the price trend. In this example, the oscillator confirmed the price trend until November (the period marked 1). Then this relationship broke down, and volume failed to confirm the upward trend. From marked period 2 until March, a declining oscillator accompanied each subsequent price rally, and a rising oscillator accompanied each price decline. This series of divergences was a warning that the stock trend was no longer healthy. Finally, at the period marked 3, the oscillator confirmed the price rally. This signaled that a new upward trend had begun. As you can see, the

---

1. Steven B. Achelis introduced a variation of the WAD in this book, *Technical Analysis from A to Z* (2001). This variation eliminates the multiplication by volume and is thus not a volume index but a price index. Achelis's variation is often incorrectly identified in software programs on price indicators as the Williams Accumulation Distribution.

relationship between volume and trend is longer-term and not something that is useful for trading.

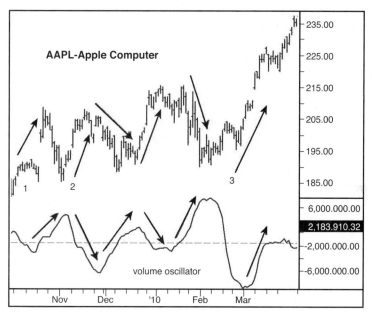

FIGURE 18.7   *Volume oscillator (AAPL daily: October 1, 2009–April 1, 2010)*

Chaikin Money Flow

The Chaikin Money Flow is an oscillator that uses the (Chaikin) AD calculation for each day. It is calculated by summing the ADs over the past 21 days and dividing that sum by the total volume over the past 21 days. This produces an oscillator that rises above zero when an upward trend begins and declines below zero when the trend turns downward.

Remember that each daily Chaikin AD calculation is based only on that particular day's high, low, and closing prices; therefore, if a gap occurs, it is not reflected in this oscillator. Another potential problem with this oscillator, as with all oscillators constructed using simple moving averages, is that simply dropping the number that occurred 21 days prior from the calculation can influence the current value of the oscillator. Remember that as an oscillator, this tool is used for confirmation, not signal generation.

Twiggs Money Flow

Colin Twiggs of www.incrediblecharts.com has adjusted the Chaikin Money Flow to account for the potential problems of gaps and the 21st-day drop-off. Twiggs eliminates the problem of gaps influencing the price strength by using Wilder's True Range, similarly to how Williams uses it in his WAD. In addition, using Wilder's calculation of an exponential moving average solves the problem of the drop-off figure affecting the current oscillator.

Chaikin Oscillator

Just to confuse things even more, Marc Chaikin invented the Chaikin Oscillator, as opposed to the Chaikin Money Flow. This oscillator is simply the ratio of the 3-day EMA of the AD to the 10-day EMA of the AD. Chaikin recommends that a 20-day price envelope, such as a Bollinger Band, also be used as an indication of when signals from the oscillator will be more reliable. Most signals are from divergences.

Figure 18.8 shows how well the Chaikin Oscillator signals short-term reversals within a trading range. The overbought and oversold levels in the chart demonstrate how the use of a standard deviation calculation for overbought and oversold can look. As with Bollinger Bands, the narrowing of the bands shows a decline in volatility. Declining volatility precedes significant price moves and is, thus, a warning of change in direction if not intensity. Notice also that when the stock price begins to trend upward, the oscillator gives premature sell signals. As mentioned earlier, this is the danger of using oscillators in a trending market.

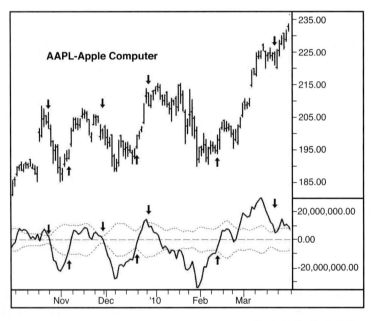

Created using TradeStation

FIGURE 18.8   Chaikin Oscillator (AAPL daily: October 1, 2009–March 30, 2010)

Money Flow Index (Oscillator)

Another method of measuring money flow into and out of a stock is the Money Flow Index. It considers "up" days and "down" days to determine the flow of money into and out of an equity. The money flow on any particular day is the day's typical, or average, price multiplied by the daily volume. The day's typical price is determined as the average of the high, low, and close. Therefore, money flow on Day i would be calculated as

$$MF_i = \{(High_i + Low_i + Close_i) / 3\} \times Volume_i$$

If Day i's average price is higher than the previous day's average price, there is positive money flow (PMF). Conversely, if Day i's average price is lower than the previous day's average price, negative money flow (NMF) occurs. The analyst chooses a specific period to consider and sums all the PMF together and all the NMF for that period. Dividing the sum of PMF by the sum of NMF results in the money flow ratio (MFR):

$$MFR = \Sigma PMF / \Sigma NMF$$

The Money Flow Index is then calculated using the formula:

$$\text{Money Flow Index} = 100 - (100 / (1 + MFR))$$

The Money Flow Index is an oscillator with a maximum of 100 and a minimum of 0. When positive money flow is relatively high, the oscillator approaches 100; conversely, when negative money flow is relatively high, the oscillator approaches 0. A level above 80 is often considered overbought and below 20 oversold. These parameters, along with the period, are obviously adjustable.

In addition, another variation of the Money Flow Index uses a ratio between positive money flow and the total dollar volume (rather than the NMF) over the specified period to calculate the money flow ratio. We used this method of calculation in Figure 18.9. Generally, the results of this method are not significantly different from the method we described earlier. In this example, we use 1.5 × standard deviation as the overbought and oversold levels, and treat it like a Bollinger Band where the signals occur in the direction of the breakout from within the band. This has mediocre results, but it does catch the beginning of the large upward trend that begins in February. As in other oscillators, it has trouble once prices begin to trend and gives premature exit signals.

Elder Force Index (EFI)

The EFI is an easy oscillator to calculate in that it uses only closing prices and daily volume. The daily price change is calculated as the daily closing price minus the previous day's closing price. This daily price change is then multiplied by the day's volume. The index is simply an exponential moving average over some specified period of the daily price change multiplied by the volume.

The purpose of this index is to measure the volume strength of a trend. The higher the level of the oscillator above zero, the more powerful the trend. A negative crossover through zero would thus indicate a weakening in trend power, and a deep negative would suggest strong power to the downside.

We have plotted the EFI in Figure 18.10. Elder suggests using either a 2-day EMA for trading or a 13-day EMA for trend determination. We used 13 days. You can see how erratic the EFI can be. In theory, a trade should be made whenever the centerline is crossed. As a mechanical method, this would have been disastrous as a number of whipsaws occurred. However, as a confirmation device, the index has merit. For example, Figure 18.10 shows a triangle pattern, a broadening pattern, a pennant, a flag, and a pennant/flag in succession. By checking the EFI each time price broke out of these patterns to see if it was confirming the direction of the breakout would have been helpful. The zigzag in late January would have caused concern, but otherwise, the EFI properly confirmed each of the subsequent breakouts.

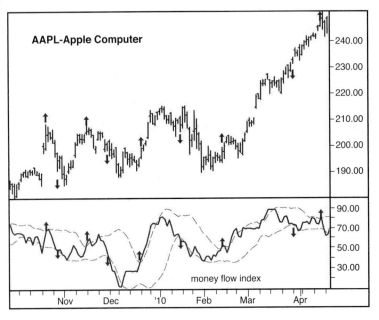

Created using TradeStation

FIGURE 18.9 Money Flow Index (AAPL daily: October 1, 2009–April 20, 2010)

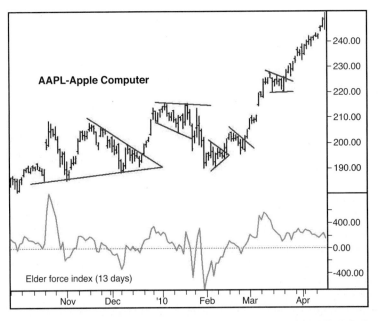

Created using TradeStation

FIGURE 18.10 Elder Force Index (AAPL daily: September 29, 2009–April 15, 2010)

Other Volume Oscillators

We have just studied the most commonly used volume oscillators. As always, a large number of variations exist, a few of which we mention here. Because these volume oscillators are variations of the more common ones we just discussed, the signals from overbought and oversold or divergences are similar.

Ease of Movement (EMV) is an oscillator developed by the volume expert Richard W. Arms. It uses a different calculation to determine daily price differences—namely, the average of the high and low for one day versus the average for the high and low of the previous day. The formula for calculating the EMV is the following:

$$EMV = [(Low_i + High_i) / 2 - (Low_{i-1} + High_{i-1}) / 2] \div Volume / [Low_i + High_i) / 2]$$

The result is a figure that measures the effect of volume on the daily range. The EMV is usually smoothed using a moving average because it can be erratic from day to day.

Volume Rate of Change is simply a ratio or percentage change between today's volume and the volume of some specified day in the past. For example, a ten-day rate of change would be today's volume versus the volume ten days ago. This method has problems because the drop-off number ten days prior, for example, will influence the current day's reading and might not have significance to recent trading. The ratio is used to identify spikes in volume (see the next section), but is not a reliable indicator by itself.

Volume Spikes

Volume spikes (not to be confused with price spikes) are most common at the beginning of a trend and at the end of a trend. The beginning of a trend often arises out of a pattern with a breakout, and the end of a trend often occurs on a speculative or panic climax. Higher-than-usual volume tends to occur with each event. By screening for volume, the trader can often find issues that are either ready to reverse or that have already reversed. The usual method of screening for a volume spike is to compare daily volume with a moving average. The trader can look for volume that is either a number of standard deviations from the average volume or a particular percentage deviation from the average. As for interpretation of the spike when it occurs, it is often difficult to determine which variety of spike has occurred until after the spike peaks and you observe the subsequent price action.

Usually there is a reason for a volume spike, but the reason for the spike might be unrelated to the technical issues of price trends and behavior. Of course, heavy trading might be related to a news announcement made about the company. Or, heavy trading volume in a stock can occur if the stock is a component of an index or basket that had a large institutional trade that day. Options expiring can also influence volume figures. In all spikes, any outside reason must first be investigated because it might have nothing to do with the issue's trend and price behavior.

Volume Spike on Breakout

Breakouts are usually obvious. High volume on a gap or on a breakout from a preexisting chart pattern is usually the sign of a valid breakout. Although breakouts do not necessarily require high volume, many analysts use a spike in volume as a confirmation of the breakout and ignore those without a volume spike.

Volume Spike and Climax

A climax usually marks the end of a trend and either a subsequent reversal or consolidation. Climaxes come in many forms, however, and are not always identifiable except in retrospect. Generally, climaxes occur with one of the short-term reversal patterns outlined in Chapter 17, "Short-Term Patterns." These typically can be price spikes or poles, one- or two-bar reversals, exhaustion gaps, key reversals, or any of the other short-term reversal patterns.

Examples of Volume Spikes

A number of volume spikes appear in Figure 18.11. The first accompanies a breakaway gap, and the second is showing that large support exists at that price level, the same level as filled the earlier gap. The third instance occurred when prices tried to break above the resistance level at $215. It ran into heavy selling and turned down. Finally, a volume spike occurred on the runaway gap in early March. The high volumes at the support and resistance levels are often important clues as to changes in direction. If price meets those levels on heavy volume and then reverses direction, those levels are extremely important and must be recorded for future use. For example, the high volume low at marker 2 provided the support that also stopped the decline at marker 3. It told of huge buying pressure at that level. Likewise, the gap in March was caused by the realization that the earlier sellers who stopped the retracement to the resistance level at $215 were gone, and the stock price was free to rise to the next level of resistance at $240.

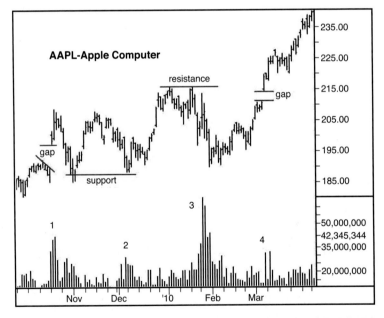

Created using TradeStation

FIGURE 18.11   Volume spikes (AAPL daily: October 1, 2009–April 15, 2010)

Shock Spiral

When we looked at the Dead Cat Bounce (DCB) in Chapter 17, we saw that a substantial volume spike occurs prior to the formation. Remember that the DCB occurs after a shocking news announcement causes a sudden and dramatic shift in price direction, usually accompanied by a large gap or a price spike. An extreme spike in volume accompanies that sudden shift. Tony Plummer (2003) uses the term "shock spiral" to describe the entire A-B-C pattern from the shock (A) to the DCB (B) to the final decline (C). The usual shock spiral is to the downside, but Plummer advocates that it can also occur on the upside.

Volume Price Confirmation Indicator (VPCI)

In a series of two articles in *Active Trader Magazine* and one in the *Journal of Technical Analysis,* Buff Dormier (2005) introduced a method of comparing a volume-weighted price moving average with a simple price moving average to determine whether volume is confirming price action. A positive deviation in the VPCI suggested that the volume was confirming the price action, and a negative deviation suggested that the volume was contradicting price action.

Volume Dips

Sharp declines in volume are usually not meaningful. The decline in volume generally indicates a decline in interest in the security, which is usually accompanied by a decline in volatility. For that reason, the issue should be ignored during the period of low volume, but the trader should be watching for an increase in volume and volatility. A volume dip is also typical for action just before a sudden expansion in price and volume, as in a breakout from a formation. Declines in volume can also occur before holidays, on summer days, and at other times when general activity is low.

OPEN INTEREST

The volume-related indexes and oscillators we have just discussed are based, in part, on the number of shares or contracts traded over a specific period of time. In the futures market, the total number of contracts outstanding is another important factor. The number of outstanding futures contracts is called "open interest."

What Is Open Interest?

In the futures markets, only contracts trade, not physical instruments or items. At the expiration of the specific futures market delivery month, the number of contracts reduces to zero as buyers and sellers "roll" their contracts into the next expiration, or make or take delivery of the product or cash as the contracts require. The number of contracts outstanding at any one time in each delivery month is its open interest. Total open interest is the number of contracts outstanding in all delivery months. It is an excellent tool in estimating the liquidity of most contracts. However, open interest is a different figure than volume. Volume is the number of contracts traded during a certain period in a specific futures market delivery month, not the number of contracts outstanding.

Although open interest is a good tool for estimating the liquidity of a contract, using it for technical trading can be a bit tricky. One problem is that open interest rises at the beginning and declines at the expiration of each contract market. This action is often unrelated to the trend. In addition, in many futures markets, the clearinghouse takes time to calculate the open interest and actual cleared volume. The figures are only available to the public on the following morning.

Open Interest Indicators

Futures contracts are created as interest develops in the specific futures market and become eliminated as interest in the futures market recedes. Thus, the conventional interpretation of open interest is that expanding open interest confirms interest in the existing trend of the futures contract price. This expansion should also be accompanied by increasing volume. Expanding open interest and volume during an upward trend, for example, suggests buyers are creating more new contracts than old contracts. When the upward trend continues but open interest and volume decline, old contract holders are selling and absorbing any new buyers, suggesting that the trend may soon reverse direction. In a correction within an upward trend, declining open interest and volume suggest that the major trend is still healthy. In this sense, open interest is used similarly to volume.

Larry Williams believes that open interest reflects the commercials because they account for such a substantial percentage of volume activity. Commercials are generally short futures contracts used to hedge against inventory. Thus, a decline in open interest, he reasons, is a sign that commercials are covering shorts and that the price will likely rise. He warns that this strategy should only be used in a trading range, and that a 30% change in open interest is necessary before action is contemplated. Colby argues that Williams' strategy does not work in the stock index futures, but he did not test the requirement for a range only.

As we know from Chapter 7, "Sentiment," the Commodity Futures Trading Commission's Commitment of Traders Reports provide breakdowns in open interest by category of trader. Some analysts have compared this data with the data reported daily by the commodity exchanges and used the resulting ratios and changes as indicators of professional and amateur trading action (Greco, 2001). These relations and calculations are complicated and go beyond our present scope.

Herrick Payoff Index (Oscillator)

John Herrick (1982) developed a complex oscillator based on price, volume, and open interest. As in many oscillators, interpretation is based on whether the index is above or below zero and whether divergences exist between volume and open interest and price velocity. Thomas Aspray (*Stocks & Commodities Magazine*, V.6:3, 115–118) has also found that in the Herrick Payoff Index, trend lines are often informative for warnings of a change in price direction, as are the penetration of support and resistance levels.

Figure 18.12 of live cattle futures displays the Herrick Payoff Index (HPI) and its 14-week EMA. Cattle has some erratic moves over the period especially in 2009, but it often shows a divergence between price and the HPI (marked with a dashed line as 1 and 2) at its peak and trough. Generally, when the HPI is above zero, prices are in an upward trend. This has not always been the case with cattle and is one reason for being skeptical about breaks above and below the zero line. Trend lines are also shown in HPI (with solid lines), as well as action price (arrow) at which they were broken. The combination of trend line breaks and divergences seems to be favorable.

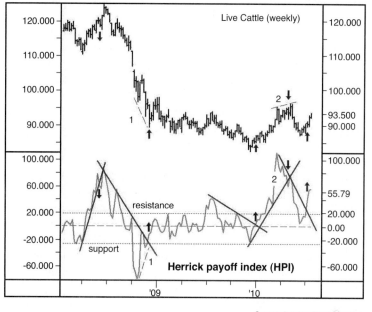

Created using TradeStation

FIGURE 18.12   Herrick Payoff Index—live cattle, perpetual contract, weekly

Other Open Interest Indicators

A number of combinations of open interest, price, and volume have been proposed. Most demonstrate what the Herrick Payoff Index displays, and the methods of analysis are the same as for other oscillators. One example is the On Balance Open Interest Indicator. William Painter proposed this indicator, which uses open interest instead of volume in an Price and Open Interest Index (POI), proposed by R. Earle Hadady (1989). This index is calculated similarly to the Price and Volume Indicator using the change in price times the change in open interest.

Price Confirmation

Confirmation is concerned with determining whether a price trend is continuing or coming to an end. One group of indicators uses measures based upon the movement of price itself to confirm the trend. Generally, these indicators are based upon the concept of momentum.

What Is Momentum?

Momentum deals with the rate at which prices are changing. For example, in an uptrend, prices are rising and the trend line slopes upward. Momentum measures how quickly the prices are rising, or how steeply the trend line is sloping. In high school calculus, you probably learned that the slope of a line is called the first derivative, and that the change in that slope is called the second derivative. Momentum is, thus, the second derivative of price action over some period.

Momentum is similar to acceleration and deceleration. For example, let us assume that a car is initially traveling at a constant speed of 30 miles per hour; at this point, the car has a constant travel slope of 30. When the car starts accelerating, it is gaining momentum, and its travel slope is increasing. At some point, the car cannot maintain the level of acceleration, and the rate of increase in speed begins to decline. The car is then said then to be decelerating, even though it is still traveling at an increasing rate of speed. The speed itself is not increasing as fast as earlier, so momentum is falling.

The same principle applies to markets. Speed is equivalent to the slope of the price trend—the number of points gained per day, for instance. Momentum is equivalent to the car's acceleration and deceleration and is the measure of the price trend's changing slope. Trend can be thought of as direction and momentum can be thought of as the rate of speed of the price change. For example, suppose that a stock is originally selling for $25 a share. If the same stock is selling for $30 a share five days later, then the stock price has increased by $5 in five days. The momentum would be $5 in five days (or $1 per day). If over the next five days, the price continues to increase to $34, the trend is still upward. However, the rate of change (or momentum) has slowed to $4 in five days.

Technical analysts have developed many indicators to measure momentum, and these measures have become leading signal generators or confirmation gauges, telling us whether the trend slope is changing. When momentum is confirming the price trend, a *convergence* or *confirmation* occurs; when momentum is failing to confirm the price trend slope by giving a warning signal, a *divergence* occurs. As a sign of price trend change then, the technical analyst often looks for a divergence.

Confirmation also is used to identify *overbought* and *oversold* conditions. Remember that prices never follow a trend in an absolute straight line. Prices oscillate about a central trend, deviating above and below the trend. When prices are considerably above the trend, the expectation is that prices will return down to the central trend and perhaps even fall below the trend line. When prices are noticeably above the central trend, an overbought condition exists. When prices are considerably below the trend, they are to be oversold and are likely to return up to the central trend and, perhaps, above.

Analysts have developed many types of oscillators to measure what is overbought and oversold. These oscillators usually are based on price but can also be based on volume or other data. Mathematically, these oscillators eliminate the trend and look only at the oscillations about the trend.

Suppose that you are watching a particular stock and notice a breakout occurring. An oscillator can be useful in determining the validity of the breakout. If an oscillator is oversold, this breakout is more likely to be valid than if the oscillator were overbought. However, in some instances, buy signals are generated from an overbought oscillator accompanied by other indicators (as we will see with the popsteckle later in this chapter).

A word of warning about using oscillators, however, is warranted. Traders often incorrectly use oscillators to generate signals without respect for the underlying trend direction. This will result in many false signals. Remember, profits are made from anticipating and riding the trend. Indicators and oscillators should only be used as secondary evidence to confirm the trend; otherwise, the analyst is likely in for trouble.

To combat the tendency to focus on overbought/oversold signals while ignoring the underlying trend, analysts have developed a number of adjustments and filters to account for trend more mechanically. Adjustments include altering the oscillator parameters, such as the period over which the oscillator is calculated and the signal levels. Other adjustments are even more sophisticated, using digital filters or other mathematical means of filtering and smoothing. The bottom line, however, is that by and large the results are the same. In fact, some analysts argue that increasing the complexity of the calculations only produces a false confidence. They also argue that complexity breeds an increase in the possibility for error when one of the parameters changes and does not allow the analyst the opportunity to gain practical experience. The indicator or oscillator becomes too mechanical. Whatever the arguments, however, even in their simplest forms, indicators and oscillators are useful as confirmation of price behavior, once the quirks are understood and the dependence upon them is secondary.

How Successful Are Momentum Indicators?

Momentum indicators are based on price information. Most academic studies of technical indicators attempt to demonstrate whether price action is random and, if not, whether this apparent nonrandomness violates some of the principles of the Efficient Markets Hypothesis. As such, these studies are usually of little use to practicing technical analysts who introduce many more variables into trading or investment decisions.

It is difficult for academics to construct tests that take into account all of the intricacies of real trading. When studying moving averages, for example, how would the requirement for protective stops around support and resistance be integrated? What kind of exit strategy should be used?

The trader must account for risk, as well as return, when considering the usefulness of an indicator. The academic concept of risk is considerably different from that which the practical investor must consider. Therefore, as we will see in Chapter 22, "System Design and Testing," when we look at testing methods, the measurements of risk provided in academic studies are not the same measures that a practitioner would use.

Finally, we will note that any method tested by academia has very likely already been discarded by the technical analysis world as outdated. By its nature, academia will always be behind the advances made in the more practical world. Nevertheless, academic studies are useful in determining the direction in which to look for means of profiting from technical analysis. For example, if a particular indicator shows no advantage over the random hypothesis, it should be treated with considerably more skepticism than one that does show some statistically relevant results.

Most academic studies of price indicators, so far, have focused exclusively on moving averages. Interestingly, there have been very few studies of standard technical indicators. The two most recent studies of indicators are Bauer and Dahlquist (1999a, 1999b) and Thomas (2003). The Bauer and Dahlquist study covered 60 technical signals, including popular oscillators, for 878 stocks over the period from 1985 through 1996, a period of generally rising stock prices. The Thomas study included price and volume oscillators for 1,750 stocks over the five-year period from 1995 through July 2001, a time during which the stock market had a significant advance and decline.

Specific Indexes and Oscillators

Remember that because momentum indexes and oscillators are based on price data, they do not add new information to the analysis. They are simply manipulations of the same data. This means that they are less informative than other indicators, such as volume, that provide new and different information. The analyst, therefore, must be careful when using price indicators, as confirmation may be more redundant than informative. This is not to say that a different manipulation of the data cannot be helpful, only that the base data itself is the same. For example, watching several different price oscillators calculated over the same period is silly because by their nature, they will be providing roughly the same results. Watching several price oscillators over different periods or including volume or some other different information would be more productive.

We describe the most common price momentum oscillators next. There are many ways of calculating momentum, but because all of them arrive at essentially the same result, we describe only the most common and most popular.

Moving Average Convergence-Divergence (MACD)

Gerald Appel, publisher of *Systems and Forecasts,* developed the Moving Average Convergence-Divergence (MACD) oscillator. A variation of the moving average crossover, the MACD is calculated using the difference between two exponential moving averages. Traditionally, a 26-period EMA is subtracted from a 12-period EMA, but these times are adjustable for shorter and longer period analysis. This calculation results in a value that oscillates above and below zero. A positive MACD indicates that the average price during the past 12 periods exceeds the average price over the past 26 periods.

The MACD line is plotted at the bottom of a price chart along with another line—the signal line. The signal line is an exponential moving average of the MACD; a nine-period EMA is the most common. A histogram of the difference between the MACD and the signal line often appears at the bottom of the chart. You can see this type of plot in Figure 18.13. The chart displays the MACD (thin black line), the signal line (thick gray line), and the histogram of the difference between the MACD and its signal line for Apple Computer over the same period as the other charts in this chapter.

The MACD is useful in a trending market because it is unbounded. When the MACD is above zero, it signals that the faster (shorter-term) moving average is above the slower (longer-term) moving average. The converse is true when the MACD is below the zero line. Crude signals occur when the MACD crosses the zero line, but these are just the same signals as would be generated from a moving average crossover.

Other information can be gleaned from the MACD, however. For example, when the MACD is above zero, suggesting an upward trend, buy signals occur when the MACD crosses from below to above the signal line. Downward crossings are not at all reliable while the trend is upward. Through experimentation to determine overbought and oversold levels, analysts can use these levels as places to generate signals for price reversion to the central trend. These extremes showed good performance results in the Thomas study of oscillators.

Additionally, some analysts compare the peaks and valleys in the MACD with the price line in a divergence analysis. Bauer and Dahlquist suggest that divergences can be useful, especially in a downward trending market. The peaks and valleys in the histogram provide two useful sets of information. They can be used for divergence analysis, and because they are sensitive to price directional change over short periods, they can also be used to signal shorter price trend changes within the longer trend.

Let us look a little more closely at Figure 18.13. A significant negative divergence developed in January when the MACD failed to confirm the new price high. A downward crossover from above the midpoint in November and January gave sell signals. The usual way to handle these is to place an entry stop just below the low of the signal bar to be executed if the price continues downward. As a protective stop, the previous high is the safest. This method would have worked well in both downward crossovers. There were also two upward crossovers from below the midpoint line, one in December and one in February. Using the same method as in the short selling on buying long instead, again both buy signals would have been profitable. Why did we not sell at the slight crossover in April? We would have placed a short entry stop at the low of the bar coinciding with the dip, but it never was triggered, leaving us still long from the buy in February.

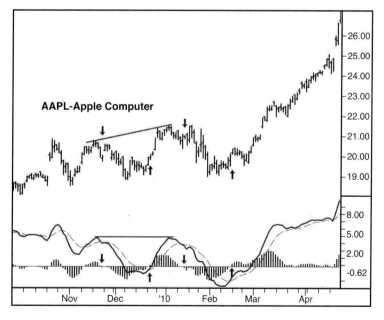

Created using TradeStation

FIGURE 18.13   Moving Average Convergence-Divergence (AAPL daily: September 28, 2009–April 23, 2010)

Rate of Change (ROC)

Rate of change (ROC) is likely the simplest oscillator. It is a measure of the amount a stock's price has changed over a given number (N) of past periods. The formula for calculating ROC is as follows:

$$ROC = \{(P_{today} - P_{N \text{ periods ago}}) / P_{N \text{ periods ago}}\} \times 100$$

With this calculation, ROC is zero if the price today is the same as it was N periods ago. It shows on a continuous basis how the current price relates to the past price.

Even though it is very simple to calculate, the ROC has many problems as an indicator. Although economists often calculate ROC using macroeconomic data, usually on an annual basis to minimize seasonality, it suffers from the drop-off effect. Only two prices, P_{today} and $P_{N \text{ periods ago}}$, appear in the calculation, and these two prices are equally weighted. Therefore, the older price that occurred N periods ago has the same effect as the current, and probably more relevant, price on the oscillator. The ROC can, thus, have a current rise or fall based solely on what number drops off in the past. Some analysts will smooth the ROC with a moving average to dampen this effect.

Analysts use the ROC in the standard four ways. Its position relative to zero can indicate the underlying trend; it can be a divergence oscillator showing when the momentum relative to the past is changing; it can be an overbought/oversold indicator; and it can generate a signal when it crosses over its zero line. In none of the instances is the signal reliable, however.

Figure 18.14 shows a graphical representation of a 14-day ROC for Apple Computer. At marker 2, we see a classic negative divergence where the ROC failed to confirm the new high in price. At marker 1, we see the variation of negative divergence called a negative reversal where the price fails to confirm a new high in the ROC. Both patterns have negative consequences, as the chart shows. We used the same trading signal method as we used in Figure 18.12 with the MACD and marked with arrows on the chart where the initial entry stops should have been placed. The only difference was that signals were generated using a filter around the midpoint line to dampen the number of false signals when the price trend was flat. This method worked equally as well with the ROC as with the MACD.

Relative Strength Index (RSI)

In June 1978, J. Welles Wilder introduced the relative strength index (RSI) in an article in *Commodities* (now known as *Futures*) magazine. The RSI measures the strength of an issue against its history of price change by comparing "up" days to "down" days. Wilder based his index on the assumption that overbought levels generally occur after the market has advanced for a disproportionate number of days, and that oversold levels generally follow a significant number of declining days.

Be careful to understand that the RSI measures a security's strength relative to its own price history, not to that of the market in general. Because of its name, a common misconception is that this indicator compares one security with other securities.

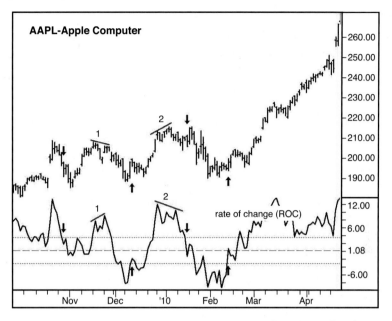

Created using TradeStation

FIGURE 18.14 Rate of change (AAPL daily: September 28, 2009–April 23, 2010)

To construct the RSI, several calculations must be made, as follows:

$$UPS = (\text{Sum of gains over N periods}) / N$$

$$DOWNS = (\text{Sum of losses over N periods}) / N$$

$$RS = UPS / DOWNS$$

$$RSI = 100 - [100 / (1 + RS)]$$

The RSI can range from a low of 0 (indicating no up days) to a high of 100.[2] In his original calculations, Wilder used 14 days as the relevant period. Although some analysts have attempted to use a time-weighted period, these methods have not been well accepted, and the 14-day period remains the most commonly used.

---

2. DOWNS is the sum of losses. In the calculation, the absolute values of the losses are added together. In other words, if a stock closes at $36 one day and $34 the next day, the loss is $2 (not a –$2 loss).

After calculating the RSI for the first 14 days, Wilder used a smoothing method to calculate RSI for future days. This process dampens the oscillations. For day 15 and after

$$\text{UPS}_{\text{day i}} = [(\text{UPS}_{\text{day i}-1} \times 13) + \text{Gain}_{\text{day i}}] / 14$$

$$\text{DOWNS}_{\text{day i}} = [\text{DOWNS}_{\text{day i}-1} \times 13) + \text{Loss}_{\text{day i}}] / 14$$

These measures for UPS and DOWNS are used to calculate RS and RSI. This method of smoothing the averages is now called the "Wilder exponential moving average" and is used in many other indicator formulas. We saw, for example, in the section on volume oscillators earlier in this chapter that the Money Flow oscillator uses the RSI formula.

The RSI has many characteristics that can generate signals. For example, when the RSI is above 50, the midpoint of the bounded range, the underlying trend in prices is usually upward. Conversely, it is downward when the RSI is below 50.

Overbought and oversold warnings are the same as with many other indicators. Wilder considered, for example, an RSI above 70 to indicate an overbought situation and an RSI below 30 to indicate an oversold condition. Analysts will often adjust these levels based on the underlying trend. Chuck LeBeau, for example, uses 75 and 25 as the overbought and oversold extremes and Brown (1999) uses 90 and 40 in an upward trend and 60 and 10 in a downward trend. She calls these new levels trend ids. Because the trend in Figure 18.15 is upward, we have drawn, in addition to the conventional overbought and oversold levels, the trend id of 90 and 40. This gives us an oversold buy signal in December and in late January that would not have been available using the conventional method.

Similar to other oscillators, RSI divergences with price often give warning of trend reversal. The RSI also appears to have patterns similar to price charts. Triangles, pennants, flags, and even head-and-shoulders patterns occur, and support and resistance levels become signal levels. The rules for breakouts from these formations are used for signals from the RSI.

Another method of signaling is **failure swings.** A failure swing occurs when the oscillator exceeds an overbought or oversold level, corrects, reverses back toward the overbought or oversold, misses, and then turns back through the correction. Two examples exit in Figure 18.15 and are marked as such. They occur at lows using the trend id method of determining the oversold level. Another short-term trading method using the RSI is to place a buy stop above the daily high when the RSI declines 10 points from a recent peak above 70. This should only be used when the trend is upward and never when a downward swing failure develops. The buy stop can be adjusted each day until either it is triggered for a day or two trade or the RSI continues to decline, suggesting that the trend is reversing downward.

There is also the method called the "RSI is wrong." In Figure 18.15, the RSI remains above or near the overbought level for a substantial period from mid-March onward, during which the AAPL price continued to rise. This method suggests that rather than looking for a top when the overbought level is penetrated, buy the issue and use a sell stop. *Active Trader Magazine* (August 2004, p 64–65) tested an "RSI is wrong" system, not optimized, on 19 futures from 1994 through 2003 with the following rules: Buy when 14-day RSI penetrates above 75; sell when RSI penetrates 25 or after 20 days. The opposite rules apply for sells using a break below the RSI 25 level as the initial short sale. The results showed a steady, straight equity curve especially for long positions.

Thomas (2003), in his testing of the RSI, found that none of the conventional signals had value except the positioning opposite from the conventional overbought/oversold levels of 70 and 30. His testing showed promise for the "RSI is wrong" thesis. Bauer and Dahlquist found that the conventional use, called a "crossover" system, of selling on a break below the over-bought 70 and buying on a break above the oversold 30 had marginal returns during the period tested. They also found that using peaks above 70 and below 30 had marginal returns, and that the opposite buying at peaks outperformed all signals. Their testing method, however, judged against the percentage of time in a position and did not account for the reduction in risk when in cash. Nevertheless, the results were "disappointing."

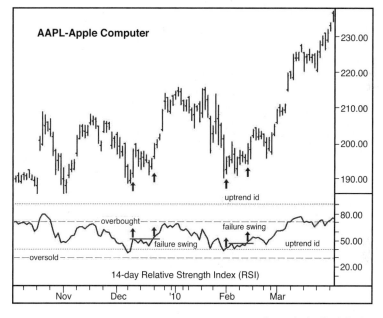

Created using TradeStation

FIGURE 18.15 RSI (AAPL daily: October 6, 2009–March 30, 2010)

As the many warnings and signals that occur in Figure 18.15 suggest, the RSI cannot be interpreted mechanically and is, perhaps, why it does not test well. However, the action is informative and useful to many traders. In a survey of traders taken in 2002 (Charleton and Earle), the most popular indicator was the RSI. In short, traders have developed many methods. If you want to use the RSI as a confirming indicator, you must learn these methods, experiment with them, and always be sure of the underlying price trend.

Stochastic Oscillator

All oscillators use a specific time over which they are calculated. The traditional periods for the MACD are 26 and 12 bars; the RSI traditionally uses 14 bars for its calculation. These oscillators depend on smoothing techniques that tend to dampen the most recent price action. The stochastic takes another tack. It looks at the most recent close price as a percentage of the price range (high to low) over a specified past "window" of time. This makes it very sensitive to recent action. Analysts use the stochastic for trading or investing when the most recent close is the most important price.

It is not absolutely clear who was the inventor of stochastics. George Lane is known for promoting the concept since 1954 (Lane, 1985), and it is sometimes referred to as Lane's Stochastic (Colby, 2003), but others apparently preceded him. Two names mentioned are Ralph Dystant and a dentist friend of his and Richard Redmont. Dystant introduced the indicator as part of an Elliott wave course through his Investment Educators, and Lane, who lectured for that firm, took it over on Dystant's death in 1978.

Not only is the inventor of stochastics unknown, the origin of the term "stochastics" is not clear. The name of this oscillator has nothing to do with the scientific term "stochastic," which means random or nondeterministic. Of course, traders would hope that this indicator did not produce random results. So, how did the name stochastic become associated with this indicator? According to Gibbons Burke (www.io.com/gibbonsb/trading/stochastic.html), Tim Slater, founder and president of CompuTrac, Inc., included this indicator in the company's software analysis program in 1978. He needed a name to attach to the indicator other than the %K and %D we will see in the indicator calculation. Slater saw a notation of "stochastic process" handwritten on the original Investment Educators literature he was using. The name stuck. Regardless of who the actual inventor might be or how it got its name, the stochastic oscillator is one of the most popular, both for long- and short-term momentum signals.

The formula for the stochastic is as follows:

$$\%K = [(C - L) / (H - L] \times 100$$

$$fast \ \%D = 3\text{-bar SMA of } \%K$$

$$slow \ \%D = 3\text{-bar SMA of } \%D$$

Where: W is the time window (that is, 14 bars)

H is the high for the window period (w)

L is the low for the window period (w)

C is the most recent bar close (w)

The "fast" stochastic, as seen in most trading software, refers to the raw stochastic number (%K) compared with a three-period simple moving average of that number (fast %D). This number is extremely sensitive to price changes. Because of the erratic volatility of the fast %D, many false signals occur with rapidly fluctuating prices. To combat this problem, analysts have created the "slow" stochastic. The slow stochastic is designed to smooth the original %D again with a three-period simple moving average. In other words, the slow stochastic is a doubly smoothed moving average, or a moving average of the moving average of %K.

Analysts often create their own variations of the stochastics formula. Lane, for example, smoothed the numerator separately from the denominator in the %K formula, and then divided each rather than smoothing the %K itself (Merrill, 1986). He also used only five days in the time window.

The question of how many periods to use in the window is problematic. The volatility and cyclical nature of the issue traded, as well as the tendency for these factors to vary, are integral to choosing a window period. Larry Williams uses a composite of different time window periods and the True Range rather than the high and low for his "Ultimate Oscillator." Others adjust the window period, as well as the number of bars used in smoothing the %K based on their interpretation of the dominant cycle in prices. Many analysts just test the results of signals over different windows to see which works best.

As in most oscillators, the stochastic works better in a trading range market but can still give valuable information in a trending market. In a trending market, divergences, trend line breaks, and swing failures generate signals. During trading ranges, crossovers and swing failures generate signals when the stochastic reaches overbought or oversold, traditionally 80 and 20. Crossovers occur when the fast stochastic crosses over the slow stochastic. Following crossovers without other confirming evidence, however, can cause whipsaws.

As in the RSI and many other oscillators, chart patterns, such as triangles and pennants, can also evolve in the stochastic oscillator. Support and resistance levels, even without swing failures, can be useful signals or warnings, and trend lines often appear to warn of potential changes in momentum. All standard technical rules apply to oscillators. However, oscillators by themselves should never be used strictly for signals. The analyst must confirm any oscillator signal with price action—a breakout or a pattern.

Academic testing of standard stochastic signals has had the same mediocre results as with other oscillators. This is not surprising, of course, because the determination of trend or trading range is rarely included in academic studies. Indeed, the fact that some positive results have occurred is encouraging, considering the primitive definitions of signals and circumstances used. Thomas (2003) found that extreme levels of overbought and oversold were somewhat predictive of future price direction but that most standard overbought/oversold interpretations failed. Bauer and Dahlquist (1999) found that acting at peaks and troughs above and below overbought and oversold respectively had better results on the long side than the short side. Unfortunately, trend was not a consideration in the testing, and the period tested (1985–1996) was one of a historically large upward trend when short signals would be expected to fail. Thus, the positive results for long signals were encouraging, considering that the signals had to keep up with the values in a generally rising market.

Figure 18.16 shows a 14-3-3 slow stochastic. This means that a 14-day time window was used; %D was smoothed once using a 3-day SMA and again using another 3-day SMA.

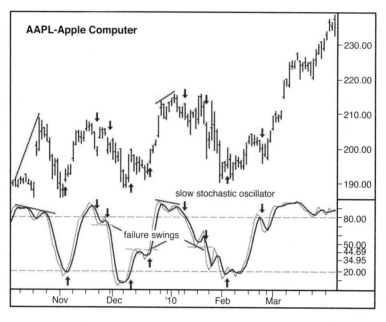

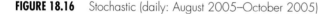

Created using TradeStation

FIGURE 18.16   Stochastic (daily: August 2005–October 2005)

AAPL is in a trending mode during the period considered but swinging in wide swings. In this case, the use of overbought and oversold levels is fruitful. Each time a buy or sell signal occurs from breaking toward the midpoint from oversold or overbought, an exit and reentry signal is given at the opposite extreme. This is not always the case. In a strong upward trend as developed during the later months of the period in Figure 18.16, the oscillator did not return to oversold. Thus, overbought breakdown sell signals in a rising trend must be suspect. They can signal the time to get out of a long trade, but they do not necessarily signal the time to enter a short trade.

In addition to the overbought/oversold signals, three failure swings occurred in late November, late December, and late January. The downward signal in late November was timely, as was the upward failure swing signal in December. The January sell signal was less profitable.

Finally, we see that before the declines in late October and early January, negative divergences developed at the peaks when the stochastic failed to confirm the new price highs.

Other Oscillators, Similar to the Stochastics

Some analysts use oscillators that are very similar to the stochastic oscillator. In particular, the Williams %R and the Commodity Channel Index are comparable indicators.

Williams %R

The Williams %R oscillator is almost identical to the stochastic. It can be thought of as an inverted stochastic. Instead of comparing the current close with the low that occurred during the time window, the Williams %R compares the current close with the high that occurred during the time window. Thus, the formula for the Williams %R is as follows:

$$\%R = [(H - C) / (H - L)] \times 100$$

The Williams %R tells whether a stock is at a relatively high point in its trading range, while the stochastic indicates whether a stock is at a relatively low point in its trading range.

Commodity Channel Index (CCI)

The Commodity Channel Index (CCI) is also very similar to the stochastic. Donald Lambert developed this indicator, describing it in the October 1980 issue of *Commodities* (now known as *Futures*) magazine. Do not be fooled by the name of the indicator; it can be used in any market, not just commodity markets. The CCI measures the deviations of a security's price from a moving average. This gives a slightly different picture than the stochastic, and in some cases, the signals are more reliable. However, the difference between the CCI and the stochastic is so miniscule that using both would be a duplication of effort and liable to create false confidence. Figure 18.17 shows how similar the CCI and the stochastic are.

The CCI is not bounded—that is, it can rise above +100 and fall below –100—as is the stochastic, and this bothers some analysts. To avoid this problem, some analysts use a stochastic calculation on the CCI, bounding the CCI to 0 to 100 and smoothing the CCI at the same time. Barbara Star reports in *Active Trader Magazine* (2004) that in trending markets, this bounded, smoothed CCI is often useful for entries in the trend direction, but not in a countertrend direction, and in trading markets, it often gives overbought and oversold signals.

Similarities Between Oscillators

Figure 18.18 shows a standard 14-day RSI compared with a 3-day to 10-day MACD. See how the two lines follow almost identical paths. It is, thus, redundant and nonproductive to use many oscillators that essentially tell the same story. This is why most analysts prefer to use just one, or perhaps two, oscillators and learn their complexities and intricacies well rather than depend on mechanical signals from many.

Combinations—Determining Trend and Trading Range

In Chapter 14, "Moving Averages," we discussed trends, moving averages, and especially the use of the ADX and its component parts, the DMI+ and DMI–. We found that moving averages were only profitable in trending markets, just as we have found in this chapter that oscillators are more profitable in trading markets. The problem, then, is to be able to determine whether a particular market is trending or trading. Usually markets rotate from one to the other, but the signals generated by moving averages and indicators are not always quick to decipher the change. Because most profits come from trending markets, analysts focus on moving averages and oscillators to determine when a trend is beginning, and the sooner they recognize the trend, the better.

The most common solution is the use of Wilder's ADX in combination with an oscillator and a moving average. Because it is smoothed through averaging, the ADX is a lagging indicator and should not be used for signals except from very low levels when a trend may be beginning. Its value is in demonstrating the degree to which prices are already trending and, by implication, suggesting what kinds of analysis—trend or trading range—should be used. It is equally adept at trend determination from very short-term intraday trading to month-to-month investing.

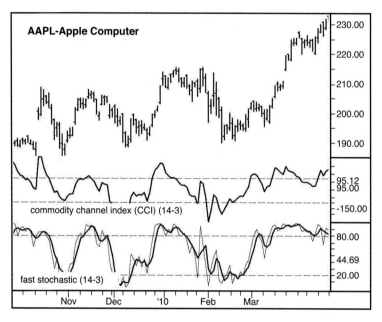

FIGURE 18.17   CCI and fast stochastic (AAPL daily: October 1, 2009–March 29, 2010)

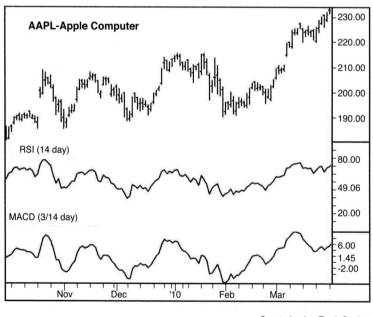

FIGURE 18.18   MACD and RSI (AAPL daily: October 1, 2009–March 29, 2010)

The use of the ADX is based on its level and its trend. The level determines the amount by which prices are trending, and the direction shows the change in that trending. Low readings (<20) suggest a trading range and low volatility in which oscillators and patterns should be used. A moderately high reading (30) indicates strong trending in which moving average crossovers and patterns should be used. A very high reading (>45) indicates a potential trend reversal in which patterns, trends, support and resistance, divergences in oscillators and volume, and oscillator failures should be used. Generally, a rising ADX reflects an increased trending, up or down, and a declining ADX reflects an approaching reversal or consolidation.

BOX 18.1 GENERAL RULES FOR USING ADX

In an article appearing in *Futures Magazine,* Ashwani Gujral provided general rules for using ADX. His guidelines include the following:

When ADX is rising and at a level

Between 15 and 25	Beginning of trending; use trending indicators.
Between 25 and 45	Definite trending; use trending indicators.
Of 45 or above	Overextended; watch for trend turning point; use price or indicator patterns.

When ADX is declining and at a level

Below 20	Low volatility; very short swings; no trend; use oscillators.
Between 20 and 30	Consolidation; use oscillators.
Between 30 and 45	Correction from extreme likely; use patterns; trending indicators.

Analysts have developed numerous methods of utilizing the ADX with oscillators and moving averages. Let us look at two of them: David Steckler's **popsteckle** and **Linda Raschke's holy grail.**

Popsteckle

In a 2000 article, appearing in *Stocks and Commodities,* David Steckler described a method of identifying stocks that are ready to "pop" upward using all three indicators. The name "popsteckle" is a contraction of "pop" and "Steckler," but Jake Bernstein (1993) is the originator of the method. Steckler's setup rules are as follows:

1. Recent price action shows low volatility (dull action).
2. 14-day ADX is below 20 (no trend).

3. Eight-day stochastic %K is greater than the day before and above 70 (upward trend beginning).

4. Eight-week stochastic %K is greater than the week before and above 50 (upward longer trend beginning).

5. Bullish market conditions exist (could be determined by market price above long-term moving average).

6. Stock breaks upward out of congestion on volume 50% above its 50-day simple moving average.

The popsteckle method monitors a low-volatility stock in a horizontal trading range for signs of positive trending action as displayed by changes in the various stochastics. No history of back testing this method is available, but the logic of the variables and indicators is consistent.

Holy Grail

Unlike the popsteckle, which looks for the beginning of a new trend, Linda Raschke's Holy Grail method takes advantage of an existing trend and uses the ADX in combination with a moving average. First, a 14-day ADX must be above 30 to indicate an existing trend. The primary trend is displayed by a 20-period EMA. An initial downturn in the ADX suggests a correction to the primary trend. When this occurs, enter in the direction of the trend when the price touches or comes close to that EMA. On the long side, the entry trigger would be a break above the high of the most recent declining bar, and it would be the opposite on the short side. The initial target that Raschke uses is the old price extreme, high or low, at which point the analyst must make a decision as to whether the price will continue in the primary trend direction or not.

CONCLUSION

To increase the odds that a technical price signal is correct, the technical analyst uses many other indicators as confirmation. The primary confirmation indicator is volume because it is a series of data independent of price. Unfortunately, volume indicators and volume itself do not always confirm a price pattern. Nevertheless, high volume at the appropriate moments does add value to the entry decision. Other means of calculating volume for comparison with past volume and price action have limited value in confirming signals, but they can provide warnings when not confirming price action. These divergences cannot be used as signals by themselves but do help the analyst by suggesting that trend change is soon likely.

The other major area of confirmation comes from momentum, or rate of price change, calculations. Strong momentum suggests a trending market, and weak momentum suggests a consolidating market. Naturally, the analyst principally looks for the beginning of a trending market, and because momentum indicators tend to lead price direction, they are often useful in warning of such a change. However, the reliability of these indicators is highly dependent upon whether the security is trading in a trend or in a trading range. By and large, these oscillators are more useful in trading ranges as overbought/oversold indications. In trending markets, they are more useful as warnings of trend change. In strong trends, they tend to be skewed in the direction of the trend and, thus, fail to provide reliable entry signals.

Some of the problems with interpreting price and volume indicators can be ameliorated with the use of the ADX or other indicators of trend strength. Combining the ADX, a moving average, and an oscillator, for example, can improve timing results considerably.

REVIEW QUESTIONS

1. General rules for interpreting volume data date back to the mid-1930s. According to these general rules, how should volume statistics be used?

2. In terms of oscillators, describe what each of the following terms means:
   a. Overbought
   b. Oversold
   c. Negative divergence
   d. Positive divergence
   e. Failure swing
   f. Negative reversal
   g. Positive reversal

3. What is meant by the term *momentum?* Looking at the prices for a hypothetical stock, XYZ, explain what is happening as far as the price trend and momentum over time. Sketch a graph of this stock's price and comment on how the curve's shape is impacted by momentum.

Day	Price of XYZ
1	28
2	28
3	29
4	30
5	32
6	35
7	39
8	43
9	47
10	51
11	54
12	57
13	59
14	60
15	61
16	61

Day	Price of XYZ
17	60
18	55
19	50
20	45
21	42
22	40
23	39
24	40
25	41
26	43

4. Gather trading information for Valero (VLO) from August 1 to October 31, 2005.

    a. Using this information, calculate the following:

        i. On-Balance-Volume

        ii. Price-volume trend

        iii. Williams Variable Accumulation Distribution

        iv. Accumulation Distribution

        v. Chaikin Money Flow

        vi. Money Flow Index (using a seven-day period)

    b. Looking at the calculations you have made, what observations can you make about Valero over the three-month period observed?

5. Look at the volume data for Valero in Question 3. Do you see any spikes or dips in volume? If so, how might these volume patterns enter into your analysis of the stock?

    a. Use the data you collect in Question 3 to calculate the following:

        i. MACD (using 12- and 26-day EMA)

        ii. 14-day rate of change (ROC)

        iii. 14-day relative strength index (RSI)

        iv. 14-3-3 stochastic

        v. Williams %R

    b. What information do you gain about Valero from these calculations? Do you see many similarities among the results of the five different calculations?

6. Most analysts will choose one oscillator to use in their analysis. Explain why using one oscillator is preferable to using the information from multiple oscillators.

7. Explain how moving averages and oscillators can be used in conjunction with each other for trading in trending and trading markets.

8. Explain what is meant by the term *confirmation*. What are some general concepts the analyst should consider when looking for confirmation?

PART VI

OTHER TECHNICAL METHODS AND RULES

CHAPTER 19 CYCLES

CHAPTER 20 ELLIOTT, FIBONACCI, AND GANN

CYCLES

CHAPTER OBJECTIVES

By the end of this chapter, you should be familiar with

- The controversy about whether cycles exist in financial market data
- How cycles are defined by their amplitude, period, and phase
- Detrending data and plotting centered moving averages
- The major methods of determining cycles in market data
- The major methods of using cycles to project future price highs and lows

Throughout this book, we have seen how prices trend, but the trend does not occur in a straight line. Prices oscillate up and down around a trend. These oscillations form the trading ranges, patterns, and channels we have discussed. Could it be that these oscillations have some sort of regularity? Believing that they do, cycle analysts look at prices as a form of complex harmonics or waves. (In physics, a harmonic is a wave whose frequency is a whole number multiple of the frequency of another wave.) Most standard patterns can be broken down into cycle layers. For example, the head-and-shoulders pattern is a combination of a long cycle peaking with several smaller cycles forming the shoulders and head. Triangles are periods within an uptrend when the amplitude of smaller cycles declines and then expands. By breaking down known patterns into harmonics, these analysts believe that the inherent oscillations are somewhat regular cycles and are, therefore, predictable.

Not surprisingly, the concept of prices oscillating in cycles is controversial. There are two basic reasons some oppose the cycle concept. First, if prices behaved in pure cycles, like radio waves or tuning forks, the numbers would easily fit into mathematical formulas that would give us precise predictions similar to what we know about ocean tides and sunrises. This has not happened. The inability to use present mathematical methods to identify specifically and precisely any existing cycles is evidence to some that there are no such cycles. These objectors claim that

449

any cycles that traders think they see are merely imaginary. As we saw in Chapter 4, "The Technical Analysis Controversy," when they discuss patterns in trading market prices, the human mind often "sees" patterns in data that do not truly exist.

Another set of objections comes from the inability to identify causes of specific cycles that many agree do exist in prices. There may be correlations between Super Bowl scores or rainfall in New York City and stock prices. However, their relationships are merely curious correlations rather than causation. There is no logical reason why these events would be causal or explanatory.

However, we do see that human behavior does strange things during different phases of the moon. For example, Al Lieber (1978) discusses changes in emotional behavior at regularly scheduled intervals correlated with phases of the moon in the *Journal of Clinical Psychology.* Yuan, Zheng, and Zhu (2006) demonstrate the correlation between lunar phases and stock prices in 48 countries. The moon rotates around the earth each 29.53 days. Thus, using a normal trading week of 4.85 days (to account for occasional holidays), we should, if there is a lunar cycle in markets, expect a cycle of approximately 20 days in stock market behavior. Does this cycle exist? Yes, it appears to. See Figure 19.1 for a demonstration of a 20-day cycle in the Standard & Poor's 500. Is this cycle related to the phases of the moon? We do not know.

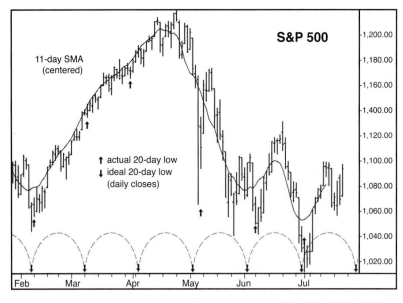

Created using TradeStation

FIGURE 19.1   20-day cycle in Standard & Poor's 500 (daily: January 27, 2010–July 22, 2010)

The astro-physical connection between market cycles and the collective human psyche is a common argument for cycle causes and has been investigated thoroughly for correlation. Some claim such correlations exist, and others say they do not. Nevertheless, this connection has led to the false accusation that technical analysts are "stargazers." Extremely few analysts have seriously made any causal connections between the planets, the moon, and the sun and market prices, and even fewer use that knowledge or presumption to act in the markets. Nevertheless, there are certain obvious planetary cycles that definitely affect prices if only by affecting supply and demand in agricultural markets.

The earth circles the sun every 365 days. Do we have an annual or seasonal cycle in market prices? Yes, of course, a very well-defined annual cycle exists in agricultural commodity prices (now being dampened by importation of agricultural products from the southern hemisphere). We also see a seasonal cycle in the stock market. (For more information about seasonal cycles in the stock market, read *Research Driven Investor* by Timothy Hayes [McGraw-Hill, New York, 2000].) Obvious causes for these cycles include change in seasons and weather. Psychologists are also learning about how sun deprivation affects human behavior, not only at different latitudes but also at different seasons of the year, and about electromagnetic effects on the brain. In addition to individual behavior, psychologists are studying crowd mood changes that might influence the markets.

There are many observed cycles in market prices. Some of them can be explained, or rationalized, and others cannot. Some, like the "presidential cycle" of four years, are thought to be synthetic; others are products of nature; and most are unexplained. There are very long-term cycles like the Kondratieff and Kuznets cycles, and very short-term ones lasting only a few minutes.

In terms of the markets, the "business cycle" is not truly a market cycle in the sense that it does not have a periodic element. However, the business cycle obviously does affect market prices, and it does have a rough periodicity of four to five years, which in turn can be affected by market prices in a feedback loop.

The important point in market cycles is that they are not truly harmonics, the mathematical description of cycles. Instead, they tend to be periodic events or extremes that can be measured in time but not necessarily in amplitude. Amplitude is a measure of the "strength" of a cycle. In markets just as in sunspots, amplitude can change and lie dormant for a while. Amplitude is related to volatility, which we know also fluctuates over time. Harmonic mathematics has not developed to the point that it can account for this conduct (it assumes a constant amplitude), and we must often rely more on observation of periodicity alone to gain insight into the cyclical timing of future market events.

Other curious aspects of market cycles are as follows: (1) They often tend to "nest" together—especially at turning points, more often at price lows—and when they do, larger events seem to occur; and (2) they tend to be fractions of larger or multiples of smaller cycles, usually by a factor of two or three. The latter is termed "harmonic" action, similar to that in music. These aspects are useful sometimes in projecting market events ahead in time. Finally, the aspect of "proportionality" suggests that longer cycles tend to have larger amplitudes. This is not always the case and can often be deceiving. Because amplitude is consistently a projection problem, the most reliable projections are made strictly on periodicity and phase.

In this chapter, we consider the description and mathematics of cycles, the ways in which analysts detect cycles, and some methods of profiting from them.

WHAT ARE CYCLES?

In mathematical terms, the cosine (and sine) function describes a cycle. Figure 19.2 shows a right-angle triangle (one with a 90-degree angle). The side across from the 90-degree angle is the hypotenuse, labeled (H). A cosine of an angle is the ratio of the adjacent side to the hypotenuse. For example, in Figure 19.2, the cosine for angle U is A/H. Thus, for every angle, there is a specific cosine value.

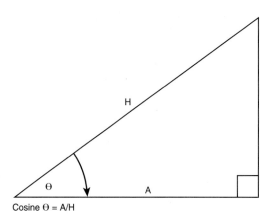

Cosine Θ = A/H

FIGURE 19.2 Triangle and cosine ratio

Within a circle (the unit circle), we can create a triangle from each point along the circle perimeter. As demonstrated in Figure 19.3, using the radius length of the circle as the hypotenuse and the length along the horizontal axis to an intersection perpendicular to the perimeter point, we can calculate the cosine of the angle between each hypotenuse and the axis line for each point along the perimeter. The cosine value is the ratio of the length along the x-axis (X') divided by the radius of the circle. The cosine value will always be one or less because X' can never be larger than the radius. As the point works its way around the circle counterclockwise, we can plot the series of cosine values in another chart with the angle (in radians) along the x-axis and the cosine value along the y-axis, as shown in Figure 19.4. As you can see in the figure, this results in a curve with values oscillating between –1 and 1. This curve is known as a cosine wave and is the basis for calculating the existence of cycles or waves in time series data.

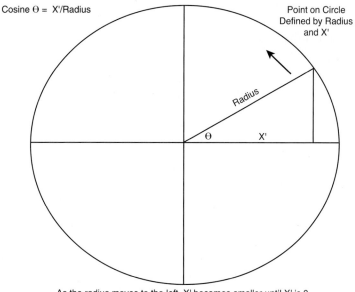

Cosine Θ = X'/Radius

Point on Circle
Defined by Radius
and X'

Radius

Θ   X'

As the radius moves to the left, X' becomes smaller until X' is 0,
and then X' becomes negative.

FIGURE 19.3 Unit circle

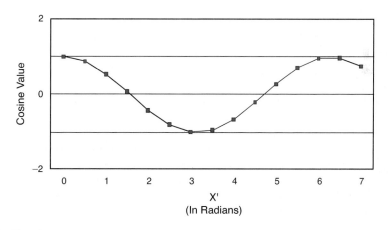

FIGURE 19.4 Plot of cosine curve

Of course, cycles can have different parameters. They can be long from bottom to bottom, high and short, and begin from different locations. The location along the cycle of each point can be defined by the following formula:

$$f(x) = a \times \cos(bx + c) + d$$

Where: a is the amplitude

bx is the period (constant b times x time in radians)

c is the phase (in radians)

d is the error factor

Rather than fully understanding the derivation of cosine waves, it is important to know the specific variables that determine the waveform. *Amplitude* is the distance from the horizontal axis to the extreme peak or trough. In Figure 19.4, it is 1. An amplitude of 2 would result in a cosine wave twice the height of the cosine waves with an amplitude of 1. *Period* s the distance between consecutive lows or consecutive highs. In our usage, the period is the time along the horizontal axis that it takes for the cycle to return to its original position. Figure 19.5 shows two cosine waves with different phases. Phase determines how far from the y-axis the particular cycle begins. It thus determines the offset between two cycles of different phases.

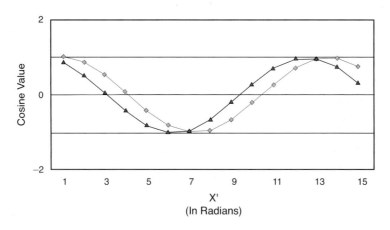

FIGURE 19.5   Cosine waves with different phases

If we know the parameter constants for each variable, we can plot any cosine wave. If there are multiple cosine waves, we can calculate each and add them together in what is called **summation.** James Hurst more thoroughly developed this idea in his book, *The Profit Magic of Stock Transaction Timing* (1970). The presumption in markets is that there is no one specific cycle but many cycles that, when summed, form the plot of prices. The forecasting problem then is to reverse the process and go from the price plot to the cosine formula to determine how many cosine waves and their parameters exist in the data. From this knowledge, presumably the direction of prices can be foretold by extrapolating the waves into the future.

Like all theories related to the markets, the theory of cycles is logical but impossible to quantify, at least with the present level of mathematics. Many methods have been invented to recognize waves in time series data, but none has been able to duplicate market price sequences with reliable accuracy. There are many reasons for this, the primary one being that the parameters in the cosine functions of market prices are not constants. Hurst calls this the principle of "variation." Amplitude and period, for example, vary over time. Most mathematical means of determining cosines from time series data assume that the parameters are constants. This does not mean that the standard methods of analysis of time series are useless, however. The changes in parameters appear to take place slowly rather than suddenly. By analyzing prices through conventional cosine analysis over specific but different periods, we can see how the parameters change. Amplitude appears to change quickly at times, but period appears to change more slowly. Thus, if we can at least estimate the period with some degree of accuracy, as analysts, we have a useful indicator. We cannot predict future price levels, but with an estimate of period, we can potentially predict the timing of future highs and lows.

Other Aspects of Cycle Analysis

There are several other aspects of cycle analysis of which the technical analysis needs to be aware. Accuracy concerns exist because cycle periods are indefinite and have error. Cycle translations and inversions make cycle analysis more difficult. However, due to harmonic properties, determining one cycle period often leads the analyst to determining cycle periods that are multiples of that initial cycle.

Accuracy

Just because the analysis of financial time series data may suggest cycles exist does not imply that the cycles are precise. As mentioned earlier, all three aspects of a wave vary over time, and as wave is added to wave, the errors become large. Because market cycles tend to synchronize at lows, the estimate of the phase is relatively easy. The analysis just begins at a major price low where presumably most cycle lows coincide. The estimate of amplitude varies too much for projection purposes. Amplitude is often called the "power" of the cycle in electronic analysis circles, where it tends to be a constant in those applications. In the financial world, power can be influenced greatly by exogenous, unpredictable events. The study of amplitude becomes nonproductive. The third aspect of the cosine wave, the period, often remains relatively constant but can sometime have large errors. Estimates are based on immediate past price history. As an example, a 20-day cycle low can occur several days before or after the expected 20 days from the last low, which itself may have been several days before or after its ideal location. The 20-day cycle, from spectral or other analysis, may only be 19.2 days, or it may be 20.4 days. Cycle periods, therefore, are indefinite and have error. This means that for investment purposes, all cycles should be used only as a guide. Even the well-established, seasonal cycle has actual high and low dates that vary considerably from year to year.

Harmonics

One of the interesting aspects of cycles first observed by Hurst in market data is that cycles tend to have period lengths a multiple of two or three longer or shorter than the next larger or smaller cycles. In other words, a cycle of 20 days will indicate that another longer cycle of either 40- or 60-days length exists and that another shorter cycle of 7 or 10 days exists. The longer is either two times or three times the observed cycle, and the shorter is either 1/3 or 1/2 the observed cycle. This observation is useful when one specific cycle is determined because it leads the analyst to what intervals to look for in longer and shorter cycles. Hurst believed that the ratio of two is more common. Others, such as Tony Plummer (2003), have hypothesized that three is the correct multiple.

In the April 1987 issue of *Technical Analysis of Stocks and Commodities Magazine,* Frank Tarkany compared his analysis of weekly market cycles with that of three other well-known analysts. Table 19.1 provides a summary of Tarkany's comparisons. All four of the analysts found 26-week cycles; this 26-week cycle is the base cycle. These analysts also noticed multiples of 26 weeks, suggesting that an autocorrelation exists between cycle periods. These cycle periods are called nominal periods because they occur regularly in most financial time series data.

TABLE 19.1   Harmonics of the 2-Week Cycle in the Stock Market

Weeks in Cycle	Gann	Garrett	Hurst	Tarkany	26-Week Harmonic	Potential Cause
234		221	234	234,237	9	Business cycle
208		214			8	Presidential cycle
182	182	178		178	7	
156	156		156	156	6	
130				134	5	
104					4	
78		78	78	78	3	18-month cycle
52	52		52		2	Seasonal cycle
26	25,26	25	26	22,23	1	Base cycle
13	12,13	10	13	12	1/2	Quarterly reports
6.5	6,7,8		6.5	6,7	1/4	
3.25	3	2	3.25	3	1/8	14-day cycle
1.625			1.625		1/16	7-day cycle

Source: Tarkany (1987)

Notice that several of the cycles appearing in Table 19.1 are stock market cycles we have mentioned in previous chapters. The well-known presidential cycle is very dependable, as is the seasonal cycle. They are both multiples of the 26-week base cycle—the seasonal cycle by two, and the presidential cycle by eight (or $2 \times 2 \times 2$). Thus, the Hurst hypothesis that cycles tend to occur in multiples of two or three seems to make sense.

Inversions

One of the most difficult observations for the analyst to face is the **inversion.** Occasionally, where a cycle low is expected, a peak occurs instead. For example, look at Figure 19.1. Where we would be expecting to see the second 20-day low, we actually see a high in this chart. This is an example of an inversion. No satisfactory explanation has been given for its existence, but several observations have been noted.

Inversions can occur at either peaks or troughs, but most often occur at peaks in harmonic cycles when the next longer cycle is at a peak. This make sense only if the next higher order cycle is a multiple of two. For example, a cycle of 20 days should make a low every 20 days. If the next higher order cycle is 40 days, synchronous with the 20-day cycle, and peaking, a 40-day peak ideally should occur just as a 20-day cycle is making a low. Thus, the 20-day cycle low is masked by the peaking of the 40-day cycle and is often difficult to decipher. When this occurs, the inverted cycle low often has just a small very short-term "dip" within the peak of the higher order cycle. This dip resembles an *M* where the small low between the two small peaks is the actual cycle low that is being overcome by the longer cycle. Proof of the low coinciding with the longer-cycle high occurs when the subsequent decline breaks below the dip. If a longer cycle is due to peak, this is the sign that its declining portion has begun.

Previously we noted that cycles are not strict harmonics but specific time-separated events. The habit of producing lows at constant intervals can be interspersed with highs at the same intervals because both are important market events. Thus, a long string of events occurring at specific intervals that is primarily dominated by low events but interspersed with occasional high events at the same periodic times can look like a harmonic wave for the period that the lows are occurring but be confusing from a cyclical standpoint. However, the progression is only a time sequence of events. Analysts thus assume inversions are anomalies within a harmonic-type wave when the wave is actually an event wave, not a true mathematically defined cycle.

TRANSLATION

The reason that we study lows in cycle analysis is because longer and shorter cycles tend to synchronize at lows. Peaks, on the other hand, almost never synchronize. Peaks, ideally, should occur at the halfway period of the cycle. A 20-day cycle, for example, should have a peak 10 days from its last low. This rarely occurs. Peaks can occur earlier or later than the halfway point. Their location away from the center point is called translation. A right translation in a cycle is when the peak is beyond the halfway point, and a left translation is when the cycle peak occurs before the halfway point. Usually, the underlying trend from a longer cycle determines the amount of translation in the shorter cycle. In Chapter 12, "Trends—The Basics," we noticed that trend directions determined the shape of the corrective trends. In an uptrend, for example, the upward trends were long and the corrections were short. These were translating right because the peaks were beyond the halfway point between the lows. If the peak had occurred at the halfway point, we would be suspicious about the continuation of the upward trend. Because cycles are nested and synchronous, the shorter cycle is dominated by the trend of the next longer cycle.

Again, let us look at Figure 19.1. The first marked low (in early February) is both a 20-day and a higher order cycle low. From that point on for more than two cycles, the trend is sharply upward. This upward strength of the longer cycle is influencing where the peak for the first, second, and third 20-day cycles will occur. As it is, the peak for the first cycle is past the midpoint of the 20-week cycle period. In the second 20-day cycle, the peak is even farther to the right of its midpoint, suggesting that the trend is becoming even steeper. This movement of the actual peak beyond the midpoint of the cycle is called right translation and is characteristic of all peaks when dominated by the strength of a longer, rising trend.

In the 20-day cycle beginning in May during the decline in prices, the peak to the cycle is only four days after the low. This cycle is left translated.

The diminution of "rightness" or "leftness" suggests that the higher order cycle is also beginning to change direction. Translation is, thus, useful in checking where the overlying longer-term cycle trend direction is headed or if it is changing direction.

How Can Cycles Be Found in Market Data?

Conventional wave-filtering mathematics has gone through tremendous growth and development in the past 50 years. Data transmission, voice and image transmission, electronic signaling, and other developments in the electronic age necessitated more sophisticated mathematics to recognize and understand waveforms. Now we have bandpass filters, digital signal processing (DSP), wavelet modeling, nonlinear spectral analysis, higher order spectral analysis (HOSA), and derivatives of each. For our purposes, however, this sophistication is unnecessary. Because waveforms in prices, if they exist, are not based on constant parameters, we need only to make initial estimates of a cycle period to satisfy our requirements. Once we have an estimate of period, we have information that is useful for projection and useful for determining the "window" or moving average length in indicators that best represents the trading period of interest.

Fourier Analysis (Spectral Analysis)

The most common and simplest method of wave analysis in a time series data is Fourier analysis. Fourier analysis, available in most mathematics software programs, has many variations. It has specific problems, however, in that it requires a large amount of data. For market forecasting, the more data that is involved, the more the waves can change and neutralize the calculations of parameters. Thus, Fourier analysis should be used only as a basic method of analyzing cycles in market time series data. A faster method, called Fast Fourier Transforms (FFTs), reduces the computation time of the analysis. A second problem with Fourier analysis is that it does not maintain the phase relationships between cycles. In other words, if one cycle crosses the horizontal axis after or before another, the difference in these phases is not recorded. This makes projection of the combination of the cycles very difficult. Figure 19.6 displays an example of spectral analysis.

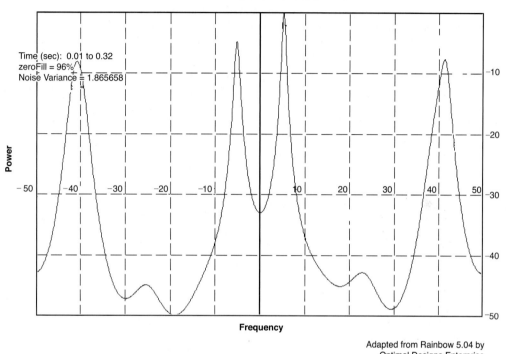

Auto-Correlation Estimate By Rainbow
Power-Spectral Density

Time (sec): 0.01 to 0.32
zeroFill = 96%
Noise Variance = 1.865658

Power

Frequency

Adapted from Rainbow 5.04 by
Optimal Designs Enterprise

FIGURE 19.6 Display of spectral analysis of time series data for cycles

Maximum Entropy Spectral Analysis

In the early 1980s, John Ehlers (2002) developed a method that attempts to solve the problems of Fourier analysis without compromising the accuracy of the results. His method, Maximum Entropy Spectral Analysis (MESA), is available through his software company, MESA Software. The method requires only a short time series to determine the inherent cycles in the data. It determines the most recent and most relevant waves for projection and records the different phases of each cycle recognized.

Simpler (and More Practical) Methods

Fourier analysis and MESA provide methods for determining cycles but depend upon complex mathematics. Often, simpler tools, such as detrending, envelopes, or centered moving averages, can help identify cycles. At times, even the naked eye can observe cycles without the aid of complicated mathematics and sophisticated computer software.

Observation

In many cases, the low points of dominant cycles in market data are obvious to the eye. The exact cyclical low can often be difficult to determine, but the general oscillation of the cycle is plain. In his book, *The Profit Magic of Stock Transaction Timing,* Hurst, the father of cycle analysis in the stock market, used a method of envelopes that he traced along the major highs and lows in a price chart. These envelopes were not predetermined like a filter but were drawn freehand on the chart. When prices touched the upper and lower edges of the band, Hurst drew an arrow at the bottom of the price chart for later inspection. When he was done with the freehand estimates, he looked at the arrows drawn and determined if any obvious stable period separated the arrows. Figure 19.7 shows what this hand-drawn method might look like.

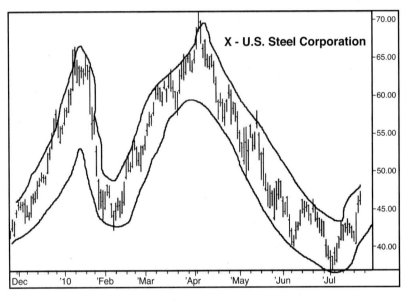

Created using TradeStation

FIGURE 19.7 Envelopes—Hurst hand-drawn method (X daily: December 14, 2009–July 22, 2010)

Of course, such methods are fraught with danger. The human mind often imagines cycles where they do not exist or invents turning points to fit a preconceived notion of an existing cycle. Hurst's method was just the beginning observation of the potential for cycles in financial data. If it appeared reasonable that cycles existed in the data, he would then use more sophisticated methods, such as Fourier analysis and moving averages, to find the specifics.

Oscillators are another method of determining with the eye if cycles exist in financial data. Many of the indicators in Chapter 18, "Confirmation," show oscillations about a central horizontal line. By observing the lows especially, because cycles tend to synchronize at lows, one can observe if the times separating each low are at regular intervals. If so, a cycle is suspected to exist in the data.

If a cycle is suspected, one way of quantifying it more accurately is to mark a dot on the bottom of the chart page just below each low. Then, using a blank piece of paper, mark a line on the edge of the paper, move the paper such that the line is placed on the first dot on the chart, and draw another line on the paper at the point where the next dot lies. This gives a measured distance between the two dots on the paper. Then move the first paper line to the second dot and draw a line on the paper where the third dot occurs on the chart. This second line should be near the earlier line for the second dot but is rarely exactly on it. Now two cycle lengths have been measured, and the difference in period can be seen immediately. Continue to move the paper across the dots, making lines to mark the length between each subsequent cycle bottom. When you're done, the paper will show the range of periods between dots and thus give an estimate of the cycle period. By placing the first line on the last dot, the range of lines from previous cycles will give an estimate of the range in which to expect the next cyclical bottom.

The eyeball measurement of cycle lengths can also be done with a ruler or a drafting divider. In this case, the distance between the first and second dot is measured and recorded; then the distance between the second and third dot is measured and recorded; and so on. Once imported into a spreadsheet, the mean, standard deviation, and other statistical measures can be determined for all the intervals.

Detrending

Because specific cycle behavior is highly dependent on the direction of the next higher order cycle, the first step in recognizing if a cycle exists in the data is to "detrend" it. Detrending is done merely by dividing the current prices by a moving average of those prices. The resulting plot will oscillate above and below a zero line, and the lows of the plot will correspond to the lows in the cycle being analyzed.

Figure 19.8 shows an example of this detrending method. The detrended line is constructed by dividing the current closing price by an 11-day SMA. The cycle with a 35-day period (slightly shorter than the ideal 40 days) shows up clearly in the plot.

As a further example, Figure 19.9 shows detrending using a six-day SMA, roughly half the length of the SMA used in Figure 19.8. The plot in Figure 19.9 shows more clearly the cycle lows 18 days apart, the half-cycle of the 35-day cycle shown in Figure 19.8.

When prices are detrended using the daily closing price as the numerator, especially as we lengthen the denominator, the plot becomes very erratic and difficult to interpret. The solution is to use a moving average in the numerator as well, but this presents some problems that must first be addressed.

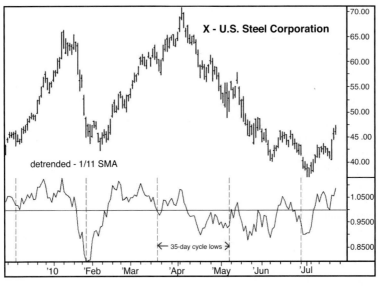

Created using TradeStation

FIGURE 19.8   Detrended plot 1- to 11-day SMA showing 35-day cycle lows (X daily: November 30, 2009–July 22, 2010)

Created using TradeStation

FIGURE 19.9   Detrended plot 1- to 6-day SMA showing 18-day cycle lows (X daily: November 30, 2009–July 22, 2010)

Centered Moving Averages

...the time relationship between the moving average and the data it smoothes is not the one that is always shown on stock price charts. In fact, the moving average data point plotted in association with the last price datum should be associated with price datum one-half the time span of the average in the past. (Hurst, 1970, p. 65)

What Hurst was saying is that a moving average is an average of both price and time. Most plots take into account the average in price but incorrectly plot that average at the time the last price of the average occurs. For example, an 11-day moving average of prices of Days 1–11 is frequently plotted at Day 11. Instead, because the moving average is also an average of the time over which the average price occurred, it should be plotted at the mean point or center of the time span of the average. In other words, the moving average of Days 1–11 should be plotted at Day 6. This plot is called a **centered moving average.** Figure 19.10 shows an 11-day centered moving average versus an 11-day moving average plotted the usual way. We use a centered moving average for the remainder of our discussion on cycles.

Created using TradeStation

FIGURE 19.10 11-day centered moving average plot versus the standard moving average plot (X daily: November 30, 2009–July 22, 2010)

Notice in Figure 19.10 that the centered moving average better reflects the price action than the conventional plot. It runs through the center of all the price oscillations and is not skewed to the right of prices, as is the conventional method. The problem of skewing to the right

becomes even more noticeable as the moving average span increases. The centered moving average plot is a better representation of prices but, of course, lags behind prices and by itself cannot be used as a signaling method. It is used to identify cycles but not to predict them.

Envelopes

As we saw in Figure 19.7, Hurst used a hand-drawn envelope about prices to get a rough estimate of the potential cycle period in the price data. Once that period could be estimated, he used moving averages to quantify the cycle more definitively.

Moving averages dampen or smooth data. In terms of cycles, a moving average represents price oscillations greater than the period of the moving average and effectively cancels out price action or oscillations less than the moving average period. Figure 19.11 includes a centered 35-day moving average overlay. The large price deviations below and above the moving average appear roughly 40 days apart. To quantify the range of price movement about this moving average, we draw an envelope parallel with the moving average. Notice that prices touch the lower envelope band about every 35 days.

FIGURE 19.11   35-day centered moving average with a 9% parallel envelope (X daily: November 30, 2009–July 22, 2010)

The next step is to draw a half-cycle centered moving average with an envelope, as shown in Figure 19.12. A half-cycle moving average in this example is 18 days. This moving average smoothes out all waves shorter than 18 days and includes waves 18 days or longer. When subtracted from the 35-day moving average, it reflects the waves that exist between 18 and 35 days, or the 35-day cycle we are investigating.

The points at which the 18-day envelope touches, or comes close to, the 35-day envelope and turns upward are the low points of the 35-day cycle. It is pure chance that the analysis results in exactly 35 days. Normally it would be close but not exact. To be more confident of the cyclicality, we should use a minimum of seven examples. We now have a well-defined 35-day cycle, and we know the days on which it bottomed and turned upward. When we later discuss the projection of cycles, we will use this data to predict when the next 35-day cycle should occur in the future.

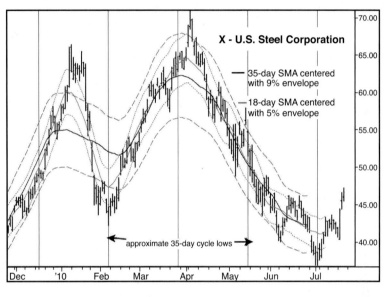

Created using TradeStation

FIGURE 19.12 Combined full-cycle period (35-day) and half-cycle (18-day) moving averages and envelopes (X daily: November 30, 2009–July 22, 2010)

Somehow we have lost precision with envelopes. This is likely because higher-order cycles are trending so strongly that the shorter cycles are being dampened out. To counter this, we return to the detrending method. Because we want to pinpoint the 35-day cycle and cycle of lesser period, we detrend the price data by plotting a line of the ratio of a 5-day SMA to the 18-day. We use the 5-day to smooth out short-term daily fluctuations and the 18-day because it should represent cycles above 18 days, namely the 35-day.

Figure 19.13 shows this detrended line with the 35-day lows clearly marked by the vertical lines exactly 35 days apart. On every line, with the exception of the inversion in May where the line peaks, a slight valley occurs that represents the 35-day low. This is fairly conclusive evidence that a periodicity of 35 days exists in the price data.

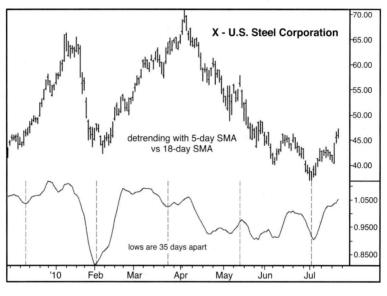

Created using TradeStation

FIGURE 19.13   Detrending using a 5-day SMA to 18-day SMA ratio (X daily: November 30, 2000–July 22, 2010)

Let us go down one more period and see if any cycle appears less than 35 days. We suspect, from Figure 19.9, the detrending exercise, that an 18-day cycle exists, but we cannot pinpoint it because we did not use a centered moving average. Remember that a moving average of roughly half the period of a cycle represents that cycle. Now we will calculate a detrended line based on the 18-day SMA which should represent the 35-day cycle and all others longer. It will screen out the motion from those longer cycle and give us more precise data for any shorter cycle than 35 days. Figure 19.14 is a plot of the ratio of the closing price to the 18-day centered SMA.

Visual inspection of Figure 19.14 shows vertical dashed lines at exact 18-day intervals beginning at the major low in February. At each of the nine dashed lines, a dip in the ratio shows that a cycle low of some nature occurred within one day of each vertical line. The one exception out of the nine shown is the inversion in late May and even on this line there is the slight dip of the *M* pattern mentioned earlier as common at inversion highs. We now have some convincing evidence that an event, usually a low, occurs in U.S. Steel stock every 18 and 35 days.

We also notice that the phase of the short cycle is out of synchronization with the 35-day cycle. This is why the actual lows in the 35-day cycles are rounded rather than sharp. If the two cycles synchronized at the lows, they would bottom at the same time and create a "V" type bottom pattern.

FIGURE 19.14   Ratio: Close to 18-day centered SMA showing short-term 18-day cycle highs and lows (X daily: November 30, 2009–July 22, 2010)

The process we just went through of deducing the cycles shorter than a known dominant cycle is called "nesting downward." We could equally as well have nested upward by again taking the dominant cycle of 35 days and deducing cycles with longer periods. This would have taken considerably more data, but it is an exercise that should be done before any trading or investing is initiated using cyclical data. When investors decide upon the period of investment, they should understand at least the next longer and shorter cycle period because these cycles will affect the behavior of the cycle of interest. In addition, the analysis should be repeated every time a cycle has completed just to be sure that the original assumptions as to cycle periods are still correct.

The preceding analysis, and all of the analysis in this chapter, can be used in any time series data regardless of the bar interval—daily, weekly, monthly, or minute-by-minute. However, as explained in Chapter 14, "Moving Averages," analysis of cycles shorter than a day must be limited to securities that trade over the complete 24 hours because the data that is shorter than daily does not account for the time between the close of one day and the open of the next day.

PROJECTIONS

We have looked at methods to determine cycles in market data. We now look at how we can use the knowledge about cycles in the data to project the next low and perhaps the next high.

Projecting Period

To project the time for the next low, we need three facts: the period length of the cycle of interest, the standard error of that cycle, and the ideal starting point from which to measure it into the future. In the example, we have found periods of 35 days and 18 days. Because we only have four cycles of the 35-day period, we cannot determine accurate projections. However, for the 18-day cycle, we have plenty of examples with apparently little error.

The first and most simple method is to use a ruler or the paper trick mentioned previously to draw points on the chart that match the periods determined from measurement. This is subject to interpretive error; in our example, the process suggested an 18-day cycle that was not borne out by further analysis.

Second, we could use the vertical line shown on the charts and project into the future. This method is accurate once we know the precise cycle periods from our analysis and the beginning point. However, it does not estimate an error range of when to expect the next turning point.

Third, we could use a linear regression model of the periods to estimate the period, the error, and the exact location for the starting point (Kirkpatrick, 1990). To begin this process, we identify the lows given by the ratio in Figure 19.14, beginning numbering with 1. Thus, the first low, which occurred on December 8, 2010, would be 1; the second low, occurring on December 31, would be 2; and so forth. Table 19.2 displays this numbering of lows under the Number column heading.

In addition, each time interval is converted to a sequence of whole numbers to eliminate the problem of weekends and to make calculation easier. In our example, for instance, the first 18-day low occurred on December 8. We record that as low Number 1 at time interval 0 because it is the beginning of our period. The next low occurred on December 31. Because this low occurred 16 trading days after low Number 1, we would label it low Number 2 and with a day number 16 days, in other words it occurred 16 days after low Number 1. From now on, all days will be measured from low Number 1. The third low occurred on January 29. We would label it low Number 3 with a period of 35 days from low Number 1. The time interval for all lows is measured from the first low. Successive lows are entered into the spreadsheet in a similar manner until the end of the period is reached, as shown in Table 19.2.

This process creates two columns in the spreadsheet. The first, the low's specific number, is the independent variable (second column in Table 19.2). The second, the low's corresponding period number, is the dependent variable (fourth column in Table 19.2).

TABLE 19.2 Kirkpatrick Linear Method of Determining the Optimal Location and Error of Cycle Periods

Column No	2	3	4	5	6	7
Date	NO (x)	Actual Period	Actual Day No.	Projected Day No.	Regression	Output
Dec 8	1		0			
Dec 31	2	16	16	16	Intercept (start day)	-1.32
Jan 29	3	19	35	34	Y (cycle period)	17.738
Feb 23	4	16	51	52	R sq (closeness of fit)	0.9996

TABLE 19.2 Continued

Column No	2	3	4	5	6	7
Date	NO (x)	Actual Period	Actual Day No.	Projected Day No.	Regression	Output
Mar 19	5	18	69	70		
Apr 19	6	20	89	87		
May 11	7	16	105	105		
Jun 7	8	18	123	123		
Jul 2	9	17	140	141		
(Jul 30)	10			158		
(Aug 25)	11			176		

We then use linear regression to determine a best fit between the cycle number and the time interval on which it occurred. The results of the linear regression suggest that the cycle period is 17.738 days, roughly 18 days, and is very reliable with an R square so close to one.

Using these numbers, we can project future lows. The best projection into the future is for the next 18-day low (Number 9) to occur 17.738 days after the model's estimate of the eighth low. As illustrated in Figure 19.15, this suggests a Number 9 projected low will occur at time interval 158, or on July 28, and the Number 10 projected low will occur on August 23 plus or minus a day or so. As it turns out, the longer 35-day cycle is due for a low around August 25.

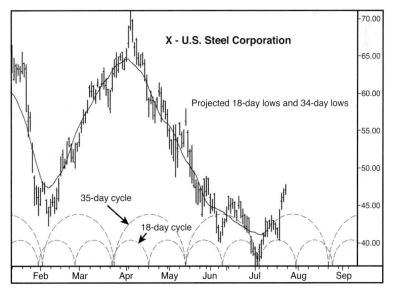

Created using TradeStation

FIGURE 19.15 Projected 18-day and 35-day cycles and lows (X daily: November 30, 2009–July 22, 2010)

Projecting Amplitude

Figure 19.14 also shows how amplitude can vary enormously. Indeed, the variation is so large that prediction is almost impossible. We can only conjecture what the future might bring in amplitude because, so far, no reasonable and consistent method exists. In this example, what can help in amplitude projection, however, is the concept of nesting. Cycles tend to oscillate within cycles. Thus, their outer boundaries, as defined by envelopes, can give us a rough estimate of what to expect for amplitude. Again, let us look at our same data example, this time shown in Figure 19.16 with a 35-day cycle envelope.

We project the next cycle lows using the linear regression method outlined previously. This gives us an idea as to when to expect cycle lows and, by inference, cycle highs. We know that the low around early July is a 35-day low. Because the envelope is bending upward, we also know that the July low is likely one of a larger cycle that is influencing the shorter cycles. It is, therefore, a powerful low, and we can expect the immediately following cycles to translate right. Right translation has already occurred in the first 18-day cycle and will likely occur in the first 35-day cycle. Because of the right translation, the peak in the 35-day cycle will likely occur during the second 18-day cycle, sometime in August.

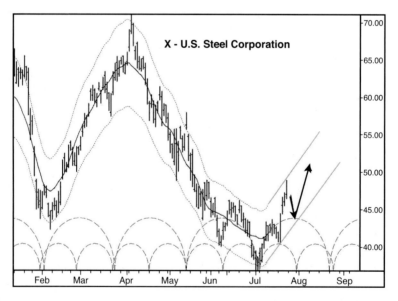

Created using TradeStation

FIGURE 19.16   Amplitude projection (X daily: November 30, 2009–July 22, 2010)

Half-Cycle Reversal

We mentioned earlier that the half-cycle, centered, moving average represents the full cycle under investigation. When the half-cycle, centered, SMA reverses, it signals that the low in the cycle of interest has occurred. Because the half-cycle, centered, moving average is plotted half its cycle back from the present, it represents what the full cycle was doing 1/4 of a cycle length back. If the full cycle was bottoming as represented by the centered moving average, we know that the full cycle still has 3/4 of its time and perhaps distance to travel. An ideal cycle will spend half its time rising and half its time declining. At 1/4 the time through the cycle we know that it has another 1/4 to go before showing signs of downward reversal. It is, thus, halfway through its advance. Being so, we can take the distance that it has traveled and assume that the price will approximately double what it did during the first quarter. We now have an estimate of the potential amplitude of the current full cycle. Of course, the amplitude also depends on the next higher order cycle. If that longer cycle is rising, we can assume the projection will be exceeded as the cycle translates to the right, and if the next higher is downward, we likely will not see an upward reversal in the centered moving average. If the next higher cycle is flat, the projection should be precise. The bottom line, then, is when one-quarter of a cycle is completed, we can begin to see what the potential shape of the full cycle will be from looking at the behavior of the half-cycle, centered moving average.

The FLD and Centered Moving Average Crossovers (The "Forward Line")

Hurst describes another interesting method of projecting prices in a cycle called the FLD line. FLD stands for "Future Line of Demarcation." It is the closing prices projected a half-cycle period forward from the current price. In Figure 19.17, for example, the cycle of interest is the 35-day cycle. Projecting closing prices a half-cycle forward, or 18 days, produces the FLD line. Several observations can be made.

First, because the projection is a half-cycle forward, its peak should appear when a low is expected and vice versa. This is because prices should rise during the first half into a cycle measured from the cycle low and should decline during the second half. Thus, the FLD high should occur at the same time as the real cycle low and vice versa. Of course, this can be upset by the influence of the next longer cycle. If prices peak after the low in the FLD, or bottom before the top in the FLD, the underlying trend is upward. Conversely, if prices bottom after the FLD peak or peak before the FLD peak, the underlying trend is downward. The location of the FLD can, thus, help us with determining the trend of the next longer cycle.

In Figure 19.17, in February, the peak in the FLD and the bottom in prices coincide precisely. In March, when a price peak is suggested by the bottoming of the FLD, prices continue higher, suggesting that the underlying trend is strong and likely to cause price to rise further. In early May, prices pay no attention to the FLD peak and continue downward, suggesting that by the next cycle low, prices will be considerably lower.

Second, by representing a half-cycle, the FLD line is declining when the cycle prices are advancing. The crossover of current prices through the FLD should occur at roughly the midpoint both time wise and pricewise in the advance or decline. In Figure 19.17, the downward crossover of prices through the FLD in February at $54.68 projected a decline of $10.66 to an estimated target of $44.02. The bottom closing price at the actual low was $44.07, only 4 cents different. In late February, prices crossed the FLD continued far beyond their projected midpoint target. This is evidence that the prior low was that from a higher-order cycle. In April, prices crossed the forward line and continued lower, telling us that the longer cycle beginning in February was over. From the 35-day cycle, the timing for the low was easily projected. The rule, then, is that when prices exceed the FLD target price after the crossover, the next higher-order cycle is strong in the direction of the price crossover. Conversely, if prices do not reach their target, or as in some cases, do not cross the FLD line, the next higher-order cycle is weak.

Third, the FLD can act as support or resistance. Notice in Figure 19.17 during the decline from April to July how many times the price touched the FLD and then reversed. This gives an example of how prices can come close to the FLD, after a cycle low or high, stop for a few bars, and either penetrate the FLD or reverse direction and fail. Thus, the FLD is an important point to watch. If prices halt at the FLD and reverse, the underlying cycle trend is not reversing on schedule. It will increase in strength in its original direction. If prices penetrate the FLD, the cycle is still intact, and prices will head for the midpoint target. Depending on whether it reaches that target or overruns it will then give clues as to the strength of the next longer cycle trend. It is, therefore, very important to watch price action when it reaches the FLD to see if it is confirming the strength or weakness of the cycle direction.

In sum, the FLD can be a useful projection device.

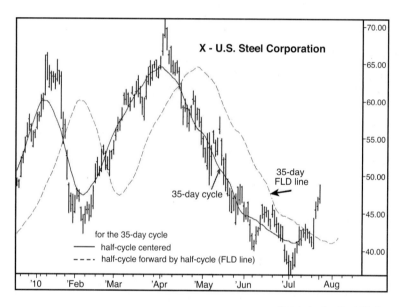

Created using TradeStation

FIGURE 19.17   Prices and the FLD line (X daily: November 30, 2009–July 22, 2010)

Because the FLD line follows price action exactly, it can give an erratic appearance and make crossovers somewhat arbitrary, based on only one or two days action. To combat this, analysts will project forward the half-cycle SMA in the same manner as the FLD. This gives a smoothed line, called the **forward** line that is easier to work with. The same rules for the FLD apply to the forward line.

The Tillman Method

Jim Tillman (1990) of Cycletrend, Inc., developed a number of methods for cycle projections. He used centered moving averages of half-cycles after having determined the dominant cycle periods.

Tillman's analysis concentrates on what he calls **focal points.** Focal points occur when three or more half-cycle, centered, moving averages cross at roughly the same location. In Figure 19.18, only crossovers of two half-cycle moving averages (9-day and 18-day) are shown, but Tillman's observations can still be made.

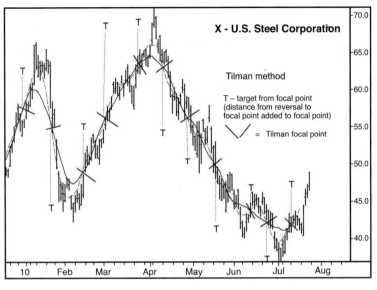

Created using TradeStation

FIGURE 19.18   Tillman SMA crossovers and focal points (X daily: November 30, 2009–July 22, 2010)

One observation is that focal points occur at roughly the halfway point of cycle advances or declines. Notice the diagonal lines at the 18-day cycle peaks, troughs, and crossovers in Figure 19.18. The crossovers occur roughly halfway between the peak and trough in points. The practical problem from this observation is that by the time the lagging half-cycle moving averages have crossed, prices have usually already reached their projection. The crossover, thus, occurs when the cycle is ending its run up or down. When you see a crossover in an upward leg of a cycle, you know that the upward leg is about to peak or already has.

In Figure 19.19, at (A), lines are drawn through the high or low of a cycle through the focal point. The upward sloping lines will continue through to the high of the cycle, and the downward sloping lines will continue through to the low of the cycle. The time from the low (high) to the focal point will equal, approximately, the time to that high (low). In our example in Figure 19.19, in January, the time from the cycle high to the focal point was 9 days, and 9 days later, the low was reached. In February–March, the rally through the focal point took 12 days. The price reached its high for the cycle 14 days. The crossover is the center of the cosine wave. It is the center in time as well as distance.

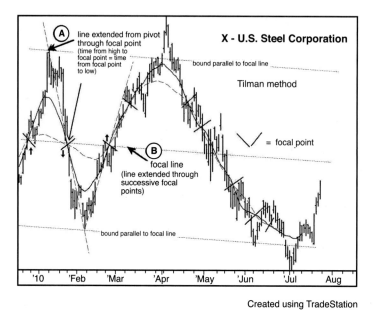

FIGURE 19.19   Lines through focal point bisecting time from low to high or high to low showing parallel boundaries (X daily: June 10, 2005–November 4, 2005)

If we then draw a trend line between two successive focal points (B), we have an estimate of the direction of the next higher-order cycle. Lines drawn parallel to that trend line to the immediate highs and lows will show that the trend is roughly midway between the parallel lines and that they represent the boundaries of the cycle (see Figure 19.19). The advantage of using these parallel lines formed from the trend between focal points is that they can be projected into the future, whereas the moving average parallel lines had to be drawn freehand as a guess.

When the parallel lines are decisively broken, we know that the next higher-order cycle has changed direction. This makes sense because the parallel lines define the boundaries of the lower-order cycle. If they are broken, it must be due to the change in direction of the next higher-order cycle.

Concept of Commonality

Another of Hurst's principles, that of "commonality," suggested that issues of the same nature tend to have the same cycles but with different amplitudes. In the stock market, this principle implies that individual stocks will have generally the same cycles as the stock market averages. The study of cycles requires the analyst's close attention and analysis. Few analysts pursue it because the conversion of the analysis to computers is difficult and requires some knowledge of applied mathematics and trigonometry. Much of the analysis must be done by hand. Because cycle analysis is intensive and very subjective, the analyst must select stocks with sufficient volatility such that the cycles of interest will have enough amplitude to become profitable if correctly timed. The same can be said of commodities in that innate volatility is a factor that should be considered when selecting an issue to trade using cycle analysis.

CONCLUSION

The possible existence of cycles or waves in financial time series data is a controversial subject that remains unresolved. The results of standard spectral methods have been unsuccessful, so far, in isolating reliable waveforms in this data. This has led many skeptics to argue that the pursuit of cycles in financial data is futile. On the other hand, cycle analysts argue that the reason cycles have not been definitively isolated is that they change their characteristics too frequently and that standard mathematics cannot adjust quickly enough. However, a simple observation of price data shows that prices oscillate. If prices oscillate in a regular manner, the preceding analysis should be sufficient to identify this regularity and to make it useful for the projection of price action in the future. The concepts of Hurst, Ehlers, Tillman, and others—mostly professional engineers—are intriguing, and even if the ideas are difficult to apply, they provide interesting insights into the workings of the financial markets.

REVIEW QUESTIONS

1. A great deal of controversy surrounds cycle theory. What are the reasons why some oppose cycle theory? How do the supporters of cycle theory respond to these criticisms?
2. Explain what each of the following terms means as it refers to cycles:
    a. Amplitude
    b. Period
    c. Phase
    d. Summation
    e. Inversion
    f. Harmonics
3. What do *left translation* and *right translation* mean? When would you expect to see each of these occurring in a cycle?
4. What is the argument for plotting a centered moving average centered over the time period in the calculation rather than plotting it at the end of the time period?

5. Download daily data for the S&P 500 for the period July 1, 2009 through July 1, 2010. (This historical data is available at http://finance.yahoo.com.)

    a. Plot this data in a chart. Are any cycles apparent in your chart?

    b. Detrend the data by creating an oscillator that is constructed using a ratio of the current close to the 11-day SMA.

    c. Does the plot of this oscillator reveal any cycle in your data?

6. Using the S&P 500 data you collected in Question 5, plot a 41-day centered SMA and a 21-day centered SMA. Explain ways in which this information might be used to determine and project cycles.

7. What is a focal point? How is it used to project cycles?

CHAPTER 20

ELLIOTT, FIBONACCI, AND GANN

CHAPTER OBJECTIVES

By the end of this chapter, you should be familiar with

- The basic tenets of and vocabulary used with the Elliott Wave Theory
- The rules and guidelines of the Elliott Wave Theory
- The construction of the Fibonacci sequence
- The derivation and characteristics of the golden ratio
- The reasons why Elliott Wave Theory can be difficult for the average analyst to apply

Perhaps there is a natural structure in markets. Structure is seen in many phenomena in nature. Although markets appear to be completely man-made, perhaps their existence, flowing from human emotion and reason, is a product of evolution and follows a natural order. After all, nature includes humans among its species. Humans like structure. Unfortunately, however, we have seen that humans tend to presume structure when perhaps it is not present. This chapter discusses those theories of market structure that assume some sort of natural order. Many technical analysts have come to accept these theories at some level, but they are not necessarily practiced.

The most widely followed theory of market structure today is the Elliott Wave Theory. We look at this theory and some of its interpretations. We also look at the mathematical basis for this theory derived from a sequence of whole numbers called the Fibonacci sequence. In addition, we consider briefly another theory of market structure by W. D. Gann.

ELLIOTT WAVE THEORY (EWT)

Devised by Ralph Nelson Elliott, the Elliott Wave Theory (EWT) is an attempt to define a structure to the stock market, and by implication, other trading markets. EWT is based upon the notion that the market behaves in an irregular cyclic manner. Proponents of EWT believe that this cyclic structure is classifiable and predictable. Defining the market structure allows the analyst to recognize where the market is within the structure and, from that, where it is proceeding next.

Because Elliott's theory defies any strict, mathematical description, except through anecdotal evidence, its existence is difficult to prove conclusively. Thus, even among practitioners of the Elliott Wave Theory, there is much disagreement about the "where are we" aspect of the theory. The basic rules are generally agreed upon, but because of the vagaries of interpretation, no agreement or consensus seems to arise as to present conditions.

In this chapter, we outline the basics of the theory, as espoused by Robert Prechter (1990), the principal proponent of the EWT. We also provide some alternate rules, when known, from some of the other leaders in the field and include some results from computer screening. However, we leave the interpretation and much detail to further study by the student. EWT is a complex subject and deserves some thought, even if a practical application can be elusive.

Ralph Nelson Elliott

Born in 1871, Ralph Nelson Elliott spent most of his business career as a railroad accountant and reorganizer in Central America. After 25 years in the railroad business, he contracted a severe illness and was forced into retirement to recover. During his recovery, Elliott decided to study the stock market, having earlier subscribed to several market letters, one by Charles Collins and the other by Robert Rhea of Dow Theory fame. At the age of 63, he began his career as a stock market technical analyst, studying the Dow Jones Averages over periods from half-hours to months.

His initial discovery of the wave principle took place in early 1934. Becoming destitute, Elliott wrote to Collins asking for an arrangement by which he could be paid for market forecasts. Collins allowed him to write to him of his opinions on the market at that time, and Elliott was amazingly correct, calling several major market turns within the hour. In 1938, Collins published the first book on the Elliott wave called *The Wave Principle.*

In the late 1930s, Elliott moved to New York and with Collins' financial assistance and investor referrals, began his business of newsletters, consulting, and money management. By now, Elliott was familiar with the Fibonacci sequence and had integrated it into his wave theory. Later in life, he wrote about all his discoveries in *Nature's Law—The Secret of the Universe,* but his advancing age affected his writing, and the book became disjointed and rambling. Elliott died in New York in 1948. Richard Martin, a former student of Collins, Hamilton Bolton, the publisher of the *Bank Credit Analyst,* and Bolton's business associate A. J. Frost were well-known for applying Elliott's theory after his death. Robert Prechter, a notable scholar of Elliott's theory, has published all his works, including magazine articles, in *The Major Works of R. N. Elliott* (1980).

Basic Elliott Wave Theory

Elliott's theory describes the market structure as a nested series of waves of various length and size. A wave is a sustained price move in one direction as determined by the reversal points that initiated and terminated the move. A wave cycle is composed of two waves—an impulse wave and a corrective wave. The impulse wave is in the direction of the current trend; the corrective wave moves against the trend's direction. During a bull market, the overall trend is called a **motive impulse wave** (upward price movement) and ends when a downtrend begins, signaling a major change in market direction.

The wave concept that a market has positive price movement followed by a correction is simple. The benefit of EWT is that it provides the analyst with more detail about these waves. Both the impulse wave and corrective waves include special subwaves. The impulse wave is always made up of five subwaves and determines the strength and trend of the wave cycle. Analysts traditionally label these waves with numbers (1, 2, 3, or I, II, III, or i, ii, iii, etc.) based on their degree relative to longer and shorter wave cycles. See waves 1 through 5, for example, in Figure 20.1. Waves 1, 3, and 5 are smaller waves that contribute to the larger wave's upward trend. Waves 2 and 4 are corrective subwaves; these corrective waves break the sustained upward movement.

The corrective wave is broken into three subwaves, rather than five. These subwaves are labeled with letters, such as A, B, and C, as shown in Figure 20.1. Waves A and C are associated with downward price movement. Wave B breaks this downward movement with an uptrend.

In describing the specific subwaves, analysts assume an upward underlying trend at the next higher degree and, thus, a rising five-wave impulse wave and a declining three-wave corrective wave. We use the same convention, but the student must be aware that in an underlying downward trend, the same relationship between impulse wave and corrective wave holds, just in the opposite direction. In other words, the downward impulse wave would include five subwaves and three subwaves in its corrective wave upward.

Look at Figure 20.1. See how the upward motive impulse wave consists of three rising impulse subwaves, coinciding with the primary trend, and the corrective wave consists of two corrective subwaves, contrary to the primary trend. This pattern can be thought of as three steps forward and two steps backward, with each step followed by a small correction.

Figure 20.1 demonstrates how the two waves of the cycle, the impulse and corrective waves, can be broken down into smaller subwaves. Each of these subwaves can be broken into separate patterns. Interestingly, the patterns of each subwave will form the same general impulse and corrective Elliott pattern with and against their trend. In other words, the patterns generated from the waves are fractal, a term we used earlier in describing how chart patterns of a specific type can exist in identical shapes in very short- as well as long-term charts. The patterns remain the same regardless of time or scale. Each series of waves will define a pattern within a pattern both up and down the scale.

Unfortunately, the patterns do not have definitive time limits. One of the major problems of the interpretation of Elliott waves is in deciding at what degree level a particular pattern exists. Often the shape of the wave can be interpreted as being part of one degree of magnitude of waves, when it really is part of a larger or smaller degree of waves. These different interpretations might have different implied consequences, making projections even more difficult.

To establish the order of the waves being analyzed, analysts generally begin with a long-term interpretation and reduce the inspection of waves through lower and lower degrees until the trading horizon is reached. Misinterpreting any of the waves between the long-term pattern and the trading horizon pattern, of course, can alter the interpretation of future prospects as well.

Elliot Wave

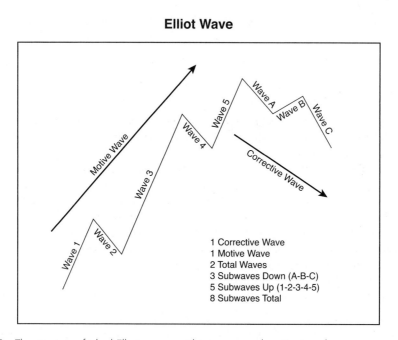

1 Corrective Wave
1 Motive Wave
2 Total Waves
3 Subwaves Down (A-B-C)
5 Subwaves Up (1-2-3-4-5)
8 Subwaves Total

FIGURE 20.1   The structure of ideal Elliott waves within an upward motive impulse wave

Each of the subwaves within either the impulse or the corrective waves can have its own peculiarities and alternative patterns. First, let us look a little more closely at the characteristics of impulse waves. Then we turn our attention to corrective waves.

Impulse Waves

Each impulse wave is composed of five subwaves. This impulse wave defines both the trend direction and the trend strength. Let's consider the basic, inviolate rules of these of these waves and some of the patterns that can develop.

Basic Rules

There are several rules regarding the characteristics of waves. These rules are inviolate. To violate a rule is to disregard the Elliott Wave Theory and, almost certainly, to arrive at an incorrect conclusion and projection. Although there are not many rules, it is important to remember that they are strict rules that cannot be violated.

The six rules for impulse waves are as follows:

- Impulse waves move in the same direction as the trend of the next higher degree wave.
- Impulse waves divide into five subwaves.

- Within an impulse wave, subwaves 1, 3, and 5 are themselves impulse waves of a lesser degree, and subwaves 2 and 4 are corrective waves.

- Within an impulse wave, subwave 1 and 5 might be either an impulse or diagonal pattern.

- Within an impulse wave, subwave 3 is always an impulse pattern.

- In cash markets, within an impulse pattern, subwave 4 never overlaps any portion of subwave 1. This is not always true for futures markets.

In addition to the inviolate rules, Elliott observed other wave characteristics that routinely occurred. Elliott's observations were made without the advantage of computer power to sift through large amounts of data, and he used only the Dow Jones Industrial Average. The observations we include in this chapter are observations from computer screens of price action in many different trading markets and over many different periods (Swannell, 2003). Most of these observations agree with Elliott's assessments, but some differ slightly. Nevertheless, the computer screens display that his observations were mostly accurate.

Impulse

Impulse patterns define the trend direction and strength. They include five subwaves, three of which move in the direction of the trend and two of which move in the direction opposite to the trend. A rising market generally has two strong subwaves: 3 and 5. In a declining market, subwave 3 is generally the strongest, and subwaves 1 and 5 are approximately equal.

Elliott Wave Theory describes the character of each subwave in more detail. The details of these subwaves are as follows:

- Wave 1 is an impulse or a leading diagonal.

- Wave 2 can be any corrective pattern but a triangle.

- Wave 2 does not retrace more than 100% of wave 1.

- Wave 3 is always an impulse.

- Wave 3 is larger than wave 2.

- Wave 3 is never shorter than waves 1 and 5.

- Wave 4 can be any corrective pattern.

- Waves 2 and 4 do not overlap in price.

- Wave 5 is an impulse or ending diagonal.

- Wave 5 retraces at least 70% of wave 4.

- In wave 5, a diagonal, extension, or truncation indicates that a major reversal is to occur soon.

Diagonals

A diagonal (see Figure 20.2) is the same as the classic wedge pattern seen in classic technical patterns. It is simply a triangle formation with both bounds headed in the same direction but at different angles so that they will meet at some point in the future.

Diagonal patterns can appear in wave 1 or wave 5. If a diagonal appears in wave 1, it is called a **leading diagonal.** A diagonal appearing in wave 5 is called an **ending diagonal.** A diagonal never occurs in wave 3. The direction of the diagonal bounds is the same direction as the trend of the higher-degree impulse wave.

A leading diagonal usually consists of five subwaves of three wavelets, each a 3-3-3-3-3 configuration converging toward an apex. Occasionally, however, the configuration is 5-3-5-3-5, just as in an impulse but with the overlapping of waves 2 and 4 (Frost and Prechter, 2000).

An ending diagonal also includes five subwaves, each of which is in turn subdivided into three smaller waves. Often, the fifth subwave will break out of the diagonal's bounds for a short period before reversing. This is called a **throw-over** (Frost and Prechter, 2000).

A throw-over is an "elongated impulse with exaggerated subdivisions" (Frost and Prechter, 2000, p. 31). Usually an extension will occur in only one of the subwaves in an impulse pattern. Thus, if waves 1 and 5 are approximately the same length, wave 3 likely will be extended. In fact, the third wave extension is the most common extended wave pattern in the stock market. In commodities, however, the extended wave is usually the fifth wave. When extended, a wave often appears to have nine subwaves rather than the usual five. This is because the extended wavelets are large enough to appear the same size as the subwaves themselves.

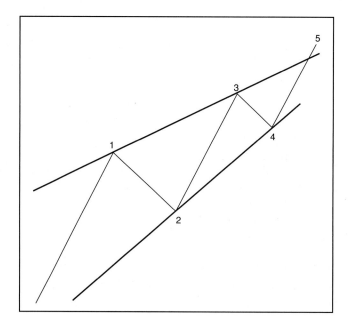

FIGURE 20.2   Diagonal leading or ending (in upward trend)

Truncation

Occasionally, the fifth wave fails to exceed the end of the third wave. This phenomenon is shown in Figure 20.3. Elliott referred to this as a "failure." Nevertheless, a truncated fifth wave will still have five subwaves.

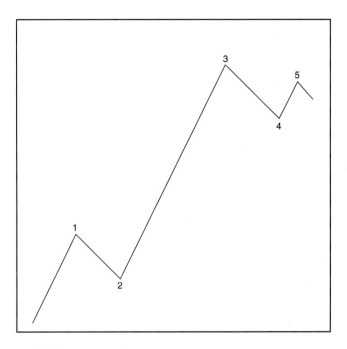

FIGURE 20.3   Truncated fifth in an uptrend

Corrective Waves

Corrective waves are unquestionably the most difficult to interpret. They can appear in many different configurations and pattern combinations. Richard Swannell and Robert Prechter have both contributed to our current understanding of corrective waves. Swannell has tested price data, searching for waves, and Prechter has interpreted Elliott's original work with some modifications. The following information about corrective waves comes from the work of these two analysts.

Corrective waves commonly occur in three subwaves (A-B-C). The direction of corrective waves is either sideways, as in a trading range, or sharply opposite to the prevailing trend of the impulse wave. Corrective waves are generalized into three categories for descriptive purposes: zigzags, flats, and triangles.

Zigzags

The single A-B-C correction in Figure 20.4 is an example of a zigzag correction. Generally, in a simple zigzag, wave A is an impulse, leading diagonal, or zigzag; wave B is any corrective pattern; and wave C is an impulse, ending diagonal, or zigzag. If wave A is a diagonal, wave C is not an ending diagonal.

In addition to this simple, single A-B-C correction, a zigzag correction can occur as a more complex double or triple zigzag pattern. The second correction pictured in Figure 20.4 shows the more complex double zigzag. Double and triple zigzags use different nomenclature for their descriptions. The double zigzag, for example, is two simple zigzags joined by a wave X. As shown in Figure 20.4, W and Y are often used to designate each simple zigzag wave within the double zigzag. When another simple zigzag is added to a double zigzag, a triple zigzag forms. The added simple zigzag is referred to as wave Z; the intervening wave is labeled XX. Fortunately, for interpretive purposes, triple zigzags are rare.

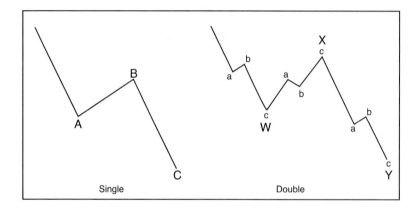

FIGURE 20.4   Single zigzag corrective pattern

Swannell (2003) provides the following characteristics for actual double zigzags:

- Wave W is a zigzag.
- Wave X is any corrective pattern other than an expanding triangle.
- Wave X is smaller than wave W.
- Wave Y is a zigzag.
- Wave Y is equal to or larger than wave X.

Triple zigzags continue with the same pattern as double zigzags; thus, wave XX is smaller than both wave Y and Z. Prechter points out that zigzags characteristically have a 5-3-5 combination of subwaves.

Flats

Sideways patterns are called flats. Flats behave very similarly to zigzags except that rather than sharp upward or downward corrections to the prevailing trend, they move sideways, and their subwaves generally overlap. The characteristics for flats are the same as for zigzags except that

- Wave B is not a triangle, retraces wave A by at least 50%, and is less than twice the length of wave A.
- Wave C overlaps wave A at some point.

The A-B-C pattern in Figure 20.5 shows a simple flat pattern. In addition to this single A-B-C pattern, flats can occur as a double or a triple. Double and triple flats have the same nomenclature as double and triple zigzags. Just like triple zigzags, triple flats are rare. The characteristics of the double and triple flats are similar to their zigzag counterparts except for the necessary adjustments needed to produce a sideways pattern. Thus, common characteristics of these multiple flat patterns are as follows:

- Waves W, X, and XX can be any corrective pattern except a triangle, a double, or a triple.
- Waves Y and Z can be any corrective pattern except a double or triple.
- Wave X retraces at least 50% of wave W.
- Wave Y is greater than wave X unless it is a triangle.
- Wave XX retraces at least 50% of wave Y.
- Wave Z is not a zigzag if wave Y is a zigzag.
- Wave Z is greater than wave XX.

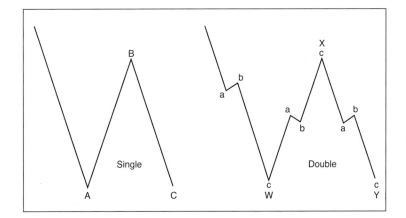

FIGURE 20.5   Single and double flat corrective patterns

Prechter points out that flats characteristically have a 3-3-5 combination of subwaves. Elliott, he argues, considered the sideways patterns as possibly including a combination of zigzag and flat, one followed by the other in a complex corrective wave. These were called doubles and triple threes. The method of designating each pattern is the same as the method used previously for double and triple sideways patterns.

Triangles

The Elliott wave triangle is identical to the standard triangle pattern we discussed in Chapter 15, "Bar Chart Patterns," with the exception that it is limited to five waves (A-B-C-D-E). Prechter points out that triangles have a 3-3-3-3-3 combination of minor waves. The Elliott wave triangle can be either a converging or a diverging triangle.

The rules for a converging triangle are as follows:

- Wave A is a zigzag or a flat.
- Wave B is only a zigzag.
- Waves C and D can be any corrective pattern except a triangle.
- Waves A, B, C, and D move within the bounds of the channel lines between A to C and B to D.
- Bounds converge (one might be horizontal), and the intersection of the bounds occurs beyond the end of wave E.
- Wave E can be a zigzag or a converging triangle.
- Either wave A or B is the longest wave.
- Wave E ends in the range of wave A.
- Wave E moves within or closes within the bounds.

Expanding triangles, although relatively rare, have generally the same rules. The exceptions are that for the expanding triangle

- Wave B is smaller than wave C but more than 40% of wave C.
- Wave C is smaller than wave D but more than 40% of wave D.
- The intersection of the bounds occurs before the formation of the triangle.
- Wave E is longer than wave D.
- Wave E ends outside the territory of wave A.
- Either wave A or B is the shortest wave.

Guidelines and General Characteristics in EWT

In addition to rules, guidelines exist within EWT. While the rules are inviolate, EWT guidelines are less definite and will not occur at all times.

Alternation

Alternation is an EWT guideline. Alternation refers to the common occurrence of one type of corrective wave occurring in wave 2 and a different type of correction occurring in wave 4. In other words, the types of corrective waves tend to alternate. If wave 2 is a flat, for example, wave 4 will likely be some other type of corrective wave, such as a zigzag or a triangle. The guideline of alternation can also occur in a corrective wave when, for example, the first part of a double is a zigzag and the second part is a flat, as shown in Figure 20.6.

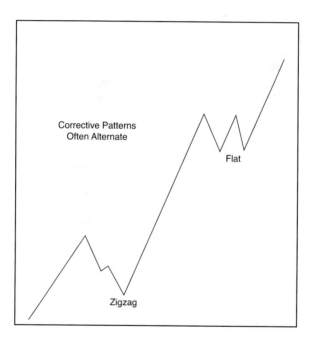

FIGURE 20.6   Example of two corrective patterns alternating in an uptrend

Equality

At least two of the three impulse subwaves in a five-wave sequence are often equal in length. Usually equality exists between wave 1 and wave 5, especially when wave 3 is extended. However, if wave 1 or wave 5 is extended, the remaining two will tend toward equality.

Channeling

Channels, similar to those we discussed in Chapter 14, "Moving Averages," are used in conjunction with EWT. To construct a channel for a five-wave impulse, draw a line between the end of wave 1 and wave 3; then draw a parallel line through the end of wave 2. Price will tend to oscillate within this channel.

Sometimes, wave 4 falls short of the lower channel line, as shown in Figure 20.7. When this occurs, draw a new line from the end of wave 2 to the end of wave 4. This line will be steeper than the original lower channel line. Then draw another parallel line running through the end of wave 3. This will give a rough approximation of where wave 5 should end. A throw-over occurs when wave 5 exceeds this second channel line and usually denotes excessive emotion in the market and possibly an extended fifth wave.

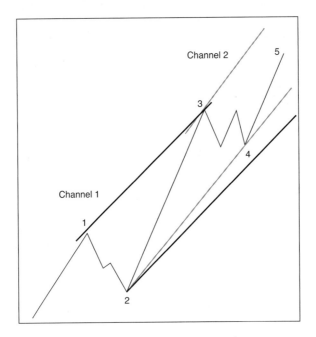

FIGURE 20.7   Channeling drawn between wave ends in an uptrend

Projected Targets and Retracements

How can EWT be used to project prices? In the next section, we discuss Fibonacci ratios and their use in projection. Because of the importance of Fibonacci numbers, we devote an entire section to their use. Right now, we mention a few other methods.

Some analysts use the channeling method for projections. These channels are useful because all price movement should lie within the channel. Prechter, however, mentions that two guidelines for target projections are available in addition to the channeling method. The first occurs in wave 4. The extent of the larger wave 4 correction should be no further than the end of wave 4 of lesser degree. In other words, the larger wave 4 should not break through the end of the minor wave 4 in the larger wave 3 preceding the larger wave 4. The fourth wave target is shown in Figure 20.8.

Figure 20.9 illustrates a projection that occurs at the end of wave 5 extensions. When wave 5 extends, the corrective wave that follows is steep and often ends either at the minor wave 2 of the extended wave 5 or at the end of wave 4. In other words, the corrective wave following an extended wave 5 often corrects all or most of the extended wave 5 move.

From his screening of actual patterns, Swannell (2003) reports that the most accurate patterns for predicted results are the triangle and ending diagonal. Their consistent behavior after their completion gives results accurate enough to be almost 90% dependable.

Other means of estimating target prices have been proposed. Hill, Pruitt, and Hill (2000), for example, estimate that in impulses, the target for wave 3 is 50% of wave 1 added to wave 1, and the target for wave 5 is 100% of wave 1 added to wave 1. Their estimates of retracements are based on the length of wave A, the first correction wave. If wave A corrects 25% to 35% of the prior impulse wave, it will likely be only a single wave correction. If wave A corrects 35% to 50%, the correction will likely be a three-wave correction, and if wave A corrects 50% to 75%, it will likely be a five-wave correction. Any reaction more than 75% suggests a possible trend change.

The most common methods of determining targets and replacements use multiples of the Fibonacci ratios. We now turn our attention to the derivation of these numbers.

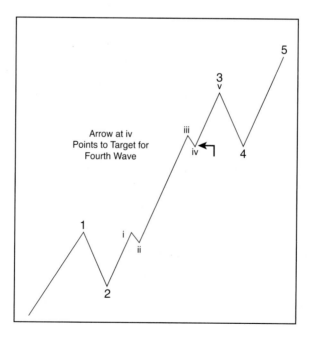

FIGURE 20.8 Fourth wave target estimate in an uptrend

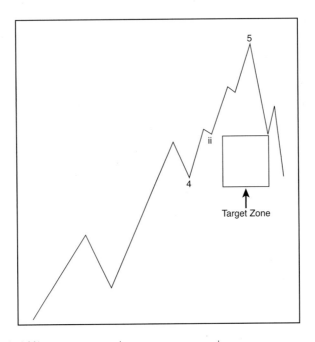

FIGURE 20.9   Extended fifth wave estimated target in an uptrend

Alternatives to EWT

As would be expected with a theory that is so difficult to apply, many analysts have differing opinions about Elliott rules and guidelines. Most of these analysts stick with the general principles of impulse waves and corrective waves and their five-wave and three-wave subdivisions, but the application of other observations in the specific waves and interpretations of Elliott can sometimes cause quite differing results.

In his book, *Mastering Elliott Wave,* Glenn Neely (1990) takes the reader from the most simple wave construction through an extremely lengthy set of rules that encompass his theory of how waves unfold. In doing so, the reader learns by practice how to set up an Elliott wave chart using the Neely method of dots rather than bar charts, how to determine monowaves and their larger patterns, and other nomenclature and idiosyncrasies of Elliott analysis.

Zoran Gayer, a student of the Neely school of Elliott analysis, has developed a sophisticated approach called bifurcation. This method is an offshoot of chaos theory, where motion goes from erratic to organized, just as prices go from consolidation to trending. In Elliott terms, this would equate to going from corrective waves to impulse waves. Zoran, as he is known, calls them directional and nondirectional moves. Directional moves are those that do not correct more than 61.8%. The bifurcation points are not necessarily the extreme high or low of a wave but can occur when the price action changes tone and direction, such as at the end of wave 3 in conventional Elliott labeling. The method becomes complicated and requires close study. Past Zoran commentaries can be seen at www.safehaven.com/archive-11.htm.

As with all the preceding methods, the assumptions underlying the market structure are that prices are determined by patterns of human nature and sentiment. Elliott believed that sentiment rose and fell in fits and starts that could be identified and labeled with his wave structure. That these fits and starts followed a mathematical sequence such as the Fibonacci sequence came as no surprise to Elliott.

However, Elliott's hypothetical structure has been analyzed by others who have used different growth structure models, even assuming that the controlling mathematics are still the Fibonacci ratios. Tony Plummer (2003), for example, hypothesizes that the growth curve of nature as well as sentiment in markets is a three-wave process influenced by shock. Shock need not be exogenous. It can be just the sudden realization that the markets have changed direction. Thus, the three-wave sequence consists of the first wave changed by natural causes and its natural completion in a normal growth curve, then a flat period as the new circumstances are evaluated, and finally the realization that the trend has changed and a second directional move. The entire cycle is composed of a zigzag up of three legs and a zigzag down, three separate cycles within the longer cycle, as illustrated in Figure 20.10. Using this method, Plummer maintains that he has been able to integrate Fibonacci, cycle analysis, and EWT into a simpler and more easily understood method of recognizing structure in the markets.

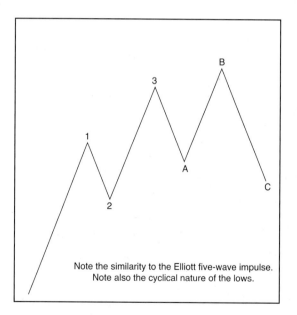

Note the similarity to the Elliott five-wave impulse. Note also the cyclical nature of the lows.

FIGURE 20.10 Plummer cycle three waves X three waves

Using EWT

Although the theory of market structure is interesting, the point in technical analysis is to use these theories to make profits. With Elliott analysis, this is difficult. The application of the rules always seems to have exceptions, the description of waves often can only be determined after the fact, and the means of projecting into the future are suspect. This is not to say that the theories do not have value. They do, and at certain instances they can be profitably utilized. To do this, the analyst must be fully trained in Elliott analysis and be patient enough to wait for an opportunity that is clearly within the realm of the implied Elliott structure. Because Elliott analysis is not easily computerized, its practical interpretation needs other technical tools before any profitable signals can be derived.

Steven Poser (2003) is correct in stating that too many Elliott analysts attempt to pick the top and bottom of moves rather than take a piece out of the middle. They overanalyze the waves and generally become overwhelmed by minutia. He suggests that at least two other technical methods must confirm any Elliott wave expectation. Other suggestions are to determine the period in which the analyst is most interested and analyze the next higher and lower degree waves to establish the context within which trading or investing will occur. Establish key price levels, he says, such as targets, retracement levels, and important reversal points based on the Elliott analysis, and use other indicators such as moving averages and oscillators to confirm action signals. For example, he looks for momentum confirmation in wave 3 and divergences in wave 5. More important, he argues, the analyst must be aware of the behavior of the market especially at certain juncture points. The Elliott Wave Theory is a model of behavior, a useful means of understanding the position of the market within itself, not a mechanical system of forecasting.

Connie Brown (1994, 1999), who worked for Prechter for a few years and is now a professional trader and adviser, has devised oscillators to confirm waves within an Elliott context. She simplifies Elliott's basic rules into a five-wave pattern, where waves 1, 3, and 5 are impulses:

- Wave 2 might not break below the origin of wave 1.
- Wave 3 cannot be the shortest wave, but it does not necessarily have to be the longest.
- Wave 4 cannot overlap the termination of wave 1.

Rather than becoming obsessed with the smaller threes and fives and other patterns, Brown claims that getting a feel for the rhythm in the market is more important. By compressing the scale in a chart, the smaller, less-important details become obscure, and attention then focuses on the market rhythm. Professional expertise is not needed to make money from this pattern. To determine the Elliott five-wave pattern, Brown begins at the middle of a pattern where the largest price move occurred and looks forward and backward (uncovering price action by widening the distance between her thumbnails that are covering price action before and after the large price move). She then uses Fibonacci ratios, Gann time, and price projections combined with oscillators based on the RSI and her composite index to estimate price projections and give action signals.

THE FIBONACCI SEQUENCE

Certain numbers and number sequences are of special interest in wave theory. Of particular importance are the Fibonacci sequence and the related golden ratio.

Fibonacci

Leonardo Pisano, better known by his nickname Fibonacci, was born in 1170 in Pisa, Italy. Fibonacci's father, Guilielmo Bonacci, was a public notary, working for the interests of the merchants of the Republic of Pisa. Because of Guilielmo's work, Fibonacci traveled with his family extensively through Northern Africa and the Mediterranean as a child. At a young age, Fibonacci was exposed to the mathematical and accounting systems of the various merchants with which his father worked. In his writings, Fibonacci recalls learning the mathematical and accounting systems of India, Egypt, Syria, Greece, Sicily, and Provence.

Around the age of 30, Fibonacci ended his travels and returned to Pisa. There he wrote a number of important texts that played an important role in reviving ancient mathematical skills. Copies of his books *Liber abaci* (1202), *Practica geometriae* (1220), *Flos* (1225), and *Liber quadratorum* (1225) still exist today. Other books written by Fibonacci, such as his book on commercial arithmetic, *Di minor guisa,* have been lost.

The writings of Fibonacci are credited with bringing the Hindu-Arabic decimal place mathematical symbols that we use today to Western Europe. Many of his works dealt with pricing issues faced by merchants. He is thought to have invented present value analysis of cash flows in contracts and a method for expressing investment returns. In addition, he solved a number of complex interest rate problems (Goetzmann, 2003). Fibonacci was likely the world's greatest mathematician in his time. Although his work formed the basis of our decimal system, and he laid the groundwork for financial mathematics, he is unfortunately remembered today almost exclusively for a small portion of his life's work—his numerical sequence.

The Fibonacci Sequence

Fibonacci derived the sequence by answering the question of how many rabbits can be produced over a year from an original pair, in an enclosed space, when all pairs give birth each month to a new pair that in turn can breed in two months. The sequence of pairs occurs in the following manner by month: 1, 1, 2, 3, 5, 8, 13, 21, 34, 55, 89, and 144. These are called Fibonacci numbers. Fibonacci numbers are simply a sequence in which the last number is added to the previous number to arrive at the next number. For example, 5 plus 3, the previous number, produces 8, the next number; next, 8 plus 5 produces 13, the next number. This sequence can continue to infinity.

The Golden Ratio

There are a number of reasons why this sequence is of interest to mathematicians and scientists. One reason is the relationship that the sequence has to the "golden ratio." Except in the very low numbers, the ratio of any number in the sequence to the next lower number is 1.618 (e.g., 144/89 = 1.61798); the ratio of any number in the sequence to the next highest number approaches 0.618 (e.g., 55/89 = 0.61798). The number 1.618, known as the golden ratio, and its reciprocal of 0.618, possess many interesting properties. For example, it is the only number that when added to 1 is the same as 1 divided by itself. Another fascinating fact is that 1.618 multiplied times 0.618 = 1. There are many more strange relationships between .618 and whole numbers; see Box

20.1 for a demonstration of the "mystery" of this number. Mathematicians use the Greek letter phi to refer to this ratio.

The golden ratio has been of interest at least since the pyramids were built and likely long before. Buildings built in proportion to the golden ratio were thought to be most pleasing to the eye. The Parthenon and the Washington Monument, for example, have dimensions based on the golden ratio. Not until relatively recently, in terms of the history of civilization, was the golden ratio derived mathematically through the Fibonacci sequence.

BOX 20.1   GOLDEN RATIO (1.618) FROM ARBITRARY WHOLE NUMBERS

Pick any two whole numbers. For this example, we picked 14 and 285, but it will work for any two numbers. Add the two numbers together. In the following example, 14 + 285 equals 299. Calculate the ratio of the sum and the second addend; in our example, this is 299/285 = 1.049. Repeat the process adding the second addend (e.g., 285) to the resulting sum (e.g., 299). As you progress through the iterations, notice how the ratio approaches 1.618.

Iteration	Result	Ratio
1. Add the two numbers together: 14 + 285	299	1.049
2. Add the result to the highest previous: 285 + 299	584	1.953
3. Add the result to the highest previous: 299 + 584	883	1.512
4. Add the result to the highest previous: 584 + 883	1467	1.661
5. Add the result to the highest previous: 883 + 1467	2350	1.602
6. Add the result to the highest previous: 1467 + 2350	3817	1.624
7. Add the result to the highest previous: 2350 + 3817	6167	1.616
8. Add the result to the highest previous: 3817 + 6167	9984	1.619
9. Add the result to the highest previous: 6167 + 9984	16151	1.618

Plato considered the golden ratio to be the "most binding of all mathematical relations, and considered it the key to the physics of the cosmos" (Frost and Prechter, 2000, p. 101). German-born, seventeenth-century mathematician, astronomer, and astrologer, Johannes Kepler likened the golden ratio to a fine jewel and claimed that it described all creation. The reason for this adoration is that the ratio appears in innumerable natural phenomena. For example, consider a spiral that has its arc length to its diameter at a ratio of 1.618; this spiral occurs in nature in comet tails, galaxy spirals, spider webs, pine cones, snail shells, ocean waves, and even the human finger when curled. It is universal. It is a growth pattern in nature, and Elliott hypothesized that it occurred in the stock market as well.

Look back at Figure 20.1; see how the number of waves, as the pattern becomes more complex, follows a Fibonacci sequence. The first waves are corrective and impulse, one and one, totaling to two. Then there are three corrective waves and five impulse waves, totaling eight waves. Each of these numbers is part of the Fibonacci sequence. If we take the progression further and include smaller and smaller waves, the number of waves continues in a Fibonacci sequence. Although this relation to Fibonacci numbers is interesting, it is portraying the ideal. But remember if you take any two whole numbers and add them together, then add to the sum the previous highest number, eventually you will arrive at *phi,* the Fibonacci ratio (1.618), between the highest number and the previous highest number. (See the example in Box 20.1.) Thus, the ratio is the universal relation rather than the numbers themselves. It is the ratio and derivatives of it that are applied to stock markets.

Price and Time Targets

Elliott wave enthusiasts, to predict retracements and price targets, as we have already seen, and to project the timing of the next series of waves, use Fibonacci ratios. For example, Prechter notes that corrective waves tend to correct approximately 61.8%, or its complement 38.2% (100%–61.8%), of their corresponding impulse waves. Prechter is quick to point out, however, that this is a tendency, not even a guideline, and is not dependable. He found that more reliable relations exist in projecting target prices for alternating waves. For example, in percentage terms, impulse waves tend to be related in some manner by 2.618, 1.618, 0.618, or 0.382. As an example, he noted that the rise in the Dow Jones Industrial from the low in 1932 to 1937, wave 1, gained 371.6%, while wave 3 from 1942 to 1966 gained 971.7%, 2.618 times as much. This relationship is pictured in Figure 20.11.

Numerous other examples of relations between waves can be cited. One common occurrence is when wave 1 and wave 5 are the same length, wave 3 is often either 1.618 or 2.681 times wave 1. In addition, in a fifth wave extension, the length of the fifth wave is frequently 1.618 times the length from the beginning to the end of wave 3. Many times in an extended wave 1, the remaining four waves end at 0.618 the length of the extended first wave. In corrective waves, wave C is often related to wave A in some Fibonacci ratio, and the wave 4 length is often related by a Fibonacci ratio or by equality to the length of wave 2.

In addition to the extent of price movements in waves being related by Fibonacci numbers, times in stock market data have also been related to the Fibonacci ratio. However, this exercise is spurious at best. Tables are often used to show the time differences between important peaks and valleys in market prices that occurred in a Fibonacci number of years, months, or days. Elliott himself used the example of the 34 months between the peak in September 1929 and the bottom in July 1932 and the 13 years between the peak in 1929 and the low in 1942 (see Figure 20.12). Although others also have seen a relation between Fibonacci time counts and important events, Hamilton Bolton, a contemporary of and correspondent with Elliott, and publisher of the *Bank Credit Analyst,* stated, "Permutations tend to become infinite" (Frost and Prechter, 2000, p. 141). One of the tenets of any technical theory is that the principles must make sense. In the case of time, which is determined somewhat arbitrarily by humans and differently over the ages, the likelihood of there being a consistent series of time intervals that follow Fibonacci sequence numbers is a little far fetched. Indeed, a comprehensive study by Herbert Riedel, PhD (1989) on 182 days of the Dow Jones Industrial Average in 1985 demonstrated that no evidence of Fibonacci ratios was present either in retracements or in timing.

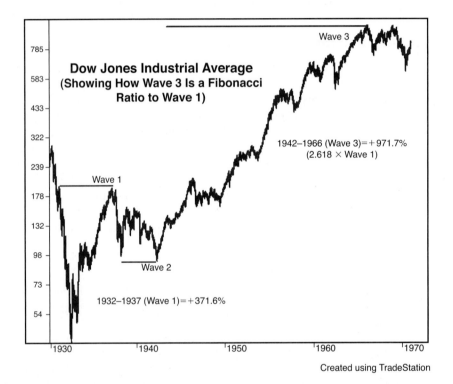

Created using TradeStation

FIGURE 20.11 Prechter interpretation of Fibonacci ratio between wave 1 and wave 3 in period 1932–1966 (monthly: 1930–1970)

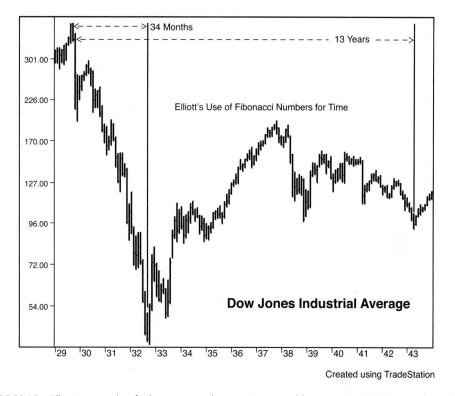

FIGURE 20.12 Elliott's example of Fibonacci numbers in time (monthly: January 1929–December 1942)

Although there is perhaps a far-too-often coincidence of waves being related to other waves by some variations of the Fibonacci ratio, the practical problem is that the relations, even if valid, are not usually known until after the fact. Thus, the relations are interesting but generally unproductive. To some extent, the same can be said about wave structure. One of the great problems with Elliott wave analysis is that the proper sequence of impulse and corrective waves is not often recognized until after the price action has completed. Even then, analysts—even those with considerable experience—will argue over whether the configuration is one type or another. For the technical analyst, especially one starting out, the concept of the Elliott Wave Theory must be understood in general terms, but the likelihood of being a seasoned practitioner is remote without considerable study, analysis, memorization of the rules and guidelines, and inspection of many long- and short-term price charts.

W. D. Gann

William Delbert Gann, born in Texas in 1878, roughly at the same time as Elliott, left his formal schooling at the age of 16 to begin his career as an itinerant salesman. Legend suggests that he made several fortunes in the commodities markets, married a number of younger women, and spent huge sums on planes, yachts, real estate, and gambling in Cuba (Costa, 2000). Some believe he was a scoundrel, that his courses on trading were full of generalities and astrology, and that he sold his advisory service several times (Williams, www.ireallytrade.com/asiseeit.htm). We do know that he died with very few assets. Nevertheless, Gann was a prolific writer, both of novels and advisory books. He published articles and sold courses on trading. Richard Wyckoff wrote an article on his trading, and Gann received considerable notoriety in his time for trading, especially in cotton. He was a superb trader, as witnessed by several independent observers. Whether or not he used the methods he proposed is uncertain.

Gann's published concept of market structure, specifically in commodity markets, encompassed time as well as price. He is known for such things as circles, squares, and triangles, all having to do with the angles of a circle. For example, he strongly believed in the seasonal cycle of approximately 360 days, the same as the number of degrees in a circle, the circle of the earth traveling around the sun. Thus, portions of a circle were important, such as 90, for 90 degrees, a quarter year, and 180, a half year; he expected that lows to highs or highs to lows would generally occur within those time periods or divisions of them. He preached that the range between tops and bottoms could be divided into zones that would project retracement levels, and he used angles drawn from tops and bottoms that when crossed, especially at the same level as his support and resistance zones, were important predictors of time and price for retracements. His concept of squares and rectangular shapes, not mathematical formulas, defined where in time and price future price motion should occur. Gann also discovered the strength of the fifth year of each decade, which since 1905 has been an up year. He claimed incorrectly to have invented swing charts, but he did successfully promote them as a method of trend following. His square of 52 is based on the 52 weeks in a year, or in a circle. His square of 144 is 12312, or the number of months in a circle. He devised spiral calculators such as the square of nine, the square of four, the 360-degree circle chart, and the hexagon chart. Gann also published a summary of 28 trading rules, all of which are still valid today.

There is no question that Gann was an inventive person. Whether his discoveries are hocus-pocus to sell his courses and books we do not know, because his methods are too vague to properly test, but even today a few analysts follow his numerological methods and claim success.

Conclusion

In this chapter, we have discussed the resemblance of stock market cycles to cycles seen occurring in nature. The basis for much of this theory goes back to the work of Ralph Elliott in the late 1930s. Elliott's work focuses on the waves in the stock market, especially how these waves are related to Fibonacci numbers and the golden ratio. His work has been thoroughly studied by subsequent analysts, especially by Robert Prechter.

The mathematical relationships and tie to nature found by these analysts can be fascinating. A basic knowledge of wave theory is a great aid to the technical analyst. However, making profitable trading decisions based primarily on wave theory is difficult. The theory is complex, requiring a great deal of study. Often waves can be found, in retrospect, which amazingly adhere to some variation of the Fibonacci sequence. However, it is often impossible to recognize these patterns and waves as they are occurring, making it difficult to use them for trading decisions.

REVIEW QUESTIONS

1. Explain the following Elliott Wave Theory terms:
    a. Motive wave
    b. Corrective wave
    c. Impulse wave
    d. Subwave
    e. Truncation
    f. Equality
    g. Alternation
    h. Rule

2. The EWT pattern is often said to be like "three steps forward and two steps back." Explain this phrase as it relates to EWT.

3. Explain what a Fibonacci number is.

4. Explain the difference between a zigzag and a flat in EWT.

5. Choose any two numbers, and go through the method shown in Box 20.1 to demonstrate how you will arrive at the golden ratio.

6. Explain why using EWT can be difficult for the average analyst.

PART VII

SELECTION

CHAPTER 21 SELECTION OF MARKETS AND ISSUES:
TRADING AND INVESTING

SELECTION OF MARKETS AND ISSUES: TRADING AND INVESTING

CHAPTER OBJECTIVES

By the end of this chapter, you should be familiar with

- The major factors to consider when choosing a security to trade
- The major factors to consider when choosing an investment security
- The relationship between hard asset and soft asset markets
- The basics of intermarket analysis
- The concept of relative strength among different investment vehicles and its implications for investors
- The basic methods of determining an individual stock's relative strength

We have now reached the stage in technical analysis where we become more practical. After learning how to analyze the long-term stock market and how to use various technical tools to determine the best entry and exit points in individual issues, we now focus on exactly what issues to consider for trading or investment goals. Those interested in using technical methods in markets must determine whether they have the time, inclination, and facilities to trade issues, or whether they want to consume less time and utilize technical methods for investing over longer periods.

WHICH ISSUES SHOULD I SELECT FOR TRADING?

Trading requires a complete commitment to the markets. It requires time every day and night, even if swing trading from day to day. Intraday trading requires constant attention, excellent execution abilities, and high-speed price reporting. It is not for everyone, and it is not advisable for people who have other jobs and limited time to commit. Trading can be accomplished through mechanical systems that are developed for that purpose, but even then, a heavy time commitment is necessary to perform the executions, to monitor the system, and perhaps to develop new systems.

The wise trader will select more than one issue to trade. In the stock market and the futures market, diversification is a necessity for many reasons. First, when a single issue becomes dormant in a small trading range and is difficult to trade, other issues with which the trader is already familiar can take its place. Second, following more than one issue increases the odds that a profitable trend will not be missed. Third, diversification, especially in issues that are not correlated, reduces risk. Thus, when screening markets with the criteria discussed next, anywhere from three to ten issues should be selected, watched, and traded. In Chapter 23, "Money and Risk Management," we will see that only a minimum commitment should be made to any one issue. Trading only one issue, and using more than the suggested initial capital in that one issue, substantially increases risk of failure.

Some traders, rather than concentrating on just a few issues, would prefer to screen through the entire marketplace for issues showing signs of an impending trend change. They program their computers to search for new highs and lows, gaps, one- and two-day reversal patterns, range and volatility changes, volume changes, moving average crossovers, and any number of other short-term indicators of possible trend change in individual stocks and contracts. From this information, they glean issues to trade over short periods and then go on to the next selected issues.

Choosing Between Futures Markets and Stock Markets

A trader must also make a choice about whether to trade in the stock market or the futures market or both. This choice is a personal one. The trader must consider a number of factors when making this decision. These factors include costs, personal risk preferences, preferred time horizon for trading, familiarity with each market, access to the proper equipment, and execution capability. Let us look at these factors in a little more detail.

Costs

Trading is a grueling, time-consuming process. It is not as glamorous as some recent movies make it out to be. Aside from the emotional strain of having to make instant decisions and instant executions, trading has many hidden costs that add up because of the many transactions necessary to profit. These transaction costs go beyond the commissions paid to the executing broker. The first cost is the initial setup of equipment. To trade, you must have not only a high-speed computer, excellent data feeds, and reliable, quick execution capability, but you must also have a backup. You cannot afford to have your system go down during a short-term, especially intraday, trade. Other costs are commissions, slippage, missing the intended price during a fast market, limit days, and unexpected events, seemingly always occurring at a critical juncture. (The dog pulls the wires out of the computer, the cat walks across the keyboard and executes several orders, and so on.)

Risk

Each trader must determine his or her own level of risk tolerance. Futures are considerably more risky than stocks because they are usually traded with high leverage. Leverage is the amount of capital that can be borrowed to initiate and carry a position. Because futures can be entered into with a relatively small amount of personal capital, a trade can lose all its capital with a small adverse move. With futures, the danger always exists that an adverse move will eliminate the trader's protective margin, requiring the trader to come up with more funds or be "stopped out."

We investigate this leverage risk more thoroughly in Chapter 23. Stocks can also be leveraged, but usually not to the degree that futures can, and are, thus, not as risky to capital. This is not to say, however, that a stock trader cannot go broke as quickly as a futures trader can. Capital risk depends on many other factors than just leverage.

Suitability

Your experience in the markets determines the issues with which you are most comfortable. For beginners in technical trading, the slowest and least risky markets are the best. Once your trading experience provides enough confidence, you can enter other faster and more risky issues. Suitability also encompasses time available, how much should be invested in fancy quote and execution equipment, and so on. It is based on personal choice and preference.

Time Horizon

Three types of trading are done by nonmarket makers—scalping, day trading, and swing trading. Scalping is taking very small profits between the bid and ask prices of a stock. It requires very close attention, excellent execution, fast-feed charting equipment, and communications, in addition to considerable experience. The competition is fierce between the scalper and the market makers, specialists, floor traders, and those others very closely connected with the issues being traded. This type of trading is not for amateurs.

Day trading is trading an issue and closing all positions by the end of the day. It has an advantage in that there is no overnight risk because no position is held overnight. A variation of day trading is called screen trading. Screen trading uses technical analysis intraday shown on a computer screen to give signals. The bar lengths are determined by the trader's ability to react quickly and accurately. Most commercial intraday technical analysis software divides trading into anywhere from single tick-by-tick, to 5-, 10-, 15-, and 60-minute bar lengths. From this data and software, almost any indicator or pattern can be programmed and used to identify opportunities. Again, however, it requires the time to watch positions all day and the equipment necessary to execute and watch entries and exits. Nevertheless, day trading has become very popular. The new automated electronic exchanges where trades are executed immediately against the trading book have revolutionized day trading and made markets more accessible to nonprofessionals. The advent of the e-mini S&P 500 futures at the Chicago Mercantile Exchange is an excellent example of a futures contract that is executed almost instantly and has a margin requirement considerably less than its earlier, larger version.

Swing trading, the third type of trading, is more easily accomplished by amateurs. It is the holding of positions over several days or weeks, attempting to catch the small trends accompanying or counter to a longer trend. The swing trader can determine entry and exit prices during non-trading hours and can judiciously place orders for the next trading day to enter or exit positions. Many swing traders watch the market throughout the day, but it is often not necessary.

Of course, professional traders are active in all the preceding trading methods because they are intimately in tune with the markets.

Volatility

As we saw in some of the short-term trading patterns, low volatility is a difficult world in which to make profits. The breakout from low volatility to high volatility is where most of the profit is derived. Therefore, futures or stocks with low volatility are generally not good choices for trading. The transaction costs of exit and entry, the possible mistakes in execution, and other costs demand that the issue traded has enough price change to make a profit despite these problems.

Liquidity

Volatility, however, must be accompanied by liquidity. Price changes may be large (high volatility), but if no size is available for trading, this volatility is of no use to the trader. Liquidity is the ability to transact a meaningful number of shares or contracts easily and without bringing about a large price change. Even volatility with heavy volume may be deceiving if the volume only occurs sporadically within the trading horizon or is the product of high-speed trading systems buying and selling the spread for large investment firms. For stocks, volatility can be measured using the ATR_{14}. A more complicated formula is necessary for futures because of the different dollar value of point moves and the different margin requirements for each market contract.

Volatility usually is related to the size of the bid and ask and the spread between bid and ask. A narrow spread does not guarantee liquidity because the bid and ask may be small. For easy entry and exit, high liquidity is a requirement. Trading is difficult enough without having to worry about whether an order will be executed close to the desired price. Each month, a section of *Technical Analysis of Stocks & Commodities* called "Futures Liquidity" shows a list of the most popular futures markets with their respective relative liquidity. These figures are based on the number of contract expirations that are traded, the total open interest, and volume. The list also displays the margin and effective margin for each contract series.

Volume

Issues with constant heavy volume are usually issues that have liquidity, but they might not have sufficient volatility to profit. Volume is, therefore, a requirement for a trading issue, but it is not the final determinant. Liquidity and volatility are also required.

WHICH ISSUES SHOULD I SELECT FOR INVESTING?

When investing, the universe of potential investments is enormous. This means that some method must be used to cull out the investments, determining those most likely to outperform the markets. Usually, the investor only goes long investments or in cash, rarely short, though in the commodities markets, long one currency, for example, may be equivalent to being short the other. Let us look at some of the items you need to consider when choosing investment securities.

In the futures markets, selection is usually based on a ratio analysis of each future versus a basket of futures or against another investment vehicle. In the stock market, selection uses two different methods. The first method is the top-down method whereby the prospects for the market are first determined, then the prospects for groups (such as industry groups or countries) are determined, and finally—after the decision is made that the market is favorable and certain groups are favorable for investment—specific stocks are selected from within the groups. This method is more common in fundamental analysis and in professional management where there may be little choice as to whether to be in the stock market or not. It is often called asset allocation, and the first step is the group selection.

The second method is the bottom-up method, whereby stocks are selected, usually based on their price behavior. This method is more technically oriented because it uses relative price strength as one of its primary selection criteria. By selecting stocks first, regardless of their group affiliations, the portfolio manager can assess what groups are performing well and whether the entire market is favorable or not. If few stocks come through the screens for performance, it is clear that the market is in difficulty, for example, and if many stocks meet the investment criteria, the market is favorable.

TOP-DOWN ANALYSIS

Top-down analysis begins with a study of the major markets such as interest rates, currencies, and stock market to determine which market has the highest possibility of profit in the future. Once a market has been selected, the next level of decision making is the groupings of issues in that market and, finally, the individual issues within those groupings. In the currency markets, the breakdown for U.S. investors is basically whether to invest in the dollar or in a foreign currency. If it is to be a foreign currency, the selection is large and can be broken into further groups—for example, the resource-producing countries and the emerging countries. If the bond market is chosen, the groupings can be on length to maturity, country and currency, and level of default risk. In the stock market, of course, industry groups are the standard sectors, but others are used such as capitalization, foreign origin, investment style, and interest-rate related. The investor must decide the long-term, secular trend in the various markets. As in trading, the trend is the most important aspect of any price change and the major determinant of whether the investor will profit from investing. Bucking the trend in investing is just as dangerous as it is in trading.

The technical method used to determine markets' relative attractiveness is called **ratio analysis.** It compares different markets with each other to see which is performing most favorably. After a market has been selected that fits the investor's objectives, further comparisons are made with components of that market, such as by industry group, capitalization, or quality.

Secular Emphasis

John Murphy, in his book *Intermarket Technical Analysis* (1991), discussed the concept of alternating emphasis in the markets on hard assets and soft assets over long secular periods. "Secular" is a term used for any period longer than the business cycle. Hard assets are solid commodities such as gold and silver; these assets traditionally are considered an inflation hedge. Soft assets are financial assets, called paper assets, that primarily include stocks and bonds.

Generally, when hard assets rise in value, soft assets decline. However, since 1998, this relationship has not always held. The reason for the inverse relationship between the value of hard assets and of soft assets is that a close correlation exists between material prices and interest rates. Inflation, or higher material prices, is generally associated with higher interest rates. When inflation becomes a threat, paper assets, which decrease in value as interest rates rise, are undesirable as investments. Likewise, when hard asset prices decline, interest rates usually decline, and soft assets increase in value.

The theory that one or the other of these kinds of assets becomes popular for substantial periods is not a new one. The principal problem with proving this theory is the lack of hard asset prices going back before the free market in gold in the late 1960s. Nevertheless, the concept likely has some validity because since then, markets have generally alternated between these two basic types. One thought is that a 16-year hard/soft asset cycle exists. If so, it appears that the markets have returned from a soft asset market to a hard asset market, as of 2002.

Gold is traditionally the measure of hard asset prices because of its universal appeal as an inflation hedge. Figure 21.1 shows the history of gold prices and the Dow Jones Industrial Average since 1973. Mostly, these two markets head in opposite directions. Gold is the hard asset; U.S. stocks are the soft assets. Notice that when gold prices rise, the stock market declines, and vice versa. This behavior led to the theory of alternating hard and soft asset markets.

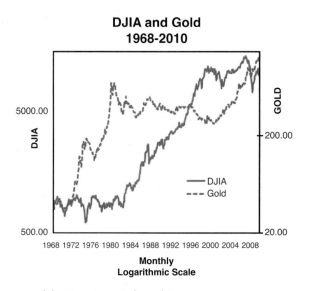

FIGURE 21.1 Gold price and the Dow Jones Industrial Average

Looking at a ratio chart of gold to the stock market, we see that clear trends develop in the relationship between these two types of assets. Figure 21.2 shows both a line for the ratio of gold to the stock market and a line for the stock market itself. A decline in the gold/stock market ratio indicates that gold is underperforming the stock market and, in relationship to the stock market, is not a wise investment.

The broad signal as to when to switch from one asset class to another is given when the ratio crosses its 48-month EMA. As seen in Figure 21.2, the last signal to switch from hard assets to soft assets occurred in June 1981, just three months after the peak in the gold price at a time when the DJIA was at 998.

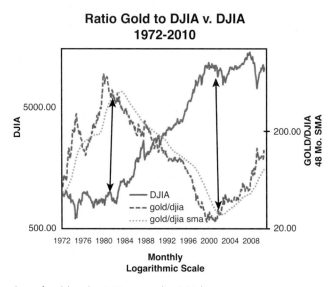

FIGURE 21.2   Ratio line of gold to the DJIA versus the DJIA line

The next switch signal came in September 2001 when the ratio crossed above its 48-month EMA, signaling a move into hard assets. Between the 1981 signal to soft assets and the 2001 signal to hard assets, gold had declined to $320 and the DJIA had advanced to 10,000. In the relatively short period since the hard asset buy signal, gold has risen to $1,200 and the DJIA has remained relatively flat with high volatility. Although these signals are not precise by any means, they do indicate over long periods in what asset type the investor should be invested. Once a definite trend toward one or the other asset type is clear, it usually remains in place for many years.

Although we have used gold as an example of a hard asset thus far, gold is not necessarily the best hard asset. Others exist such as silver, oil, copper, and aluminum. These are called "industrial raw materials" and are normally associated with the business cycle. Along with gold, these industrial prices have a long-term component that follows the gold price and gives more options for investment during a period of hard assets types.

Figure 21.3 shows the relationship between industrial raw material prices and the stock market since 1973. As you can see, the moving average crossovers in the ratio occur at approximately the same time as those for the gold market alone did in Figure 21.2. Thus, when we see the ratio of gold or industrial raw material prices to the stock market cross its 48-month EMA, we know that a long-term shift is occurring in the investment emphasis from hard assets to soft assets or vice versa.

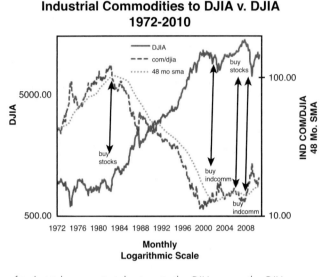

FIGURE 21.3   Ratio of industrial raw material prices to the DJIA versus the DJIA

What does this mean for investment selection? Being in the time period following the 2001 signal for the switch to hard assets suggests that analysis should be concentrated on those investments concerned with hard asset prices. Those investments could be in futures or spot markets of the hard assets themselves; however, this group also includes stocks of mining, oil- or forest product-producing companies, or currencies in countries like Australia or Canada that are involved in exporting raw materials. There are many choices, but the emphasis should be placed on those investments that will gain from increases in industrial materials and gold prices. When the tide turns the other way, and soft assets appear more promising, emphasis should be placed on commodity users, not producers, consumer staples, anything related to interest rates, bonds and stocks, or currencies of consuming nations.

Cyclical Emphasis

Within the longer secular economic trend are a number of business cycles. These business cycles are of varying length but usually average around four to five years. These business cycles are the normal horizon for most economists, business managers, and investors. It is well recognized that leadership in the trading markets often switches within the business cycle. There appears to be a standard pattern that is worth watching. Murphy maintains that although the markets may appear independent, they are interrelated and follow certain patterns. For that reason, he suggests that investors should be aware of all these markets and their interactions. The activity in all of these markets might offer suggestions about investment prospects.

Martin Pring (2002) classifies investment markets into three categories: commodities, bonds, and stocks. Murphy adds currencies and, to some extent, foreign stock markets, to this list. The business cycle affects each of these markets but in different ways. Let us look at the normal sequence of leadership among these investments and see how to recognize when a change in leadership has occurred. We will look in sequence at the dollar exchange rate to gold, using gold as a proxy for inflation and commodity prices, gold to the long-term note (U.S. Treasury 10-year note), a proxy for interest rates, the long-term note to the stock market (Dow Jones Industrial—DJIA), and, finally, the stock market back to the dollar exchange rate (NYBOT U.S. Dollar Index—DXY).

U.S. Dollar and Gold

Murphy maintains that currency rates influence industrial prices but sometimes with a considerable lead. The dollar is important in that it is the pricing currency for many of the world's raw materials such as oil, gold, and other precious metals. When the dollar declines, it makes these commodities cheap in foreign currencies but expensive in dollar terms. Thus, there is a leading inverse relationship between the U.S. dollar and raw materials prices in the United States. In Figure 21.4, we use gold as a proxy for industrial prices because gold has a well-defined price, whereas most indexes of material prices have different weightings for their components and are, thus, biased toward the interest of the respective index compilers. Figure 21.4 shows the ratio of the dollar to gold and gold itself. When the ratio is rising, or the dollar is stronger than gold, gold tends to decline, and vice versa.

FIGURE 21.4 Ratio of U.S. dollars to gold versus gold, monthly

In the business cycle, we use the 18-month SMA as the signal line. In Figure 21.4, this signal line crossed downward in September 2001, suggesting a rise in gold versus the dollar. The signal line, as a proxy for commodity prices, suggested investment in industrial raw materials, including gold, raw materials, energy, and any other inflation-affected securities. In October, the signal line crossed upward, and gold declined for a few months, but then in May 2009, the signal line broke down again, signaling the time to buy gold versus the dollar.

Gold and Bonds (Long-Term Interest Rates)

The next sequence is typically for industrial prices to lead long-term U.S. interest rates. By taking a ratio of the gold price to the U.S. Treasury ten-year note, we see that at certain times, a signal is given by the ratio as to when to enter or exit the long-term bond market. The ratio is shown in Figure 21.5. In December 2001, the ratio crossed above its 18-month SMA, suggesting that material prices were outperforming financials. That relationship held for almost seven years. A flip-flop occurred in the debt crisis of 2008–2009 but as of May 2009, the ratio was back above its moving average and suggesting that materials were still advantageous over bonds.

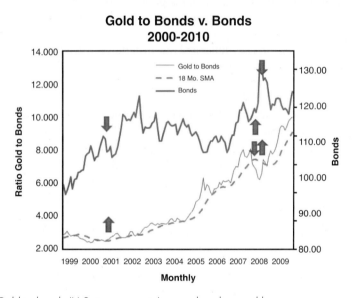

FIGURE 21.5   Gold to bonds (U.S. ten-year note) versus bonds, monthly

Bond Market and Stock Market

Ideally, the next switch in markets is from the bond market to the stock market. As Chapter 10, "Flow of Funds," demonstrated, the lead-lag relationship has not been a successful one since 1998. Murphy argues that this is because for the first time since the 1930s, actual deflation has become a threat and has upset the previous balance between interest rates and the stock market. Nevertheless, a plot of the ratio of bonds to stocks, as shown in Figure 21.6, shows very definite times when one or the other has the advantage.

This chart shows that even if we had owned bonds, despite what the commodity markets were suggesting, they should have been switched to the stock market around August 2003. From that point to February 2008, when the ratio crossed below its moving average, the U.S. ten-year note only rose from 112.3 to 188.6 (+5.6%) while the DJIA rose from 6416 to 11237 (+75%). Then, following the crossover below the moving average in February, the relationship caught the stock market decline (relative to bonds) into July 2009. As of mid-2010, the ratio is approaching its moving average again from below. A positive crossover would be bearish for the stock market.

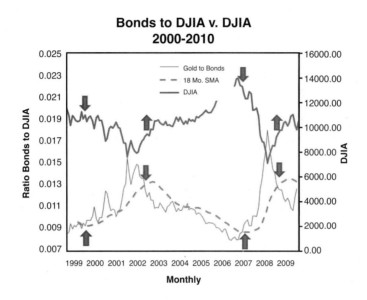

FIGURE 21.6   Ratio of bonds (U.S. Treasury 10-year note) to the DJIA versus the DJIA

Stock Market and the U.S. Dollar

The final analysis is to return to the beginning and see how the dollar and the stock market have interacted. Generally, the two markets are so out of sync that a ratio analysis will lag beyond the investment period desired. The dollar usually leads the industrial raw material market, which in turn generally leads the bond market, which in turn leads the stock market. By connecting the loop, nothing is accomplished because there seems to be only a slight relationship between the stock market and the dollar. This is born out in Figure 21.7, which compares the DJIA with the U.S. dollar. The signal to buy the DJIA in preference to the dollar is late. The percentage returns since are still favorable for the investor in the stock market but only partially favorable for the earlier investment in the dollar. This is a good example of why the analyst must always be aware of the absolute prices as well as the relative ones.

Implications of Intermarket Analysis

From the previous analysis, it appears that around 2001, the investor should have been looking at the raw materials markets and the stock market. Because both markets appeared favorable, the raw material market stocks would likely have been the best investments. The signals given by the various ratios are usually long-term signals, in the sense that they are operating within the business cycle. They are neither trading signals nor mechanical signals. Their purpose is to inform the investor in which markets to invest solely from how the marketplaces are behaving. When certain sectors become strong, they tend to remain strong, just as when a trend begins, it tends to remain. Eventually these ratios will suggest changes in the investment mix, but only rarely do they err, and often that miscalculation comes from the investor impatience and greed, treating the signals as mechanical rather than waiting to be sure they are real.

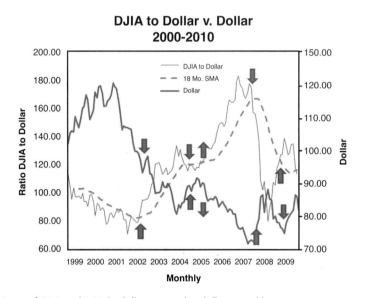

FIGURE 21.7   Ratio of DJIA to the U.S. dollar versus the dollar, monthly

One important caveat is that the signals come from ratios, not raw figures. Raw figures should always be used as a backup. It is possible that sometime in the future all markets will decline. In that case, the investor may find the "best" market but still lose money—perhaps not as quickly as in other markets, but still lose. For this reason, the absolute value of markets must never be overlooked. Many investors are happy with a relative return rather than an absolute return even in a declining market. This is a major mistake because the law of percentages suggests that to make back any actual loss is considerably more difficult than to make back a relative loss.

BOX 21.1   LAW OF PERCENTAGES

A relative loss of 20% can be made back with a relative gain of 20%, but an absolute 20% loss requires a 25% gain to break even. This is called the "law of percentages." In investing, it suggests that all absolute losses must be kept to a minimum. As the old adage goes, "You can't spend a relative return." For example, if you have $100 in capital and sustain a 20% loss, you are left with $80. You must earn a 25% return on the $80 to return to the break-even level of $100. For any particular loss amount, the percentage amount that must be gained to break even is calculated using the formula % gain necessary = % loss ÷ (1–% loss). As an extreme example, a 50% loss requires a 100% gain to break even. Considering the difficulty of investing for a 100% gain, the investor is better off cutting losses before reaching such an extreme that is unlikely to be recouped.

Finally, this analysis is not intended to forecast the economy. It is useful primarily in determining where the best market for investment might be at any time and for enough time for investment. Because most indicators lead the economy, forecasting the economy is unfruitful. From this information, certain aspects of the economy are obvious, but investment is best left to the analysis of price than to the analysis of the lagging economy.

Stock Market Industry Sectors

Some analysts have proposed theories of industry group and sector rotation during the stock market cycle. These rule definitions, however, are too strict, and often the markets do not accommodate them. For example, some models suggest that utilities, generally considered interest-related stocks, should be bought at certain stages of the market cycle when interest rates are expected to decline. However, as we have seen previously, when an inflationary environment exists, anything to do with interest rates will generally underperform. In other words, any system of following specific models of business cycles is not flexible enough to account for changes in the major market segments.

For some individuals, like stock mutual fund managers, investment in the stock market is a requirement. In these instances, the best manner of screening out the most likely sectors to outperform is the use of ratio analysis between the sector performance and the stock market as a whole. For example, Figure 21.8 shows a three-point, point-and-figure plot of the (a) S&P Utility Sector and the (b) S&P Financials Sector to the S&P 500, and Figure 21.9 shows a three-point, point-and-figure plot of the S&P (a) Energy Sector and the (b) S&P Materials Sector to the S&P 500.

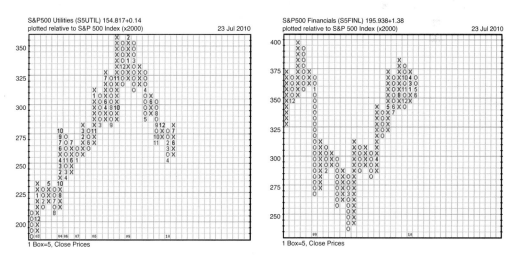

Source: Investors Intelligence

FIGURE 21.8 Point-and-figure chart of the ratio of the (a) S&P Utility Sector and the (b) S&P Financials Sector to the S&P 500

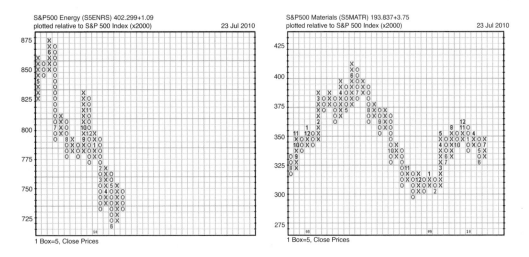

FIGURE 21.9   Point-and-figure chart of the ratio of the (a) S&P Energy Sector and the (b) S&P Materials Sector to the S&P 500

Plotting the relative strength ratio of an industry and often a stock to some underlying average, we often see an irregular line that is difficult to interpret. By plotting these ratios on a point-and-figure chart, the minor, less significant oscillations are eliminated, and the overall relationship of the two indices becomes more obvious. In Figure 21.8a, for example, it is clear that underperformance of utility stocks began in 2009. These charts are much more informative than a line chart. Remember, however, when deciding whether to act on any of the ratio analyses, the absolute price action of the stock in the numerator always must be analyzed as well. When both charts demonstrate a trend, one can act with more confidence.

BOTTOM UP—SPECIFIC STOCK SELECTION AND RELATIVE STRENGTH

At present, almost 8,000 stocks trade in the active stock markets in the United States. This number is too large for an analyst to screen at frequent intervals. Some technical analysts briefly inspect the chart of every stock in their universe, using either a bar, candlestick, or point-and-figure chart. This is a laborious process and far from objective. Others screen through relative strength ratio charts. The least time-consuming and most objective method is to screen all stocks on a periodic basis for relative price strength using one of the methods described next. Relative strength provides evidence that a particular stock is outperforming the market and is very likely in a strong, upward trend. These methods have also been used successfully in mutual funds, ETFs, industry group selection, commodities, and foreign securities.

Relative Strength

Most technical screening methods use a concept called relative strength to judge which securities have the most promise. Relative strength is a reliable concept that has been demonstrated academically and practically to have value. Indeed, because the method is so successful, it is the primary argument against the Random Walk and Efficient Markets Hypotheses. The presumption behind the concept of relative strength is that strength will continue, similar to how trends will continue, and that by recognizing the strongest trends, an edge can be obtained by investing in them until their strength abates. If the strongest stocks remain strong, the market cannot be random or efficient.

The most common means of establishing relative strength is called the ratio method. It is merely the ratio between two investments, sectors, industry groups, averages, commodities, and so on, to see which is outperforming the other. Usually a line chart is drawn that shows the item of interest, say a steel stock, and a ratio of the item to an average, say a steel industry average. If the line of the ratio is rising, it is simply showing that the particular stock is stronger than its industry average. Interpretations of behavior are similar to those used in price and other oscillators. Divergence analysis, trend lines, and even patterns appear in the ratio lines. The item can also be plotted in a point-and-figure chart along with a point-and-figure chart of the ratio similar to what is shown in the sector charts shown in Figures 21.8 and 21.9.

Academic Studies of Relative Strength

In 1967, Robert Levy, PhD, published a paper in the *Journal of Finance* in which he argued that relative price strength tended to remain for a long-enough period that it could be profitable and that the concept of random walk was, therefore, dead. His paper received considerable opposition at that time when the Efficient Markets Hypothesis and the Random Walk Hypothesis were relatively new and highly favored among academics.

Not until 1993 was another major paper published on the subject of relative price strength, or "momentum" as it is commonly called. This paper, "Returns to Buying Winners and Selling Losers: Implications for Stock Market Efficiency," was also published in the *Journal of Finance*. The authors, Professors Narishimhan Jegadeesh and Sheridan Titman, demonstrated how stocks with high returns over a 3- to 12-month period earned excess profits of about 1% per month for the following year. However, they also found that these stocks on average had losses 13 to 60 months later, thus proposing the theory that relative price strength was not permanent but more likely a temporary phenomenon. They clearly stated that the t-test statistical evidence forced them "to conclude that the hypothesis of market efficiency can be rejected at even the most conservative levels of significance."

In a study of 150 momentum (relative strength) and contrarian strategies, Conrad and Kaul (1998) also found that the optimum profit occurred during the 3- to 12-month horizon. In addition, they found that a contrarian strategy (buying the lows) only had statistically significant profits during the period 1926 through 1947.

Of course, other academics immediately criticized the study for any number of possible reasons, but by the time of Conrad and Kaul's paper, other doubts about market efficiency had also been demonstrated, and the evidence was not rejected immediately as it had been with Levy in the 1960s. Since then, the basis of their paper has been proven correct not only in foreign countries but also in the period following the original paper in the United States, as reported in a subsequent paper by Jegadeesh and Titman in 2001 in the *Journal of Finance.*

In 1998, Professor K. G. Rouwenhorst showed that momentum was successful in 12 European stock markets, and in 1999, he demonstrated that momentum was most strong in emerging markets. Other studies confirm the existence of profitability from relative strength in China, Germany, 8 different Asian markets (without Japan), and Switzerland. Even Professor Eugene Fama, one of the originators of the Efficient Markets Hypothesis, found that momentum was the only anomaly to survive a multitude of tests (Fama and French, 1996). Academia has, thus, concluded that the theory of relative price strength shows success not only in producing profits but also in debunking part of the Efficient Markets Hypothesis.

Various reasons have been proposed for the existence of relative strength, none of which has been proven. The most logical has to do with behavioral tendencies of investors and the flow of information. An excellent discussion of the behavioral model describing investor underreaction and overreaction is Barberis, Shleifer, and Vishny (1997). However, we are not concerned with why relative strength is valid. Our only concern is that over a period of three to six months, using relative strength is a viable strategy and is, thus, a reliable means of selecting stocks.

Measuring Relative Strength

Given the importance of relative strength, the technical analyst needs a method for measuring it. A number of methods of measuring relative strength exist, the most popular being the percentage change, the alpha, the trend slope, and the Levy methods.

Percentage Change Method

In their study, Jegadeesh and Titman used a six-month price change as their basic lookback calculation. "Lookback" is the period over which relative price strength is calculated. The stocks then were sorted based on these rates of change. They found that the higher decile stocks continued to be strong for the next three to ten months. Their sample included both large capitalized and thinly capitalized and both high-priced and low-priced stocks. All performed similarly both in the original experiment and in the subsequent out-of-sample tests.

BOX 21.2 CALCULATION OF ALPHA FOR AAPL

The graph in Figure 21.10 shows the scatter plot of weekly changes in AAPL (Apple Computer stock) and the S&P 500 index. The linear regression line through the scatter plot can be defined by its beta (1.60) and its alpha (1.55). Beta represents how volatile AAPL is relative to the S&P. AAPL's beta of 1.6 implies that AAPL stock will oscillate on a weekly basis 60% more than the S&P. The alpha of 1.55 indicates that AAPL has been outperforming the S&P by 1.55% on average over the 52 weeks in the plot. It thus has a positive alpha and is a strong stock. Comparing AAPL's alpha to that of other stocks is a way to determine which are the strongest and best candidates for investment. For a more thorough explanation of linear regression, see Appendix A, "Basic Statistics."

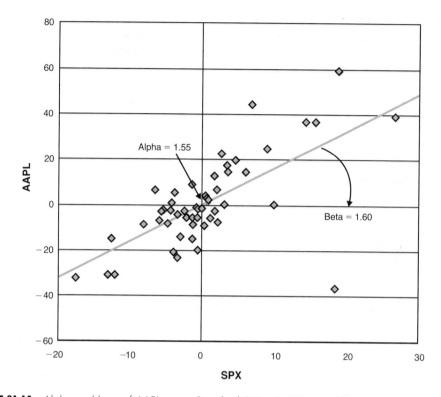

FIGURE 21.10   Alpha and beta of AAPL versus Standard & Poor's 500, weekly

Alpha Method

A number of different methods of calculating relative strength have been developed. One is the alpha method. In the beta theory of Modern Portfolio Theory (MPT), stock prices are compared with an average, usually the S&P 500, weekly, over a year (and sometimes with different time intervals and period). The weekly percentage change in the stock price is plotted versus the weekly percentage change in S&P 500, and a linear regression line is drawn through these plots on a best-fit basis. The line so defined is expressed using the slope of the line, called the **beta,** and the intercept with the vertical axis, called the **alpha.** Thus, each stock over a specified period has an alpha and a beta. Traditionally, beta has been used as a measure of volatility relative to the S&P 500 and considered a definition of volatility risk. Stocks that oscillated widely have a high beta representing a steep slope in their regression line and, thus, demonstrate a proclivity to swing widely about the S&P. The alpha describes the value when the regression line crosses the 0% change in the S&P and is, thus, a measure of the trend relative to the S&P 500. MPT suggested that high beta stocks would be more profitable but would also be more risky. What they missed is that high beta stocks could also have negative alphas, suggesting that, while more volatile, their trends relative to the S&P could be downward. In MPT, the alpha must always either approach or be close to zero because, in theory, no systemic gain can come from the market (the S&P 500) itself. In other words, a stock's price motion is determined by beta, not alpha.

Alpha is not considered of any importance. However, in actual markets, alpha does not remain at the zero level and has, thus, become a measure of how much better or worse the stock is performing relative to the S&P. When alpha is compared among stocks, it provides a relative strength measure, and stock lists can be ranked by alpha to show which issues are the strongest. Alpha will change more frequently and more widely than beta, but beta is somewhat irrelevant to the relative price strength and has been largely discarded, even as a measure of volatility.

Trend Slope Method

Rather than go through the more complicated calculation of alpha and beta, another method of screening for relative price strength is to calculate the slope of the price curve in percentage terms over a specified period through a linear regression formula for each stock. The stocks can then be ranked by the slopes of their price curves. This method is similar to the alpha method and to the Jegadeesh and Titman method. It is easier to calculate than the alpha method and does not suffer from the drop-off effect of a rate-of-change calculation beginning at an arbitrary price.

Levy Method

Robert Levy introduced a method of calculating relative strength in his 1965 paper. Levy first calculated the ratio of the stock's current price to its 131 trading-day moving average. He then ranked this ratio against the same ratio for all other stocks.

Levy found, as did Jegadeesh and Titman later, that the screen for relative strength should be calculated on performance of the stock over a six-month lookback period. Anything shorter tended to give multiple whipsaws in postcalculation performance, and anything longer tended to be too close to when the performance began to regress back to its mean. Levy also found that when the overall stock market headed downward into a lengthy bear market, relative strength continued to be reliable but gradually lost its ability to pick winning stocks, and when the final decline, the washout, occurred, those stocks having been relatively the strongest usually declined the most. In his estimation, relative strength was, thus, a bull market selection process and should not be used when the stock market declines.

One of the authors has tested the method live over 17 years (Kirkpatrick, 2007) using 26-weeks as the lookback period and found it still provides a consistent list of winning stocks. 26 weeks is close enough to Levy's original 131 days and can be substituted in the ratio to make the calculation easier.

EXAMPLES OF HOW SELECTED PROFESSIONALS SCREEN FOR FAVORABLE STOCKS

Different analysts develop different methods for screening for favorable stocks. Let's look at ways a few selected professionals go about this task.

William O'Neil CANSLIM Method

CANSLIM is an acronym for a method of picking stocks to buy, devised by William O'Neil (2002), publisher of *Investor's Business Daily*. The data and ratings for each stock are included in a subscription to that newspaper. The breakdown of CANSLIM is as follows:

C—Current quarterly earnings per share versus a year earlier

A—Annual earnings increases

N—New products, management, and stock price highs

S—Supply and demand of stock

L—Leader or laggard

I—Institutional sponsorship

M—Market direction

We, as technical analysts, are only concerned with L and M. The other selection criteria are useful but not in the domain of this book. To determine L, leader or laggard, O'Neil calculates the 12-month percentage price change of every stock, weighted more heavily over the most recent 3 months, and ranks each stock in percentiles from 99 to 0, with 99 being the strongest. He has not divulged the exact formula, but as we know from academic studies and others, the exact calculation is less important than the lookback time over which price change is measured. This method is on the long side at 12 months, about the time when a strong stock begins to revert to its moving average. The weighting over the past 3 months reduces the overall time for comparison and, therefore, improves the prospects of price strength continuing. O'Neil found that the average relative strength percentile, by his calculation, was 87 before large upward moves.

For M, market direction, O'Neil refuses to listen to newsletters and "gurus" and refuses to use economic data because it lags behind the market. He has a number of specific indicators and patterns he watches for signs that a market is bottoming. He believes that the buy-and-hold method is faulty because the widely held belief that all stocks will recover after a bear market is a myth.

James P. O'Shaughnessy Method

Not surprisingly, James O'Shaughnessy, the president of O'Shaughnessy Capital Management in Greenwich, Connecticut, found in studying 43 years of fundamental and price data that most investment strategies are mediocre at best and that traditional investment management does not work. He studied market capitalization, price-to-earnings ratios, price-to-book ratios, price-to-cash flow ratios, price-to-sales ratios, dividend yields, earnings changes, profit margins, and return on equity. He found that relative price strength, out of all the possible variables, fundamental and technical, was the only "growth variable that consistently beats the market" (1997).

O'Shaughnessy's calculation of relative strength is similar to O'Neil's in that it takes a ratio of the year-end price to the price one year prior. It is, thus, a 12-month relative price strength measure, a slightly longer-term calculation considering the history of relatively strong stocks remaining strong. O'Shaughnessy developed from his testing of data from December 31, 1954, through December 31, 1995, a multifactor investment strategy model called the Cornerstone Growth Strategy. It includes a primary screen for stocks with a price-to-sales ratio below 1.5, earnings greater than the previous year, and of those selected so far, the top 50 stocks in relative price strength.

Charles D. Kirkpatrick Method

Charles Kirkpatrick (2002), coauthor of this book, has long had a model similar to that of O'Shaughnessy. The principal differences are threefold. First, in working with Robert Levy in the late 1960s, he discovered the importance of relating all ratios to each other. Thus, in using the price-to-sales ratio, he calculates the relative price-to-sales ratio of all stocks. Second, Kirkpatrick uses the Levy calculation of relative price strength over six months in line with Levy's original work and that of later studies showing the importance of that period for postcalculation continuation of price strength (see Figure 21.11). A multifactor investment strategy is developed using the relative rankings of each of the preceding factors. This method has outperformed the S&P 500 over the past 27 years in live weekly reporting by better than four to one.

Value Line Method

The Value Line Ranking System (www.valueline.com) has an extraordinary history of outperforming the stock market. Value Line claims that its Timeliness Ranking system has outperformed the Standard & Poor's 500 by 16 to 1 since 1965. Although the company will not divulge its method of calculation, it does admit that a significant portion of it includes a calculation of relative price strength. Other factors include earnings trends, recent earnings, and earnings surprises. Value Line charges a fee for its stock services.

Richard D. Wyckoff Method

A method of profiting from the stock market using technical analysis and relative price strength that has stood the test of over 80 years is the method taught by Richard DeMille Wyckoff beginning in 1931.

Richard Wyckoff, now considered a legend and one of the most important proponents of technical analysis, began his long career in Wall Street as a runner in 1888 when he was only 15 years old. He organized his own brokerage firm by the time he was 25. From his brokerage firm, he published a daily newsletter that evolved into a magazine called the *Magazine of Wall Street*. Motivated by seeing "appalling losses in securities suffered annually by millions of people who do not realize what they are risking and have an amazingly small knowledge of the market" (Hutson, 1986), in 1910, under the pen name "Rollo Tape," Wyckoff described many important aspects of the stock market in a book titled *Studies in Tape Reading*. His observations then are still valid today. Before retiring for health reasons in 1928, his subscriber list exceeded 200,000 names, and later, when he returned to Wall Street in the early 1930s, he wrote many books on the subject of profiting from the stock market and developed a correspondence course.

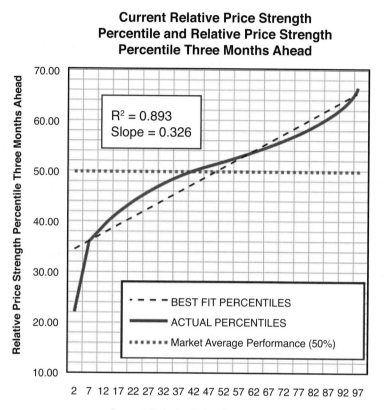

Current Relative Price Strength Percentile and Relative Price Strength Percentile Three Months Ahead

$R^2 = 0.893$
Slope = 0.326

- - - - BEST FIT PERCENTILES
——— ACTUAL PERCENTILES
•••••• Market Average Performance (50%)

Current Relative Price Strength Percentile

Chart of the relationship between the current relative price strength percentile (independent variable) and relative price strength percentile three months later (dependent variable). The relationship is strong. The dark, straight line (actual data) fits closely to the dark, dashed line (expected data) and has a relatively steep slope of 0.326. This suggests that for every increased point in relative price strength percentile, the results increased by close to a third of a point. Its R^2 is high at 0.893, suggesting that the relationship is relatively close to perfect, which would be 1.000. It is positive, which suggests the higher the current relative price strength percentile, the higher will be the relative price strength percentile three months later. The best three-month performance comes from the highest level of current relative price strength percentile.

Source: Kirkpatrick (2009)

FIGURE 21.11   Relative three-month performance of stocks selected by relative price strength using the Kirkpatrick (2009) method.

Wyckoff believed most strongly that stock prices were determined solely by "supply and demand." He had little use for "tips, rumors, news items, earnings analyses, financial reports, dividend rates, and the myriad of other sources of information" or the "half-baked trading theories expounded in boardrooms and popular books on the stock market" (Wyckoff in Hutson, 1986). He was a true technical analyst, and a very successful one. He believed that the markets were influenced mostly by wealthy individuals and informed insiders. Substituting "institutions" today for these players, we find that the situation has not changed. By understanding what these capital pools were doing in the markets, one could profit by following them. Their capital moved the markets, right or wrong, and the small investor could take advantage of this movement by understanding how to gauge it.

Wyckoff's tools were many of the methods described in this book. He used bar charts (called "vertical charts") and point-and-figure charts (called "figure charts"). He measured relative strength for both long and short positions, used volume as a means of testing the best time to consider acting, required stop orders be entered with any action order, used trend lines to determine direction, used composite indexes, used group indexes, and believed that timing of entry and exit was the most important variable in success. Support and resistance, reversal points (called "danger points"), and horizontal counts from figure charts were important to his method. In short, he used about everything you have learned so far. He believed that attempting to fit the market into a formula or specific pattern was futile because no two markets are the same. The market, he believed, traveled in waves—small ones evolving into larger ones in either direction—and that these waves could be detected and even anticipated, but they followed no certain, mathematical path. Consequently, although his method had some organization, it required judgment and experience.

Wyckoff's progression of selecting stocks was as follows:

1. To determine the direction of the entire market, Wyckoff devised an index called the Wyckoff Wave that was a composite of the most widely held and active stocks. This was his proxy for the market. Preferably, the stocks in the index were the ones that the investor or trader was interested in trading. His concept of trend was to watch trend lines drawn on the Wave chart and on charts of the composite market.

2. To select the stocks in harmony with the market, Wyckoff selected stocks that were strong in upward trends and weak in downward trends. He believed that it was futile to act against the trend. His calculation of relative price strength used the percentage changes from wave highs to lows and lows to highs of each stock versus those of the Wyckoff Waves. Those stocks that consistently outperformed in each Wave in the direction of the longer Wave trend were the ones to analyze further.

3. To determine the potential of those selected so far, Wyckoff used the point-and-figure horizontal count. At the same time, a stop level was established, and for the stock to be considered further, a three-to-one ratio of potential gain to potential stop loss was necessary.

4. To determine if the stock is ready to move, shorter-term considerations were needed to analyze the nature of its price action. To do this, Wyckoff relied on volume, range, and to some extent, short-term momentum. This portion of his method relied heavily on experience and judgment.

5. To time the entry, Wyckoff based his decision on the turning in the overall market. His basis for this principle was that most stocks move with the market direction, and to time with the market change just reduces the risk of error.

CONCLUSION

Trading is often focused on very few issues because each must be watched very closely and intently. Selecting the issues most suitable for a trader depends on many factors having to do with the trader's time horizon, liquidity, volatility, preferred market, technical methods, operating costs, and risk tolerance. Those traders who look for special opportunities in the market rather than concentrate on a small number of issues are often swing traders who hold their positions for a few days or weeks. They use screens based principally on technical action such as patterns, gaps, breakouts from prior highs and lows, and changes in volume or volatility to select issues. Their equipment is able to scan through large numbers of issues looking for such indications of trend change. As might be expected, these methods are not often used by amateurs because they must be followed each day all day, though swing trading setups can often be recognized at night and orders placed for the next day while the trader is otherwise occupied.

In investment selection, as in fundamental screening for issues in which to invest, technical screening can begin with the overall picture, the top-down approach, or it can begin right with the individual issues in the markets that the investor is most interested in, the bottom-up approach. Of course, rather than analyze economics and company financial data, the technical analyst regards the price action of the areas of interest. In the top-down approach, the analyst begins with the long, secular period of economic activity and studies the relative action of the four basic investment segments—currencies, materials prices, interest rates, and stock markets. From the results of that analysis, the analyst can then further analyze the sectors of those markets showing the most promise. At all times, focus is placed on the best-acting areas for investment because they have consistently been shown to continue with such strength, similar to the behavior of trends on an absolute basis. The bottom-up approach is most often accomplished specifically for the stock markets because they have so many different issues from which to choose. This analysis is likewise centered around what is called relative strength to determine the best acting issues over a specified past lookback period, usually around six months, with anticipation that those selected issues will continue to outperform over the following year. Relative strength has been widely tested both in academia and in practice and has shown consistent reliability.

REVIEW QUESTIONS

1. Explain the differences among scalping, day trading, and swing trading.
2. A trader should consider a particular instrument's volatility, liquidity, and volume when choosing instruments to trade. Explain why each of these three characteristics is an important component of the trader's decision.
3. Explain the difference between a hard asset market and a soft asset market.
4. Explain the basic premise of secular analysis and its importance to the investor.
5. Explain the basic principle behind cyclical analysis and its importance to the investor.

6. Lauren inherited $10,000 and immediately invested the money in the stock market. Unfortunately, she lost 30% of her investment. Explain why she will have to have a return greater than 30% to get back to her initial capital level of $10,000.

7. Explain what is meant by the term *relative strength* in this chapter and the implications of a stock's relative strength for the investor.

8. Andrew has been following the performance of the stock of his favorite company, Back Country Driving Equipment (BCDE). He has plotted the ratio of BCDE to the S&P 500 for the past year, and he has found a strongly upward-sloping line. He thought that this meant that BCDE was a relatively strong stock; however, he noticed that investors in BCDE have lost money over the past year. He is confused as to how investing in a relatively strong stock could result in a loss. Explain how this could happen.

PART VIII

SYSTEM TESTING AND MANAGEMENT

CHAPTER 22 SYSTEM DESIGN AND TESTING

CHAPTER 23 MONEY AND RISK MANAGEMENT

SYSTEM DESIGN AND TESTING

CHAPTER OBJECTIVES

By the end of this chapter, you should be familiar with

- The importance of using a system for trading or investing
- The difference between a discretionary and a nondiscretionary system
- The mind-set and discipline required to develop and trade with a system
- The basic procedures for designing a system
- The role that risk management plays in system design
- How to test a system
- Standard measures of system profitability and risk

We have covered most of the methods used by technical analysts to analyze the trading markets. We now enter into the field of how to utilize this knowledge to produce profits and reduce risk. Any constant and consistent management of assets requires money management, which we cover in the next chapter, and some type of system. Haphazardly investing or trading on intuition, rumor, or untested theories is a road to disaster. It is why most amateur traders and investors lose money.

A fundamental investor may use price-to-earnings, debt ratios, and so forth, whereas a technical investor will likely use relative strength, price trend, or volatility, and both investors will believe they are doing the correct analysis. They are not. In both cases, the methods may be correct, but making money requires a tested system. There are many myths in investing, and most investors succumb to them without further analysis. To trade or invest successfully, we need to know not only how profitable a method has been, but also what the risks of capital loss were. Not having an understanding of tested methods is flying blind in the financial markets. How do we test these methods? We create a system. The system must include not only the method for profit but also the means of controlling risk of loss. Both aspects of investing are extremely important. Some would argue that controlling loss is even more important than the profit method, that by buying and selling at the flip of a coin, one could make a decent return just by controlling risk of loss.

Let us begin this chapter by looking a little more closely at what a system is. Then, we focus on what risk is and how to control losses. Once we have these foundations, we can focus on the mechanics of developing a system and testing investment strategies.

WHY ARE SYSTEMS NECESSARY?

No stock market goes up forever. Indeed, most world stock markets have declined to zero at one time or another. The buy-and-hold strategy so popular in the U.S. today is based on a statistical anomaly. It is a strategy based on a survival bias in the U.S. and the U.K. markets, the only countries in history, so far, whose markets have not completely disappeared at some time (Burnham, 2005). This has caused a misleading assumption that U.S. stocks and stocks in general will necessarily continue to rise. "It would be naïve to expect the future of U.S. stocks to be as bright as the past" (Burnham, 2005, p 175).

We certainly know that individual stocks can go to zero. How about buggy whips in 1910, or canals in 1830, or bowling in 1950, or junk bonds and REITs in 1980, or more recently the autos and the banks? Thus, a long-term plan that excludes a means of controlling risk is eventually doomed.

On the other hand, most technical and fundamental methods, by themselves, are not profitable over time either. Some of the exceptions have been covered earlier in this book, but these methods primarily depend upon the market circumstances at the time, on the method used, and on controlling risk. Traders' and investors' greatest misconception is that the market has order and that by finding and acting on that order, profits will be consistent and large. It presumes that a magic formula exists somewhere that can predict markets. This belief is not true. In looking at the previous studies in this book, there is no magic order to the markets beyond the fact that they sometimes trend and, more often, remain in trading ranges. The money made is based on the use of well-controlled entries and exits, especially those that limit the amount of loss that can occur and that will react to changing conditions in the market. A system will aid the investor or trader in timing these market entries and exits.

Discretionary Versus Nondiscretionary Systems

Systems are the next step in the development of an investment plan after understanding the methods of either technical or fundamental investing. Systems can be discretionary, nondiscretionary, or a combination of both. In discretionary systems, entries and exits are determined by intuition; in other words, the trader or investor exercises some discretion in making trades. Nondiscretionary systems are those in which entries and exits are determined mechanically by a computer.

Think for a minute of the stereotypical discretionary trader. Imagine the ultimate discretionary trader behaving like the man in the antacid advertisement with two or three phones yelling, "buy" in one, "sell" in another, with computer screens showing prices and charts of securities all over the world, with ringing phones, with news broadcasts from financial TV stations, and with a large contact list of people in different specialties. This type of trader is generally looking for the home run. It is a great image, one that has in it a bit of the swashbuckler, the gunslinger, and so on. In fact, many truly exceptional traders are like this. They have the gifted intuition to be able to do this consistently and profitably.

Most people, however, do not have the time, the knowledge, the contacts, the equipment, the quickness of thought, or the stomach to do this. In fact, most people who attempt to trade like this either burn out or go broke. They have no way of evaluating what they are doing except from the equity in their account at the end of the day. It is as if the excitement is more important than making profits.

The nondiscretionary trader, on the other hand, is usually calm, calculating, and likely bored. The majority of successful traders and investors use nondiscretionary systems (Etzkorn interview of Babcock, 1996). Some have been engineers; others have that type of mind, familiar with statistics and systems. They have studied the markets, the methods of profit making—both fundamental and technical—and have tested the techniques using modern statistical methods. They understand that nothing is perfect and that markets change character over time. However, by testing their methods and strategies, they have derived a mechanical system that minimizes risk of loss and maximizes return.

Rules are the structure of a system. An example of a rule would be "buy when one moving average crosses above another." Variables are the quantities used in the rules—two moving averages, and parameters are the actual values used in the variables—two days and seven days. A system will include all these factors, and their usefulness is determined by testing different rules, variables, and parameters over varied markets and market conditions.

A purely nondiscretionary system is one that runs by itself on market data that is continually fed into it. If our rule is to buy when the two-day moving average crosses above the seven-day moving average, for example, a buy order automatically is placed when this occurs. Once the trader has determined the rule to follow, the system is on autopilot and the trader does not make decisions.

A trader or investor can also choose to use a partial discretionary system. The partial discretionary system is one that generates signals that then are acted upon by the investor based on personal confidence in them and experience with them. By having some discretion, however, the system cannot be tested accurately because emotion can enter into the trading decisions and cause unquantifiable errors.

Is it always better to choose a nondiscretionary, mechanical system over a discretionary one? Let us look at some of the advantages and disadvantages of this approach.

Benefits of a Nondiscretionary, Mechanical System

A nondiscretionary, mechanical system provides a mathematical edge as determined by testing and adjusting. This is the principle behind the casino and an insurance business, both of which profit from many small profitable trades and occasional losses.

Using a nondiscretionary system avoids emotion. This is an advantage because traders often lose money due to emotional decisions. The nondiscretionary system also reduces other trading pitfalls—overtrading, premature action, no action, and constant decision making. Trading with a properly designed mechanical system also prevents large losses and risk of ruin, which most traders have never quantified or understood. In fact, risk control can be one of the most important advantages of a mechanical system.

Trading with a nondiscretionary system also provides certainty, develops confidence, and produces less stress. Anxiety comes from uncertainty. Although a nondiscretionary system cannot predict the future, it can structure how to react to possible outcomes. It gives a list of responses to events beyond one's control.

Pitfalls to a Nondiscretionary, Mechanical System

Though there are many benefits to a nondiscretionary, mechanical system, pitfalls also exist. For one, extrapolating will not have the same results as tests; history does not repeat itself precisely. The more a system is optimized or curve-fitted, the less reliable it will be in the future. In fact, in their book, *The Ultimate Trading Guide,* Hill, Pruitt, and Hill (2000) suggest that you should generally expect half the profits and twice the drawdowns as shown in tests of past data. Having been tested, the system designer expects results that are often unrealistic. The designer must be careful not to lose confidence when unrealistic expectations are not achieved.

Nondiscretionary systems often will make profits in clumps, especially if it is a trend-following system. The trader then loses small amounts waiting for the next clump and protecting from large losses. In other words, great creativity may have gone into inventing the system, but its operation is boring. In addition, some system designs allow large drawdowns but still eventually produce profits. The emotional problem for the user is the wait for the drawdown to be recovered and meanwhile the possible loss of confidence in the system. A loss of confidence results in fiddling with the rules or giving up just as the system is about to kick in.

Although a good system adjusts to a changing market, it does require periodic updates. This can often be a source of confusion for the designer. Is it time to update an underperforming system because of a changing marketplace? Alternatively, is the lackluster performance period a time for the trader to sit by patiently waiting for the system to kick in? The answers to these questions are not always obvious.

Remember that the system falls apart if it is not followed precisely. This is what the testing was for, and violations of the rules established from the testing negate the value of the system. This requires considerable discipline.

Using a nondiscretionary, mechanical system is not easy—otherwise, everyone would do it. There is a lot of work in coming up with a system, testing it, adjusting it, and trying it correctly and convincingly. The tendency for many people is to "wing it" and see if it works. That method leaves the trader nowhere.

How Do I Design a System?

Now you are convinced that you need to design a system for trading. However, how do you do that? Let us look at some of the requirements and steps involved in creating an effective system.

Requirements for Designing a System

What is needed to design a successful system? Before even considering the components of a system, we must begin with something even more basic—designing a workable, profitable system begins with some basic personal attitudes. Some of the characteristics of the necessary mind-set include the following:

- Understand what a discretionary or nondiscretionary system will do—be realistically knowledgeable, and lean toward a nondiscretionary, mechanical system that can be quantified precisely and for which rules are explicit and constant.

- Do not have an opinion of the market. Profits are made from reacting to the market, not by anticipating it. Without a known structure, the markets cannot be predicted. A mechanical system will react, not predict.

- Realize that losses will occur—keep them small and infrequent.

- Realize that profits will not necessarily occur constantly or consistently.

- Realize that your emotions will tug at your mind and encourage changing or fiddling with the system. Such emotions must be controlled.

- Be organized—winging it will not work.

- Develop a plan consistent with one's time available and investment horizon—daily, weekly, monthly, and yearly.

- Test, test, and test again, without curve-fitting. Most systems fail because they have not been tested or have been overfitted.

- Follow the final tested plan without exception—discipline, discipline, discipline. No one is smarter than the computer, regardless of how painful losses may be, and how wide spreads between price and stops may affect one's staying power.

Understanding Risk

When we set out to create a system, we are usually concentrating on profits. Remember our underlying objective is to make profits. However, we must be careful not to focus so much on earning profits that we forget about the critical concept of risk.

The amateur investor or trader usually uses a discretionary system. Testing and analyzing and evolving a workable nondiscretionary system takes too much time, knowledge, experience, and thought. Most people would rather just take the word of others and act spontaneously. Profitable professionals, however, always have a system. Although they may use a discretionary system, professionals know the results of investment action from experience and know the risks. Successful professionals always apply some form of risk control, even if it is just a series of mental stop-loss levels. Considering risk marks the difference between amateurs and professionals. Those who consider profit potential and not risk are mostly amateurs, even if they think they are professionals, and generally have or manage portfolios that considerably underperform the markets over the long term.

Risk is a vital concept, but what exactly is it? Academics have long characterized risk as equivalent to volatility. As seen in Appendix A, "Basic Statistics," the Capital Asset Pricing Model (CAPM) and options theory consider volatility not only an important variable in markets, but also a measure of risk. These ideas are partially correct, but as anyone who has operated in the markets knows, the real definition of risk is: "How much money am I going to lose?" This is how the technical analyst focuses on risk.

The amount of money lost, or potentially lost, is called *drawdown*. It is defined as that amount by which the equity in an account declines from a peak. In other words, a drawdown is how much investors would suffer if they became invested in an account at its peak value. In a specific trade, the drawdown also can be defined as the amount that the trade value declines between the entry and the exit, even if the exit is above the entry and produces a final profit. Drawdown is sometimes referred to as the "pain" of holding a position. Although volatility can contribute to drawdown, as we will see later in looking at the smoothness of equity curves, the major concern for any investor or trader is the amount that can be lost.

Remember how we saw in Chapter 21, "Selection of Markets and Issues: Trading and Investing," that a 50% decline requires a 100% advance to return to even and that a 100% gain can be wiped out with only a 50% loss. We can see a bit more of the mathematics of this phenomenon in Appendix A where we consider the geometric mean, which in this case would be 0%. This law of percentages is against the investor. Thus, a profit and a loss are not equivalent. A minor loss always requires a larger gain to offset it. The purpose in quantifiable systems is to minimize that potential loss.

Risk to the investor or trader in the markets also includes many intangibles. Loss comes not only from asset loss but also from emotional loss. Nothing is more disturbing to the psyche than losing money and at the same time being proven wrong. Both these risks can be reduced by systems. Losing money can be prevented through proper exit strategies, and the emotional loss can be alleviated through the confidence that although one may make small mistakes, one's equity curve continues upward. A well-devised and well-understood system can produce that confidence, making small losses just an inconvenience rather than a traumatic event.

Initial Decisions

Once you are committed to the mind-set and discipline of creating a system, you must make certain decisions about the characteristics of your system. The actual fundamental or technical method used as the basis for the system is relatively unimportant. What is important is that whatever is used can be defined precisely. Most fundamental and technical methods, by themselves, have a sketchy record of performance. Performance in the system will depend more on filters, adjustments, and the entry and exit strategies than the method itself. This does not mean that any old method will work. Pick one that is familiar, comfortable, sensible, and has a decent record; then concentrate on the process.

Most systems designers argue that the simpler the system, the better. A system can become bogged down with large numbers of conditions and statistically will lose degrees of freedom, requiring more data and more signals to establish its significance. Some designers such as Richard Dennis argue against simplicity (Collins, 2005), but they have enormous computer power and knowledge behind them. Hill and others argue that even with modern technology and mathematics, the success of systems now is no greater than the classic systems designed with a hand or crank calculator.

The first decision that must be made is that of trading philosophy and premises. In other words, you must decide what kind of input and method is to be used to generate signals. Some investors depend on fundamental information; most traders depend on technical methods. Others use a combination. The important aspect is to have a clear understanding of the system's premises and to know that the rules will be easily quantifiable and precise. Specificity is much easier to use and to test than generality. You must also understand the logic of the system and be sure that it suits your style of trading or investing.

Second, you must decide on which markets to focus. Is the market suitable for the intended system? Are there opportunities for diversification between markets or instruments? How much volatility and liquidity is required, and what specific instruments will be traded?

Third, you must establish the time horizon for the system. For example, most trend-following systems work better over longer periods, but most pattern systems work in hours and days. Does the system intend to scalp trades, swing trade, or long-term invest? In addition, what is the psychologically best-suited time not only for system logic but also for ease of use? Do you have time to spend all day with the system, or can you monitor the system only daily, weekly, or monthly?

Fourth, you must have a risk control plan; otherwise, you will not know what to do when markets change. Understand that losses are inevitable, but be sure to keep them under control. Admitting losses separates the professional from the amateur. Rationalizing or excusing losses never helps. The market is never wrong—get out, the quicker the better. To do this, devise a stop-loss strategy—"no clinging to the mast of the sinking ship." This strategy should include protective and trailing stops, price targets, and adjustments for volatility, type of market, and any other state that the market might be in. Otherwise, the account may suffer a larger loss. Emotions and judgment become adversely affected, causing missed opportunities, selling profitable positions to get even, and other mistakes. Stop-losses free up nonproductive capital and cause less stress once accepted. A good rule of thumb for maximum risk per trade is 2% of capital. This 2% is the difference between the entry price and the stop price.

Fifth, establish a time routine, which should include when to update the system and necessary charts, plan new trades, and update exit points for existing trades. As part of your system administration, maintain a trader's notebook, a trader's diary, and a daily equity chart.

Types of Technical Systems

Technical analysts use a number of types of technical trading systems. Although there are numerous systems, they can be divided into four main categories: trend following, pattern recognition, countertrend, and exogenous signals systems.

Trend Following

From our knowledge of technical systems, we understand that markets trend at times and trade in a range at other times. The most profitable background is a trending background because the moves are larger and generate fewer transaction costs. It is no wonder, then, that trend-following nondiscretionary systems have been the most productive. Most large-scale mechanical system hedge funds and commodity trading advisors use trend-following systems. Rather than attempting to catch the peaks and valleys, the trend-following system acts in the direction of the trend as soon after it has begun as can be reliably detected. Contrary to the buy low and sell high philosophy, the trend-following system will buy high and sell higher. Schwager believes that slower, longer trend systems work better because the gains are larger, though less frequent, and the whipsaws are minimal. Most trend-following systems add a trend indicator such as the ADX to their set of rules to be sure that a trend is in existence. However, as we know from earlier studies on trends, the performance of a trend-following system can suffer during a trading range market.

Moving Average Systems

The classic trend-following system is composed of two moving averages that generate signals when they cross over each other. In his book, *The Definitive Guide to Futures Trading,* Larry Williams discusses how as early as the 1940s, Donchian demonstrated the validity of this method and showed that it was more successful than the older system of using price versus a single moving average.

If two moving averages are better than one, would three be even better? No, studies have shown that adding more moving averages weakens performance because of the increased number of rules required. Although practitioners frequently report success using moving averages, we must mention that academic studies have shown that moving average crossover systems, even with simple filters, are generally unprofitable. However, academics have not used any kind of risk control in their experiments. Without the use of these important risk-control strategies, the academic studies are not a true measure of the profitability of using a moving average crossover system.

Breakout Systems

A variation of the trend-following system is the breakout system. These systems generate buy and sell signals when price moves out of a channel or band. The most popular of these systems is based on a variation of the Donchian channel breakout system or some kind of volatility breakout system using Bollinger Bands or other measures of range volatility. The breakout system can be long term and use weekly figures, or short term, such as the open range breakout systems used intraday.

Problems with Trend-Following Systems

Given their profitability, the moving average and breakout strategies are popular. Because many of these trend-following systems are being traded, many others will receive the same signal at roughly the same time and price you will. Liquidity can become strained, and slippage costs from wider spreads and incomplete fills will increase the transaction costs over what may have been anticipated. The solution to this problem is to devise an original system or to spread out or scale entry orders.

Another problem with trend-following systems is that whipsaws are common, especially during a trading range market, as the system attempts to identify the trend. In fact, trend-following systems often produce less than 50% wins because of the many whipsaws during ranging markets. This problem can be reduced with the use of confirmations, such as special price requirements (penetration requirement, time delay, and so on), once a signal has been given, or through filters and diversification into uncorrelated markets.

Inevitably, to avoid whipsaws, a trend-following system will be late in the trend and will thus miss profit potential at both ends of the trend. Unfortunately, this is the cost of a trend-following system. If an attempt is made to clip more profit at each end of the trend, the number of losses will increase from the ranging nature of the trend at its terminal points. On the exit side of a trend, specific trailing stops or such can be used to receive better prices, but again there is the risk of missing another leg in the trend by exiting prematurely.

Losses occur primarily in the trading range preceding the establishment of a trend, as the system tries to identify the next trend as closely as possible. One strategy to combat this is to use a countertrend system at the same time, even if it is not as profitable as the trend-following system. The gains from the countertrend system will offset some of the losses of the trend-following system, and the overall performance results will improve over the trend-following system alone.

Moving-average and breakout systems are usually limited to a one-directional signal only. Part of the advantage in following a trend is to pyramid in the direction of the trend as evidence of its viability becomes stronger. To accomplish this in a trend-following system, other indicators must be used, thus increasing the complexity and decreasing the adaptability of the system.

The greatest fault with trend-following systems is the large percentage of consecutive small losses that produce significant drawdowns. For example, let us say that the system suffers ten small losses in a row while in a trading range. The drawdown to the equity of the account accumulates during this period from the peak of the equity to the subsequent cumulative loss. A series of losses that cause a large drawdown affect not only the pocketbook but also the confidence in the system and often lead to further complications. One strategy to lessen a sequence of losses is the strategy mentioned previously of using a countertrend system. Another is to initiate only small positions on a signal until the trend is well established. Yet another is to run another trend-following system parallel that has a longer or shorter period.

Because a trend-following system often is characterized by clumps of large profits from the trend and many small losses from the trading range, extreme volatility occurs in equity. We will look at this later when we study equity curve smoothness, but the most-often-used countermeasure is to diversify into other markets or systems.

As with most mechanical systems, a trend-following system can work well during testing and then bomb in practice. In most cases, this is due to improper testing and adjusting. Sometimes the improper testing is due to unrealistic assumption about transactions costs. Unrealistic assumptions including spreads during fast markets, limit days in the futures market, and other possible anomalies may have given false results during the testing stage of the system under consideration. Remember that the popularity of trend-following systems can affect slippage; this fact often is erroneously ignored in the testing phase.

Occasionally, substantial parameter shifts will occur that the adaptive system will not be able to recognize and accommodate. Again, by diversifying by using more than one system, or using market character adjustments to volatility, such problems can be reduced.

Pattern Recognition Systems

"Every ship at the bottom of the sea had plenty of charts" is attributed to noted systems trader Jon Najarian (Patel, 1997). Using patterns requires considerable testing and overcoming the problem of defining patterns. Larger patterns do not succumb to easy computer recognition because of their variable nature. System traders such as Larry Williams, Larry Connor, and Linda Raschke use short patterns, some of which we discussed in Chapter 17, "Short-Term Patterns," and limit their exposure with specific position stops and price or time targets. Generally, such systems are partially discretionary because they require some interpretation during the trade entry.

Countertrend Systems

Countertrend systems are based on the buy-low-sell-high philosophy within a trading range. This type of system requires a certain amount of volatility between the peaks and valleys of ranges; otherwise, transaction costs, missing limits, and being stopped out on false moves chew up any potential profits. Generally, these systems are discretionary. They profit from fading minimum moves against a trend and using oscillator indicators such as the stochastic, RSI, the MACD, or cycles. The largest potential problem in trading with one of these systems is the possibility of a trend developing that creates the risk of unlimited losses. Protective stops are a necessity.

Generally, this type of system does not perform well. A number of publicly available tests, for example, of buying and selling within Bollinger Bands have been conducted, and invariably the best performance comes from buying and selling on breakouts from the bands rather than trading within them. The major use of countertrend systems is to run coincident with trend-following systems to dampen the series of losses in the trend-following system during a trading range.

Exogenous Signal Systems

Some systems generate signals from outside the market being traded. Intermarket systems, such as gold prices for the bond market, would be an example of an exogenous signal system. Other examples are sentiment such as the VIX for S&P futures, volume, or open interest warnings of activity that trigger price systems or act as confirmation of price systems, or fundamental signals such as monetary policy or consumer prices.

Which System Is Best?

Which type of system is the best? John R. Hill and George Pruitt, whose business is to test all manner of trading systems (www.futurestruth.com), maintain that the best and most reliable systems are trend-following systems. Within trend-following systems, the breakout systems have the best characteristics, specifically the Bollinger Band breakout systems, and the Donchian, or channel, breakout systems. Closely behind are the moving-average crossover systems.

How Do I Test a System?

Not surprisingly, for an accurate evaluation of any system, the data must be impeccable. Without the correct data, the system tests are useless. Data should always be the same as what will be used when the system is running in real time. Not only the data but also the data vendor should be the same source as what will be used in practice. Different vendors receive different data feeds. This is especially a problem in short-term systems, where the sequence of trades is important for execution and for pattern analysis.

The amount of data required depends on the period of the system. A general rule of thumb is that the data must be sufficient to provide at least 30 to 50 signals and cover periods where the market traveled up, down, and sideways. This will ensure that the test has enough history behind it and enough exposure to different market circumstances.

The real-time trader has enough difficulty with "dirty" data on a live feed, and this becomes just as crucial when testing back data. Cleanliness of data is another very necessary requirement. Any anomalies or mispriced quotes will have an effect on the system test and will skew the results in an unrealistic manner. Cleaning of data is not an easy task and often must be relegated to the professional data providers.

Special Data Problems for Futures Systems

Although stock data has a few historical adjustments such as dividend payments, splits, offerings, and so on, the futures market has another more serious problem: which contract to test. Most futures contracts have a limited life span that is short enough not to be useful in testing most systems. The difficulty comes from the difference in price between the price at expiration and the price of the nearest contract on that date. Those prices are rarely the same and are difficult to splice into something realistic that can be used for longer-term price analysis. To test a daily system, for example, two years or more of daily data is required at the very least, but no contract exists that runs back for two years. Of course, testing can be done on nearest contract series, but it is limited to the contract length. This is satisfactory if the system trades minute by minute but not for daily signals in a longer-term system.

To rectify this problem, two principal methods of splicing contract prices of different expirations together in a continuous stream have been used. These methods are known as *perpetual contracts* and *continuous contracts*. Neither is perfect, but these methods are the ones most commonly used in longer-term price studies.

Perpetual contracts, also called *constant forward contracts,* are interpolations of the prices of the nearest two contracts. Each is weighted based on the proximity to expiration of the nearest contract to the forward date—say a constant 90 days. As an example, assume that today is early December, only a few days from expiration of the December contract of a commodity future and a little over three months from the expiration of the March contract, the next nearest. The 90-day perpetual would be calculated by proportioning each contract's current price by the distance each is in time from the date 90 days from now. This weighting in early December favors the March contract price, and each day as we approach the December expiration, the December contract receives less weight until expiration when the perpetual is just the March contract price. The following day, however, the March contract price begins to lose weighting as the June contract price begins to increase its weighting. This process gives a smooth but somewhat unrealistic contract price; it eliminates the problem of huge price gaps at rollover points, but you cannot literally trade a constant forward series. As Schwager points out, "the price pattern of a constant-forward series can easily deviate substantially from the pattern exhibited by the actual traded contracts—a highly undesirable feature" (1996, p. 664).

The continuous, or spread adjusted, contract is more realistic, but it suffers from the fact that at no time is the price of the continuous contract identical to the actual price because it has been adjusted at each expiration or each rollover date. The continuous contract begins at some time in the past with prices of a nearby contract. A rollover date is determined based on the trader's usual rollover date—say ten days before expiration. Finally, a cumulative adjustment factor is determined. As time goes on and different contracts roll over to the next contract, this spread between contracts is accumulated and the continuous contract price adjusted accordingly. With this method, the continuous prices are exactly what would have been the cost to the trader had the system signals been followed when they occurred. There is no distortion of prices. Price trends and formations occur just as they would have at the time. The only difference is that the actual prices are not those in the continuous contract. Percentage changes, for example, are not accurate. Nevertheless, the method demonstrates exactly what would have happened to a system during the period of the continuous contract, precisely what the systems designer wants to know.

As Schwager points out, "a linked futures price series can only accurately reflect either price *levels,* as does the nearest futures, or price *moves* as does continuous futures, but not both…" (1996, p. 669). Students interested in trading futures can refer to the book, *Schwager on Futures: Technical Analysis,* to learn more about these techniques.

Testing Methods and Tools

Fortunately, the wheel need not be reinvented when it comes to testing software. Many trading software products include a testing section. Some are reliable; however, some are not. Before purchasing any such software, you should understand the testing methods and resulting reports of the software. Almost all such programs leave out crucial analysis data and may often define terms and formulas differently from others. For example, the term "drawdown" has different meanings, depending on intraday data, closing data, trade close data, and so forth. You must understand the meaning of all terms in any software program to correctly interpret tests performed by it. With this in mind, the systems analyst must establish exactly what information is desired, what evaluation criteria would be useful, and how the results should be presented.

Test Parameter Ranges

The initial test of a system is run to see if the system has any value and, if so, where the problem areas might lie. When the testing program is run, the parameters selected initially should be tested to see if they fall in a range or are independent spikes that might or might not occur in the future. A parameter range, called the parameter set, that gives roughly the same results bolsters confidence in the appropriateness of the parameter value. If, when the parameter value is changed slightly, the performance results deteriorate rapidly, the parameter will not likely work in the future. It is just an aberration. When the results remain the same, or similar, the parameter set is said to be stable—obviously a desirable characteristic.

BOX 22.1   DESIGNING A SYSTEM—THE "NERVES OF STEEL SYSTEM"

Let us look at a simple case study of how to develop a trading system. Suppose we decide that we will trade U.S. Steel Corporation common stock (X), traditionally a less volatile blue chip. We also decide that we will start with a simple Donchian channel breakout system on weekly highs and lows data.

Looking at the monthly chart of X (see Figure 22.1) from 2000 through mid-2010, we see many periods of upward and downward trends and trading ranges. This is an ideal history to analyze and test because it includes the three possible trends in any market: up, down, and sideways. It also covers a period more than nine years, roughly 500 weeks, enough to give us plenty of signals.

Created using TradeStation

FIGURE 22.1   U.S. Steel Corporation common stock price (monthly: January 2000–July 2010)

continues

continued

The Donchian channel breakout system gives a buy signal when the weekly closing price breaks above the highest price over the past 4 weeks. The sell signal occurs when the weekly closing price breaks below the lowest price over the past 4 weeks. Some public systems use 20 trading days, an approximation of 4 weeks, but we will be more conservative and wait for the weekly signals. We will use 4 weeks initially, the standard starting point in this system. We will trade 100 shares of stock in each entry and exit. There will initially be no stops or any other exit criteria other than the opposite signal. This is called a "Stop and Reverse" (SAR) system, and funds are invested at all times, either long or short.

The equity curve for this system is shown in Figure 22.2. An *equity curve* is a chart of the equity in the account (vertical axis) versus time measured either by trade number or by time (horizontal axis). In Figure 22.2, time is along the horizontal axis. Looking at the chart, we can see that system was unsuccessful for many years and only caught on in 2007 when the equity curve rose to the right as the theoretical portfolio gained from the signals. It was not a steady ride, however, as several large drawdowns occurred, and a majority of the profits came from one relatively short series of trades in 2008. We would like to develop a variation of this method that gives us less drawdowns, perhaps more profit, and a steady climb in profits over time. One of the difficulties of a widely swinging equity curve is that the investor doesn't know if the adverse swing is temporary or an indication that something is wrong with the system. It is preferable, therefore, to dampen the swings using various methods of capital risk control.

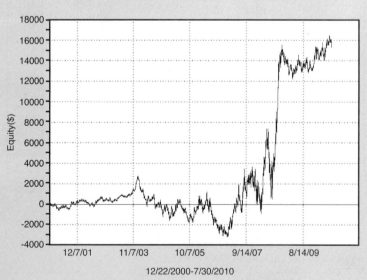

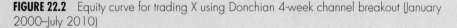

FIGURE 22.2   Equity curve for trading X using Donchian 4-week channel breakout (January 2000–July 2010)

Some tabulated data from the initial test is shown in Table 22.1.

TABLE 22.1   Nerves-of-Steel System Initial Test Statistics

Trades	All	Long	Short
Net profit	$15,529.00	$9,205.00	$6,324.00
Gross profit	$35,578.00	$17,378.00	$18,200.00
Gross loss	($20,049.00)	($8,173.00)	($11,876.00)
Profit factor	1.77	2.13	1.53
Number of trades	74	37	37
Percent profitable	39.2%	51.35%	27.03%
Average trade net profit	$209.85	$248.78	$170.92
Largest winner as a % of gross profit	35.75%	30.36%	69.88%
Largest loser as a % of gross loss	10.90%	26.75%	16.71%
Maximum consecutive losing trades	6	3	1
Average weeks in winning position	12.6	12.7	12.4
Average weeks in losing position	4.6	4.9	4.4
Buy-and-hold return	154.27%		
Return on account	275.63%		
Monthly average return	$404.75		
Standard deviation of monthly return	$1,986.58		
Sharpe ratio	(0.3)		
Maximum drawdown (intraday)	($6,832.00)	($5,832.00)	($8,115.00)
Maximum trade drawdown	($2,186.00)	($2,186.00)	($1,985.00)
Net profit as a % of drawdown	275.63%	605.01%	88.11%

Source: TradeStation

Let's look at some of these statistics and learn what they tell us about the Nerves-of-Steel system so far:

- **Net profit** is the difference between gross profit and gross loss. It is positive for this system and gives the impression that the system has some merit.

- **Gross profit and gross loss** are the totals under each category for each trade. Gross profit is the total profit from profitable trades; gross loss is the total from all losing trades.

- The **profit factor** is the absolute value of the ratio of gross profit to gross loss. It shows the profitability of the system. In this case, for every dollar of loss, 1.77 dollars of profit are generated. If the profit factor is less than one, the system is losing (and net profit would be negative).

continues

continued

- Looking at the **number of trades,** this system generated 74 trades: 37 long trades and 37 short trades. This is a large enough number of trades for reliable statistics. Generally, at least 30 to 50 trades are required to test a system.

- **Percent profitable** is the percent of all trades that were profitable. In our example, only 39.2% of the trades were profitable. It is typical for a trend-following system to have less than 50% of the trades profitable. When a low percentage of the trades is profitable, it suggests many small losses and large drawdowns—in other words, high risk. If we can increase the percentage of profitable trades, we can lower the risk profile and reduce the risk of ruin.

- **Average trade net profit** is the average profit received per trade. If this is particularly small, it suggests that the system is vulnerable to transaction costs. In this system, the average profit should cover any incidental costs.

- The **largest winner or loser versus gross profit or gross loss** figure gives a hint as to whether the gain or loss was accounted for by only one trade. In this case, the largest winning trade accounted for 36% of the total gross profit. On the short side, the largest winner accounted for almost 70% of the gross profit. Although this is characteristic of trend-following systems, which tend to make profits in large but few clumps, it suggests that the system is highly dependent on finding that one or two hugely profitable trades. Over a period of nine years, it means that a lot of waiting will be done by the system user.

- The **maximum consecutive losing trades** is important because a long string of consecutive losses invariably causes a large drawdown and, thus, a high potential risk for the system. In this case, the number of successive losses is six trades in a row. In trend-following systems, the number of successive losses is usually high and is one reason that the systems user must have complete confidence in the system.

- Considering the **average weeks in winning and losing positions**, there is not much question that the Nerves-of-Steel system has produced many profits and short-term losses but most likely for less than a year. From a capital gains tax standpoint, this could cause an extra tax burden.

- **Buy-and-hold return (154%)** is the return gained if the investor bought the stock on the first day and held it for the entire time period through all its gyrations.

- **Return on account (276%)** is the total return on the minimum account size as determined by the maximum drawdown. It should be compared to the buy-and-hold return to see if the system outperforms a do-nothing approach. In this case, the system exceeded the do-nothing approach, which is a favorable sign. Of course, such comparisons are not as easy as they look because the concept of risk has not been introduced to either method. The buy-and-hold method has infinite risk because the drawdown can be 100%, while the risk of the system has been limited to a much smaller percentage.

- **Average monthly return and standard deviation** of the monthly return are used to determine the volatility of returns. The average monthly return for this system is $404.75, but it is highly volatile with a standard deviation of $1,986.58. Ideally, a system should have a standard deviation less than five times the monthly return. In this case, it is 4.90 times, just under the limit.

- The **Sharpe ratio** is a common measure of the return versus risk of a portfolio or system. As we saw in Chapter 21, it is a ratio of return—in this case, adjusted for the risk-free return of T-bills, to the standard deviation of return, a proxy for risk. As we stated earlier, however, risk is not just variability, but is also the risk of capital loss. The Sharpe ratio fails to account for drawdown and fails to account for skewed deviations of return. An investment that deviates more to the upside, for example, will not be fairly represented by the Sharpe ratio, which assumes a normal distribution. These problems are why system designers shy away from the Sharpe ratio and have designed other ratios of return to risk that are more realistic. In this system, the Sharpe ratio is close to zero, suggesting that the return does not exceed the risk-free return of T-bills.

- **Maximum drawdown** is the maximum amount that the equity curve corrected from a peak. Assuming the future returns remain similar to the period tested, it is the likely maximum risk of capital loss from the system.

- Naturally, one wants a system that has no drawdown, but barring that, one wants a system that has profits considerably higher than any drawdown potential. The current case has a percentage of 276%, a particularly favorable ratio considering that this is the first try at the system. The standard is anything above 200%, depending on the length of the period studied. In the current case, the period is particularly long, and a higher net profit to maximum drawdown should be expected. It, thus, becomes a gauge for comparing systems, and a common ratio for that is the **Net Profit as Percentage of Maximum Intraday Drawdown** (see Table 22.1).

The Nerves-of-Steel system shows promise. It has returned, in its raw state, over 1.8 times the buy-and-hold. However, it also has some problems, namely that took a long time to get going, and once it did it was volatile and suffered from some large drawdowns. We look next at ways to improve this system.

OPTIMIZATION

Once you determine that the parameters in your system are valid, you may optimize the system. *Optimizing* is simply changing the parameters of a system to achieve the best results. The most important benefit of optimization is that the designer may find parameters that do not work under any circumstances. If parameters do not work with the past data, it is highly likely they will not work in the future. Thus, optimizing can eliminate useless rules and parameters.

Optimizing is also useful in determining whether certain types of stops are useful. Often the designer finds that there is a limit—for example, to a protective stop—beyond which the stop does not add to the system performance. Often, the distance of trailing stops is too close to the last price, causing premature exits. These determinations can be analyzed more closely with optimization.

Although it can be beneficial, optimization does come with hazards. With modern computers and sophisticated software, we can take any series of prices and find the best parameters for any predefined system. The problem is that by doing such an optimization, we are just fitting the data to a curve of results and have no idea whether the parameters we have derived will perform in the future. Because the future is what we are attempting to control, most optimization is useless and even dangerous because it gives us a false sense of confidence.

The principal concern with optimization is the tendency to "curve-fit." Curve-fitting occurs when the optimization program finds the absolute best set of parameters. What the program is really doing is fitting the parameters to the data that is being tested. Thus, it is forming a mathematical model of that data and fitting parameters to that particular time in history. The only way that the parameters will work in the future is if the future exactly duplicates the history that was optimized. Of course, we know this will never happen and, thus, the parameters determined by optimization will be useless in the future. Any system could be made to look profitable if optimized; this is a problem that buyers of systems must face when considering purchasing an existing system for investing or trading. The trick is to optimize over a certain period and then test the parameters derived through optimization on a period in which no optimization has been conducted. This is called out-of-sample (OOS) testing. Invariably we will find that the results in the optimization will overstate the results in the out-of-sample period and, thus, the optimized parameters should never be used to evaluate the system's usefulness. Optimization should be kept simple. Fine-tuning the system just increases the level of false confidence that eventually will be dashed in real time when the system fails.

There is, thus, some controversy about the use of optimization in arriving at workable mechanical systems. The basic principles of realistic optimization are to keep it simple, test out-of-sample data against in-sample optimization results, preferably use baskets of securities, determine parameter sets instead of single parameters, understand that the best results are high profits with minimal risk, and do not expect to find the Holy Grail. Next, we discuss some optimization methods and some tests for statistical significance to perform after the most realistic parameter sets have been determined.

Methods of Optimizing

As a general rule, an optimization should be done over a considerable period of price data and include those periods when the prices are in trends and in trading ranges. We do not know ahead of time whether the future will be similar, but we do know that there will be trends and trading ranges. Any system must be able to deal with both of these situations and have developed adjustable parameter sets or rules that will account for them. Parameters determined in this manner should be suitable for future conditions.

Whole Sample

One method of optimizing is to take the entire price sample and run an optimization of the parameters. This is usually frowned upon because it is the closest to curve-fitting. To avoid this, the optimization is on a basket of securities—either futures or stocks—rather than a market average or single issue and over a long enough period to generate a large number of trades. The diversification of securities reduces the likelihood that any results are solely the result of peculiarities in a particular security, and the large number of signals increases the statistical significance of the results. After determining the optimal parameter sets, those that are consistent and give decent results (but not necessarily the best results), the next step is to divide the optimization period roughly into tenths and run a test on each period using the derived parameter sets. The results from these ten different periods then can be analyzed for consistency to see if the system generated similar results under all conditions. Things to look for are the amount of drawdowns, the number of signals, the number of consecutive losses, the net profit as a percentage of maximum drawdown, and so on. The actual amount of net profit is less important for each stage than are the determinants of risk and the consistency of results (Ruggiero, 2005). If the results are not consistent, the system has a major problem and should be optimized using other means or discarded.

Out-of-Sample Optimization (OOS)

This is a method most often used in neural network and regression studies. We do not cover these particular methods because they are more useful with other data series. They can be used in market analysis, and some people, such as Lou Mendleson (www.profittaker.com), claim to have successfully been able to correlate different markets using neural network patterns. However, for purposes of this study of optimization, we ignore neural networks, multiple regressions, and others such as genetic algorithms, expert systems, and artificial intelligence. Instead, we focus on the most common and productive methods, those used by the majority of systems designers.

One variation of OOS that is commonly used is to take the entire price data series to be optimized and divide it into sections, one of 70%–80% of the data to be used to develop the system called the "in-sample" data, and one of 20%–30% called the "out-of-sample" data. The out-of-sample data can include the first small portion of the total period and the last, or just the last, most recent data. As with all other test methods, the sample must include bull, bear, and consolidation periods. The total amount of data necessary is large in all optimization processes. This is especially true for daily data since the beginning of the stock market rise in the early 1980s to 2000. The trend then was so strongly upward that systems designed using that data for optimizing often fell apart during the decline from 2000 to 2002. This was because the tested data did not include many examples of declining or trading markets. All must be included so that the system can learn to adjust to any future change in direction or habit.

This method of OOS optimizes the in-sample data and then tests it on the out-of-sample data. The out-of-sample results are theoretically what the system should expect in real time. Invariably, the out-of-sample performance will be considerably less than the performance generated in the optimization. If the out-of-sample results are unsatisfactory, the method can be repeated, but the more that the out-of-sample results are used as the determinant of parameter sets, the more that the objectivity of the optimization is compromised and the closer to curve-fitting the process becomes. Eventually, if continued in this manner, the out-of-sample data becomes the same as the sample data, and the optimization is just curve-fitting. One other method of reducing the effect of curve-fitting is to use more than one market as the out-of-sample test. It is difficult to have the same parameter set in different markets and at the same time curve-fit. This appears counterintuitive because most analysts would think that each market is different, has its own personality, and requires different parameters. Indeed, when looking at publicly available systems for sale, one method of eliminating a system from consideration is if it has different parameters for different markets. This usually indicates that the results are from curve-fitting, not real-time performance. A reliable system should work in most markets.

Walk Forward Optimization

Walk forward optimization is also an OOS method that uses roughly the same kind of price data series as the one described previously. In the walk forward method, the in-sample data is also 70% to 80% of the entire series but is usually the first portion of the series, and the more recent 20% to 30% is the out-of-sample data. Although there are many variations of this method, the most common procedure is to optimize the in-sample data and then test it on a small period of the out-of-sample date—for example, in daily data anywhere from one month to one year. The results of this test are recorded, and another window of data is optimized—this time, the in-sample data used earlier less the amount of time taken for the test, a month up to a year, plus the data used in the test. Again, the results are recorded, and the window moved forward another period until the test reaches the most recent data and a series of test recordings is available. Each optimization, thus, has an out-of-sample test. The results from all the recordings are then analyzed for consistency, profit, and risk. If some parameter set during the walk forward process suddenly changes, the system is unlikely to work in the future. The final decision about parameter sets is determined from the list of test results.

Optimization and Screening for Parameters

We look next at all the different summaries and ratios that a system designer considers in measuring *robustness* (the ability of the system to adjust to changing circumstances), but first we must mention those that are used to screen out the better systems during optimization.

When optimization is conducted on a price series, the results will show a number of different parameter sets and a number of results from each parameter set. We can look at the net profit, the maximum drawdown, and any of the other statistics shown in Box 22.1. Many analysts screen for net profit, return on account, or profit factor as a beginning. They look at the average net profit per trade to see if the system generates trades that will not be adversely affected by transaction costs, and, most important, they look at the net profit as a percentage of the maximum drawdown. The means of profiting from a system, any system of investing, are determined by the amount of risk involved. Remember the law of percentages. Risk of capital loss is the most important determinant in profiting. The net profit percentage of maximum drawdown describes quickly the bottom-line performance of the system. Unfortunately, the optimizing software of some commercial systems fails to include this factor and it must be calculated from other reported statistics.

Measuring System Results for Robustness

When analyzing a system, we look at the system components, the profit, the risk, and the smoothness of the equity curve. We want to know how robust our results are. Robustness simply means how strong and healthy our results are; it refers to how well our results will hold up to changing market conditions. It is important that our system continues to perform well when the market changes because although markets trend and patterns tend to repeat, the future market conditions will not exactly match the past market conditions that were the basis for our system design.

Components

The most important aspect of the optimization and testing process is to be sure that all calculations are correct. This sounds simple, but it is surprising how often this is overlooked and computer program errors have led to improper calculations. The next aspect is to be sure that the number of trades is large enough to make the results significant. The rule of thumb is between 30 and 50 trades, with 50 or more being the ideal. We have mentioned previously that the comparisons between in-sample and out-of-sample results should differ in performance but should not materially differ in average duration of trades, maximum consecutive winners and losers, the worst losing trade, and the average losing trade. We should also be aware of the average trade result in dollars and the parameter stability. We could apply a student t test to the parameters and their results to see if their differences are statistically significant, and we should test for brittleness, the phenomenon when one or more of the rules are never triggered. Once we are satisfied that the preceding inspection shows no material problems, we can look at the performance statistics more closely.

Profit Measures

Remember that the point of practicing technical analysis is to make money—or profit. On the surface, it seems as if this is a simple concept: If I end up with more money than I began with, then the system is profitable. Actually, measuring and comparing the profitability of various potential systems is not quite so straightforward. There are several ways in which analysts will measure the profitability of systems. The major ways are as follows:

- Total profit to total loss, called the **profit factor,** is the most commonly used statistic to screen for systems from optimization. It must be above 1.0, or the system is losing. Although a high number suggests greater profits, we must be wary of overly high numbers; generally, a profit factor greater than ten is a warning that the system has been curve-fitted. As a measure of general performance, the profit factor only includes profits and losses, not drawdowns. It, therefore, does not represent statistics on risk.

- **Outlier-adjusted profit** to loss is a profit factor that has been adjusted for the largest profit. Sometimes a system will generate a very large profit or loss that is an anomaly. If the profit factor is reduced by this anomaly and ends up below 1.0, the system is a bust because it depended solely on the one large profit. The largest winning trade should not exceed 40% to 50% of total profit.

- **Percentage winning trades** is a number we use in the next chapter on the makeup of risk of ruin. Obviously, the more winning trades there are, the less chance of a run of losses against a position. In trend-following systems, this percentage is often only 30% to 50%. Most systems should look for a winning trade percentage greater than 60%. Any percentage greater than 70% is suspect.

- **Annualized rate of return** is used for relating the results of a system against a market benchmark.

- The **payoff ratio** is a calculation that is also used in the risk of ruin estimate. It is a ratio of the average winning trade to average losing trade. For trend-following systems, it should be greater than 2.0.

- The **length of the average winning trade** to average losing trade should be greater than 1. Otherwise, the system is holding losers too long and not maximizing the use of capital. Greater than 5 is preferable for trend-following systems.

- The **efficiency factor** is the net profit divided by the gross profit (Sepiashvili, 2005). It is a combination of win/loss ratio and wins probability. Successful systems usually are in the range of 38% to 69%—the higher the better. This factor is mostly influenced by the win percentage. It suggests that reducing the number of losing trades is more effective for overall performance than reducing the size of the losses, as through stop-loss orders.

For a system to be robust, we should not see a sudden dip in profit measures when parameters are changed slightly. Stability of results is more important than total profits.

Risk Measures

What happens if you find a system that has extraordinarily high profit measures? Chances are you have a system with a lot of risk. Remember, high profits are good, but we must balance them against any increased risk. Some of the major ways that analysts will measure the risk within their system are as follows:

- The **maximum cumulative drawdown** of consecutive losing trades from peak equity can also be thought of as the largest single trade paper loss in a trade. The maximum loss from an equity peak is the most common usage. The rule of thumb is that a maximum drawdown of two times that found in optimizing should be expected and used in anticipated risk calculations.

- The **net profit to drawdown ratio** is the same as net profit as a percentage of maximum drawdown. It is also called the **recovery ratio,** and it is the best method of initially screening results from optimization. In any system, it should be above 2.0.
- **Maximum consecutive losses** often affect the maximum drawdown. When this number is large, it suggests multiple losses in the future. It is imperative to find out what occurred in the price history to produce this number if it is large.
- **Large losses** due to price shocks show how the system reacts to price shocks.
- The **longest flat time** demonstrates when money is not in use. It is favorable in that it frees capital for other purposes.
- The **time to recovery** from large drawdowns is a measure of how long it takes to recuperate losses. Ideally, this time should be short and losses recuperated quickly.
- **Maximum favorable and adverse excursions** from list of trades informs the system's designer of how much dispersion exists in trades. It can be used to measure the smoothness of the equity curve but also give hints as to where and how often losing trades occur. Its primary use is to give hints as to where trailing stops should be placed to take advantage of favorable excursions and reduce adverse excursions.
- The popular **Sharpe ratio** has severe problems when applied to trading systems. First, it does not include the actual annual return but only the average monthly return. Thus, irregularities in the return are not recognized. Second, it does not distinguish between upside and downside fluctuations. As a result, it penalizes upside fluctuations as much as downside fluctuations. Finally, it does not distinguish between intermittent and consecutive losses. A system with a dangerous tendency toward high drawdowns from consecutive losses would not be awarded as high a risk profile as others with intermittent losses of little consequence.

Individual analysts will choose, and even create, the measure of risk that is most important to their trading objectives. Some of the other measures of risk mentioned in the literature are as follows:

- **Return Retracement ratio**—This is the average annualized compounded return divided by MR (maximum of either decline from prior equity peak [i.e., worst loss from buying at peak] or worst loss at low point from any time prior).
- **Sterling ratio** (over three years)—This is the arithmetic average of annual net profit divided by average annual maximum drawdown; it is similar to the gain-to-pain ratio.
- **Maximum loss**—This is the worst possible loss from the highest point; using this measure by itself is not recommended because it represents a singular event.
- **Sortino ratio**—This is similar to the Sharpe ratio, but considers only downside volatility. It is calculated as the ratio of the monthly expected return minus the risk-free rate to the standard deviation of negative returns.

Smoothness and the Equity Curve

Some analysts prefer to analyze risk in a graphic, visual manner. Two graphs commonly are used as a visual analysis of a system's performance: the **equity curve** and the **underwater curve.**

An equity curve chart is shown in Figure 22.2. It shows the level of equity profit in an account over time. Ideally, the line of the equity profits should be straight and run from a low level at the lower-left corner to a high level at the upper-right corner. Dips in the line are losses either taken or created by drawdowns.

The common measure of smoothness is the standard error of equity values about the linear regression trend drawn through those equity values. Smoothness of a system usually is affected more by changes in the entry parameters or adjustments, such as filters. Because the majority of price action has occurred by the exit, the exit parameters and stops have little effect on smoothness.

The second type of graph used to look at system performance is the underwater curve chart. An example of this type of chart is shown in Figure 22.3. This displays the drawdown from each successively higher peak in equity. It is calculated in percentages and gives a representation not only of how much drawdown occurred, but also of how much time passed until equity recovered from that drawdown. As Figure 22.3 shows, the maximum percentage drawdown in the initial Nerves-of-Steel system was a little over 7%. This chart helps us to see that a major problem with the system is not the size of the drawdowns but the time it takes for the system to recover. In Box 22.2, we outline a method for improving the system.

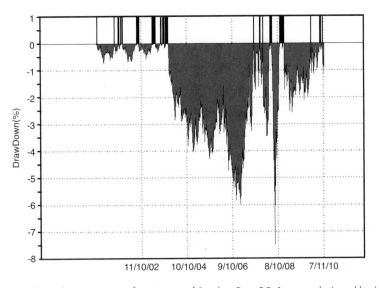

FIGURE 22.3 Weekly underwater curve for Nerves-of-Steel in Box 22.1 example (weekly: January 7, 2000–July 30, 2010)

BOX 22.2   UPGRADE IN THE NERVES-OF-STEEL SYSTEM

Now it is time to upgrade our system, based upon the results of our initial testing. To show the power of stop orders, at least in this instance, we institute several kinds of stops to limit losses. This will not necessarily reduce drawdown, however. Sometimes it will increase drawdown because while the individual losses will be smaller, the number of losing trades will increase. To see how the results can change by introducing new factors, a two-point protective stop and a 3.4% trailing stop once the stock had gained 0.2 percent are added.

Some tabulated data from the second test is as follows:

Trades	All	Long	Short
Net profit	$48,553	$28.944	$19,609
Gross profit	$57,266	$33,374	$23,892
Gross loss	($8,713)	($4,430)	($4,283)
Profit factor	6.57	7.53	5.58
Number of trades	300	182	118
Percent profitable	82.33%	87.62%	78.81%
Average trade net profit	$161.84	$159.03	$166.18
Largest winner as a % of gross profit	3.46%	4.49%	8.28%
Largest loser as a % of gross loss	2.55%	5.01%	5.18%
Maximum consecutive losing trades	3	2	5
Average weeks in winning position	1.15	1.19	1.09
Average weeks in losing position	1.39	1.48	1.29
Buy-and-hold return	154.27%		
Return on account	6,023.95%		
Monthly average return	$833.43		
Standard deviation of monthly return	$721.39		
Sharpe ratio	0.62		
Maximum drawdown (intraday)	($924)	($570)	($1587)
Maximum trade drawdown	($210)	($210)	($200)
Net profit as a % of drawdown	6,023.92%	5,077.89%	1,766.58%

Source: TradeStation

Look at how the system improves with the addition of the stops. The improvement is so large that it is likely untrustworthy, especially because we have no idea as to whether this performance will continue into the future. In reality, we would change each variable and rule one by one to see the effect on results. Rather than go through each change individually, we show the results after all changes, for demonstration purposes.

continues

continued

Figure 22.4 shows the new equity curve for the system. Notice how smooth the curve is now and how it never was in the loss column. Because stop orders increase the number of trades that are exited and then entered again, the turnover increased from 74 to 300 trades and were not evenly divided between short and long positions as in a pure reversal system. This gives us plenty of sample trades. Notice also that the percentage of profitable trades increased significantly even with the higher turnover. The profit per trade declined, of course, but was still reasonable enough to cover any unforeseen expenses, and the profit factor, the total profit to loss increased substantially. There were no extraordinary winners or losers, meaning that the system was not influenced by only one or two large trades, but the trades were only held for a little more than a week, making the profits all short-term for tax purposes. The largest improvement came in the return—a whopping 6,023.95% over the buy-and-hold 154.27%. This gain came from reducing losses with the stops and shows how the law of percentages can be fought successfully with capital risk management. The higher turnover with less capital risk produced a higher average monthly return and a standard deviation of less than the return, well below the standard of 5.0 times. This accounts for the smoothed equity curve.

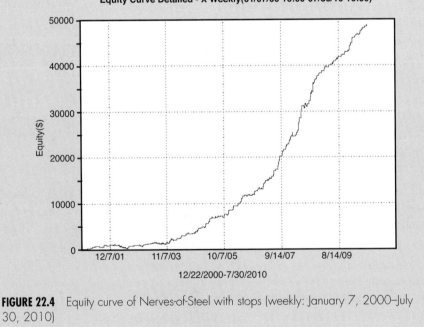

FIGURE 22.4 Equity curve of Nerves-of-Steel with stops (weekly: January 7, 2000–July 30, 2010)

The underwater curve in Figure 22.5 shows the drawdown for the improved Nerves-of-Steel system in percentage terms. This too improved except for one outlier in the late spring of 2002 when the percentage drawdown reached as low as 13%. Otherwise, the drawdowns remained in the 2% to 6% range, a level that most traders can live with.

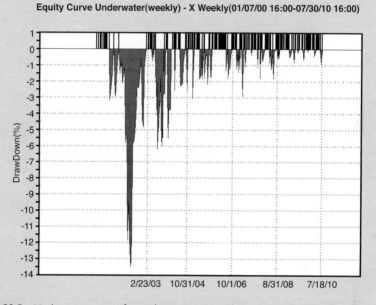

FIGURE 22.5 Underwater curve for trailing stops (weekly: January 7, 2000–July 30, 2010)

Do not use this system as it stands in any stock. It is presented only as an example of the process of looking for parameters, variables, and rules in a system development.

However, we hope that you can see the process of developing a reliable and profitable system and some of the types of adjustments that can be applied to systems, especially the use of stops, to improve performance and reduce risk. System development is a very difficult and time-consuming task.

BOX 22.3   WHAT IS A GOOD TRADING SYSTEM?

In his book, *Beyond Technical Analysis,* Tushar Chande discusses the characteristics of a good trading system. Chande's Cardinal Rules for a good trading system are the following:

- **Positive expectation**—Greater than 13% annually
- **Small number of robust trading rules**—Less than ten each is best for entry and exit rules
- **Able to trade multiple markets**—Can use baskets for determining parameters, but rules should work across similar markets, different stocks, different commodities futures, and so on
- **Incorporates good risk control**—Minimum risk as defined by drawdown should not be more than 20% and should not last more than nine months
- **Fully mechanical**—No second-guessing during operation of the system

---

CONCLUSION

Throughout this book, we have looked at a number of technical indicators to guide our buying and selling of securities in reaction to particular market conditions. In this chapter, we turned our attention to mechanizing these reactions. A system is simply a plan or set of rules of when to buy and sell securities. A system lets us determine *a priori* how we will react to particular market situations. Having a system in place helps us to follow a well-thought-out plan and prevents us from haphazardly trading based on emotion.

Of course, our basic objective in creating a system is to make a profit. Although this sounds like a straightforward goal, the goal of making a profit is not as simplistic as it sounds. Of course, we test our system to see how well it performs. But—and this is an important but—just because a system performs well using past, historical data in a trial situation does not guarantee that we will have the same stellar results in future, real-time trading. The most basic reason for this performance differential is that the market never repeats itself exactly; the system is operating in a different market environment than the one in which it was tested. There are also some system design and testing issues of concern. The system designer must be careful about data choice and not to overfit the data in the sample period. As we have seen in this chapter, even a system that has a high net profit in a test period is not necessarily a system that will perform well in the future. The system designer must consider a host of statistics about the system performance to determine whether the system is suitable for future trading. By following the guidelines laid out in this chapter, you should be ready to design systems and test them to determine their appropriateness for your trading situation.

REVIEW QUESTIONS

1. Explain the difference between a discretionary and nondiscretionary system.

2. What are the advantages and disadvantages of a nondiscretionary system?

3. How would you describe the discipline and mind-set necessary to develop and follow a trading or investing system?

4. Your brother is a physician who does not have the time to manage his own money. Knowing that you have an interest in investments and have taken a class in technical analysis, he asks you to develop a trading system for him. Before you agree to take on this job, you want to make sure that he understands the concept of risk. How would you explain risk to him, especially as it is related to using a system for investing?

5. After you explain the concept of risk to your brother, he still wants you to develop a trading system. In fact, he has done some reading and is convinced that a trend-following moving-average crossover system is the way to go. He even knows what stock he wants to trade using the system—his favorite pharmaceutical company, High Profit Pharmaceuticals (HPP). You do some initial investigation, and you think that HPP is currently in a trading range. Explain to your brother why you think it would be unwise to attempt to trade HPP using a moving-average crossover system at this point. (Be sure to explain the concept of a whipsaw in your explanation.)

6. Your brother, eager to develop the "perfect" system to trade HPP, has developed a system, tested it, and optimized it. His results show that he would have quadrupled his money last year trading his system! He is ready to put the system in place to trade HPP this year, expecting to quadruple his money. What questions would you have about his testing and optimization procedures, and what warnings would you want to give him?

7. Two of your friends, Jennifer and Michael, have developed systems to trade IBM. During the test period, Jennifer's system had a net profit of $9,578, while Michael's system had a net profit of only $8,993. Explain why this information alone is not enough to determine that Jennifer's system is superior to Michael's.

MONEY AND RISK MANAGEMENT

CHAPTER OBJECTIVES

After reading this chapter, you should be familiar with

- Definitions and measurements of risk as it relates to money management
- The martingale betting strategy
- Diversifiable versus correlated risk
- Methods for testing money-management strategies
- The use of various types of stops to manage risk
- Methods for determining the minimum capital needed for a system
- Methods for determining the percentage of capital to allocate toward one system

They [great traders] have all been humbled by the market early on in their careers. This creates a definite respect for Mr. Market. Until one has this respect indelibly engraved in their (sic) makeup, the concept of money management and discipline will never be treated seriously. (Cooper, 2004)

Money management is the next and final step in portfolio design after having established a reliable system or systems. We have concentrated on the reward side of investment because that is the more interesting and the part that most investors or traders find enjoyable. Unfortunately, the reward side is only half of the portfolio equation. The other half is money management, a much-neglected aspect of portfolio management that should receive as much attention as the reward side. We can refer to money management as the risk side of investment, the means of preventing financial ruin. It is principally concerned with how to measure and manage risk of loss and, therefore, how to utilize one's capital most efficiently. In most aspects of investing, there is a trade-off between reward and risk. Neither can be measured precisely, and the amount of risk to reward is a personal decision based on one's tolerance for risk. Everyone is happy with reward, but different investors have different thoughts on what they can accept as risk. Unfortunately, reward is not guaranteed, but risk is. A system might not return profits, but a system will always have losses. Just how much risk is acceptable, how to measure it, and how to control it is the subject of this chapter.

RISK AND MONEY MANAGEMENT

"Risk is the amount and probability of an adverse or series of adverse events occurring" (Rotella, 1992). Substituting "losses" for "adverse events" results in the following: *Risk is the amount and probability of a loss or series of losses occurring.* Note that the probability of occurrence is as important as the total amount.

There has never been a system that was 100% profitable, that never took a loss on any trade or investment. Although such a system is the ideal, it has never been achieved despite the brilliant minds, sophisticated mathematics and theories, and superfast computer abilities that have addressed methods of investment. It likely never will be achieved. The search for such a perfect strategy can become an obsession but is genuinely futile, and losses are, therefore, inevitable in investing and trading.

Ruin is also very likely. Every day some traders and investors are wiped out, largely because they did not utilize a portfolio method that included an assessment and control of risk. The area between perfection and ruin is a compromise between the gains and losses, known more commonly as "rewards and risks," of a system or portfolio strategy. As can be imagined, the possibilities between perfection and ruin are limitless and have much to do with personal preference for risk. The reward side of a strategy we can fairly well quantify, as was shown in the previous chapter on systems, but the risk side is not so easily understood. The trade-off between the two will affect the ultimate success or failure of a portfolio strategy. That is the essence of money management—to maximize return at minimum risk. No home runs, no Holy Grails, no perpetual money machines—just plain and simple, consistent profits with minimum chance of losing all of one's capital. The extremes, of course, range between highly leveraged options or futures contracts in a seat-of-the-pants, untested, untried system, and on the opposite side, strictly cash. The cash investment theoretically has no risk, whereas hotshot investments and systems are likely doomed. (A cash position does not have the risk of losing capital. Economists, however, will consider the inflation risk—the risk of the cash position losing purchasing power during inflationary periods.)

Ironically, a good system can lose money if it is not applied with concern for risk. Money management can turn it into a profitable, reliable system, but money management cannot help a system that does not work. Thus, as we covered in the last chapter, the first step in creating a portfolio strategy is to find a workable system, preferably more than one. It need not be a supersystem, just one that consistently shows higher profits than losses. It can be based on fundamentals, technicals, or both. If you read interviews with successful traders and investors, you will find every one of them has a different method or system of entering the markets, but they all have in common a money-management system to protect against loss. Indeed, most will admit that money management is more important than any system. The second step is to decide on what markets and in which issues the system will trade or invest. The third step is to combine these systems and issues into a portfolio strategy. At this point, the subject of money management arises.

Because the theories of money management largely concern price and size, the evaluation and control of risk are technical. Fundamental investors cannot assess risk in the marketplace with fundamentals alone. What should be the initial capital? What should be the trade size in contracts, shares, or dollars? What should be the risk strategies applied to these positions? What should be the execution style? Should the strategies be combined into one portfolio system, or should each system be treated separately? All these questions must be answered to manage the portfolio successfully, and all of them rely on technical studies and use of price action and signals. Generally, the systems will take care of themselves if properly tested and will give adequate entry signals, leaving the investor with the problem of how to best position from those signals and what exit strategies to use. The object of money management is to maximize the best situations and avoid or minimize those situations that can cause capital loss.

Because money management has much to do with determining the size of positions, it has also been called "position sizing." However, there is more to it than just sizing. The parameters for risk avoidance, such as stops and exit strategies, are also important, as are diversification and execution methods. We cover some of the principal money-management strategies you should know and demonstrate methods of testing for and reducing the risk of ruin.

TESTING MONEY-MANAGEMENT STRATEGIES

We covered the standard method of testing a system in Chapter 22, "System Design and Testing," but now we are looking at complete portfolio systems that include, hopefully, many subsystems and many issues traded using each subsystem with different objectives that satisfy the requirement for diversification. Of course, we should already have tested each subsystem by itself with a diversified number of issues and have confidence in its results alone. By merging it into a portfolio system, however, we now need a method to test the entire model. We will see that the model often will produce better results than any of the separate subsystems do individually. To test the model, we can use the same methodology as used in Chapter 22, or we can use what is called a Monte Carlo simulation.

Because the testing system in Chapter 22 is plagued with the risk of curve-fitting and the inability to determine the success or failure of the system under varying circumstances, we need a testing method that looks at a multiple set of possibilities and tells us how well the rule, variables, and parameters in the combined subsystems handle change. The Monte Carlo simulation is one of the better and more often used testing methods of portfolio risk.

Without discussing the mathematics behind a simulation (because it can become very complicated), we instead just outline what it does. A simple simulation can be performed on a spreadsheet, with considerable work, and a more sophisticated software program called Equity Monaco is available from www.tickquest.com for free. More sophisticated software is available elsewhere for a fee. More information on the mathematics of Monte Carlo simulations can be seen at www.montecarlosimulations.org.

As we will see later in this chapter, with the martingale betting system, a system may be profitable but the bettor must be able to withstand a long series of losses (a large drawdown). This means that the trading system results, even if spectacular from the optimization tests, could be just the result of chance or luck.

In the martingale betting system, the system is profitable only as long as the bettor is able to withstand a long series of losses, a large drawdown. To measure whether the system is valuable in all circumstances and what the odds of failure from a series of losses might be, especially because the trader usually has limited capital, the trader (or investor) needs to test for as many different circumstances as possible. The Monte Carlo simulation does not use the rule, variables, or parameters in the original trading system. It uses only the actual trades, entry and exit, and the profit or loss from each. It looks at the sequence of these trades from various angles to see what the probability of a series of losses leading to ruin exists in the system. It, thus, is a money-management test rather than a system test, though obviously the system determines the trades. If the money-management test fails by showing a high probability of ruin, the original system must be discarded, adjusted to improve these results, or other safeguards installed to prevent such a possible disaster.

The simulation takes the original trade data, profits, and losses and scrambles them in a random manner. This is done many times, usually at least 100 times and better if 1,000 or 2,000 times. An equity curve is then created for each scrambled sequence of trades. The results from each equity curve are then assembled to give the results and related to a normal distribution curve. The simulation is testing to see if the system is random and by how much. The less the system is random, the more likely it will be profitable with minimum risk of failure.

MONEY-MANAGEMENT RISKS

We have defined risk in many ways in earlier chapters. Variability of returns, amount of loss per trade, beta, maximum amount of loss per trade, drawdown, maximum drawdown, and volatility of prices have all been used. In Appendix A, "Basic Statistics," we cover some of the statistical principles associated with risk measurement in Modern Portfolio Theory. One of the principal difficulties in the use of standard linear statistics in evaluating markets is that it assumes that each price, each trade, and each profit or loss is independent. In other words, it stands by itself and is not related to any other price, trade, or trade return. When using such statistics, one must, therefore, be careful not to believe absolutely in what the statistical tests might show.

Concepts

For our purposes, the important risk consideration is loss of capital. This comes from losses on trades, realized or unrealized, and, thus, we will use drawdowns as the best definition of risk. Because drawdowns, if not controlled, can lead to ruin, our intention in this chapter is to develop means that will keep us from losing all our capital.

Drawdown and Maximum Drawdown

When we discussed drawdowns in the previous chapter, we found that more than one drawdown can occur, and it may result from one trade or many trades. If we look at all the drawdowns over a period, the one that has the highest intrapeak equity percentage loss is called the maximum drawdown (MDD). The MDD is the worst case that occurred in the system and often is used as an estimate of the worst case that can occur in the future. Of course, it could have been a fluke and exaggerate potential drawdowns in real trading, or it could underestimate and make drawdowns appear less damaging than they would be in real trading. We will find that we can reduce risk of loss on single trades with stops, but we cannot reduce the risk from a series of losses. All we can do is find a realistic estimate of the odds of a long run of losses against us and then take our chances or change the system. Even assuming a large MDD, we must design the money-management strategy such that enough capital is always available to withstand a loss in the magnitude of the known MDD. Otherwise, the system goes broke.

Drawdowns, for statistical purposes, are not independent, especially if the loss occurs in multiple systems at one time based on some adverse news. Uncontrollable loss, called "an act of God" in the insurance industry, or a "Black Swan" after the subject of the book by that name by Nassim Taleb (2010), cannot be anticipated and thus is never included in any estimate of risk. These events, however, usually only affect a single trade rather than a series of trades.

Theory of Runs

A drawdown is usually the result of a series of losses. We can estimate the chances of a series of losses using the theory of runs. This theory states that the probability of a series of independent events is the product of the probability of each event occurring. Thus, if a system has a losing percentage of 40%, the odds of a run of five losses in a row are $(0.40 \times 0.40 \times 0.40 \times 0.40 \times 0.40)$ = .01 or 1%. If a system has a losing percentage of 60%, the odds of a run of five losses in a row are 8%. Although this calculation does not account for money lost in each transaction, it does suggest that to avoid a series of losses, the lower the losing percentage of the system, the better. Even so, a large number of losses together may not be harmful to a system specifically—many trend-following systems have long runs of losses—but create an additional risk of loss of confidence in the system and the potential premature abandonment just before it becomes profitable. Psychology is a major component in trading, and confidence is usually fragile when trades are going against the trader.

Martingale Betting System

A martingale betting system often is used in a situation where the bet size can be changed but the odds are relatively even, such as gambling at a roulette wheel. The basis for the method is the theory of runs and the odds against a long series of losses when probability is about even. The method is to double up on the next bet after a loss, and return to the standard bet after a win. Eventually, a winning bet will cover all the previous losses and return a profit on the original bet. Unfortunately, the system requires substantial capital to withstand an unexpectedly long series of losses in a row.

For example, assume you make a $100 standard bet that takes the $100 bet and either returns the bet plus $100 on a win or pays nothing on a loss with even odds of winning or losing

(50% win percentage). After a run of five successive losses occurs, using a martingale system, the next bet will require $3,200 above the $3,100 that has already been lost ($100 + $200 + $400 + $800 + $1,600 = $3,100). Thus, to bet the sixth time after five successive losses would require $6,300, hoping for a win that would net $100 above our previous commitment. It is a tough way to make $100. Nevertheless, as long as the bettor can ante up the funds for the next bet in a losing series of bets, he or she will profit eventually by the amount of the original bet ($100) when the final winning bet occurs.

If the payoff ratio is greater than one-for-one and the win percentage is greater than 50%, the martingale approach may be profitable in the trading markets, but that long series of losses is always hanging out in space somewhere waiting to occur. Furthermore, in the trading markets, the profit from each bet is not constant. It could, for example, be larger for losses than for gains. Of course, a maximum loss or stop can be used to get out of the game, but by then so much capital has been lost that the chances of recovery are slim. Needless to say, the martingale approach rarely is used in trading markets.

Reward to Risk

The objective in all investment is to have a high reward to risk. Return on investment, or ROI, is the standard calculation of reward. ROI is calculated as net profit divided by initial capital at the beginning of the measured period. We have gone into more detail in Appendix A on statistics.

The standard method for analyzing portfolios and systems for reward and risk is to calculate the ratio of ROI to the MDD. This is called the Sterling ratio and is how we initially evaluated the system design parameters in Chapter 22. Some analysts use other ratios. The profit/loss ratio, also called the *profit factor,* is commonly used, and the *payoff ratio,* which is the average gain per profitable trade to the average loss per unprofitable trade, is often used. Other methods of measuring specific aspects of a system or portfolio reward-to-risk are the Sharpe ratio, mentioned in Chapter 22 and Appendix A, and percent of winning trades.

A recent myth about MDD, derived from the risk-reward relationship in Modern Portfolio Theory, is that a higher MDD suggests a higher return. This is not true. Capital risk and reward are not proportional. MDD cannot be greater than 100%, but return can theoretically be infinite.

Normal Risks

The most important aspect of money management, beyond establishing where and what kind of stops to use to protect capital, is the determination of position size for each trade. Too much in a position can incur unwarranted risks in case of failure, including complete ruin, and too little can reduce profit potential beyond the risk-free rate. Position size is directly related to capital risk, the amount of money that can be lost, and it is the aspect of money management that most traders and investors overlook.

Position Size

By "position size," we mean the amount of capital committed to a system or investment that incurs a specific risk. This is usually based on the difference between the entry price and exit price multiplied by the number of shares or contracts. As an example, let us assume we can only risk $500 in a trade. We have a breakout system that will buy a stock at $50. We place a protective sell stop at $45. This $5 difference in price is the capital risk we are taking per share. The entire position is not at risk because it will be liquidated on the stop. Without a stop, of course, we have no idea what risk we are taking. This is one reason fundamental analysis has trouble controlling capital risk. It has no means of determining when to exit a position. Knowing we have a $5 dollar per share risk, however, we know we can buy 100 shares for a total capital risk of our limit of $500.

In systems, position size has two levels of importance. The first is the determination of the minimum size of account required to trade a system with a minimum level of potential risk of ruin. The second is the determination of the optimal size of each position taken in a system that meets the predetermined risk level of the system owner. Generally, the position size in either determination is based on the maximum drawdown of the system and the margin required for a futures contract or price of a stock.

Number of Shares or Contracts

In the stock market, the question of how many shares to use in a system is relatively easy because margin requirements are comparatively small and the number of shares flexible. In the futures markets, however, the number of contracts to use can become a problem. Margin requirements frequently change. The two standard methods of determining the number of contracts are either to use the system on a fixed number of contracts or to determine the risk as a percentage of the trading account and divide that by the margin required for each contract. After a successful series of trades, if the account capital has increased, a decision must be made as to whether to continue with a set number of contracts or continue with the percentage risk proportion on a continuous capital adjustment. Some traders use a capital step process whereby the number of contracts is only adjusted when the account capital reaches certain thresholds.

Evstigneev and Schenk-Hoppe (2001) argue that constant proportion strategies produce wealth more rapidly than other proportional methods. This is an outgrowth of the Kelly formula discussed next and implies that keeping a portfolio equally proportionally invested is the best method of accumulating profits. This concept goes against the grain of some analysts. They maintain that while the system is working, the accumulation of profits is favorable, but at some time, a significant series of losses will occur, when the capital is larger than its initial size, and the losses will be proportionately larger because they depend on the proportion of the capital in the account. For now, we will go with the statistical evidence from Evstigneev and Schenk-Hoppe. They are not alone in their conclusions. As such, we will look for the optimal proportion of capital to invest in a system that will avoid the risk of total loss of capital. This sometimes is referred to as the "fixed fractional" method.

Determining Optimal Position Size

There are three methods of determining the position size: (1) Risk of Ruin formula, (2) Theory of Runs formula, and (3) Optimal f or Kelly formula. To calculate the best position size, all three formulas should be used, and that formula with the smallest percentage of capital to be risked should be the one used in the system or model.

Risk of Ruin Formula

The Risk of Ruin (ROR) formula uses three pieces of data from the historical or testing data: (1) the probability of success or the percentage of wins; (2) the payoff ratio, or average win trade amount divided by the average loss trade amount; and (3) the fraction exposed to trading.

The risk of ruin formula (Kaufman, 1998) is

ROR = $((1-ta)\div(1+ta))^{cu}$

Where: ROR is the risk of ruin

ta is the trading advantage (percent wins minus percent losses)

cu is the number of trading units, shares, or contracts

Because the ratio is always less than one, the greater "cu" is, the less chance of ruin using a fixed dollar amount. In addition, the greater the "ta," the less chance of ruin. The risk of ruin, therefore, is proportional to the percentage wins. The formula demonstrates that trend-following systems with a high percentage of losses often should end in ruin. This formula, however, fails to account for the amount of each win and loss.

To determine the optimal percentage of capital to use in any system with win and loss amounts, use this formula:

PCT = $([(A + 1) \times p] - 1) / A$

Where: PCT is the percentage of capital to use

A is the average payoff ratio

p is the percentage of wins

BOX 23.1   OPTIMAL PERCENTAGE OF CAPITAL TO AVOID RISK OF RUIN

Using the figures from the example in Chapter 22, let us calculate the percentage of capital to use from the risk of ruin formula.

Data

(p) Percent profitable trades (profitable trades) = 82.33%

Average win trade amount = $231.85

Average loss trade amount = $170.84

(A) Average payoff ratio (average win/average loss) = 1.357

Formula

Optimal percentage of capital = $\{[(A + 1) \times p] - 1\}\div A$

Substituting

Optimal percentage of capital = $\{[(1.357 + 1) \times .8233] - 1\}\div 1.357 = 69.3\%$

That is, any amount over 69.3% of capital in this system has a high chance of ending in ruin. The high percentage suggests that the risk of ruin is low for normal commitments of 2%.

Theory of Runs

The chance of going broke from a series of losses is the amount of trading times the percentage of losses to the power of the largest string of losses. Most analysts will assume a minimum run of ten consecutive losses as the baseline. In any case, most calculations end with a maximum suggested percentage investment of around 2% to avoid the risk of going broke.

Optimal f and the Kelly Formula

The Kelly formula was invented by John L. Kelly, Jr. of Bell Labs in the early 1940s to measure long-distance telephone noise and was later adopted by gamblers to determine optimal betting sizes. Its application to the trading markets is somewhat tenuous because it does not account for MDD and, thus, risk of ruin. However, it is used in conjunction with other position-size calculations to determine the optimal size of a position relative to capital. In any profitable system, capital growth increases in proportion to the percentage of capital risked. After a certain threshold in the percentage, however, the rate of growth decreases and eventually reaches zero. The Kelly ratio or optimal f is the threshold of maximum growth. Optimal f is, therefore, a method of determining the optimal percentage of capital that should be invested in a particular system.

The optimal f percentage = (percentage of wins × (profit factor + 1) – 1) / profit factor

Where: Percentage of wins is the percentage of winning trades

Profit factor is the ratio of total gains over total losses

Once f is determined, it is multiplied times capital for the amount to be used in each position. This amount can be divided by the contract margin requirement for each contract to determine the number of contracts. In the stock market, the amount for each position can be divided by the price of the shares to determine the number of shares. Because this method often suffers from extraordinary drawdowns, the percentage of capital is usually limited to 0.8 of optimal f, or a maximum optimal f of 25%.

To account for MDD that is otherwise not in the f formula, another method called the *secure f* (Zamansky and Stedhahl, 1998) is to divide the MDD by optimal f to determine the amount that can be risked on one contract or convert this amount to a percentage of capital for stock shares. The Larry Williams formula for the number of contracts to trade is to take the amount of money at risk (account balance times risk percent from whatever formula) divided by the largest single loss. A loss in the future can be controlled by stops.

BOX 23.2   CALCULATING OPTIMAL F

Again, using the system developed in Chapter 22, let us calculate the optimal f.

Formula

Optimal f = (percentage of wins × (profit factor + 1) −1) / profit factor

Data

Percentage of wins = 82.33%

Profit factor   = 5.81

Substituting

Optimal f   = (.8233 × (5.81 + 1) −1) / 5.81

                = 79.2%

This is the maximum percentage to invest any capital account in the Nerves-of-Steel system developed in Chapter 22.

Final Position Size

The smallest percentage of capital suggested by the three formulas is used as the final percentage to use in trading the specified system. Generally, because the theory of runs limits the percentage to around 2%, most professional traders use this figure, or less, as a maximum commitment to any system. In the Nerves-of-Steel system, however, the percentage of losses is so small, the odds of a run of five losses is almost negligible. Thus, the other methods should take precedence, and each shows that a substantial portion of assets could have been invested in the system.

Initial Capital

The reason for concern about initial capital requirements is the risk of a series of losses right in the beginning of the system use. The problem at start-up is not the problem of individual loss in a trade. That can be controlled with stops. The problem is the risk of complete loss of capital. This problem is related to the possibility of a run of losses that wipes out capital and eliminates the trader from being able to reenter the system. Later, when profits have accrued, the accumulated profit cushion lessens the risk of losing all, but at the start, the risk of being wiped out is the highest.

A general rule of thumb for initial capital is to have at least three times the margin required for a single contract for each contract traded, or at least two times the amount of the MDD plus the initial margin for stocks and contracts. A more precise number can be determined from the Monte Carlo simulation described previously, estimating the odds of complete failure of the system using history. As in any simulation, the levels determined from the test should be doubled or tripled as a precaution against extraordinary initial surprises.

BOX 23.3 INITIAL CAPITAL—MONTE CARLO SIMULATION

In Chapter 22, we developed the Nerves-of-Steel trading system. Now, using a Monte Carlo simulation of the Nerves-of-Steel system, let us look at a chart of the distribution of terminal equity for the total number of tests. The test period was nine years, seven months, and five days, and 300 positions were taken for an average of 46 per year. The initial price of U.S. Steel was $17.45, and we assume all trades are 100 shares. From our earlier calculations of maximum capital to risk on this system, the lowest was 69%. Taking the first position of 100 shares at $17.45 and dividing by 69% gives us $2,500, the amount of ideal starting capital based on those calculations. We set the maintenance capital at $1,000. This is the level below which our system goes broke. (We need the remaining $1,000 to close up shop and go home.) We then run the simulation to see if the system can withstand a series of adverse runs within a year.

The lower line in Figure 23.1 shows the results for an initial capital of $2,500. At the 50% vertical line, the upper line appears at $9,700. This means that 50% of the upper tests beginning with $2,500 had ending equity of $9,700 or less. At no time in the 2,000 simulations did the Nerves-of-Steel go broke within the first year.

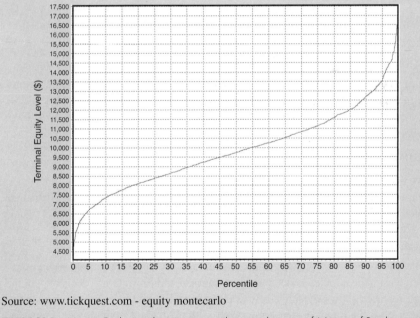

Source: www.tickquest.com - equity montecarlo

FIGURE 23.1 Monte Carlo simulation projected terminal equity of Nerves-of-Steel system

Leverage

Leverage, or the borrowing of capital to increase the potential for gain, of course, also increases the risk. Leverage generally increases the volatility of the portfolio or system and, thus, magnifies all those dangerous possibilities from increased volatility, including larger drawdowns and more potential for complete failure.

Risk is proportional to leverage. If we find that our system or combination of systems produces an MDD that is unacceptably high, we can adjust the portfolio mix to include a risk-free investment, such as Treasury bills, in the proportion necessary to bring down the potential MDD. For example, if the model estimates a 40% MDD, and we will only accept a 20% MDD, we can adjust the model to invest 50% of the capital in risk-free investments and the remainder in the systems. On the other hand, if the systems suggest a 10% MDD, and we are willing to accept a 20% MDD, we can borrow 100% of the model's capital and double our return as well as our risk.

Pyramiding

Pyramiding is a more complicated method of adding leverage to a position. It consists of adding to a profitable position to gain leverage. Of course, the risks are not as clear because gaining size in the position after it is profitable may result in a larger position just as the inevitable drawdown begins. The best manner of pyramiding is to test it within the system as a set of rules. Specific rules of thumb for pyramiding include the following:

1. Never adding to a position until its profit becomes positive
2. Placing stops at the break-even level as size increases
3. Entering the largest positions first and diminishing the size of subsequent entries
4. Being sure that the position risk is still within the limits established by the system and by the maximum acceptable position size

Unusual Risks

Before we become involved in standard portfolio risks, we must be aware of other risks that we have some control over but that will not usually show up in standard tests of performance. These are outlined next.

Psychological Risk

As we have mentioned many times earlier, trading and investing are largely psychological. The motion of investment vehicles is due largely to rational and to irrational decisions on the part of buyers and sellers. Taking advantage of this price motion through technical analysis is an emotional exercise for the trader or investor as well. The participant in the markets must be careful not to be swept up in the emotion of the crowd; indeed, in many instances, he or she must act against the crowd and, thus, against human nature. Many inputs can affect the psychological stability of the trader. Lack of sleep, family fight, sickness, or any other nonstandard outside intervention can upset one's attitude and ability to act successfully. Unfortunately, once lack of success begins, lack of confidence also begins, and lack of confidence can cause even more errors in judgment. The purpose in designing a nondiscretionary system is to reduce those outside emotional effects and let the system operate by itself. However, a losing system or series of losses can cause even the slightest override of the system; simply a change in orders, a wait after a breakout, or any other minor action unknowingly can upset the expected results even more. Many system overrides are not even recognized by the trader—just a little change here and there. Thus, there is a constant battle between the psyche and the markets. A supersystem will not avoid one's own nature. Only oneself can control one's nature. It is a risk that cannot be eliminated by a computer, only reduced, and the system must be followed religiously. Some writers argue that the psychology of trading accounts for better than 70% of success. This is likely true, but unfortunately, it is perverse and unquantifiable.

Knowledge of the Market

"I didn't realize that option expired today" or "I didn't realize that contract traded at night in Singapore" can be costly mistakes. The trader or investor must be fully aware of the markets being traded, their history, their method of execution, their various peculiarities, their people, their structure, and their operation. There is no excuse for losing money from simple ignorance. Most investors learn from experience about the oddities of particular markets, but that experience can be costly.

Diversifiable Risk

Diversification is a complex subject. As we saw in Chapter 22, the complexity has to do with the weighting amount of different vehicles or systems in a portfolio, as well as whether the behaviors of the components are similar or different from each other. Various mathematical models have been developed; but as we said before, diversification is the commonsense approach of "not putting all your eggs in one basket" that is needed. Obviously, if different vehicles or systems are used, they should not act in concert. Otherwise, they are essentially the same system, and risk has not been diversified away.

Risk is both correlated and uncorrelated. Correlated risk cannot be eliminated through diversification. We must use other means. This nondiversifiable, or market, risk is the risk generated by the overall market itself and accounts for a large portion of portfolio risk. Uncorrelated risk, however, can be reduced through diversification. Uncorrelated risk comes from the effects of all sorts of exogenous variables on individual issues and has more to do with the risk of the individual issue than the overall market. Uncorrelated risk can be reduced by diversification into dissimilar or uncorrelated issues or systems.

An example of correlated, nondiversifiable risk would be the risk that the Federal Reserve tightening the money supply will have a widespread impact on security values and impact almost any stock in a portfolio. On the other hand, the risk that a Vioxx lawsuit will decrease the value of Merck stock is uncorrelated, diversifiable risk. The lawsuit would not impact the stocks of other companies.

Reduction in uncorrelated risk can reduce MDD and enhance ROI. Indeed, the results of a diversified portfolio are often superior to the results from the best individual system by itself. The Capital Asset Pricing Model suggests that a properly structured 9-stock portfolio reduces the uncorrelated risk to that of one-third the risk of a single stock. A 16-stock portfolio can reduce uncorrelated risk to one-fourth that of a single stock. The relationship is based on the inverse square root of the number of stocks in the portfolio. As such, the portfolio can never eliminate uncorrelated risk, but with just a few different issues or systems, it can reduce it enough to make it irrelevant. The real problem then becomes the effect of correlated risk as in the debt crisis in 2008–2009 when many investments that had earlier been uncorrelated suddenly became correlated and declined together. What constitutes correlation in investments or systems, then, is a subject equally difficult to assess. Some investors believe that diversification detracts from performance because it dilutes reward along with risk. Using specific selection methods to concentrate on the investments with the most potential, they use exit strategies in individual issues to reduce uncorrelated risk and market timing for the entire portfolio to reduce correlated risk. (For more details on the mathematics behind diversification and portfolio theory, refer to Appendix A.)

One further complication in the subject of correlations is that often a lead-lag relationship occurs that is invisible to the system tester, and most correlations themselves change over time. Efficient diversification is, thus, a useful and important subject but not a simple one.

Trade Frequency

Ten losing trades in different markets is the same as ten consecutive losses in one market. The drawdown is the same. Thus, diversification can bring problems as well as reduce risk. The frequency of trading in different markets will increase the risk of a series of losses across markets.

Temporal

Risk increases with time. The longer a position is held, the more risky it becomes. This is why long-term interest rates are usually higher than short-term rates. On the other hand, in the markets, reward does not increase with time. Thus, to reduce risk, a position should not be held beyond the time that reward ends. Then, only risk remains.

Security Quality

If given the choice of trading a high-quality issue (as determined by some financial rating service) that has the same market characteristics as a low-quality issue, including volatility, liquidity, and volume, which would you choose? The high-quality issue, of course. Erroneously, quality is a concept that normally is not addressed and certainly is not a factor in most systems models.

Money-Management Risk Strategies

In addition to determining the optimal position size, optimal initial capital, and leverage, risk strategies include the timing and placement of exits.

Entry strategies carry no risk until executed. An entry can be made at any time, when the situation or setup is right, or not at all. Perhaps you would rather go to the beach. Because you must now watch your investment, you cannot go to the beach. Once entered into a position, however, an exit strategy is necessary because the position is now at risk. It is the most important action decision in any system.

Exit strategies are usually twofold: prevention of loss of capital or closing at a target profit or price. Prevention of capital loss can come after a loss, as in a protective stop, or after a profit, as in a trailing stop. There is always a trade-off between potential reward and potential risk. An exit stop placed too tightly to the trading price prevents a single large loss, but many small losses that are equally devastating can occur instead. An exit stop can also be too loose, resulting in a larger-than-necessary loss. It must be wide enough to avoid being triggered by random noise and intrinsic volatility of the issue but not sacrifice too many profitable trades. At other times, a profit may have accrued, and rather than a risk of loss, the question of stop placement or target exit is necessary. All these decisions, naturally, should be tested before the situation arises. There are advantages and disadvantages to all of them.

Slippage is a problem with stops. Any stop that suggests an exit in the direction of the short-term trend rarely will be executed at the same price as the system test suggests. A volatility stop, for example, often will occur when price volatility exceeds the estimated volatility, and a technical stop at a specific price, depending on where it is located within a price pattern, may occur along with many others and receive a poor execution. A target exit often receives a better execution and less slippage because the trend is directed into the target limit. However, it might not be executed at all if the price fails to reach the target, or the price might roar through the target and lose profit opportunity. There is no easy answer about slippage except that these potential problems should be addressed in the testing of a system.

Protective Stop

All entries must have a protective stop under all circumstances, and that stop must be inviolate. The protective stop is placed at the level of maximum limit of loss from entry, accounting for the maximum loss that the trader can allow on any one position on any one trade. It is often called a "money-management" stop because it prevents the complete loss of capital. It is determined by the level of risk that the trader is willing to take with his capital in any one position on any one trade. There are numerous methods of determining where the protective stop should be placed.

Hard Money or Dollar Stop

When we decide how much money we are willing to risk in a trade, we can place a protective money stop at a price level that reflects that potential loss and no more. In the earlier example of position size risk, we considered a stock trading at $50 and the maximum amount we wanted to risk was $500. We can buy 100 shares at $50 and place a sell stop at $45, or we can buy 200 shares at $50 and place a sell stop at $47.50. The same dollar risk appears to be present in each transaction. This is not accurate, however, because the odds of being triggered at $47.50 are higher than at $45. The consideration of where to place the stop, therefore, should be one based on the best price rather than on how many shares can be bought. Once the price is determined, the amount of shares to purchase can be adjusted accordingly. Let us say there is a large support level at $46. It would be wiser to use the $45 stop than the $47.50 stop, even though fewer shares are originally purchased, because the support level has a better chance of holding the stock from falling through $45 and triggering the stop. Furthermore, as technical traders, we know that if the support level at $46 is broken, we do not want to own the stock. At $47.50, we do not know anything about the stock prospects, and the market does not care.

Maximum Winning Adverse Excursion

The protective stop is placed to prevent loss if something goes wrong with the system. A method of determining when the system is going wrong is called the maximum adverse excursion method. Taking each winning trade in the system test or from the past real-time use of the system, one plots the frequency of adverse excursions. These are the amounts by which the value of the entered position in each trade goes against the initial value before it is closed at a profit. It is similar to a drawdown except limited to winning trades. If an entry is made and the trade eventually is a profitable one, the adverse excursion is the amount of money that the trade was in the hole before it turned profitable. Some profitable trades immediately profit. These are not a problem. Looking at those winning trades that do have initial problems, you will find that over time, the excursion from entry value reaches a limit. If the system is trouble free, that price is the level beyond which a profitable trade should not go in the future. A price just beyond that level is where the protective stop should be placed. Losing trade adverse excursions are not considered because they will become a problem and will be stopped out at the protective stop. Once the maximum adverse excursion from winning trades is established, it also determines how many contracts or shares can be entered on the system entry signal. If the maximum adverse excursion for one contract is greater than the maximum limit of loss allowed by the trader, the position should not be taken. Otherwise, the number of shares or contracts can be determined by dividing the maximum adverse excursion by the margin required for the contract or the price of the shares. The maximum winning adverse excursion should be recalculated periodically to maintain consistent with any changes in the market or the system.

Trailing Stop

With the protective stop in place and inviolate, the market issue will either trigger that stop or will begin to profit. Once a certain amount of profit in the trade has occurred, the next problem for the system is to maximize the profit without giving up too much of what has been gained. A trailing stop is used most frequently to lock in the gain.

Breakeven Level and Breakeven Stop

A trailing stop often is not placed until a certain gain level is accumulated. This is called the breakeven level, the profit level at which a stop can be placed at the entry price to lock in a breakeven on the trade but not be triggered by noise. In the preceding example, we bought the stock at $50, and after a little erratic motion, the stock rose to $55. The ATR (Average True Range) is $1.50. If we had earlier set three times the ATR, or $4.50, as the break-even level, then when the stock reached $54.50 ($50 + $4.50), we would automatically raise the protective stop to a break-even stop at the entry price of $50. This eliminates the risk of any loss on the transaction from now on. At the same time as the break-even stop is placed, a trailing stop strategy is initiated.

Another method of handling the break-even level is to exit half the position when the profit has reached the break-even level. The break-even stop is then raised to the entry price. This method locks in a profit, keeps a portion of the position open, and cannot lose capital once it is entered. The potential for profit is reduced, but a smaller profit has already been stashed, and the risk of loss is zero on the remaining portion. A trailing stop strategy then is applied to the remaining position.

Technical Point Versus Money Point

The decision about a trailing stop usually centers on whether to use a technical point or a money point. A money point stop is similar to a hard money stop described previously, only in this case it defines the amount that the trade should not lose from its maximum profit level. If $500 is the money point stop, the stop-price level changes with the value change in the market issue, such that if a correction of more than $500 occurs from the maximum unrealized profit, the system will exit the trade. A technical stop is one that is placed at a price that represents a technical level beyond which it is obvious that the trade is reversing direction. It is sometimes called a critical threshold stop (Katz and McCormick, 1998) because breaking the specified stop level is critical to the trade. Technical points often are used more in investment and swing trading trailing stops. Money point stops are used more in short-term trading, where price action is often more erratic. The market itself does not accommodate a money point stop because that level is unrelated to the market price and is a matter of the personal risk decision of the trader, but the market does respect the technical stop if properly placed.

Volatility Stop

We discussed volatility stops in Chapter 13, "Breakouts, Stops, and Retracements." A trailing stop is placed at a certain level based on the historical volatility of the issue. As such, the stop price will adjust to changes in volatility, and loosen when volatility increases and tighten when volatility decreases. It is commonly used for this reason.

Maximum Winning Favorable

A maximum winning favorable excursion, as opposed to the adverse used in establishing stops, also can be used to establish a trailing stop. The maximum favorable excursion is the highest amount that a profitable trade reaches before it is exited. It is similar to a target. A fraction of this calculation is added to the entry price, and the fraction is increased over time.

Trend Line

A trend line stop can be used because a trend line follows the price action. As a technical point stop, it has advantages in that a bunching of orders at a critical level, such as a support or resistance zone, usually is not seen along a trend line, such that when triggered, the execution of the exit will be less influenced by competing orders.

Adaptive

Special formulas, such as Wilder's parabolic, can be used. These formulas follow the price trend and adjust to market conditions along the way. They and volatility stops also are called adaptive stops, and their details can be complicated.

Other Kinds of Stops

We have just considered a number of protective and trailing stop strategies, which are generally based on price action. Other exit strategies may be employed, such as those based on a particular technical signal or those based on time.

Signal

One obvious stop is the signal stop. This occurs when the system gives a signal to enter a position in the opposite direction from the existing position. It is part of a stop-and-reverse system.

Time

Because of the multidimensional aspect of time and reward versus risk, a time stop often is used in short-term trading when time, cost of money, and opportunity cost are important. This stop is placed to exit the position a certain time after the entry. If a profit has not been gained within the time specified, the odds of it not occurring in the future increase and the position is best closed to avoid further risk. A variation of the time stop is to reduce the position size as certain time passes. This reduces the risk but leaves room for some further gain. Time stops are also used in swing trading where the trade horizon is only a few days.

Targets

In our look at point-and-figure charts and, in some instances, at bar chart patterns, a price target often is established. Exiting at a target can be an exit strategy. In short-term trading, money targets are often used: "If I make $500 on this trade, I'm out." Targets can be tested as long as the target calculation method is easily quantified. At a target, especially a longer-term target, position size may be reduced or trailing stops tightened using technical barriers, a money stop, or volatility adjustment. In addition, once a target is reached, the system might have a reentry signal that enters the position again if the target is exceeded by a certain amount or the trend continues. Finally, a combination of target and time stop can adjust the target prices as time moves along. This reduces the possibility of the added risk with time affecting profits. All target limits should be accompanied by a trailing stop to avoid losing any profits already gained in case a target is not reached.

Execution

Execution risk strategies are useful in short-term trading where profit margin often is related to executed prices and slippage. Entry execution in most instances is related to when the system gives a signal. A breakout system often has competition at the breakout level, for example. Exit execution, on the other hand, can be controlled through experiment. A short-term system must establish, when the system is not a stop-and-reverse, the time at which a better exit can be obtained. Should the trade exit on the close for the day, the opening of the next day, or at some time between when volatility usually declines? The opening is usually emotional and can be both an advantage or disadvantage. The closing is used in most systems because it is the most rational and eliminates overnight risk.

Another means of executing an entry or exit is scaling. This is done more by institutions, which have large positions they need to accumulate or distribute, but it can equally be useful for the smaller-sized trader or investor, who can accommodate more than one standard position size. Scaling is the entering or exiting a position over time in small pieces. The initial execution accomplishes part of the goal of the system, and over time, entries may be added at more advantageous prices. If they do not, at least a small position has been entered.

MONITORING SYSTEMS AND PORTFOLIOS

All systems and portfolios must be monitored for changes in behavior. The obvious change is when the system is running a series of losses larger than usual. There are methods of monitoring the system that will warn of changes, however, before any substantial loss is incurred.

Bryant (2001) suggests the following methods. Calculate the average profit factor over a moving number of trades—say the last 20 trades—just as in an oscillator such as the stochastic. Plot this calculation and then run a moving average through the plot and watch the behavior of the profit factor window to its moving average. The profit factor should always be above 1.0, and minor oscillations should be ignored. Any drift lower, however, is a warning of something potentially wrong. The recent calculation of a profit factor window should be compared with the entire history of profit factors with a t-test to see if the deviation from the moving average is significant.

Perform a test run to see if the strings of wins and losses are within a normal distribution—that is, if they are random or not. If no dependency is present, smaller size positions should be traded after a win and larger after a loss. If the test shows a positive dependency, the run streak is significant and positions should be reduced until the last trade is a win, at which point position size can be increased.

The equity curve of the system should be checked periodically. One method is to sum the profits and losses over a specified number of trades—say 30—and plot this figure in time. The sum should remain positive, or equity momentum is declining. Another common method of watching the equity curve is to calculate a moving average of equity. Breaking of the moving average is not necessarily a signal for action but is a warning. If a forward line is calculated or a trend line plotted and broken, action likely should be taken, as the system performance is deteriorating for some reason. Often when these signals of danger arise, the position size in the system is reduced until evidence of recovery is seen or the problem resolved.

The sum or average of the percent of winning trades over a specified number of trades will tell if there is a change in runs. A z-test can test whether the differences in proportions or percentages are significant and worth investigating further.

IF EVERYTHING GOES WRONG

Occasionally a portfolio model breaks down completely. Murphy's Law takes hold, and everything that can go wrong does. At that point, the remedy is to close down the system and exit all positions. A standard for closing the entire portfolio model is a dollar or percentage stop, usually around 20%. No system should sustain that amount of loss without adjustment.

CONCLUSION

It pays to understand that trading and investing are not just a matter of entry into positions. Technical signals are useful for entry, but technical understanding of risk is even more important. Remember the law of percentages and how difficult it is to recover from losses. Investing and trading are a matter of determining and controlling loss of capital. Entry is easy; best exit is difficult. Money management consists of a number of ways to measure and to protect from the risk of loss either in individual trades or in complete systems. Exit strategies and the principles of position size are likely the most important aspects of any portfolio model. Amateur investors and traders do not often utilize these risk control measures, but if they did, considerably fewer disasters to pride and portfolios would result.

REVIEW QUESTIONS

1. You have tested a system and find that it has a losing percentage of 25%.
    a. What is the chance of having a run of three losses?
    b. What is the chance of having a run of four losses?
    c. What is the chance of having a run of five losses?
2. Explain what is meant by the *martingale betting system.*
3. You have tested a system, and it has an MDD of 30%. You are willing to have a 45% drawdown. How might you use leverage with this system to maximize your return, given the level of risk you are willing to take?
4. You are employed as a money manager and know you will lose your job if your drawdown exceeds 15%. However, you have a system with a 30% MDD that you would like to use. How can you structure your strategy to use the system, but at the same time not exceed a 15% drawdown?
5. A phrase heard frequently in finance is "more risk, more return." If I invest my entire portfolio in one stock, High Growth Energy Corporation (HGEC), I am taking substantial risk because "all my eggs are in one basket." Should I expect a higher return than I would if I had diversified my portfolio because I am taking so much risk? Explain.
6. Explain the difference in correlated (market) risk and uncorrelated (diversifiable) risk.
7. Explain how each of the following items would impact the percentage of capital you would want to allocate to a particular system:
    a. Average winning trade amount
    b. Average losing trade amount
    c. Percent of trades that are profitable
8. In the words of a Kenny Roger's song, "You've got to know when to hold 'em, know when to fold 'em." How could these words be applied to money management?
9. Explain how stops are an important part of risk management.
10. Explain the meaning of the phrase, "Entry strategies carry no risk until executed."

PART IX

APPENDICES

APPENDIX A BASIC STATISTICS

APPENDIX B TYPES OF ORDERS AND OTHER TRADER TERMINOLOGY

BASIC STATISTICS

This appendix was written by Richard J. Bauer, Jr., PhD, CFA, CMT, Professor of Finance, Bill Greehey School of Business, St. Mary's University, San Antonio, Texas.

APPENDIX OBJECTIVES

By the end of this appendix, you should be familiar with

- The difference between descriptive and inferential statistics
- How to calculate common measures of central tendency and dispersion
- The process of regression
- The basic premises and statistics related to MPT

Because financial asset prices are numbers that often change with high frequency, it is not surprising that statistical techniques, which primarily concern the analysis of numerical data, have been applied to investing in a variety of ways. According to Lind, Marchal, and Wathen (2002), statistics is "the science of collecting, organizing, presenting, analyzing, and interpreting data to assist in making more effective decisions" (p. 3). In this appendix, we examine the major statistical and quantitative techniques that have been used in connection to stock analysis, although some of the techniques also apply to other assets. The primary goal of the appendix is to acquaint you with these methods, not present them in detail.

RETURNS

In finance, we often refer to an investment's return. Suppose that we buy a stock for $50, hold it for one year while earning a $2 dividend, and then sell it for $53. We calculate the stock's return as follows:

$$R = \frac{(53 + 2 - 50)}{50} = 0.10 = 10\%$$

More generally, we can express the formula for returns as the following:

$$R = \frac{(P_t + D_t - P_{t-1})}{P_{t-1}}$$

This formula can apply to bonds, options, futures, and so on. The only difference is that the term for dividends would be replaced with interest or any other additional inflow over the period.

We usually talk about return, even though the return might not represent a realized gain. Even if we continue to hold a stock, we can still talk about our return over the previous year; essentially, we assume that we did sell it and calculate the return based on that assumption. There are some important reasons for focusing on returns rather than prices. We learn about them later in this appendix.

PROBABILITY AND STATISTICS

The foundation behind most of statistics is probability. Probability is concerned with the question: Is it likely that the observed outcome occurred purely by chance? The notion of chance is tricky. It is a topic that can lead to deep philosophical debates. For example, we could ask, "Did life on earth appear purely accidentally (by chance), or was it somehow determined through another mechanism?" If something is not random, then we say it comes about through a deterministic process.

We can think about stock prices in terms of random versus deterministic. Are stock prices random? Alternatively, are stock returns random? On the other hand, are the deviations from an average return random, while the average return is stable? As we saw in Chapter 4, "The Technical Analysis Controversy," researchers have debated these questions and continue to debate these questions. Regardless of your viewpoint, probability concepts and statistical concepts are widely used in the study of investments.

One key concept in statistics is called ***independence***. If two events are independent, then whatever outcome there is from the first event does not affect the probability of the outcome for the second event. Suppose you start flipping a coin that is perfectly weighted so that the probability of a tail is 1/2 and the probability of a head is 1/2. You flip the coin five times and get five heads in a row. What is the probability of a head on the next flip? It is tempting to say that there is a greater probability of a tail than a head because flipping six heads in a row happens only rarely; however, heads is just as likely as tails on the next flip. The events of the six flips are all independent; later outcomes are not affected by earlier outcomes. If you are performing statistical tests to analyze investments, you have to consider the concept of independence. Many statistical tests assume that the events are independent.

Two mathematical/statistical terms that are relevant to investing are ***permutations*** and ***combinations***. Let us assume that we are considering investing in five different stocks: Coca-Cola (KO), Pepsico (PEP), IBM (IBM), Microsoft (MSFT), and McDonald's (MCD).

Permutations deal with rearrangements of items. Instead of listing the five stocks as KO, PEP, IBM, MSFT, MCD, we could list them as IBM, KO, MCD, MSFT, PEP. With five unique items, 120 different sequences could be listed. If we are going to buy some of each of the five stocks, the order should not make a difference; therefore, we are not as interested in permutations.

The concept of combinations has more application in investments. With combinations, the sequence is not important. A portfolio consisting of KO and MSFT is the same as a portfolio consisting of MSFT and KO. With five stocks, there are five different one-stock portfolios we could form, ten different two-stock portfolios, ten different three-stock portfolios, five different four-stock portfolios, and only one five-stock portfolio. It does not take very many stocks to generate many different possible portfolios. Using 100 stocks as the universe to choose from, there are 75,287,500 5-stock portfolios that could be formed. Using 500 stocks (for example, the S&P 500) as the universe, there are 245,810,588,801,891,000,000 possible 10-stock portfolios.

In the previous discussion, we have assumed equally weighted amounts of the stocks. For example, the amount invested in each of two stocks would be 50% of the total dollar amount invested. If we consider unequal weightings, such as 78% of MSFT and 22% of KO, the number of possible portfolios is limitless (assuming we can buy fractional amounts of each stock). You can see how different investors could decide to hold very different portfolios, even if they are choosing stocks from the same set, such as the Dow Jones Industrial stocks.

DESCRIPTIVE STATISTICS

In statistics, a distinction is made between ***descriptive statistics*** and ***inferential statistics***. Descriptive statistics, as the name suggests, merely tries to describe or characterize data in a shorthand manner. Inferential statistics tries to infer various statements about data based on observed outcomes or assumptions about outcomes. We first examine descriptive statistics.

How would you describe a set of outcomes? How similar are the items in the set of outcomes? Are the outcomes generally high or low? How are two or more sets of outcomes related to each other? Do they tend to be alike or different? Do the outcomes seem to be linked to time? In other words, are outcomes later generally different from outcomes at earlier times? We try to answer some of these questions with descriptive statistics.

Measures of Central Tendency

A logical starting point in describing a set of data is to ask: What is the typical outcome? In statistics jargon, typical outcome is called ***central tendency***. There are several different measures of central tendency, each one approaching things from a slightly different perspective.

To illustrate the different measures, assume that we have the following monthly return data for nine months (January–September 2004) for PepsiCo (PEP): 1.4%, 9.8%, 4.1%, 1.2%, –2.1%, 1.4%, –7.2%, 0.0%, –2.2%.

Mean

The first measure of central tendency (and the one most frequently used) is the ***mean***. This is what we would normally refer to as the average. To calculate the mean, we would total the values for the nine months and divide by 9:

$$\text{Mean} = \frac{(1.4\% + 9.8\% + 4.1\% + 1.2\% + -2.1\% + 1.4\% + -7.2\% + 0.0\% + -2.2\%)}{9}$$

Notice that the average value, 0.7%, is not one of the observed values, even though we are in effect saying that it is average outcome.

Median

The second measure of central tendency is the ***median***. To calculate the median, we must first arrange all the outcomes in rank order (this just means that we list them from lowest to highest). The outcome that divides the list into two equal parts is the median. In this case, the median is 1.2%. Half of the outcomes are above 1.2%, while the other half are below 1.2%. The median often is used when either the distribution of outcomes is *skewed* to more high values or more low values, rather than being *symmetric*.

Mode

The third measure of central tendency is the ***mode***. The mode is the outcome that occurs with the highest frequency. In the preceding list, the mode is 1.4%. If the figures had more decimals, like 1.368%, there would likely not be any outcome that occurred more than once. In that case, the mode would not be meaningful. This is why it is unlikely that someone would refer to the mode when analyzing stock return data.

Geometric Mean

The three measures of central tendency just described are standard in statistics textbooks. However, there is another measure of the mean that often is used in finance: the ***geometric mean.*** The mean described earlier is called the ***arithmetic mean.*** To illustrate the difference between the arithmetic mean and the geometric mean, consider a four-year investment asset with annual returns of 90%, –40%, 60%, and –50%. The arithmetic mean is calculated by adding the four outcomes and dividing by 4. Doing this, we get a value of 15%, which sounds quite good as an annual return. However, consider someone who had started with $1,000 and invested in the asset. After year 1, he/she would have $1,900. After year 2, the investment would be worth $1,140. After year 3, it would be worth $1,824. Finally, at the end of year 4, he/she would have only $912. What happened to the 15% return of the arithmetic mean? Well, this example illustrates the weakness of arithmetic means, especially when used with percentages.

The geometric mean in this example would be calculated by taking the fourth root (due to four outcomes) of (1.90) (0.60) (1.60) (0.50), subtracting 1, and getting –2.3%. The 1.90 comes from adding 1 to the decimal representation of 90%. By multiplying the initial investment of $1,000 by (1.90) (0.60) (1.60) (0.50), we get $912, which was the ending value of the investment, referred to as terminal wealth. When we compute the terminal wealth divided by the initial investment, we take the *n*th (where *n* is the number of outcomes) root of that number, and then subtract 1 to get the geometric mean. If we were using a financial calculator, we could find the geometric mean by putting the terminal value of $912 into the FV register, 4 into the n register, $1,000 into the PV register, and then solving for the %i, or interest rate. Therefore, the geometric mean return is the same as what is called the ***compound rate of return.***

It is important to understand the difference between the arithmetic mean, which is the "average" we usually hear quoted, and the geometric mean. The geometric mean has a more direct bearing on how much you will actually earn over the life of an investment. The geometric mean will always be less than the arithmetic mean, with one minor exception: They will be equal if the return is identical in every period. The greater the variability in the returns, the greater the difference will be between the two measures. The previous example, with returns changing from −50% to +90% over just a four-year period, illustrates this point. Because investors are probably more interested in a high geometric mean return than a high arithmetic mean return, a good investment maxim is: Beware of Volatility!

You will probably have minimal use for the mode in analyzing stock returns. However, the arithmetic mean, median, and geometric mean all have their uses. The mean, either arithmetic or geometric, is the most common measure.

Measures of Dispersion

In finance, there are many ways to think about the term "risk." One way is to view risk as uncertainty about outcomes. If there is more variability in outcome set A than in outcome set B, we usually consider A to be the riskier choice. From the previous discussion about geometric mean, we know that it will be harder to reach a certain level of terminal wealth with a highly volatile investment.

The two main measures of volatility are the ***variance*** and ***standard deviation.*** These are closely related because the standard deviation is the square root of the variance. The standard deviation is used more frequently because it has the advantage of being in the same units as the mean; the variance (being equal to the squared standard deviation) is in units that are difficult to interpret.

For simplicity, let us assume that we have only four years of annual returns and want to calculate the standard deviation. Assume that the returns are 12%, −5%, 21%, and 12%. We can easily add these four numbers and divide by 4 to get the mean of 10%. Next, we compute the squared deviations from the mean and total them. Finally, we divide by 3 and take the square root. This is shown next (where σ is used to denote standard deviation):

$$\sigma = \sqrt{\frac{(12 - 10)^2 + (-5 - 10)^2 + (21 - 10)^2 + (12 - 10)^2}{3}}$$

$$= \sqrt{\frac{(4 + 225 + 121 + 4)}{3}} = 10.86$$

You might be wondering, as most people do, why we divided by 3 instead of 4. We could divide by 4 depending on how we interpret what we are doing. In statistics, we talk about a ***sample*** versus the ***population.*** The population is the entire set of possible outcomes or entire set of entities. For example, we can think of the adult population in the United States. A sample is when we examine a few outcomes or a few of the entities in the set and try to make inferences from them about the entire population. For example, we could conduct a survey of 1,000 randomly chosen adults in the United States as our sample. Therefore, in our numerical example, we could divide by 4, if we are assuming that these outcomes represent the entire set of outcomes. However, because we are probably interested in what outcomes may occur for many periods in the future, we can interpret the three outcomes as a sample of the population. For some complex reasons, we divide by 3 instead of 4 to get what is called an ***unbiased estimate.*** The number 3 in this case is referred to as ***degrees of freedom.***

Initially, there were 4 degrees of freedom. However, when we calculate the mean, which we need for the standard deviation, we are said to have used up 1 degree of freedom. Because we have $4 - 1 = 3$ degrees of freedom remaining, we use that in the denominator. In our case of only 4 outcomes, the choice of 3 or 4 makes a significant difference in the answer. However, if we had, say, 101 observations, the choice of dividing by either 101 or 100 would not make much difference. It is probably wise not to worry too much about whether or not you use n (the number of observations) or $n - 1$ in the denominator; usually it will not make much difference.

With the concept of standard deviation in hand, we can now see a situation where using returns leads you to a different place than using prices. Suppose we observe the following prices for a given stock: 40.00, 44.00, 48.40, and 53.24. If we compute the mean, we get 46.41 with a standard deviation of 5.70. However, if we ignore any possible dividends and compute returns, they are 10%, 10%, and 10%. Notice that when we compute returns, we end up with one less observation because we use up one observation by focusing on changes in price. We need a beginning price to compute the first period's return. Alternatively, we need an ending period price to calculate the return in the last period. Using returns, we have a mean of 10% and a standard deviation of 0%.

If we think of risk as volatility, we now have a slight dilemma. If we focus on prices, we say that the stock is risky due to the variability, which is measured by the standard deviation of 5.70. However, if we focus on return, we might say there is no risk at all because there is no volatility in the returns, and we have a standard deviation of 0%. Which view is correct? Note that the lack of volatility is due to a strong upward trend in the price. Remember the saying, "The trend is your friend"? We have just illustrated a possible statistical justification for that statement. There is no one correct view; you just have to be aware of what is happening and the implications of it for returns compared with prices.

Relationships Between Variables

Up to this point, we have considered statistics for just one variable. It is now time to broaden our perspective and consider more than one variable. As we could expect, things start getting more complicated.

With one variable, we had a measure of variation called *variance*. The two-variable version of variance is *covariance*. It is calculated in a manner similar to variance. Let us use four months of stock returns for PepsiCo (PEP) and Coca-Cola (KO) to illustrate the calculation. PEP's returns for January–April 2004 were 1.4%, 9.8%, 4.1%, and 1.2%. The returns for KO over the same period were −3.0%, 1.5%, 1.2%, and .05%. The mean return for PEP over the period was 4.125% (with standard deviation of 4.008%), while the mean return for KO was 5.0% (with standard deviation of 2.076%). To calculate covariance, we subtract the mean from each PEP observation, subtract the mean from the corresponding KO observation, multiply the results, add them together, and divide by the number of observations minus 1. So, we get (the covariance between i and j is denoted as cov_{ij}):

$$cov_{pep/ko} = \frac{(1.4 - 4.125)(-3.0 - 0.05) + (9.8 - 4.125)(1.5 - 0.05) + (4.1 - 4.125)(1.2 - 0.05) + (1.2 - 4.125)(0.5 - 0.05)}{3}$$

$$= \frac{(8.311 + 8.229 - 0.029 - 1.316)}{3} = \frac{15.195}{3} = 5.065$$

We saw that a major problem with variance was that the units of measurement were not meaningful. The same problem exists with covariance; the covariance value is hard to interpret. With variance, we solved the problem by taking the square root of the variance. With covariance, we solve it in a different manner—we divide the covariance by each of the standard deviations. This produces a number that can only range from −1 to +1. We call this number the ***correlation coefficient.*** Using the example from the previous covariance calculation, we get the following:

$$r = \frac{\sigma_{im}}{\sigma_i \sigma_m} = \frac{\sigma_{pep/ko}}{\sigma_{pep} \sigma_{ko}} = \frac{5.065}{(4.008)(2.076)} = 0.609$$

This result means that PEP and KO were positively correlated to a reasonably strong degree over the period.

If we have observations of a variable at consecutive time intervals, we refer to the variable as a ***time series variable, time series data,*** or just ***time series.*** If the correlation coefficient between two variables is +1, the two variables are perfectly correlated. In this case, when variable X goes up, Y goes up. When X is down, Y is down. If the variables are perfectly negatively correlated with a correlation coefficient of −1, the opposite is true—when X is up, Y is down, and vice versa. What does a correlation coefficient of 0 mean? It means that there is no discernible relationship between the two variables. If X is up, there is nothing meaningful that you can say about the value of Y; it could be up or down, or stay the same.

There are two basic ways to picture time-series correlation relationships between two variables. The first is to graph the two variables against time; the second is to plot one on the x-axis and the other on the y-axis. Figure A.1 shows an example of the first type using monthly returns for Coke (ticker = KO) and PepsiCo (PEP) from January 2000 through December 2004. The second method is shown in Figure A.2.

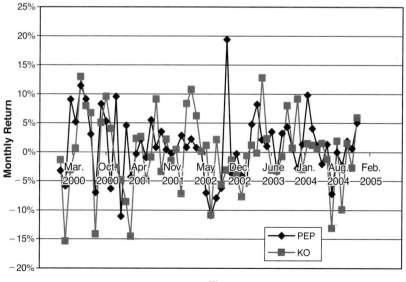

FIGURE A.1   Monthly returns for KO and PEP (January 2000–December 2004)

Look at Figure A.1. Notice that there is a general tendency for KO to be up when PEP is up, and for KO to be down when PEP is down. If the two stocks had been negatively correlated, they would have generally been moving in opposite directions. The actual correlation coefficient for the two stocks during this time was 0.489. If we draw two stocks at random from the S&P 500 and measure the correlation coefficient for their returns, a typical value would be for about 0.2 to 0.5, which we would call weak positive correlation. We would expect a higher value for KO and PEP, compared with two randomly chosen stocks, owing to the fact that they are in the same industry.

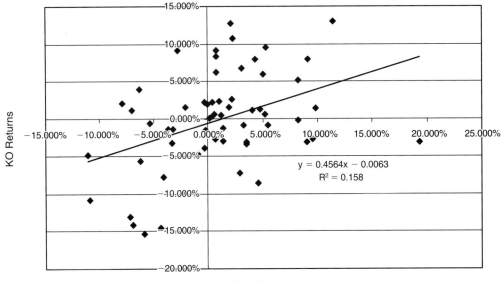

FIGURE A.2   Monthly returns of KO versus PEP (January 2000–December 2004)

Now, consider Figure A.2. In this case, we see the positive correlation from the fact that a line of best fit (to be explained shortly) drawn through the returns slopes from the southwest quadrant to the northeast quadrant. If the stocks were negatively correlated, the line would go from northwest to southeast. What if the correlation was 0? In that case, the scatter of points would look like a shotgun scatter around the center; there would be no discernible relationship, and the best-fitted line would be horizontal.

In the previous discussion about correlation, we spoke of a *line of best fit.* We were intimating about doing a *linear regression least-squares fit* through the points. Suppose we had the same data points as we had in Figure A.2 for two variables, X and Y. If we were to draw a line such that the sum of the squared difference between the actual data points and our line was minimized (in other words, the line in question produced a lower sum than every other conceivable straight line), we would call it the *least-squares regression line,* or *line of best fit.* Statisticians have worked out the equation for such a line, so that you can calculate the intercept and slope of the least-squares regression line without actually having to plot the data and experiment with various lines. The equation for a line is often denoted as Y = a + bX. Using this notation, the equations for the line are as follows:

$$b = \frac{n(\sum_{i=1}^{n} X_i Y_i) - (\sum_{i=1}^{n} X_i)(\sum_{i=1}^{n} Y_i)}{n(\sum_{i=1}^{n} X_i^2) - (\sum_{i=1}^{n} X_i)^2}$$

$$a = \frac{\sum_{i=1}^{n} Y_i}{n} - b\frac{\sum_{i=1}^{n} X_i}{n}$$

where *n* is the number of observations, and X_i is the ith observation of the X variable. The summation symbol, $\sum_{i=1}^{n} X_i$, simply means to add up all the X observations. The other summations work in a similar manner.

This can all be done extremely easily in Excel. There are several different ways to have Excel do regression calculations, but one easy method is to have it put the line and equation on a chart of the data, as was done in Figure A.2. Because we are using the KO/PEP data, we would interpret this equation as saying, "KO's returns can be estimated by taking the return for PEP in a given month, multiplying PEP's return by 0.4564 (the slope), and adding –0.0063 (the intercept)."

There is a very nice side benefit to the correlation coefficient. If we square it, we get a value called the ***r-squared*** or ***coefficient of determination.*** Because the correlation coefficient can only have values between –1 and +1, the r-squared value will be between 0 and 1 (because squaring results in a nonnegative number). Furthermore, this value is a measure of the goodness-of-fit. If we get an r-squared of 0.45, we are explaining 45% of the variability in KO's returns through its relationship with PEP's returns. The higher the r-squared, the better the fit. In our case, the r-squared value is 0.158, saying that we have explained 15.8% of the variation in KO's returns with our equation. This might sound extremely low to you. However, remember that we said typical correlation coefficients between two stocks at random are usually between 0.2 and 0.5? That means that one stock's returns can typically explain about 4%–25% (obtained by squaring 0.2 and 0.5) of another stock's returns. In many cases, the correlation coefficient is even less than 0.2, meaning that the r-squared may be close to 0.

Before moving on, it is worthwhile to pause and think about what we just said about typical correlations between stock returns. Stocks do generally tend to move up and down together, as evidenced by positive correlation. However, the relationships are not hard and fast, but quite loose. Sometimes people refer to stock prices as being very noisy. By this, they mean that any relationships are subtle and tenuous. In communication theory, people talk about the signal-to-noise ratio. Imagine listening to a radio broadcast of a speech. With no interference and perfect transmission, the words in the speech, which correspond to the signal, are easily identified and understood. If there is heavy interference—because the radio station is far away, there is bad weather, or someone is using a poor hair dryer in the house—there is much noise. The more noise, the lower the signal-to-noise ratio and the harder it is to understand what is being said. Similarly, stock prices are noisy with a low signal-to-noise ratio. Any patterns or relationships that do exist are not easy to discern.

The portion of the unexplained Y variable in each period is called the ***error term*** or ***residual.*** Let us examine a specific case to illustrate this. In May 2000, PEP's return was 11.414%, while KO's was 12.963%. Using the regression line equation in Figure A.2, we would estimate KO's return as 4.579% (0.4564 × 11.414% – 0.63%). Note that we changed the intercept value of –0.0063 to percentage notation of –0.63%. The error in our estimate is 8.384% (12.963% – 4.579%). When we perform regression, we implicitly assume that the error terms are random and have no relationship with each other. However, particularly using time series data, the error terms themselves may be correlated with each other, which is called ***autocorrelation*** or ***serial dependence.*** There is a statistical test called the Durbin-Watson test that helps detect autocorrelation. If autocorrelation is present, the fitted regression line may be inaccurate.

In a regression, the variable being explained is called the ***dependent variable.*** The variable doing the explaining is called the ***independent variable,*** or ***explanatory variable.*** We can extend the idea of regression to more than one independent variable. This is called ***multiple regression.*** Logically, two explanatory variables are better than one, three are better than two, and so on. In fact, virtually any additional explanatory variable we include in a regression will improve the r-squared. For example, we might include monthly average temperature in Paris as an additional series to help explain stock returns. This would not make logical sense, and the temperature in Paris would not have causal relationship to stock returns, but the r-squared would probably increase. When using more than one independent variable, researchers examine what is known as the adjusted r-squared. The adjusted r-squared value penalizes the r-squared value as more independent variables are added to the regression equation. In effect, it helps balance benefit versus cost; is it beneficial to add a particular variable?

One frequently encountered problem in performing multiple regressions is what is called ***multicollinearity.*** This occurs when there is reasonably strong correlation between two or more of the independent variables. Suppose, for example, that we were trying to understand the factors that affected the stock returns during 2005 of all the S&P 500 stocks. Suppose that for each stock, we had values of changes (2005 values minus 2004 values) in assets, sales, earnings, and shareholder's equity. There would probably be strong links between most of these variables, so that there would be a high degree of multicollinearity. Several problems are caused by multicollinearity, however. One of the main problems is that it clouds the picture concerning which independent variables are statistically significant.

The term **statistically significant** revolves around the idea: How likely is it that I would observe this outcome purely based on chance alone? Consider a coin-flipping contest. Imagine that 80,000 spectators in a football stadium are asked to stand up and flip a quarter. If it lands heads, they stay standing. If not, they sit down. After the first toss we would expect that approximately 40,000 people would still be standing. After the next toss we would expect about 20,000 to remain standing. It would probably take us about 16 tosses to identify the champion coin-tosser. So if someone in the crowd were to flip 16 heads in a row, we shouldn't be surprised.

A threshold of 5% is often used to signify statistical significance. If we observe something that we would expect to see less than 5% of the time based strictly on chance alone, then it might be deemed statistically significant. If we demanded a more stringent test, then we might use a threshold of 1%. But, just because something is statistically significant that does not mean it is economically significant. A statistician might say that tests of a certain trading rule show that a statistically significant relationship has been found. However, a trader might say: "Yes, that's great, but due to transactions costs and other factors I can't make money with this rule."

INFERENTIAL STATISTICS

With inferential statistics, we try to use observed data to infer things about general characteristics of the observed data or characteristics of additional observations. We often test whether a certain hypothesis is true or false. A hypothesis might be something like, "The slope of this line is 1." To test hypotheses, we must make some assumptions. The most critical assumptions are the assumptions we make about what is known as the ***probability distribution.***

The most well-known of all probability distributions is the ***normal distribution,*** also referred to as a ***Gaussian distribution*** because it was first formulated by Karl Gauss, the eighteenth-century German mathematician. It is also known as the ***bell curve,*** due to its bell shape. It only takes two parameters—the mean and standard deviation—to describe a given normal distribution; there are infinitely many normal distributions due to an infinite number of combinations of values for the mean and standard deviation. The normal distribution has three important characteristics:

- It is bell-shaped, with its peak at the center. The mean, median, and mode are all located at the peak.

- It is symmetric about the mean.

- It approaches the horizontal axis asymptotically at the left and right tails of the bell curve. It extends infinitely in both directions.

The normal distribution also has special importance due to what is called the ***central limit theorem.*** If we take repeated samples from a population, calculate the mean of each sample, and then plot the distribution of the sample means, they will approximate a normal distribution. As the sample size increases, the approximation will improve. The central limit theorem has important implications for a wide variety of statistical tests.

There are two rule-of-thumb values concerning the normal distribution that are useful to memorize. First, approximately two-thirds of the outcomes will lie (either above or below) within one standard deviation of the mean. Second, approximately 95% of the outcomes will lie within two standard deviations from the mean.

Are stock prices normally distributed? No, you cannot have negative prices, and with any normal distribution, every number is possible, both positive and negative, even though some values are highly improbable as outcomes. Are stock returns normally distributed? No, because we cannot have a return lower than –100%, but we can have returns greater than 100%. However, returns come much closer to being normally distributed than do stock prices. Looking at PEP's monthly returns from January 2000 through December 2004, we see what is displayed in Figure A.3.

This graph is a histogram. There are various "buckets" for counting returns. Here, the buckets are in intervals of 5.0%. Over the 60-month period, 26 returns fell in the interval from 0.0% to 5.0%. The size of the buckets will have an impact on the appearance; too few will clump everything together, while too many will produce a very flat histogram. In this example, we can see that PEP's returns do not look like a perfect normal distribution, but they do generally follow a bell shape. There are formal statistical tests designed to assess whether a given sample of outcomes can reasonably be said to follow a normal distribution.

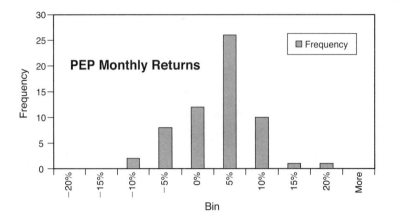

FIGURE A.3   Histogram of PEP monthly returns (January 2000–December 2004)

Stock returns cannot logically be expected to exactly follow a normal distribution due to the impossibility of returns less than –100%. However, what if we take the change in the logarithm (or log) of the prices? These are called log-returns. Do these numbers follow a normal distribution? If they do, we say that the data follows a log-normal distribution. Taking the log produces numbers that range from 0 to ∞. For stock returns, log-normality is a more reasonable assumption. However, the exact distribution of stock returns has been tough to pin down. Finance researchers are still arguing over the best distribution to use for stock returns, as we saw in our discussion in Chapter 4.

Earlier in this appendix, we used the term "degrees of freedom" when discussing standard deviation. This term also surfaces in descriptions of probability distributions. The easiest way to think of it is just as a parameter needed to specify the distribution. For the normal distribution, we needed two parameters, due to the need to specify the mean and standard deviation.

Three very important distributions are the Chi-Square, t, and F distributions. All of these are based on various manipulations of standard normal variables. A ***standard normal variable*** is one that follows a normal distribution with a mean of 0 and a standard deviation of 1. We can easily transform most variables into standard normal variables. Suppose that we observe a value of 24 from a sample that has a mean of 20 and a standard deviation of 5. First, we calculate how far the observation is from the mean. We do this by subtracting the mean of 20 from the value of the observation of 24, leaving us a value of 4. Next, we divide the standard deviation into our number, which gives us 0.8 (4/5). This tells us that the observation is 0.8 standard deviations from the mean.

The Chi-Square distribution is based on the sums of standard normal variables. If it is based on the sum of two standard normal variables, we say that it has two degrees of freedom. If it is based on the sum of three, it has three degrees of freedom. As the number of degrees of freedom increases, the distribution begins to approach the shape of a normal distribution. The Chi-squared distribution primarily is used for goodness-of-fit tests. The term "test statistic" refers to a value computed from a sample that is used to test a particular hypothesis. A hypothesis could be something like: "Are all the colors of M&M candies in a bag equally likely to occur?" Many test statistics are known to follow a Chi-Square distribution, so this distribution has many applications.

The t distribution or Student's t (Student was a pen name used by the person who first worked out its applications) is used often in statistics. The t distribution applies when the true standard deviation is unknown (which is most of the time) and is especially important for small samples. The t distribution converges to the normal distribution as the number of degrees of freedom (the sample size minus 1) increases. It closely approximates a normal distribution by 30 degrees of freedom. The t distribution is symmetric, similar in shape to the normal distribution but with wider tails. It commonly is used to test the statistical significance of regression coefficients (such as the intercept and slope). An application of the t statistic is shown later.

The last major commonly used distribution is the F distribution. The F distribution is based on the ratio of two variables, each of which follows a Chi-Square distribution. It primarily is used to test whether samples have the same variance. It is used in regression as an overall measure of goodness-of-fit because it is the ratio of explained variation to unexplained variation.

Now let us see how some of these things come together in looking at some output from a linear regression. Let us use PEP's monthly returns as the Y variable and the S&P 500 monthly returns as the X variable over the 2000–2004 period. We can use Excel to run the regression. Table A.1 displays the output, with the values of primary importance shaded in gray.

TABLE A.1   Excel Regression Output for PEP Monthly Returns from 2000 to 2004

Summary Output

Regression Statistics

Multiple R	0.2733
R-Square	0.0747
Adjusted R-Square	0.0588
Standard Error	0.0550
Observations	60

ANOVA

	df	SS	MS	F	Significance F
Regression	1	0.0142	0.0142	4.6828	0.0346
Residual	58	0.1753	0.0030		
Total	59	0.190			

	Coefficients	Standard Error	t Stat	P-Value	Lower 95%	Upper 95%	Lower 95.0%	Upper 95.0%
Intercept	0.0096	0.0071	1.3540	0.1810	−0.0046	0.0238	−0.0046	0.0238
X Variable 1	0.3321	0.1535	2.1640	0.0346	0.0249	0.6394	0.0249	0.6394

Let us start with the intercept and slope of the regression. The intercept, which is clearly labeled, is 0.0096. The slope is labeled X Variable 1 under Coefficients and has a value of 0.3321. The slope is approximately the beta of the stock, which is explained later. Technically, monthly returns on the risk-free asset (T-bills or T-bonds might be used) should have been subtracted from each variable, but we are trying to keep things simple. As a practical matter, in many cases it won't matter much if we don't subtract risk-free asset returns. The beta, a measure of risk, for an average stock is 1. We see that PEP's beta is less than that of an average stock. We also see the r-squared value, which is labeled R-Square of 0.0747. This means that our regression explains 7.47% of the variation in PEP's returns over this period. Below the slope value of 0.3321, we see the t statistic value of 2.1640. As a rule of thumb, t values over 2 are statistically significant, so this exceeds that hurdle. The item labeled P-Value shows the probability that we would observe the given value strictly by chance alone. The P-value of the slope t value is 0.0346, which says that the probability that this t value happened purely by chance was only 3.46%. In most academic research, P-values less than 5% (or sometimes 1%) are considered statistically significant. Analyzing this information is called a t test. Finally, let us consider the F value of 4.6828. This has a significance value of 0.0346, the same as the t value. It essentially tells you the same information as the t in this case. Unless you are performing a multiple regression, the P-value of the t of the slope and the significance value of the F statistic will be the same. The other numbers on the output have their uses, which you can learn from a standard statistics textbook.

What do the results tell us? The results show that our regression equation does seem to explain part of the variation in PEP's returns. The results are significant from a statistical point of view. However, we are only explaining 7.47% of the variation in PEP's returns. Whether this is useful from a practical point of view depends on other factors.

MODERN PORTFOLIO THEORY

We all learned portfolio theory as children: Don't put all your eggs in one basket! However, MPT began in 1952 with the work of Harry Markowitz. He worked out many mathematical relationships between groups of stocks, or portfolios. Some of the key results are as follows:

- The mean return of a portfolio is a simple weighted average of the mean returns of the individual stocks.
- The standard deviation (of returns) of a portfolio is a quadratic function.
- The standard deviation of a portfolio is almost always less than a simple weighted average of the individual stock standard deviations.
- Even with weak positive correlation, there are significant benefits to diversification.
- If an investor is only concerned with the mean return and standard deviation of a portfolio, it is possible logically to eliminate many portfolios from consideration.
- For large portfolios, the variance of each stock contributes little to the overall portfolio variance. However, the covariance of each stock's returns with the returns of all the other stocks is quite important.

We will flesh out these points as we go along.

Consider combinations (or portfolios) of two stocks, X and Y. Assume that we have esti-mates of the expected return (mean) and standard deviation of returns for each stock. We can cal-culate the expected return of a portfolio of X and Y by taking a simple weighted average of the individual expected returns. Thus, denoting the expected return on the portfolio as R_p, we have the following:

$$R_p = w_x R_x + w_y R_y$$

How about the standard deviation of a portfolio of X and Y? That is more complicated. The formula involves a squared term (therefore, it is a quadratic equation) and looks like this:

$$\sigma_p = \sqrt{w_x^2 \sigma_x^2 + w_y^2 \sigma_y^2 + 2 w_x w_y \sigma_x \sigma_y r_{xy}}$$

The r_{xy} term in this equation is the correlation between stock X and stock Y. If this value was equal to 1 (perfect correlation), this equation would simplify to the following:

$$\sigma_p = \sqrt{\sigma_x^2 + \sigma_y^2 + 2 w_x w_y \sigma_x \sigma_y} = \sqrt{(w_x \sigma_x + w_y \sigma_y)^2} = w_x \sigma_x + w_y \sigma_y$$

However, perfect correlation is virtually impossible in the real world. With $r_{xy} < 1$, the standard deviation of the portfolio is always less than a simple weighted average of the two indi-vidual standard deviations. This means that there are significant benefits to diversification in terms of risk reduction.

We can see how portfolios look in what is called ***risk-return space*** in Figure A.4. This fig-ure is based on annualized monthly returns for PEP and KO over the 2000–2004 period. Note the curved line, which shows the quadratic nature of the standard deviation relationship. Also, note that a portfolio consisting of 80% KO and 20% PEP is a better choice than KO by itself. Why do we say this? We say it because points that are to the northwest are preferable because they offer more return for less risk. The correlation of returns between the two stocks was 0.489 over this period. Therefore, we see that there are significant benefits to diversification, even if the two stocks have weak positive correlation.

How would the curve change if the correlation was greater? The line between the two ends, representing 100% of one of the stocks, would become straighter. If the correlation was perfect (+1), it would be a completely straight line. How would the curve change if the correla-tion was smaller? It would bend more toward the vertical axis. In the extreme case of perfect negative correlation (−1), there would actually be one portfolio possibility that would touch the vertical axis with a standard deviation of 0. However, the most common case, as stated earlier, is correlation between 0.2 and 0.5. Therefore, the curve in Figure A.4 is typical in terms of its gen-eral shape.

When we extend our calculations to more than two stocks, the expected return is still a simple weighted average of the individual returns, while the standard deviation has terms con-taining the variance of each stock plus cross-terms (similar to $2 w_x w_y \sigma_x \sigma_y r_{xy}$). When we graph possible portfolio combinations for three stocks, we get a picture like the one in Figure A.5.

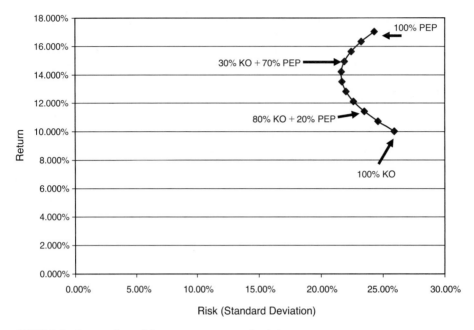

FIGURE A.4   Two-stock portfolio return versus standard deviation

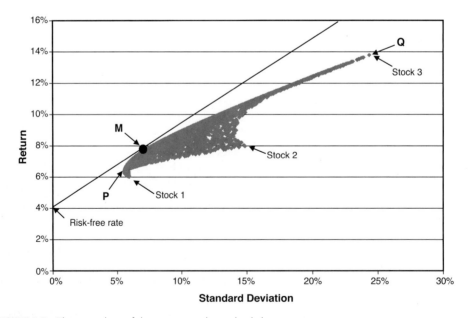

FIGURE A.5   Three stock portfolios return and standard deviation

    Some aspects of Figure A.5 we discuss later. For now, let us focus on the points of possi-
ble portfolios using stocks 1, 2, and 3. This figure was drawn using 1,000 different possible portfolios. If we extended the number of points, the blank spots gradually would be filled in.
Therefore, instead of a curved line of possible portfolios, we have a curved region.

If we were to extend our set of possible stocks to four, the variance of the portfolio would be calculated by adding up all the terms in the following matrix and dividing by 3 (see Figure A.6).

The terms along the diagonal, shown inside the smaller boxes in Figure A.6, are the variances of each of the four stocks. The off-diagonal terms are covariance terms. Because the covariance of stock 1 with stock 2 is the same as the covariance between stock 2 and stock 1, the matrix is actually symmetric around the diagonal. Notice that there are four variance terms and 12 covariance terms. The covariances are roughly three times (12 to 4) as important in the portfolio variance calculation. As the number of stocks under consideration grows, the individual variance terms become less and less important. For example, consider adding a fifth stock. The matrix would expand to 25 cells. The variance of stock 5 would be one of the 25 cells. However, there would be eight additional covariance terms added to the matrix, representing stock 5's covariances with the other four stocks. For large portfolios, the variance of each stock is relatively unimportant; what is important is how each stock co-varies with the rest of the stocks in the portfolio. This idea hints at what is called the ***Capital Asset Pricing Model (CAPM)***, to be discussed shortly.

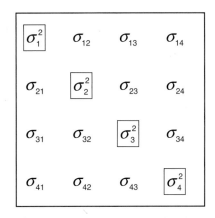

FIGURE A.6   Variances of four stocks

Let us return to Figure A.5. Which portfolio would we actually want to hold? Before we answer that question, we need to look at another concept. Consider the diagram in Figure A.7 that shows estimates of the mean and standard deviation for the returns on five stocks. Which investment(s) is/are the most attractive? To begin, we assume that investors will not bear more risk without the likelihood of more return. In investments jargon, we are assuming that investors are risk-averse. With this assumption, it becomes clear that we would prefer points to the northwest on the diagram. Stock A is preferable to Stock B because it has higher return for the same risk. The same argument can be made concerning C and D. We can also argue that A is preferable to C because it has less risk for the same return. In portfolio theory-speak, we say that A dominates B, B dominates C, and A dominates C. That leaves us with A and E. There is no clear way to say which one an investor would prefer. It depends on his/her tolerance for bearing risk. A more aggressive investor would opt for E, while a less aggressive investor would opt for A. The fact that A and E dominate the others means that they form what is called the ***efficient set.***

We can extend the efficient set concept to what is called the ***efficient frontier.*** Let us return to Figure A.5 once again, focusing on some additional aspects of it. Portfolios along the upper edge of the curve from P to Q (which is the point at stock three) represent the efficient frontier. These portfolios have either the highest return for any given value of standard deviation, or the lowest standard deviation for any given level of return. These are the portfolios that would be of most interest to rational investors. The particular portfolio along P–Q that an investor would choose would depend on his/her risk tolerance. We are assuming that investors only care about two things: expected return and standard deviation. This perspective is called a ***mean-variance framework.***

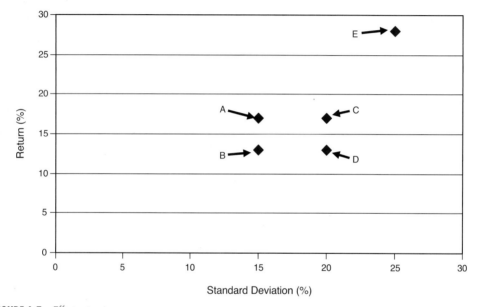

FIGURE A.7   Efficient set

Portfolio theory was all fine and good, but there were still two important hurdles in applying the equations. First, Markowitz did not specify how to get the inputs. In other words, he offered no prescribed method for coming up with the estimates of expected return and standard deviation. Of course, one could use historical data to come up with estimates, but how much data would be needed? Sixty months of monthly returns? Fifty-two weeks of daily returns? There was no clear answer. Second, as the portfolio size increased, the number of inputs became exponentially large. For a 100-stock portfolio, an investor would need 100 expected returns, 100 standard deviations, and 4,950 correlation coefficients. With today's computing power, it would not be difficult to calculate these inputs from a given sample of historical data, but in the early 1960s, this was a formidable computing task.

By 1964, a computationally easier method, with some added theory, had been developed. William Sharpe has received most of the credit for this. The theory became known as the Capital Asset Pricing Model, or CAPM. This theory was based on several simplifying assumptions, such as no transactions costs, no taxes, and other assumptions. However, the most important assumption was that of homogeneous expectations. This means that all investors view the inputs to portfolio theory in the same manner, and that they agree on the expected returns and standard deviations of all stocks and their correlations (or covariances). With this assumption, all investors identify the same efficient frontier. Next, we add the assumption that a risk-free asset (like U.S. Treasury bills) exists.

Returning (for the last time) to Figure A.5, consider the line that starts at the risk-free rate and is just tangent to the efficient frontier. The point of tangency is labeled as portfolio M. The question "which portfolio should I hold?" now becomes "what combination of the risk-free asset and portfolio M do I want to own?" That is true because combinations of the risk-free asset and portfolio M lie along the line from the risk-free rate to portfolio M and beyond. Portfolios on this line dominate (in portfolio theory-speak) all those that lie below. This means that this line has now become the efficient frontier. Portfolio M has now taken on some special significance. Every investor wants to hold the risky portfolio. This means that all investors own a chunk of M, which is a portfolio consisting of all stocks (because every stock must be held by someone, everyone has to hold some of every stock). Investors willing to bear more risk might put all of their money in M. Investors who are more cautious might put only 30% of their money in M and 70% in the risk-free asset (T-bills). Either way, both hold the stocks in M in the same proportions.

From these ideas, it can be shown (we will not go through a tedious derivation) that the expected return r_i on any stock i is given by the following equation, which we will call the CAPM equation:

$$r_i = r_f + \beta_i (r_m - r_f)$$

$$\text{where } \beta_i = \frac{cov_{im}}{(var_i)(var_m)} = \frac{\sigma_{im}}{\sigma_i \sigma_m} = r_{im} \frac{\sigma_i}{\sigma_m} (\frac{1}{\sigma_i \sigma_m}) = r_{im} \frac{\sigma_i}{\sigma_m}$$

This means that β is the product of the correlation coefficient between the stock and the market as a whole times the standard deviation of the stock relative to that of the market. So, if the stock's correlation with the market is 0.4 and its standard deviation is three times that of the market, then its β is 1.2 (0.4 × 3).

For many years, investors had thought about expected return like this:

Expected return = risk-free return + risk premium

For example, the expected return on a corporate bond would be the yield on a U.S. Treasury bond, a risk-free asset (risk-free in terms of default risk) of the same maturity, plus a premium for default risk, plus possibly a premium for liquidity risk. To calculate the expected return on the stock of that same company, an extra risk premium would be added for the fact that common stockholders have a residual claim and, thus, common stock has higher risk than the company's bonds.

Therefore, the CAPM equation has the same basic structure that people had been using for many years. The difference is that the risk premium is quantifiable. Note that all of the risk comes about through the relationship between the stock and the market. This is risk that cannot be diversified away, referred to as ***nondiversifiable risk.*** It is also called ***systematic risk. Beta*** is a measure of systematic or systemwide risk. All companies have some similar risk because they operate under the same laws, the same tax structure, the same political leadership, the same monetary policy, and so on. However, these things will affect different stocks differently. Companies will also have higher systematic risk, or betas, if they have more debt or have a cost structure with higher fixed costs (as opposed to variable costs).

Does the CAPM work? Yes and no. There have been many debates about how to test the CAPM. The evidence in support of the CAPM is mixed. Individual stock betas tend to be highly unstable. For example, remember that we calculated the beta for PEP over the 1995–1999 period using monthly returns. The beta we got was 1.466. When we did the same calculation over the 2000–2004 period, we got 0.332. (Remember that we performed this calculation in the earlier discussion about regression.) It is possible that if we did some in-depth analysis of PEP over this period, we could rationalize the difference. However, sometimes company betas seem to change from one period to another without an obvious reason. However, portfolio betas tend to be more stable. If a particular mutual fund has a beta of 1.18 and the stock market is generally up over a certain period, the return on that mutual fund would most likely exceed that of the S&P 500. If the market were down, the fund's performance would probably be worse than that of the market. In spite of the various problems with betas, they are heavily quoted and used. This is partly because there is no good alternative.

What is the beta for the market as a whole? Because the covariance of an asset with itself is the same as the asset's variance, and the correlation of any asset with itself is 1, the expression for $\beta, r_{im} \frac{\sigma_i}{\sigma_m}$ simplifies to 1. In practice, the S&P 500 is often used to represent the market portfolio. A stock with a beta greater than 1 is an above-average risk stock. If the stock's beta is less than 1, its risk is below average.

PERFORMANCE MEASUREMENT

Performance measurement can refer to calculations done at what we will call the microlevel or at what we call the macrolevel. At the microlevel, in Chapter 22, "System Design and Testing," we discussed various measures for assessing the performance of a particular trading strategy.

Now we need to look at the macrolevel. We address things at the macrolevel by posing the question, "How do we tell whether an investor's overall investment performance has been good or bad?" This is of particular interest to people who are hiring someone else to manage their money, such as a mutual fund portfolio manager. We want to determine whether the performance is adequate given the risk.

One simple method of assessing performance is to measure reward per unit of risk. Because we can earn the risk-free return by investing in a risk-free asset, like Treasury bills, it makes sense to focus on the reward in excess of the risk-free return per unit of risk. Therefore, we simply subtract the risk-free return from the average return from the investment and divide by the standard deviation of the returns over the period of measurement. If fund ABC earned an average return of 12% over the period with a standard deviation of 20%, while the risk-free return was 4%, our performance measure would be 0.4 (calculated as (12 – 4) / 20)). This measure is called the ***Sharpe performance measure*** or ***Sharpe ratio,*** because it was first suggested by William Sharpe.

Putting the same idea in CAPM terms, a logical measure is excess return per unit of beta, which is known as the ***Treynor measure of performance.*** Suppose that in the previous example, the beta of fund ABC was 1.1. This would lead to a Treynor measure of 7.27. (First subtract 4% from 12%, yielding 8%; then divide 1.1 into 8%.)

Another measure related to beta is what is called ***Jensen's alpha.*** Let us assume that we are estimating the market risk premium, which is $R_m – R_f$, as 6%. Let us use the same numbers for fund ABC that we used before. With these estimates, we would estimate the fund's expected return as 10.6% (4% + 1.1 × 6%). We would next subtract the 10.6% from the actual return of 12% to get 1.4%, which would be the fund's alpha. Therefore, alpha is a measure of excess return, return beyond what we expect based upon the CAPM. Fund managers are sometimes said to be "searching for alpha."

Geometrically, we can see the Treynor and Jensen measures in Figure A.8. Suppose that you use the Treynor and Jensen measures to rank two investments, X and Y. It is possible that investment X will have the highest Treynor measure but the lower Jensen alpha. However, in most cases, the ranking will be the same. There is some irony in the fact that the two performance measures based on the CAPM's beta don't bear the name of Sharpe, who developed the CAPM.

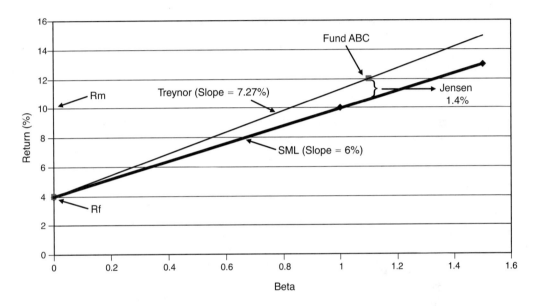

FIGURE A.8 Treynor and Jensen performance measures

Geometrically, the Sharpe measure would look similar to the Treynor measure line drawn in Figure A.8. The difference is that standard deviation would be used in place of beta on the x-axis.

A relatively new (developed in 1994 by J.P. Morgan Co.) measure that is used to summarize risk, especially at the overall firm level, is Value-at-Risk, known as VaR. Banks commonly use this measure, and it is even used for regulatory purposes. VaR tells us in one simple number the maximum loss that will occur (with 95% confidence under normal conditions) over a given period, such as one day. Because no one can foresee the future, the phrase "will occur" is based on certain assumptions. Let us say a certain investment firm is holding various U.S. and foreign stocks. Consider the risk along three dimensions: the risk of holding U.S. equities, the risk of holding foreign stocks, and the exchange rate risk. With VaR, you would analyze the variability in these three components (you could divide it more finely into more components) and the correlations between them. You would then roll all this information into a complex computer program that would perform the VaR calculation and give you one number as the result. For example, the VaR might be $3.6 million, meaning that there is less than a 5% chance that the firm would suffer a one-day loss greater than $3.6 million. Due to the complexity of the calculations, this measure would normally only be used by financial institutions.

ADVANCED STATISTICAL METHODS

Some researchers have applied some very sophisticated statistical techniques to investment analysis. It is beyond the scope of this book to go into detail concerning some of these advanced methods. However, we try to provide a qualitative understanding of some of the major techniques.

We used the term "time series" earlier in this appendix. It merely refers to data for which we have observations in consecutive periods. *Time series modeling* refers to statistical techniques for analyzing time series data.

When a researcher begins to analyze a given time series, the first question to ask is usually this: "Is the series stationary?" You can think of stationary as being generally stable, with some degree of structure. Stock prices are usually nonstationary because they are usually trending up or down, or fluctuating with trends.

Earlier in this appendix, we talked about how returns are often used rather than prices. Returns are often stationary. The stationarity of returns is a major advantage. It is not possible to make statements that are very meaningful about a nonstationary series. Stationarity is tested using what is called a *unit root test*. If the series has a unit root, it is not stationary. Therefore, you hope to be able to reject the hypothesis that the series has a unit root.

It is possible for two series to both be nonstationary but for some mathematical (linear) combination of the two series to be stationary. If this occurs, we say that the two series are cointegrated. Cointegration analysis techniques have been applied in several areas of finance, but there is probably great potential for additional applications of this method.

Major buzzwords in the finance academic community over the past 10 to 15 years are the acronyms ARCH and GARCH. Because ARCH is a subset of GARCH, we focus just on it. GARCH stands for *generalized autoregressive conditional heteroscedasticity*. This sounds extremely complicated, and it is to some degree. However, the basic idea behind it is simple—ordinary regression breaks down when you analyze many financial time series because the volatility of the series changes over time.

When the volatility (you can think of this as the standard deviation of stock returns, for example) of a series is not constant (not precisely constant, but at least generally constant or consistent), we say it is heteroscedastic. If we think of periods like that before and soon after the market crash of 1987 or the Internet bubble of the late 1990s, it is easy to imagine that volatility changes over time.

Methods such as ARCH and GARCH are used to estimate volatility. There are three major reasons why volatility estimates have increased in importance, as follows:

- The use of options contracts has increased dramatically in the past few decades. The key input into option pricing models is an estimate of the asset's volatility.

- There have been significant periods of changing volatility over the past few decades. Examples are the stock market crash of 1987, the Asian financial crisis of 1997, the Russian moratorium of government debts, the financial insolvency of Long Term Capital Management (LTCM) in 1998, the World Trade Center attack in 2001, the accounting manipulations of Enron and other companies in 2002, and the 2008–2009 financial crisis.

- There has been increased use of VaR, which requires volatility estimates.

One other term you may encounter is **maximum likelihood.** With maximum likelihood, you work backward from the observed data to make inferences about the probability distribution that produced those outcomes. You try to find the distribution that was most likely to be the source of the outcomes. Maximum likelihood techniques can be applied to many different statistical problems. It can even be an alternative to least squares in performing regression.

ARTIFICIAL INTELLIGENCE

The term artificial intelligence (AI) refers to using computers to mimic intelligent processes found in the natural world. Researchers in AI have often overestimated their ability to produce intelligent behavior or thought processes with machines. However, AI has definitely had some success and will probably continue to exert greater impact on our society in the future. You only have to look at the latest robotic devices in an electronics store to glimpse some of the potential. We only briefly describe three of the major developments in AI: expert systems, neural networks, and genetic algorithms.

To build an expert system, you need a cooperating expert. An expert system tries to model the thinking process of someone who is an expert on a particular subject. For example, programmers might interview a doctor at length, trying to build various rules for decision making. For example, the doctor might say that the first thing to do is take the patient's temperature. If the patient has a fever, you proceed along one set of steps. If the patient does not have a fever, you proceed along another set of steps. As you can imagine, the list of steps would be extremely long to diagnose many different illnesses. Some steps might lead to a dead end, where the system would indicate that a doctor would need to be consulted; the situation would be beyond the capability of the expert system. If you had an expert investor like Warren Buffett, you could potentially build a system that would mimic his stock selection process. However, researchers have found that it is extremely difficult to encode the decision-making process of many experts. Experts often seem to have a sixth sense in many situations that cannot be modeled.

The basic idea behind neural networks is to model, in a computer program, the network of neurons that continually "fire" in our brains, causing us to sense, think, feel, and act. A neural network consists of an input layer, an output layer, and some hidden layers in between. The designer of the neural network decides how many layers should be between the input and output layers and how the layers interact. In an investments application, company financial and stock price data might be inputs, while buy/sell decisions would be outputs. Critics have complained that neural networks are too much like a black box. You put in certain inputs and get out certain outputs, but it is not very clear what is happening in the middle. This criticism does have some validity; building a neural network is done more by trial and error than referring to an architectural or engineering blueprint. Defenders of neural networks counter that it is possible to dissect a neural network and uncover the inner structure.

Genetic algorithms (GAs) derive their name from the fact that they mimic certain genetic processes such as mutation. GAs are optimization algorithms. They try to maximize or minimize what is referred to as "fitness."

Problems are mapped into strings of 1s and 0s. For example, let us consider stock selection strategies. Positions 1 and 2 in the string might correspond to quartiles of ROE. A value of 00 might mean that you pick stocks that are in the lowest quartile of ROE for a given group of stocks. Similarly, values of 01, 10, and 11 would represent the other three quartiles. If we continued this scheme for other variables, we might be able to say that a certain string (pattern of 1s and 0s) would mean that we select stocks that are in the highest quartile of ROE, highest quartile of EPS growth, lowest quartile of P/E ratio, highest quartile of relative price strength, and so on.

Genetic algorithms typically start with a randomly generated population of strings. The strings then undergo various genetic operations, such as mutation and crossover (where two strings swap tails), and the population gradually evolves. The evolution is driven toward higher values of fitness. In an investing application, fitness could be the return earned from pursuing a certain strategy.

There are two major hurdles in using GAs: (1) mapping your problem into a string, the process of problem representation, can be difficult; and (2) sometimes, particularly in investing applications, seemingly obvious fitness values (called "fitness functions") can produce poor results because the system evolves toward a solution driven by uncommon quirks in the test data. New refinements to the basic technique, such as genetic programming, may lead to useful applications in the investing world.

REVIEW QUESTIONS

1. Explain the difference between descriptive and inferential statistics.
2. The monthly closing prices for VLO and TSO for the year 2005 are given in Table A.2. (The closing prices are adjusted for stock splits and dividends.)

TABLE A.2 Monthly Closing Prices for VLO and TSO

Date	VLO Adj. Close*	Volume	TSO Adj. Close*	Volume
3-Jan-05	25.89	6,327,590	31.71	1,156,805
1-Feb-05	35.49	11,433,242	36.78	1,283,473
1-Mar-05	36.5	14,312,645	36.87	1,496,781
1-Apr-05	34.14	19,363,771	37.79	1,944,952
2-May-05	34.24	15,281,285	43.48	1,586,209
1-Jun-05	39.47	11,828,418	46.39	1,481,663
1-Jul-05	41.3	11,438,900	48.09	1,213,225
1-Aug-05	53.2	18,753,469	57.69	1,948,447
1-Sep-05	56.48	24,614,095	67.12	3,366,504
3-Oct-05	52.57	23,972,552	61.04	3,137,700
1-Nov-05	48.1	17,303,419	55.07	2,545,585
1-Dec-05	51.6	11,718,461	61.55	1,698,647

Source: http://finance.yahoo.com

   a. Calculate the monthly return for each of these stocks.

   b. Calculate the following for each of these stocks:

      i. Arithmetic mean of the monthly returns

      ii. Median monthly return

      iii. Geometric mean monthly return

   c. Explain why the mode is not a meaningful statistic for this data set.

3. Calculate the standard deviation of the monthly return for both VLO and TSO using the data provided in Question 2. Explain how the standard deviation relates to risk.

4. What is the correlation coefficient for VLO and TSO? Explain what the correlation coefficient means.

5. Plot the monthly returns using TSO as the dependent variable and VLO as the independent variable.

   a. Calculate the least-squares regression line.

   b. What is the r-squared for the regression line? How is this number interpreted?

   c. If the monthly return for VLO was 3.4%, given the regression equation, what would be your best estimate of the monthly return for TSO?

TYPES OF ORDERS AND OTHER TRADER TERMINOLOGY

In the second half of this book, we cover strategies and tactics that can be used with technical analysis systems and patterns. Many of these strategies require knowledge of trading terms and how to tell a broker in trader language what to do. Here are some of the common terms used universally in the markets:

All or None (AON) Execute the entire order or none of it, but not some fraction.

Ask The price at which a seller is willing to sell.

Bid The price at which a buyer is willing to buy.

Day Order An order that, if not executed, expires at the end of the day. Most orders are assumed to be day orders unless otherwise specified.

Downtick A downtick is the opposite of an uptick in that the next previous different price was above the current price.

Fill or Kill (FOK) Execute an order immediately and completely, or cancel it.

Good 'Til Canceled Order (GTC) or Open Order An order that remains in effect until executed or cancelled. It usually has a time limit of several days to up to a month, at which time it must be renewed.

Immediate or Cancel (IOC) An order that must be executed immediately or it becomes void.

Leaves The unexecuted balance of an order.

Limit, Limited Order, or Limited Price Order An order to execute a stated amount at a specific or better price.

Liquidity The ability of the market to absorb a reasonable amount of transactions with a minimum effect on prices.

Long As opposed to short, a position of ownership. "I am long 100 shares of XYZ" means I own 100 shares of XYZ. "I am going long" means I am buying.

Market on Close (MOC) Execute at the close as near to the last sale as possible.

Market Order An order to execute a stated amount at the bid or offer price currently available in the marketplace. All orders are assumed to be market orders unless otherwise stated.

Not Held The broker is not "held" to the transactions on the tape. He can "work" the order.

Odd Lot Usually fewer than 100 shares.

Offer The price at which a seller is willing to sell.

Opening Only or OPG An order to be executed on the opening only and if not executed to be cancelled. This is valid for market and limit orders.

Pegged Market An order is pegged to buy on the best offer and sell on the best bid.

Pull Back An order to withdraw a current bid or offer.

Quote The highest bid and the lowest offer in a given market at a given time, sometimes including the volume at the bid and offer—usually called a "quote in size."

Relative Allows the customer to enter a more aggressive price than the current market price, and have the entered price stay within a fixed interval to the market should prices deteriorate.

Round Lot Usually 100 shares.

Scale An order to execute in increments—to sell into a rising market or buy into a declining market.

Scale Order A specific order to scale a specified amount at specific price variations.

Seat A membership in an exchange.

Short One has sold the security and owes it to the lender. "I am short 100 shares of XYZ" means I have borrowed and sold 100 shares of XYZ and at some time must buy it back and return it to the lender. "I am going short" means I am selling the security in anticipation of its price declining.

Short Covering Buy stock to return stock previously borrowed to make delivery on a short sale.

Short Sale A sale of a security that is not owned, usually entered in anticipation of a decline in price. A short sale, because the security is not owned but must be delivered to the buyer, requires that the security be borrowed (usually arranged by the broker) and at some time returned. When the security is "covered" with a "buy to cover" order, the security is returned, and the profit or loss in the position is determined by the difference between the price at which the security was bought and sold. Sometimes, the broker cannot borrow the stock, for a multitude of reasons, and the order to sell short will be denied.

Stock Ahead Other orders at the same price were placed on the book earlier and are ahead of the current order. Precedence for orders is based on when they were placed. These earlier orders may be executed without execution of the current order.

Stop Limit Order A stop order that becomes a limit order once the stop price is reached.

Stop Order An order to execute once a price reaches a certain level away from current price. A stop order becomes a market order once the specified price is reached. It may not be executed at the stop price. An example is "Buy 100 shares XYZ at 52 stop." Presumably, XYZ is trading below 52 currently, and the order states that should the price reach 52, then enter a market order to buy 100 shares. This type of order is principally used as protection against a sudden decline (a sell stop). For example, say you own 100 shares of XYZ at 50 and believe it will rise. To protect yourself from a major loss, you place a "sell 100 shares XYZ at 48 stop" to sell out your position at 48 or below when 48 is reached. Thus, if you are correct and XYZ rises, you profit, but if XYZ declines, you limit your loss to approximately two points. A stop order can also be entered if there is no current position, but if the analyst believes that a certain price is crucial and wants to enter a position once that price is reached. The stop order is the most important order of all orders because it can either enter a potential winning position or limit one's risk.

Time in Force The time limit for the order to be entered or cancelled.

Uptick or Plus Tick A term used to designate that the last price is above the next earlier price. A Zero Plus Tick is a term that designates the last price that is the same as the next earlier price but still above the last different price. Short sales of stocks usually must be executed on an uptick, though this rule may change soon. ETF short sales do not require an uptick, and neither do any futures markets. A downtick is the opposite of an uptick in that the next previous different price was above the current price.

VWAP The Volume Weighted Average Price for a stock. VWAP is calculated by adding the dollars traded for every transaction in that stock and dividing the total shares traded. It is used by institutions to measure the effectiveness of executions and as a target for daily executions.

AN ORDER TICKET

An order ticket, whether on the Internet or on the broker's desk pad, usually includes the following:

    Contract Description:
        Underlying
        Exchange
        Security Type: Stock, Option, Future, Future Option, Warrant, Cash, Index, Bond
        Currency
        Expiration Date
        Strike Price
        Option Type: Call/Put

Action:

    Buy/Sell

Order Description:

    Order Type: Limit, Stop, Stop Limit, Market, MOC, MOO, IOC, FOK, AON, and so on.

    Quantity

    Limit Price

    Stop Price

Time in Force:

    Day/GTC

    Good after Time

    Expiration Date and Time

    Regular Trading Hours Only?

Many other conditions can be added, depending on the complexity of the order, and not all the categories mentioned are necessarily required. They depend on the type of security and what the trader desires to do.

BIBLIOGRAPHY

Aby, Carroll D. J. *Point & Figure Charting: The Complete Guide.* Greenville, SC: Traders Press, Inc., 1996.

Achelis, Steven B. *Technical Analysis from A to Z.* New York, NY: McGraw-Hill, 2001.

Afolabi, M. O., and O. Olude. "Predicting Stock Prices Using a Hybrid Kohonen Self Organizing Map (SOM)." Proceedings of the Fortieth Annual Hawaii International Conference on System Sciences, (2007): 48.

Ahamed, Liaquat. *Lords of Finance: The Bankers Who Broke the World.* New York, NY: Penguin, 2009.

Alexander, S. "Price Movements in Speculative Markets: Trends or Random Walks." *Industrial Management Review* 2 (1961): 7–26.

Allen, Fredrick Lewis. *Only Yesterday.* New York, NY: First Perennial Classics, 2000.

Alphier, James. "The Tragic Neglect of the Old Masters." *Technical Analysis of Stocks & Commodities* 6, no. 10 (1988): 395–396.

———, and B. Kuhn. "A Helping Hand from the Arms Index." *Technical Analysis of Stocks & Commodities* 5, no. 4 (1987): 142–143.

Amyx, Jennifer. *Japan's Financial Crisis: Institutional Rigidity and Reluctant Change.* Princeton, NJ: Princeton University Press, 2004.

Anderson, John A. "Point and Figure Charting: A Computational Methodology and Trading Rule Performance in the S&P 500 Futures Market." Working paper, Queensland University of Technology, Brisbane, Queensland, undated.

Angell, George. *Winning in the Futures Markets: A Money-Making Guide to Trading, Hedging and Speculating.* Revised Edition. New York, NY: McGraw-Hill, 1990.

Antonacci, Gary S. "Modern Portfolio Theory in Managed Futures, Part 2." *Technical Analysis of Stocks & Commodities* 5, no. 4 (1987): 239–241.

Appel, Gerald, and Fred Hitschler. *Stock Market Trading Systems: A Guide to Investment Strategy for the 1980s*. Homewood, IL: Dow Jones-Irwin, 1980.

Appel, Gerald. *Technical Analysis: Power Tools for Active Investors*. Short Hills, NJ: FT Press, 2005.

Arms, Richard W., Jr. *Profits in Volume*. 2nd ed., New York, NY: Marketplace Books, John Wiley & Sons, Inc., 1998.

———. *The Arms Index: An Introduction to the Volume Analysis of Stock and Bond Markets*. Homewood, IL: Dow Jones-Irwin, 1989.

Arnold, Tom, John Earl, David North. "Are Cover Stories Effective Contrarian Indicators?" *Financial Analysts Journal* 63, no. 2 (2007): 70-75.

Aronson, David R. "Moving-Window Correlation Stability and Its Use in Indicator Evaluation." *Journal of Technical Analysis* (formerly *The Market Technicians Association Journal*), Spring 1992.

———. *Evidence-Based Technical Analysis: Applying the Scientific Method and Statistical Inference to Trading Signals*. New York, NY: John Wiley & Sons, Inc., 2006.

Aspray, Thomas E. "Payoff Index." *Technical Analysis of Stocks & Commodities* 6, no. 3 (1988): 115–118.

Ayres, Leonard P. *Turning Points in Business Cycles*. New York: The Macmillan Company, 1940.

Bachelier, Louis. "Theorie de la speculation." Thesis, Annales Scientifiques de l'École Normale Superieure, 1900. I I I–17, 21–86. Translated by Cootner (ed.) as "Random Character of Stock Market Prices." (Massachusetts Institute of Technology, 1964: 17–78 or Haberman S., and Sibett T. A. (eds.) as "History of Actuarial Science." (London: VII, 1995: 15–78).

———. "Theorie des probabilities continues." *Journal des Mathematiques Pures et Appliquees*, 1906.

———. "Les probabilities cinematiques et dynamiques." *Annales de l'Ecole Normale Superieure*, 1913.

Barber, B., and T. Odean. "Boys Will Be Boys: Gender, Overconfidence, and Common Stock Investment." *Quarterly Journal of Economics* 116 (2001): 261–292.

Barberis, Nicholas, A. Shleifer, and Robert W. Vishny. "A Model of Investor Sentiment." Working paper no. 5926, National Bureau of Economic Research, Cambridge, MA, 1997.

Bask, Michael, and Jarko Fidrmac. "Fundamentals and Technical Trading: Behavior of Exchange Rates in the CEEC's" *Open Economies Review* 20 (2006): 589–605.

Bauer, Richard, and Julie Dahlquist. *Technical Market Indicators: Analysis and Performance*. New York, NY: John Wiley & Sons, Inc., 1999.

———. "Technical Indicators for Individual Stocks: The Quality Versus Quantity Tradeoff." *MTA Journal* 51 (Winter–Spring 1999): 67–71.

Baum, Caroline. "Just in Time to Come Crashing Down." *Los Angeles Business Journal*, January 3, 2000.

Belford, Peter. "Candlestick Stock Analysis with Genetic Algorithms." Proceedings of the Eighth Annual Conference on Genetic Evolutionary Computation, Association for Computing Machinery, (2006): 1851–1852.

Bell, D. "Regret in Decision Making Under Uncertainty." *Operations Research* 30, no. 5 (1982): 961–981.

Berg, Joyce, Robert Forsythe, Forrest Nelson, and Thomas Rietz. "Results from a Dozen Years of Election Futures Markets Research." College of Business Administration, University of Iowa, Iowa City, IA, 2000.

Berstein, Jake. *Investor's Quotient*. New York, NY: John Wiley & Sons, Inc., 1993.

Bjorgen, Eric, and Steve Leuthold. "Corporate Insiders' Big Block Transactions." *Journal of Technical Analysis* (formerly *The Market Technicians Association Journal*) 57 (2002): 26–29.

Black, Fisher. "Noise." *Journal of Finance* 41 (1986): 529–544.

Blanchet-Scalliet, Christophette, Awa Diop, Rajna Gibson, Denis Talay, and Etienne Tanre. "Technical Analysis Compared to Mathematical Models Based Methods Under Parameters Mis-Specification." *Journal of Banking & Finance* 31, no. 5 (2007): 1351–1373.

Bloomberg News. "Analyst Rates Tyco 'Hold.'" *New York Times*, January 9, 2002, c2.

Blume, L., D. Easley, and M. O'Hara. "Market Statistics and Technical Analysis: The Role of Volume." *Journal of Finance* 49 (1994): 153–181.

Blumenthal, Earl. *Chart for Profit Point and Figure Trading*. Larchmont, NY: Investors Intelligence, 1975.

Bollinger, John. *Bollinger on Bollinger Bands*. New York, NY: McGraw-Hill, 2002.

Boucher, Mark. *The Hedge Fund Edge*. New York, NY: John Wiley & Sons, Inc., 1999.

Boxer, C. *The Dutch Seaborne Empire, 1600–1800*. New York, NY: Penguin (Non-Classics), 1965.

Braudel, F. *Civilization & Capitalism 15th–18th Century, Volume I, The Structures of Everyday Life*. New York, NY: Harper & Row Publishers, 1981. Translated from French by Kochan, M., and revised by Reynolds, S., 1979, Les Structures du Quotidien: Le Possible et L'Impossible, Librarie Armand Colin, Paris.

———. *Civilization & Capitalism 15th–18th Century, Volume II, The Wheels of Commerce*. New York, NY: Harper & Row Publishers, 1982. Translated by Reynolds, S., 1979, Les Jeux de l'Exchange, Librarie Armand Colin, Paris.

Brecht, Kira McCaffrey. "Understanding Futures Margin." *Active Trading Magazine* (January 2003): 64–65.

Bressert, Walter. *The Power of Oscillator/Cycle Combinations*. Tucson, AZ: Walter Bressert and Associates, 1991.

Brock, W., J. Lakonishok, and B. LeBaron. "Simple Technical Trading Rules and the Stochastic Properties of Stock Returns." *Journal of Finance* 47 (1992): 1731–1764.

Brown, Constance W. "The Derivative Oscillator: A New Approach to an Old Problem." *Journal of Technical Analysis* (formerly *The Market Technicians Association Journal*) (Winter–Spring 1994): 45–61.

———. *Technical Analysis for the Trading Professional*. New York, NY: McGraw-Hill, 1999.

———. *Fibonacci Analysis*. New York, NY: Bloomberg Press, 2008.

Brown, D., and R. Jennings. "On Technical Analysis." *Review of Financial Studies* 2 (1989): 527–552.

Bruce, Brian. "Stock Analysts: Experts on Whose Behalf, Editorial Commentary." *Journal of Psychology and Financial Markets* 3, no. 4 (2002): 198–201.

Bruner, Robert F. and Sean D. Carr. *The Panic of 1907: Lessons Learned from the Market's Perfect Storm*. New York, NY: John Wiley & Sons, Inc., 2009.

Bryant, Michael R. "Money Management Indicators." *Technical Analysis of Stocks & Commodities* 19, no. 10 (2001): 42–50.

Bulkowski, Thomas N. "Bulkowski's Free Pattern Research," http://www.thepatternsite.com, 2010.

———. *Encyclopedia of Chart Patterns*. 2nd ed. New York, NY: John Wiley & Sons, Inc., 2005.

———. *Trading Classic Chart Patterns*. New York, NY: John Wiley & Sons, Inc., 2002.

———. *Encyclopedia of Candlestick Charts*. New York, NY: John Wiley & Sons, Inc., 2008.

Burke, Michael L. *Three Point Reversal Method or Point and Figure Construction and Formations*. Larchmont, NY: Chartcraft, Inc., 1990.

Burnham, Terry. *Mean Markets and Lizard Brains*. New York, NY: John Wiley & Sons, Inc., 2005.

Busby, Thomas L. and Patsy Busby Dow. *The Markets Never Sleep: Global Insights for More Consistent Trading*. New York, NY: John Wiley & Sons, 2007.

Caginalp, Gunduz, and H. Laurent. "The Predictive Power of Price Patterns." *Applied Mathematical Finance* 5 (1998): 181–205.

Caginalp, Gunduz, David Porter, and Vernon Smith. "Financial Bubbles: Excess Cash, Momentum, and Incomplete Information." *Journal of Psychology and Financial Markets* 2, no. 2 (2001): 80–99.

Campbell, J., A. Lo, and C. MacKinlay. *The Econometrics of Financial Markets*. Princeton, NJ: Princeton University Press, 1997.

Carlson, John A., and Carol L. Osler. "Rational Speculators and Exchange Rate Volatility." *European Economic Review* 44, no. 2 (2000): 231–253.

Carr, Michael J. *Smarter Investing in Any Economy: The Definitive Guide to Relative Strength Investing*. Cedar Falls, IA: W & A Publishing, 2008.

Carr, Thomas K. *Trend Trading for a Living: Learn the Skills and Gain the Confidence to Trade for a Living*.

Carriere, C. *Negociants Marseilles au XVIIIe siecle, Volume I*. Marseille, 1973.

Carroll, Paul. "The Haurlan Index." *Technical Analysis of Stocks and Commodities* 12, no. 1 (January 1994): 23–25.

Case, K., and R. Shiller. "The Behavior of Home Buyers in Boom and Post Boom Markets" (1988). In R. Shiller. *Market Volatility*. Cambridge, MA: MIT Press, 1989.

Chiarella, Carl, Xue-Zhong He, and Cars Hommes. "A Dynamic Analysis of Moving Average Rules." *Journal of Economic Dynamics and Control* 30, no. 9–10 (2006): 1729–1753.

Chan, K., Y. Peter Chung, and W. Fong. "The Informational Role of Stock and Option Volume." *The Review of Financial Studies* 15, no. 4 (2002): 1049–1075.

Chande, Tushar S. *Beyond Technical Analysis*. New York, NY: John Wiley & Sons, Inc., 2001.

———, and Stanley Kroll. *The New Technical Trader: Boost Your Profit by Plugging into the Latest Indicators*. New York, NY: John Wiley & Sons, Inc., 1994.

Chang, P. H. K., and C. L. Osler. "Methodical Madness: Technical Analysis and the Irrationality of Exchange-Rate Forecasts." *The Economic Journal* 109, no. 458 (1999): 636–661.

Chang, Yung-Ho, Massoud Metghalchi, and Chia-Chung Chan. "Technical Trading Strategies and Cross-National Information Linkage: The Case of Taiwan Stock Market." *Applied Financial Economics* 16, no. 10 (2006): 731–743.

Charleton, William T., and John H. Earl, Jr. "The State of Technical Analysis in Practice and in College Curriculums: A Survey of Technical Analysts," *Journal of Technical Analysis* (Summer-Autumn 2002): 5–9.

Chavarnakul, Thira, and David Enke. "Intelligent Technical Analysis Based Equivolume Charting for Stock Trading Using Neural Networks." *Expert Systems with Applications* 34, no. 2 (2008): 1004–1017.

Chen, Ceng-Wei, Chin-Sheng Huang, and Hung-Wei Lai. "The Impact of Data Snooping on the Testing of Technical Analysis: An Empirical Study of Asian Stock Markets." *Journal of Asian Economics* 20, no. 5 (2009): 580–591.

Chen, J., H. Hong, and J. Stein. "Forecasting Crashes: Trading Volume, Past Returns and Conditional Skewness in Stock Prices." *Journal of Financial Economics* 61 (2001): 345–381.

Chesler, Daniel. "Trading False Moves with the Hikkake Pattern." *Active Trader Magazine* 5, no. 4 (April 2004): 42–46.

Cheung, Y. W., and C. Y. P. Wong. "A Survey of Market Practitioners' Views on Exchange Rate Dynamics." *Journal of International Economics* 51 (2000): 401–419.

Cheung, Y. W., and M. D. Chinn. "Currency Traders and Exchange Rate Dynamics: A Survey of the U.S. Market." *Journal of International Money and Finance* 20 (2001): 439–471.

Cheung, Y. W., M. D. Chinn, and I. W. Marsh. "How Do UK-based Foreign Exchange Dealers Think Their Market Operates?" Working paper no. 7524, National Bureau of Economic Research, Cambridge, MA, 2000.

Cheung, William, Keith S. K. Lam, and HangFai Yeung. "Intertemporal Profitability and Stability of Technical Analysis: Evidences from the Hong Kong Stock Exchange." *Applied Economics* (2009): 1466–4283.

Chong, Terence Tai-Leung, and Wing-Kam Ng. "Technical Analysis and the London Stock Exchange: Testing the MACD and RSI Rules Using the FT30." *Applied Economic Letters* 15, no. 14 (2008): 1111–1114.

Clarke, Roger, Scott Krase, and Meir Statman. "Tracking Errors, Regret and Tactical Asset Allocation." *Journal of Portfolio Management* 20, no. 3 (Spring 1994): 16–23.

Cobleigh, Ira and Peter DeAngelis. *When to Sell Stocks and Pin Down Your Profits.* Grifo Publishing, 1983.

Cohen, Abe. *The Chartcraft Method of Point and Figure Trading.* Larchmont, NY: Chartcraft, 1960.

Colby, Robert and Thomas Meyers. *The Encyclopedia of Technical Market Indicators.* New York: McGraw Hill, 1988.

Colby, Robert W. *The Encyclopedia of Technical Market Indicators.* New York, NY: McGraw-Hill, 2003.

Cole, George. *Graphs and Their Application to Speculation.* Peoria, IL: Bernbee Press, 1936.

Collins, Art. "The Legend and the Lore of Richard Dennis." *Technical Analysis of Stocks & Commodities* 23, no. 4 (April 2005): 46–53.

Connors, Laurence A. *Connors on Advanced Trading Strategies.* Malibu, CA: M. Gordon Publishing Group, 1998.

———. "Larry Connors on How the Markets Really Work." Interview by Editor Jayanthi Gopalakrishnan. *Technical Analysis of Stocks & Commodities* 22, no. 12 (2004): 74–79.

———, and Linda Bradford Raschke. *Street Smarts: High Probability Trading Strategies for the Futures and Equity Markets.* Malibu, CA: M. Gordon Publishing Group, 1995.

———, and Conor Sen. *How Markets Really Work: A Quantitative Guide to Stock Market Behavior.* Sherman Oaks, CA: Trading Markets Publishing Group, 2004.

Conrad, Jennifer, and Guatam Kaul. "The Anatomy of Trading Strategies." *The Review of Financial Studies* 11, no. 3 (1998): 489–519.

Cooper, Jeff. *Hit and Run Trading II: Capturing Explosive Short-Term Moves in Stocks*. Columbia, MD: Marketplace Books, 2004.

Cootner, Paul, ed. *The Random Character of Stock Market Prices*. Cambridge, MA: MIT Press, 1964.

———. "Stock Prices: Random vs. Systematic Changes." *Industrial Management Review* 3 (1962): 24–45.

Costa, Neil A. "W. D. Gann—The Market Master." *Australian Technical Analysts' Association Journal* (July–August 2000).

Covel, Michael. *Trend Following: How Great Traders Make Millions in Up or Down Markets*. Upper Saddle River, NJ: Financial Times Prentice Hall, 2004.

———. *The Complete TurtleTrader: How 23 Novice Investors Became Overnight Millionaires*. New York, NY: Harper Paperbacks, 2009.

Cowles, Alfred 3rd. "Can Stock Market Forecasters Forecast?" *Econometrica* 1, no. 3 (1933): 309–324.

———. "A Revision of Previous Conclusions Regarding Stock Price Behavior." *Econometrica* 28 (1960): 909–915.

———, and H. Jones. "Some A Posteriori Probabilities in Stock Market Action." *Econometrica* 5 (1937): 280–294.

Crabel, Toby. "Inside Day Patterns in the S&P." *Technical Analysis of Stocks & Commodities* 7, no. 11 (1989): 387–389.

———. "2-bar NR and ORB." *Technical Analysis of Stocks & Commodities* 8, no. 2 (1990): 70–73.

———. "Opening Range Breakout, Parts 1–8." *Technical Analysis of Stocks & Commodities* (1989–1990). The parts are in separate issues: 6, no. 9 (pp. 337–339); 6, no. 10 (366–368); 6, no. 12 (456–458); 7, no. 2 (47–49); 7, no. 4 (119–120); 7, no. 5 (161–163); 7, no. 6 (188–189); 7, no. 7 (208–210).

Cross, J. G. *A Theory of Adaptive Economic Behavior*. Cambridge, MA: Cambridge University Press, 1983.

Dahlquist, Julie, "Blue Monday Goes Green," *Active Trader*, November 2009.

Davis, Ned. *Being Right or Making Money*. Venice, FL: Ned Davis Research, Inc., 2000.

———. *The Triumph of Contrarian Investing*. New York, NY: McGraw-Hill, 2003.

Davis, Robert Earl. *Profit and Profitability: Technical Analysis of the Price Fluctuations of Common Stocks by the Point and Figure Method*. West Lafayette, IN: Dunn & Hargitt's Financial Service, 1965.

————, and C. C. Thiel. *Point and Figure Commodity Trading: A Computer Evaluation.* West Lafayette, IN: Dunn & Hargitt's Financial Service, 1970.

De Bondt, W. F. M. "Betting on Trends: Intuitive Forecasts of Financial Risk and Return." *International Journal of Forecasting* 9 (1993): 355–371.

————, and R. Thaler. "Does the Stock Market Overreact?" *Journal of Finance* 40 (1985): 793–805.

Desmond, Paul F. "Identifying Bear Market Bottoms and New Bull Markets." *Journal of Technical Analysis* (formerly *The Market Technicians Association Journal*) 57 (2002): 38–42.

Detry, P. J., and Philippe Gregoire. "Other Evidences of the Predictive Power of Technical Analysis: The Moving Averages Rules on European Indexes." European Finance Management Association Meeting, Lugano, Switzerland, 2001, http://ssrn.com/abstract=269802.

De Veaux, Richard D., and Paul F. Velleman. *Intro Stats.* Boston, MA: Pearson-Addison Wesley, 2004.

deVilliers, Victor. *The Point & Figure Method of Anticipating Stock Price Movements.* New York, NY: Windsor Books, reprint of 1933 edition.

————, and Owen Taylor. *De Villiers and Taylor on Point and Figure Charting.* Short Hills, NJ: FT Prentice Hall, 2000.

deZwart, Gerben, Thijs Markwat, Laurens Swinkels, and Dick van Dijk. "The Economic Value of Fundamental and Technical Information in Emerging Currency Markets." *Journal of International Money and Finance* 28, no. 4 (2009): 581–602.

Dewey, Edward R. *Cycles: The Mysterious Forces That Trigger Events.* New York, NY: Hawthorne Books, 1971.

Dewey, Edward R., and Edwin F. Dakin. *Cycles: The Science of Prediction.* New York: NY: Henry Holt & Company, Inc., 1947.

Dice, Charles A., and Wilford J. Eiteman. *The Stock Market.* New York, NY: McGraw-Hill, Inc., 1941.

Dines, James. *How the Average Investor Can Use Technical Analysis for Stock Profits: An In-Depth Work on Stock Market Technical Analysis, Mob Psychology, and Fundamentals.* Belvedere, CA: Dines Chart Corporation, 1972.

Dormeier, Buff. "The Volume Price Confirmation Indicator." *Active Trader Magazine* 6, no. 2 (February 2005): 21.

Dorsey, Thomas J. *Point and Figure Charting: Essential Applications for Forecasting and Tracking Market Prices.* New York, NY: John Wiley & Sons, Inc., 2001.

Downs, Walter T. "Combining Statistical and Pattern Analysis." *Technical Analysis of Stocks & Commodities* 16, no. 10 (1998): 447–456.

Dreman, David. "Bubbles, and the Role of Analysts' Forecasts." *Journal of Psychology and Financial Markets* 3, no. 1 (2002): 4–14.

———, and Michael A. Berry. "Analyst Forecasting Errors and Their Implications for Security Analysts." *Financial Analysts Journal* 51, no. 3 (May–June 1995): 30–41.

Duddella, Suri. *Trade Chart Patterns Like the Pros: Specific Trading Techniques.* Privately published, 2007.

du Plessis, Jeremy. *The Definitive Guide to Point and Figure.* Hampshire, Great Britain: Harriman House Ltd., 2005.

Dutta, Goutam, Pankaj Jha, Arnab Kumar Laha, and Neerj Mohan. "Artificial Neural Network Models for Forecasting Stock Price Index in the Bombay Stock Exchange." *Journal of Emerging Market Finance* 5, no. 3 (2006): 283–295.

Edwards, Robert, John Magee, and W. H. C. Bassetti. *Technical Analysis of Stock Trends*, 9th ed. Boca Raton, FL: St. Lucie Press, 2007.

Ehlers, John. "MESA Adaptive Moving Averages." *Technical Analysis of Stocks and Commodities* 19, no. 9 (September 2001): 30–35.

———. *MESA and Trading Market Cycles.* New York, NY: John Wiley & Sons, Inc., 2002.

Elder, Alexander. *Trading for a Living.* New York, NY: John Wiley & Sons, Inc., 1993.

———. *Come into My Trading Room.* New York, NY: John Wiley & Sons, Inc., 2002.

Eng, William F. *The Technical Analysis of Stocks, Options, & Futures.* Chicago, IL: Probus Publishing, 1988.

Etzkorn, Mark. "Bruce Babcock: Market Realities." *Futures Magazine* (December 1996): 36–42.

Evstigneev, Igor V., and Klaus Reiner Schenk-Hoppe. "From Rags to Riches: On Constant Proportions Investment Strategies." Working paper no. 89, Institute for Empirical Research in Economics, University of Zurich, 2001.

Faith, Curtis. *Way of the Turtle: The Secret Methods that Turned Ordinary People into Legendary Traders.* New York, NY: McGraw-Hill, 2007.

Fama, E.F. and K. R. French, "Multifactor explanations of asset pricing anomalies," *Journal of Finance* 51 (1996): 55–84.

Fama, Eugene. "The Behavior of Stock-Market Prices." *The Journal of Business* 38, no. 1 (1965): 34–105.

———. "Efficient Capital Markets: A Review of Theory and Empirical Work." *Journal of Finance* 25 (1970): 383–417.

———. "Efficient Capital Markets: II." *Journal of Finance* 46 (1991): 1575–1617.

Farmer, D. "Some Price Fluctuations in Angevin, England." *Economic History Review* (1956): 3–28.

Fischoff, B., and P. Slovic. "A Little Learning…: Confidence in Multicue Judgment Tasks." In R. Nickerson (ed.), *Attention and Performance*, VIII. Erlbaum, Hillsdale, NJ: Erlbaum, 1980.

Fisher, Kenneth L., and Meir Statman. "The Sentiment of Investors, Large and Small." *Financial Analysts Journal* 56 (2000): 16–23.

Fisher, Mark B. *The Logical Trader*. New York, NY: John Wiley & Sons, Inc., 2002.

Flanagan, Mike, PhD. "Developing an Expert System to Forecast the Stock Market." *Technical Analysis of Stocks & Commodities* 12, no. 11 (1994): 463–468.

Flanegin, Frank, and Denis P. Rudd. "Should Investments Professors Join the 'Crowd?'" *Managerial Finance* 31, no. 5 (2005): 28–37.

Fosback, Norman. *Stock Market Logic: A Sophisticated Approach to Profits on Wall Street*. Chicago, IL: Dearborn Financial Publishing, Inc., 1976 (1993 edition).

Friesen, Geoffrey C., Paul Weller, and Lee M. Dunham. "Price Trends and Patterns in Technical Analysis: A Theoretical and Empirical Examination." *Journal of Banking & Finance* 33, no. 6 (2009): 1089–1100.

Frost, A. John, and Robert R. Prechter. *Elliott Wave Principle: Key to Market Behavior, 20th Anniversary Edition*. Gainesville, GA: New Classics Library, 2000.

Galbraith, John K. *A Short History of Financial Euphoria*. New York, NY: Penguin, 1994.

Gann, W. D. *The Truth of the Stock Tape*. New York, NY: Financial Guardian Publishing Company, 1923.

Gartley, H. M. *Profits in the Stock Market*. 3rd ed. (1981). Pomeroy, WA: Lambert-Gann Publishing Co., 1935.

Gehm, Ralph. *Quantitative Trading and Money Management*. New York, NY: John Wiley & Sons, Inc., 1983.

Gehrig, Thomas, and Lukas Menkhoff. "Extended Evidence on the Use of Technical Analysis in Foreign Exchange." *International Journal of Finance & Economics* 11, no. 4 (2006): 327–338.

Gentile, Tom. "Explore Your Options." *Technical Analysis of Stocks and Commodities* 22, no. 11 (November 2004): 101.

Gervais, S., and T. Odean. "Learning to Be Overconfident." *Review of Financial Studies* 14 (2001): 1–27.

Goepfert, Jason. "Mutual Fund Cash Reserves, the Risk-Free Rate and Stock Market Performance." *Journal of Technical Analysis* (formerly *The Market Technicians Association Journal*) (October 2004): 1–5.

Goetzmann, William N. "Fibonacci and the Financial Revolution." Working paper no. 03-28, Yale International Center for Finance, Yale School of Management, New Haven, CT, 2003.

Graham, Benjamin, and D. Dodd. *Security Analysis: Principles and Technique.* 3rd ed. New York, NY: McGraw-Hill, 1951.

Graifer, Vadym and Christopher Schumacher. *Techniques of Tape Reading.* New York, NY: McGraw-Hill, 2003.

Granville, Joseph E. *Strategy of Daily Stock Market Timing for Maximum Profit.* Englewood Cliffs, NJ: Prentice-Hall, Inc., 1960.

————. *A New Strategy of Daily Stock Market Timing for Maximum Profit.* Englewood Cliffs, NJ: Prentice-Hall, Inc., 1976.

Greco, Sal. "New Applications for Open Interest in U.S. Treasury Bond Futures: A Money Flow vs. Breadth Approach." *Journal of Technical Analysis* (formerly *The Market Technicians Association Journal*) (Spring–Summer 2001): 9–15.

Grossman, S. "On the Efficiency of Competitive Stock Markets Where Trades Have Diverse Information." *Journal of Finance* 31 (1976): 573–585.

————, and J. Stiglitz. "On the Impossibility of Informationally Efficient Markets." *American Economic Review* 70 (1980): 393–408.

Gujral, Ashwani. "ADX: The Key to Market Trends." *Futures Magazine* (May 2005): 34–36.

Hadady, R. Earl. "The POI Index." *Journal of Technical Analysis* (formerly *The Market Technicians Association Journal*) (May 1989): 32–44.

Hamilton, W. *The Stock Market Barometer: A Study of its Forecast Value Based on Charles H. Dow's Theory of the Price Movement, reprint of 1922 edition.* New York, NY: John Wiley & Sons, Inc., 1998.

Harlow, Charles V. *An Analysis of the Predictive Value of Stock Market 'Breadth' Measurements.* Larchmont, NY: Investors Intelligence, 1968.

Harris, Larry. *Trading and Exchanges: Market Microstructure for Practitioners.* New York, NY: Oxford University Press, 2002.

Harris, Michael. *Short-Term Trading with Price Patterns.* Greenville, NC: Traders Press, Inc., 2000.

Hartle, Thom. Interview: Van K. Tharp, *Technical Analysis of Stocks & Commodities* 17, no. 4 (1999): 186–192.

————. "James B. Stack, Big Sky Investor," *Technical Analysis of Stocks and Commodities* 12, no. 7 (July 1994): 294–302.

————. "Retracement Tendencies." *Active Trader Magazine* 5, no. 3 (March 2004): 32.

Hasanhodzic, Jasmina, Andrew W. Lo, and Emanuele Viola. "Is It Real, or Is It Randomized?: A Financial Turing Test." Unpublished manuscript, 2010 (available at http://web.mit.edu/alo/www/papers/arorassrn.pdf)

Haurlan, P. N. *Measuring Trend Values.* La Canada, CA: Trade Levels, Inc., 1968.

Hauschild, K., and Michael Winkelmann. "Kapitalmarketeffizienz und Point and Figure Analyse." *Kredit Und Kapital* (1985): 18.

Hawawini, G., and D. Keim. "On the Predictability of Common Stock Returns: World-wide Evidence." In R. A. Jarrow, V. Maksimovic, and W. T. Ziemba, eds, Finance (1994), in the Handbook series, North Holland.

Hayes, Timothy W. "Momentum Leads Price: A Universal Concept with Global Applications." *Journal of Technical Analysis* (formerly *The Market Technicians Association Journal*) (Winter–Spring 2004): 19–24.

———. *Research Driven Investor*. New York, NY: McGraw-Hill, 2000.

Herrick, John. "Cyclic Timing." *Technical Analysis of Stocks & Commodities* 1, no. 3 (1982): 52–57.

Higgins, Robert C. *Analysis for Financial Management*. 3rd ed. New York, NY: McGraw-Hill Higher Education, 1992.

Hill, John R., George Pruitt, and Lundy Hill. *The Ultimate Trading Guide*. New York, NY: John Wiley & Sons, Inc., 2000.

Holt, Laurence. *Stikky Stock Charts: Learn the 8 Major Stock Chart Patterns Used by Professionals and How to Interpret Them to Trade Smart—in One Hour, Guaranteed*. Laurence Holt Books, 2004.

Hoyle. *The Game in Wall Street and How to Play It Successfully*. New York, NY:: J. S. Ogilvie Publishing Co. (reprinted by Fraser Publishing Co., Burlington VT, 1968), 1898.

Hsu, Po-Hsuan, Yu-Chin Hsu, and Chung-Ming Kuan. "Testing the Predictive Ability of Technical Analysis Using a New Stepwise Test Without Data Snooping Bias." *Journal of Empirical Finance* 17, no. 3 (2010): 471–484.

Huberman, G., and T. Regev. "Contagious Speculation and a Cure for Cancer: A Nonevent That Made Prices Soar." *Journal of Finance* 56 (2001): 387–396.

Hubner, Manifred. "SENTIX: Behavioral Indices, a Behaviourally Oriented Development of the TA Tool-Kit" *International Federation of Technical Analysts Journal* (2008): 26–31.

Hughes, James F. "The Birth of the Climax-Breadth Method." *Analysts Journal*, 3rd quarter (1951): 25–35.

Hurst, James M. *The Profit Magic of Stock Transaction Timing*. Englewood Cliffs, NJ: Prentice-Hall, 1970.

Hutson, Jack K. *Charting the Stock Market: The Wyckoff Method*. Seattle, WA: Technical Analysis, Inc., 1986.

Ince, Huseyin, and Theodore B. Trafalis. "Short-Term Forecasting with Support Vector Machines and Application in Stock Price Prediction." *International Journal of General Systems* 37, no. 6 (2007): 677–687.

———. "Kernal Principal Component Analysis and Support Vector Machines for Stock Price Prediction." *IIE Transactions* 39, no. 6 (2007): 629–637.

Jackwerth, Jens Carsten, and Mark Rubinstein. "Recovering Probability Distributions from Options Prices." *Journal of Finance* 51 (1996): 5.

Jacobs, Bruce I. *Capital Ideas and Market Realities: Option Replication, Investor Behavior, and Stock Market Crashes.* Malden, MA: Blackwell, 1999.

Jegadeesh, Narisimhan, and Sheridan Titman. "Returns to Buying Winners and Selling Losers: Implications for Stock Market Efficiency." *Journal of Finance* 48 (1993):65–91.

———. "Profitability of Momentum Strategies: An Evaluation of Alternative Explanations." *Journal of Finance* 56 (2001): 699–720.

Jiler, William. *How Charts Can Help You in the Stock Market.* New York, NY: Commodity Research Corporation, 1962.

Johansen, Anders, and Didier Sornette. "Large Stock Market Price Drawdowns Are Outliers." *Journal of Risk* 4, no. 2 (2002): 69–110.

Johnson, Spencer. *Who Moved My Cheese?* New York, NY: Penguin Putnam, 1998.

Jordan, Douglas, and J. David Diltz. "The Profitability of Day Traders." *Financial Analysts Journal* (November–December 2003): 85–95.

Kaeppel, Jay. "The Put/Call VXO." *Active Trader Magazine* (August 2004): 28–31.

Kahneman, D., and A. Tversky. "Prospect Theory: An Analysis of Decision Under Risk." *Econometrica* 47 (1979): 263–291.

Kahneman, D. "Variants of Uncertainty." In *Judgment Under Uncertainty: Heuristics and Biases* (512), D. Kahneman, P. Slovic, and A. Tversky, eds., Cambridge University Press, Cambridge, 1982.

Kamich, Bruce M. *How Technical Analysis Works.* New York, NY: New York Institute of Finance, 2003.

Katz, Jeffrey and Donna McCormick. "Barrier Stops and Trendlines," *Technical Analysis of Stocks and Commodities* (July 1998): 44–49.

———. "Evaluating Trading Systems with Statistics, Part I." *Technical Analysis of Stocks & Commodities* 15, no. 7 (1997): 311–317.

———. "Using Statistics with Trading Systems, Part II." *Technical Analysis of Stocks & Commodities* 15, no. 8 (1997): 347–352.

Kaufman, Perry J. *Trading Systems and Methods.* 3rd ed. New York, NY: John Wiley & Sons, Inc., 1998.

Kaufman, S. Kris and Marc Chaikin. "The Use of Price-Volume Crossover Patterns in Technical Analysis," *Journal of Technical Analysis* (formerly *Market Technicians Association Journal*) 37 (Spring 1991): 35–41.

Kellenbenz, H. "Introduction to Confusion de Confusiones." In M. Fridson (Ed.), *Confusion de Consusiones*, 125–146. New York, NY: John Wiley & Sons, Inc., 1957/1996.

Keltner, Chester W. *How to Make Money in Commodities*. Kansas City, MO: Keltner Statistical Service, 1960.

Kindleberger, Charles P. *Manias, Panics, and Crashes: A History of Financial Crises*. New York, NY: John Wiley & Sons, Inc., 2005.

King, Wilford I. "Forecasting Methods Successfully Used Since 1928." *Journal of the American Statistical Association* 27, no. 179 (1932): 315–319.

Kirkpatrick, Charles D. "Linear Regression Projection of Periodicity." *Journal of Technical Analysis* (formerly *The Market Technicians Association Journal*) (Summer 1990): 26–32.

———. "Stock Selection: A Test of Relative Stock Values Reported over 17 ½ Years." *Journal of Technical Analysis* (May 2007).

———. *Beat the Market: Invest by Knowing What Stocks to Buy and What Stocks to Sell*. Short Hills, NJ: FT Press, 2008.

Knapp, Volker. "The RSI Trend System." *Active Trader Magazine* 5, no. 8 (August 2004): 64–65.

Koch, Rene, PhD. "Creating Your Own Trading System." *Technical Analysis of Stocks & Commodities* 22, no. 7 (July 2004): 24–35.

Kondratieff, Nicolas D. *The Long Wave Cycle* (translated by Guy Daniels). New York, NY: Richardson and Snyder, 1984.

Krausz, Robert. *A W.D. Gann Treasure Discovered*. New York, NY: Marketplace Books, John Wiley & Sons, Inc., 1998.

Kurczek, Dion. "Basic Pullback Buyer." *Active Trader Magazine* 4, no. 3 (March 2003): 9.

———. "Two-Bar Breakout System." *Active Trader Magazine* 4, no. 11 (November 2003): 56.

———, and Volker Knapp. "Four-Week Breakout System." *Active Trader Magazine* 4, no. 11 (September 2003): 74.

Laibson, David I. "Golden Eggs and Hyperbolic Discounting." *Quarterly Journal of Economics* 112, no. 2 (May 1997): 443–478.

Landry, David. *Dave Landry's 10 Best Swing Trading Patterns and Strategies*. Los Angeles, CA: M. Gordon Publishing Group, 2003.

———. *David Landry on Swing Trading*. Los Angeles, CA: M. Gordon Publishing Group, 2003

Lane, George C. "Lane's Stochastics: The Ultimate Oscillator." *Journal of Technical Analysis* (formerly *The Market Technicians Association Journal*) (May 1985).

Larson, A. "Measurement of Random Processes in Futures Prices." *Food Research Institute* 1 (1960): 313–324.

LeBaron, Blake. "Technical Trading Rule Profitability and Foreign Exchange Intervention." *Journal of Economics* 49 (1999): 125–143.

Lebeau, Charles and David Lucas. *Technical Traders Guide to Computer Analysis of the Futures Markets*. New York, NY: McGraw-Hill, 1991.

Lefevre, Edwin. *Reminiscences of a Stock Operator*. Burlington, VT: Fraser Publishing, 1987.

Leiber, Alan. "Human Aggression and Lunar Synodic Cycle." *Journal of Clinical Psychology* 39, no. 5 (1978): 385.

Leroy, S. "Risk Aversion and the Martingale Property of Stock Returns." *International Economic Review* 14 (1973): 436–446.

Levy, Robert A. "Relative Strength as a Criterion for Investment Selection." *Journal of Finance* 22, no. 4 (1967): 595–610.

————. *The Relative Strength Concept of Common Stock Price Forecasting*. Larchmont, NY: Investors Intelligence, 1968.

————. "Predictive Significance of Five Point Chart Patterns." *Journal of Business* 44, no. 3 (1971): 316–323.

Lictenstein, S., B. Fischoff, and L. D. Phillips. "Calibration of Probabilities: The State of the Art to 1980." In Kahneman, D, P. Slovic, and A. Tversky (eds.). *Judgment Under Uncertainty: Heuristics and Biases*, 306–334. Cambridge, MA: Cambridge Press, 1982.

Lim, Kian-Ping, and Robert Brooks. "The Evolution of Stock Market Efficiency Over Time: A Survey of the Empirical Literature." *Journal of Economic Surveys* (2010).

Lind, Douglas A., William G. Marchal, and Samuel Adam Wathen. *Basic Statistics for Business and Economics*. New York, NY: McGraw-Hill, 2002.

Liu, James N. K., and Raymond W. M. Kwong. "Automatic Extraction and Identification of Chart Patterns Toward Financial Forecast." *Applied Soft Computing* 7, no. 4 (2007): 1197–1208.

Liu, Wei, and Jing Wang. "Some Properties of Technical Analysis Indicators Based on Stochastic Volatility Model." *Mathematica Applicata* (2010).

Livermore, Jesse L. *How to Trade in Stocks*. New York, NY: McGraw-Hill, 2006.

Lo, Andrew W. "The Adaptive Markets Hypothesis: Market Efficiency from an Evolutionary Perspective." *Journal of Portfolio Management* 30 (2004): 15–29.

————, and A. Craig MacKinlay. "Stock Market Prices Do Not Follow Random Walks: Evidence from a Simple Specification Test." *Review of Financial Studies* 1 (1988): 41–66.

————. *A Non-Random Walk Down Wall Street*. Princeton, NJ: Princeton University Press, 1999.

————, Harry Mamaysky, and Jiang Wang. "Foundations of Technical Analysis: Computational Algorithms, Statistical Inference, and Empirical Implementation." *Journal of Finance* 55 (2000): 4.

————, and Jasmina Hasanhodzic. *The Evolution of Technical Analysis: Financial Prediction from Babylonian Tablets to Bloomberg Terminals*. New York, NY: John Wiley & Sons, Inc., 2010.

Loomis, Carol. Interview with Warren Buffett, as reported by the Los Angeles Chinese Learning Center (2001), http://chinese-school.netfirms.com/Warren-Buffett-interview.html, original from *Fortune Magazine* reporting on a speech at the Allen & Co.'s annual Sun Valley meeting for corporate executives.

Lowenstein, Roger. *When Genius Failed: The Rise and Fall of Long-Term Capital Management*. New York, NY: Random House, 2000.

Lucas, R. "Asset Prices in an Exchange Economy." *Econometrica* 46 (1978): 1429–1446.

————. "The Usefulness of Historical Data in Selecting Parameters for Technical Trading Systems." *Journal of Futures Markets* 9 (1989): 55–65.

Lui, Y. H., and D. Mole. "The Use of Fundamental and Technical Analyses by Foreign Exchange Dealers: Hong Kong Evidence." *Journal of International Money and Finance* 17, no. 3(1998): 535–545.

Lukac, Louis P., and B. Wade Brorsen. "The Value of Optimization." *Technical Analysis of Stocks & Commodities* 6, no. 7 (1988): 262–264.

————, and Scott H. Irwin. "A Test of Futures Market Disequilibrium Using Twelve Different Technical Trading Systems." *Applied Economics* 20 (1988): 623–639.

Lukeman, Joshua. *The Market Maker's Edge: A Wall Street Insider Reveals How to: Time Entry and Exit Points for Minimum Risk, Maximum Profit; Combine Fundamental and Technical Analysis; Control Your Trading Every Day, Every Trade*. New York, NY: McGraw-Hill, 2003.

MacDonald, Ronald, Lukas Menkhoff, and Rafael R. Rebitzky. "Exchange Rate forecasters' Performance: Evidence of Skill?" *CESifo Working Paper Series No. 2615* (2009), Department of Economics, University of Glasgow.

Mackay, Charles. *Extraordinary Popular Delusions and the Madness of Crowds*. Petersfield, Hampshire, UK: Harriman House, 2003.

Malkiel, Burton. *A Random Walk Down Wall Street*. Princeton, NJ: Princeton University Press, 1966.

Mandelbrot, Benoit B. "The Variation of Certain Speculative Prices." *Journal of Business* 36 (1963): 394–419.

————. *Fractals and Scaling in Finance: Discontinuity, Concentration, Risk*. New York, NY: Springer-Verlag, 1997.

Maremont, Mark. "Tyco Seems to Back Off from Breakup—CEO Says the Spinoff Plan May Be Pared in Face of Unfavorable Market." *Wall Street Journal*, February 14, 2002, A3.

Markowitz, Harry. "Portfolio Selection." *Journal of Finance* 7, no. 1 (1952): 77–91.

Markstein, David L. *How to Chart Your Way to Stock Market Profits*. New York, NY: Arco Publishing, 1972.

Marshall, Ben R., Rocheter H. Cahan, and Jared M. Cahan. "Does Intraday Technical Analysis in the U.S. Equity Market Have Value?" *Journal of Empirical Finance* 15, no. 2 (2008): 199–210.

Maschke, E. "Deutshe Stadte am Ausgang des Mittelalters." *Die Stadt am Ausgang des Mittelalters* (1974), edited by Rausch, W., offprint, Lintz.

May, Christopher. *Nonlinear Pricing: Theory and Applications*. New York, NY: John Wiley & Sons, Inc., 1999.

McClellan, Sherman and Marian. *Patterns for Profit*. La Canada, CA: Trade Levels Inc., 1970.

McLaren, William, with Matthew Foreman. *Gann Made Easy: How to Trade Using the Methods of W. D. Gann*. Corpus Christi, TX: Gann Theory Publishing, 1986.

McMillan, Lawrence G. *McMillan on Options*. New York, NY: John Wiley & Sons, Inc., 1996.

Menkhoff, Lukas. "Examining the Use of Technical Analysis." *International Journal of Finance and Economics* 2 (1997): 307–318.

———."The Use of Technical Analysis by Fund Managers: International Evidence." *Journal of Banking & Finance* (2010): to be published.

———, Rafael R. Rebitzky, and Michael Schroder. "Heterogeneity in Exchange Rate Expectations: Evidence on the Chartist-Fundamentalist Approach." *Journal of Economic Behavior & Organization* 70, no. 1–2 (2009): 241–252.

———, and Mark P. Taylor. "The Obstinate Passion of Foreign Exchange Professionals: Technical Analysis." *Journal of Economic Literature* 45, no. 4 (2007): 936–972.

Merrill, Arthur A. "Advance-Decline Divergences as an Oscillator." *Stocks & Commodities Magazine* 6, no. 9 (September 1988): 354–355.

———. *Behavior of Prices on Wall Street*. Published privately by the author, 1997.

———. *Filtered Waves*. Published privately by the author, 1997.

———. "Negative Volume Divergence Index," *Technical Analysis of Stocks and Commodities*, vol. 8, no. 10 (1990): 396–397.

———. "Retracement Percentage," *Journal of Technical Analysis* (Formerly the *Market Technicians Association Journal*), 33 (August 1989): 38–45.

———. "Stochastics ???" *Journal of Technical Analysis* (formerly *The Market Technicians Association Journal*) (February 1986).

Meyers, Dennis, PhD. "The Siren Call of Optimized Trading Systems." *Technical Analysis of Stocks & Commodities* 14, no. 10 (1996): 415–418.

———. "Walk Forward with the XAU Bond Fund System." *Technical Analysis of Stocks & Commodities* 15, no. 5 (1997): 199–205.

Miner, Robert C. *Dynamic Trading: Dynamic Concepts in Time, Price & Pattern Analysis with Practical Strategies for Traders and Investors.* Cedar Falls, IA: Trader's Press, 2002.

———. *High Probability Trading Strategies: Entry to Exit Tactics for the Forex, Futures, and Stock Markets.* New York, NY: John Wiley & Sons, Inc., 2008.

Mishkin, F. *The Economics of Money, Banking, and Financial Markets.* 7th ed. Boston, MA: Addison-Wesley, 2004.

Mitra, Subrata Kumar. "How Rewarding Is Technical Analysis in the Indian Stock Market?" *Quantitative Finance* (May 2010): 1469–7688.

Modelski, George, and William R. Thompson. *Leading Sectors and World Powers: The Coevolution of Global Economics and Politics.* Columbia, SC: University of South Carolina Press, 1996.

Momsen, John. *Superstar Seasonals: 18 Proven-Dependable Futures Trades for Profiting Year after Year.* Brightwaters, NY: Windsor Books, 2004.

Munro, John. "Dutch Banking and Finance in the 17th and 18th Centuries." Economics 301Y1 (2005), Lecture Topic No 24, Department of Economics, University of Toronto, http://www.economics.utoronto.ca/munro5/.

Murphy, John J. *Intermarket Technical Analysis.* New York, NY: John Wiley & Sons, Inc., 1991.

———. *Technical Analysis of the Financial Markets.* New York, NY: New York Institute of Finance, 1999.

Nassar, David, and William S. Lupien. *Market Evaluation and Analysis for Swing Trading: Timeless Methods and Strategies for an Ever-Changing Market.* New York, NY: McGraw-Hill, 2004.

Neely, Christopher J., Paul A. Weller, and Joshua M. Ulrich. "The Adaptive Markets Hypothesis: Evidence from the Foreign Exchange Market." *Journal of Financial and Quantitative Analysis* 44 (2009): 467–488.

Neely, Christopher, Paul Weller, and Rob Dittmar. "Is Technical Analysis in the Foreign Exchange Market Profitable? A Genetic Programming Approach." *Journal of Financial and Quantitative Analysis* 32 (1997): 405–426.

Neely, Glen. *Mastering Elliott Wave.* Brightwaters, NY: Windsor Books, 1990.

Neftci, S. "Naïve Trading Rules in Financial Markets and Wiener-Kolmogorov Prediction Theory: A Study of 'Technical Analysis,'" *Journal of Business* 64 (1991): 549–572.

Neill, Humphrey B. *The Art of Contrary Thinking.* Caldwell, ID: Caxton Printers, 1997.

Nelson, S. *The A B C of Stock Speculation, 1902.* Burlington, VT: Fraser Publishing Co., 1964 reprint.

Niederhoffer, V., and M. Osborne. "Market Making and Reversal on the Stock Exchange." *Journal of the American Statistical Association* 61 (1966): 897–916.

Nison, Steve. *Japanese Candlestick Charting Techniques*. New York, NY: New York Institute of Finance, 2001.

O'Neil, William J. *How to Make Money in Stocks*. 3rd ed. (2002). New York, NY: McGraw-Hill, 1988.

O'Shaughnessy, James P. *What Works on Wall Street*. New York, NY: McGraw-Hill, 1997.

Odean, T. "Are Investors Reluctant to Realize Their Losses?" *Journal of Finance* 53 (1998): 1775–1798.

Olsen, Luke. "Why Be Normal?" Society for Amateur Scientists, e-bulletin (November 21, 2003).

Osborne, M. "Periodic Structure in the Brownian Motion of Stock Prices." *Operations Research* 10 (1962): 345–379.

Osler, Carol L. "Identifying Noise Traders: The Head-and-Shoulders Pattern in U.S. Equities." *Federal Reserve Bank of New York* Staff Report No. 42, February, 1998.

———. "Currency Orders and Exchange-Rate Dynamics: Explaining the Success of Technical Analysis." FRB of New York Staff Report No. 125, April 2001.

———. "Support for Resistance: Technical Analysis and Intraday Exchange Rates." *Economic Policy Review,* FRB of New York, 6, no. 2 (2000): 53-68.

———. "Currency Orders and Exchange Rate Dynamics: An Explanation for the Predictive Success of Technical Analysis." *Journal of Finance* 58, no. 5 (2003): 1791–1820.

Oz, Tony. *The Stock Trader: How I Make a Living Trading Stocks*. Goldman Brown Business Media, 2000.

———. *Stock Trading Wizard: Advanced Short-Term Trading Strategies for Swing and Day Trading*. Tony Oz Publications, 1999.

Painter, William M. "On Balance Open Interest Indicator." *Journal of Technical Analysis* (formerly *The Market Technicians Association Journal*) (Fall–Winter 1995): 48–56.

Park, Cheol-Ho, and Scott H. Irwin. "The Profitability of Technical Analysis: A Review." University of Illinois at Urbana-Champaign, AgMAS Project Research Report 2004-04, 2004.

———."A Reality Check on Technical Trading Rule Profits in the U. S. Futures Markets." *Journal of Futures Markets* 30, no. 7 (2009): 633–659.

Patel, Alpesh. *The Mind of the Trader*. London, UK: Financial Times/Pitman, 1997.

Pau, L. "Technical Analysis for Portfolio Trading by Syntactic Pattern Recognition." *Journal of Economic Dynamics and Control* 15 (1991): 715–730.

Pesavento, Larry and Leslie Jouflas. *Trade What You See: How to Profit from Pattern Recognition*. New York, NY: John Wiley & Sons, Inc., 2007.

Peterson, P. E., and R. M. Leuthold. "Using Mechanical Trading Rules to Evaluate the Weak-Form Efficiency of Futures Markets." *Southern Journal of Agricultural Economics* (1982): 14.

Peterson, Richard L. *Inside the Investor's Brain: The Power of Mind Over Money*. New York, NY: John Wiley & Sons, Inc., 2007.

Plummer, Tony. *The Psychology of Technical Analysis*. Chicago, IL: Probus Publishing Company, 1989.

———. *Forecasting Financial Markets: The Psychology of Successful Investing*. 4th ed. London, UK: Kogan Page, 2003.

Poser, Steven W. *Applying Elliott Wave Theory Profitably*. New York, NY: John Wiley & Sons, Inc., 2003.

Prechter, Robert R. *The Major Works of R. N. Elliott*. Gainesville, GA: New Classics Library, Inc., 1980.

———. *Elliott Wave Principle: Key to Stock Market Profits*. Gainesville, GA: New Classics Library, Inc., 1990.

Pring, Martin J. "The Summed Rate of Change." *Technical Analysis of Stocks and Commodities* (September 1992): 10.

———. *Martin Pring on Market Momentum*. Homewood, IL: Irwin Professional Publishing, 1993.

———. *Technical Analysis Explained*. 4th ed. New York, NY: McGraw-Hill, 2002.

Qi, M., and Y. Wu. "Technical Trading-Rule Profitability, Data Snooping, and Reality Check: Evidence from the Foreign Exchange Market." *Journal of Money, Credit and Banking* 38 (December 2005): 2135–2158.

Reinhard, Carmen M. and Kenneth Rogoff. *This Time is Different: Eight Centuries of Financial Folly*. Princeton, NJ: Princeton University Press, 2009.

Rhea, Robert. *The Dow Theory: An Explanation of Its Development and an Attempt to Define Its Usefulness as an Aid to Speculation,* reprint of 1932 Barron's Publishing edition by Fraser Publishing Co., Burlington, VT, 1993.

Ricard, J. *Le Negoce d'Amsterdam contenant tout ce uie doivent savoir les marchands et banquires, tant ceux qui sont etablis a Amsterdam que ceux des pays etrangers*. Amsterdam, 1722.

Riedel, Herbert. "Do Stock Prices Reflect Fibonacci Ratios?" *Technical Analysis of Stocks and Commodities* 7, no. 12 (December 1989): 433–436.

Rode, David, Yolanda Friedman, Satu Parikh, and Jerimiah Kane. "An Evolutionary Approach to Technical Trading and Capital Market Efficiency." Working paper, Wharton School, 1995.

Roscoe, Philip, and Carole Howorth. "Identification Through Technical Analysis: A Study of Charting and UK Non-professional Investors." *Accounting, Organizations and Society* 34, no. 2 (2009): 206–221.

Ross, Joe. *Trading by the Book*, 5th edition. Ross Trading, 1994.

Rotella, Robert P. *The Elements of Successful Trading*. New York, NY: NY Institute of Finance, 1992.

Ruggiero, Murray A., Jr. "Walking Before You Run with System Optimization." *Futures Magazine*. February 2005.

———. "Out of Sample, Out of Mind." *Futures Magazine*. April 2005.

Samuelson, Paul. "Proof That Properly Anticipated Prices Fluctuate Randomly." *Industrial Management Review* 6 (1965): 41–49.

Sapori, A. *Una Compagnia di Calimala ai primi del Trecento*. Florence, 1932.

Savin, N Eugene, Paul A.Weller, and Janis Zvingelis. "The Predictive Power of 'Head and Shoulders' Price Patterns in the U. S. Stock Market." *Journal of Financial Econometrics* 5, no. 2 (2007): 243–265.

Schabacker, R. *Stock Market Theory and Practice*. New York, NY: B.C. Forbes Publishing Company, 1930.

———. *Technical Analysis and Stock Market Profits*. New York, NY: Pitman Publishing, 1932.

———. *Stock Market Profits*. New York, NY: B.C. Forbes Publishing Company, 1934.

Schade, George A., Jr. "Forecasting Like the Technical Masters: Edson Gould's 'Three Steps and a Stumble Rule' Could Prove Timely." *Stocks, Futures & Options Magazine* www.sfomag.com. (September 2004): 68–72.

Schnapper, B. *Les Rentes au XVIe siècle, Histoire d'un instrument de crédit*. Paris, 1957.

Schulmeister, Stephan. "Profitability of Technical Stock Trading: Has It Moved from Daily to Intraday Data?" *Review of Financial Economics* 18, no. 4 (2009): 190–201.

———. "Components of the Profitability of Technical Currency Trading." *Applied Financial Economics* 18, no.11 (2008): 917–930.

Schultz, Harry D., and Samson Coslow (eds). *A Treasury of Wall Street Wisdom*. Palisades park, NJ: Investor's Press, 1966. Reprinted by Traders Press, Inc., Greenville, SC, 2001.

Schultz, Henry. "Forecasting Security Prices." *Journal of American Statistical Association* 20, no. 150 (1925): 244–249.

Schwager, Jack D. *Market Wizards*. New York, NY: New York Institute of Finance, 1989.

———. *The New Market Wizards: Conversations with America's Top Traders, New Edition*. New York, NY: John Wiley & Sons, Inc., 1995.

———. *Schwager on Futures: Technical Analysis*. New York, NY: John Wiley & Sons, Inc., 1996.

———. *Technical Analysis*. New York, NY: John Wiley & Sons, Inc., 1996.

———. *Getting Started in Technical Analysis*. New York, NY: John Wiley & Sons, Inc., 1999.

Schwartz, Martin. *Pit Bull: Lessons from Wall Street's Champion Day Trader*. New York, NY: Harper Paperbacks, 1999.

Schwartz, R., and D. Whitcomb. "The Time-Variance Relationship: Evidence on Autocorrelation in Common Stock Returns." *Journal of Finance* 32 (1977): 41–55.

Seamans, George (pseudonym for Ely Bramson). *This Is the Road to Stock Market Success*. Chicago, IL: Seamans-Blake, Inc., 1946.

———. *100 Rules on How to Trade Profitably*. Brightwaters, NY: Windsor Books, 1983.

Sepiashvili, David, PhD. "How to Best Evaluate System Performance." *Futures Magazine*. March 2005.

Sharpe, William, and G. Alexander. *Investments*. 4th ed. Englewood Cliffs, NJ: Prentice-Hall, 1990.

Shaw, Alan. *Technical Analysis*, reprinted by the Market Technicians Association from the *Financial Analysts Handbook*. Homewood, IL: Dow Jones-Irwin, 1988.

Shefrin, M., and M. Statman. "The Disposition to Sell Winners Too Early and Ride Losers Too Long: Theory and Evidence." *Journal of Finance* 40 (1985): 777–790.

Shiller, Robert J. *Irrational Exuberance* 2nd ed. New York, NY: Broadway Books, 2001.

Shimizu, S. *The Japanese Chart of Charts*. Tokyo, 1986 (as translated from Japanese by Nicholson, G.).

Shleifer, A. *Inefficient Markets: An Introduction to Behavioral Finance*. New York, NY: Oxford University Press Inc., 2000.

Sieveking, H. *Wirtschaftgeschichte*, in *Enzyklopadie der rechts und Staatswissenschaft. Bd. 47* (nr. 2725) 1935.

Skinner, B. F. "Superstition in the Pigeon." *Journal of Experimental Psychology* 38 (1947): 168–172.

Smith, Edgar L. *Common Stocks as Long-Term Investments, 1928*. Reprint by Kessinger Publishing Company, Whitefish, Montana, 2003.

———. *Tides in the Affairs of Men*. New York, NY: MacMillan Company, 1939.

Sobel, Robert. *Panic on Wall Street: A History of America's Financial Disasters*. New York, NY: Macmillan, 1968.

Solt, M. E., and M. Statman. "How Useful Is the Sentiment Index?" *Financial Analysts Journal* (September–October 1988): 45–55.

Sornette, Didier. "Critical Market Crashes." *Physics Reports* 378, no. 1 (2003): 1–98.

———. *Why Stock Markets Crash: Critical Events in Complex Financial Systems*. Princeton, NJ: Princeton University Press, 2003.

Sperando, Victor. *Trader Vic: Methods of a Wall Street Master.* New York, NY: John Wiley & Sons, Inc., 1993.

Sprandel, R. Der stadtische Rentenmarkt in Nordwestdeutschland im Spatmittelatler, *Offenliche Finanzen und privates Kapital im spaten Mittelalter und der ersten Halfte des 19. Jahrhunderts.* ed H. Kellerbenz (Stuttgart, 1971) 14–23.

Staff. "Futures Insight: Crude Oil." *Active Trader Magazine* 5, no. 7 (July 2004): 70.

———. "The Trading System Lab." *Active Trader Magazine* 4, no. 7 (July 2003): 42.

———. "Gann's 28 Trading Rules." *Technical Analysis of Stocks and Commodities* 10, no. 6 (June 1992): 268–271.

Star, Barbara. "The CCI Stochastic." *Active Trader Magazine.* September 2004, 52–54.

Steckler, David. "Trading Stochastic Pops." *Technical Analysis of Stocks & Commodities* 18: 8 (2000): 30–41.

Steenbarger, Brett N. *The Psychology of Trading: Tools and Techniques for Minding the Markets.* New York, NY: John Wiley & Sons, Inc., 2002.

Steidlmayer, J. Peter, and Steven B. Hawkins. *Steidlmayer on Markets: Trading with Market Profile.* Hoboken, NJ: John Wiley & Sons, Inc., 2003.

Stephen J. Brown, William Goetzmann, and Alok Kumar. "The Dow Theory: William Peter Hamilton's Track Record Re-Considered." *Journal of Finance* 53: 4 (August 1998): 1311–1333.

Steiger, W. "A Test of Nonrandomness in Stock Price Changes." In P. Cootner (ed.), *The Random Character of Stock Market Prices.* Cambridge, MA: MIT Press, 1964.

Stottner, R. "P&F-Filteranalyse, Averaging-Strategie und Buy & Hold—Anlageregel." Jahrb.f.National, u. Stat. (1990): 207.

Stringham, Edward. "The Extralegal Development of Securities Trading in Seventeenth-Century Amsterdam." *The Quarterly Review of Economics and Finance* 43 (2003): 321–344.

Strong, Robert A. "A Behavioral Investigation of Three Paradigms in Finance." *Northeast Journal of Business and Economics* (Spring–Summer 1988).

Swannell, Richard. "Elliott Waves Vary Depending on the Time Frame and Direction of the Pattern." *Journal of Technical Analysis* (formerly *The Market Technicians Association Journal*) (Summer–Fall 2003): 17–24.

Szala, Ginger, and James T. Holter. "Storm Warning! How Social Mood Drives Markets." *Futures* (Nov. 2004).

Taleb, Nassim N. *The Black Swan: Second Edition: The Impact of the Highly Improbable: With a New Section: On Robustness and Fragility.* New York, NY: Random House, 2010.

Tarkany, Frank. "Weekly Price Cycles: Evidence of Auto-Correlation." *Technical Analysis of Stocks & Commodities* 5, no. 4 (1987): 127.

Taylor, George Douglass. *The Taylor Trading Technique*. Greenville, NC: Traders Press, Inc., 2000. Reprint of 1950 edition.

Taylor, M. P., and H. Allen. "The Use of Technical Analysis in the Foreign Exchange Market." *Journal of International Money and Finance* 11 (1992): 304–314.

Taylor, S. J. "Trading Futures Using a Channel Rule: A Study of the Predictive Power of Technical Analysis with Currency Examples." *Journal of Futures Markets* (1993): 14.

Teixeira, Lamartine Almeida, and Adriano Lorena Inacio. "A Method for Automatic Stock Trading Combining Technical Analysis and Nearest Neighbor Classification." *Expert Systems with Applications* 37, no. 10 (2010): 6885–6890.

Tharp, Van K. *Super Trader: Make Consistent Profits in Good and Bad Markets*. New York, NY: McGraw-Hill, 2009.

Thomas, James D. "News and Trading Rules." PhD thesis, School of Computer Science, Computer Science Department, Graduate School of Industrial Administration, Carnegie Mellon University, January 2003.

Tillman, Jim. "Practical Application of Cycles to Investment Markets." *Journal of Technical Analysis* (formerly *The Market Technicians Association Journal*) (Summer 1990).

Treynor, J., and R. Ferguson. "In Defense of Technical Analysis." *Journal of Finance* 40 (1985): 757–773.

Tversky, A., and D. Kahneman. "Extensional vs. Intuitive Reasoning: The Conjunction Fallacy in Probability Judgment." *Psychological Review* 90, no. 4 (1983): 293–315.

van Daele, Marco. "Investor Sentiment, Stock Returns, and Volatility in Germany," dissertation, Universität Maastricht, May 2005.

Velez, Oliver, and Greg Capra. *Tools and Tactics for the Master Day Trader*. New York, NY: McGraw-Hill, 2000.

Vervoort, Sylvain. *Capturing Profit with Technical Analysis: Hands-on Rules for Exploiting Candlestick, Indicator, & Money Management Techniques*. Glenelg, MD: Marketplace Books, 2009.

Vince, Ralph. *Portfolio Management Formulas*. New York, NY: John Wiley & Sons, Inc., 1990.

———. *The Mathematics of Money Management*. New York, NY: John Wiley & Sons, Inc., 1992.

von Ronik, Wolf. "Statistics: Your Crash Potential." *Technical Analysis of Stocks & Commodities* 19, no. 7 (2001): 20–24.

Wang, Changyun. "Investment Sentiment, Market Timing, and Future Returns," *Applied Financial Economics* 13, no. 12 (December 2000): 871–878.

Wang, Jar-Long, and Shu-Hui Chan. "Stock Market Trading Rule Discovery Using Pattern Recognition and Technical Analysis." *Expert Systems with Applications* 33, no. 2 (2007): 304–315.

Weber, Heinrich, and Kermit Zieg. *The Complete Guide to Point-and-Figure Charting.* Petersfield, Hampshire, UK: Harriman House Ltd., 2003.

Wheelan, Alexander H. *Study Helps in Point and Figure Technique.* New York, NY: Morgan, Rogers, and Roberts, 1954.

Wicker, Elmus. *Breaking Panics of the Guilded Age.* UK: Cambridge University Press, 2008.

Wilder, J. Welles Jr. *New Concepts in Technical Trading Systems.* Greensboro, SC: Trend Research, 1978.

Williams, Larry. *How I Made One Million Dollars Last Year Trading Commodities.* Brightwaters, NY: Windsor Books, 1979.

———. *The Definitive Guide to Futures Trading.* Brightwaters, NY: Windsor Books, 1988.

———. *Futures Millionaire.* Manual published by Karol Media, Wilkes-Barre, PA, 1995.

———. *Long-Term Secrets to Short-Term Trading.* New York, NY: John Wiley & Sons, Inc., 1999.

———. *Day Trade Futures Online.* New York, NY: John Wiley & Sons, Inc., 2000.

———. *The Right Stock at the Right Time.* New York, NY: John Wiley & Sons, Inc., 2003.

Wyckoff, Richard D. *Studies in Tape Reading* (under the pseudonym Rollo Tape). New York, NY: Traders Press, 1910. Reprinted in 1982 by Fraser Publishing Company, Burlington, VT.

———. "How I Trade and Invest in Stocks & Bonds." New York, NY: Magazine of Wall Street, 1924. Reprinted in 1983 by Fraser Publishing Company, Burlington, VT.

———. *Stock Market Technique, 2 vols.* New York, NY: Richard D. Wyckoff, 1933. Reprinted in 1984 by Fraser Publishing Company, Burlington, VT.

Yen, Stephane Meng-Feng, and Ying-Lin Hsu. "Profitability of Technical Analysis in Financial and Commodity Futures Markets—A Reality Check." *Decision Support Systems* (August 2010): accepted but not published.

Yuan, Kathy, Lu Zheng, and Qiaoqiao Zhu. "Are Investors Moonstruck? Lunar Phases and Stock Returns." *Journal of Empirical Finance* 13, no. 1 (January 2006): 1–23.

Zamansky, Leo and David Stendahl. "Secure Fractional Money Management," *Stocks and Commodities Magazine* 15, no. 7 (July 1998): 318–323.

Zamansky, Leo, PhD, and James Goldcamp. "Walking a Fine Line." *Futures Magazine.* October 2001.

Zhu, Yingzi, and Guofu Zhou. "Technical Analysis: An Asset Allocation Perspective on the Use of Moving Averages." *Journal of Financial Economics* 92, no. 3 (2009): 519–544.

Zieg, K. C., and P. J. Kaufman. *Point-and-Figure Commodity Trading Techniques.* Larchmont, NY: Investors Intelligence, 1975.

Zweig, Martin E. *Martin Zweig's Winning on Wall Street.* 4th ed. New York, NY: Warner Books, Inc., 2007.

INDEX

A

A/D line. *See* advance-decline line
AA (Alcoa Corporation)
  daily bar chart, 210
  daily candlestick chart, 212
line chart of daily closing prices, 207
  stock price data in tabular form, 203
  weekly bar chart, 211
AAPL (Apple Computer)
  alpha calculation, 518
  gaps and classic patterns, 368-370
ABC (American Bread Company), 63
absolute breadth index, 144-145
Aby, Carroll, 339
academic criticisms of technical analysis
  behavioral finance, 49-50
  EMH (Efficient Markets Hypothesis)
    arbitrage and price equilibrium, 47-48
    *economic theory of competitive markets,
      41-42*
    explained, 40-41
    new information, 42-46
    origins and development, 41
    rationality of investors, 46-47
  explained, 33-34
  pragmatic criticisms, 50-51
  RWH (Random Walk Hypothesis)
    drawdowns, 37-38
    explained, 35
    fat tails, 36
    origins and development, 35
    proportions of scale, 39-40
accelerating trend lines, 240-241
Accumulation Distribution (AD), 419
accuracy of cycles, 455-456

Achelis, Steven B., 420
action points in one-box reversal point-and-
  figure charts, 344-345
AD (Accumulation Distribution), 419
Adaptive Markets Hypothesis, 18
*The Adaptive Markets Hypothesis: Market
  Efficiency from an Evolutionary Perspective*
  (Lo), 46
adaptive stops, 575
advance, 133
advance-decline line (A/D line), 27, 134-136
  advance-decline line to its 32-week simple
    moving average, 139
  advance-decline moving average, 138
  advance-decline ratio, 146-147
  traditional advance-decline methods, 138-139
advisory opinion polls, 103-105
Advisory Service Sentiment survey, 103-105
ADX, 290, 441-444
AI (artifical intelligence), 603-604
AIG, 31
Alcoa Corporation. *See* AA
All or None (AON), 607
alpha method, 519-520, 600
alternation, 487
American Association of Individual Investors
  poll, 105
American Bread Company (ABC), 63
American Misery Index, 189
Amibroker, 203
amplitude, projecting, 454
  commonality, 474-475
  FLD (Future Line of Demarcation), 471-472
  half-cycle reversal, 470-471
  Tillman method, 472-474

Amsterdam Exchange, 24
analysis
    confirmation analysis
        classic patterns, 411
        crossovers, 411
        divergences, 409-410
        explained, 408
        failure swings, 409
        overbought/oversold, 408-409
        reversals, 410
        trend IDs, 410-411
    cycle analysis
        accuracy, 455-456
        centered moving averages, 463-464
        detrending, 461
        envelopes, 464-467
        Fourier analysis (spectral analysis), 458
        harmonics, 456-457
        inversions, 457
        Maximum Entropy Spectral Analysis
          (MESA), 459
        observation, 460-461
        translation, 457-458
Anderson, John, 339
Andrews pitchfork, 249-250
Andrews, Alan, 249
annualized rate of return, 550
anticipating breakouts, 262
AON (All or None), 607
Appel, Gerald, 29, 432
Apple Computer (AAPL)
    alpha calculation, 518
    gaps and classic patterns, 368-370
arbitrage and price equilibrium, 47-48
ARCH, 602-603
Argus Research Group, 118
arithmetic mean. *See* mean
arithmetic moving averages, 278
arithmetic scale, 213, 220
Arms Index, 149-151
Arms, Richard W. Jr., 149
artificial intelligence (AI), 603-604
ascending triangle pattern, 317

ascending triple top and descending triple
    bottom pattern, 350-351
ask price, 59
assumptions of technical analysis, 3
asymmetric information, 43
ATR (Average True Range), 29, 259-260
auction markets, 59
autocorrelation, 590
Average True Range (ATR), 29, 259-260
averages
    equally weighted (geometric) averages, 72
    market capitalization weighted averages,
        71-72
    moving averages. *See* moving averages
    price-weighted averages, 70
Ayres, Leonard P., 27, 136

B

Bachelier, Louis, 35
bands
    Bollinger Bands, 292-293
    explained, 292
    Keltner Bands, 293
    STARC Bands, 293
    trading strategies, 294-295
Bandwidth Indicators, 295
bank loans, 184
bar charts
    explained, 210-211
    patterns, 307-308
        ascending triangle, 317
        broadening, 320
        descending triangle, 315-316
        diamond top, 321-322
        double top and double bottom, 309-310
        flags and pennants, 329-331
        head-and-shoulders, 326-329
        rectangle, 310-313
        rounding top and rounding bottom,
          325-326
        standard triangle, 314-315
        symmetrical triangle, 317-318
        triple top and triple bottom, 313-314
        wedge and climax, 322-325

bear markets, 80

bearish resistance lines, 248

"The Behavior of Stock Market Prices"
(Fama), 35

Behavioral Finance, 30, 49-50, 304-305

bell curve, 591-592

Bergstresser, Charles, 26

beta, 259, 519

　average beta, 594

　defined, 599-600

　Treynor measure of performance, 600

Beyond Technical Analysis (Chande), 556

bias and decision making, 92-94

bid price, 59

bid-ask spread, 59

bids, 607

bigcharts.com, 203

Black Monday, 36-37

Black-Scholes option-pricing model, 101

Blumenthal, Earl, 218, 339

Bollinger Bands, 292-293

Bolton, Hamilton, 478, 496

Bonacci, Guilielmo, 493

bonds, 512

Bosco, Bartolomo de, 24

bounded oscillators, 408

bowl pattern, 325-326

box pattern, 310-313

box size (point-and-figure charts), 217-218

breadth. *See* market breadth, measuring

break-even level, 574

break-even stops, 574

breakaway gaps, 364

breakouts

　anticipating, 262

　breakout gaps, 364

　breakout systems, 237, 536

　calculating risk/return ratio for breakout
　　trading, 271

　combining with stops, 269

confirming

　close filter, 256-257

　intra-bar breakouts, 256-257

　Pivot Point Technique, 260-262

　point or percent filter, 258

　time, 258

　volatility, 259-260

　volume, 259

explained, 255-256

false ("specialist") breakouts, 272-273

false/premature breakouts, 311

setting price targets with, 309

volume spikes, 425

broadening pattern, 320

brokered markets, 58

Brown, Connie, 492

bubbles, 94

Buffett, Warren, 168

Bulkowski ranking of candlestick patterns,
401-402

Bulkowski, Thomas N., 302

bull markets, 80

bullish support lines, 248

bullish triangle and bearish triangle
pattern, 352

Burke, Gibbons, 438

Burke, Michael, 339

buyer expectations, 17

C

Calahan, Edward A., 201

candlestick patterns

　Bulkowski ranking of candlestick patterns,
　　401-402

　dark cloud cover, 395-397

　doji, 391-392

　engulfing, 394-396

　evening star, 397-398

　explained, 211-213, 390-391

　hammer, 393

　hanging man, 393-394

　harami, 392-393

　inverted hammer, 394-395

morning star, 397-398

piercing line, 395-397

shooting star, 394-395

three black crows, 398-399

three inside down, 399-400

three inside up, 399-400

three outside down, 400

three outside up, 400

three white soldiers, 398-399

windows, 392

CANSLIM method, 521

capital, initial, 568-569

CAPM (Capital Asset Pricing Model), 571, 598-600

Carroll, Paul, 141

cash markets, 60-61

catapult pattern (three-point reversal point-and-figure charts), 354-355

CBOT (Chicago Board of Trade), 63

CCI (Commodity Channel Index), 441

CDO (credit default options), 66

centered moving averages, 463-464

central limit theorem, 591

central tendency, measuring, 583-585

CFTC (Commodity Futures Trading Commission), 122

Chaikin Money Flow, 421

Chaikin Oscillator, 422

Chaikin, Marc, 419

Chande, Tushar, 556

channeling (EWT), 487-488

channels, 237, 243-244, 295

Chartcraft (Cohen and Blumenthal), 218

Chartcraft Service, 339

Chartered Market Technician (CMT), 7

charts

bar charts. *See* bar charts

benefits of, 200

candlestick charts, 211-213

data requirements, 204-205

explained, 199-200

history of, 201-204

line charts, 207-209

patterns. *See* patterns

point-and-figure charts, 335

arithmetic scale, 220

box size, 217-218

continuous price flow, 336-337

explained, 215-216

history of, 337-339

logarithmic scale, 220

multibox reversal, 217-218

old versus new methods, 337

one-box reversal, 216-217, 339-345

three-point reversal, 345-357

time, 218

time and volume omission, 336

trend lines, 248

scale

arithmetic scale, 213

semi-logarithmic scale, 214

volume

bar/candle charts, 412-413

equivolume, 412-413

point-and-figure, 414

Chesler, Daniel, 379

Chi-Square distributions, 592

Chicago Board of Trade (CBOT), 63

Chicago Mercantile Exchange (CME Group), 63

Citigroup, 31

CLB (Core Laboratories), 276-277

climaxes, 107-108, 373, 426

close breakouts, 256-257

CME Group (Chicago Mercantile Exchange), 63

CMT (Chartered Market Technician), 7

coefficient of determination, 589

Cohen, Abe, 218, 339

coil triangle pattern, 317-318

cointegration, 602

Colby, Robert, 156

Collins, Charles, 478

combinations, 583

Commitment of Traders (COT) reports, 122-124

Commodity Futures Trading Commission (CFTC), 122
commodity markets. *See* **futures markets**
common gaps, 367
Common Stocks as Long-Term Investments **(Smith), 168**
commonality, 474-475
competitive markets, economic theory of, 41-42
components, measuring for robustness, 549
compound rate of return, 584
computers and pattern recognition, 305-306
CompuTrac, Inc., 438
confirmation
  analysis methods
    classic patterns, 411
    crossovers, 411
    divergences, 409-410
    explained, 408
    failure swings, 409
    overbought/oversold, 408-409
    reversals, 410
    trend IDs, 410-411
  in Dow Theory, 82-83
  momentum (price confirmation)
    Commodity Channel Index (CCI), 441
    determining trend and trading range, 441-444
    explained, 430-431
    Moving Average Convergence-Divergence (MACD), 432-433
    Rate of Change (ROC), 434-435
    Relative Strength Index (RSI), 434-437
    similarities between oscillators, 441-442
    Stochastic oscillator, 437-440
    success of momentum indicators, 431-432
    Williams %R oscillator, 440-441
  open interest
    explained, 427-428
    indicators, 428-429
  overview, 407-408
  volume confirmation. *See* volume

confirming breakouts
  close filter, 256-257
  intra-bar breakouts, 256-257
  Pivot Point Technique, 260-262
  point or percent filter, 258
  time, 258
  volatility, 259-260
  volume, 259
congestion areas. *See* **trading ranges**
Connor, Larry, 382-386, 538
Consensus Bullish Sentiment Index, 106
consolidation areas. *See* **trading ranges**
constant forward contracts, 539
Consumer Confidence Index, 106
continuous contracts, 206, 539
continuous price flow, 336-337
contracts
  cash markets, 60-61
  constant forward contracts, 539
  continuous contracts, 539
  derivative markets
    counterparty risk, 62
    defined, 62
    futures markets, 63-65
    option markets, 65-66
    underlying, 62
  explained, 59
  linked contracts, 205-206
  number of, 565
  perpetual contracts, 539
  swaps and forwards, 66
contrarian investing, 90-91
contrary opinion, 96
Cootner, Paul, 35
Coppock, E. S. C., 29
Core Laboratories (CLB), 276-277
corrective waves, 483
  flats, 485-486
  triangles, 486
  zigzags, 484
correlation, 586-590
cosine waves, 452-455

costs
    of funds, 185
    futures versus stock markets, 504
COT (Commitment of Traders) reports, 122-124
count
    in one-box reversal point-and-figure charts, 341-343
    in three-point reversal point-and-figure charts, 347-348
counterparty risk, 62
countertrend systems, 538
covariance
    calculating, 586
    variance versus, 597
Cowles, Alfred III, 35, 76
Crabel, Tony, 377, 388
crashes, 94
credit default options (CDO), 66
criticisms of technical analysis
    behavioral finance, 49-50
    EMH (Efficient Markets Hypothesis)
        arbitrage and price equilibrium, 47-48
        economic theory of competitive markets, 41-42
        explained, 40-41
        new information, 42-43, 46
        origins and development, 41
        rationality of investors, 46-47
    explained, 33-34
    pragmatic criticisms, 50-51
    RWH (Random Walk Hypothesis)
        drawdowns, 37-38
        explained, 35
        fat tails, 36
        origins and development, 35
        porpotions of scale, 39-40
crossovers, 411
crowd behavior and concept of contrary opinion, 96
cup pattern, 325-326
current advances in technical analysis, 30-31
curves, 302

cycles
    accuracy, 455-456
    amplitude, 470-475
    controversy about, 449-451
    cosine waves, 452-455
    defined, 452-455
    harmonics, 456-457
    identifying
        centered moving averages, 463-464
        detrending, 461
        envelopes, 464-467
        Fourier analysis (spectral analysis), 458
        Maximum Entropy Spectral Analysis (MESA), 459
        observation, 460-461
    inversions, 457
    projections
        amplitude, 470-475
        periods, 468-469
    temporal patterns/cycles
        34-year historical cycles, 166-168
        decennial pattern, 168-169
        election year pattern, 171-172
        event trading, 175
        explained, 163-164
        four-year or presidential cycle, 170-171
        January barometer, 174
        January effect, 174
        Kondratieff waves (K-waves), 164-166
        seasonal patterns, 172-174
    translation, 457-458
Cycletrend, Inc., 472
cyclical emphasis (ratio analysis), 510-511
    bond market to stock market, 512
    gold to bonds, 512
    implications of intermarket analysis, 513-515
    stock market to U.S. dollar, 513-514
    U.S. dollar to gold, 511

D

dark cloud cover candlestick pattern, 395-397
Davis, Robert Earl, 339
day orders, 607

DCB (Dead Cat Bounce), 371-373
dealer markets, 58
decelerating trend lines, 241-242
decennial pattern, 168-169
decision making
 and sentiment. *See* sentiment
 effect of bias on, 92
decline, 133
deductive reasoning, 50
The Definitive Guide to Futures Trading
 (Williams), 536
definition of technical analysis, 3
degrees of freedom
 defined, 585
 in probability distributions, 592-593
DeMark, Tom, 232
DeMark-Williams reversal points, 232-233
dependent variables, 590
derivative markets
 counterparty risk, 62
 defined, 62
 futures markets, 63-65
 option markets, 65-66
 underlying, 62
descending triangle pattern, 315-316
descriptive statistics
 central tendency measurement, 583-585
 defined, 583
 multiple variables, 586-590
 volatility measurement, 585-586
designing systems
 countertrend systems, 538
 exogenous signal systems, 538
 initial systems, 534-535
 pattern recognition systems, 537-538
 reliability, 538
 requirements, 532-533
 risk, 533-534
 trend-following systems
  breakout systems, 536
  explained, 535-536
  moving average systems, 536
  problems with, 536-537

Desmond, Paul F., 152
determining
 price extremes, 287
 support and resistance, 286
 trends, 227-229, 285
deterministic, 582
detrending, 461
Devoe, Raymond Jr., 371
Dewey, Edward R., 164
diagonals, 482
diamond top pattern, 321-322
direct search markets, 58
directional movement
 calculating, 288-289
 Directional Movement concept, 29
 DMIs (directional movement indicators),
  289-291
directional trends
 defined, 238
 uptrends, identifying, 238
  regression lines, 239
  trend lines, 239-244
discretionary systems, 530-531
distributions, 582-583, 591-594
divergence, 409-410
 defined, 132-133
 double divergences, 137
 double negative divergence, 136-137
 negative divergence, 132
 positive divergence, 132
 reversal, 133
diversifiable risk, 571-572
diversification, 595
DJIA. *See* Dow Jones Industrial Average
DMIs (directional movement indicators),
 289-291
doji candlestick pattern, 391-392
doji star, 397
dollar stops, 573
dollars
 stock market to U.S. dollar ratio analysis,
  513-514
 U.S. dollar to gold ratio analysis, 511

Donchian channel, 295

Donchian, Richard, 29, 237

Dormier, Buff, 427

Dorsey, Thomas, 218, 339

double divergences, 137

double negative divergence, 136-137

double top and double bottom pattern, 309-310, 349

Dow Jones Industrial Average
  34-year historical cycle, 166-167
  historical drawdowns, 38
  history of, 26-27

Dow Theory, 225-226
  confirmation, 82-83
  criticisms of, 85
  economic rationale, 78
  history of, 27
  idea market picture, 78
  minor trends, 82
  origins and development, 76-78
  primary trends, 80-81
  secondary trends, 81
  theorems, 78-79
  volume of transactions, 84

*The Dow Theory: An Explanation of Its
  Development and an Attempt to Define
  Its Usefulness as an Aid to Speculation*
  (Rhea), 76

Dow, Charles H., 4, 16-17, 26, 70, 75-76, 230, 337, 407

Dow, Jones & Company, 26

Downs, Walter, 383

downtick, 609

downtrends, 11. *See also* trends

drawdowns, 37-38, 563

Drew, Garfield, 29

Dystant, Ralph, 438

E

early financial markets and exchanges, 23-25

Ease of Movement (EMV), 425

eccentric sentiment indicators, 117

economic rationale, 78

economic theory of competitive markets, 41-42

Edison Telegraph Printer, 201

Edison, Thomas, 201

Edwards, Robert D., 3, 28

efficiency factor, 550

efficient frontier, 598

Efficient Markets Hypothesis (EMH), 17, 30

efficient set, 597-598

EFI (Elder Force Index), 423-424

Ehlers, John, 285

EHM (Efficient Markets Hypothesis), 17, 30

80/60 rule, 158

Elder Force Index (EFI), 423-424

election year pattern, 171-172

Elliott Wave Theory. *See* EWT

Elliott, Ralph Nelson, 477-478

EMA (Exponentially Smoothed Moving
  Average), 282-285

EMH (Efficient Markets Hypothesis)
  economic theory of competitive markets, 41-42
  explained, 40-41
  new information, 42-43
  origins and development, 41

emotional feedback, 19

emotions. *See* sentiment

empirical support for technical analysis, 52

EMV (Ease of Movement), 425

Encyclopedia of Chart Patterns
  (Bulkowski), 302

*The Encyclopedia of Technical Market
  Indicators* (Colby and Meyers), 156

ending diagonals, 482

engulfing candlestick pattern, 394-396

Enron, 43-44

entry (patterns), 302

entry stops, 263-264

entry strategies, 572

envelopes, 464-467

equality (EWT), 487

equally weighted (geometric) averages, 72

equity curve, 552

equity lines, 142

equivolume, 412-413

error term, 590

ETFs (exchange-traded funds), 61-62

evening star candlestick pattern, 397-398

event declines, 372

event trading, 175

EWT (Elliott Wave Theory)

    alternation, 487

    alternatives to, 490-491

    channeling, 487-488

    corrective waves, 483

        flats, 485-486

        triangles, 486

        zigzags, 484

    equality, 487

    explained, 477-480

    impulse waves

        basic rules, 480-481

        diagonals, 482

        impulse patterns, 481

        truncation, 483

    origins and development, 478

    practical interpretation, 491-492

    projected targets, 488-490

ex-dividend gaps, 367

exchange-traded funds (ETFs), 61-62

execution risk strategies, 576

exhaustion gaps, 367

exit (patterns), 302

exit stops, 263-264

exit strategies, 573

exogenous signal systems, 538

expectations, 17

expected return, 599

expert systems, 603

expiration

    of futures, 65

    of options, 65

explanatory variables, 590

explosion gap pivot, 364

Exponentially Smoothed Moving Average (EMA), 282-283

F

F distributions, 593

failure swings, 409, 436

failures, 303

false ("specialist") breakouts, setting stops for, 272-273

false breakouts, 311

FAMA (Following Adaptive Moving Average), 285

Fama, Eugene, 17, 35, 41

fan lines

    defined, 241

    Gann fan lines, 250-251

Fast Fourier Transforms (FFTs), 458

fat tails, 36

Federal Open Market Committee (FOMC), 191

Federal Reserve System, 60

    FOMC (Federal Open Market Committee), 191

    monetary policy

        explained, 190-191

        Fed policy futures, 191

        Three Steps and a Stumble indicator, 193-194

        valuation model, 192

        yield curve, 194

FFTs (Fast Fourier Transforms), 458

Fibonacci sequence

    explained, 493

    golden ratio, 493-495

    origins and development, 493

    price and time targets, 495-497

Fill or Kill (FOK), 607

finance.yahoo.com, 203

financial markets. *See* markets

Fisher, Mark, 388

fitness, 603-604

flags and pennants pattern, 329-331

flats, 485-486

FLD (Future Line of Demarcation), 471-472

flow of funds
  bank loans, 184
  cost of funds, 185
  explained, 177-178
  Fed policy
    explained, 190-191
    Fed policy futures, 191
    Three Steps and a Stumble indicator,
      193-194
    valuation model, 192
    yield curve, 194
  household financial assets, 182
  long-term interest rates, 187
  margin debt, 179-180
  Misery Index, 188-189
  money market funds, 178-179
  money supply, 183-184
  money velocity, 187, 189
  secondary offerings, 180-181
  short-term interest rates, 185-186
FOK (Fill or Kill), 607
Following Adaptive Moving Average
  (FAMA), 285
FOMC (Federal Open Market Committee),
  191
formations. *See* **patterns**
forward market, 24
forwards, 66
4-week rule, 29
four-year cycle, 170-171
Fourier analysis, 458
fractal nature of patterns, 18, 303
fractal nature of trends, 15-16, 225
freestockcharts.com, 203
Frost, A. J., 478
fulcrum in one-box reversal point-and-figure
  charts, 344
funds
  bank loans, 184
  cost
    long-term interest rates, 187
    Misery Index, 188-189
    money velocity, 187-189
    short-term interest rates, 185-186
  ETFs (exchange-traded funds), 61-62

  Fed policy
    explained, 190-191
    Fed policy futures, 191
    Three Steps and a Stumble indicator,
      193-194
    valuation model, 192
    yield curve, 194
  household financial assets, 182
  margin debt, 179-180
  money market funds, 178-179
  money supply, 183-184
  secondary offerings, 180-181
fungibility, 58
funnel pattern, 320
Future Line of Demarcation (FLD), 471-472
futures markets, 63-65
  choosing between futures markets and
    stock markets
    costs, 504
    liquidity, 506
    risks, 505
    suitability, 505
    time horizon, 505-506
    volatility, 506
    volume, 506
  data problems, 539-540
  Fed policy futures, 191

G
Gammage, Kennedy, 157
Gann fan lines, 250-251
Gann two-day swing method, 233-234
Gann, William Delbert, 28, 233, 250, 497-498
gaps
  breakaway gaps, 364
  common gaps, 367
  ex-dividend gaps, 367
  exhaustion gaps, 367
  explained, 363-364
  opening gaps, 365-367
  pattern gaps, 367
  runaway gaps, 367
  stops and, 269-270
  suspension gaps, 367

GARCH (generalized autoregressive conditional heteroscedasticity), 602-603

Gartley, H. M., 415

GAs (genetic algorithms), 603-604

Gauss, Karl, 591

Gaussian distributions, 591-592

Gayer, Zoran, 490

General Electric, 36

generalized autoregressive conditional heteroscedasticity, 602-603

genetic algorithms (GAs), 603-604

geometric averages, 72

geometric mean, 584-585

GMA (Geometric Moving Average), 284

Goepfert, Jason, 108

gold

gold to bonds ratio analysis, 512

Hulbert Gold Sentiment Index, 128

U.S. dollar to gold ratio analysis, 511

golden ratio, 493-495

Good 'Til Canceled Order (GTC), 607

Gould, Edson, 248

Granville, Joseph, 28, 416

Grossman, Stanford, 42

GTC (Good 'Til Canceled Order), 607

H

Hadady, R. Earle, 429

half-cycle reversal, 470-471

Hamilton, William Peter, 17, 27, 76-77, 230

hammer candlestick pattern, 393

hanging man candlestick pattern, 393-394

harami candlestick pattern, 392-393

hard money stops, 573

harmonics of cycles, 456-457

Haurlan Index, 140-141

Haurlan, Peter N., 140

head-and-shoulders pattern, 326-329, 343

hemlines as sentiment indicator, 117

herding, 46

Herrick Payoff Index (HPI), 428-429

Herrick, John, 428

High Growth Stock Investors, 203

high volume method of identifying reversal points, 234

high-low logic index, 156

hikkake reversals, 379-380

Hilbert's Transform, 285

Hill, John R., 538

Hindenburg Omen, 157

Hirsch, Yale, 171

histograms, 591

historical indicators, 117-118

history

of charts, 201-204

of EWT (Elliott Wave Theory), 478

of point-and-figure charting, 337-339

of technical analysis

early financial markets and exchanges, 23-25

modern technical analysis, 26-30

Hitschler, Fred, 29

Holy Grail method, 444

Honma, Sokyu, 24-25, 201

hook reversals, 379

horizontal count in three-point reversal point-and-figure charts, 347

horn pattern, 375

household financial assets, 182

HPI (Herrick Payoff Index), 428-429

Hughes, James F., 136-137

Hulbert Financial Digest, 128

Hulbert Gold Sentiment Index, 128

Hulbert, Mark, 128

Hurst, James, 454, 460

hyperbolic discounting, 47

I

ideal market picture (Dow Theory), 78

identifying

cycles

centered moving averages, 463-464

detrending, 461

envelopes, 464-467

Fourier analysis (spectral analysis), 458

Maximum Entropy Spectral Analysis (MESA), 459

observation, 460-461

trends, 12-13
  linear least-squares regression, 12-13
  trend lines, 13-14
IFTA (International Federation of Technical Analysts, Inc.), 7
Immediate or Cancel (IOC), 607
implied volatility, 101
impulse waves
  basic rules, 480-481
  diagonals, 482
  impulse patterns, 481
  truncation, 483
independence, 582
Independence Day pattern, 175
independent variables, 590
indexes
  Accumulation Distribution (AD), 419
  Commodity Channel Index (CCI), 441
  explained, 408
  On-Balance-Volume (OBV), 416-417
  Price Volume Trend, 418
  Relative Strength Index (RSI), 434-437
  Williams Accumulation Distribution (WAD), 420
  Williams Variable Accumulation Distribution (WVAD), 418-419
inductive reasoning, 50
inferential statistics
  defined, 583, 591
  probability distributions, 591-594
information, 42-43
informed investors, 69
informed players, sentiment of
  explained, 91-92
  measuring, 118-124
initial capital, 568-569
initial system design decisions, 534-535
inside bars, 376-378
insiders, measuring sentiment of
  COT (Commitment of Traders) reports, 122-124
  Investors Intelligence, 119-120
  large blocks, 121-122

secondary offerings, 119
Sell/Buy ratio, 118-119
interest rates
  long-term interest rates, 187
  short-term interest rates, 185-186
Intermarket Technical Analysis **(Murphy), 507**
intermediate trends, 16, 81
internal trend lines, 244
International Federation of Technical Analysts, Inc. (IFTA), 7
intra-bar breakouts, 256-257
intraday patterns, 386-389
intraday trends, 16
introduction to technical analysis, 3-5
inversions of cycles, 457
inverted hammer candlestick pattern, 394-395
inverted triangle pattern, 320
inverted yield curve, 194
investment securities, 506-507
investors
  informed investors, 69
  investor psychology, 89, 226-227
  investors as their own worst enemies, 93
  liquidity players, 69
  noise players, 46, 69
  rationality of, 46-47
  sentiment
    crowd behavior and concept of contrary opinion, 96
    human bias and decision making, 92-94
    neurochemistry effect on human thinking, 92
  short-term traders, 51
Investors Intelligence
  Advisory Service Sentiment survey, 103-105
  measuring sentiment with, 119-120
IOC (Immediate or Cancel), 607
irrational exuberance, 48
Irwin, Scott, 52
island reversals, 373
Isosceles triangle pattern, 317-318

J

Jackwerth, Jens Carsten, 36
January barometer, 174
January effect, 174
Japanese Candlestick Charting Techniques (Nison), 211, 390
Jegadeesh, Narishimhan, 517
Jensen's alpha, 600
JNJ (Johnson & Johnson), 207-209
Jones, Edward, 26
Jones, Herbert E., 35

K

K-waves (Kondratieff waves), 164-166
Kahneman, Daniel, 47
KAMA (Kaufman Adaptive Moving Average), 285
kasakasa pattern, 393
Kato, Kosaku, 24
Kaufman Adaptive Moving Average (KAMA), 285
Kelly formula, 567-568
Keltner Bands, 293
Keltner, Chester, 293
Kepler, Johannes, 494
key reversal bars, 373
Kirkpatrick, Charles D., 522-523
knockout pattern, 381
knowledge of market, 571
Kondratieff waves (K-waves), 164-166
Kondratieff, Nicolas D., 164

L

Lambert, Donald, 441
Landry, David, 364, 381
Lane, George, 438
large blocks, measuring sentiment with, 121-122
large losses, 551
leading diagonals, 482

Leading Sectors and World Powers: The Coevolution of Global Economics and Politics (Modelski and Thompson), 165
least-squares regression line, 588
leaves, 607
LeBeau, Chuck, 436
legislation
    Securities Act of 1933, 28
    Securities Exchange Act of 1934, 28
length
    of average winning trade, 550
    of moving averages, 279-280
    of trends, 15-16
leptokurtic distribution, 36
leverage, 570
Levy method, 520
Levy, Paul, 35
Levy, Robert, 308, 517, 520
Lieber, Al, 450
limits, 607
Lindsay, George, 29
line charts, 207-209
line formation, 230
line of best fit, 588
linear regression, 239
    linear regression least-squares fit, 12-13, 588
    probability distributions and, 593-594
Linearly Weighted Moving Average (LWMA), 282
linked contracts, 205-206
liquidity
    defined, 607
    futures versus stock markets, 506
liquidity players, 69, 91
Lo, Andrew W., 18, 39, 46, 50
loans, 184
log-returns, 592
logarithmic scale, 220
long, 607
long tail pattern (three-point reversal point-and-figure charts), 355

long-range bar, 370
Long-Term Capital Management (LTCM), 48-49
long-term interest rates, 187
The Long Wave Cycle (Kondratieff), 164
longest flat time, 551
Lonja, 24
LTCM (Long-Term Capital Management), 48-49
LWMA (Linearly Weighted Moving Average), 282

M
MACD (Moving Average Convergence-Divergence), 29, 432-433
MacKinlay, A. Craig, 39
Magee, John, 3, 28, 32
Malkiel, Burton, 35
MAMA (MESA Adaptive Moving Average), 285
management. *See* money management
Mandelbrot, Benoit, 36
manias
    book recommendations, 95
    books about, 95
    defined, 94
margin balances, 110-111
margin debt, 179-180
market breadth, measuring
    absolute breadth index, 144-145
    advance-decline line to its 32-week simple moving average, 139
    advance-decline ratio, 146-147
    breadth line (advance-decline line), 134-136
    breadth thrust, 147-148
    definition of breadth, 133
    double negative divergence, 136-137
    Haurlan Index, 140-141
    McClellan Oscillator, 142-143
    McClellan Ratio-Adjusted Oscillator, 143
    McClellan summation index, 144
    overview, 148
    plurality index, 144

traditional advance-decline methods, 138-139
    unchanged issues index, 145
market capitalization weighted averages, 71-72
Market on Close (MOC), 607
market orders, 608
market selection
    explained, 503-504
    futures versus stock markets
        costs, 504
        liquidity, 506
        risks, 505
        suitability, 505
        time horizon, 505-506
        volatility, 506
        volume, 506
    investment securities, 506-507
    ratio analysis
        bond market to stock market, 512
        cyclical emphasis, 510-511
        gold to bonds, 512
        implications of intermarket analysis, 513-515
        secular emphasis, 507-510
        stock market industry sectors, 515-516
        stock market to U.S. dollar, 513-514
        U.S. dollar to gold, 511
    relative strength
        academic studies of, 517-518
        explained, 517
        measuring, 518-520
    screening for favorable stocks: case studies, 520
        Charles D. Kirkpatrick method, 522-523
        James P. O'Shaughnessy method, 521-522
        Richard D. Wyckoff method, 522-524
        Value Line Ranking System, 522
        William O'Neil CANSLIM method, 521
market sentiment. *See* sentiment
market strength, measuring
    absolute breadth index, 144-145
    advance-decline line to its 32-week simple moving average, 139
    advance-decline ratio, 146-147

Arms Index, 149-151
breadth and new highs to new lows, 159-160
breadth line (advance-decline line), 134-136
breadth thrust, 147-148
double negative divergence, 136-137
explained, 131-133
Haurlan Index, 140-141
high-low logic index, 156
Hindenburg Omen, 157
McClellan Oscillator, 142-143
McClellan Ratio-Adjusted Oscillator, 143
McClellan summation index, 144
modified Arms Index, 151
moving averages, 157-158
net ticks, 160
new highs versus new lows, 155
NPDD (ninety percent downside days), 152
plurality index, 144
10-to-1 up volume days and 9-to-1 down
    volume days, 153-154
traditional advance-decline methods, 138-139
unchanged issues index, 145
Market Vane polls, 106
markets
auction markets, 59
breadth. *See* market breadth, measuring
brokered markets, 58
cash markets, 60-61
dealer markets, 58
defined, 58
derivative markets
    counterparty risk, 62
    defined, 62
    futures markets, 63-65
    option markets, 65-66
    underlying, 62
direct search markets, 58
economic theory of competitive markets,
    41-42
history of, 23-25
how markets work, 66-68
knowledge of, 571
market structure and pattern recognition, 306

measurements
    equally weighted (geometric) averages, 72
    explained, 69-70
    market capitalization weighted averages,
        71-72
    price-weighted averages, 70
players, 69
selection. *See* market selection
sentiment. *See* sentiment
stock market, 60
strength. *See* market strength, measuring
structure
    concepts of W. D. Gann, 497-498
    EWT (Elliott Wave Theory), 478-492
swaps and forwards, 66
MarketWatch, 128
Markowitz, Harry, 594
Martin, Richard, 478
martingale betting system, 563-564
Mastering Elliott Wave (Neely), 490
maximum adverse excursion method, 574
maximum consecutive losses, 551
maximum cumulative drawdown, 550
maximum drawdowns (MDD), 563
Maximum Entropy Spectral Analysis
    (MESA), 459
maximum favorable and adverse
    excursions, 551
maximum likelihood, 603
maximum loss, 551
maximum winning favorable excursion, 575
McClellan Market Report, **123**
McClellan Oscillator, 142-143
McClellan Ratio-Adjusted Oscillator, 143
McClellan summation index, 144
McClellan, Marian, 142-144
McClellan, Sherman, 142-144
McClellan, Tom, 123
MDD (maximum drawdowns), 563
mean
calculating, 583
geometric mean versus, 584-585
mean-variance framework, 598

measuring

gaps, 367

market movement

equally weighted (geometric) averages, 72

explained, 69-70

market capitalization weighted averages, 71-72

price-weighted averages, 70

market strength

absolute breadth index, 144-145

advance-decline line to its 32-week simple moving average, 139

advance-decline ratio, 146-147

Arms Index, 149-151

breadth and new highs to new lows, 159-160

breadth line (advance-decline line), 134-136

breadth thrust, 147-148

double negative divergence, 136-137

explained, 131-133

Haurlan Index, 140-141

high-low logic index, 156

Hindenburg Omen, 157

McClellan Oscillator, 142-143

McClellan Ratio-Adjusted Oscillator, 143

McClellan summation index, 144

modified Arms Index, 151

moving averages, 157-158

net ticks, 160

new highs versus new lows, 155

NPDD (ninety percent downside days), 152

plurality index, 144

10-to-1 up volume days and 9-to-1 down volume days, 153-154

traditional advance-decline methods, 138-139

unchanged issues index, 145

relative strength

alpha method, 519-520

Levy method, 520

percentage change method, 518-519

trend slope method, 520

sentiment of informed players

COT (Commitment of Traders) reports, 122-124

Investors Intelligence, 119-120

large blocks, 121-122

secondary offerings, 119

Sell/Buy ratio, 118-119

sentiment of uninformed players

advisory opinion polls, 103, 105

American Association of Individual Investors poll, 105

buying and selling climaxes, 107-108

combining put/call ratio and volatility, 102

Consensus Bullish Sentiment Index, 106

Consumer Confidence Index, 106

eccentric sentiment indicators, 117

historical indicators, 117-118

margin balances, 110-111

Market Vane polls, 106

money market fund assets, 111-112

mutual fund statistics, 108-109

odd-lot short selling, 115

option trading and sentiment, 97-98

overview, 97

put-call ratios, 98-100

relative volume, 112-113

Rydex funds, 109-110

Sentix Index, 106

uninformed short selling, 113-115

unquantifiable contrary indicators, 116-117

volatility, 100-101

system results for robustness

components, 549

profit measures, 549-550

risk measures, 550-551

smoothness and equity curve, 552

median, 584

megaphone pattern, 320

mercato a termine, 24

Merrill, Arthur, 122, 139, 246, 308

MESA (Maximum Entropy Spectral Analysis), 459
  MAMA (MESA Adaptive Moving Average), 285
Metastock, 203
Meyers, Thomas, 156
Mikkea, Jim, 157
minor trends, 82
miscalibration of probabilities, 47
Misery Index, 188-189
MOC (Market on Close), 607
mode, 584
Modelski, George, 164
Modern Portfolio Theory (MPT), 594-600
modified Arms Index, 151
momentum
  Commodity Channel Index (CCI), 441
  explained, 29, 430-431
  Moving Average Convergence-Divergence (MACD), 432-433
  Rate of Change (ROC), 434-435
  Relative Strength Index (RSI), 434-437
  similarities between oscillators, 441-442
  Stochastic oscillator, 437-440
  success of momentum indicators, 431-432
  Williams %R oscillator, 440-441
money
  bank loans, 184
  cost of funds, 185
  explained, 177-178
  Fed policy
    explained, 190-191
    Fed policy futures, 191
    Three Steps and a Stumble indicator, 193-194
    valuation model, 192
    yield curve, 194
  household financial assets, 182
  long-term interest rates, 187
  management. *See* money management
  margin debt, 179-180
  Misery Index, 188-189
  money market funds, 178-179

  money stops, 269
  money supply, 183-184
  secondary offerings, 180-181
  short-term interest rates, 185-186
  velocity, 187-189
Money Flow Index (Oscillator), 422-424
money management
  determining optimal position size
    optimal f and Kelly formula, 567-568
    Risk of Ruin (ROR) formula, 565-566
    theory of runs, 567
  explained, 559-560, 564-565
  if everything goes wrong, 577
  monitoring systems and portfolios, 577
  risk strategies
    execution, 576
    explained, 530, 572-573
    protective stops, 573-574
    signal stops, 576
    targets, 576
    time stops, 576
    trailing stops, 574-575
  risks
    diversifiable risk, 571-572
    drawdowns, 563
    explained, 560-561
    initial capital, 568-569
    knowledge of market, 571
    leverage, 570
    martingale betting system, 563-564
    maximum drawdowns (MDD), 563
    number of shares or contracts, 565
    optimal f and Kelly formula, 567-568
    position size, 564-568
    psychological risks, 570-571
    pyramiding, 570
    reward to risk, 564
    Risk of Ruin (ROR) formula, 565-566
    security quality, 572
    temporal, 572
    theory of runs, 563, 567
    trade frequency, 572
  testing money management strategies, 561-562

money market funds, 111-112, 178-179

money market managers, 126-127

money point, 575

money stops, 269

money supply, 183-184

monitoring systems and portfolios, 577

Monte Carlo simulations, 562, 569

Montgomery, Paul Macrae, 116

morning star candlestick pattern, 397-398

Most, Nathan, 61

motive impulse wave, 479

Moving Average Convergence-Divergence (MACD), 432-433

moving averages, 157-158, 536

   advance-decline moving average, 138

   bands

      Bollinger Bands, 292-293

      explained, 292

      Keltner Bands, 293

      STARC Bands, 293

      trading strategies, 294-295

   calculating, 276-278

   centered moving averages, 463-464

   channels, 295

   defined, 275-276

   directional movement

      calculating, 288-289

      DMIs (directional movement indicators), 289-291

   Exponentially Smoothed Moving Average (EMA), 282-283

   Following Adaptive Moving Average (FAMA), 285

   Geometric Moving Average (GMA), 284

   Kaufman Adaptive Moving Average (KAMA), 285

   length of, 279-280

   Linearly Weighted Moving Average (LWMA), 282

   MESA Adaptive Moving Average (MAMA), 285

   multiple moving averages, 280-281

number of stocks above their 30-week moving average, 157-158

percentage envelopes

      explained, 291-292

      trading strategies, 294-295

triangular moving averages, 285

usage strategies

      determining price extremes, 287

      determining support and resistance, 286

      determining trend, 285

      giving specific signals, 288

variable EMAs, 285

Volume-Adjusted Moving Average, 285

Wilder's moving average, 284

moving averages crossovers, 29

Moving-Average Convergence/Divergence (MACD), 29, 432-433

moving-average envelopes, 29

MPT (Modern Portfolio Theory), 594-600

MTA (Market Technicians Association), 7

multibox reversal point-and-figure charts, 217-218

multicollinearity, 590

multiple bar patterns

   knockout, 381

   Oops!, 382

   shark, 383-384

   trend correction, 380-381

multiple moving averages, 280-281

multiple regression, 590

multiple variables in descriptive statistics, 586-590

Murphy, John, 507

mutual funds

   mutual fund cash as percentage of assets, 108-109

   statistics, 108

N

Najarian, Jon, 537

naked bar upward reversals, 379

narrow-range bar, 385-386

Nature's Law—The Secret of the Universe (Elliott), 478

nearest future method, 205
Neely, Glenn, 490
negative divergence, 132, 410
negative failure swings, 409
negative reversals, 133, 410
Nelson, A. C., 76
Nelson, S. A., 27
Nerves-of-Steel system
    design, 541-545
    Monte Carlo simulation, 569
    upgrading based on results of initial testing,
        553-555
net profit to drawdown ratio, 551
net ticks, 160
neural networks, 603
neurochemistry effect on human thinking, 92
neurofinance, 17
neutral areas, 225
New Concepts in Technical Trading Systems
    (Wilder), 288
new highs versus new lows, 155
*A New Strategy of Daily Stock Market Timing
    for Maximum Profit* (Granville), 416
9-to-1 down volume days, 153-154
Nison, Steve, 30, 211, 390
noise players, 46, 69
nondiscretionary systems
    benefits of, 531-532
    explained, 530-531
    pitfalls of, 532
nondiversifiable risk, 599
nonrandom nature of price, 18
normal distributions, 36, 591-592
normal risks
    initial capital, 568-569
    leverage, 570
    number of shares or contracts, 565
    optimal f and Kelly formula, 567-568
    position size
        determining optimal position size, 565-568
        explained, 564-565
        final position size, 568
    pyramiding, 570

Risk of Ruin (ROR) formula, 565-566
    theory of runs, 567
not held, 608
NPDD (ninety percent downside days), 152
number of shares or contracts, 565

O

O'Neil, William, 521
O'Shaughnessy, James P., 521-522
observing cycles, 460-461
OBV (On-Balance-Volume), 416-417
odd lots, 608
odd-lot short selling, 115
offers, 608
Okum, Arthur, 188
On Balance Open Interest Indicator, 429
*On the Impossibility of Informationally
    Efficient Markets* (Grossman and
    Stiglitz), 42
On-Balance-Volume (OBV), 416-417
one-box reversal point-and-figure charts,
    216-217, 373
    action points, 344-345
    consolidation area, 340
    determining count in, 341-343
    explained, 339
    fulcrum, 344
    head-and-shoulders pattern, 343
    trend lines, 340-341
one-day change in advance-decline line, 138
Oops! pattern, 382
OOS (out-of-sample) optimization, 547-548
open interest
    explained, 427-428
    indicators, 428-429
open orders, 607
opening gaps, 365-367
OPG (Opening Only), 608
optimal f, 567-568
optimal position size, determining
    optimal f and Kelly formula, 567-568
    Risk of Ruin (ROR) formula, 565-566
    theory of runs, 567

optimizing systems
  explained, 546
  measuring system results for robustness
    components, 549
    profit measures, 549-550
    risk measures, 550-551
    smoothness and equity curve, 552
  out-of-sample (OOS) optimization, 547-548
  screening for parameters, 548-549
  walk forward optimization, 548
  whole sample, 547
option trading, 65-66, 97-98
order tickets, 609-610
oscillators
  analysis methods
    classic patterns, 411
    crossovers, 411
    divergences, 409-410
    failure swings, 409
    overbought/oversold, 408-409
    reversals, 410
    trend IDs, 410-411
  bounded/unbounded, 408
  Chaikin Money Flow, 421
  Chaikin Oscillator, 422
  defined, 139
  Ease of Movement (EMV), 425
  Elder Force Index (EFI), 423-424
  explained, 408
  Herrick Payoff Index (HPI), 428-429
  McClellan Oscillator, 142-143
  McClellan Ratio-Adjusted Oscillator, 143
  Money Flow Index (Oscillator), 422-424
  Moving Average Convergence-Divergence
    (MACD), 432-433
  Rate of Change (ROC), 434-435
  similarities between, 441-442
  Stochastic oscillator, 437-440
  Twiggs Money Flow, 421
  volume oscillator, 420-421
  Volume Rate of Change, 425
  Williams %R oscillator, 440-441
out-of-sample (OOS) optimization, 547-548

outlier-adjusted profit, 550
outside bars, 379-380
overbought level, 408-409
overconfidence, 46
overreaction, 46
oversold level, 408-409

P

panics, 94-95
paper umbrella pattern, 393
Parabolic SAR, 267
Parabolic System, 29
parameters
  screening for, 548-549
  test parameter ranges, 540
Park, Cheol-Ho, 52
pattern gaps, 367
pattern recognition systems, 537-538
patterns
  ascending triangle, 317
  ascending triple top and descending triple
    bottom, 350-351
  assumptions about, 18
  bar charts and patterns, 307-308
  book recommendations, 307
  broadening, 320
  bullish triangle and bearish triangle, 352
  candlestick
    Bulkowski ranking of candlestick patterns,
      401-402
    dark cloud cover, 395-397
    doji, 391-392
    engulfing, 394-396
    evening star, 397-398
    explained, 390-391
    hammer, 393
    hanging man, 393-394
    harami, 392-393
    inverted hammer, 394-395
    morning star, 397-398
    piercing line, 395-397
    shooting star, 394-395
    three black crows, 398-399

three inside down, 399-400
three inside up, 399-400
three outside down, 400
three outside up, 400
three white soldiers, 398-399
windows, 392
catapult, 354-355
characteristics of, 302-303
construction and determination, 362
Dead Cat Bounce (DCB), 371-373
defined, 302
descending triangle, 315-316
diamond top, 321-322
double top and double bottom, 309-310, 349
entry/exit, 302
existence of, 303-304
failures, 303
flags and pennants, 329-331
fractal nature of, 18, 303
fulcrum, 344
gaps
  Apple Computer (AAPL) case study,
    368-370
  breakaway gaps, 364
  common gaps, 367
  ex-dividend gaps, 367
  exhaustion gaps, 367
  explained, 363-364
  opening gaps, 365-367
  pattern gaps, 367
  runaway gaps, 367
  suspension gaps, 367
head-and-shoulders, 326-329, 343
intraday patterns, 386-389
island reversals, 373
multiple bar patterns
  knockout, 381
  Oops!, 382
  shark, 383-384
  trend correction, 380-381
one- and two-bar reversal patterns
  hikkake reversals, 379-380
  hook reversals, 379
  horn, 375

inside bars, 376-378
naked bar upward reversals, 379
one-bar reversals, 373
outside bars, 379-380
two-bar breakouts, 375
two-bar reversals, 373-375
pattern recognition
  behavioral finance and, 304-305
  computers and, 305-306
  market structure and, 306
patterns with best performance and lowest risk
  of failure, 332
profitability of, 308-309
pullbacks, 303
rectangle, 310-313
rising and declining trend lines, 352-354
rising bottom and declining top, 349-350
rounding top and rounding bottom, 325-326
shakeout, 356-357
short- versus long-term patterns, 359-362
spikes, 355-356, 370-371
spread triple top and spread triple bottom,
  351-352
standard triangle, 314-315
symmetrical triangle, 317-318
temporal patterns/cycles
  decennial pattern, 168-169
  election year pattern, 171-172
  event trading, 175
  explained, 163-164
  four-year or presidential cycle, 170-171
  January barometer, 174
  January effect, 174
  Kondratieff waves (K-waves), 164-166
  seasonal patterns, 172-174
  34-year historical cycles, 166-168
throwbacks, 303
triple top and triple bottom, 313-314, 350
validity of, 303-304
volatility patterns
  narrow-range bar, 385-386
  VIX, 386
  wide-range bar, 384-385
wedge and climax, 322-325

payoff ratio, 550, 564

peaks, 228-229

pegged market, 608

pennants, 329-331

percent breakout filter, 258

percentage change method, 518-519

percentage envelopes
    explained, 291-292
    trading strategies, 294-295

percentage method of identifying reversal
    points, 233

percentage of gain, setting trailing stops
    with, 268

percentage winning trades, 550

performance measurement statistics, 600-601

periods, 454, 468-469

permutations, 582

perpetual contracts, 205, 539

piercing line candlestick pattern, 395-397

pipe formation, 373-375

Pisano, Leonardo ("Fibonacci"), 493

Pivot Point Technique, 260-262

pivots, 364

Plato, 494

players
    informed players, 69, 92
    investor psychology, 89, 226-227
    investors as their own worst enemies, 93
    liquidity players, 69
    noise players, 69

Plessis, Jeremy du, 339

Plummer, Tony, 456, 491

plurality index, 144

plus tick, 609

POI (Price and Open Interest Index), 429

Poincare, Henri, 35

Point and Figure Charting (Dorsey), 218

*The Point and Figure Method of Anticipating
    Stock Price Movements* (De Villiers), 338

point-and-figure charts
    arithmetic scale, 220
    box size, 217-218
    continuous price flow, 336-337

explained, 215-216, 335, 414

history of, 337-339

logarithmic scale, 220

multibox reversal, 217-218

old versus new methods, 337

one-box reversal
    action points, 344-345
    consolidation area, 340
    determining count in, 341-343
    explained, 216-217, 339
    fulcrum, 344
    head-and-shoulders pattern, 343
    trend lines, 340-341

three-point reversal
    *ascending triple top and descending triple
        bottom, 350-351*
    bullish triangle and bearish triangle, 352
    catapult, 354-355
    double top and double bottom, 349
    explained, 345
    horizontal count, 347
    rising and declining trend lines, 352-354
    rising bottom and declining top, 349-350
    shakeout, 356-357
    spike, 355
    *spread triple top and spread triple bottom,
        351-352*
    trend lines, 346-347
    triple top and triple bottom, 350
    vertical count, 348

time, 218

time and volume omission, 336

trend lines, 248

point breakout filter, 258

polls, 102
    advisory opinion polls, 103-105
    American Association of Individual
        Investors, 105
    Consensus Bullish Sentiment Index, 106
    Consumer Confidence Index, 106
    Market Vane polls, 106
    Sentix Index, 106

Poor, Henry, 27

popsteckle, 443-444
population, 585
portfolios, monitoring, 577
Poser, Steven, 492
position sizing. *See* money management
positive divergence, 132, 410
positive failure swings, 409
positive reversals, 133, 410
pragmatic criticisms of technical analysis,
    50-51
Prechter, Robert, 483
predictive technical analysis, 4
premature breakouts, 311
presidential (four-year) cycle, 170-171
price
    arbitrage and price equilibrium, 47-48
    ask price, 59
    bid price, 59
    confirmation. *See* price confirmation
    as determined by supply and demand, 17
    history of price reporting, 27
    nonrandom nature of, 18
    normal distributions and, 591
    price discount assumption, 17
    price extremes, 287
    price flow, 336-337
    price targets, setting with breakout price, 309
    returns versus, 581-582, 586
    standard deviation of price, 259
    trends. *See* trends
Price and Open Interest Index (POI), 429
price confirmation
    determining trend and trading range, 441-444
    momentum
        Commodity Channel Index (CCI), 441
        explained, 430-431
        Moving Average Convergence-Divergence
            (MACD), 432-433
        Rate of Change (ROC), 434-435
        Relative Strength Index (RSI), 434-437
        similarities between oscillators, 441-442
        Stochastic oscillator, 437-440
        success of momentum indicators, 431-432
        Williams %R oscillator, 440-441

Price Volume Trend, 418
price-weighted averages, 70
primary bear markets, 80
primary bull markets, 80
primary dealer positions (Treasury Bonds),
    125-126
primary trends, 16, 80-81
Pring, Martin, 510
probability distributions, 582-583, 591-594
profit
    measuring profitability of systems, 549-550
    profit factor, 549, 564
    profit/loss ratio, 564
    profitability of patterns, 308-309
    profiting from technical analysis, 10-11
    trends as key to profits, 224-225
The Profit Magic of Stock Transaction Timing
    (Hurst), 454, 460
program trading, 412
progressive stops. *See* trailing stops
projected targets (EWT), 488-490
projecting
    amplitude
        commonality, 474-475
        FLD (Future Line of Demarcation),
            471-472
        half-cycle reversal, 470-471
        Tillman method, 472-474
    periods, 468-469
proportions of scale, 39-40
protective stops, 264-265
    hard money or dollar stops, 573
    maximum adverse excursion method, 574
Pruitt, George, 538
psychological accounting, 46
psychological risks, 570-571
pullbacks, 247, 303, 608
put/call ratio
    measuring sentiment with, 98-102
    Treasury Bond COT data, 125
    Treasury Bond futures put/call ratio, 124
pyramiding, 570

Q

quadratic equation, standard deviation as, **595**
Quantitative Analysis Services, Inc., **100**
quotes, **608**

R

r-squared, **589**
random, deterministic versus, **582**
The Random Character of Stock Market Prices
   (Cootner), **35**
A Random Walk Down Wall Street
   (Malkiel), **35**
Random Walk Hypothesis (RWH)
   drawdowns, 37-38
   explained, 35
   fat tails, 36
   origins and development, 35
   proportions of scale, 39-40
range trading, **236-237**
ranges
   defined, 210
   True Range, 420
Raschke, Linda Bradford, **386, 444, 538**
RASI (ratio-adjusted summation index), **144**
rate of change (ROC), **29, 133, 434-435**
ratio analysis, **517**
   bond market to stock market, 512
   cyclical emphasis, 510-511
   gold to bonds, 512
   implications of intermarket analysis, 513-515
   secular emphasis, 507-510
   stock market industry sectors, 515-516
   stock market to U.S. dollar, 513-514
   U.S. dollar to gold, 511
ratio-adjusted summation index (RASI), **144**
rationality of investors, **46-47**
reactive technical analysis, **4**
recovery ratio, **551**
rectangle formation. *See* trading ranges
rectangle pattern, **310-313**
Redmont, Richard, **438**

regression
   calculating, 588-590
   linear regression, 239, 593-594
   regression lines, 239
relative strength
   academic studies of, 517-518
   explained, 517, 608
   measuring
      alpha method, 519-520
      Levy method, 520
      percentage change method, 518-519
      trend slope method, 520
   RSI (relative strength index), 29, 434-437
relative volume, **112-113**
reports, COT (Commitment of Traders)
   reports, **122-124**
Research Driven Investor (Hayes), **451**
residual, **590**
resistance
   causes of, 230-232
   determining, 286
   resistance points, 230
   resistance zones, 230, 234-236
retracements
   explained, 245-246
   waiting for, 270
return on investment (ROI), **564**
Return Retracement ratio, **551**
returns
   expected return, 599
   normal distributions and, 591
   prices versus, 581-582, 586
   risk versus return, 597
   ROI (return on investment), 564
   stationarity of, 602
Returns to Buying Winners and Selling Losers:
   Implications for Stock Market Efficiency
   (Levy), **517**
reversals
   explained, 133, 410
   hikkake reversals, 379-380
   hook reversals, 379

horn pattern, 375
inside bars, 376-378
island reversals, 373
naked bar upward reversals, 379
one-bar reversals, 373
outside bars, 379-380
reversal points, determining
  DeMark or Williams method, 232-233
  Gann two-day swing method, 233-234
  high volume method, 234
  percentage method, 233
reversal amount, 337
reversal bars, 373
reversal size, 337
two-bar breakouts, 375
two-bar reversals, 373-375
reverse triangle pattern, 320
reward to risk, 564, 597, 600-601
Rhea, Robert, 17, 27, 76, 478
rising and declining trend lines pattern, 352-354
rising bottom and declining top pattern, 349-350
rising wedge pattern, 323
Risk of Ruin (ROR) formula, 565-566
risk/return ratio, 271, 595
risks. *See also* **volatility**
  beta, 599-600
  counterparty risk, 62
  diversifiable risk, 571-572
  drawdowns, 563
  explained, 560-561
  futures versus stock markets, 505
  initial capital, 568-569
  knowledge of market, 571
  leverage, 570
  martingale betting system, 563-564
  maximum drawdowns (MDD), 563
  measuring, 550-551
  money-management risk strategies
    execution, 576
    explained, 530, 572-573

  if everything goes wrong, 577
  monitoring systems and portfolios, 577
  protective stops, 573-574
  signal stops, 576
  targets, 576
  time stops, 576
  trailing stops, 574-575
nondiversifiable risk, 599
number of shares or contracts, 565
optimal f and Kelly formula, 567-568
patterns with best performance and lowest risk of failure, 332
position size
  determining optimal position size, 565-568
  explained, 564-565
  final position size, 568
psychological risks, 570-571
pyramiding, 570
reward to risk, 564, 597, 600-601
Risk of Ruin (ROR) formula, 565-566
risk/return ratio, 271, 595
security quality, 572
and system design, 533-534
temporal, 572
theory of runs, 563, 567
trade frequency, 572
robustness, measuring system results for
  components, 549
  profit measures, 549-550
  risk measures, 550-551
  smoothness and equity curve, 552
ROC (rate of change), 29, 133, 434-435
ROI (return on investment), 564
ROR (Risk of Ruin) formula, 565-566
Rotnem, Ralph, 117
round lots, 608
round numbers in trading ranges, 232
rounding top and rounding bottom pattern, 325-326
Rouwenhorst, K. G., 518
RSI (relative strength index), 29, 434-437
Rubenstein, Mark, 36

rules of trading, 297
runaway gaps, 367
RWH (Random Walk Hypothesis)
    drawdowns, 37-38
    explained, 35
    fat tails, 36
    origins and development, 35
    proportions of scale, 39-40
Rydex Global Advisors, 109

S
sample, population versus, 585
Samuelson's Dictum, 42
Samuelson, Paul, 35, 42
saucer pattern, 325-326
scale
    arithmetic scale, 213, 220
    defined, 608
    logarithmic scale, 220
    proportions of scale, 39-40
    scale orders, 608
    semi-logarithmic scale, 214
    trend lines, 240
Schabacker, Richard W., 28
Schumpeter, Joseph A., 164
Schwager on Futures: Technical Analysis, **540**
Schwager, Jack, 200
screening for parameters, 548-549
seasonal patterns, 172-174
seats, 608
secondary offerings, 119, 180-181
secondary trends, 16, 81
secular emphasis (ratio analysis), 507-510
Securities Act of 1933, 28
Securities and Exchange Commission, 60
Security Analysis (Graham and Dodd), **28**
security quality, 572
selecting markets
    explained, 503-504
    futures versus stock markets
        costs, 504
        liquidity, 506
        risks, 505
        suitability, 505

        time horizon, 505-506
        volatility, 506
        volume, 506
    investment securities, 506-507
    ratio analysis
        bond market to stock market, 512
        cyclical emphasis, 510-511
        gold to bonds, 512
        implications of intermarket analysis, 513-515
        secular emphasis, 507-510
        stock market industry sectors, 515-516
        stock market to U.S. dollar, 513-514
        U.S. dollar to gold, 511
    relative strength
        academic studies of, 517-518
        explained, 517
        measuring, 518-520
    screening for favorable stocks: case studies, 520
        Charles D. Kirkpatrick method, 522-523
        James P. O'Shaughnessy method, 521-522
        Richard D. Wyckoff method, 522-524
        Value Line Ranking System, 522
        William O'Neil CANSLIM method, 521
Sell/Buy ratio, 118-119
seller expectations, 17
semi-logarithmic scale, 214
sentiment
    crowd behavior and concept of contrary opinion, 96
    defined, 89
    Hulbert Gold Sentiment Index, 128
    human bias and decision making, 92-94
    of liquidity players, 91
    measuring for informed players, 118-124
        COT (Commitment of Traders) reports, 122-124
        explained, 91-92
        Investors Intelligence, 119-120
        large blocks, 121-122
        secondary offerings, 119
        Sell/Buy ratio, 118-119

measuring for uninformed players
   advisory opinion polls, 103-105
   American Association of Individual
     Investors poll, 105
   buying and selling climaxes, 107-108
   combining put/call ratio and volatility, 102
   Consensus Bullish Sentiment Index, 106
   Consumer Confidence Index, 106
   eccentric sentiment indicators, 117
   explained, 91
   historical indicators, 117-118
   margin balances, 110-111
   Market Vane polls, 106
   money market fund assets, 111-112
   mutual fund statistics, 108-109
   odd-lot short selling, 115
   option trading and sentiment, 97-98
   overview, 97
   put-call ratios, 98-100
   relative volume, 112-113
   Rydex funds, 109-110
   Sentix Index, 106
   uninformed short selling, 113-115
   unquantifiable contrary indicators,
     116-117
   volatility, 100-101
neurochemistry effect on human thinking, 92
T-bill rate expectations by money market fund
   managers, 126-127
theory of contrarian investing, 90-91
Treasury Bond COT data, 125
Treasury Bond futures put/call ratio, 124
Treasury Bond primary dealer positions,
   125-126
Sentix Index, 106
serial dependence, 590
shadows, 213
shakeout pattern (three-point reversal
   point-and-figure charts), 356-357
shares, number of, 565
shark pattern, 383-384
Sharpe ratio, 551, 600
Sharpe, William, 598, 600

Sherwell, Chris, 371
Shiller, Robert, 48
shock spiral, 427
shooting star candlestick pattern, 394-395
short, 608
short covering, 608
Short Interest Ratio, 113
short selling
   defined, 608
   odd-lot short selling, 115
   uninformed short selling, 113-115
short-term interest rates, 185-186
short-term patterns
   Dead Cat Bounce (DCB), 371-373
   explained, 359-362
   gaps
     Apple Computer (AAPL) case study,
      368-370
     breakaway gaps, 364
     common gaps, 367
     ex-dividend gaps, 367
     exhaustion gaps, 367
     explained, 363-364
     opening gaps, 365-367
     pattern gaps, 367
     runaway gaps, 367
     suspension gaps, 367
   intraday patterns, 386-389
   island reversals, 373
   multiple bar patterns
     knockout, 381
     Oops!, 382
     shark, 383-384
     trend correction, 380-381
   one- and two-bar reversal patterns
     hikkake reversals, 379-380
     hook reversals, 379
     horn pattern, 375
     inside bars, 376-378
     naked bar upward reversals, 379
     one-bar reversals, 373
     outside bars, 379-380
     two-bar breakouts, 375
     two-bar reversals, 373-375

pattern construction and determination, 362

spikes, 370-371

volatility patterns

  narrow-range bar, 385-386

  VIX, 386

  wide-range bar, 384-385

short-term traders, 51

signal stops, 576

Skinner, B. F., 304

Slater, Tim, 438

slippage, 573

Smith, Edgar Lawrence, 168

**"Some A Posteriori Probabilities in Stock
    Market Action" (Cowles and Jones), 35**

Sornette, Didier, 36

Sortino ratio, 551

**SPDR (Standard & Poor's Depository
    Receipt), 61**

specialist breakouts, setting stops for, 272-273

spectral analysis, 458

speed lines, 248-249

spikes, 355, 370-371

  climaxes, 426

  explained, 425-426

  on breakout, 425

  shock spiral, 427

  volume dips, 427

  Volume Price Confirmation Indicator
      (VPCI), 427

**spread triple top and spread triple bottom,
    351-352**

Spyder, 61

Stack, John, 139

stagflation, 188

**Standard & Poor's Depository Receipt
    (SPDR), 61**

Standard and Poor's, 27

standard deviation

  calculating, 585-586

  normal distributions and, 591

  of price, 259

  as quadratic equation, 595

standard normal variables, 592

Standard Statistics, 27

standard triangle pattern, 314-315

Star, Barbara, 441

STARC Bands, 293

stationarity of returns, 602

statistical significance, 590

statistics

  advanced statistics overview, 602-603

  descriptive statistics

    central tendency measurement, 583-585

    defined, 583

    multiple variables, 586-590

    volatility measurement, 585-586

  inferential statistics

    defined, 583, 591

    probability distributions, 591-594

  MPT (Modern Portfolio Theory), 594-600

  for performance measurement, 600-601

  probability and, 582-583

  returns versus prices, 581-582

  statistical significance, 590

  volume statistics

    Accumulation Distribution (AD), 419

    Chaikin Money Flow, 421

    Chaikin Oscillator, 422

    climaxes, 426

    Ease of Movement (EMV), 425

    Elder Force Index (EFI), 423-424

    interpreting, 415-416

    Money Flow Index (Oscillator), 422-424

    On-Balance-Volume (OBV), 416-417

    Price Volume Trend, 418

    Twiggs Money Flow, 421

    value of, 414-415

    volume oscillator, 420-421

    Volume Rate of Change, 425

    volume spikes, 425-427

    *Williams Accumulation Distribution
        (WAD), 420*

    *Williams Variable Accumulation
        Distribution (WVAD), 418-419*

Steckler, David, 152, 443

Sterling ratio, 551

Stiglitz, Joseph, 42

Stochastic oscillator, 437-440

stock ahead, 608

The Stock Market Barometer (Hamilton), 76

"Stock Market Prices Do Not Follow Random
  Walks: Evidence from a Simple
  Specification Test" (Lo and MacKinlay), 39

Stock Market Profits (Schabacker), 28

Stock Market Techniques No. 2 (Wyckoff), 338

Stock Market Theory and Practice
  (Schabacker), 28

Stock Market Trading (Blumenthal), 339

stock markets, 60
  bond market to stock market ratio
    analysis, 512
  choosing between futures markets and
    stock markets
    costs, 504
    liquidity, 506
    risks, 505
    suitability, 505
    time horizon, 505-506
    volatility, 506
    volume, 506
  industry sectors, 515-516
  stock market to U.S. dollar ratio analysis,
    513-514

StockCharts.com, 203

StockCube Ltd, 339

Stoller Average Range Channel (STARC), 293

Stoller, Manning, 293

stops
  calculating risk/return ratio for breakout
    trading, 271
  changing stop orders, 264
  combining with breakouts, 269
  defined, 263, 609
  entry stops, 263-264
  exit stops, 263-264
  gaps and, 269-270
  money stops, 269
  placing for false ("specialist") breakouts,
    272-273

protective stops, 264-265
  hard money or dollar stops, 573
  maximum adverse excursion method, 574
  signal stops, 576
  stop limit orders, 608
  time stops, 268-269, 576
  trailing stops
    adaptive stops, 575
    break-even level and break-even stops, 574
    defined, 265-266
    *maximum winning favorable
      excursion, 575*
    setting with Parabolic SAR, 267
    setting with percentage of gain, 268
    setting with trend lines, 266-267
    technical point versus money point, 575
    trend line stops, 575
    volatility stops, 575
  waiting for retracement, 270

Stowell, Joe, 379

strength of market, measuring. *See* market
  strength, measuring

Strong, Robert, 34

Student's t distributions, 593

Study Helps in Point and Figure Technique
  (Whelan), 216

suitability, futures versus stock markets, 505

supply and demand, 14-17

support
  causes of, 230-232
  determining, 286
  support points, 230
  support zones, 234-236

suspension gaps, 367

Swannell, Richard, 483

swaps, 66

symmetrical triangle pattern, 317-318

systematic risk, 599

systems
  Chande's Cardinal Rules for a good trading
    system, 556
  design
    countertrend systems, 538
    exogenous signal systems, 538

initial systems, 534-535

Nerves-of-Steel system case study, 541-545

pattern recognition systems, 537-538

reliability, 538

requirements, 532-533

risk, 533-534

trend-following systems, 535-537

discretionary, 530-531

monitoring, 577

necessity of, 530

nondiscretionary

benefits of, 531-532

explained, 530-531

pitfalls of, 532

optimization

explained, 546

measuring system results for robustness, 549-552

out-of-sample (OOS) optimization, 547-548

screening for parameters, 548-549

walk forward optimization, 548

whole sample, 547

overview, 529

testing

methods and tools, 540

overview, 538-539

special data problems for futures systems, 539-540

test parameter ranges, 540

T

t distributions, 593

T-bill rate expectations by money market fund managers, 126-127

Tabell, Edmund, 29

targets, 576

Tarkany, Frank, 456

Taylor, Owen, 338

Technical Analysis (Schwager), 200

Technical Analysis and Market Profits (Schabacker), 28

Technical Analysis from A to Z (Achelis), 420

Technical Analysis of Stock Trends (Edwards and Magee), 3, 28

technical point, 575

temporal patterns/cycles

decennial pattern, 168-169

election year pattern, 171-172

event trading, 175

explained, 163-164

four-year or presidential cycle, 170-171

January barometer, 174

January effect, 174

Kondratieff waves (K-waves), 164-166

seasonal patterns, 172-174

34-year historical cycles, 166-168

temporal risk, 572

10-to-1 up volume days, 153-154

terminal wealth, 584

testing money management strategies, 561-562

testing systems

methods and tools, 540

Nerves-of-Steel system case study, 541-545

overview, 538-539

special data problems for futures systems, 539-540

test parameter ranges, 540

theorems of Dow Theory, 78-79

A Theory of Adaptive Economic Behavior (Cross), 43

theory of contrarian investing, 90-91

Theory of Contrary Opinion, 96

theory of runs, 563, 567

"The Theory of Speculation" (Bachelier), 35

thepatternsite.com, 302

34-year historical cycles, 166-168

Thompson, William, 164

three black crows candlestick pattern, 398-399

three inside down candlestick pattern, 399-400

three inside up candlestick pattern, 399-400

three outside down candlestick pattern, 400

three outside up candlestick pattern, 400

three-point reversal point-and-figure charts

ascending triple top and descending triple bottom, 350-351

bullish triangle and bearish triangle, 352

catapult, 354-355

double top and double bottom, 349

explained, 345

horizontal count, 347

rising and declining trend lines, 352-354

rising bottom and declining top, 349-350

shakeout, 356-357

spike, 355

spread triple top and spread triple bottom, 351-352

trend lines, 346-347

triple top and triple bottom, 350

vertical count, 348

Three Steps and a Stumble indicator, 193-194

three white soldiers candlestick pattern, 398-399

throw-overs, 482

throwbacks, 247, 303

thrust, 147-148

ticker tape, 202

ticks, 160, 202

Tides and the Affairs of Men **(Smith), 168**

Tillman method, 472-474

Tillman, Jim, 472

time

omission from point-and-figure charts, 336

point-and-figure charts, 218

time stops, 268-269

time breakout filter, 258

time horizon, 505-506

time in force, 609

time series modeling, 602

time series variables, 587

time stops, 268-269, 576

Titman, Sheridan, 517

Tower, Ken, 100

trade frequency, 572

TradeStation, 203

Trading Classic Chart Patterns **(Bulkowski), 302**

trading ranges. *See also* **rectangle pattern**

breakout trading, 237

defined, 225

determining, 441-444

explained, 230

in one-box reversal point-and-figure charts, 340

range trading, 236-237

reversal points, determining

DeMark or Williams method, 232-233

Gann two-day swing method, 233-234

high volume method, 234

percentage method, 233

round numbers, 232

support and resistance

causes of, 230-232

resistance points, 230

resistance zones, 230, 234-236

support points, 230

support zones, 234-236

trading rules, 297

trading systems. *See* **systems**

trailing stops

adaptive stops, 575

break-even level and break-even stops, 574

defined, 265-266

maximum winning favorable excursion, 575

setting with Parabolic SAR, 267

setting with percentage of gain, 268

setting with trend lines, 266-267

technical point versus money point, 575

trend line stops, 575

volatility stops, 575

transaction volume, 84

translation in cycles, 457-458

Treasury Bonds

COT data, 125

futures put/call ratio, 124

primary dealer positions, 125-126

trend correction patterns, 380-381

trend-following systems

breakout systems, 536

explained, 535-536

moving average systems, 536

problems with, 536-537

trend IDs, 410-411

trend lines, 13-14
    accelerating trend lines, 240-241
    Andrews pitchfork, 249-250
    channels, 243-244
    decelerating trend lines, 241-242
    Gann fan lines, 250-251
    identifying uptrends with, 239-240
    internal trend lines, 244
    in one-box reversal point-and-figure charts, 340-341
    on point-and-figure charts, 248
    rules for, 242
    scale, 240
    setting trailing stops with, 266-267
    speed lines, 248-249
    stops, 575
    in three-point reversal point-and-figure charts, 346-347
trend slope method, 520
trends. *See also* **cycles; moving averages**
    breakouts
        anticipating, 262
        calculating risk/return ratio for breakout trading, 271
        combining with stops, 269
        confirming, 256-262
        explained, 255-256
        false/premature breakouts, 311
        setting price targets with, 309
    defined, 11, 79
    determining, 227-229, 285, 441-444
    directional trends, 238
    Dow Theory, 225-226
    downtrends, 11
    effect of investor psychology on, 226-227
    explained, 9-10, 227
    fractal nature of, 15-16, 225
    identifying, 12-13
        linear least-squares regression, 12-13
        trend lines, 13-14
    importance of, 10-11
    intraday trends, 16

    as key to profits, 224-225
    minor trends, 82
    neutral areas, 225
    peaks and troughs, 228-229
    primary trends, 16, 80-81
    pullbacks, 247
    relationship with supply and demand, 14-15
    retracements, 245-246
    secondary trends, 16, 81
    throwbacks, 247
    trading ranges
        breakout trading, 237
        defined, 225
        explained, 230
        range trading, 236-237
        resistance zones, 234-236
        reversal points, determining, 232-234
        round numbers, 232
        support and resistance, 230-232
        support zones, 234-236
    trend lengths, 15-16
    trend correction patterns, 380-381
    trend-following systems
        breakout systems, 536
        explained, 535-536
        moving average systems, 536
        problems with, 536-537
    trend IDs, 410-411
    trend lines
        accelerating trend lines, 240-241
        Andrews pitchfork, 249-250
        channels, 243-244
        decelerating trend lines, 241-242
        Gann fan lines, 250-251
        identifying uptrends with, 239-240
        in one-box reversal point-and-figure charts, 340-341
        in three-point reversal point-and-figure charts, 346-347
        internal trend lines, 244
        on point-and-figure charts, 248
        rules for, 242

scale, 240

setting trailing stops with, 266-267

speed lines, 248-249

uptrends, identifying, 238

defined, 11

regression lines, 239

trend lines, 239-244

William Hamilton's thoughts on, 79

Treynor measure of performance, 600

triangle patterns, 486

ascending triangle, 317

descending triangle, 315-316

standard triangle, 314-315

symmetrical triangle, 317-318

trading triangles, 319

triangular moving averages, 285

**triple top and triple bottom pattern,
313-314, 350**

troughs, 228-229

True Range, 420

truncation, 483

Tulip Bulb Mania, 24

Tversky, Amos, 47

Twain, Mark, 18

Twiggs Money Flow, 421

two-bar breakouts, 375

two-bar reversals, 373-375

Two Tumbles and a Jump indicator, 193

Tyco, 31

U

The Ultimate Trading Guide **(Hill, Pruitt, and
Hill), 532**

unbiased estimate, 585

unbounded oscillators, 408

unchanged issues index, 145

unchanged stock, 133

underlying, 62

underwater curve, 552

uninformed players, measuring sentiment of

advisory opinion polls, 103-105

American Association of Individual
Investors poll, 105

buying and selling climaxes, 107-108

combining put/call ratio and volatility, 102

Consensus Bullish Sentiment Index, 106

Consumer Confidence Index, 106

eccentric sentiment indicators, 117

explained, 91

historical indicators, 117-118

margin balances, 110-111

Market Vane polls, 106

money market fund assets, 111-112

mutual fund statistics, 108-109

odd-lot short selling, 115

option trading and sentiment, 97-98

overview, 97

put-call ratios, 98-100

relative volume, 112-113

Rydex funds, 109-110

Sentix Index, 106

uninformed short selling, 113-115

unquantifiable contrary indicators, 116-117

volatility, 100-101

uninformed short selling, 113-115

unit root tests, 602

unquantifiable contrary indicators, 116-117

unusual risks

diversifiable risk, 571-572

knowledge of market, 571

psychological risks, 570-571

security quality, 572

temporal, 572

trade frequency, 572

unweighted index, 72

up and down volume indicators

Arms Index, 149-151

explained, 149

modified Arms Index, 151

NPDD (ninety percent downside days), 152

10-to-1 up volume days and 9-to-1 down
volume days, 153-154

uptick, 609

uptrends, identifying, 238. *See also* **trends**
    regression lines, 239
    trend lines, 239-240
        accelerating trend lines, 240-241
        decelerating trend lines, 241-242
        internal trend lines, 244
        rules for, 242
        scale, 240

V

valuation model (Federal Reserve), 192
Value Line averages, 72
Value Line Ranking System, 522
VaR (Value-at-Risk) method, 601
variable EMAs, 285
variables
    dependent variables, 590
    explanatory variables, 590
    independent variables, 590
    multiple variables, 586-590
    standard normal variables, 592
    time series variables, 587
variance
    calculating, 585-586
    covariance versus, 597
variation, 455
velocity of money, 187, 189
vertical count, 348
Vickers Stock Research Corporation, 118
Villiers, Victor De, 338
VIX pattern, 386
volatility. *See also* **risks**
    breakout filter, 259-260
    estimating, 602-603
    futures versus stock markets, 506
    implied volatility, 101
    measuring, 585-586
    measuring sentiment with, 100-102
    volatility patterns
        narrow-range bar, 385-386
        VIX, 386
        wide-range bar, 384-385
    volatility stops, 575

volume
    defined, 411-412
    futures versus stock markets, 506
    high volume method of identifying reversal
        points, 234
    indexes
        Accumulation Distribution (AD), 419
        On-Balance-Volume (OBV), 416-417
        Price Volume Trend, 418
        Williams Accumulation Distribution
          (WAD), 420
        Williams Variable Accumulation
          Distribution (WVAD), 418-419
    interpreting changes in volume, 415-416
    omission from point-and-figure charts, 336
    oscillators
        Chaikin Money Flow, 421
        Chaikin Oscillator, 422
        Ease of Movement (EMV), 425
        Elder Force Index (EFI), 423-424
        Money Flow Index (Oscillator), 422-424
        Twiggs Money Flow, 421
        volume oscillator, 420-421
        Volume Rate of Change, 425
    portrayal in charts
        bar/candle charts, 412-413
        equivolume, 412-413
        point-and-figure, 414
    transaction volume, 84
    up and down volume indicators
        Arms Index, 149-151
        explained, 149
        modified Arms Index, 151
        NPDD (ninety percent downside
          days), 152
        10-to-1 up volume days and 9-to-1 down
          volume days, 153-154
    value of volume statistics, 414-415
    volume breakout filter, 259
    volume dips, 427
    volume oscillator, 420-421

volume spikes
- *climaxes, 426*
- *explained, 425-426*
- *on breakout, 425*
- *shock spiral, 427*
- *volume dips, 427*
- *Volume Price Confirmation Indicator (VPCI), 427*
- VPCI (Volume Price Confirmation Indicator), 427
- VWAP (Volume Weighted Average Price), 609

Volume-Adjusted Moving Average, 285
volume breakout filter, 259
volume oscillator, 420-421
Volume Price Confirmation Indicator (VPCI), 427
Volume Rate of Change, 425
Volume Weighted Average Price (VWAP), 609
VPCI (Volume Price Confirmation Indicator), 427
VWAP (Volume Weighted Average Price), 609

W

WAD (Williams Accumulation Distribution), 420
waiting for retracement, 270
walk forward optimization, 548
Ward, Kenneth, 29
The Wave Principle **(Collins), 478**
waves (EWT)
- corrective waves, 483
  - *flats, 485-486*
  - *triangles, 486*
  - *zigzags, 484*
- defined, 478
- explained, 479-480
- impulse waves
  - *basic rules, 480-481*
  - *diagonals, 482*
  - *impulse patterns, 481*
  - *truncation, 483*
- motive impulse wave, 479

wedge and climax pattern, 322-325

Whelan, Alexander, 216
whipsaw, 263
whole sample optimization, 547
Why Stock Markets Crash: Critical Events in Complex Financial Systems **(Sornette), 36**
wide-range bar, 370, 384-385
Wilder's moving average, 284
Wilder, J. Welles Jr., 29-30, 284, 288, 420, 434
Williams %R oscillator, 440-441
Williams Accumulation Distribution (WAD), 420
Williams, Larry, 232, 379, 382, 428, 439, 536, 538
windows candlestick pattern, 392
women's hemlines as sentiment indicator, 117
Worden, D. G., 29
WVAD (Williams Variable Accumulation Distribution), 418-419
Wyckoff, Richard D., 27, 498, 522-524

X-Y-Z

yield curve (Federal Reserve), 194

zigzags, 484
Zweig, Martin, 29, 148

FINANCIAL TIMES

In an increasingly competitive world, it is quality
of thinking that gives an edge—an idea that opens new
doors, a technique that solves a problem, or an insight
that simply helps make sense of it all.

We work with leading authors in the various arenas
of business and finance to bring cutting-edge thinking
and best-learning practices to a global market.

It is our goal to create world-class print publications
and electronic products that give readers
knowledge and understanding that can then be
applied, whether studying or at work.

To find out more about our business
products, you can visit us at www.ftpress.com.